# Guide to
# UNIX System Administration

Jason W. Eckert
M. John Schitka

THOMSON

COURSE TECHNOLOGY

Australia • Canada • Mexico • Singapore • Spain • United Kingdom • United States

## Guide to UNIX System Administration

is published by Course Technology

**Senior Editor:**
William Pitkin III

**Senior Product Manager:**
Laura Hildebrand

**Developmental Editor:**
Dave George

**Production Editor:**
Molly Applegate, MacAllister
Publishing Services

**Technical Editor:**
Walter Merchant

**Reviewers:**
Robert Koch, Randy Weaver,
Elsa Lankford, Kofi Obiri-Yeboah

**Manufacturing Coordinator:**
Trevor Kallop

**Product Marketing Manager:**
Jason Sakos

**Associate Product Managers:**
Tim Gleeson, Nick Lombardi

**Editorial Assistant:**
Christy Urban

**Cover Design:**
Abby Scholz

**Text Designer:**
GEX Publishing Services

**Compositor:**
GEX Publishing Services

# BRIEF
# Contents

# TABLE OF
# Contents

# Preface

*UNIX is simple. It just takes a genius to understand its simplicity.*

—Dennis Ritchie, co-creator of UNIX

As Dennis Ritchie points out, UNIX was designed from simple principles. These principles, however, have been continuously improved upon since the late 1960s. Today, UNIX is known not only as the grandfather of all modern operating systems, but also as one of the most highly refined and developed operating systems in existence. Its development has shaped computer science for the past three decades and will continue to influence the computing industry in the future. As a result, there is always a demand for UNIX-educated users, administrators, developers, and advocates.

This book uses carefully constructed examples, questions, and practical exercises to prepare readers with the necessary information to understand the basics of the UNIX operating system and its major flavors: HP-UX, Solaris, and SCO UnixWare. Key to demonstrating UNIX ability is the certification process. This book helps prepare the user for the widely recognized SCO CSA exam.

Topics covered in each chapter are as follows:

**Chapter 1**, "Introduction to UNIX" introduces operating systems as well as the features, benefits, uses, and various flavors of the UNIX operating system. As well, this chapter discusses the history and development of UNIX, SCO certification, and Internet resources.

**Chapter 2**, "Installing the UNIX Operating System" discusses the hardware and software information needed prior to UNIX installation, as well as methods that can be used to collect it. Next, the chapter explores the steps involved in installing UnixWare 7 given the hardware and software information collected previously.

**Chapter 3**, "Accessing a UNIX System" describes how to interact with UNIX shells via a terminal. More specifically, it discusses basic shell commands, shell metacharacters, and command help. In addition, it discusses the CDE desktop environment, the SCO Admin, and SCO Help tools, as well as proper shutdown procedures.

**Chapter 4**, "Managing Files and Directories" outlines the UNIX filesystem structure, and the type of files that can be found on it. As well, this chapter discusses commands that can be used to locate, view, link, and manage files and directories on the UNIX filesystem.

**Chapter 5**, "Working with Text Files" covers those commands that can be used to view the contents of text files and search for text within them that match a regular expression. Furthermore, this chapter examines the features and usage of the pico and vi text editors.

**Chapter 6**, "File and Directory Security" discusses how to interpret and set file and directory permissions and ownership. As well it discusses the default permissions given to files and directories upon creation and how to modify the Access Control List on a file.

**Chapter 7**, "Administering UNIX Filesystems" examines common UNIX filesystems and how to create, mount, manage, and monitor them. This chapter also discusses the structure of the /dev directory and the device files used to refer to device drivers in the UNIX kernel. As well, this chapter discusses the usage of the Device Database when locating information about devices on the system.

**Chapter 8**, "System Initialization, Runlevels, and SAF" covers the major steps needed to initialize a UNIX system. More specifically, it examines the Boot Command Processor, daemon initialization, runlevels, daemon management, and the System Access Facility.

**Chapter 9**, "The Shell Environment" outlines the different shells available on a UNIX system and the features of each. It also examines command input and output redirection, piping, variables, aliases, and environment files that are used to create variables upon shell startup.

**Chapter 10**, "Process Administration" covers the different types of processes, as well as how to view their attributes, change their priority, and kill them using command line and graphical utilities. Furthermore, this chapter discusses how to schedule processes to occur at a future time.

**Chapter 11**, "Package and Logfile Management" covers the installation and management of software packages and package sets. Additionally, this chapter discusses common logfiles, logfile management, and the System Logs Daemon.

**Chapter 12**, "Archiving and Compressing User Data" describes utilities such as compress, tar, cpio, and vxdump that are commonly used to compress and back up files on a UNIX filesystem. In addition, this chapter introduces common devices used to store archives and their management.

**Chapter 13**, "User and Group Administration" focuses on user and group creation and management using both command line and GUI utilities. As well, this chapter discusses user authentication and the different files and databases involved in storing user and group information on the system.

**Chapter 14**, "Printer Administration" discusses the print process as well as the command line and graphical utilities that may be used to create printers on a UNIX system. As well, this chapter discusses how to create print jobs and manage jobs in the print queue.

## The Intended Audience

Simply put, this book is intended for those who wish to learn the UNIX operating system and how to administer it. You need not have UNIX experience prior to reading this book, however basic knowledge of computer hardware and operating systems is assumed. As well, this book covers most of the topics presented on the SCO CSA certification exam. The remainder of these topics are covered in the "Guide to Advanced UNIX Administration" text. Also, the topics introduced in this book and the certification exam are geared towards systems administration, yet are also well suited for those who will use or develop programs for UNIX systems.

## Features

To ensure a successful learning experience, this book includes the following pedagogical features:

- Chapter Objectives: Each chapter in this book begins with a detailed list of the concepts to be mastered within that chapter. This list provides you with a quick reference to the contents of that chapter, as well as a useful study aid.

- Illustrations and Tables: Numerous illustrations of server screens and components aid you in the visualization of common setup steps, theories, and concepts. In addition, many tables provide details and comparisons of both practical and theoretical information and can be used for a quick review of topics.

- End-of-Chapter Material: The end of each chapter includes the following features to reinforce the material covered in the chapter:

- Summary: A bulleted list is provided which gives a brief but complete summary of the chapter.

- Key Terms List: A list of all new terms and their definitions

- Review Questions: A list of review questions tests your knowledge of the most important concepts covered in the chapter.

- Hands-on Projects: Hands-on projects help you to apply the knowledge gained in the chapter.

- Discovery Exercises are study projects designed to challenge you and build upon the basics discussed in the book.

## Text and Graphic Conventions

Additional information and exercises have been added to this book to help you better understand what's being discussed in the chapter. Icons throughout the text alert you to these additional materials. The icons used in this book are described below.

 The Note icon is used to present additional helpful material related to the subject being described.

 Tips garnered from the authors' experience are included to provide extra information about how to attack a problem, or what to do in certain real-world situations.

 Cautions are included to help the reader anticipate potential mistakes or problems to help prevent them from happening.

 Each Hands-on Project in this book is preceded by the Hands-on icon and a description of the exercise that follows.

## Instructor's Resources

The following supplemental materials are available when this book is used in a classroom setting. All of the supplements available with this book are provided to the instructor on a single CD-ROM.

**Electronic Instructor's Manual.** The Instructor's Manual that accompanies this textbook includes additional instructional material to assist in class preparation, including suggestions for classroom activities, discussion topics, and additional projects.

**Solutions** to all end-of-chapter material, including the Review Questions, and where applicable, Hands-on Projects, and Discovery Exercises.

**ExamView®** This textbook is accompanied by ExamView, a powerful testing software package that allows instructors to create and administer printed, computer (LAN-based), and Internet exams. ExamView includes hundreds of questions that correspond to the topics covered in this text, enabling students to generate detailed study guides that include page references for further review. The computer-based and Internet testing components allow students to take exams at their computers, and also save the instructor time by grading each exam automatically.

**PowerPoint presentations.** This book comes with Microsoft PowerPoint slides for each chapter. These are included as a teaching aid for classroom presentation, to make available to students on the network for chapter review, or to be printed for classroom distribution. Instructors, please feel at liberty to add your own slides for additional topics you introduce to the class.

**Figure Files:** All of the figures in the book are reproduced on the Instructor's Resources CD, in bit-mapped format. Similar to the PowerPoint presentations, these are included as a teaching aid for classroom presentation, to make available to students for review, or to be printed for classroom distribution.

# ACKNOWLEDGMENTS

Firstly, we wish to thank our Project Manager, Laura Hildebrand, for her coordination and insight, as well as our Developmental Editor, Dave George, for working through all of our comments and code samples to transform the text into its current state. Their support, wisdom, and insight were invaluable to the creation of this book, made it a truly enjoyable writing experience for us, and resulted in a textbook that takes a fundamentally different approach than traditional textbooks. As well, we wish to thank Digital Content Factory for their advice and guidance, as well as Frank Gerencser and Stuart Bentley of TriOS College for freeing us up to write this book.

*Jason W. Eckert:* I must take this time to thank my co-author, M. John Schitka for the hard work, long hours, and dedication he spent on this book. As well, I thank the Starbucks Coffee company for keeping me on schedule, and, most importantly, my daughter, Mackenzie, for providing me with many of the examples used in the textbook and teaching me that having fun playing a Harry Potter game is more important than writing a textbook.

*M. John Schitka:* First, I have to thank my mentor, friend, and co-author, Jason W. Eckert, for his insight, support, patience, and wisdom during the long days and late nights that went into the creation of this book. More importantly I must thank my family: my wife Jill, and children Kyra, Luke, and Noah for their sacrifice, tolerance, patience, and encouragement during the time it took to write the book. They have no idea how important and appreciated it all was. It is truly hoped that the readers will find this book an enlightening and beneficial part of their educational journey.

Finally, we must both acknowledge Rev. Frank J. Quinto for his expertise and guidance. Were it not for him, our roads would be darker and not as well ruled.

Readers are encouraged to e-mail comments, questions, and suggestions regarding *Guide to UNIX System Administration* to the authors:

- Jason W. Eckert: jasonec@trios.com
- M. John Schitka: johnsc@trios.com

## Before You Begin

UNIX can be a large and intimidating topic if poorly organized. As a result, each concept introduced in this book has been carefully planned and introduced in sequence. To ensure that you gain a solid understanding of core UNIX concepts, you must read this book in consecutive order, since each chapter builds upon previous ones. As well, we recommend that you explore the Internet for Web sites and newsgroups that will help expand your knowledge of UNIX.

## Lab Requirements

The following hardware is required for the Hands-on Projects at the end of each chapter and should be listed on the Hardware Compatibility List available at *www.sco.com*.

- Pentium processor or higher CPU
- 64 MB RAM
- 4 GB hard disk
- CD-ROM Drive
- 3.5-inch floppy diskette drive
- All peripheral devices (such as video cards, disk controllers and network interface cards) must be UnixWare compliant. (See *www.sco.com*)
- An Internet connection for the Discovery Exercises at the end of each chapter is assumed

Similarly, the following lists the software required for the Hands-on Projects at the end of each chapter:

- SCO UnixWare 7.1.1—a UnixWare 7.1.1 Media Kit may be purchased from the vendor at *www.sco.com*.

# 1

# INTRODUCTION TO UNIX

**After reading this chapter and completing the exercises, you will be able to:**

- ◆ Understand the purpose of an operating system
- ◆ Outline the key features and uses of the UNIX operating system
- ◆ Describe the origins of the UNIX operating system
- ◆ Identify and describe common UNIX flavors
- ◆ Use the Internet to find UNIX resources
- ◆ Outline the benefits of UNIX certification

With over 30 years of growth, UNIX is one of the oldest and most highly developed operating systems in use today. This chapter introduces you to operating systems and operating-system-related terminology, followed by a discussion of the features and uses of the UNIX operating system. Next, this chapter examines the development of the UNIX operating system and discusses common UNIX flavors. Finally, this chapter outlines valuable UNIX Internet resources and UNIX certification.

## OPERATING SYSTEMS

Every computer has two fundamental components: hardware and software. The term **hardware** refers to the physical components inside a computer. These components are electrical in nature, and contain a series of circuits that are used to manipulate the flow of information. A computer can have many different pieces of hardware, including the following:

- A processor that computes information. This is also known as the central processing unit (CPU).

- Physical memory stores information needed by the processor. This is also known as random access memory (RAM).

- Hard disk drives that store most of your information

- Floppy disk drives, which store information on floppy disks

- CD-ROM drives, which read information from CD-ROM disks

- Sound cards, which provide sound to external speakers

- Video cards, which display results to the computer monitor

- Network interface cards (NICs), which transmit information to other computers across a computer network

- Circuit boards (also known as mainboards or motherboards), which hold and provide electrical connection between various hardware components

**Software**, on the other hand, refers to the sets of instructions (programs) that understand how to use the hardware of the computer in a meaningful way; more specifically, software programs use hardware to manipulate data (or files) and perform useful tasks. For instance, when a bank teller types information into the computer behind the counter at a bank, the bank teller is using a program that understands what to do with your bank records (data).

Programs and data are usually stored on hardware media such as CD-ROMs, hard disks, or floppy disks, although they can also be stored on other media or even embedded in computer chips. These programs are loaded into various parts of your computer hardware (such as your computer's memory and processor) when you first turn your computer on, and when you start additional software such as word processors or Internet browsers. After a program is executed and running on your computer's hardware, that program is referred to as a process.

Thus, the difference between a program and a process is small. A **program** is a file stored on your computer, whereas a **process** is that file in action, performing a certain task.

Two different types of programs are executed on a computer:

- **Applications**, which are programs designed for a specific use and that we commonly interact with, such as word processors, computer games, graphical manipulation programs, and computer system utilities

- The **operating system (OS)** software, which consists of a series of software components used to directly control the hardware of your computer. Without an operating system, you would not be able to use your computer. Turning on a computer loads the operating system into computer hardware, which then loads and centrally controls all other application software in the background. Applications take your information and relay that information to the operating system. The operating system then uses the computer hardware to carry out the requests.

Figure 1-1 depicts the relationship between these components.

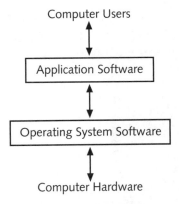

**Figure 1-1**   The role of operating system software

The operating system carries out many different tasks by interacting with many different types of computer hardware. In order for the operating system to accomplish this, it must contain the appropriate **device driver** software for every hardware device in your computer. Each device driver tells the operating system how to use that specific device. In addition, the operating system provides a **user interface**, which is an application program that accepts user input indicating what is to be done, forwards this input to the operating system for completion, and, once this is completed, gives the results back to the user.

The user interface can be a command-line prompt where you must type a command to tell the operating system what to do, or it can be a **graphical user interface (GUI)**, which consists of a series of visual depictions of tasks known as icons that you may use to control the operating system. Finally, operating systems offer **system services**, which are programs that handle system-related tasks such as printing, scheduling programs, and accessing the network. These system services determine most of the functionality that is seen by the user of an operating system. Different operating systems offer different system services, and many operating systems enable users to customize the services they offer.

## The UNIX Operating System

**UNIX** is an operating system that runs a variety of different applications. Similar to other operating systems, the UNIX operating system loads into computer memory when you first power on your computer and initializes all the hardware components. Next, the operating system loads the programs required to give you an interface from which you may enter commands that cause the operating system to perform specific tasks. The operating system then uses the computer hardware to perform the tasks required by the applications.

### UNIX Provides a Standard Interface

The standard GUI in UNIX is the Common Desktop Environment (CDE); however, some UNIX flavors may use other GUIs instead such as MOTIF, **GNU Object Model Environment (GNOME)**, and **K Desktop Environment (KDE)**. Figure 1-2 depicts an example of the CDE interface.

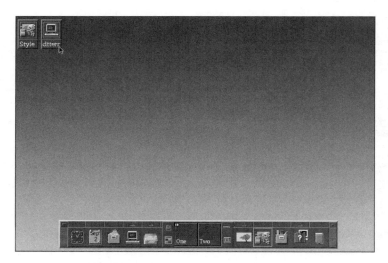

**Figure 1-2**    The CDE interface

In addition, all UNIX flavors offer a text-based **command-line interface** where you may type commands that ultimately perform useful commands on the system. Figure 1-3 shows an example of this type of interface.

The UNIX operating system enables multiple users to access the system simultaneously using different user interfaces; hence, we refer to UNIX as a **multiuser** operating system.

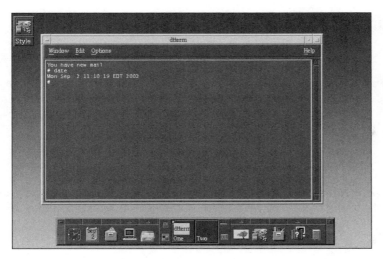

**Figure 1-3**   A command-line interface

## UNIX Runs Many Applications

From its conception, UNIX was designed as a powerful application **server** that can run for long periods of time without being shut down. It has the capability to manage thousands of applications at the same time; as a result, it is referred to as a **multitasking** operating system. Furthermore, these applications may be run locally or across a network to provide services for other client computers.

The most common applications used on UNIX computers include the following:

- Databases
- Scientific/engineering software
- Regression analysis software
- Graphic-rendering software
- File Transfer Protocol (FTP) services
- Web services
- Domain Name Space (DNS) services
- Internet firewalls and proxy services
- Newsgroup services
- Network management software
- E-mail services

## UNIX Is Customizable

UNIX supports the Shell and Perl programming languages, which can be utilized to automate tasks or create custom tasks that are then invoked as needed. Consider a company that needs an application that copies a database file from one computer to another, yet also requires that the database file is manipulated in a specific way, tested by another program for duplicate records, summarized, and then printed as a report. To this company, it may seem like a task that would require expensive software; however, in UNIX you can simply write a short Perl script that uses common UNIX commands and programs together to achieve this task in only a few minutes.

Customization via scripts is invaluable to companies as it enables them to combine several existing applications together to perform a certain task, which may be specific only to that company and hence not previously developed by another free software developer. Most UNIX configurations present hundreds of small utilities, which, when combined with Shell or Perl programming, can quickly and easily make new programs that meet many business needs.

## UNIX Supports Many Hardware Architectures

Another important feature of UNIX is its support for a variety of hardware architectures. Different **hardware architectures** (also called **hardware platforms**) have different CPUs that ultimately determine the processing capability of the computer.

CPUs are categorized based on the types of instructions they execute; the two main categories are **Complex Instruction Set Computing (CISC)** processors and **Reduced Instruction Set Computing (RISC)** processors. CISC processors normally execute more complex commands than RISC processors; however, since complex commands take longer to execute on a processor, RISC processors tend to be faster than CISC processors. As a result, RISC processors are more expensive and often found only in scientific, academic, engineering, and business environments.

Table 1-1 shows some common hardware architectures that are used by UNIX as well as their types.

**Table 1-1**    Common UNIX hardware architectures and processor types

| Architecture | Type |
| --- | --- |
| Alpha | RISC |
| Advanced RISC Machine (ARM) | RISC |
| IBM RS/6000 Series | RISC |
| Intel | CISC |
| Microprocessor without Interlocked Pipeline Stages (MIPS) | RISC |
| Motorola 68000 Series | RISC |
| Precision Architecture-RISC (PA-RISC) | RISC |

**Table 1-1**    Common UNIX hardware architectures and processor types (continued)

| Architecture | Type |
| --- | --- |
| PowerPC | RISC |
| Scalable Processor Architecture (SPARC) and Ultra SPARC | RISC |

**NOTE**

Another more recent variant of the processor types shown in Table 1-1 is the Intel Itanium processor, which uses CISC technology in parallel. As a result, it is commonly termed the **Explicitly Parallel Instruction Computing (EPIC)** architecture.

Regardless of the hardware architecture, the key software elements of the UNIX operating system are the same; thus, software created for a specific hardware architecture can be adapted to other architectures with little difficulty. This feature of UNIX is known as **application independence** and is attractive to many commercial software developers.

## UNIX Is Scalable

Many companies and institutions use computers to perform extraordinarily large calculations that would be unsuitable for most computers. To satisfy these tasks, companies may purchase computers with multiple CPUs, which can work together to distribute the load and perform the same tasks faster. The ability for a computer to increase workload as the number of processors increases is known as **scalability**.

UNIX can take advantage of several different processors in a single computer using one of two methods: **symmetric multiprocessing (SMP)** and **asymmetric multiprocessing (ASMP)**. SMP allows the same operating system and memory use of both processors simultaneously for any task, whereas ASMP refers to a system where each processor is given a certain role or set of tasks to complete independent of the other processors.

## UNIX May Be Clustered

Although it may seem logical to purchase computers that have a large number of processors, the performance of a computer relative to the number of processors decreases as you add processors to a computer. In other words, a computer with 64 processors does not handle 64 times as much work as one processor due to physical limitations within the computer hardware itself; a computer with 64 processors may only perform 50 times as much work as a single processor.

As a result of this limitation, many companies cluster several smaller computers together to work as one large computer. This **cluster** approach results in much better scalability; 64 computers with one processor each working toward a common goal can handle close to 64 times as much as a single processor. One example of this approach to computing is the movie industry. DreamWorks SKG has used clusters of UNIX computers to create animated movies in much less time than previous films of the same nature. Another example is Shared Hierarchical Academic Research Computing Network (SHARCnet) in Ontario, Canada, where several universities develop and use clusters of UNIX computers for calculating scientific and engineering data.

## UNIX Roles

All of the features of the UNIX operating system enable it to function in different environments in a variety of roles, including:

- Network/Internet server
- File and print server
- Application server
- Supercomputer
- Scientific workstation
- Office workstation

## THE HISTORY OF UNIX

Much of the research and development that led to the UNIX operating system came from the Multiplexed Information and Computing Service (MULTICS) project that was started in 1965 by the Massachusetts Institute of Technology (MIT), General Electric (GE), and AT&T Bell Laboratories. The MULTICS project used a GE645 mainframe computer to reveal better ways of developing operating systems that regulate the amount of time each process has to use the processor. (Operating systems that do this today are referred to as time-sharing operating systems.) Unfortunately, the project was too costly to pursue and it was abandoned in 1969.

Ken Thompson, one of the original researchers on the MULTICS project, continued to experiment with operating system development after the project was abandoned. In 1969, he developed an operating system that ran on the Digital Equipment Corporation (DEC) PDP-7 computer. Thompson affectionately called this operating system UNICS, because it was based on MULTICS, but was much less complex. This name was later changed to UNIX.

Shortly thereafter, Dennis Ritchie invented the C programming language that was used on Ken Thompson's UNIX operating system. The C programming language was a revolutionary language at the time. Most programs at the time needed to be written specifically for the hardware of the computer, which involved referencing volumes of information regarding the hardware in order to write a simple program. However, the C programming language was much easier to use to write programs, and it was possible to run a program on several different machines without having to rewrite the code. The UNIX operating system was rewritten in the C programming language in 1973. By the late 1970s, the UNIX operating system ran on different hardware platforms, which was something that the computing world had never seen until that time. Because UNIX could be used on multiple hardware platforms, it was called a portable operating system.

Unfortunately, the company Ken Thompson and Dennis Ritchie worked for, AT&T Bell Laboratories, was restricted by a federal court order from marketing UNIX. Instead, AT&T Bell Laboratories continued to develop new versions of UNIX and sold the rights to use them to several different companies that in turn marketed their own type of UNIX; these types are commonly referred to as different **UNIX flavors**.

At the same time, AT&T also gave free copies to universities, which displayed great interest in UNIX during the early 1970s. One such university was the University of California at Berkeley, which released its own flavor of UNIX called Berkeley Software Distribution (BSD) in 1974.

By the late 1970s, BSD UNIX was adopted as the primary operating system for the U.S. Department of Defense Advanced Research Projects Agency (DARPA). Around the same time, AT&T's sixth version of UNIX was developed into the first commercially available version of UNIX. By 1980, thousands of commercial UNIX systems existed worldwide mainly running on DEC PDP-11 and VAX computers. Figure 1-4 depicts a magazine advertisement from this time period marketing version 7 of AT&T Bell UNIX.

In 1982, AT&T released System III UNIX (System I and II never existed), and the University of California at Berkeley released BSD UNIX version 3. Both of these new versions of UNIX were based on version 7 of the AT&T Bell UNIX, but they were very different in philosophy and appearance. Sun Microsystems Inc. also formed in 1982 to develop and sell BSD UNIX in the corporate and academic markets on their own hardware architecture.

By 1983, AT&T released System V UNIX (System IV was never released), resulting in two distinct streams of UNIX at the time: the AT&T System V stream and the BSD stream. Companies that developed and marketed UNIX took direction from one of these two streams. However, the differences between these two streams diminished over time as features from one stream were incorporated into the other, and vice versa. The most prominent example of this was when Sun Microsystems and AT&T combined many of the benefits of System V UNIX and BSD UNIX to develop System V Release 4 in 1989.

In addition, the Institute of Electrical and Electronics Engineers, Inc. (IEEE) created a standard called **Portable Operating System Interface (POSIX)** in 1986 to address how operating systems interface with application programs and to provide a way to standardize many of the different UNIX flavors that appeared during this time. The *X* in the name POSIX reflects that it was heavily influenced by the UNIX operating system. Most UNIX flavors, regardless of their stream, have adhered to POSIX standards since the late 1980s.

In 1991, a Finnish student named Linus Torvalds released a free version of UNIX called **Linux**. Since then, Linux has been freely and aggressively developed by volunteers worldwide and is one of the most common UNIX operating systems used today. Linux was not based on the original AT&T UNIX source code, and, as a result, it is not a true UNIX flavor. However, it is commonly considered its own flavor of UNIX since it has incorporated many of the features used in both BSD and System V UNIX.

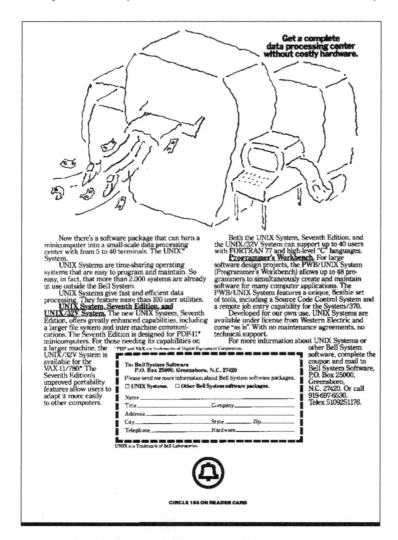

**Figure 1-4**    Marketing AT&T version 7 UNIX

By 1993, two free versions of BSD UNIX called FreeBSD and NetBSD appeared on the scene due to the closing of the BSD project at the University of California at Berkeley. In 1998, System V Release 5 evolved with the introduction of Santa Cruz Operations (SCO) UnixWare 7, and, in 2000, Apple Computers Inc. introduced the first user-friendly version of UNIX called OS/X.

Figure 1–5 depicts a timeline representing the development of the different streams of UNIX.

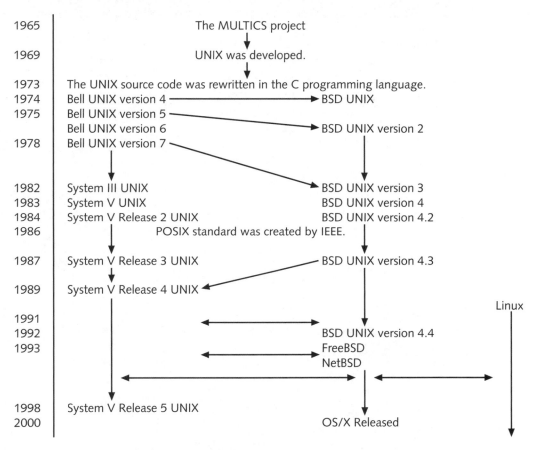

**Figure 1-5**   The UNIX development timeline

All mainstream flavors of UNIX today are POSIX compliant, and the differences between Linux, BSD, and System V UNIX today are minimal—filesystem features and the syntax of a few commands being among the most visible differences. System V UNIX is much more common today than BSD UNIX, and many UNIX flavors such as Solaris and Irix were initially BSD and later switched to System V. Table 1-2 lists some common flavors of UNIX, their manufacturers, and types.

**Table 1-2**   Common UNIX flavors

| Flavor | Manufacturer | Architectures |
|--------|--------------|---------------|
| A/UX | Apple Computer Inc. | Motorola 68000 Series |
| AIX | International Business Machines (IBM) | IBM RS/6000 Series |

**Table 1-2**   Common UNIX flavors (continued)

| Flavor | Manufacturer | Architectures |
|---|---|---|
| Digital UNIX (formerly OSF/1) | DEC | Alpha |
| FreeBSD | BSD | Intel and Alpha |
| Hewlett-Packard UNIX (HP-UX) | Hewlett-Packard Inc. | PA-RISC and Intel |
| Irix | Silicon Graphics Inc. | MIPS |
| Mac OS/X | Apple Computer Inc. | PowerPC |
| Linux | Not applicable | Intel, Alpha, ARM, SPARC, Ultra SPARC, MIPS, PowerPC, Motorola 68000 Series, PA-RISC, and RS/6000 |
| NetBSD | BSD | Intel, Alpha, ARM, SPARC, Ultra SPARC, MIPS, PowerPC, and Motorola 68000 Series |
| NCR MP-RAS | NCR Corporation | Intel |
| Openserver | Formerly SCO and Caldera International, now the SCO Group | Intel |
| SCO UNIX | SCO | Intel |
| Solaris | Sun Microsystems Inc. | SPARC, Ultra SPARC, and Intel |
| TRU64 | Formerly DEC and Compaq, now owned by Hewlett-Packard | Alpha |
| Ultrix | Formerly DEC and Compaq, now owned by Hewlett-Packard | Alpha |
| UnixWare | Formerly Novell, Unix Systems Laboratories (USL), SCO, and Caldera International, now owned by the SCO Group | Intel |
| XENIX | Formerly Microsoft and SCO | Intel |

# UNIX FLAVORS IN MORE DETAIL

As mentioned previously, few differences exist between UNIX flavors today due to POSIX standards and the sharing of features during UNIX development. Over 95% of all concepts introduced throughout this text are identical across all UNIX systems. These similarities include most user interfaces, file locations, and file formats, among others.

Most differences between UNIX flavors relate to different hardware architectures; for example, the system startup procedure is almost always specific to the hardware. For the relatively cheap and popular Intel platform, a **basic input/output system (BIOS)** program is available that lies in an **electrically erasable programmable read-only memory (EEPROM)** computer chip on the system motherboard. The BIOS stores system configuration information and locates the operating system stored on a hard disk inside the computer. An Intel BIOS typically consists of several user-friendly menus that enable users to configure Integrated Development Environment/Small Computer Systems Interface (IDE/SCSI) hard disks and other peripheral devices that can be changed during system startup by pressing Delete.

Like the Intel architecture, non-Intel architectures have an EEPROM computer chip that stores system configuration information as well as a program that locates the operating system on a hard disk in the computer; this program is commonly called a **bootstrap program**. The bootstrap program typically has another component called a **monitor** that runs continuously and can stop an operating system if it detects any software or hardware problems.

Like a BIOS, a bootstrap program can be configured. However, this configuration is usually done via an interactive command prompt that may host upwards of 500 commands specific to the hardware itself. As a result, bootstrap programs are versatile yet difficult to use. In addition to this, all hardware names used in the bootstrap program will have a format determined by the hardware manufacturer. For example, the third SCSI disk on the first SCSI controller of a SPARC computer may be called `/sbus@1,180000/ebus4,8000/sd1,3:a`, whereas the same disk in the bootstrap program of an Alpha computer could be named `dka500.5.0.1.1`. Thus, when using specific hardware architecture, ensure that you thoroughly understand the hardware before administrating the UNIX operating system on that architecture.

## UnixWare

Although it resembles all other versions of System V Release 4 UNIX, UnixWare was the first System V Release 5 UNIX in existence and is one of the most popular UNIX flavors in business because it runs on the widely available and inexpensive Intel platform. It is developed today by the SCO Group (formerly Caldera International) and focuses on integrating UNIX and Linux systems together in business environments.

 **NOTE** The flavor of UNIX that is demonstrated in this text is UnixWare, because it is widely available on the common Intel platform. In addition to this, any differences between UnixWare and other UNIX flavors will be identified when they arise. Because covering the differences between all UNIX flavors is impractical for any text, this discussion is limited to UnixWare, Solaris, and HP-UX UNIX because they are commonly used in industry today.

## Solaris

Solaris is one of the oldest UNIX flavors available. Bill Joy, the co-founder of Sun Microsystems, was the original developer of BSD UNIX in the 1970s. Solaris was initially called the SunOS when it was released by Sun Microsystems in 1982 and is widely used in academic and business environments today, primarily on the SPARC and Ultra SPARC architectures. Sun Microsystems and Solaris have achieved great fame in the past two decades for creating technologies that have become standard across all UNIX; two of these include the **Network File System (NFS)** for sharing data files between UNIX computers and the **Network Information System (NIS)** for sharing configuration files between UNIX computers.

## Hewlett-Packard UNIX (HP-UX)

Since HP-UX was first released in 1986, it has become one of the most popular UNIX flavors in large-scale computing environments. HP-UX runs primarily on the PA-RISC architecture, but newer versions also run on the Intel Itanium architecture.

## UNIX RESOURCES

Continuous development has made UNIX a powerful and versatile operating system. However, this development has also increased the complexity of UNIX and UNIX resources available on the Internet. Newcomers to UNIX may find this bounty of resources intimidating, but there are some simple rules that make finding particular types of UNIX resources easier. Understanding how to navigate the Internet to find these resources is a valuable skill to develop.

By far, the easiest way to locate resources on any topic is by using a **search engine** such as *www.google.com* where you can simply put in a phrase representing what you are searching for and receive a list of Web sites that contain relevant material. Because a plethora of UNIX-related Web sites is available on the Internet, a search of the word "UNIX" yields thousands of results. You may find that you need to narrow down and be more specific in your search in order to obtain a list of Web sites that likely contain the information you desire. Therefore, it is very important to approach UNIX documentation by topic; otherwise, you may be searching for hours through several Web sites to find the resources you need. In addition, specifying a certain flavor of UNIX in a search engine also reduces the number of results displayed.

Each UNIX flavor is maintained by a certain company or organization as discussed earlier in this chapter. These companies or organizations often host valuable UNIX information and documentation on their own Web site. For example, to find documentation on Solaris UNIX, you can visit *www.sun.com* since Solaris is developed by Sun Microsystems. Similarly, *www.sco.com* and *www.hp.com* host information about SCO UnixWare and HP-UX, respectively.

Because UNIX has been common in academic environments since the 1970s, most university Web sites offer UNIX tutorials and other useful information such as **Frequently Asked Questions (FAQs)**. Visiting a university Web site and searching for the word "UNIX" often displays links to this information.

Also, many UNIX magazines are available on the market today for administrators, users, and developers. Often these magazines host Web sites of the same name that have links to other UNIX resources as well. For example, the SysAdmin magazine can be accessed on the Internet at *www.sysadminmag.com*.

Web sites host valuable information, but most do not provide any means for users to communicate with each other. This functionality is provided by **Usenet**, which enables users to post messages in forums called **newsgroups** and enables other users to read and reply to those messages. Newsgroups are sometimes referred to as computer bulletin boards and are similar to bulletin boards found around a school campus and in other public places.

Newsgroup forums are grouped according to topic. Posting to a newsgroup is often a very quick way to find the solution to a problem, because people who read the posting are likely to have had the same problem and found a solution. Some newsgroup forums are moderated by a specific person or group. The moderators edit messages before they are posted to ensure they fit the forum's theme. This ensures proper newsgroup etiquette, which dictates that before posting a question, you must search previous postings to ensure that the question has not already been asked and answered, and that only messages relevant to the newsgroup topics are posted.

You can learn more about using Usenet newsgroups by visiting *www.usenet.org* or searching the Usenet newsgroups available on the Internet at *groups.google.com*.

## UNIX CERTIFICATION

As technology advances, so does the need for educated people to manage technology. One of the principal risks that companies take is the hiring of qualified people to administer, use, or develop programs for UNIX, and different people have different skill levels. To lower this risk, companies seek people who have demonstrated proficiency in certain technical areas. Although this proficiency may be demonstrated in the form of practical experience, practical experience alone is often not enough for companies when hiring for certain technical positions.

Certification exams have become a standard benchmark for technical ability and are sought after by many companies. The format of these **certification exams** can vary based on the technical complexity of the subject area, but usually the exams involve a multiple-choice computer test administered by an approved testing center. Hundreds of thousands of computer-related certification exams are written worldwide each year, and the certification process is likely to increase in importance in the future.

**TIP**  It is critical to recognize that certification does not replace ability, but demonstrates it. An employer may have 30 qualified applicants and part of the hiring process will likely be a demonstration of ability. It is unlikely the employer will incur the cost and time it takes to test all 30; it is more likely that the employer will look for benchmark certifications that indicate a base ability and then test this smaller subgroup.

Furthermore, certifications are an internationally administered and recognized standard. Although an employer may not be familiar with the criteria involved in achieving a computer science degree from a particular university in Canada or a certain college in Texas, certification exam criteria is well published on Web sites and hence well known. In addition, it does not matter in which country the certification exam is taken as the tests are standardized and administered by the same authenticating authority using common rules.

Certifications come in two broad categories: vendor specific and vendor neutral. For **vendor-specific** certifications, the vendor of a particular operating system or program sets the standards to be met and creates the exams. Obtaining one of these certifications demonstrates knowledge of a particular product or operating system. For example, Microsoft, Novell, Sun, Hewlett-Packard, and Oracle all have vendor-specific certifications for their products.

**Vendor-neutral** exams demonstrate knowledge in a particular area, but not for any specific product or brand of product. In either case, the organizations that create the certification exams and set the standards strive to ensure that the exams are of the highest quality and integrity to be used as a true benchmark worldwide.

Many UNIX vendors offer vendor-specific certification exams; however, since most UNIX knowledge is transferable from one UNIX flavor to another, UNIX certification is seen as somewhat vendor neutral by the computer industry. Thus, anyone who has taken the tests for Solaris certifications have demonstrated enough UNIX ability such that they may also be hired to administer OpenUNIX or HP-UX systems.

Most UNIX certification exams have multiple parts—there are typically systems administration examinations and network administration examinations. One certification track that is offered by the SCO Group for UnixWare is the Master Advanced Certified Engineer (ACE) program, which consists of three certifications:

- Certified Systems Administrator (CSA)—formerly Certified Unix Systems Administrator (CUSA)
- ACE
- Master ACE

The CSA certification tests normal systems administration tasks, whereas the ACE tests network administration tasks. The Master ACE certification can be taken on one of two topics: Shell programming or clustering. This textbook focuses on topics that are included on the CSA certification test.

1

## CHAPTER SUMMARY

❏ Operating systems control the hardware of a computer, execute applications, and provide user interfaces.

❏ UNIX is a multiuser, multitasking, and scalable operating system that is available for most hardware architectures.

❏ UNIX was developed in 1969 from the MULTICS project headed by AT&T. UNIX development has since divided into two streams: AT&T System V and BSD.

❏ Several different flavors of UNIX have been developed in the past two decades; they differ in manufacturer, hardware architecture, and stream.

❏ POSIX and the sharing of ideas have standardized most features of different UNIX flavors; as a result, most knowledge is transferable from one UNIX flavor to another.

❏ Often the largest differences between UNIX flavors relate to system hardware terminology, whereas most commands are identical between UNIX flavors.

❏ A wide variety of documentation and resources is available for UNIX in the form of Internet Web sites, FAQs, and newsgroups.

❏ Certification is a valuable means of demonstrating knowledge and ability to industry.

## KEY TERMS

**application** — Software that runs on an operating system and provides the user with specific functionality, such as word processing or financial calculation.

**application independence** — A program's capability to be easily adapted to hardware platforms other than the one for which it was originally written.

**asymmetric multiprocessing (ASMP)** — The process by which an operating system uses multiple processors yet assigns different tasks to each.

**basic input/output system (BIOS)** — A program used to locate and initialize the operating system on an Intel computer.

**bootstrap program** — A program used to locate and initialize the operating system on a non-Intel computer.

**certification exam** — A standard benchmark of technical ability administered by an authorized testing center, recognized in industry, and sought after by many companies.

**cluster** — Several smaller computers linked together to function as one large supercomputer.

**command-line interface** — A text-based user interface that requires that the user type commands to instruct the operating system.

**Complex Instruction Set Computing (CISC)** — The hardware architecture type commonly used by the Intel architecture.

**device driver** — Software that contains instructions that the operating system uses to control and interact with a specific type of computer hardware.

**electrically erasable programmable read-only memory (EEPROM)** — A specialized chip that is able to retain information in the absence of power and whose information store can be altered. Also referred to as nonvolatile RAM (NVRAM).

**Explicitly Parallel Instruction Computing (EPIC)** — A hardware architecture type that computes all tasks in parallel.

**Frequently Asked Questions (FAQs)** — A list, usually posted on a Web site, where answers to commonly posed questions can be found.

**GNU Object Model Environment (GNOME)** — One of the GUI environments that is available on some flavors of UNIX.

**graphical user interface (GUI)** — The GUI is the component of an operating system that provides a user-friendly interface, comprising graphics or icons to represent desired tasks. Users can point and click to execute a command rather than having to know and use proper command-line syntax.

**hardware** — The tangible parts of a computer, such as the network boards, video card, hard disk drives, printers, and keyboards.

**hardware architecture** — A configuration of computer hardware that has a specific type of CPU; three types of hardware architectures are available: RISC, CISC, and EPIC.

**hardware platform** — *See also* Hardware architecture.

**K Desktop Environment (KDE)** — One of the GUIs available for some flavors of UNIX.

**Linux** — A widely used UNIX flavor originated by Linus Torvalds.

**monitor** — The part of the bootstrap program that halts an operating system if any hardware or software problems are detected.

**multitasking** — An operating system's capability to run two or more tasks at one time; the operating system then regulates the time each process has to execute on the processor.

**multiuser** — An operating system's capability to allow access by more than one user at a time.

**Network File System (NFS)** — A distributed file system designed by Sun Microsystems that allows computers to share data stored on them with other computers on the network.

**Network Information System (NIS)** — A network service designed by Sun Microsystems that enables UNIX computers to share configuration information with other computers on the network.

**newsgroup** — A group of messages that users may add or respond to. The worldwide collection of newsgroups is called Usenet.

**operating system** — Software used to control and directly interact with computer hardware components.

**Portable Operating System Interface (POSIX)** — An IEEE standard that has led to the standardization of many operating systems including most UNIX flavors.

**process** — A program loaded into memory and running on the processor performing a specific task.

**program** — Sets of instructions that understand how to interact with the operating system and computer hardware to perform specific tasks; they are stored as a file on media, such as a hard disk drive.

**Reduced Instruction Set Computing (RISC)** — A hardware architecture type that is commonly used today on computers that require high performance.

**scalability** — The ability for a system to increase its performance as the number of processors increase.

**search engine** — An Internet Web site such as *www.google.com* or *www.dogpile.com* where a person types in a phrase representing what is being searched for and receives a list of Web sites that contain relevant material.

**server** — A computer configured with network services. Other computers may access these services from across a computer network.

**software** — Programs stored on a storage device in a computer that provide a certain function when executed.

**symmetric multiprocessing (SMP)** — The process by which an operating system uses multiple processors to perform a single task.

**system services** — Applications that are integral to the operating system and enable it to perform specialized tasks.

**UNIX flavors** — Different versions of the UNIX operating system.

**UNIX** — The first true multitasking, multiuser operating system, developed by Ken Thompson and Dennis Ritchie.

**Usenet** — A worldwide system used to exchange ideas and information in forums called newsgroups.

**user interface** — The program that a human uses to interact with an operating system.

**vendor-neutral certification** — Certification that is broad based and not restricted to one type of operating system.

**vendor-specific certification** — Certification that is focused and restricted to one type of operating system.

---

# REVIEW QUESTIONS

1. Computers consist of physical components and logical components. The logical components of a computer that understand how to work with the physical components are referred to as _____.

    a. hardware

    b. records

    c. software

    d. processors

2. Operating system software is necessary for a computer to function. True or False?

3. UNIX is a _____ and _____ operating system.

   a. production, stable

   b. multiuser, multitasking

   c. processing, operating

   d. large, useful

4. Which of the following people is credited with creating the UNIX operating system? (Choose all that apply.)

   a. Dennis Ritchie

   b. Richard Stallman

   c. Linus Torvalds

   d. Ken Thompson

5. Which standard GUI environment is available on most UNIX systems?

   a. GNOME

   b. CDE

   c. KDE

   d. RPM

6. Which of the following is the best definition of certification?

   a. an accurate measure of practical performance

   b. a globally recognized benchmark that is used by companies when hiring staff

   c. a test that must be taken to become a member of the UNIX newsgroup

   d. a list of supported hardware available for a particular flavor of UNIX

7. Which of the following is a general type of certification? (Choose all that apply.)

   a. vendor neutral

   b. globally unique

   c. vendor specific

   d. vendor unique

8. In what year was the UNIX operating system developed?

   a. 1961

   b. 1969

   c. 1973

   d. 1980

1

9. Which of the following is a common method of obtaining support for UNIX?

   a. documents that shipped with the software when it was bought

   b. the software vendor's Web site

   c. searching the Internet for information related to your concern and flavor of UNIX via a search engine

   d. Internet newsgroups

   e. all the above

10. In what advanced language was UNIX rewritten?

   a. POSIX

   b. C

   c. C++

   d. Perl

11. UNIX was developed as a result of the _____ project.

   a. UNICS

   b. MULTICS

   c. UNISYS

   d. BSD

12. What term describes multiple computers configured and joined together to act as one large supercomputer?

   a. grouping

   b. cluster

   c. SMP

   d. hive

   e. flock

13. What computer chip stores system hardware configuration information and is used to locate the operating system files during computer startup?

   a. EEPROM

   b. CMOS

   c. BIOS

   d. CISC

14. What is one of the largest differences among UNIX flavors?

   a. the hardware architecture used

   b. the GUI used

   c. the commands used to perform system tasks

   d. the formats used by configuration files

15. What generic term is used to refer to the sets of instructions that understand how to use the hardware of a computer?

    a. process

    b. software

    c. POSIX

    d. program

16. Which of the following user interfaces is available in UNIX? (Choose all that apply.)

    a. command line

    b. preprocessor

    c. GUI

    d. menu based

17. Which of the following is the standard that defines how operating systems interact with applications programs to which most major flavors of UNIX have adhered?

    a. System V

    b. BSD

    c. GNOME

    d. POSIX

    e. RICS

18. Which of the following refers to an operating system's capability to use more than one processor to improve performance?

    a. spatial architecture

    b. application independence

    c. scalability

    d. clustering

19. Which of the following streams of UNIX emerged in the early 1980s? (Choose all that apply.)

    a. System V

    b. version 7

    c. BSD

    d. POSIX

20. Which of the following refers to the ease of writing applications for several platforms?

    a. spatial architecture

    b. application independence

    c. scalability

    d. clustering

1

## DISCOVERY EXERCISES

1. The project organizer for a university computer science fair contacts you and asks you to organize a forum that discusses the origins of the UNIX operating system. Topics should include how it has evolved and split into competing flavors, how it maintains common standards and structure, and how it continues to develop. Prepare a bulleted list of the major topics that you will discuss and write down some sample questions that you anticipate from the participants as well as your responses.

2. Provided you have a functional Web browser and an Internet connection, research three different flavors of UNIX on the Internet. Record where you went to obtain your information, and compare and contrast the different flavors with regards to the strengths of each. Once you are finished, locate and visit at least two UNIX newsgroups. How did you locate them and what topics are available on each? Find two questions per newsgroup posted by a user in need of a solution to a problem and follow the thread of responses suggested by others to solve that problem.

3. In 1993, AT&T sold its UNIX source code to another company. Since then, it has been sold again. Provided you have Internet access and a functional Web browser, search the Internet to find out who currently owns the rights to the original AT&T source code.

4. Use the Internet or any other source of information to research the POSIX standard. Summarize its purpose and features in a small report. When you are finished, use the Internet or any other source of information to research a new standard called Unix98. Compare and contrast the POSIX standard with the Unix98 standard.

5. Provided you have an Internet connection and a functional Web browser, research some of the differences between BSD and System V UNIX.

6. While out to dinner with friends, conversation turns to the topic of careers. Your friends understand your desire to work with computers and applaud your desire to learn new topics; however, some of them do not understand why you spend time, energy, and money on certification. How would you explain the process and benefits of certification to your friends, with reference to UNIX certification?

# 2

# INSTALLING THE UNIX OPERATING SYSTEM

**After reading this chapter and completing the exercises, you will be able to:**

♦ Gather the appropriate hardware and software information necessary to install UNIX

♦ Install the UnixWare 7 operating system using good practices

In this chapter, you will examine a typical UNIX installation using UnixWare 7 on the Intel hardware architecture. You will learn about the information that you need prior to beginning a UNIX installation, as well as the methods that can be used to obtain this information. Next, you will explore the steps involved during a UnixWare 7 installation, where you will use the information gathered earlier.

# GATHERING PRE-INSTALLATION INFORMATION

Prior to purchasing and installing the UNIX operating system, you should gather several pieces of information regarding the hardware in your computer and the software settings that you require for the UNIX system. Because there are many pieces of hardware and software information to document, it is good form to complete a **pre-installation checklist**, which contains all important installation information. Table 2-1 shows a typical pre-installation checklist; the items in this checklist will be discussed throughout this chapter.

**Table 2-1**    Sample pre-installation checklist

| CPU (type and MHz) | Intel Pentium III 800 MHz |
|---|---|
| RAM (MB) | 256MB |
| Keyboard model and layout | 101-key U.S. keyboard |
| Mouse model and device | 2-button Microsoft Intellimouse connected to PS/2 port |
| Hard disk type (IDE primary master, SCSI Disk 3, and so on) | IDE primary master |
| Hard disk size (MB)<br>Size of UNIX partition<br>/ filesystem size<br>swap slice size<br>/home filesystem size | 40GB<br>40GB<br>20GB<br>500MB<br>10GB |
| System node name | unix1 |
| Network card Internet Protocol (IP) configuration (IP address, netmask, default router, Domain Name Service [DNS] servers, and domain name) | DHCP:  not used<br>IP address:  3.4.5.6<br>Netmask:  255.0.0.0<br>Default router:  3.0.0.1<br>DNS servers:  192.168.1.5, 10.5.22.1<br>Domain name:  course.com |
| Packages to install | All available packages |
| Number of users | 35 |
| Video card make and model | Cirrus Logic GD 5446—Revision u |

## Gathering Hardware Information

All operating systems require a minimum amount of computer hardware (such as RAM, hard disk space, and CPU type) to function properly because operating systems are a series of software programs that interact with and control computer hardware. Although most hardware purchased today is sufficient to run the UNIX operating system, it is nonetheless important to ensure that a computer meets the minimum hardware requirements before performing an installation.

These minimum hardware requirements can be obtained from several sources. If the operating system was obtained on CD-ROM, a printed manual or file on the CD-ROM may specify these requirements. You can also find the minimum hardware requirements for most operating systems on the operating system's official Web sites. For the UnixWare 7 operating system, you can find the minimum and recommended hardware requirements on the Internet at *www.sco.com* or in Table 2-2.

**Table 2-2**   UnixWare 7 minimum and recommended hareware requirements

| CPU processor | Minimum: 486DX<br>Recommended: Pentium processor or higher |
| --- | --- |
| Physical memory (RAM) | Minimum: 16MB<br>Minimum for GUI: 32MB<br>Recommended for GUI: 64MB |
| Disk space free (hard disk drive) | Minimum: 500MB free space<br>Recommended: 1GB free space<br>Additional free space is required for any file storage or the installation of other software programs. |
| Additional drives | CD-ROM drive<br>3.5-inch floppy disk drive |
| Peripheral devices | All peripheral devices (such as video cards, disk controllers, and network cards) must be UnixWare compliant. |

Furthermore, each operating system supports only particular types of hardware components. To find out whether your hardware will work with UNIX, simply consult the manual that was shipped with the hardware, the hardware manufacturer's Web site, or the UNIX vendor's Web site. Many companies consult these resources prior to purchasing hardware for UNIX to avoid hardware support problems.

**NOTE**

To find out what hardware is supported by UnixWare 7, visit the SCO **Compatible Hardware Web Pages (CHWP)** on the Internet at *www.sco.com/chwp*.

You can use several tools and resources to fill in the hardware information sections of the pre-installation checklist. The computer manuals that are shipped with the computer system are examples of one such resource. Most computer manuals have the specifications of each computer component listed in a table at the end of the book or inside the front cover.

In addition, if you are planning to install UNIX on the Intel, MIPS, or Alpha architecture, the Windows operating system may already be present on the computer. In this case, you can use common Windows utilities to view hardware information. The most comprehensive of these utilities is the System Information tool, shown in Figure 2-1.

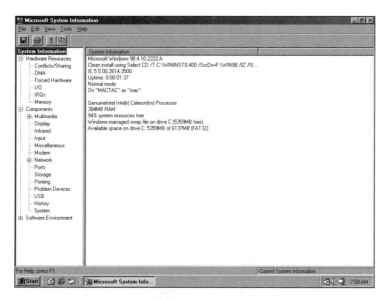

**Figure 2-1**    The Windows System Information tool

**NOTE**
To access the Windows System Information tool, simply navigate to the Windows Start Menu, Programs, Accessories, System Tools, System Information.

The Windows Device Manager (in the System applet of the Windows Control Panel) is another utility that can display most hardware information, as shown in Figure 2-2.

**NOTE**
To access the Windows 95/98/ME Device Manager, simply navigate to the Windows Start Menu, Settings, Control Panel, System, Device Manager. To access the Windows 2000/XP (Classic View) Device Manager, simply navigate to the Windows Start Menu, Settings, Control Panel, System, Hardware, Device Manager.

Another Windows utility that is useful for gaining hardware information regarding your video card and monitor is the Display applet of the Windows Control Panel, as shown in Figure 2-3.

**NOTE**
To access the Windows Display applet information regarding your video card and monitor, simply navigate to the Windows Start Menu, Settings, Control Panel, Display, Settings, Advanced.

Of course, other sources of the hardware information are available. For instance, the Intel architecture stores configuration information in a complementary metal-oxide semiconductor (CMOS) chip on the computer mainboard. The information in the CMOS chip is read by the BIOS when the computer is first turned on in order to initialize peripherals and perform a **power–on self test (POST)**. The POST displays output similar to Figure 2-4 when you first turn on the computer.

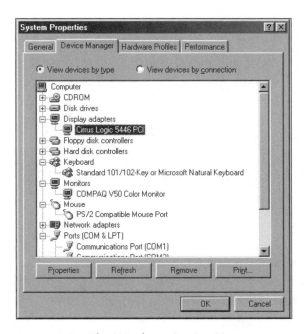

**Figure 2-2**    The Windows Device Manager

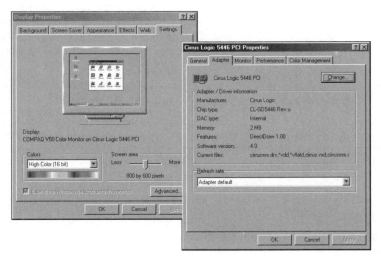

**Figure 2-3**    The Windows Display applet

```
Award Modular BIOS v4.51PG, AN Energy Star Ally
Copyright © 1984-98, Award Software, INC.


ASUS P2L-B ACPI BIOS Revision 1008


Award Plug and Play BIOS Extension v1.0A
Initializing Plug and Play Cards
Card-01: D-Link DE-220P PnP ISA Card
Card-01: Creative SB AWE64 PnP


PNP Init Completed


Detecting HDD Primary Master   ... QUANTUM FIREBALL CX6.4A
Detecting HDD Primary Slave    ... None
Detecting HDD Secondary Master ... ATAPI CDROM
Detecting HDD Secondary Slave  ... None




Press DEL to enter SETUP
01/28/99-i440LX-<P2L-B7>
```

**Figure 2-4**    A sample system startup screen

After the POST has completed, the BIOS looks for an operating system on a floppy, CD-ROM, or hard disk. Most settings used by the BIOS are configurable because they are stored on the CMOS chip, and most BIOSs enable you to choose these settings or view hardware information after the POST has completed by pressing Delete, as shown in Figure 2-4. If a user enters the BIOS setup utility, a screen such as the one shown in Figure 2-5 appears where you can configure devices and observe useful hardware information.

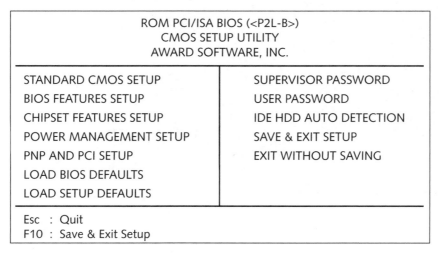

**Figure 2-5**    A typical system BIOS

The system BIOS setup utility looks very different from manufacturer to manufacturer; however, each utility roughly contains the same general types of information and configurations.

## Gathering Software Information

In addition to identifying hardware components to ensure that they are supported by the UNIX operating system and meet the minimum requirements, you should also identify the software components that will be used in the UNIX operating system. The UNIX installation program prompts you for these settings during the initial stages of the installation. This includes the filesystem configuration, system node name, Internet or network configuration parameters, required software packages, and security settings, as well as the number of users who are able to log in and use the system simultaneously for licensing purposes.

### Filesystem Configuration

UNIX systems organize the hard disk into sections called **partitions**. Hard disks can contain a maximum of four partitions. The table of all partition information for any particular hard disk is stored in the first readable sector outside all partitions. The partition information is called the **Master Boot Record (MBR)**.

The UNIX term "partition" is analogous to the Windows term "primary partition."

The MBR is also sometimes referred to as the Master Boot Block (MBB).

Each partition is then divided into smaller, more manageable sections called **slices**; a single partition may have up to 184 slices. The table of all slice information for a certain partition is called the **Volume Table of Contents (VTOC)**, which is stored in a special slice within the partition.

The UNIX term "slice" is analogous to the Windows term "logical drive."

Each slice in a partition can then store data directly on the hard disk for the system to read, or it can store information in unique files that the operating system can access by filename.

If slices must contain information in a file format, you must be prepared to store the files. To do this, create a **filesystem** on the slice that specifies how data should reside on the slice itself. UNIX can then access each filesystem if they are attached (or mounted) to a certain directory. When the computer stores data in that particular directory, it is physically stored on the respective filesystem on the hard drive.

In the Windows operating system, each drive letter (C:, D:, and E:) may correspond to a separate filesystem (such as FAT or NTFS) that resides on a partition on the hard drive. In UNIX, certain directories represent different filesystems that are stored on slices within a UNIX partition.

Many different types of filesystems are available to UNIX systems. Each one has different features and is specialized for a different use. Table 2-3 lists the commonly used UNIX filesystems and the flavors that support them.

**Table 2-3**    Common UNIX filesystems

| Filesystem | UNIX Flavors |
| --- | --- |
| Boot Filesystem (BFS) | UnixWare |
| CD-ROM Filesystem | UnixWare, Solaris, and HP-UX |
| DOS FAT Filesystem | UnixWare, Solaris, and HP-UX |
| High Performance Filesystem (HFS) | HP-UX |
| Journaled Filesystem (JFS) | HP-UX |
| NetWare-UNIX Client Filesystem (NUCFS) | UnixWare |
| Network Filesystem (NFS) | UnixWare, Solaris, and HP-UX |
| System V Filesystem (S5) | UnixWare, Solaris, and HP-UX |
| UNIX Filesystem (UFS) | UnixWare and Solaris |
| Veritas Filesystem (VxFS) (It is called the Journaled Filesystem [JFS] in HP-UX.) | UnixWare and HP-UX |

The default filesystem used in UnixWare 7 and HP-UX is the **Veritas Filesystem (VxFS)**; the default filesystem used in Solaris is the **UNIX Filesystem (UFS)**.

UNIX systems have a certain number of slices that must be created at minimum; some of these slices contain a filesystem and some of them do not. For UnixWare 7, only two slices must contain a filesystem: the slice that is mounted to the root directory in UNIX (/) and that can contain all of the files used by the operating system, applications, and users, and the slice that is mounted to the /stand directory in UNIX containing files that are used to load the UNIX operating system.

Not all UNIX flavors use the /stand filesystem.

As a general rule of thumb, the / filesystem should be double the size of the amount of packages to be installed. This ensures that enough working space is available for the operating system as well as room to add more files. In addition, the /stand filesystem should be at least 20MB.

Creating extra slices that contain filesystems makes UNIX more robust against filesystem errors; if the filesystem on one partition encounters an error, only data on one part of the system is affected, not the entire system (other filesystems). Because some directories in UNIX are used vigorously and, as a result, are more prone to failure, it is good practice to mount these directories to their own filesystem. Directories that are commonly mounted to separate slices include /home (for user home directories), /usr (for operating-system-related programs), /var (for system log files and temporary files), /tmp (for temporary files), and /opt (for additional programs).

UNIX requires some slices that do not contain a filesystem. These slices are never mounted to a directory and are used by the operating system only. A typical UnixWare 7 installation creates a slice that contains the VTOC and information used to boot the system (the BOOT slice), a slice that records any unusable sectors on the hard disk due to physical malfunction (the **ALTS TABLE**), and a slice used for **virtual memory** (also known as swap memory).

Virtual memory consists of an area on the hard disk that can be used (much like Windows uses its swap file or page file system) to store information that normally resides in physical memory (RAM) if the physical memory is being used excessively. Information is continuously swapped from physical memory to virtual memory on the hard disk and vice versa when programs are executed that require a great deal of resources on the computer. Typically, a swap slice should be at least the size of the physical RAM, but it can be larger if the UNIX system is intended to run large applications; many users make the swap partition twice the size of physical RAM to avoid any problems after installation.

To simplify filesystem administration, it is good form to create one partition that spans the entire hard disk and then divide that partition into the number of slices that are needed. Figure 2-6 depicts this approach.

Furthermore, the partition that contains the / filesystem must be marked active in the MBR; the active partition in the MBR is the partition that is searched at boot time for an operating system.

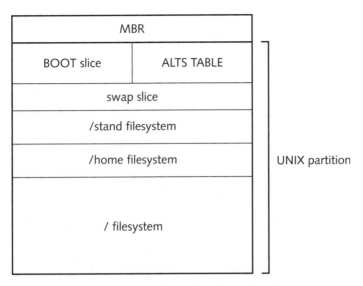

**Figure 2-6**  A typical UNIX hard disk configuration

## System Network Configuration

If you are installing a UNIX system to use or provide network services, then the installation program will prompt you for the necessary values to complete the configuration of the **network interface card (NIC)** in the computer. These values are usually assigned by the network administrator or Internet service provider (ISP) for the company. The following list summarizes these settings:

- **System node name**—Also known as the hostname of a computer, it is the name of the computer that is registered in DNS such that others can connect to it by name.

- **Domain name**—The name of the domain that is registered in DNS of which the computer is a part. The system node name and the domain name together make up the **Fully Qualified Domain Name (FQDN)**; a computer with the system node name of "www" and a domain name of "sco.com" would have the FQDN of "www.sco.com".

- **IP address**—This is the unique number assigned to the computer that enables it to participate on an IP network such as the Internet.

- **Netmask**—Also known as the network mask or subnet mask, this specifies which portion of the IP address identifies which logical network the computer is on.

- **Default router**—Also known as the default gateway or gateway of last resort, this specifies the address of a computer that accepts information from the local computer and sends it to other computers if the local computer cannot.

- **DNS servers**—These servers resolve FQDNs, such as *www.sco.com*, to IP addresses such that other computers can connect to them across the Internet. You can list more than one DNS server. The local computer will then try the second server in the list if the first one is unavailable, and so on.

You can configure the previous settings manually or have most of the settings automatically configured provided a **Dynamic Host Configuration Protocol (DHCP) server** exists on the network. Not all UNIX flavors allow this to be chosen during installation; if you are able to select the option to use DHCP during installation, the UNIX computer will attempt to get these settings from a DHCP server on the network. Alternatively, you can choose to configure the aforementioned network settings manually or by using DHCP after the installation has been completed.

## Package Selection

It is important to know which software packages are needed to customize the UNIX system to perform certain tasks before installation. These software packages require disk space, and, as a result, you should keep available disk space in mind when choosing software packages. For instance, in UnixWare, an installation may place over 500Mb of data on the hard disk. Regardless of the UNIX flavor, you are always prompted during installation to select a set of commonly used packages grouped by function; however, you can choose to customize this list and select only the individual packages needed. In addition, you can choose to install only the bare minimum set of packages and then add to them afterwards to avoid installing unnecessary packages; this is known as installing a **small footprint server** in UnixWare 7.

Regardless of the packages selected, most UNIX systems come with the following standard system packages:

- FTP server and client
- Telnet server and client
- LP printing service
- CDE
- NFS server
- E-mail server
- Web server

## Security Settings

Several hundred parameters that alter the security of a system can be set on a UNIX computer; the minimum password length required for user accounts and the decision to allow incoming FTP traffic are two examples. To simplify the selection of each of these parameters, most UNIX systems enable you to select a specific level of security called a **security profile**, which selects commonly used values for these parameters automatically. UnixWare 7 has four security profiles:

- Low—This profile sets parameter values for systems that have little need for security.

- Traditional—This profile sets parameter values that are commonly used.

- Improved—This profile sets parameter values that meet the minimum **C2** security requirements set by the U.S. Department of Defense Trusted Computer System Evaluation Criteria (TCSEC).

- High—This profile sets parameter values that meet the maximum C2 security requirements.

Many of the parameters that are discussed later in this textbook have different default values depending on the security profile chosen during installation.

# Purchasing UNIX

Once the hardware and software requirements have been identified, you should purchase the UNIX operating system from the appropriate vendor. Most UNIX vendors have different prices for different operating system uses. For example, you will not require a great deal of hardware or user support for a UNIX system that will be used as an e-mail server for a small company; thus, you may purchase a UNIX flavor that ships with only the software required for an e-mail server at a lower cost.

When purchasing UnixWare 7, you are given the option to purchase a **license** that is suited to your needs. This license is called an **edition license**. Each type of edition license supports only a certain number of concurrent users, hardware, and software. Table 2-4 lists the different UnixWare 7 edition license types.

**Table 2-4**   UnixWare 7 editions

| Edition Type | Supported Users | Supported Hardware | Supported Software |
|---|---|---|---|
| Base | 1 user | Up to 1 CPU and 1GB of memory | Standard UNIX software only |
| Business | 5 users | Up to 1 CPU and 4GB of memory | Standard UNIX software as well as Windows integration software (VisionFS) and network backup software (ARCServe) |
| Messaging | 1 user | Up to 2 CPUs and 4GB of memory | Standard UNIX software as well as Windows integration software (VisionFS), network backup software (ARCServe), and e-mail server software (Netscape Mail Server) |
| Departmental | 25 users | Up to 2 CPUs and 4GB of memory | Standard UNIX software as well as Windows integration software (VisionFS) and network backup software (ARCServe) |
| Enterprise | 50 users | Up to 4 CPUs and 16GB of memory | Standard UNIX software as well as Windows integration software (VisionFS), network backup software (ARCServe), and filesystem management tools (Online Data Manager) |
| Data Center | 150 users | Up to 8 CPUs and 32GB of memory | Standard UNIX software as well as Windows integration software (VisionFS), network backup software (ARCServe), filesystem management tools (Online Data Manager), and logging tools |

# PERFORMING THE UNIX INSTALLATION

**NOTE**

Although the UNIX operating system has many standard features across different flavors, the installation procedure may vary greatly from flavor to flavor since each UNIX vendor creates their own installation program specific to their supported hardware. However, all UNIX installations prompt the user for the same information, and once you are familiar with the installation procedure for one UNIX flavor, it is easy to transfer that knowledge to other flavors. Although most UNIX vendors enable you to install the operating system from shared files on a server across a computer network, this chapter examines the steps necessary to install a UnixWare 7 system from CD-ROM.

**NOTE** If you are installing UnixWare on a system that has SCSI hard disks, ensure that the / filesystem is configured on the first SCSI hard disk on the first SCSI controller to avoid problems.

Before installing UnixWare on a computer that has IDE hard disk controllers, you must take the following precautions:

- Ensure that the CD-ROM drive is not configured as an IDE secondary slave; UnixWare is unable to perform a file copy during the installation from a secondary slave device.

- If the secondary IDE controller does not have any devices on it, simply disable the secondary IDE controller in the computer's BIOS; otherwise, you will receive a controller timeout error immediately following the installation.

To install UnixWare 7 from CD-ROM, simply place the first UnixWare CD-ROM in the CD-ROM drive and turn on the computer; most computers automatically search for a startup program on the CD-ROM immediately after being turned on, which can then be used to start the installation of UnixWare. However, if the installation of UnixWare does not start when the CD-ROM is placed in the CD-ROM drive during computer startup, then you should first check to make sure that the system BIOS settings allow the CD-ROM to be searched at boot time. However, if the system BIOS allows booting from the CD-ROM and the UnixWare installation program still fails to start, you must create two installation floppy diskettes as well as a **host bus adapter (HBA) diskette**; the HBA diskette contains UnixWare device drivers that will be required during the installation.

Many Intel computers contain the Windows operating system on them before UNIX is installed. If this is the case with your system, note that you can use a Windows utility called the **ezcp utility** in the info\images directory on the first UnixWare 7 installation CD-ROM to create the three floppy diskettes required for installation. The ezcp program requires an image file that will be used to create the floppy boot disk; UnixWare supplies the following images:

- boot1.img is used to create the first floppy boot diskette.

- boot2.img is used to create the second floppy boot diskette.

- hba.img is used to create the HBA diskette.

To create these floppy diskettes from inside the Windows operating system, perform the following steps:

1. Insert the first UnixWare 7.1.1 installation CD-ROM disk into your CD-ROM drive.

2. Open a command prompt.

3. At the command prompt, type **d:** (if d: represents your CD-ROM drive).

4. At the command prompt, type **cd info\images** to change the current directory to the info\images directory.

5. At the command prompt, type **ezcp imagefile** (where *imagefile* is either boot1.img, boot2.img, or hba.img).

Regardless of whether you start the installation from the CD-ROM or from floppy disks, the remainder of the installation is the same. SCO distinguishes five general stages to installing UnixWare 7, which occur in the following order:

1. Interview—The user is prompted to configure most hardware and software settings.

2. Media extraction—Selected software packages are copied to the hard disk.

3. Software loading—Selected software packages are configured using the information specified during this stage.

4. Initial hard disk boot—The UnixWare 7 system is loaded for the first time using the configuration specified during the interview stage. At this point, you must configure the mouse settings.

5. Updates and layered products installation—You can configure any additional packages that are to be installed from the second and third UnixWare 7 CD-ROMs. The second UnixWare 7 CD-ROM is always required as it contains some mandatory UnixWare packages.

## The Interview Stage

The interview stage involves the most user interaction. It consists of the following substages:

- Language, keyboard, and license configuration
- Hardware configuration
- System node name and installation method selection
- Hard disk configuration
- Software selection
- Network configuration
- Time and security profile settings
- User account configuration

The following sections discuss each substage.

### Language, Keyboard, and License Configuration

After the first UnixWare 7 CD-ROM has been inserted into the CD-ROM drive of the computer, you will see the screen depicted in Figure 2-7 while waiting for a small copy of the UnixWare 7 operating system and installation program to be loaded into memory.

**Figure 2-7**    The UnixWare 7 splash screen

After the installation program has been loaded, you are then prompted for the language that will be used for the remainder of the installation process, as shown in Figure 2-8.

Upon pressing Enter, a welcome screen appears, as shown in Figure 2-9, that indicates the function keys used to maneuver the remainder of the installation process. Useful function keys and their definitions are listed at the bottom of most installation screens for the remainder of the installation.

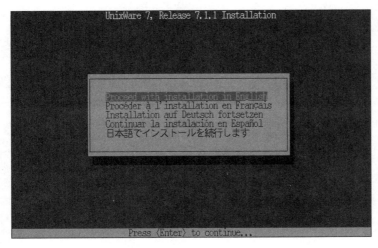

**Figure 2-8**    Choosing an installation language

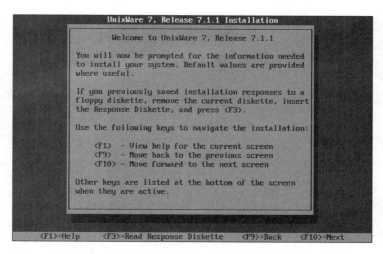

**Figure 2-9**    The installation welcome screen

Following this, you are prompted for information regarding the **locale**, which determines the character set (format of characters) that will be used when text is displayed on the screen in UnixWare. Because many choices are available, you are prompted to narrow down the selection by selecting the appropriate zone, as shown in Figure 2-10.

If you select the zone called Americas (Latin-1), then the choices for locales shown in Figure 2-11 appear. If you are unsure about which locale to choose, select the generic C (English) locale.

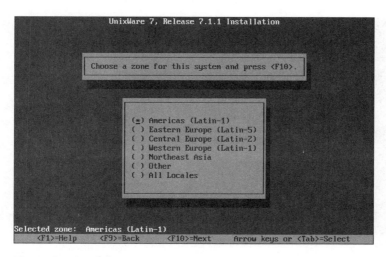

**Figure 2-10**    Selecting a zone

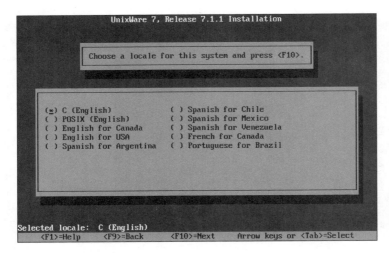

**Figure 2-11**    Selecting a locale

After the locale has been chosen, you are prompted for the type of keyboard that will be used with the character set, as shown in Figure 2-12.

Next, you must supply the appropriate license information that was purchased from SCO; this consists of a License Number, License Code, and optional License Data, as depicted in Figure 2-13. The License Number indicates the UnixWare edition that has been purchased. If you use the F8 key to defer licensing, you will receive a 60-day evaluation Business edition license.

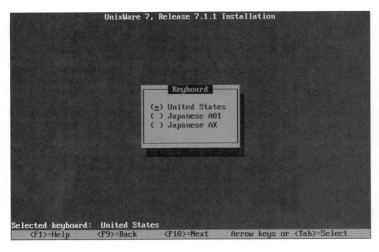

**Figure 2-12**    Selecting a keyboard type

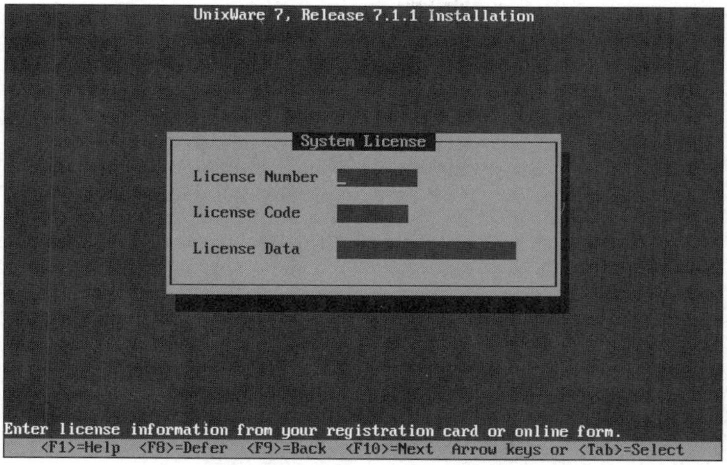

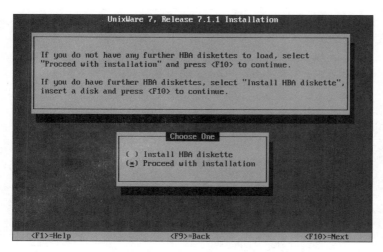

**Figure 2-13**    Supplying license information

## Hardware Configuration

The next stage is to configure the hardware information for UnixWare. If you have used floppy disks to start the installation, you will be prompted to insert the HBA diskette to load hardware device drivers into memory; otherwise, these device drivers are automatically loaded from the installation CD-ROM. When completed, you will be prompted to insert any additional HBA diskettes that have been provided by hardware manufacturers, as shown in Figure 2-14.

**Figure 2-14**    Configuring additional HBA diskettes

If you select Proceed with installation in Figure 2-14, the drivers that were loaded into memory previously will be activated by the operating system and you will then be asked to either configure hardware settings (such as interrupt request [IRQ] and input/output [I/O] address) manually using the Device Configuration Utility (DCU) or have UnixWare automatically detect them, as shown in Figure 2-15.

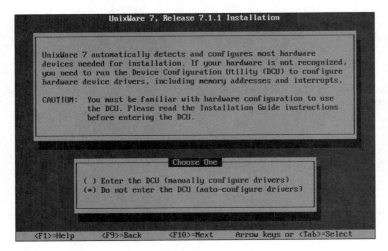

**Figure 2-15**   Configuring device drivers

 Although you may navigate back to previous screens during the installation, you may only enter the DCU once during an installation.

**NOTE**

If you choose to Enter the DCU in Figure 2-15, the screen shown in Figure 2-16 will appear.

**Figure 2-16**   The DCU

To configure hardware device settings, choose Hardware Device Configuration from Figure 2-16. This lists the configuration of all components, as shown in Figure 2-17. You may then configure the IRQ, I/O address range, memory address range, and direct memory access (DMA) for detected devices.

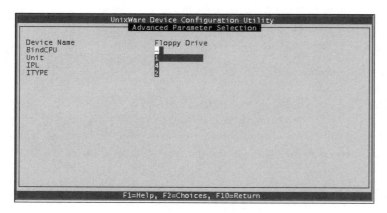

```
                  UnixWare Device Configuration Utility
                    Hardware Device Configuration
         Device Name        IRQ   IOStart   IOEnd    MemStart   MemEnd     DMA
       ================      ===   =======   =====    ========   ======     ===
   Y   Parallel Port         7     378       37f                                
   Y   Floppy Drive          6     3f0       3f7                             2  
   Y   I2O IOP               -     -         -                                  
   Y   Real Time Clock       8     -         -                                  
   Y   Keyboard & Display    1     60        62       a0000      bffff          
   Y   Keyboard & Display    -     64        64                                 
   Y   Direct Memory Access  -     0         1f                                 
   Y   Direct Memory Access  -     c0        df                              0  
   Y   Direct Memory Access  -     80        9f                                 
   Y   CMOS RAM              -     70        7f                                 
   Y   AT Platform (UP)      -     -         -                                  
   Y   UNKNOWN               -     -         -                                  
   Y   UNKNOWN               -     -         -                                  
   Y   PCI IDE               14    1f0       1f7                                
   Y   PCI IDE               15    170       177                                
   Y   UNKNOWN               0     -         -                                  
   Y   UNKNOWN               -     -         -        f8000000   fbffffff       
                    (Page Up/Page Down for more)
   TAB/arrow=Move, F1=Help, F2=Choices, F4=Verify, F6=Info, F7=Adv, F10=Return
```

**Figure 2-17**    Configuring hardware settings

**NOTE**    It is recommended that you manually configure parameters using the DCU if you have an older SCSI adapter in your computer; often the IRQ setting for these adapters is detected incorrectly.

In addition, pressing F7 while the cursor is on a certain hardware device enables you to configure advanced configuration parameters such as CPU to bind the hardware to if there are multiple CPUs in the computer (BindCPU), the IRQ priority (IPL), instance of the controller (unit), and the number used for IRQ sharing (ITYPE). Figure 2-18 shows the configuration of the advanced parameters for the floppy disk drive.

```
                  UnixWare Device Configuration Utility
                      Advanced Parameter Selection

   Device Name            Floppy Drive
   BindCPU                
   Unit                   1
   IPL                    4
   ITYPE                  2









                     F1=Help, F2=Choices, F10=Return
```

**Figure 2-18**    Configuring advanced hardware settings

The DCU also enables you to activate and deactivate device drivers that are currently loaded by the operating system; to do this, simply choose Software Device Drivers from Figure 2-16 and you will receive a list of device driver types, as shown in Figure 2-19. If you choose All Software Device Drivers from this screen, a list similar to that depicted in Figure 2-20 will appear. From this list, you can alter device driver support. An asterisk indicates that the device driver is loaded into the operating system.

**Figure 2-19**    Configuring software device drivers

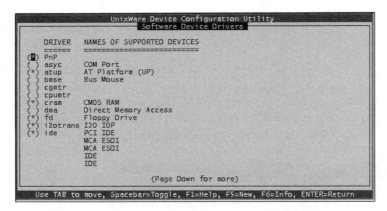

**Figure 2-20**    Selecting software device drivers

Regardless of whether you choose to configure device drivers manually using the DCU or automatically, they are tested after their configuration and any unused device drivers are removed from memory. If you selected incorrect parameters for a device in the DCU, you will receive an error message at this point to that nature.

## System Node Name and Installation Method Selection

After the hardware has been successfully configured, you are prompted for the system node name (also known as the hostname), as shown in Figure 2-21.

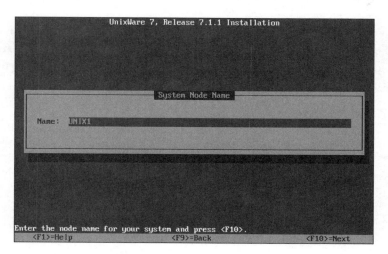

**Figure 2-21** Selecting a system node name

The system node name cannot start with a number and can contain only numbers and case-insensitive letters. The system node name can be up to 63 characters long; however, it is common practice to limit it to 7 characters or less to maintain compatibility with older UNIX computers.

Following the selection of the system node name, the UnixWare installation program prompts you for the source of the installation packages, as shown in Figure 2-22.

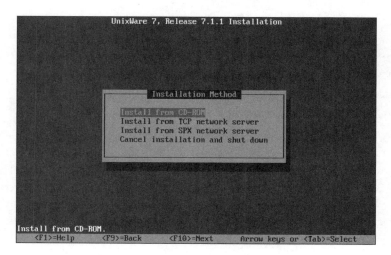

**Figure 2-22** Selecting an installation method

If your CD-ROM is not indicated in this list, it is likely configured as an IDE secondary slave.

**NOTE**

Although you can install from a computer on the network that is running either the **Internet Packet Exchange/Sequenced Packet Exchange (IPX/SPX) protocol** or Transport Control Protocol/Internet Protocol (TCP/IP) network protocols, these installation methods are beyond the scope of this text.

## Hard Disk Configuration

Following the selection of an installation method, you are required to configure the partitions, slices, and MBR of the hard disk. The first screen, shown in Figure 2-23, prompts you to choose the partition configuration for the first hard disk in the system.

 If you have more than one hard disk, you may configure up to two of them during installation.

**NOTE**

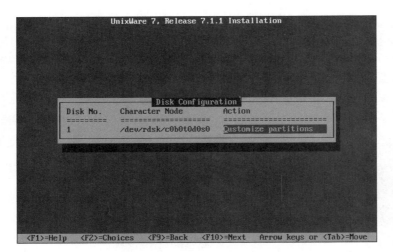

**Figure 2-23**    Configuring disk partitions

Upon pressing F2 at the screen shown in Figure 2-23, you are given the choice to create one UNIX partition that spans the entire hard disk automatically (Use whole disk for UNIX) or to manually create a UNIX partition (Customize partitions), as shown in Figure 2-24.

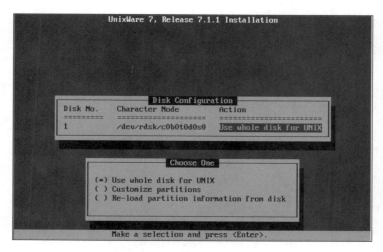

**Figure 2-24**    Partition options

If you choose Customize partitions in Figure 2-24, you will be taken to the screen depicted in Figure 2-25 where you may manually configure up to four partitions; at minimum, you must have one active UNIX partition.

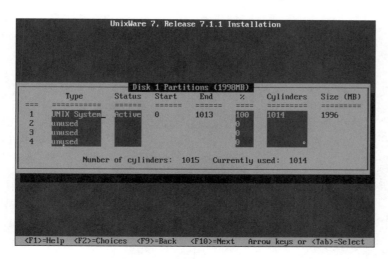

**Figure 2-25**    Manually configuring partitions

**NOTE**    If you are not using the whole disk for UNIX, ensure that the UNIX partition starts before the 1024th cylinder (the 8GB mark on most hard disks). If you don't, the system might not be able to find the UNIX operating system.

Following the creation of an active UNIX partition, you are prompted to either accept the default slices and filesystems created by the installation program inside this partition, or customize them, as shown in Figure 2-26.

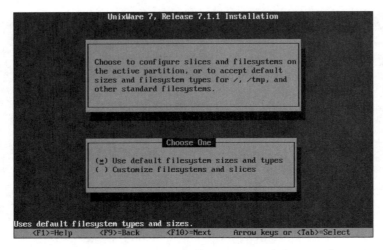

**Figure 2-26**    Selecting default filesystem and slice configuration

If you choose to Customize filesystems and slices from Figure 2-26, you will be given a screen similar to Figure 2-27 that has default values for most slices as well as the recommended filesystems and filesystem sizes for those slices.

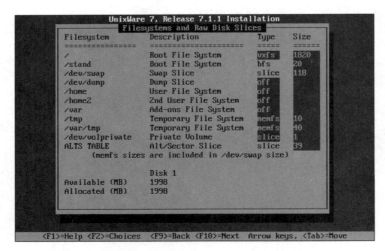

**Figure 2-27**    Customizing filesystems and slices

The /stand filesystem, ALTS TABLE, and swap slice are mandatory; thus, only their size may be changed. For all other slices or filesystems, their type and size may be changed.

To avoid using them in addition to the / filesystem, simply ensure that their type is set to off, as shown with the /home, /home2, and /var filesystems in Figure 2-27.

Most filesystems shown in Figure 2-27 enable the user to select between only the VxFS and UFS filesystems. However, the /tmp and /var/tmp filesystems allow the choice of memfs for their filesystem. The memfs filesystem is contained in physical and swap memory. Their contents are deleted when the system is shut down.

 **NOTE** Also notice from Figure 2-27 that the Dump Slice is disabled (this is the default setting). It contains the state of the operating system in memory in the case of an operating system failure. If you enable this slice, it should be at least the same size as the RAM in your computer. In addition, some programs require certain slices for their own use; one example of this is the Online Data Manager in UnixWare, which uses the Private Volume shown in Figure 2-27 to store configuration information.

 **NOTE** It is important to use memfs for the /tmp and /var/tmp filesystems if you want to use system recovery utilities later on.

 **NOTE** If you increase the size of one filesystem, you must decrease the size of another filesystem since the system initially allocates all space to slices within the UNIX partition.

After the slices and filesystems within the UNIX partition have been configured, you must choose disk options, as shown in Figure 2-28.

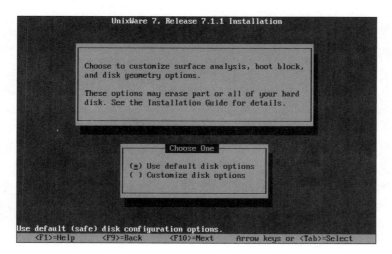

**Figure 2-28**  Selecting default disk options

If you choose the default disk options, the system will not scan the hard disk for bad blocks (damaged areas of the physical hard disk) and will install a new MBR that indicates the location of the active UNIX partition. If you choose to customize the disk options, you may alter the default disk options and reset the physical disk geometry, as shown in Figure 2-29. If you choose to reset the physical disk geometry, the MBR (and all partitions that are on the hard disk) will be destroyed and the installation will be restarted. Only choose this option if you want to erase data that is on the hard disk before installing UnixWare on it.

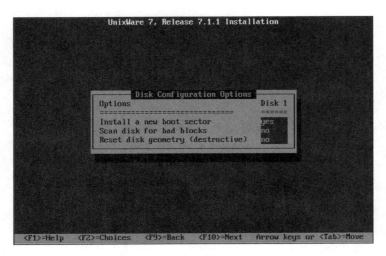

**Figure 2-29**    Customizing disk options

 Always ensure that the UnixWare installation program installs a new MBR; otherwise, you will not be able to boot the UnixWare operating system after installation.

**NOTE**

## Software Selection

After the disk options have been selected, you are prompted to choose the software that will be installed as part of the installation process, as shown in Figure 2-30. The default software that you are allowed to install is known as the **system profile** and depends on the UnixWare edition chosen. In addition, this software does not include any optional software packages that exist on the second and third installation CD-ROMs.

The system profiles in Figure 2-30 enable you to select the most common software packages for the edition (License-Based Defaults), all software packages (Full), or the bare minimum set of UNIX packages (Small Footprint Server). Alternatively, you can add or remove individual packages from the License-Based Defaults by choosing Customize Installation of Packages.

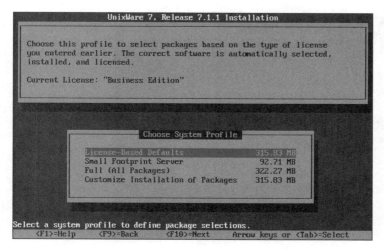

**Figure 2-30**    Selecting a system profile

 The GUI is not installed with the Small Footprint Server.

**NOTE**

## Network Configuration

The next few screens following the software package selection may vary depending on the NIC hardware in the computer. If your NIC was detected automatically by the installation program, a screen similar to Figure 2–31 will appear; however, if your NIC was not automatically detected, you will be prompted to configure your NIC manually and select its model from a list, as shown in Figures 2–32 and 2–33, respectively. Alternatively, you may choose to defer the configuration of the NIC in the computer.

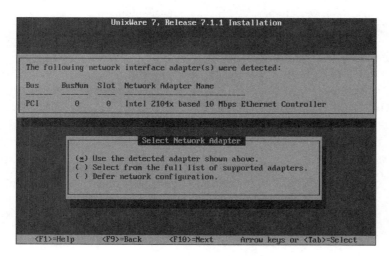

**Figure 2-31**    Selecting a detected NIC

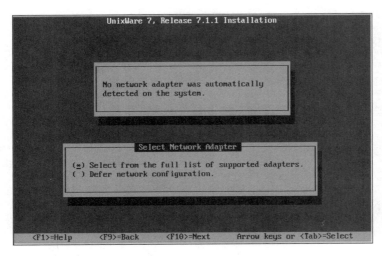

**Figure 2-32**    Manually selecting a NIC

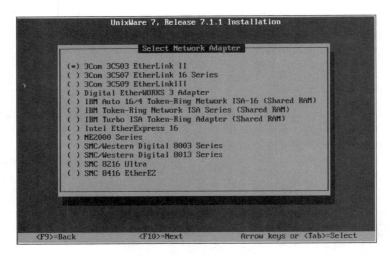

**Figure 2-33**    Manually selecting a NIC type

 If you manually configure your NIC during installation, you may also be prompted for other configuration parameters such as the IRQ and I/O address or media type.

**NOTE**

If a NIC has been configured, you are then prompted to configure the **TCP/IP protocol** that will be used with the NIC, as shown in Figure 2-34. The System IP Address, System Netmask, and Frame Type are mandatory; however, all other parameters are optional. The Broadcast Address is automatically calculated from the System IP Address and System Netmask.

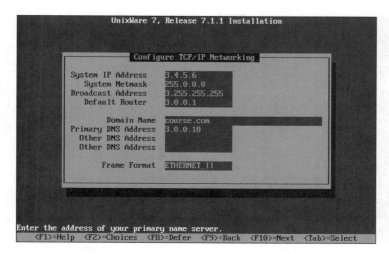

**Figure 2-34**   Configuring the TCP/IP protocol

After configuring TCP/IP, you can optionally configure the IPX/SPX network protocol as well, as shown in Figure 2-35. Unless this protocol is used on your network, defer this configuration by pressing F8 to avoid unnecessary network traffic.

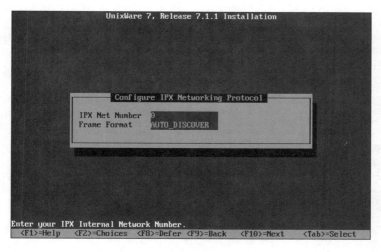

**Figure 2-35**   Configuring the IPX/SPX protocol

Next, you are prompted to configure the **Network Information Service (NIS)**, as depicted in Figure 2-36. NIS is a service that enables multiple UNIX computers to share common configuration files. The particulars of its configuration are beyond the scope of this text. If NIS is not required, you must use the F8 key to defer its configuration.

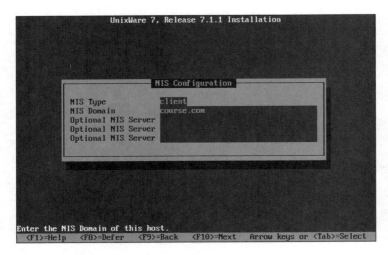

**Figure 2-36**    Configuring NIS

## Time and Security Profile Settings

After the network has been configured or deferred, you are prompted to confirm the time and date settings set by your computer BIOS as well as select a time zone so that the system time can be automatically adjusted in the future, as shown in Figure 2-37.

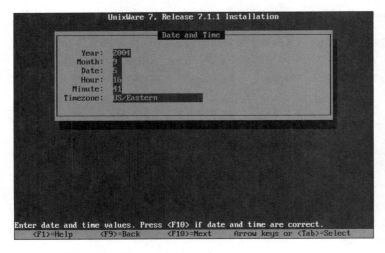

**Figure 2-37**    Selecting a date and time

Following this, the security profile for the system must be chosen, as shown in Figure 2-38. Unless the computer is on a public network, the traditional security profile is a suitable choice for security on most systems.

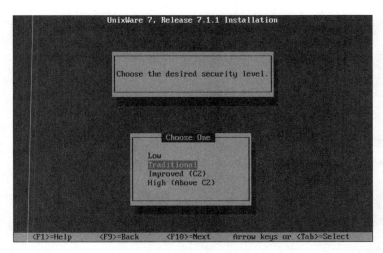

**Figure 2-38**    Selecting a security profile

## User Account Configuration

The final substage within the interview stage is configuring the user accounts that will be created. These accounts let you log into and use the system following installation. One user account has all privileges to the UNIX system. This user is called root and must be given a password during installation. In addition, another user account, called the system owner account, can perform some administration tasks from the GUI. This user account must be given a name and a password during installation.

You are first prompted to supply the appropriate information for the system owner including the name (description), login name, unique user ID (UID), and password, as shown in Figure 2-39.

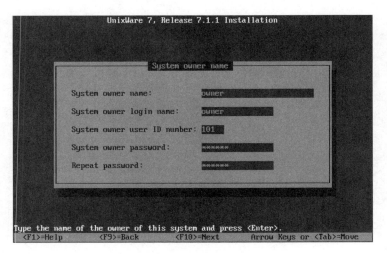

**Figure 2-39**    Configuring the system owner user account

Finally, you must supply the password for the root account, as shown in Figure 2-40.

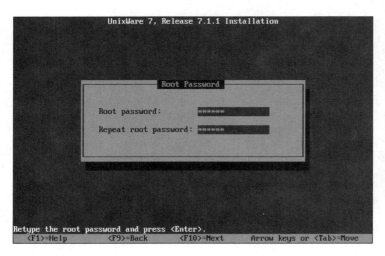

**Figure 2-40**   Configuring the root user account

## The Media Extraction and Software Loading Stage

After the root password has been supplied during the interview stage, you must accept the license agreement, as shown in Figure 2-41, and press F10 at the confirmation screen, as shown in Figure 2-42. Then you can proceed to create the partitions, slices, and filesystems on the hard disk, extract the media to the hard disk, and then configure it for use.

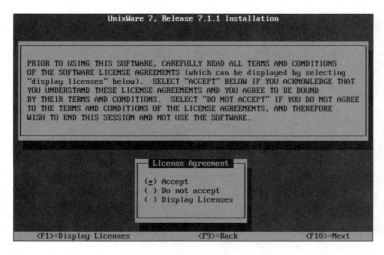

**Figure 2-41**   Accepting the license agreement

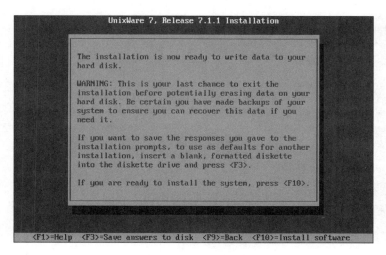

**Figure 2-42**    Starting the media extraction

While the software is being extracted and installed, you will see progress bars on the screen for each software package, as shown in Figure 2-43. This procedure is not interactive and may take anywhere from fifteen minutes to one hour, depending on the speed of the computer.

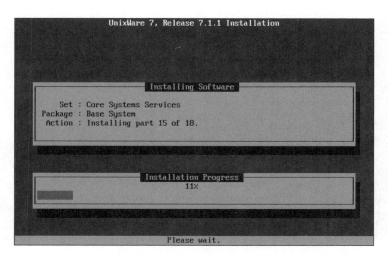

**Figure 2-43**    Extracting the media and loading the software

## The Initial Hard Disk Boot Stage

After the system has extracted and configured all the software, you will be prompted to remove the first UnixWare 7 CD-ROM and any floppy disks, and restart the computer, as shown in Figure 2-44.

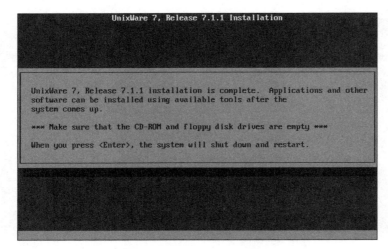

**Figure 2-44**    Performing the initial hard disk boot

When the computer restarts, the UnixWare operating system is loaded from the hard disk for the first time, and the system configures the network and adds the root and system owner user accounts to the system. Following this, you are prompted to configure the mouse settings, as depicted in Figure 2-45.

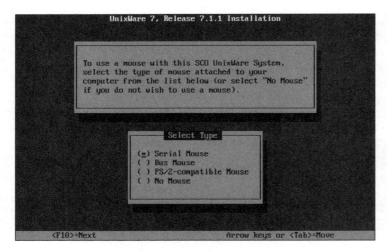

**Figure 2-45**    Configuring the mouse

If you choose a bus or PS/2 mouse, then you are prompted to indicate the number of mouse buttons; you will also be asked to indicate the serial port and mouse protocol if you choose a serial mouse.

If you do not choose a mouse, the installation will complete, but the GUI will not be displayed until a mouse is configured.

If a mouse is configured, the system configures the mouse and prompts you to test the mouse to ensure that you have chosen the correct mouse settings, as shown in Figure 2-46.

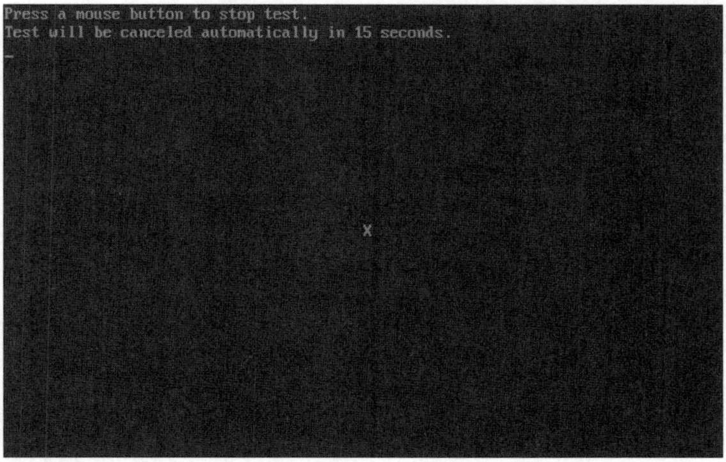

```
Press a mouse button to stop test.
Test will be canceled automatically in 15 seconds.

                              x
```

**Figure 2-46**   Testing the mouse configuration

## The Updates and Layered Products Installation Stage

After the mouse has been configured or deferred, you are prompted to insert the second UnixWare installation CD-ROM and install optional packages from it, as shown in Figures 2-47 and 2-48, respectively.

```
To continue installing the system, please insert
CD-ROM #2 and press <F10>.




                      <F10>=Continue
```

**Figure 2-47**   Inserting the second CD-ROM

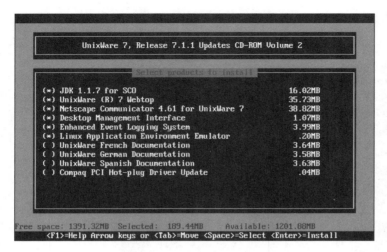

**Figure 2-48**    Selecting optional software packages

Some packages such as documentation and graphical interfaces are not displayed in Figure 2-48. Yet, these packages are mandatory and must be installed. After these packages and the packages chosen in Figure 2-48 have been installed, you are prompted to insert the third UnixWare installation CD-ROM and install more optional software packages, as shown in Figure 2-49. Because all software is optional on the third CD-ROM, you can choose to defer this step.

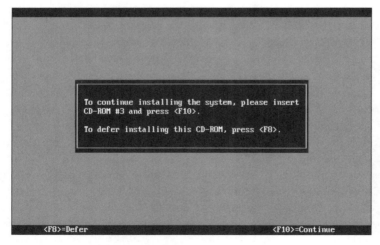

**Figure 2-49**    Inserting the third CD-ROM

After all software has been installed, the system starts any remaining services and allows users to log in.

## Chapter Summary

❑ The installation program for UNIX is different between different UNIX flavors; however, all UNIX installations use similar procedures and require similar information.

❑ Before installing UNIX on a computer, you should verify that the computer hardware meets the minimum requirements and is supported by the UNIX flavor being installed.

❑ Proper installation preparation involves planning the filesystem structure, network configuration, software packages, and security settings.

❑ UNIX systems divide hard disks into partitions that contain slices; each slice may contain a filesystem that is accessed via a certain directory in UNIX.

❑ A pre-installation checklist may be created to summarize the different hardware and software information required prior to installation.

❑ Before installing UnixWare, you must purchase a UnixWare edition license that is suited for the needs of the system.

❑ A typical UnixWare installation has five stages: interview, media extraction, software loading, initial hard disk boot, and updates and layered products installation.

## Key Terms

**ALTS TABLE** — The slice on a UNIX partition that is used to record any bad blocks on the physical hard disk so that they are not used in the future.

**C2** — A level of security defined by the U.S. Department of Defense Trusted Computer System Evaluation Criteria (TCSEC).

**Compatible Hardware Web Pages (CHWP)** — An Internet resource provided by SCO that lists hardware that is compatible with the UnixWare operating system.

**default router** — Also known as the default gateway or gateway of last resort, this is where information is sent on a network that is not destined for the local network.

**domain name** — The name of the network, company, or organization that is registered on a DNS server.

**Domain Name Service (DNS) server** — A server on a computer network that resolves names to IP addresses.

**Dynamic Host Configuration Protocol (DHCP) server** — A server on a computer network that can assign most TCP/IP configuration settings to other computers.

**edition license** — A license that determines the hardware, software, and user support for the UnixWare operating system.

**ezcp utility** — A Windows utility provided on the first UnixWare 7.1.1 CD-ROM that can be used to create installation floppy disks.

**filesystem** — The way in which a slice is formatted to enable data to reside on the physical media.

**Fully Qualified Domain Name (FQDN)** — The full name used to identify a computer on networks such as the Internet; it consists of the system node name and domain name of a computer.

**host bus adapter (HBA) diskette** — A diskette that contains UNIX device drivers used during the installation process.

**Internet Protocol (IP) address** — The unique number that each computer participating on the Internet must have.

**Internet Packet Exchange/Sequence Packet Exchange (IPX/SPX) protocol** — A method used to format information for use on a computer network commonly used on Novell networks.

**license** — Information that enables you to use an operating system.

**locale** — Refers to the world region that determines the character set that an operating system will use to display text characters.

**Master Boot Record (MBR)** — The area of a hard disk outside of a partition that stores partition information.

**netmask** — Also known as the network mask or subnet mask, this specifies which portion of the IP address identifies the logical network the computer is on.

**Network Information Service (NIS)** — A service that enables multiple UNIX computers to share configuration information across a computer network.

**network interface card (NIC)** — Hardware device used to connect a computer to a network of other computers and communicate or exchange information on it.

**partitions** — Used to divide up a hard disk into smaller areas for ease of use. There may be four partitions per hard disk.

**power-on self test (POST)** — The initialization of hardware components by the BIOS when the computer is first turned on.

**pre-installation checklist** — A list of hardware and software information useful during a UNIX installation.

**security profile** — Indicates a general selection of security-related system parameters.

**slice** — Used to divide up a UNIX partition into smaller areas for ease of use. There may be 184 slices per UNIX partition.

**small footprint server** — A system profile that consists of the bare minimum set of software packages in a UnixWare system.

**system node name** — Also known as a hostname, this is the logical identifier given to a computer.

**system profile** — The system software chosen for a UnixWare installation.

**TCP/IP protocol** — A method used to format information for use on a computer network; this is the most common protocol used on computer networks and the protocol used on the Internet.

**UNIX Filesystem (UFS)** — The default filesystem used by Solaris.

**Veritas Filesystem (VxFS)** — The default filesystem used by UnixWare and HP-UX.

2

**virtual memory** — An area on a hard disk (swap partition) that can be used to store information that normally resides in physical memory (RAM) if the physical memory is being used excessively.

**Volume Table of Contents (VTOC)** — The area of a BOOT slice that contains slice information for a particular UNIX partition.

## REVIEW QUESTIONS

1. How many times can you enter the DCU during a UnixWare installation?

    a. once

    b. twice

    c. an unlimited number of times

    d. none of the above—the DCU must be run after installation.

2. What is the minimum disk free space required for a UnixWare installation?

    a. 100MB

    b. 500MB

    c. 1GB

    d. 1.2GB

3. Which of the following are valid methods for locating compatible hardware?

    a. the UNIX vendor's Web site

    b. printed documentation

    c. the hardware manufacturer's Web site

    d. the Windows operating system

    e. all of the above

4. Hard disks are divided into _____, which are then divided further into _____.

    a. slices, partitions

    b. filesystems, slices

    c. partitions, slices

    d. slices, filesystems

5. A slice must always contain a filesystem. True or False?

6. Which area of the hard disk contains a map of bad blocks?

    a. ALTS TABLE

    b. BOOT slice

    c. / filesystem

    d. swap slice

7. Which area of the hard disk is used for virtual memory?

   a. ALTS TABLE

   b. BOOT slice

   c. / filesystem

   d. swap slice

8. Which area of the hard disk contains partition information?

   a. MBR

   b. VTOC

   c. BOOT

   d. ALTS

9. Which area of the hard disk contains slice information?

   a. MBR

   b. VTOC

   c. BOOT

   d. ALTS

10. What is the default filesystem used on UnixWare 7?

    a. UFS

    b. VxFS

    c. S5

    d. BFS

11. Which of the following refers to the bare minimum set of packages required for the UnixWare operating system?

    a. Enterprise edition license

    b. small footprint server

    c. traditional security profile

    d. Business edition license

12. Which UnixWare 7 edition is licensed for 25 users and up to 2 CPUs?

    a. Base

    b. Business

    c. Departmental

    d. Enterprise

2

13. Before installing UnixWare on IDE hard disks, ensure that the CD-ROM drive is not configured as a _____.

    a. primary master

    b. primary slave

    c. secondary master

    d. secondary slave

14. Which Windows utility can be used to create installation floppy disks in case the CD-ROM is not bootable?

    a. mkbootdisk

    b. ezcp

    c. diskadd

    d. install_disk

15. The second UnixWare installation CD-ROM can be deferred. True or False?

16. Which of the following is not a general UnixWare installation stage?

    a. interview

    b. software loading

    c. mouse configuration

    d. media extraction

17. When are you first prompted for mouse configuration?

    a. at the beginning of the installation

    b. on the first reboot after the installation

    c. after the installation has completed

    d. never

18. The UNIX partition should start before the 1024th cylinder of the hard disk. True or False?

19. What can be used to configure hardware device settings as well as software device drivers in the UnixWare operating system?

    a. VxFS

    b. DCU

    c. ezcp

    d. System Configurator

20. The set of software packages selected in noun is known as the _____.

    a. security profile

    b. system profile

    c. edition

    d. software update

21. Which of the following user accounts requires a password configured during UnixWare installation? (Choose all that apply.)

    a. root

    b. system owner

    c. LP service account

    d. user1

22. Which of the following are valid security profiles? (Choose all that apply.)

    a. low

    b. secure

    c. traditional

    d. high

23. If you choose Customize filesystems and slices during the installation of UnixWare 7 and increase the size of the /var filesystem, what must you do afterwards?

    a. Click the Commit Changes button.

    b. Reduce the size of another filesystem.

    c. Select a filesystem of type VxFS.

    d. Activate the change in the DCU.

24. How many hard disks can be configured during installation?

    a. one

    b. two

    c. four

    d. unlimited

25. If you choose to configure a dump slice during installation, how large should it be?

    a. at least the same size as your RAM

    b. half the size as your RAM

    c. 20MB

    d. at least 1GB

## HANDS-ON PROJECTS

These projects should be completed in the order given. The hands-on projects should take a total of three hours to complete. The requirements for this lab include:

   ❒ A UnixWare 7.1.1 CD-ROM installation set (three CD-ROMs)

❐ An Intel architecture computer that meets the minimum UnixWare 7 installation requirements and contains UnixWare 7 supported hardware components, including a NIC and CD-ROM drive

❐ Optional access to a functional Web browser and an Internet connection

## Project 2-1

In this hands-on project, you will fill in a pre-installation checklist.

1. Fill in the following pre-installation checklist by supplying the appropriate information.

| CPU (type and MHz) | |
| --- | --- |
| RAM (MB) | |
| Language support | English |
| Keyboard model and layout | |
| Mouse model and device | |
| Hard disk type (primary master and so on) | |
| Hard disk size (MB) | |
| System node name | unix1 |
| Network card IP configuration (IP address, netmask, default router, DNS servers, and domain name) Note, these values here are usually assigned by your ISP. | |
| Time zone | |
| Root password | secret |
| System owner account name | user1 |
| System owner account password | secret |
| Packages to install | All packages |
| Video card make and model | |

2. For any hardware components listed previously, ensure that the hardware is listed on the CHWP available on the Internet at *www.sco.com/chwp* (provided that you have a functional Web browser and Internet access).

## Project 2-2

In this hands-on project, you will install UnixWare 7 on a computer.

1. Turn on the computer and place the first UnixWare 7.1.1 installation CD-ROM in the CD-ROM tray. The UnixWare 7 splash screen should appear after a few seconds.

If the UnixWare 7 splash screen does not appear, ensure that your CD-ROM is listed in the boot order in your computer's BIOS settings. If the CD-ROM is listed and still fails to display the UnixWare 7 splash screen, create the necessary floppy disks using the instructions provided earlier in this chapter and repeat Step 1 with the first installation floppy disk in the floppy disk drive.

2. At the first installation screen, ensure that **Proceed with installation in English** is selected and then press **Enter**.

3. At the Welcome screen, read the text on the screen and press **F10**.

4. When prompted to choose a zone, ensure that **Americas (Latin-1)** is selected and press **F10**.

5. When prompted to choose a locale, ensure that **C (English)** is selected and press **F10**.

6. At the Keyboard screen, ensure that **United States** is selected and press **F10**.

7. At the System License screen, press **F8** to defer licensing. When prompted to use an evaluation license, select **Yes, use an evaluation license.** and press **Enter**.

8. When prompted to install another HBA diskette, ensure that **Proceed with installation** is selected and press **F10**.

9. When prompted to configure device drivers, ensure that **Do not enter the DCU (auto-configure drivers)** is selected and press **F10**.

10. At the System Node Name screen, enter the name **unix1** and press **F10**.

11. At the Installation Method screen, ensure that **Install from CD-ROM** is selected and press **F10**.

12. At the Disk Configuration screen, press **F2** and observe your choices. Ensure that **Use whole disk for UNIX** is selected and press **Enter**. Next, press **F10**.

13. When prompted to use the default filesystem sizes and types, select **Customize filesystems and slices** and press **F10**.

14. At the Filesystems and Raw Disk Slices screen, observe the default entries. Is there a /home filesystem defined? Navigate to the Type for the /home filesystem and press **F2** to select a VxFS filesystem for this slice. Next, ensure that the size of the /home filesystem is 50MB. What do the Available and Allocated entries indicate at the bottom of the screen? Reduce the size of the / filesystem by 50MB to counteract the change. When you are finished, press **F10**.

15. When prompted to choose disk options, ensure that **Use default disk options** is selected and press **F10**.

16. At the Choose System Profile screen, select **Full (All Packages)** and press **F10**.

17. The next few screens will differ depending on the NIC hardware inside your computer. Follow the prompts to supply the appropriate information about your NIC.

18. At the Configure TCP/IP Networking screen, enter the information from the pre-installation checklist in Project 2-1. When you are finished, press **F10**.

2

19. At the Configure IPX Networking Protocol screen, press **F8** to defer the config-uration of IPX/SPX.

20. At the NIS Configuration screen, press **F8** to defer the configuration of NIS.

21. At the Date and Time screen, verify that the information is correct and press **F10**.

22. When prompted to choose the security profile, ensure that **Traditional** is selected and press **F10**.

23. When prompted to configure the system owner user account, enter the following information:

    System owner name: **owner**

    System owner login name: **owner**

    System owner password: **secret**

    Press **F10** when you are finished.

24. When prompted for the password for the root user account, type **secret** in the areas provided and press **F10**.

25. At the License Agreement screen, observe the screen and press **F10**.

26. When prompted to install the system, read the information displayed and press **F10**. The media extraction and software loading should take fifteen minutes to one hour depending on the speed of your computer.

27. When prompted to restart the computer, remove any CD-ROMs and floppy disks from the system and press **Enter**. The initial hard disk boot should take two to fifteen minutes, depending on the speed of your system.

28. When prompted to configure the mouse, select the appropriate mouse from the list and press **F10**. Specify additional information about your mouse when asked and follow the prompts to test your mouse (you must press a mouse button to end the test).

29. When prompted, place the second UnixWare 7.1.1 CD-ROM in CD-ROM drive of the computer and press **F10**. When the default optional software packages are displayed, observe the entries and press **Enter**. The installation of these packages should take fifteen minutes to one hour depending on the speed of your computer.

30. When the installation of these packages has completed, press **F10** to confirm the results.

31. When prompted, place the third UnixWare 7.1.1 CD-ROM in CD-ROM drive of the computer and press **F8** to defer.

32. The following step will be fully explained in the next chapter: When the UnixWare system has fully loaded, press **Ctrl+Alt+F2** and log in as the user **root** with the password **secret**. When you receive a command prompt, type the command **shutdown -y** and press **Enter**. If you are prompted to turn off the power, you may safely turn off the computer.

## DISCOVERY EXERCISES

1. You work for the Albus Corporation as a network administrator. You have been instructed to install UnixWare 7 on a 4-processor computer that will support 40 users. What edition license should be purchased? The computer has a DLink NE2000-compatable NIC. Will this be supported? Provided that you have a functional Web browser and an Internet connection, where on the Internet could you go to confirm this? List two Internet sources for information on this issue.

2. You are asked to install UNIX on a computer in your office to provide file and print services. The IT manager is unfamiliar with UNIX and purchases a computer without checking the specific hardware inside because the company has purchased several of these computers in the past and has had no problems with the Windows operating system automatically detecting the hardware inside them. Prepare a list of reasons that you could give the IT manager outlining why understanding the hardware components of a computer is valuable for a UNIX installation. What problems might you encounter when installing on this hardware? Furthermore, design an installation checklist and fill in sample values that are reasonable for a file and print server that will support 100 users. On this sample checklist, state the rationales for each choice (processor, memory, disk space, packages, and so on) given your knowledge of each of these requirements.

3. Provided that you have a functional Web browser and an Internet connection, research the individual installation steps for a typical HP-UX and Solaris installation. How do they compare to the UnixWare installation that you performed in this chapter? Do these installations look similar? Do these installations prompt the user for the same information? Prepare a short summary of the similarities and differences between installing UnixWare, HP-UX, and Solaris.

# 3

# ACCESSING A **UNIX** SYSTEM

> **After reading this chapter and completing the exercises, you will be able to:**
>
> ♦ Describe the difference between shells, terminals, and the UNIX kernel
> ♦ List common shells that are used by UNIX
> ♦ Use commands to perform UNIX tasks
> ♦ Use the CDE to perform UNIX tasks
> ♦ Identify and protect shell metacharacters
> ♦ Obtain help using the manual pages and SCOhelp
> ♦ Use SCO Admin to perform system administration tasks
> ♦ Shut down a UNIX system using good practices

In the previous chapter, you installed a UNIX system. In this chapter, you will learn about interacting with a UNIX system after installation. First, this chapter discusses UNIX user interface concepts and describes the different types of user interfaces available for UNIX systems. Next, you will explore the features and usage of command-line interfaces including how to find help, use the SCO Admin utility, and shut down the system. Finally, you will learn about the use of graphical interfaces and the SCOhelp utility.

## LOGGING INTO THE SYSTEM

Once the UNIX operating system has been installed, you must log into the system with a valid username and password, and interact with the user interface to perform useful tasks. Thus, it is essential to understand the different types of user interfaces that exist and their structure.

Recall that an operating system is merely a collection of software that enables you to use your computer hardware in a meaningful fashion. Every operating system has a core component, which loads all other components and serves to centrally control the activities of the computer. This component is called the **kernel**. In UNIX, it is a file usually called unix (UnixWare), genunix (Solaris), or vmunix (HP-UX) located on the hard drive that is loaded when you first turn your computer on.

When users interact with their computer, they are interacting with the kernel of the computer's operating system. However, this interaction cannot happen directly; it must have a channel through which it can access the kernel and a user interface that passes user input to the kernel for processing. The channel that enables a certain user to log in is called a **terminal**. Many terminals in UNIX enable you to log into the computer locally or across a network. Furthermore, terminals may offer a command-line interface or a GUI; as a result, these terminals are referred to as **command-line terminals** or **graphical terminals**, respectively.

After logging into a command-line terminal, the user receives a user interface called a **shell**, which then accepts input from the user and passes this input to the kernel for processing. Many different shells are available for UNIX systems. Although all shells can access the same UNIX utilities, each offers special features that other shells might not have. Table 3-1 lists some common UNIX shells and their descriptions.

**Table 3-1**    Common UNIX shells

| Shell | Description |
| --- | --- |
| Bourne shell (sh) | The original AT&T shell developed by Steve Bourne. It is available on all UNIX systems and is the default shell for Solaris systems and the root user in UnixWare. |
| POSIX shell (sh) | A POSIX-improved version of the Bourne shell. It is the default shell for users in HP-UX. |
| Korn shell (ksh) | A shell developed by David Korn that has many more features than the Bourne Shell. It is the default shell for regular users in UnixWare. |
| C shell (csh) | A shell developed by the University of California at Berkeley. It is the default shell on BSD UNIX systems. |
| BASH shell (bash) | An improved version of the Bourne shell (BASH stands for Bourne Again Shell). It is the default shell on Linux systems. |

The shell that is given to the user upon login is the one that is specified in the properties of the user account; thus, one user may log into a terminal on a UNIX system and receive the Bourne shell, whereas another user may log into a terminal on the same UNIX system and receive a Korn shell. Figure 3-1 shows the relationship between terminals, shells, and the UNIX kernel.

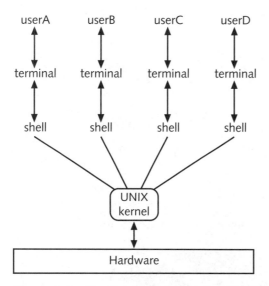

**Figure 3-1**   Terminals, shells, and the kernel

As mentioned earlier, UNIX is a multiuser and multitasking operating system, and as such can allow for thousands of terminals; each terminal could represent a separate logged-in user who has his or her own shell. The four different channels in Figure 3-1 could be different users logged into the same UNIX computer; two users could be logged in locally to the server (seated at the server itself) and the other two could be logged in across a network, such as the Internet.

When a user logs into a graphical terminal, the system also provides a shell for the user; however, a program called **X Windows** is loaded on top of that shell to provide graphical functionality and a **desktop environment** is loaded on top of X Windows to standardize the look and feel of X Windows. Figure 3-2 depicts the difference between graphical and command-line terminals; userA is logged into a graphical terminal while userB, userC, and userD are logged into command-line terminals.

A typical command-line terminal login screen looks like:

```
Welcome to UnixWare 7, Release 7.1.1
The system's name is unix1.

Console Login:
```

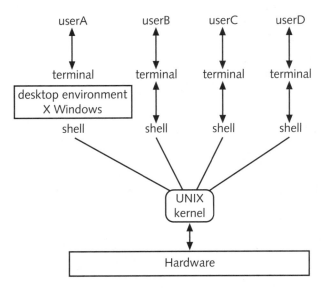

**Figure 3-2**   Logging into a graphical terminal

Figure 3-3 depicts a typical graphical terminal login screen for UNIX.

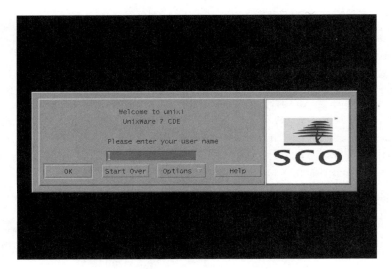

**Figure 3-3**   A graphical terminal login screen

To access a terminal device from across the network, you may use a utility such as tel-net or ssh to obtain a command-line terminal or an X Windows client such as Hummingbird Exceed to obtain a graphical terminal. Many utilities such as these are available, and some such as telnet are included with most operating systems today. You may also access terminals while seated at the local UNIX system. These terminals are commonly called **virtual terminals** and may be accessed by pressing a combination of keys such as Ctrl+Alt+F1. Table 3-2 shows a list of local UnixWare terminals, and their names and types.

**Table 3-2**    UnixWare virtual terminals

| Terminal Name | Key Combination | Type |
|---|---|---|
| Virtual terminal 01 (vt01) | Ctrl+Alt+F1 | Graphical |
| vt02 | Ctrl+Alt+F2 | Command line |
| vt03 | Ctrl+Alt+F3 | Command line |
| vt04 | Ctrl+Alt+F4 | Command line |
| vt05 | Ctrl+Alt+F5 | Command line |
| vt06 | Ctrl+Alt+F6 | Command line |
| vt07 | Ctrl+Alt+F7 | Command line |
| vt08 | Ctrl+Alt+F8 | Command line |

## USING A COMMAND-LINE TERMINAL

Once you are logged into a command-line terminal, you will receive a shell and a shell prompt where you can enter in commands. If you log in as the root user (the administrator), a # prompt will be used, whereas all other user accounts receive a $ prompt. The only exception to this is the C shell. If you log in as the root user to a C shell, a # prompt will be used, whereas all other user accounts receive a % prompt.

### Basic Shell Commands

When using a command-line terminal, the shell ultimately interprets all information the user enters onto the command line. This information includes the command itself, as well as options and arguments. **Commands** indicate the name of the program to execute and are case sensitive. **Options** are specific letters that start with a dash (-) and appear after the command name to alter the way the command works. In addition, options are specific to the command in question; the person who developed the command determined which options to allow for that command.

**NOTE**

Some options start with two dashes (--); these options are referred to as POSIX options and are usually comprised of a whole word, not just a letter.

**Arguments** also appear after the command name, yet do not start with a dash. They specify the parameters that the command works upon, which are not predetermined by the person who developed the command. Say, for example, that you wanted to list all of the files in the /var/adm/acct directory on the hard drive. You could use the **ls** command with the **-a** option (which tells the `ls` command to list all files) and the /var/adm/acct argument (which tells `ls` to look in the /var/adm/acct directory), as shown in the following example:

```
# ls -a /var/adm/acct
.        ..          fiscal   nite     sum
# _
```

Once you type the command and press Enter in the previous output, the `ls` command shows you that there are three files in the /var/adm/acct directory and returns your command prompt so that you can enter another command.

Commands, options, and arguments are case sensitive; an uppercase letter (*A*) is treated differently than a lowercase letter (*a*).

Always put a space between the command name, options, and arguments; otherwise, the shell will not understand that they are separate and your command might not work as expected.

Although you may pass options and arguments to commands, not all commands need to have arguments or options supplied on the command line to work properly; the **date** command is one example that just prints the current date and time:

```
# date
Tue Sep 10 19:54:35 EDT 2002
# _
```

Table 3-3 provides a short list of some common UNIX commands that you may use.

**Table 3-3**   Some common UNIX commands

| Command | Description |
|---|---|
| banner *string* | Prints a text banner on the terminal screen for the *string* argument provided |
| cal | Displays the calendar for the current month |
| clear | Clears the terminal screen |
| date | Displays the current date and time |
| finger | Displays information on system users |
| id | Displays the numbers associated with the user account name and group names. These are commonly referred to as user IDs (UIDs) and group IDs (GIDs). |
| uname -a | Displays all information about the system |
| w | Displays currently logged in users and their tasks |
| who | Displays currently logged in users |
| exit | Exits out of the current shell |

## Shell Metacharacters

Another important feature of the shell is the use of shell **metacharacters**, which are keyboard characters that have special meaning. One of the most commonly used metacharacters is the $ character, which tells the shell that the following text refers to a variable. A variable is a piece of information that is stored in memory; variable names are typically uppercase words and most variables are set by the UNIX system automatically when you log in. For example, you may use the $ metacharacter to refer to a variable by using the echo command (which prints text to the terminal screen):

```
# echo Hi There!
Hi There!
# echo My shell is $SHELL
My shell is /sbin/sh
# _
```

Notice from the previous output that $SHELL was translated into its appropriate value from memory (/sbin/sh, the Bourne shell) because the shell recognized SHELL as a variable since it was prefixed by the $ metacharacter.

Table 3-4 shows a list of the common shell metacharacters that will be discussed throughout this textbook.

**Table 3-4**    Common shell metacharacters

| Metacharacter(s) | Description |
| --- | --- |
| $ | Shell variable |
| & | Background command execution |
| ; | Command termination |
| < << > >> | I/O redirection |
| \| | Command piping |
| * ? [ ] | Shell wildcards |
| ' " \ | Metacharacter quotes |
| ` | Command substitution |
| ( ) { } | Command grouping |

It is good practice to avoid metacharacters when typing commands unless you need to take advantage of their special functionality, as the shell will readily interpret them, which may lead to unexpected results.

**NOTE**

If you accidentally use one of these characters and your shell does not return you to the normal shell prompt, press Delete (or on some terminals, Ctrl+c) and your current command will be cancelled.

In some circumstances, you may need to use a metacharacter in a command to prevent the shell from interpreting its special meaning. To do this, enclose the metacharacters in single quotes (' '). Single quotes protect those metacharacters from being interpreted specially by the shell (that is, a $ will be interpreted as a $ character and not a variable identifier). You may also use double quotes (" ") to perform the same task; however, double quotes do not protect the $, \, and ` characters. If only one character needs to be protected from shell interpretation, you may precede that character by a \ rather than enclosing it within quotes. The following shows an example of this type of quoting:

```
# echo My shell is $SHELL
My shell is /sbin/sh
# echo 'My shell is $SHELL'
My shell is $SHELL
# echo "My shell is $SHELL"
My shell is /sbin/sh
# echo My shell is \$SHELL
My shell is $SHELL
# _
```

As shown in Table 3-4, not all quote characters protect characters from the shell. The backquote characters (` `) may be used to perform command substitution; anything between backquotes is treated as another command by the shell and its output will be substituted in place of the backquotes. Take the expression `` `date` `` as an example:

```
# echo Today is `date`
Today is Wed Aug 16 15:09:01 EDT 2002
# _
```

## Obtaining Command Help

Most flavors of UNIX contain more than 1000 different UNIX commands in common configurations, so it would be impractical to memorize the syntax and use of each command. Fortunately, UNIX stores documentation for each command in central locations so that they may be accessed easily. The most common form of documentation for UNIX commands are **manual pages** (commonly referred to as man pages). Just type the **man** command followed by a command name and extensive information about that UNIX command will appear page by page on the terminal screen. This information includes a description of the command and its syntax, as well as the available options, related files, and commands. For example, to receive information on the format and usage of the **date** command, you could do the following:

```
# man date
```

The manual page then appears page by page on the terminal screen; you may use the Enter key and the spacebar on the keyboard to scroll through the information line by line or page by page, respectively, or use the q key to exit. The first screen of the manual page for the **date** command is:

```
                                            date(1)
```

```
    date -- print and set the date

Synopsis

    date [-u] [+format]

    date [-u] [[mmdd]HHMM _ mmddHHMM[[cc]yy]]

    date [-a [-]sss.fff]

Description

    If no argument is given, or if the argument begins with
    +, the current date and time are printed. Otherwise, the
    current date is set for the real-time clock and the
    system clock if the user is a privilege user.

    Supplementary code set characters in + format (see
    below) are recognized and displayed according to the
    locale specified in the LC_CTYPE environment variable
    (see LANG on environ(5)). Month and weekday names are
    recognized according to the locale specified in the
:q
# _
```

Notice that the **date** command is displayed as **date(1)** in the previous manual page output. The (1) denotes a section of the manual pages; section (1) means that date is a command that may be executed by any user. All manual pages contain certain section numbers that describe the category of the command in the manual page database; Table 3-5 lists the common manual page section numbers.

**Table 3-5**   Manual page section numbers

| Manual Page Section | Description |
| --- | --- |
| 1<br>1M<br>X1M | Commands that any user may execute<br>Commands that only the root user may execute<br>X Windows commands that only the root user may execute |
| 2 | System calls |
| 3<br>3M<br>3F | Library routines and functions<br>Mathematical functions<br>FORTRAN functions |

**Table 3-5**    Manual page section numbers (continued)

| Manual Page Section | Description |
| --- | --- |
| 4 | File formats |
| 5 | Miscellaneous |
| 6 | Games |
| 7 | Device drivers and interfaces |

The manual page sections listed in Table 3-5 are the most commonly used today; however, manual page sections may have a wide variety of characters prefixed or appended to them to customize their meaning. For example, 1bsd refers to a BSD command that any user may execute.

Sometimes more than one command, library routine, or file has the same name; if you run the **man** command with that name as an argument, UNIX will return the manual page with the lowest section number. Say there was a file called date as well as a command named date; if you type **man date**, the manual page for the **date** command (section 1 of the manual pages) would appear. To show the manual page for the date file format (section 4 of the manual pages) instead, you would type **man 4 date**.

Recall that many commands are available to the UNIX user; thus, it may be cumbersome to find the command that you need to perform a certain task without using a UNIX command dictionary. Fortunately, you have the ability to search the manual pages by keyword. Say, for example, that you want to find a command that shows your username; to find all of the commands that have the word "username" in their name or description, type the following:

```
# man -k username
NWGetBannerUserName (3nw) - returns user name printed on banner pages
NWSetBannerUserName (3nw) - sets user name printed on banner pages
rusersd (1Mtcp)          - network username server
whoami (1)               - display the effective current username
# _
```

Notice from the previous output that the **whoami** command performs the desired task. Once you find the command needed, you may run the **man** command on that command without the **-k** option to find out detailed information about the command; in this case, you could run the command **man whoami** to view the syntax of the **whoami** command.

You may also use the `apropos username` command to perform the same function as the `man -k username` command. Both commands yield the exact same output on the terminal screen.

## Administrative Tools

You may perform any administrative task on a UNIX system provided you know the command or commands that must be used as well as any required options or arguments. Since administrators typically perform several tasks, UNIX flavors usually offer a menu-based tool that can perform common administrative tasks such as adding user accounts or creating printers; this tool is called SCO Admin in UnixWare, admintool in Solaris, and sam (System Administration Manager) in HP-UX. To invoke these tools, type their name at a command prompt and an interactive menu will appear that can perform several different administrative tasks via a series of administrative managers. Typing `scoadmin` at a command prompt results in the screen depicted in Figure 3-4.

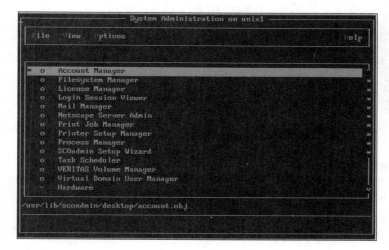

**Figure 3-4**    The SCO Admin CHARM interface

A text-based menu interface, such as the one depicted in Figure 3-4, is often called a Character Motif (CHARM) interface.

**NOTE**

Only a subset of all administrative tasks can be completed using SCO Admin.

**NOTE**

Each manager in Figure 3-4 is prefixed by the **o** character and may be navigated to by using the keyboard cursor keys and opened by pressing Enter. Any names that are prefixed with a - character are folders that contain more managers; press Enter to open these folders. You may also use the F10 key to navigate to the menus at the top of the screen; the Exit entry on the File menu can be used to exit the SCO Admin utility.

Each manager simplifies a specific area of administration and will have different menus than other managers. Figure 3-5 depicts the screen that appears when you open the Account Manager from Figure 3-4.

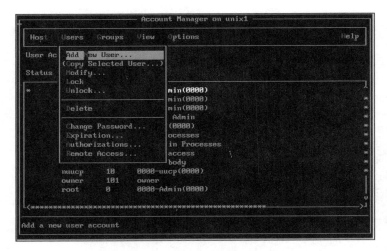

**Figure 3-5**    SCO Admin Account Manager CHARM interface

If you already know which SCO Admin manager you want to use, you may start that manager directly from the command line; executing the command **scoadmin  acc** starts the SCO Admin Account Manager immediately since Account Manager is the only SCO Admin manager that starts with the letters *acc*. To see a list of manager names in SCO Admin that you may access, use the **-t** option with the **scoadmin** command:

```
# scoadmin -t
Account Manager
Address Allocation Manager
Application Installer
Audio Configuration Manager
Client Manager
Device Configuration Utility (DCU)
DHCP Server Manager
Dialin Services Manager
Dialup Systems Manager
DNS Manager
Filesystem Manager
FTP Server Manager
Hotplug Manager
Install Server
International Settings Manager
Intranet Manager
LDAP Manager
License Manager
```

3

```
     Login Session Viewer
     Mail Manager
     Modem Manager
     Netscape Server Admin
     NetWare Settings
     NetWare Setup
     Network Configuration Manager
     Packet Filter Manager
     PnP Configuration Manager
     Print Job Manager
     Printer Setup Manager
     Process Manager
     Reports Manager
     SCOadmin Setup Wizard
     Security Profile Manager
     Serial Manager
     SNMP Agent Manager
     System Defaults Manager
     System Information
     System Logs Manager
     System Monitor
     System Shutdown Manager
     System Time Manager
     System Tuner
     Task Scheduler
     VERITAS Volume Manager
     Video Configuration Manager
     Virtual Domain User Manager
     # _
```

## Shutting down the UNIX System

Since the operating system handles writing data from computer memory to the disk drives in a computer, simply turning off the power to the computer may damage user and system files. Thus, it is important to prepare the operating system for shutdown before turning off the power to the hardware components of the computer. To do this, you may issue the **shutdown command**. The `shutdown` command is standard across most UNIX flavors; you may consult the manual page for the `shutdown` command to find any subtle variations. In UnixWare, the `shutdown` command prompts the user to continue and begins the shutdown process immediately by default. However, you may specify the `-y` (yes) option to the `shutdown` command to prevent it from prompting you to continue, and the `-g` (grace time) option followed by the number of seconds to wait before beginning the shutdown process. For example, to shut down the system in two minutes, execute the following command:

```
# shutdown -g120 -y
UX:shutdown: INFO:
Shutdown started.     Thu Sep 12 14:31:08 EDT 2002
```

If the system is not powered off automatically at the end of the shutdown procedure, then the UnixWare system will display a message indicating that it is safe to power off the computer.

The **shutdown** command broadcasts a message to all users who are currently logged into the system that the system is shutting down; however, you may want to send a customized message instead using the **wall (warn all) command**. When the **wall** command is executed, you are given a secondary prompt to enter a message that will be broadcast to all users. When you are finished entering in the lines of text, use the Ctrl+d key combination to send the message:

```
# wall
The system will be shut down for maintenance in 20 minutes.
Please save your work and log off before then.
Thankyou.
Ctrl-d

Broadcast Message from root (console) on unix1 Sun Sep 15 08:19:48...
The system will be shut down for maintenance in 20 minutes.
Please save your work and log off before then.
Thankyou.
# _
```

Furthermore, the **shutdown** command can be used to reboot the system; this is often needed when you make a major change to the system configuration and want it to take effect immediately. To reboot a system, just add the **-i6** (initstate 6) option to the **shutdown** command; this will begin the shutdown process normally, yet restart the system after it has completed. Initstates are discussed later in Chapter 8 of this book.

## USING A GRAPHICAL TERMINAL

If you choose to log into a graphical terminal as depicted in Figure 3-3 instead of a command-line terminal, then X Windows and a desktop environment will be loaded on top of a shell to provide a different user interface.

X Windows was jointly developed by DEC (Digital Equipment Corporation) and MIT (Massachusetts Institute of Technology) in 1984. Then, it was code-named Project Athena and was released in 1985 as X Windows in hopes that a new name would be found to replace the X. Shortly after, X Windows was sought after by many UNIX vendors and by 1988 MIT released version 11 release 2 of X Windows (X11R2). Since 1988, X Windows has been maintained by The Open Group, which released version 11 release 6 of X Windows (X11R6) in 1995.

**NOTE**

To find out more about X Windows, visit The Open Group on the Internet at *www.x.org*.

Although X Windows performs most of the graphical functions in a GUI, a desktop environment also exists to modify the look and feel of X Windows. Desktop environments come with a full set of GUI tools designed to be packaged together, including Web browsers, file managers, and drawing programs. Most versions of UNIX ship with the **Common Desktop Environment (CDE)**; however, you may choose from other desktop environments that vary from UNIX flavor to UNIX flavor. For example, UnixWare enables you to choose the Panorama desktop environment from the graphical terminal login screen, as shown in Figure 3-6.

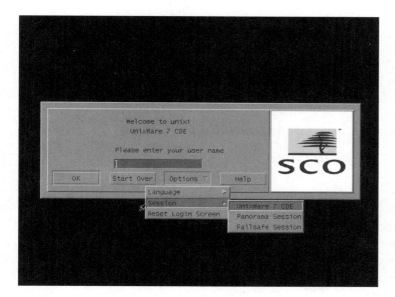

**Figure 3-6**    Choosing a desktop session

The **Panorama desktop environment** is a legacy desktop that uses less memory than the CDE. It enables multiple separate desktops to be displayed and managed via a tool at the bottom of the desktop screen called a panner. Figure 3-7 provides an example of a Panorama desktop environment.

The remainder of this book focuses on the CDE. The computer icon on the toolbar at the bottom of the CDE desktop can be used to open a command-line shell, as depicted in Figure 3-8, where you can use any command that can be typed in a command-line terminal.

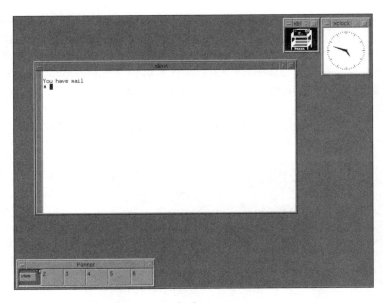

**Figure 3-7**    The Panorama desktop

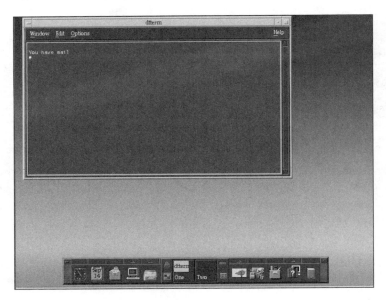

**Figure 3-8**    A CDE shell prompt

The CDE toolbar can also be used to open application programs such as SCO Admin; these are often contained on menus that can be opened from the toolbar, as shown in Figure 3-9.

**Figure 3-9**    Starting SCO Admin

Many applications, such as Netscape, can only be run from within a desktop environment. Other applications can be run in either a command-line terminal or desktop environment. Recall that SCO Admin uses a CHARM interface when executed in a command-line terminal; when it is opened in the CDE, it uses X Windows to draw the interface, as shown in Figure 3-10.

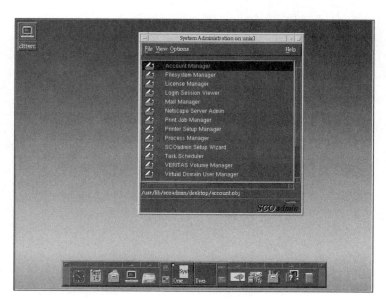

**Figure 3-10**    SCO Admin

You may also start SCO Admin by typing the `scoadmin` command in a shell inside the CDE.

Each graphical application such as SCO Admin has a minimize button that places an icon on the desktop that represents the program, as well as a maximize button that maximizes the application's screen area and a window menu that enables you to resize, move, or close the window, as shown in Figure 3-11.

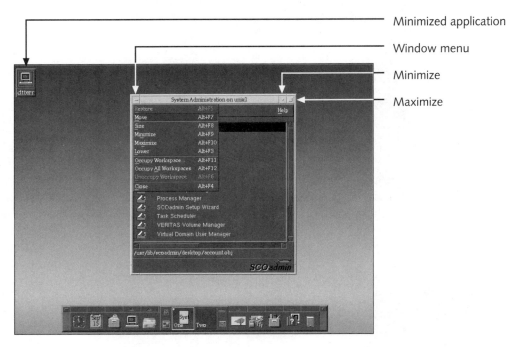

**Figure 3-11**    Window properties

Regardless of its appearance, the graphical SCO Admin interface offers the same functionality as the CHARM interface, as shown with the SCO Admin Account Manager in Figure 3-5 and in Figure 3-12.

Some managers in SCO Admin require the Netscape Web browser; these managers are not available in the CHARM interface.

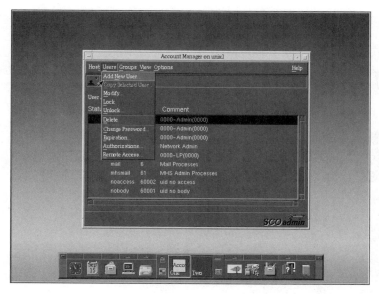

**Figure 3-12**    SCO Admin Account Manager GUI interface

For the root user, the CDE offers two different methods for administering the system: using commands at a shell prompt and using SCO Admin. During installation, however, you are prompted to create a system owner user account; this account can perform system administration using SCO Admin only. Thus, if the system owner needed to power down the system, that user is restricted to using the Shutdown Manager in the System folder of SCO Admin, as shown in Figure 3-13.

**Figure 3-13**    SCO Admin System Shutdown Manager

When using a graphical terminal, you may still use the **man** command at a shell prompt to search the manual pages for command documentation. However, the CDE desktop often includes a more comprehensive graphical help utility. For UnixWare, this utility is called SCOhelp and runs on its own Web server on port 457. To start the SCOhelp utility, type the **scohelp** command at a shell prompt or select it from the list shown in Figure 3-14.

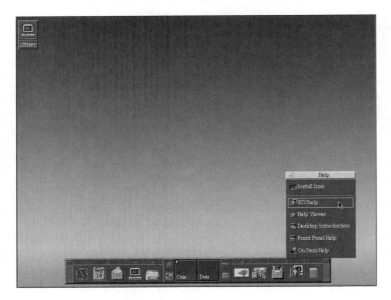

**Figure 3-14**    Starting SCOhelp

Once SCOhelp is started, the Netscape Web browser will be started to provide the contents of SCOhelp, as shown in Figure 3-15.

**NOTE**    If the SCOhelp utility fails to start, you will need to run the command /etc/scohelphttp start at a shell prompt to start the SCOhelp Web server.

**NOTE**    Since SCOhelp requires the Netscape Web browser, it is not available in a command-line terminal. However, it may be accessed by other computers that have Web browsers across the network. Simply point the Web browser to the URL *<IP address of UnixWare server>*:457.

SCOhelp consists of a series of Hypertext Markup Language (HTML) Web pages that contain hyperlinks to documentation for common UNIX tasks organized by topic. You may browse though this SCOhelp documentation using the links shown in Figure 3-15, or you may search the SCOhelp documentation for a specific keyword using the Verity search engine, as shown in Figure 3-16. To access the Verity search engine, click on the Search button at the bottom of Figure 3-15.

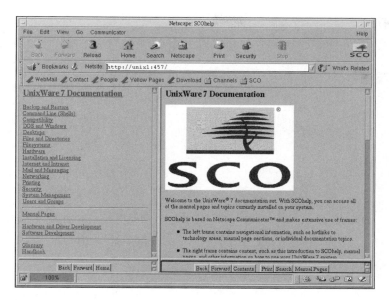

**Figure 3-15**    SCOhelp

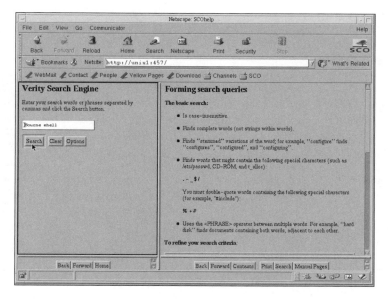

**Figure 3-16**    The Verity search engine

Entering a search string in Figure 3-16 will return hyperlinks to documents that contain the same string, as shown in Figure 3-17.

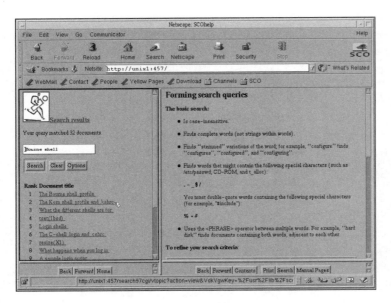

**Figure 3-17** Obtaining search results

If you do not receive a list of results when using the Verity search engine, your SCOhelp documentation has likely not been indexed for searching yet. To index the SCOhelp documentation after a UnixWare installation, type the command `/usr/man/bin/config_search -f` at a shell prompt.

**NOTE**

The contents of the System Handbook printed documentation that is shipped with UnixWare 7 is also contained in the SCOhelp documentation.

**NOTE**

In addition to displaying SCOhelp documentation, SCOhelp enables you to access the manual page database. To do this, press the Manual Pages button at the bottom of the SCOhelp screen and you will receive the screen shown in Figure 3-18, where you may search for manual pages by name and section.

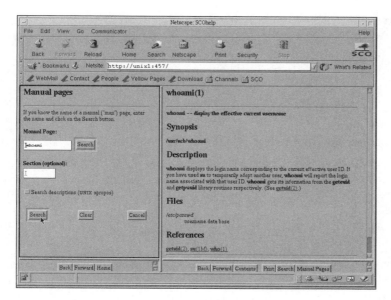

**Figure 3-18**   Searching manual pages in SCOhelp

## CHAPTER SUMMARY

- Users log into a terminal to obtain a UNIX user interface that may be used to interact with the UNIX kernel.

- Many users may be logged into different terminals simultaneously on the same UNIX system.

- The command-line UNIX user interface is called a shell; many different shells are available for UNIX users.

- UNIX shells interpret special characters that may need to be protected in certain situations.

- X Windows and a desktop environment comprise the GUI in UNIX; the standard UNIX desktop environment is the CDE.

- System and command documentation may be obtained using the manual pages or the SCOhelp utility.

- SCO Admin can be used to simplify some administrative tasks; it is available in both graphical and CHARM interfaces.

## KEY TERMS

**argument** — Text that appears after a command name, does not start with a dash (-) character, and specifies information the command requires to work properly.

**command** — A program that may be executed when typed on the command line.

**command-line terminal** — An interface that enables a user to interact with a command-line shell.

**Common Desktop Environment (CDE)** — One of the two default desktop environments provided with SCO UnixWare 7.1.1; it is also the standard desktop environment on UNIX.

**desktop environment** — A set of programs that provide a standard appearance for X Windows.

**graphical terminal** — An interface that enables a user to log in and start X Windows and a desktop environment.

**kernel** — The core component of the UNIX operating system.

**manual pages** — The most common set of local command syntax documentation, available by typing the man command-line utility—also known as man pages.

**metacharacter** — A single character that is interpreted by the shell as having specific or special meaning; the shell interprets several metacharacters specially.

**options** — Specific letters that start with one dash (-) or two dashes (--) and appear after the command name to alter the way the command works.

**Panorama desktop environment** — One of the two default desktop environments provided with SCO UnixWare 7.1.1.

**shell** — A user interface that accepts input from the user and passes the input to the kernel for processing.

**shutdown command** — A command used to safely shut down the UNIX operating system.

**terminal** — A channel that enables a user to log in and gain access to a UNIX system.

**virtual terminals** — Terminals located and accessed locally on the UNIX server.

**wall (warn all) command** — A command used to send a message to all users currently logged into the system.

**X Windows** — The component of the UNIX GUI that displays graphics to windows on the terminal screen.

## REVIEW QUESTIONS

1. Which of the following commands can you use to safely shut down the UNIX system in one minute?

    a. shutdown -g1 -y

    b. shutdown -g60

c. down

d. halt

e. crash stop

2. Both SCOhelp and SCO Admin have a CHARM interface when used in a command-line terminal. True or False?

3

3. Which of the following commands is equivalent to the man -k *keyword* command?

a. find *keyword*

b. man *keyword*

c. apropos *keyword*

d. appaloosa *keyword*

4. UNIX commands entered via the command line are not case sensitive. True or False?

5. Which of the following commands blanks the terminal screen, erasing previously displayed output?

a. erase

b. clean

c. blank

d. clear

6. When sitting at a computer running UNIX, what key combination is pressed to open the graphical terminal?

a. Ctrl+Alt+F1

b. Ctrl+Alt+7

c. Ctrl+Alt+F2

d. Ctrl+7

7. Which of the following is the default shell for normal users in UnixWare 7?

a. Bourne

b. Korn

c. BASH

d. C

8. When logging into a terminal, a user receives a user interface called a _____.

a. GUID

b. shell

c. text box

d. command screen

9. Which of the following manual page sections identifies commands that can only be run by the root user?

   a. M

   b. 1

   c. 3M

   d. 1M

10. How can you protect a metacharacter (such as the $ character) from shell interpretation?

    a. Precede it with a /.

    b. Follow it with a \.

    c. Precede it with a $.

    d. It cannot be done as metacharacters are essential.

    e. Precede it with a \.

11. The SCOhelp documentation in UnixWare 7.1.1 is automatically indexed after installation. True or False?

12. You know that there is a UNIX command that will perform a desired function for you, but you cannot remember the full name of the command. You do remember it will flush a variable from your system. Which of the following commands, when typed at a command prompt, shows a list of commands that will likely contain the one you desire?

    a. man -k flush

    b. man -k find all

    c. man flush

    d. man -key flush

13. Running SCO Admin from a command-line interface and a GUI terminal results in exactly the same display. True or False?

14. Which of the following commands can be used to send a message to all users on the system?

    a. wall

    b. net send

    c. console message

    d. update

15. Which of the following are shells available to users in UNIX? (Choose all that apply.)

    a. Dash

    b. Corn

c. BASH

d. Bourne

16. Which of the following command components is normally preceded by a dash?

   a. argument

   b. option

   c. modifier

   d. switch

17. Which of the following UNIX commands displays a calendar showing the current month?

   a. calendar

   b. date

   c. cal

   d. date –month

18. Which of the following command prompts signifies that a user is logged in as the root user?

   a. %

   b. #

   c. $

   d. @

19. Which of the following commands shows the users who are currently logged into the UNIX system?

   a. finger

   b. who

   c. id

   d. date

20. Which of the following desktop environments is provided by default with UnixWare 7.1.1? (Choose all that apply.)

   a. GNOME

   b. CDE

   c. X Windows

   d. Panorama

   e. Pandora

   f. KDE

21. X Windows was jointly developed by _____.
    a. AT&T Laboratories and MIT
    b. DEC and GNU Foundation
    c. University of California at Berkeley and Bell Laboratories
    d. DEC and MIT

22. The channel that allows a certain user to log in is called a _____.
    a. terminal
    b. interface
    c. shell
    d. GUI

23. What is the core component of the UNIX operating system referred to as?
    a. core
    b. root
    c. kernel
    d. interface

24. Which of the following manual page sections refers to device drivers and interfaces?
    a. X1M
    b. 3R
    c. 4
    d. 7

25. Which of the following commands shows the manual page for the date file?
    a. man -k date
    b. man date 4
    c. man sec 4 date
    d. man 4 date

# HANDS-ON PROJECTS

These projects should be completed in the order given. The hands-on projects should take a total of three hours to complete. The requirement for this lab includes:

❏ A UnixWare 7 system installed according to Project 2-2

## Project 3-1

In this hands-on project, you will interact with different shells on command-line terminals.

1. Once your UNIX system has been loaded, you will be placed at a graphical terminal (vt01). Switch to a command-line terminal (vt02) by pressing **Ctrl+Alt+F2**, and log into the terminal using the username **root** and the password **secret**. Which prompt did you receive and why?

2. At the command prompt, type **date** and press **Enter** to view the current date and time. Now, type **Date** and press **Enter**. Why did you receive an error message? Can you tell which shell gave you the error message? Type **echo $SHELL** at the command prompt and press **Enter** to confirm the shell that you are using.

3. Switch to a different command-line terminal (vt05) by pressing **Ctrl+Alt+F5**, and log into the terminal using the username **owner** and the password **secret**. Which prompt did you receive and why?

4. At the command prompt, type **who** and press **Enter** to view the users logged into the system. Who is logged in and on which terminal?

5. Switch back to the terminal vt02 by pressing **Ctrl+Alt+F2**. Did you need to log in? Are the outputs from the date and Date commands still visible?

6. Try typing in each command listed in Table 3-3 in order (pressing **Enter** after each one) and observe the output. What did the last command (exit) do?

7. Switch to the terminal tty5 by pressing **Ctrl+Alt+F5**, and type the command **ksh** and press **Enter**. What does this command do? Next, type **echo $SHELL** at the command prompt and press **Enter**. What shell are you using now?

8. At the command prompt, type **csh** and press **Enter**. What does this command do? Did your prompt change? Next, type **echo $SHELL** at the command prompt and press **Enter**. What shell are you using now?

9. Type **exit** at the command prompt and press **Enter** to log out of your shell. Which shell was exited? Type **echo $SHELL** to verify your answer.

10. Type **exit** at the command prompt and press **Enter**. Which shell was exited this time? Type **echo $SHELL** to verify your answer.

11. Type **exit** at the command prompt to log out of your shell. What happened and why?

## Project 3-2

In this hands-on project, you will log into a graphical terminal in UnixWare 7 and interact with the Panorama and CDE desktops.

1. Switch to the graphical terminal (vt01) by pressing **Ctrl+Alt+F1**, and log in using the username **root** and the password **secret**. Which desktop starts and why?

2. Observe the CDE desktop. Are there any minimized applications? Double-click on the minimized application in the upper-left corner of the screen. What application is it? What prompt do you receive and why?

3. At the command prompt, type **who** and press **Enter** to view the users logged into the system. Who is logged in and on which terminal? X Windows is typically started as the system console, whereas each shell started within the CDE desktop is termed a pseudo terminal session (pts) when viewed with the who command.

4. At the command prompt, type **echo $SHELL** and press **Enter** to view your current shell. Is this shell the same shell used for command-line terminals?

5. Click on the exit sign icon on the toolbar and press **OK** when prompted to confirm the logout request.

6. At the graphical login screen, use your mouse to select the **Options** menu, and choose **Session** and then **Panorama Session** from that menu. What appears near the top of the graphical login screen? Log in as the user **root** and use the password **secret**.

7. Observe the Panorama desktop. Is a shell prompt available? Use your mouse to click on the blue background and select **Quit pmwm**. When prompted to confirm the action, press **OK**.

# Project 3-3

In this hands-on project, you will use and protect shell metacharacters.

1. Switch to a command-line terminal (vt02) by pressing **Ctrl+Alt+F2**, and log into the terminal using the username **root** and the password **secret**.

2. At the command prompt, type **date;who** and press **Enter** to run the date command immediately followed by the who command. Use the information in Table 3-4 to describe the purpose of the ; metacharacter.

3. At the command prompt, type **echo This is OK** and press **Enter** to show a message on the terminal screen.

4. At the command prompt, type **echo Don't do this** and press **Enter**. Which character needs to be protected in the previous command? Press **Del** to cancel your command and return to a shell prompt.

5. At the command prompt, type **echo "Don't do this"** and press **Enter**. What appears on the terminal screen?

6. At the command prompt, type **echo Don\'t do this** and press **Enter**. What appears on the terminal screen?

7. At the command prompt, type **echo $SHELL** and press **Enter** to view the contents of the variable SHELL using a shell metacharacter. Next, type **echo $TEST** and press **Enter** to find out what happens when a variable that does not exist is used in a command. What appears?

8. At the command prompt, type **echo You have $4.50** and press **Enter**. What appears? Why? Which character needs to be protected in the previous command? What are two different ways that you can protect this character from interpretation by the shell?

> If you are prompted to accept a Netscape License Agreement, press **Accept** to continue.
>
> **NOTE**

9. At the command prompt, type **echo 'You have $4.50'** and press **Enter**. What appears on the terminal screen? Did the single quotes protect this metacharacter from shell interpretation?

10. At the command prompt, type **echo "You have $4.50"** and press **Enter**. What appears on the terminal screen? Did the double quotes protect this metacharacter from shell interpretation?

11. At the command prompt, type **echo You have \$4.50** and press **Enter**. What appears on the terminal screen? Did the backslash protect this metacharacter from shell interpretation?

12. At the command prompt, type **uname** and press **Enter**. What appears?

13. At the command prompt, type **echo I am using `uname`** and press **Enter**. What function do the backquotes perform?

14. Type **exit** and press **Enter** to log out of your shell.

**HANDS-ON PROJECTS**

# Project 3-4

In this hands-on project, you will find information about commands using online help utilities.

1. Switch to a command-line terminal (vt02) by pressing **Ctrl+Alt+F2**, and log into the terminal using the username **root** and the password **secret**.

2. At the command prompt, type **man -k cron** and press **Enter** to view a list of manual pages that have the word **cron** in the name or description. Use Table 3-5 to determine what type of manual pages appears. How many manual pages are there for cron? Are they different types of manual pages?

3. At the command prompt, type **man cron** and press **Enter** to view the manual page for the cron command. Observe the description of cron, press **q**, and then press **Enter** when finished to exit the manual page and return to your command prompt.

4. At the command prompt, type **man 4 cron** and press **Enter** to view the manual page for the cron file. Observe the syntax of the cron file format, and press **q** when finished to exit the manual page and return to your command prompt.

5. At the command prompt, type **scohelp** and press **Enter**. What error message did you receive? Why?

6. Type **exit** and press **Enter** to log out of your shell.

7. Switch to the graphical terminal (vt01) by pressing **Ctrl+Alt+F1**, and log into the terminal using the username **root** and the password **secret**.

8. Click on the arrow above the question mark icon on the CDE toolbar and select **SCOhelp**. What other methods can be used to start SCOhelp?

**NOTE**  If the SCOhelp documentation does not appear, open a shell prompt by clicking on the computer icon on the CDE toolbar and enter the command /etc/scohelphttp start.

9. Observe the SCOhelp window. Next, maximize the SCOhelp screen by clicking on the upper-right box of the window.

10. Click on the **Manual Pages** button at the bottom right of the screen. Enter the word **cron** in the Manual Page box and **4** in the Section box, and click on the **Search** button. Do you recognize this manual page?

11. Click on the **Search** button at the bottom right of the screen. Enter the word **cron** in the Verity Search Engine box and press the **Search** button. Were any results shown from the SCOhelp documentation? Why?

12. Minimize the SCOhelp application using the button second from the right in the upper-left corner of the window. Where does SCOhelp appear on the desktop?

13. Click on the computer icon on the CDE toolbar to open a shell prompt.

14. At the command prompt, type **/usr/man/bin/config_search -f** and press **Enter** to index the SCOhelp Web pages. This process should take approximately three minutes. When it is finished, type **exit** and press **Enter** to close the shell.

**NOTE**  You may need to press **Enter** to get your prompt back when the config_search command has completed.

15. Maximize the SCOhelp application by double-clicking on the appropriate icon on your desktop. Enter the word **cron** in the Verity Search Engine box if it is not already there and press the **Search** button. Were any results shown from the SCOhelp documentation? Why?

16. Open the window menu by clicking on the upper-left corner of your window and select **Close** to close the SCOhelp utility.

17. Click on the exit sign icon on the CDE toolbar and click **OK** when prompted to log out of the CDE desktop environment.

**HANDS-ON PROJECTS**

## Project 3-5

In this hands-on project, you will use the SCO Admin utility in both CHARM and graphical interface modes, and properly shut down your system.

1. Switch to the graphical terminal (vt01) by pressing **Ctrl+Alt+F1**, and log into the terminal using the username **owner** and the password **secret**.

2. Click on the arrow above the SCO bonsai tree icon on the CDE toolbar and select **SCO Admin** from the list. What managers are listed? What other method can be used to open SCO Admin?

3. Navigate to the **System** folder at the bottom of the list and open it by double-clicking on it. Next, double-click the **System Shutdown Manager**.

4. View the System Shutdown Manager. By default, how long must you wait before the shutdown process begins? Change the number to **0** in the Minutes box. Next, select the **Reboot after Shutdown** button. Next, select the **Shutdown** menu and click on the **Begin Shutdown** button. When prompted to shut down, press **OK**.

5. When your system has rebooted, switch to a command-line terminal (vt02) by pressing **Ctrl+Alt+F2**, and log into the terminal using the username **root** and the password **secret**.

6. At the command prompt, type **scoadmin -t** and press **Enter**. How many SCO Admin managers start with the word **System**?

7. At the command prompt, type **scoadmin system shut** and press **Enter**. What appears and why?

8. In the System Shutdown Manager, press **Enter** to open the Host menu, select **Exit**, and press **Enter** to exit the System Shutdown Manager. When prompted to save your changes, select **No** and press **Enter**.

9. At the command prompt, type **shutdown –g0 –y** and press **Enter**. What does this command do? If prompted that it is safe to power off the computer, turn off the power to your computer.

---

## DISCOVERY EXERCISES

1. You are the network administrator for Polupaski Inc., a peripheral device company. The network uses UNIX and you need help information on some commands to perform your job. Open the manual pages and find all the commands that have the word "zone" in their name or description. What command did you use to accomplish this task? Are there any commands in this list that only a root user can execute? How are they indicated? Select any two of them and compare their manual pages. Access and read the manual pages on three other commands that interest you either by using the command name or searching for them by related keyword (try using apropos).

2. Use the SCOhelp utility to obtain help on how to configure an NIC in UnixWare. How did you find the answer? Were there any links to manual pages? Were there any hyperlinks to other useful information?

3. Provided you have a functional Web browser and Internet connection, research the history of the CDE. When did it become the standard UNIX desktop and which UNIX vendors first implemented it? Also research the more recent GNOME and KDE desktops, and compare them to the CDE desktop. Where are these desktops used?

4. Identify the errors with the following commands and indicate possible solutions. *Hint*: Try typing them out at a shell prompt to view the error message.

Echo "This command does not work properly"

date –z

apropos man –k

finger route

shutdown –g

echo "I would like lots of $$$"

man 6 date

# 4

# MANAGING FILES AND DIRECTORIES

> **After reading this chapter and completing the exercises, you will be able to:**
>
> ♦ Understand the UNIX directory structure and Filesystem Hierarchy Standard (FHS)
>
> ♦ Navigate the UNIX directory structure using relative and absolute pathnames
>
> ♦ Describe the various types of UNIX files
>
> ♦ View filenames and file types
>
> ♦ Use shell wildcards to specify multiple filenames
>
> ♦ Use standard UNIX commands to manage files and directories
>
> ♦ Find files and directories on the filesystem
>
> ♦ Understand and create linked files

An understanding of the structure and commands surrounding the UNIX filesystem is essential for effectively using UNIX to manipulate data. In the first part of this chapter, you will explore the UNIX filesystem hierarchy by changing your position in the filesystem tree and listing different filenames. Next, you will learn about shell wildcard metacharacters and the common commands used to manage files and directories. Finally, you will explore commands that can be used to locate and link files on a filesystem.

## THE UNIX DIRECTORY STRUCTURE

Understanding how UNIX stores files on the hard drive is fundamental to using the UNIX operating system. Typical UNIX systems could have thousands of data and program files on the hard drive, so a structure that organizes those files is necessary to make it easier to find and manipulate data and run programs. UNIX uses a logical directory tree to organize files into different directories. Directories are also called folders since they hold files much like the folders inside a filing cabinet. When you store files in a certain directory, they are physically stored in the filesystem of a certain slice in the UNIX partition on a hard disk inside the computer.

UNIX shares many similarities to the Windows operating system with respect to filesystem structure; both operating systems use directories to store files, yet use slightly different nomenclature when identifying those files. In the Windows operating system directory tree structure shown in Figure 4-1, each filesystem on a hard drive partition is referred to by a drive letter (such as C: or D:) and has a root directory (indicated by the \ character) containing subdirectories that together form a hierarchical tree.

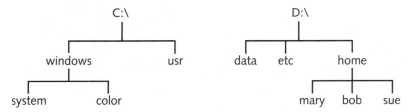

**Figure 4-1**    A Windows directory tree

It is important to describe directories in the directory tree properly; the **absolute pathname** to a file or directory is the full pathname of a certain file or directory starting from the root directory. In Figure 4-1, the absolute pathname for the color directory is C:\windows\color and the absolute pathname for the sue directory is D:\home\sue. In other words, C:\windows\color refers to the color directory below the windows directory below the root of the C: drive; similarly, D:\home\sue refers to the sue directory below the home directory below the root of the D: drive.

UNIX uses a similar directory structure; however, there are no drive letters. There is a single root (referred to using the / character), and different filesystems on hard drive slices are mounted to different directories on this directory tree such that filesystems are transparent to the user. Figure 4-2 shows an example of a UNIX directory tree equivalent to the Windows directory tree shown in Figure 4-1.

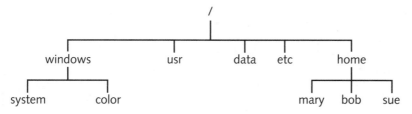

**Figure 4-2**   A UNIX directory tree

In Figure 4-2, the absolute pathname for the color directory is /windows/color and the absolute pathname for the sue directory is /home/sue. In other words, the /windows/color directory refers to the color directory below the windows directory below the root of system (the / character); similarly, the /home/sue directory refers to the sue directory below the home directory below the root of the system.

## Changing Directories

When users log into their UNIX system, they are placed in their **home directory**, which is a unique place for users to store their personal files. Regular users usually have a home directory named after their user account under the /home directory, as in /home/sue. The root user, however, uses the / directory as the home directory. You can confirm the directory that you are currently in on the system by observing the name at the end of the shell prompt or by typing the **pwd (print working directory) command** at a command-line prompt and pressing Enter. If you are logged in as the root user, the following output appears on the terminal screen:

```
# pwd
/
#_
```

However, if you are logged in as the user sue, you will receive the following output:

```
$ pwd
/home/sue
$_
```

To change directories, you can issue the **cd (change directory) command** with an argument specifying the destination directory. If you do not specify a destination directory, the cd command simply returns you to your home directory:

```
# cd /home/mary
# pwd
/home/mary
# cd /etc
# pwd
/etc
# cd
```

```
# pwd
/
# _
```

In the examples discussed earlier, the argument specified after the **cd** command is an absolute pathname to a directory; the system has all the information it needs to find the destination directory as the pathname starts from the root (/) of the system. However, in order to avoid typing in the entire pathname each time, you may use a relative pathname in place of an absolute pathname in most UNIX commands. A **relative pathname** is the pathname of a target file or directory relative to your current directory in the tree. To specify a directory underneath your current directory, refer to that directory by name (do not start the pathname with a / character). To refer to a directory closer to the root of the tree (also known as a parent directory), use two periods (**..**). The following is an example of using relative pathnames to move around the directory tree:

```
# cd /home/mary
# pwd
/home/mary
# cd ..
# pwd
/home
# cd mary
# pwd
/home/mary
# _
```

In this example, .. was used to move up one parent directory and the word "mary" was used to specify the mary **subdirectory** relative to our current location in the tree; however, you may also move more than one level up or down the directory tree:

```
# cd /home/mary
# pwd
/home/mary
# cd ../..
# pwd
/
# cd home/mary
# pwd
/home/mary
# _
```

**NOTE**

You may also use one period (.) to refer to the current directory. Although this is not useful when using the **cd** command to change directories, it will be useful later on in the textbook.

Although absolute pathnames are straightforward enough to use as arguments to commands when specifying the location of a certain file or directory, relative pathnames can save you a great deal of typing and reduce the potential for error if your current directory is far away from the root directory. Say, for example, that the current directory is /home/sue/projects/acme/plans and you want to change this to the /home/sue/projects/acme directory. Using an absolute pathname, you would type cd /home/sue/projects/acme. However, by using a relative pathname, you would only need to type cd .. to perform the same task since the /home/sue/projects/acme directory is one parent directory above the current location in the directory tree.

**4**

## THE FILESYSTEM HIERARCHY STANDARD (FHS)

A typical UNIX system has thousands of files that are logically organized into directories in the UNIX directory tree. This complexity also enables different UNIX flavors to place files in different places; as a result, a great deal of time can be spent searching for a common configuration file on a foreign UNIX system. To solve this problem, the **Filesystem Hierarchy Standard (FHS)** was created.

The FHS defines a standard set of directories for use by all UNIX systems, as well as the file and subdirectory contents of each directory. This ensures that a Solaris user will find the correct configuration file on a UnixWare or HP-UX system with little difficulty, as the **filename** and location follow a standard convention. The FHS also gives UNIX software developers the ability to locate files on a UNIX system regardless of the flavor and hence create software that is not flavor specific.

A comprehensive understanding of the standard types of directories found on UNIX systems is valuable when locating and managing files and directories. Table 4-1 lists some standard UNIX directories and their descriptions as defined by the FHS. These directories will be discussed throughout this chapter and following chapters.

**NOTE**

You can read the complete FHS definition at *www.pathname.com/fhs/*.

**Table 4-1** Directories defined by the FHS

| Directory | Description |
|-----------|-------------|
| /bin | Contains binary commands for use by all users |
| /dev | Contains device files |
| /etc | Contains system-specific configuration files |
| /home | Default location for user home directories |
| /lib | Contains shared program libraries (used by the commands in /bin and /sbin) |
| /mnt | Empty directory used for accessing (mounting) disks such as floppy disks and CD-ROMs |
| /opt | Stores additional software programs |

**Table 4-1**    Directories defined by the FHS (continued)

| Directory | Description |
|-----------|-------------|
| /proc | Stores process and kernel information |
| /root | The root user's home directory |
| /sbin | Contains system binary commands (used for administration) |
| /tmp | Holds temporary files created by programs |
| /usr | Contains most system commands and utilities—commonly contains the following directories: <br>/usr/bin — user binary commands<br>/usr/games — educational programs and games<br>/usr/include — C program header files<br>/usr/lib — libraries<br>/usr/local — local programs<br>/usr/sbin — system binary commands<br>/usr/share — files that are architecture independent<br>/usr/src — source code<br>/usr/X11R6 — the X Window System |
| /var | Contains log files and spools |

## VIEWING FILES AND DIRECTORIES

Once a directory structure exists to organize files into an easy-to-use format, you can list directory contents to locate the files users may need to execute, view, or edit. On a similar note, you must also understand the various types of files and filenames that can be listed, as well as the different commands used to select filenames for viewing.

### File Types

It is important to have a solid understanding of the various types of files present on most UNIX systems when viewing files and directories. Several different types of files can exist on a UNIX system. The most common include:

- **Text files**
- **Binary data files**
- **Executable program files**
- **Directory files**
- **Linked files**
- **Special device files**
- **Named pipes** and **sockets**

4

Most files on a UNIX system that contain configuration information are text files. Programs are also files that exist on the hard drive before they are executed in memory to become processes, and are usually associated with several supporting binary data files that store information such as common functions and graphics. Directories are just special files that serve as placeholders to organize other files; when you create a directory, a file is placed on the hard drive to represent that directory. Linked files are files that have an association with one another; they can represent the same data or can point to another file (also known as a shortcut file). These files are discussed in more detail later in this chapter in the section headed Linking Files.

Special device files are less common than the other file types that have been mentioned, but they are important for system administrators as they represent different devices on the system such as hard disks and serial ports. These device files are used in conjunction with commands that manipulate devices on the system. Special device files are typically found only in the /dev directory. These files will be discussed in later chapters of this textbook. As with special device files, named pipe files are uncommon and used primarily by administrators. Named pipes identify a channel that passes information from one process in memory to another and, in some cases, can be mediated by files on the hard drive; one process writes to the file while another process reads from it to achieve this passing of information. Another variant of a named pipe file is a socket file that enables a process on another computer to write to a file on the local computer while another process reads from that file.

## Filenames

Files are recognized by their filename, which are rarely longer than 20 characters on most UNIX systems, even though they can include up to 255 characters. Filenames are typically comprised of alphanumeric characters, the underscore (_), the dash (-), and the period (.).

**NOTE**

It is important to avoid using the shell metacharacters discussed in the previous chapter when naming files. Using a filename that contains a shell metacharacter (such as my$file.txt) as an argument to a UNIX command might produce unexpected results.

**NOTE**

Filenames that start with a period (.) are referred to as **hidden files**; they require a special command to be seen. These are covered in the next section of this chapter.

Although filenames used by the Windows operating system typically end with a period and three characters that describe the file type as in document.txt (text) and server.exe (executable program), most files on the hard drive of a UNIX system do not follow this pattern. However, some files on the UNIX filesystem do contain characters at the end of the filename that indicate the file type. These characters are commonly referred to as

**filename extensions**. Table 4-2 shows some common filename extensions and their associated file types.

**Table 4-2**    Common filename extensions

| Metacharacter | Description |
| --- | --- |
| .c | C programming language source code files |
| .cc<br>.cpp | C++ programming language source code files |
| .html<br>.htm | HTML files |
| .ps | Files formatted for printing with PostScript |
| .txt | Text files |
| .tar | Archived files (contain other files within) |
| .gz<br>.bz2<br>.Z | Compressed files |
| .tar.gz<br>.tgz<br>.tar.Z | Compressed archived files |
| .conf<br>.cfg | Configuration files (contain text) |
| .so | Shared object (programming library) files |
| .o | Compiled object files |
| .pl | Practical Extraction and Report Language (PERL) programs |
| .tcl | Tool Command Language (TCL) programs |
| .jpg<br>.jpeg<br>.png<br>.tiff<br>.xpm<br>.gif | Binary files that contain graphical images |
| .sh | Shell scripts (contain text that is executed by the shell) |

## Listing Files

UNIX hosts a variety of commands that can be used to display files and their types in various directories on filesystems. The most common method for displaying files is by using the **ls command**. The following is a sample file listing in the /projects directory that will be used throughout this chapter for demonstration only:

```
# pwd
/projects
```

```
# ls
Newfiles project   project12 project2 project4
myscript project1  project13 project3 project5
# _
```

The `ls` command shows all the files in the current directory in columnar format; however, you may also pass an argument to the `ls` command indicating the directory to be listed if the current directory listing is not required. In the following example, the files underneath the /home/bob directory are listed without changing the current directory:

```
# pwd
/projects
# ls /home/bob
assignment1 file1 letter letter2 project1
# _
```

Recall from the previous chapter that you can use switches to alter the behavior of commands. To view a list of files and their type, use the `−F` switch to the `ls` command:

```
# pwd
/projects
# ls -F
Newfiles/ project@ project12 project2 project4*
myscript* project1 project13 project3 project5
# _
```

The `ls −F` command appends a special character at the end of each filename to indicate the type of file. In the previous output, note that the filenames myscript, Newfiles, project, and project4 have special characters appended to their names. The @ symbol indicates a linked file, the * symbol indicates an executable file, the / character indicates a subdirectory, and the | character indicates a named pipe. All other file types do not have a special character appended to them and could be text files, binary data files, or special device files.

**NOTE** It is a common convention to name directories starting with an uppercase letter such as *N* in the Newfiles directory shown in the previous output. This ensures that directories are listed at the beginning of the `ls` command output and enables you to quickly determine which names refer to directories when running the `ls` command without any options that specify file type.

Although the `ls −F` command is a quick way of getting file type information in an easy-to-read format, there are times when you will need to obtain more detailed information about each file. The `ls −1` command can be used to provide a long listing for each file in a certain directory:

```
# pwd
/projects
# ls -l
total 158
drwxr-xr-x  2 root  sys      96 Sep 17 19:55 Newfiles
```

```
-rwxr-xr-x  1 root  sys     188 Sep 17 19:57 myscript
lrwxrwxrwx  1 root  sys       8 Sep 17 19:57 project -> project1
-rw-r--r--  1 root  sys     145 Sep 17 19:55 project1
-rw-r--r--  1 root  sys     613 Sep 17 19:57 project12
-rw-r--r--  1 root  sys     681 Sep 17 19:57 project13
-rw-r--r--  1 root  sys     145 Sep 17 19:55 project2
-rw-r--r--  1 root  sys      74 Sep 17 19:55 project3
-rwxr-xr-x  1 root  sys   74312 Sep 17 20:15 project4
-rw-r--r--  1 root  sys       0 Sep 17 20:14 project5
#  _
```

Each file listed in this example has eight components of information listed in columns from left to right:

1. A file type character
   - The *d* character represents a directory.
   - The *l* character represents a symbolically linked file (discussed later).
   - The *b* or *c* characters represent special device files (discussed later).
   - The *p* character represents a named pipe.
   - The – character represents all other file types (text files and binary data files).

2. A list of permissions on the file (also called the **mode** of the file)

3. A hard link count (hard links are discussed later)

4. The **owner** of the file (discussed later)

5. The **group** owner of the file (discussed later)

6. The file size

7. The most recent modification time of the file

8. The filename (some files are shortcuts or pointers to other files, which are indicated with an arrow -> as with the file called project in the previous output; these are known as **symbolic links**, which are discussed later)

The file named project1 in the previous example is a regular file as the long listing of it begins with a – character, the permissions on the file are rw-r--r--, the hard link count is 1, the owner of the file is the root user, the group owner of the file is the sys group, the size of the file is 145 bytes, and the file was modified last on September 17th at 7:55 P.M.

Many UNIX systems offer shorter alternatives to commonly used commands. For UnixWare, the **l command** gives a listing similar to an `ls -l` command and the `lf` command gives a listing similar to an `ls -F` command.

The `ls -F` and `ls -l` commands are valuable to a user who wants to display file types; however, neither of these commands can display all file types using special characters. To show the file type of any file, you can use the **file command**; just give the `file` command an argument specifying what file to analyze. You may also pass multiple files as arguments or use the * metacharacter to refer to all files in the current directory. The following is an example of using the `file` command in the root user's home directory:

```
# pwd
/projects
# file project1
project1:        ascii text
# file Newfiles myscript
Newfiles:        directory
myscript:        commands text
# file *
Newfiles:        directory
myscript:        commands text
project:         ascii text
project1:        ascii text
project12:       ascii text
project13:       ascii text
project2:        ascii text
project3:        ascii text
project4:        ELF 32-bit LSB executable 80386 Version 1
project5:        Empty file
# _
```

As shown in this example, the `file` command can also identify the differences between the types of executable files. The myscript file is a text file that contains executable commands (also known as a shell script), whereas the project4 file is a 32-bit executable compiled program. In addition the `file` command also identifies empty files such as project5 in the previous example.

Some filenames represent important configuration files or program directories. Since these files are rarely edited by the user and might clutter up the listing of files, they are normally hidden from view when the `ls` and `file` commands are used. Recall from earlier that their filenames start with a period (.). To view them, pass the `-a` option to the `ls` command. Home directories typically contain many hidden files; the following output lists those in the home directory for the user mary:

```
# pwd
/home/mary
# ls
# ls -a
.                   .Xauthority  .login         .sh_history
..                  .dt          .profile       .vtlrc
.UpgradeVer7.1.1 .dtprofile     .scoadmin.pref
#_
```

As discussed earlier, . refers to the current working directory and .. refers to the parent directory relative to your current location in the directory tree; each of these pointers is seen as a special (or fictitious) file when using the `ls  -a` command, as they each start with a period.

In addition, you may specify several options simultaneously for most commands on the command line and receive the combined functionality of all the options. For example, to view the hidden files in mary's home directory and their file types, type the following:

```
# pwd
/home/mary
# ls -aF
./                      .Xauthority  .login            .sh_history
../                     .dt/         .profile          .vtlrc
.UpgradeVer7.1.1 .dtprofile*  .scoadmin.pref
#
```

The aforementioned options to the `ls` command (`-l`, `-F`, and `-a`) are the most common options used when navigating the UNIX directory tree; however, many options that alter the listing of files on the filesystem are available in the `ls` command. Table 4-3 describes these options.

**Table 4-3** Common options to the `ls` command

| Option | Description |
|--------|-------------|
| -a | Lists all filenames |
| -A | Lists most filenames (excludes the . and .. special files) |
| -C | Lists filenames in column format (default action) |
| -d | Views directory filenames only (not their contents) |
| -F | Lists filenames classified by file type |
| -l | Lists filenames in long format |
| -i | Lists the inode number for each file and directory (inode numbers are discussed later in the chapter in the section entitled Linking Files) |
| -r | Lists filenames reverse sorted |
| -R | Lists filenames in the specified directory and all subdirectories |
| -s | Lists filenames and their associated size in blocks (typically, 1 block = 1KB) |
| -t | Lists filenames sorted by modification time |
| -u | Lists filenames sorted by the most recently accessed time |
| -x | Lists filenames in rows rather than in columns |

## Wildcard Metacharacters

In the previous section, the * metacharacter was used to indicate or match all the files in the current directory much like a wildcard matches certain cards in a card game. As a result, the * metacharacter is called a **wildcard metacharacter**; these characters can simplify commands that specify more than one filename on the command line as shown with the `file` command earlier. These wildcard metacharacters are interpreted by the shell and can be used with most common UNIX filesystem commands, including a few that have already been mentioned (`ls`, `file`, and `cd`). These metacharacters match

certain portions of filenames or the entire filename itself. Table 4-4 describes the wildcard metacharacters.

**Table 4-4** Wildcard metacharacters

| Metacharacter | Description |
|---|---|
| * | Matches zero or more characters in a filename |
| ? | Matches one character in a filename |
| [aegh] | Matches one character in a filename—provided this character is either an a, e, g, or h |
| [a-e] | Matches one character in a filename—provided this character is either an a, b, c, d, or e |
| [!a-e] | Matches one character in a filename—provided this character is *not* an *a, b, c, d,* or *e* |

Wildcards can be demonstrated well using the `ls` command. The following list of commands
provides examples of using wildcard metacharacters to narrow down the listing produced by
the `ls` command:

```
# pwd
/projects
# ls
Newfiles    project   project12 project2 project4
myscript    project1  project13 project3 project5
# ls project*
project     project12 project2 project4
project1    project13 project3 project5
# ls project?
project1  project2 project3 project4 project5
# ls project??
project12  project13
# ls project[135]
project1  project3 project5
# ls project[!135]
project2  project4
# _
```

# MANAGING FILES AND DIRECTORIES

As mentioned earlier, using a UNIX system involves navigating around several directories
and manipulating the files inside them. Thus, an efficient UNIX user must understand how
to create directories as needed, copy or move files from one directory to another, and
delete files and directories; these tasks are commonly referred to as file management tasks.

Take, for example, the /projects directory contents shown earlier in this chapter:

```
# pwd
/projects
# ls -F
Newfiles/ project@ project12 project2 project4
myscript* project1 project13 project3 project5
# _
```

As shown in the previous output, there is only one directory (Newfiles), an executable shell script (myscript), and several project-related files (project*). Although this directory structure is not cluttered and appears in an easy-to-read fashion on the terminal screen, typical directories on a UNIX system contain many more files. As a result, it is good form to organize these files into subdirectories based on the file's purpose. Since the /projects directory in the previous output has several project files, a subdirectory called proj_files could be created to contain the project-related files and decrease the size of the directory listing. To do this, use the mkdir command, which takes arguments specifying the absolute or relative pathnames of the directories to create. To create a proj_files directory underneath the current directory, use the mkdir command with a relative pathname:

```
# mkdir proj_files
# ls -F
Newfiles/     proj_files/ project1   project13 project3 project5
myscript*     project@    project12 project2  project4*
# __
```

Now you can move the project files into the proj_files subdirectory by using the mv (move) command. The mv command requires two arguments at minimum: the **source file/directory** and the **target file/directory**. If several files are to be moved, specify several source arguments; the last argument then becomes the target directory. Both the source(s) and destination may be absolute or relative pathnames, and the source might contain wildcards if several files are to be moved. For example, to move all of the project files to the proj_files directory, you could type mv with the source argument project* (to match all files starting with the letters "project") and the target argument proj_files (the relative pathname to the destination directory), as shown in the following output:

```
# mv project* proj_files
# ls -F
Newfiles/     myscript*  proj_files/
# ls -F proj_files
project@      project12 project2 project4*
project1      project13 project3 project5
# _
```

In the previous output, the current directory listing does not show the project files anymore, yet the listing of the proj_files subdirectory indicates that they were moved successfully.

Since the mv command moves the location of a file, be sure not to forget the new file location.

If the target is the name of a directory, then the mv command will move those files to that directory. If the target is a filename of an existing file in a certain directory and there is one source file, then the mv command will move that file to the target directory and rename it the target filename. If the target is a filename of a nonexistent file in a certain directory, then the mv command will create a new file with that filename in the target directory and move the source file to that file.

Another important use of the mv command is to rename files, which is simply moving a file to the same directory but with a different filename. To rename the myscript file from earlier examples to myscript2, use the following mv command:

```
# ls -F
Newfiles/     myscript*     proj_files/
# mv myscript myscript2
# ls -F
Newfiles/     myscript2*     proj_files/
#
```

Similarly, the mv command can rename directories. If the source is the name of an existing directory, it will be renamed to whatever directory name is specified as the target.

The mv command works similar to a cut-and-paste operation in which the file is copied to a new directory and deleted from the source directory. There may be times, however, when the file in the source directory should be maintained; this is referred to as copying a file and can be accomplished using the cp command. Much like the mv command, the cp command takes two arguments at minimum; the first argument specifies the source file/directory to be copied and the second argument specifies the target file/directory. If several files need to be copied to a destination directory, specify several source arguments and the last argument on the command line becomes the target directory. Each argument may be an absolute or relative pathname and may contain wildcards or the special metacharacters . (which specifies the current directory) and .. (which specifies the parent directory). For example, to make a copy of the file /etc/hosts in the current directory (/projects), specify the absolute pathname to the /etc/hosts file (/etc/hosts) and the relative pathname indicating the current directory (.):

```
# cp /etc/hosts .
# ls -F
```

```
Newfiles/     hosts        myscript2*     proj_files/
# _
```

You can also make copies of files in the same directory; to make a copy of the hosts file called hosts2 in the current directory, type the following command:

```
# cp hosts hosts2
# ls -F
Newfiles/     hosts     hosts2     myscript2*     proj_files/
#_
```

One notable difference between the **mv** and **cp** commands aside from their purpose is that they work on directories differently. The **mv** command renames a directory, whereas the **cp** command creates a whole new copy of the directory and its contents. To copy a directory full of files in UNIX, you must tell the **cp** command that the copy will be **recursive** (involve files and subdirectories too) by using the **-r** option. The following example demonstrates copying the proj_files directory and all of its contents to the /home/mary directory with and without the **-r** option:

```
# ls -F
Newfiles/     hosts          hosts2 myscript2* proj_files/
# ls -F /home/owner
# cp proj_files /home/owner
UX:cp: ERROR: <proj_files> is a directory
# cp -r proj_files /home/owner
# ls -F /home/mary
proj_files/
# _
```

**NOTE**

When copying or moving files, if the target is a file that exists, the mv and cp commands will overwrite the target file without prompting the user. If you suspect that files may be overwritten during a copy or move, just use the -i(interactive) option to either the cp or mv command and the system will prompt you to confirm any overwriting.

Creating directories, and copying and moving files are file management tasks that preserve or create data on the hard disk. To remove files or directories, you must use either the **rm** command or the **rmdir** command.

The **rm** command takes a list of arguments specifying the absolute or relative pathnames of files to remove. As with most commands, wildcards can be specified to simplify specifying the multiple files to remove. Once a file has been removed from the filesystem, it cannot be recovered. Like the **cp** and **mv** commands, the **rm** command also accepts the **-i** option to prompt the user to confirm each file deletion. The following shows an example demonstrating the use of the **rm** command to remove the hosts2 file:

```
# ls -F
Newfiles/     hosts  hosts2     myscript2*     proj_files/
# rm hosts2
```

```
# ls -F
Newfiles/    hosts  myscript2* proj_files/
# _
```

To remove a directory, you could use the **rmdir** command; however, the **rmdir** command will only remove a directory if there are no files within it. To remove a directory and the files inside, you must use the **rm** command and specify that a directory full of files should be removed. Recall from earlier that you need to use the recursive option (**-r**) with the **cp** command to copy directories; to remove a directory full of files, you can also use a recursive option (**-r**) with the **rm** command. Say, for example, that the root user wanted to remove the proj_files subdirectory of /project and all of the files within it without being prompted to confirm each file deletion; the command **rm -r proj_files** must be used to do this as illustrated below:

```
# pwd
/projects
# ls -F
Newfiles/     hosts      myscript2*     proj_files/
# rm -r proj_files
# ls -F
Newfiles/  hosts  myscript2*
# _
```

In most commands, such as rm and cp, both the -r and the -R options have the same meaning (recursive).

**NOTE**

The -r option to the rm command is dangerous if you are not sure what files exist in the directory to be deleted recursively. As a result, the -r option to the rm command is commonly referred to as the -resume option, because if you use it incorrectly, you might need to prepare your resume.

**NOTE**

It is important to note that the aforementioned file management commands are commonly used by UNIX users, developers, and administrators alike. Table 4-5 summarizes these common file management commands.

**Table 4-5**   Common UNIX file management commands

| Command | Description |
|---------|-------------|
| mkdir | Creates directories |
| rmdir | Removes empty directories |
| mv | Moves / renames files and directories |
| cp | Copies files and directories full of files (with the -r option) |
| rm | Removes files and directories full of files (with the -r option) |

## Finding Files

Before using the file management commands mentioned in the last section, you must know the locations of the files involved. One of the most versatile methods for locating files on the filesystem is using the `find` command. The `find` command searches the directory tree recursively starting from a certain directory for files that meet certain criteria. The format of the `find` command is as follows:

find *<start directory>* -criteria *<what to find>*

For example, to find any files named inittab underneath the /etc directory, use the command `find /etc -name inittab`. You will receive the following output:

```
# find /etc -name inittab
/etc/inittab
# _
```

You can also use wildcard metacharacters with the `find` command; however, because they must only be interpreted by the `find` command, these wildcards must be protected from shell interpretation. To do this, ensure that any wildcard metacharacters are enclosed within quote characters. The following output shows an example of using the `find` command with wildcard metacharacters to find all files that start with the word "host" underneath the /etc directory:

```
# find /etc -name "host*"
/etc/inst/save/etc/net/ticlts/hosts
/etc/inst/save/etc/net/ticots/hosts
/etc/inst/save/etc/net/ticotsord/hosts
/etc/mail/hoststat
/etc/inet/hosts
/etc/inet/hosts.allow
/etc/inet/hosts.deny
/etc/net/ticlts/hosts
/etc/net/ticots/hosts
/etc/net/ticotsord/hosts
/etc/hosts
# _
```

Although searching by name is the most common criterion used with the `find` command, many other criteria may be used with the `find` command as well. To find all files starting from the /var directory that have a size greater than 1024KB, use the following command:

```
# find /var -size +2048
/var/sadm/install/contents
# _
```

The size of a file must be specified in 512-byte blocks (1/2KB); thus, the number 2048 in the previous example indicates 1024KB.

In addition, if you wanted to find all the directories only underneath the /dev directory, type the following command:

```
# find /dev -type d
/dev
/dev/dsk
/dev/kd
/dev/rdsk
/dev/sad
/dev/byte
/dev/byte/dec
/dev/byte/hex
/dev/byte/octal
/dev/term
/dev/tp
/dev/pts
/dev/X
/dev/inet
/dev/NVT
/dev/vx
/dev/hba
/dev/cdrom
/dev/rcdrom
/dev/fd
/dev/_tcp
# _
```

Table 4-6 provides a list of some common criteria used with the **find** command.

**Table 4-6**    Common criteria used with the **find** command

| Criteria | Description |
|---|---|
| -atime -x<br>-atime +x | Searches for files that were accessed less than x days ago<br>Searches for files that were accessed more than x days ago |
| -fstype x | Searches for files if they are on a certain filesystem x (where x could be ext2, ext3, and so on) |
| -group x | Searches for files that are owned by a certain group or GID (x) |
| -inum x | Searches for files that have an inode number of x |
| -mtime -x<br>-mtime +x | Searches for files that were modified less than x days ago<br>Searches for files that were modified more than x days ago |
| -name x | Searches for a certain filename x (x may contain wildcards) |
| -size -x<br><br>-size x<br>-size +x | Searches for files with a size less than x, where x is the number of 512-byte blocks<br>Searches for files with a size of x, where x is the number of 512-byte blocks<br>Searches for files with a size greater than x, where x is the number of 512-byte blocks |

**Table 4-6** Common criteria used with the `find` command (continued)

| Criteria | Description |
|---|---|
| -type x | Searches for files of type x, where x is:<br>• *b* for block files<br>• *c* for character files<br>• *d* for directory files<br>• *p* for named pipes<br>• *f* for regular files<br>• *l* for symbolic links (shortcuts)<br>• *s* for sockets |
| -user x | Searches for files owned by a certain user or UID (x) |

Although the `find` command can be used to search for files based on many criteria, it may take several minutes to complete the search if the number of directories and files being searched is large. To reduce the time needed to search, narrow down the directories searched by specifying a subdirectory when possible. It takes less time to search the /usr/local directory and its subdirectories than it does to search the /usr directory and all of its subdirectories. In addition, if the filename that you are searching for is an executable file, then that file can likely be found in less time using the `type` command. The `type` command only searches directories that are listed in the **PATH variable** in the current shell. Before exploring the `type` command, you must understand the usage of PATH.

Executable files may be stored in directories scattered around the directory tree; recall from the discussion on FHS that most executable files are stored in directories named /bin or /sbin, yet over 30 /bin and /sbin directories are scattered around the directory tree after a typical UNIX installation. The special PATH variable is placed into memory each time you log into the UNIX system so that they do not need to specify the full pathname to commands such as `ls` (which is the executable file /usr/bin/ls). Recall from Chapter 3, "Accessing a UNIX System," that you can see the contents of a certain variable in memory by using the $ metacharacter with the `echo` command:

```
# echo $PATH
/sbin:/usr/sbin:/usr/bin:/etc:/usr/ccs/bin
# _
```

The PATH variable lists directories that are searched for executable files if a relative or absolute pathname was not specified when executing a command on the command line. In the previous output, when you type the `ls` command on the command line and press Enter, the system recognizes that the command was not an absolute pathname (that is, /usr/bin/ls) or relative pathname (that is, ../../usr/bin/ls) and proceeds to look for the `ls` executable file in the /sbin directory, then the /usr/sbin directory, then the /usr/bin directory, and so on. If all the directories in the PATH variable are searched and no `ls` command is found, then the shell sends an error message to the user stating that the command was not found. In the previous output, the /usr/bin directory is in the PATH variable and thus the `ls` command will be found and executed, but not until the previous directories in the PATH variable are searched first.

To search the directories in the PATH variable for the file called grep, you could use the word "grep" as an argument for the `type` command. You will receive the following output:

```
# type grep
grep is /sbin/grep
# _
```

If the file being searched does not exist in the PATH variable directories, then the `type` command lets you know which directories it was not found in as illustrated here:

```
# type rep
rep not found
# _
```

Some commands are not files that reside on the hard disk and are executed; these commands are shell functions that are built into the shell and placed in memory when the shell is first started. The `cd` command is a built-in shell function. Using the `type` command to locate the `cd` command produces the following output:

```
# type cd
cd is a shell builtin
# _
```

## LINKING FILES

Recall that files may be linked to one another. This linking can happen in one of two ways: one file may be a pointer or shortcut to another file (known as a symbolic link or symlink), or two files may share the same data (known as a **hard link**).

To better understand how files are linked, you must understand how files are stored on a filesystem. On a structural level, a filesystem has three main sections:

- The superblock
- The inode table
- Data blocks

The **superblock** is the section that contains information about the filesystem in general such as the number of **inodes** and data blocks, as well as how much data a data block stores in kilobytes. The **inode table** consists of several inodes (information nodes); each inode describes one file or directory on the filesystem and contains a unique inode number for identification. More importantly, the inode stores information such as the file size, data block locations, last date modified, permissions, and ownership. When a file is deleted, only its inode (which serves as a pointer to the actual data) is deleted. The data that makes up the contents of the file as well as the filename are stored in **data blocks** that are referenced by the inode.

 Each file and directory must have an inode. All files except for special device files also have data blocks associated with the inode. Special device files are discussed later in Chapter 7 of this textbook.

 Recall that directories are just files that are used to organize other files; they also have an inode and data blocks, but their data blocks contain a list of filenames that are located within the directory.

Hard linked files are direct copies of one another as they share the same inode and inode number. All hard linked files have the same size, and when one file is modified, the other hard linked files are updated as well. Figure 4-3 illustrates the relationship between hard linked files. You can hard link a file an unlimited number of times; however, the hard linked files must reside on the same filesystem. This is because inode numbers are unique only on the same filesystem and hard links are recognized by ignoring this rule.

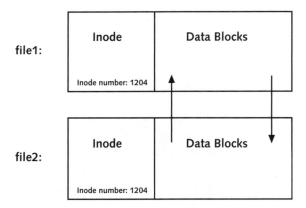

**Figure 4-3**    Hard linked files

To create a hard link, you must use the `ln` (link) command and specify two arguments: the existing file to hard link and the target file that will be created as a hard link to the existing file. Each argument may be the absolute or relative pathname to a file. Take, for example, the following contents of the /sample directory:

```
# cd /sample
# ls -F
file1 file3
# _
```

If you want to make a hard link to file1 called file2, as shown in Figure 4-3, issue the command `ln file1 file2` at the command prompt. A file called file2 will be created and hard linked to file1. To view the hard linked filenames after creation, use the `ls -l` command:

```
# ls -l
total 2
-r--r--r--        1 root    sys             188 Sep 19 16:23 file1
-r--r--r--        1 root    sys            3204 Sep 19 16:26 file3
# ln file1 file2
# ls -l
total 4
-r--r--r--        2 root    sys             188 Sep 19 16:23 file1
-r--r--r--        2 root    sys             188 Sep 19 16:23 file2
-r--r--r--        1 root    sys            3204 Sep 19 16:26 file3
# _
```

Notice from this long listing that file1 and file2 share the same inode as they have the same size, permissions, ownership, modification date, and so on. Also note that the link count (the number after the permission set) for file1 has increased from the number 1 to the number 2 in this output. A link count of 1 indicates that only one inode is shared by the file. A file that is hard linked to another file shares two inodes and thus has a link count of 2. Similarly, a file that is hard linked to three other files shares four inodes and thus has a link count of 4.

Although hard links share the same inode, deleting a hard linked file does not delete all the other hard linked files as well. Removing a hard link can be achieved by removing one of the files, which will then lower the link count.

To view the inode number of hard linked files to verify that they are identical, you could use the `-i` option to the `ls` command in addition to any other options; the inode number is placed on the left of the directory listing on each line, as shown in the following output:

```
# ls -li
total 4
35278 -r--r--r-- 2 root    sys             188 Sep 19 16:23 file1
35278 -r--r--r-- 2 root    sys             188 Sep 19 16:23 file2
35382 -r--r--r-- 1 root    sys            3204 Sep 19 16:26 file3 #
# _
```

**NOTE**

Directory files are not normally hard linked, as the result would consist of two directories that contain the same contents; however, the root user has the ability to hard link directories in some flavors of UNIX such as Linux.

Symbolic links (see Figure 4-4) are different than hard links in that they do not share the same inode and inode number with their target file; one is merely a pointer to the other and thus both files also have different sizes. The data blocks in a symbolically linked file contain only the pathname to the target file. When you edit a symbolically linked file, you are actually editing the target file. Thus, if the target file is deleted, then the symbolic link serves no function as it points to a nonexistent file.

Symbolic links are sometimes referred to as soft links.

**NOTE**

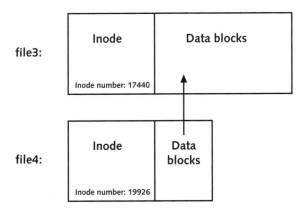

**Figure 4-4**   Symbolically linked files

To create a symbolic link, use the **-s** option to the **ln** command. To create a symbolic link to file3 called file4, as shown in Figure 4-4, type **ln  -s  file3  file4** at the command prompt. As with hard links, the arguments specified may be absolute or relative pathnames. To view the symbolically linked filenames after creation, use the **ls  -l** command as demonstrated here:

```
# ln -s file3 file4
# ls -l
total 12
-r--r--r--    2 root   sys      188 Sep 19 16:23 file1
-r--r--r--    2 root   sys      188 Sep 19 16:23 file2
-r--r--r--    1 root   sys     3204 Sep 19 16:26 file3
lrwxrwxrwx    1 root   sys        5 Sep 19 16:26 file4 -> file3
# _
```

Notice from the previous output that file4 does not share the same inode as the permissions, size, and modification date are different from file3. Symbolic links are also easier to identify than hard links; the file type character (before the permissions) is l, which indicates a symbolic link, and the filename points to the target using an arrow. The **ls -F** command indicates symbolic links by appending the @ symbol as shown in the following output:

```
# ls -F
file1  file2  file3  file4@
# _
```

Another difference between hard links and symbolic links is that symbolic links need not reside on the same filesystem as their target; they point to the target filename and do not require the same inode as seen in the following output:

```
# ls -li
total 12
35278 -r--r--r--    2 root    sys     188 Sep 19 16:23 file1
35278 -r--r--r--    2 root    sys     188 Sep 19 16:23 file2
35382 -r--r--r--    1 root    sys    3204 Sep 19 16:26 file3
35411 lrwxrwxrwx    1 root    sys       5 Sep 19 16:26 file4 -> file3
# _
```

Unlike hard links, symbolic links are commonly made to directories to simplify navigating the filesystem tree. In addition, symbolic links made to directories are typically used to maintain compatibility with other UNIX systems; on UnixWare, the /usr/tmp directory is symbolically linked to the /var/tmp directory for this reason.

## CHAPTER SUMMARY

- ❏ The UNIX filesystem is arranged hierarchically using a series of directories to store files, and the location of these directories and files can be described using absolute or relative pathnames.

- ❏ The UNIX directory tree obeys the FHS, which gives UNIX users and developers the ability to locate system files in standard directories.

- ❏ Many types of files may exist on the UNIX filesystem such as text files, binary data files, executable programs, directories, linked files, and special device files.

- ❏ The ls command can be used to view filenames and offers a wide range of options to modify this view.

- ❏ Wildcard metacharacters can be used to simplify the selection of several files when using common UNIX file commands.

- ❏ Many file management commands are available to create, change the location of, or remove files and directories. The most common of these include cp, mv, rm, rmdir, and mkdir.

- ❏ Although you may use the type command to find executable files using the PATH variable, the most versatile command used to find files is the find command, which searches for files based on a wide range of criteria.

- ❏ Files can be created as pointers to other files or as linked duplicates of other files. These are called symbolic and hard links, respectively.

## KEY TERMS

**.** — A special metacharacter used to indicate the user's current directory in the directory tree.

**..** — A special metacharacter used to represent the user's parent directory in the directory tree.

**absolute pathname** — The full pathname to a certain file or directory starting from the root directory.

**binary data file** — A file that contains machine language (binary 1s and 0s) and stores information (such as common functions and graphics) used by binary compiled programs.

**cd (change directory) command** — The command used to change the current directory in the directory tree.

**data blocks** — These store the information of a certain file and the filename.

**directory file** — A special file on the filesystem used to organize other files into a logical directory tree structure.

**executable program file** — A file that can be executed by the UNIX operating system to run in memory as a process and perform a useful function.

**file command** — The command that displays the file type of a specified filename.

**filename** — The user-friendly identifier given to a file.

**filename extension** — A series of identifiers following a period (.) at the end of a filename used to denote the type of file; the filename extension .txt denotes a text file.

**Filesystem Hierarchy Standard (FHS)** — A standard outlining the location of set files and directories on a UNIX system.

**group** — When used in the mode of a certain file or directory, this refers to group ownership of that file or directory.

**hard link** — A file joined to other files on the same filesystem that share the same inode.

**hidden files** — Files that are not normally revealed to the user via common filesystem commands.

**home directory** — A directory on the filesystem set aside for users to store personal files and information.

**inode** — The portion of a file that stores information on the files attributes, access permissions, location, ownership, and file type.

**inode table** — The collection of inodes for all files and directories on a filesystem.

**linked file** — Files that represent the same data.

**l command** — An equivalent to the ls -l command; it gives a long file listing.

**ls command** — The command used to list the files in a given directory.

**mode** — The part of the inode that stores information on access permissions.

**named pipe** — A temporary connection that sends information from one command or process in memory to another; it can also be represented by a file on the filesystem.

**owner** — The user whose name appears in a long listing of a file or directory and who has the ability to change permissions on that file or directory.

**PATH variable** — A variable that stores a list of directories that will be searched in order when commands are executed without an absolute or relative pathname.

**pwd (print working directory) command** — The command used to display the current directory in the directory tree.

**recursive** — Referring to itself and its own contents. A recursive search includes all subdirectories in a directory and their contents.

**relative pathname** — The pathname of a target directory relative to your current directory in the tree.

**socket** — A named pipe connecting processes on two different computers; it can also be represented by a file on the filesystem.

**source file/directory** — The portion of a command that refers to file or directory from which information is taken.

**special device file** — A file used to identify hardware devices such as hard disks and serial ports.

**subdirectory** — A directory that resides within another directory in the directory tree.

**superblock** — The portion of a filesystem that stores critical information such as the inode table and block size.

**symbolic link** — A pointer to another file on the same or another filesystem; commonly referred to as a shortcut.

**target file/directory** — The portion of a command that refers to the file or directory to which information is directed.

**text file** — A file that stores information in a readable text format.

**wildcard metacharacters** — Metacharacters used to match certain characters in a file or directory name; they are often used to specify multiple files.

## REVIEW QUESTIONS

1. A directory is a type of file. True or False?

2. What is at the beginning of every directory structure (or directory tree)?

   a. trunk directory

   b. main directory

   c. base directory

   d. root directory

3. UNIX files can use filename extensions to indicate file types; however, these filename extensions are optional. True or False?

4. What command would you type on the command line to find out what directory in the directory tree you are currently in?

   a. pd

   b. cd

   c. where

   d. pwd

5. Which of the following is an absolute pathname? (Choose all that apply.)

   a. Home/resume

   b. C:\myfolder\resume

   c. resume

   d. /home/resume

   e. C:home/resume

6. A special device file is used to _____.

   a. Enable proprietary custom-built devices to work with UNIX.

   b. Represent hardware devices such as hard disk drives and ports.

   c. Keep a list of devices settings specific to each individual user.

   d. Do nothing in UNIX.

7. If your current directory is /home/mary/project1, which command could you use to move to the /etc directory directly under the root?

   a. cd ..

   b. cd /home/mary/etc

   c. cd etc

   d. cd /etc

   e. cd \etc

8. You type the l command at a UnixWare command prompt to see a long listing of files in your current directory. What other command performs the same function as l?

   a. ls -l

   b. file

   c. lf

   d. ls -F

9. After typing the ls -a command, you notice that there is a file whose filename begins with a period (.). What does this mean?

   a. It is a binary file.

   b. It is system file.

   c. It is a file in the current directory.

   d. It is hidden file.

10. After typing the ls -F command, you notice a filename that ends with an asterisk (*). What does this mean?

    a. It is a hidden file.

    b. It is a linked file.

    c. It is a special device file.

    d. It is an executable file.

11. When using the UNIX operating system, the root directory is represented by a _____ character. When using a Microsoft operating system, the root directory is represented by a _____ character.

    a. / , \

    b. \ , /

    c. / , /

    d. \ , \

12. If resume is the name of a file in the home directory of the root of the filesystem and your present working directory is home, what is the relative name for the file named resume?

    a. /home/resume

    b. /resume

    c. resume

    d. \home\resume

13. What will the following wildcard regular expression return: file[a–c]?

    a. filea–c

    b. filea and filec

    c. filea, fileb and filec

    d. fileabc

14. UNIX has only one root directory per directory tree. True or False?

15. Using wildcard metacharacters, how can you indicate a character that is *not* an *a, b, c,* or *d*?

    a. [^abcd]

    b. not [a–d]

    c. [!a–d]

    d. !a–d

16. A user typed in the command pwd and saw the output /home/jim/sales/pending. How could that user navigate to the /home/jim directory?

    a. cd ..

    b. cd /jim

    c. cd ../..

    d. cd ./.

17. Sue's current directory in the directory tree is /home/classmarks/unix-am. She then types the command cd .  and presses Enter. What directory will appear if Sue types the pwd command?

    a. /

    b. /home/classmarks

    c. \home\classmarks\unix-am

    d. /home/classmarks/unix-am

18. A symbolic link is also known as a soft link and is depicted by a @ at the beginning of the filename when viewed using the ls -l command. True or False?

19. What was created to define a standard directory structure and common file location for UNIX?

    a. FSH

    b. X.500

    c. FHS

    d. root directory

20. Which of the following is the folder where administrative commands can be found?

    a. /bin

    b. \sbin

    c. /root

    d. /superuser

    e. /sbin

21. All files have a _____.

    a. superblock

    b. inode

    c. PATH

    d. home directory

22. What must you do to run cp or mv interactively and be asked if you want to overwrite an existing file?

    a. There is no choice as the new file will overwrite the old one by default.

    b. Type interactive cp or interactive mv.

    c. Type cp –i or mv–i.

    d. Type cp –interactive or mv – interactive.

    e. Just type cp or mv as they run in interactive mode by default.

23. What will be the result of the cp /etc/hosts . command?

    a. The same as the cp /etc/hosts ..

    b. Copy the /etc/hosts file to the clipboard.

    c. Create a copy of the file hosts in the /etc directory.

    d. Create a copy of the hosts file from /etc to the current directory.

24. Under which directory would you find commands and supporting files needed by users on a regular basis? (Choose all that apply.)

    a. /bin

    b. /sbin

    c. /lib

    d. /root

    e. /usr

25. As hard linked files share the same inode and data, when one of the files hard linked together is deleted, they are all deleted. True or False?

26. When you change the data in a file that is hard linked to three others, _____.

    a. Only the data in the file you modified is affected.

    b. Only the data in the file you modified and any hard linked files in the same directory are affected.

    c. The data in the file you modified and the data in all hard linked files are modified as they have different inodes.

    d. The data in the file you modified and the data in all hard linked files are modified as they share the same data, and all have the same inode and file size.

27. What does the /var directory contain?

    a. various additional programs

    b. spools and log files

    c. temporary files

    d. files that are architecture independent

    e. local variance devices

28. What does the mv command do? (Choose all that apply.)

    a. Makes a volume

    b. Makes a directory

    c. Moves a directory

    d. Moves a file

29. The type command _____.

    a. Can only be used to search for executables

    b. Searches for a file in all directories starting from the root

    c. Is not a valid UNIX command

    d. Searches for a file only in directories that are in the PATH variable

30. Hard links need to reside on the same filesystem as the target, whereas symbolic links need not be on the same filesystem as the target. True or False?

31. Which command do you use to rename files and directories?

    a. cp

    b. mv

    c. rn

    d. rename

32. What command would be used to remove jobs, a directory that contains several files and subfolders?

    a. rm jobs

    b. remdir jobs

    c. It cannot be done; the directory must be empty so you have to delete the contents first.

    d. rm -r jobs

33. What command is used to create a new directory or subdirectory?

    a. None; the FHS is a set standardized directory structure that cannot be modified.

    b. /mnt/dir *directory name*

    c. mkdir *directory name*

    d. make dir *directory name*

34. Given the following output from the ls command, how many files are linked with file1?

```
drwxr-xr-x    3 root     root        4096 Apr  8 07:12 Desktop
-rw-r--r--    3 root     root         282 Apr 29 22:06 file1
-rw-r--r--    1 root     root         282 Apr 29 22:06 file2
-rw-r--r--    4 root     root         282 Apr 29 22:06 file3
-rw-r--r--    2 root     root         282 Apr 29 22:06 file4
-rw-r--r--    1 root     root         282 Apr 29 22:06 file5
-rw-r--r--    1 user1    sys          282 Apr 29 22:06 file6
```

a. none

b. one

c. three

d. four

## HANDS-ON PROJECTS

These projects should be completed in the order given. All hands-on projects should take a total of three hours to complete. The requirement for this lab includes:

❏ A computer with UnixWare 7 installed according to Project 2-2

### Project 4-1

In this hands-on project, you will log into the computer and navigate the file structure.

1. Turn on your computer. Once your UNIX system has been loaded, you will be placed at a graphical terminal (vt01). Switch to a command-line terminal (vt02) by pressing **Ctrl+Alt+F2**, and log into the terminal using the username **root** and the password **secret**.

2. At the command prompt, type **pwd** and press **Enter** to view the current working directory. What is your current working directory?

3. At the command prompt, type **cd** and press **Enter**. At the command prompt, type **pwd** and press **Enter** to view the current working directory. Did your current working directory change? Why or why not?

4. At the command prompt, type **cd .** and press **Enter**. At the command prompt, type **pwd** and press **Enter** to view the current working directory. Did your current working directory change? Why or why not?

5. At the command prompt, type **cd ..** and press **Enter**. At the command prompt, type **pwd** and press **Enter** to view the current working directory. Did your current working directory change? Why or why not?

6. At the command prompt, type **cd home** and press **Enter**. At the command prompt, type **pwd** and press **Enter** to view the current working directory. Did your current working directory change? Where are you now? Did you specify a relative or absolute pathname to your home directory when you used the cd home command?

7. At the command prompt, type **cd etc** and press **Enter**. What error message did you receive and why?

8. At the command prompt, type **cd /etc** and press **Enter**. At the command prompt, type **pwd** and press **Enter** to view the current working directory. Did your current working directory change? Did you specify a relative or absolute pathname to your home directory when you used the cd /etc command?

9. At the command prompt, type **cd /** and press **Enter**. At the command prompt, type **pwd** and press **Enter** to view the current working directory. Did your current working directory change? Did you specify a relative or absolute pathname to the / directory when you used the cd / command?

10. At the command prompt, type **cd home/owner** and press **Enter**. At the command prompt, type **pwd** and press **Enter** to view the current working directory.

11. Currently, you are in the home directory for the user owner two levels below the root of the filesystem tree. To go up two parent directories to the / directory, type **cd ../..** and press **Enter** at the command prompt. Next, type **pwd** and press **Enter** to ensure that you are in the / directory.

12. At the command prompt, type **cd /etc/inet** and press **Enter** to change the current working directory using an absolute pathname. Next, type **pwd** and press **Enter** at the command prompt to ensure that you have changed to the /etc/inet directory. Now type in the command **cd ../conf** at the command prompt and press **Enter**. Type the **pwd** command and press **Enter** to view your current location. Explain how the relative pathname shown in the cd ../conf command specified your current working directory.

13. At the command prompt, type **cd ../../home/owner** and press **Enter** to change your current working directory to the home directory for the user owner. Verify that you are in the target directory by typing the **pwd** command at a command prompt and pressing **Enter**. Would it have been more advantageous to use an absolute pathname to change to this directory instead of the relative pathname that was used?

14. Type **exit** and press **Enter** to log out of your shell.

**HANDS-ON PROJECTS**

# Project 4-2

In this hands-on project, you will examine files and file types using the ls and file commands.

1. Switch to a command-line terminal (vt02) by pressing **Ctrl+Alt+F2**, and log into the terminal using the username **root** and the password **secret**.

2. At the command prompt, type **cd /var** and press **Enter**. Verify that you are in the /var directory by typing **pwd** at the command prompt and pressing **Enter**.

3. At the command prompt, type **ls** and press **Enter**. Do any of the files have extensions? What is the most common extension you see and what does it indicate? Is the list you are viewing on the screen the entire contents of /var?

4. At the command prompt, type **cd** and press **Enter**. At the command prompt, type **pwd** and press **Enter**. What is your current working directory? At the command prompt, type **ls** and press **Enter**. What directories do you see? How many of these are defined in FHS?

5. At the command prompt, type **ls /var** and press **Enter**. How does this output compare with what you saw in Step 3? Has your current directory changed? Verify your answer by typing **pwd** at the command prompt and pressing **Enter**.

4

Notice that you were able to list the contents of another directory by giving the absolute name of it as an argument to the ls command without leaving the directory you are currently in.

6. At the command prompt, type **ls /etc/skel** and press **Enter**. Did you see a listing of any files? At the command prompt, type **ls –a /etc/skel** and press **Enter**. What is special about these files? What do the first two entries on the list (. and ..) represent?

7. At the command prompt, type **ls –aF /etc/skel** and press **Enter**. Which file types are available in the /etc/skel directory?

8. At the command prompt, type **ls –F /usr/sadm/bin** and press **Enter**. Which file types are present in this directory?

9. At the command prompt, type **ls /stand** and press **Enter**. Next, type **ls –l /stand** and press **Enter**. What additional information is available on the screen? Which file types are available in the /stand directory? At the command prompt, type **l /stand** and press **Enter**. Is the output any different from that of the ls –l /stand command you just entered? Why or why not?

10. At the command prompt, type **file /etc** and press **Enter**. What kind of file is /etc?

11. At the command prompt, type **file /etc/inittab** and press **Enter**. What type of file is /etc/inittab?

12. At the command prompt, type **file /stand/\*** to see the types of files in the /stand directory. Is this information more specific than the information you gathered in Step 9?

13. Type **exit** and press **Enter** to log out of your shell.

**HANDS-ON PROJECTS**

# Project 4-3

In this hands-on project, you will use the ls command alongside wildcard metacharacters in your shell to explore the contents of your home directory.

1. Switch to a command-line terminal (vt02) by pressing **Ctrl+Alt+F2**, and log into the terminal using the username **root** and the password **secret**.

2. At the command prompt, type **cd /stand** and press **Enter**.

3. At the command prompt, type **ls**. How many files with a name beginning with the letter *b* exist in /stand?

4. At the command prompt, type **ls \*** and press **Enter**. What is listed and why?

5. At the command prompt, type **ls b\*** and press **Enter**. What is listed and why?

6. At the command prompt, type **ls boot?** and press **Enter**. What message do you receive and why?

7. At the command prompt, type **ls boot????** and press **Enter**. What is listed and why?

8. At the command prompt, type **ls \*.blm** and press **Enter**. What is listed and why?

9. At the command prompt, type **ls stage[135].blm** and press **Enter**. What is listed and why?

10. At the command prompt, type **ls stage[!135].blm** and press **Enter**. What error do you receive and why?

11. Type **exit** and press **Enter** to log out of your shell.

## Project 4-4

In this hands-on project, you will create new directories.

1. Switch to a command-line terminal (vt02) by pressing **Ctrl+Alt+F2**, and log into the terminal using the username **root** and the password **secret**.

2. At the command prompt, type **mkdir mysamples** and press **Enter**. Next, type **ls –F** at the command prompt and press **Enter**. Is the new directory listed?

3. At the command prompt, type **cd mysamples** and press **Enter**. Next, type **ls –F** at the command prompt and press **Enter**. What are the contents of the subdirectory mysamples?

4. At the command prompt, type **mkdir undermysamples** and press **Enter**. Next, type **ls –F** at the command prompt and press **Enter**. What are the contents of the subdirectory mysamples?

5. At the command prompt, type **mkdir todelete** and press **Enter**. Next, type **ls –F** at the command prompt and press **Enter**. Does the subdirectory todelete you just created appear listed in the display?

6. At the command prompt, type **cd ..** and press **Enter**. Next, type **ls –R mysamples** and press **Enter**. Notice that the contents of the subdirectory mysamples and its subdirectories undermysamples and todelete are displayed. You have used the recursive option with the ls command.

7. Type **exit** and press **Enter** to log out of your shell.

## Project 4-5

In this hands-on project, you will copy files using the cp command.

1. Switch to a command-line terminal (vt02) by pressing **Ctrl+Alt+F2**, and log into the terminal using the username **root** and the password **secret**.

2. Next, type **ls –F** at the command prompt and press **Enter**. How many files are listed and what are their names?

3. At the command prompt, type **cp /etc/issue** and press **Enter**. What error message is sent and why?

4. At the command prompt, type **cp /etc/issue newissue** and press **Enter**. Next, type **ls –F** at the command prompt and press **Enter**. How many files are there and what are their names? Why?

5. At the command prompt, type **cp newissue mysamples/newissue2** and press **Enter**. Next, type **ls –F** at the command prompt and press **Enter**. How many files are there and what are their names? Why?

6. At the command prompt, type **cd mysamples** and press **Enter**. Next, type **ls –F** at the command prompt and press **Enter**. Was newissue copied successfully?

7. At the command prompt, type **cp /etc/inittab .** and press **Enter**. Next, type **ls –F** at the command prompt and press **Enter**. How many files are there and what are their names? Why?

8. At the command prompt, type **cp inittab ..** and press **Enter**. Next, type **cd ..** at the command prompt and press **Enter**. At the command prompt, type **ls –F** and press **Enter**. Was the inittab file copied successfully?

9. At the command prompt, type **cp /etc/hosts /etc/issue /etc/inittab mysamples** and press **Enter**. Were you prompted to overwrite the inittab file that existed in mysamples previously? Why?

10. At the command prompt, type **cp –i /etc/hosts /etc/issue /etc/inittab mysamples** and press **Enter**. Were you prompted to overwrite the inittab file this time? Type **y** and press **Enter** to confirm the overwriting of the file.

11. Next, type **cp mysamples mysamples2** at the command prompt and press **Enter**. What error message did you receive? Why?

12. At the command prompt, type **cp –r mysamples mysamples2** and press **Enter**. Next, type **ls –F** at the command prompt and press **Enter**. Was the directory copied successfully? Type **ls –F mysamples2** at the command prompt and press **Enter**. Were the contents of mysamples copied to mysamples2 successfully?

13. Type **exit** and press **Enter** to log out of your shell.

**HANDS-ON PROJECTS**

## Project 4-6

In this hands-on project, you will use the mv command to rename files and directories.

1. Switch to a command-line terminal (vt02) by pressing **Ctrl+Alt+F2**, and log into the terminal using the username **root** and the password **secret**.

2. At the command prompt, type **cd mysamples** and press **Enter**. Next, type **ls –F** at the command prompt and press **Enter**. How many files are listed and what are their names?

3. At the command prompt, type **mv inittab** and press **Enter**. What error message is sent and why?

4. At the command prompt, type **mv inittab inittab2** and press **Enter**. Next, type **ls –F** at the command prompt and press **Enter**. How many files are listed and what are their names? What happened to inittab?

5. At the command prompt, type **mv inittab2 undermysamples** and press **Enter**. Next, type **ls –F** at the command prompt and press **Enter**. How many files are there and what are their names? Where did inittab2 go?

6. At the command prompt, type **cd undermysamples** and press **Enter**. Next, type **ls –F** at the command prompt and press **Enter**. Notice that the inittab2 file you moved in Step 5 was moved here.

7. At the command prompt, type **cd ..** and press **Enter**.

8. At the command prompt, type **mv –i newissue2 undermysamples/inittab2** and press **Enter**. What message appears on the screen and why? Press **n** and then **Enter** to prevent the inittab2 file from being overwritten.

9. At the command prompt, type **mv –i newissue2 newissue** and press **Enter**. Why were you not prompted to continue?

10. At the command prompt, type **mv undermysamples samples** and press **Enter**. Why did you not need to specify the recursive option to the **mv** command to rename the undermysamples directory to samples?

11. Type **exit** and press **Enter** to log out of your shell.

**HANDS-ON PROJECTS**

## Project 4-7

In this hands-on project, you will make and view links to files and directories.

1. Switch to a command-line terminal (vt02) by pressing **Ctrl+Alt+F2**, and log into the terminal using the username **root** and the password **secret**.

2. At the command prompt, type **cd mysamples** and press **Enter**. Next, type **ls –F** at the command prompt and press **Enter**. What files do you see? Now, type **ls –l** at the command prompt and press **Enter**. What is the link count for the newissue file?

3. At the command prompt, type **ln newissue hardlinksample** and press **Enter**. Next, type **ls –F** at the command prompt and press **Enter**. Does anything in the terminal output indicate that newissue and hardlinksample are hard linked? Next, type **ls –l** at the command prompt and press **Enter**. Does anything in the terminal output indicate that newissue and hardlinksample are hard linked? What are their sizes? What is the link count for newissue and hardlinksample? Next, type **ls –li** at the command prompt and press **Enter** to view the inode numbers of each file. Do the two hard linked files have the same inode number?

4. At the command prompt, type **ln newissue hardlinksample2** and press **Enter**. Next, type **ls –l** at the command prompt and press **Enter**. What is the link count for the files newissue, hardlinksample, and hardlinksample2? Why?

5. At the command prompt, type **ln –s newissue symlinksample** and press **Enter**. Next, type **ls –F** at the command prompt and press **Enter**. Does anything in the terminal output indicate that newissue and symlinksample are symbolically linked? Which file is the target file? Next, type **ls –l** at the command prompt and press **Enter**. Does anything in the terminal output indicate that newissue and symlinksample are symbolically linked? What are their sizes? Next, type **ls –li** at the command prompt and press **Enter** to view the inode numbers of each file. Do the two symbolically linked files have the same inode number? Explain.

6. At the command prompt, type **ln -s /etc/conf/ config** and press **Enter**. Next, type **ls -F** at the command prompt and press **Enter**. What file type is indicated for config? Now, type **cd config** at the command prompt and press **Enter**. Type **pwd** at the command prompt and view your current directory. What is your current directory? Next, type **ls -F** at the command prompt and press **Enter**. What files are listed? Next, type **ls -F /etc/conf** at the command prompt and press **Enter**. Note that your config directory is merely a pointer to the /etc/conf directory. How can this type of linking be useful?

7. Type **exit** and press **Enter** to log out of your shell.

## Project 4-8

In this hands-on project, you will find files on the filesystem using the find and type commands.

1. Switch to a command-line terminal (vt02) by pressing **Ctrl+Alt+F2**, and log into the terminal using the username **root** and the password **secret**.

2. At the command prompt, type **find / -name "newissue"** and press **Enter**. Did the find command find the file? How quickly did it find it? How long did the command take to complete executing? Why?

3. At the command prompt, type **find /mysamples -name "newissue"** and press **Enter**. Did the find command find the file? How quickly did it find it? Why?

4. At the command prompt, type **type newissue** and press **Enter**. Did the type command find the file? Why? Type **echo $PATH** at the command prompt and press **Enter**. Is the /mysamples directory listed in the PATH variable? Is the /sbin directory listed in the PATH variable?

5. At the command prompt, type **type grep** and press **Enter**. Did the type command find the file? Why?

6. At the command prompt, type **find /etc -name "host*"** and press **Enter**. What files are listed? Why?

7. At the command prompt, type **find /mysamples -type l** and press **Enter**. What files are listed? Why?

8. At the command prompt, type **find /var/spool -size 0** and press **Enter**. What files are listed?

9. Type **exit** and press **Enter** to log out of your shell.

## Project 4-9

In this hands-on project, you will delete files and directories using the rmdir and rm commands.

1. Switch to a command-line terminal (vt02) by pressing **Ctrl+Alt+F2**, and log into the terminal using the username **root** and the password **secret**.

2. At the command prompt, type **cd mysamples** and press **Enter**. At the command prompt, type **ls –R** and press **Enter**. Which two directories exist? What are their contents?

3. At the command prompt, type **rmdir samples todelete** and press **Enter**. Did the command work? Why? Next, type **ls –F** at the command prompt and press **Enter**. Were both directories deleted successfully?

4. At the command prompt, type **rm hardlinksample** and press **Enter**. Next, type **ls –F** and press **Enter**. Were the other hard links removed as well? Why or why not?

5. At the command prompt, type **rm symlinksample** and press **Enter**. Next, type **ls –F** and press **Enter**. Was the target file removed as well? Why or why not?

6. At the command prompt, type **cd ..** and press **Enter**. Next, type **rmdir mysamples** at the command prompt and press **Enter**. What error message do you receive and why?

7. At the command prompt, type **rm –r mysamples** at the command prompt and press **Enter**. Next, type **ls –F** at the command prompt and press **Enter**. Was the mysamples directory and all files within it deleted successfully?

8. Type **exit** and press **Enter** to log out of your shell.

## DISCOVERY EXERCISES

1. Use the ls command with the –F option to explore directories described in the FHS starting with /bin. Do you recognize any of the commands in /bin? Explore several other FHS directories and note their contents. Refer to Table 4-1 for a list of some directories to explore. Furthermore, visit *www.pathname.com/fhs/* and read about the FHS. What benefits does it offer UNIX?

2. Write the commands required for the following tasks. Try out each command on your system to ensure that it is correct:

   a. Make a hierarchical directory structure under **/** that consists of one directory containing three subdirectories.

   b. Copy two files into each of the subdirectories.

   c. Create one more directory with three subdirectories beneath it and mv files from the subdirectories containing them to the counterparts you just created.

   d. Hard link three of the files. Examine their inodes.

   e. Symbolically link two of the files and examine their link count and inode information.

   f. Make symbolic links from your home directory to two directories in this structure and examine the results.

   g. Delete the symbolic links in your home directory and the directory structure you created under /.

3. Write the command below that can be used to answer the following questions: (*Hint*: Try each out on the system to check your results.)

   a. Find all files on the system that have the word "test" as part of their filename.

   b. Search the PATH variable for the pathname to the awk command.

   c. Find all files in the /usr directory and subdirectories that are larger than 50KB in size.

   d. Find all files in the /usr directory and subdirectories that are less than 70KB in size.

   e. Find all files in the / directory and subdirectories that are symbolic links.

   f. Find all files in the /var directory and subdirectories that were accessed less than six days ago.

   g. Find all files in the /home directory and subdirectories that are empty.

   h. Find all files in the /etc directory and subdirectories that are owned by the group bin.

4. You are the system administrator for a scientific research company that employs over 100 scientists who write and run UNIX programs to analyze their work. All of these programs are stored in each scientist's home directory on the UNIX system. One scientist has left the company and you are instructed to salvage any work from that scientist's home directory. When you enter the home directory for that user, you notice that there are very few files and only two directories (one named projects and one named lab). List the commands that you would use to navigate through this user's home directory and view filenames and file types.

5. When you type the pwd command, you notice that your current location on the UNIX filesystem is the /usr/adm directory. Answer the following questions assuming that your current directory is /usr/adm for each question:

   a. Which command could you use to change to the /usr directory using an absolute pathname?

   b. Which command could you use to change to the /usr directory using a relative pathname?

   c. Which command could you use to change to the /usr/adm/log directory using an absolute pathname?

   d. Which command could you use to change to the /usr/adm/log directory using a relative pathname?

   e. Which command could you use to change to the /etc directory using an absolute pathname?

   f. Which command could you use to change to the /etc directory using a relative pathname?

6. Use wildcard metacharacters and options to the ls command to view:

   a. All the files that end with .tab under the /etc directory

   b. All hidden files in the /home/owner directory

   c. The directory names that exist under the /var directory

   d. All the files that start with the letter *a* underneath the /usr/ccs/bin directory

   e. All the files that have exactly three letters in their filename in the /usr/ccs/bin directory

   f. All files that have exactly three letters in their filename and end with either the letter *t* or the letter *c* in the /usr/ccs/bin directory

# 5

# WORKING WITH TEXT FILES

> **After reading this chapter and completing the exercises, you will be able to:**
> ◆ Display the contents of text files and binary files
> ◆ Search text files for regular expressions using the grep command
> ◆ Use the pico editor to manipulate text files
> ◆ Use the vi editor to manipulate text files

Most of the configuration of a UNIX system exists within text files. Thus, to effectively administer a UNIX system, you must understand how to view, search, and edit text files. In this chapter, you will be introduced common text utilities that can be used to view and search text files using regular expression metacharacters. Finally, this chapter concludes with an introduction to the vi text editor.

# DISPLAYING THE CONTENTS OF TEXT FILES

By far the most common file type that a user displays is a **text file**. These files are usually small files that contain configuration information or instructions that the shell interprets (called a shell script). They can also contain other forms of text, such as the text in e-mail letters. To view an entire text file on the terminal screen (also referred to as **concatenation**), use the **cat command**. The following is an example of using the cat command to display the contents of an e-mail message (in the file project2):

```
# ls
Newfiles    project     project12   project2    project4
myscript    project1    project13   project3    project5
# cat project2
Hi there, I hope this day finds you well.

Unfortunately we were not able to make it to your dining
room this year while vacationing in Algonquin Park - I
especially wished to see the model of the Highland Inn
and the train station in the dining room.

I have been reading on the history of Algonquin Park but
nowhere could I find a description of where the Highland
Inn was originally located on Cache Lake.

If it is no trouble, could you kindly let me know such that
I need not wait until next year when I visit your lodge?

Regards,
Mackenzie Elizabeth
# _
```

If the file is very large and you only want to view only the first few lines of it, you can use the **head command**. By default, the head command displays the first 10 lines (including blank lines) of a text file on the terminal screen, but it can also take a numeric option specifying a different number of lines to display. The following is an example of using the head command to view the top of the project2 file:

```
# head project2
Hi there, I hope this day finds you well.

Unfortunately we were not able to make it to your dining
room this year while vacationing in Algonquin Park - I
especially wished to see the model of the Highland Inn
and the train station in the dining room.

I have been reading on the history of Algonquin Park but
nowhere could I find a description of where the Highland
Inn was originally located on Cache Lake.
```

The following is an example of using the head command to view the top three lines of the project2 file:

```
# head -3 project2
Hi there, I hope this day finds you well.

Unfortunately we were not able to make it to your dining
#
```

Just as the head command can be used to display the beginning of text files, the **tail command** can be used to display the end of text files. By default, the tail command displays the last 10 lines of a file, but it can also take a numeric option specifying the number of lines to display to the terminal screen, as shown with the project2 file:

```
# tail project2

I have been reading on the history of Algonquin Park but
nowhere could I find a description of where the Highland
Inn was originally located on Cache Lake.

If it is no trouble, could you kindly let me know such that
I need not wait until next year when I visit your lodge?

Regards,
Mackenzie Elizabeth
```

The following is an example of using the tail command to view the bottom two lines of the project2 file:

```
# tail -2 project2
Regards,
Mackenzie Elizabeth
#
```

The tail command also accepts another option specifying which line number to start at when displaying text to the terminal screen. For example, to display the end of a text file starting from line 10 and continuing on until the end of the file, use the +10 option to the tail command:

```
# tail +10 project2
Inn was originally located on Cache Lake.

If it is no trouble, could you kindly let me know such that
I need not wait until next year when I visit your lodge?

Regards,
Mackenzie Elizabeth
#
```

Although some text files can be displayed completely on the terminal screen, you may encounter text files that are too large to be displayed. In this case, the `cat` command will display the entire file contents in order to the terminal screen and the top of the file will not be displayed, as there is not enough screen area to do so. Thus, it is useful to display text files in a page-by-page fashion by using either the **pg command** or **more command**.

The `pg` command displays a text file page by page on the terminal screen starting at the beginning of the file; pressing the spacebar or Enter will display the next page and so on. The file project12 is an excerpt from Shakespeare's tragedy *Macbeth* and is too large to be displayed fully on the terminal screen using the `cat` command. Using the `pg` command to view its contents results in the following output:

```
# pg project12
Go bid thy mistress, when my drink is ready,
She strike upon the bell. Get thee to bed.
Is this a dagger which I see before me,
The handle toward my hand? Come, let me clutch thee.
I have thee not, and yet I see thee still.
Art thou not, fatal vision, sensible
To feeling as to sight? or art thou but
A dagger of the mind, a false creation,
Proceeding from the heat-oppressed brain?
I see thee yet, in form as palpable
As this which now I draw.
Thou marshall'st me the way that I was going;
And such an instrument I was to use.
Mine eyes are made the fools o' the other senses,
Or else worth all the rest; I see thee still,
And on thy blade and dudgeon gouts of blood,
Which was not so before. There's no such thing:
It is the bloody business which informs
Thus to mine eyes. Now o'er the one halfworld
Nature seems dead, and wicked dreams abuse
The curtain'd sleep; witchcraft celebrates
Pale Hecate's offerings, and wither'd murder,
Alarum'd by his sentinel, the wolf,
:
```

Note from the previous output that the `pg` command displays the first page without returning the user to the shell prompt; instead, the `pg` command displays a : prompt at the bottom of the terminal screen. At this prompt, the user can press the spacebar to advance one whole page or press Enter to advance to the next line. The `pg` command also enables other user interaction at this prompt; pressing h at the prompt displays a help screen, as shown in the following output, and pressing **q** exits out of the **pg** command completely without viewing the remainder of the file:

```
------------------------------
  h                      help
  q or Q                 quit
  <blank> or <newline>   next page
  l                      next line
  d or <^D>              display half a page more
  . or <^L>              redisplay current page
  f                      skip the next page forward
  n                      next file
  p                      previous file
  $                      last page
  w or z                 set window size and display next page
  s savefile             save current file in savefile
  /pattern/              search forward for pattern
  ?pattern? or
  ^pattern^              search backward for pattern
  !command               execute command

Most commands can be preceeded by a number, as in:
+1<newline> (next page); -1<newline> (previous page); 1<newline> (page 1).

See the manual page for more detail.
------------------------------
  :
```

The **more** command does more than the **pg** command, as it displays the next complete page of a text file if you press the spacebar, but only displays the next line of a text file if you press Enter. In that way, you can browse the contents of a text file page by page or line by line. Viewing the file project12 with the **more** command results in the following output:

```
# more project12
Go bid thy mistress, when my drink is ready,
She strike upon the bell. Get thee to bed.
Is this a dagger which I see before me,
The handle toward my hand? Come, let me clutch thee.
I have thee not, and yet I see thee still.
Art thou not, fatal vision, sensible
To feeling as to sight? or art thou but
A dagger of the mind, a false creation,
Proceeding from the heat-oppressed brain?
I see thee yet, in form as palpable
As this which now I draw.
Thou marshall'st me the way that I was going;
And such an instrument I was to use.
Mine eyes are made the fools o' the other senses,
```

```
Or else worth all the rest; I see thee still,
And on thy blade and dudgeon gouts of blood,
Which was not so before. There's no such thing:
It is the bloody business which informs
Thus to mine eyes. Now o'er the one halfworld
Nature seems dead, and wicked dreams abuse
The curtain'd sleep; witchcraft celebrates
Pale Hecate's offerings, and wither'd murder,
Alarum'd by his sentinel, the wolf,
project12 (71%)
```

Note from the previous output that the **more** command displays a prompt at the bottom of the terminal screen that indicates how much of the file is displayed on the screen as a percentage of the total file size. In this example, 71% of the project12 file is displayed. At this prompt, you can press the spacebar to advance one whole page or press Enter to advance to the next line. Similar to the **pg** command, pressing **h** at the **more** command prompt displays a help screen, as shown in the following output, and pressing **q** exits out of the **more** command completely without viewing the remainder of the file:

```
Commands flagged with an asterisk (``*'') may be preceeded by a number.
Commands of the form ``^X'' are control characters, i.e. control-X.

h                 Display this help.

f, ^F, SPACE * Forward  N lines, default one screen.
b, ^B        * Backward N lines, default one screen.
j, CR        * Forward  N lines, default 1 line.
k            * Backward N lines, default 1 line.
d, ^D        * Forward  N lines, default half screen or last N to d/u.
u, ^U        * Backward N lines, default half screen or last N to d/u.
g            * Go to line N, default 1.
G            * Go to line N, default the end of the file.
p, %         * Position to N percent into the file.

r, ^L          Repaint screen.
R              Repaint screen, discarding buffered input.

m[a-z]         Mark the current position with the supplied letter.
'[a-z]         Return to the position previously marked by this letter.
''             Return to previous position.

/pattern     * Search forward  for N-th line containing the pattern.
/!pattern    * Search forward  for N-th line NOT containing the pattern.
more.help (62%)
```

The `pg` and `more` commands can also be used in conjunction with the output of commands if that output is too large to fit on the terminal screen. To do this, use the | metacharacter after the command followed by either the `pg` or `more` command as illustrated here:

```
# cd /var
# ls -l | more
total 24
drwxrwxr-x    8 root     sys        1024 Sep 17 20:10 adm
drwxrwx---    3 root     audit        96 Sep  1 19:40 audit
drwxr-xr-x    2 root     sys          96 Sep  2 10:50 cron
drwxrwxrwx    4 root     sys        1024 Sep 17 19:51 dt
drwxrwxr-x    3 root     sys          96 Sep  1 19:24 iaf
drwxrwxr-x    2 root     sys          96 Sep  1 19:37 ldap
drwxrwxr-x    3 lp       lp           96 Sep  1 19:19 lp
drwxrwxrwt    2 bin      bin          96 Sep  2 10:50 mail
lrwxrwxrwx    1 root     sys           9 Sep  1 19:22 motd -> /etc/motd
drwxr-xr-x    2 bin      bin          96 Sep  1 19:23 netls
drwxrwxr-x    2 root     sys          96 Sep 17 19:49 netware
drwxrwxrwt    2 bin      bin          96 Sep  1 19:19 news
drwxrwxr-x    3 root     sys          96 Sep  1 19:44 opt
drwxrwxr-x    2 root     sys        2048 Sep  2 10:08 options
drwxr-xr-x    3 bin      bin          96 Sep  1 19:19 pmd
drwxrwxrwt    2 bin      bin          96 Sep  1 19:19 preserve
drwxr-xr-x    6 root     root         96 Sep  1 21:59 sadm
drwxr-xr-x    6 root     sys        1024 Sep 17 19:50 saf
drwxrwxr-x   16 root     sys        1024 Sep 14 18:42 spool
drwxrwxrwt    2 bin      bin          31 Sep 17 20:30 tmp
drwxrwxr-x   10 uucp     uucp       1024 Sep  1 19:19 uucp
Standard input
```

In this example, the output of the `ls -l` command was redirected to the `more` command that displays the first page of output on the terminal; you can then advance through the output page by page or line by line. This type of redirection will be discussed later in Chapter 9 of this textbook.

## DISPLAYING THE CONTENTS OF BINARY FILES

It is important to employ text file commands such as `cat`, `head`, `tail`, `pg`, and `more` only on files containing text; otherwise, you may find yourself with random output on the terminal screen or even a dysfunctional terminal.  To view the contents of binary files, you typically use the program that was used to create the file; however, some commands can be used to safely display the contents of most binary files.

The **strings command** searches for text characters in a binary file and outputs them to the screen; in many cases, these text characters may indicate what the binary file is used for. For example, to find the text characters inside the /bin/date binary executable program, you could use the following command:

```
# strings /bin/date
uxcore.abi
UX:date
/etc/TIMEZONE
0123456789
/var/adm/wtmp
:142:Cannot adjust date: %s
CFTIME
:1119:Usage:
date [-u] [+format]
date [-u] [[mmdd]HHMM _ mmddHHMM[[cc]yy]]
date [-a [-]sss.fff]
/var/adm/utmp
/var/adm/utmpx
/var/adm/wtmp
/etc/.initpipe
old time
new time
:8:Incorrect usage
:144:Bad conversion
TZ=GMT
TZ=GMT
# _
```

Although this output might not be easy to read, it does contain portions of text that could point a user in the right direction to find out more about the /bin/date command. Other commands that are safe to use on binary files and text files include the **od command**, which displays the contents of the file in octal format (numeric base 8 format), and the **hd command**, which displays the contents of the file in hexadecimal format (numeric base 16 format). The following are some examples of using the od and hd commands to display the contents of the file /etc/hosts:

```
# od /etc/hosts
0000000 064443 062544 072156 021011 024100 024443 067550 072163
0000020 004563 027061 021062 021412 062151 067145 020164 022042
0000040 062510 062141 071145 020072 071457 071555 071457 067151
0000060 074151 032526 032056 071545 071057 071543 071457 034461
0000100 063055 066165 027554 071565 027562 071163 027543 066543
0000120 027544 066543 026544 067151 072145 062457 061564 064057
0000140 071557 071564 073054 030440 030456 034440 027461 031060
0000160 031057 020070 033061 031472 035060 031063 061440 071543
0000200 042440 070170 022040 005042 005043 020043 067111 062564
0000220 067162 072145 064040 071557 020164 060564 066142 005145
0000240 005043 031061 027067 027060 027060 004461 067554 060543
0000260 064154 071557 004564 067165 074151 005061
0000274
```

```
# hd /etc/hosts
0000    23 69 64 65 6e 74 09 22    40 28 23 29 68 6f 73 74    #ident."@(#)host
0010    73 09 31 2e 32 22 0a 23    69 64 65 6e 74 20 22 24    s.1.2".#ident "$
0020    48 65 61 64 65 72 3a 20    2f 73 6d 73 2f 73 69 6e    Header: /sms/sin
0030    69 78 56 35 2e 34 65 73    2f 72 63 73 2f 73 31 39    ixV5.4es/rcs/s19
0040    2d 66 75 6c 6c 2f 75 73    72 2f 73 72 63 2f 63 6d    -full/usr/src/cm
0050    64 2f 63 6d 64 2d 69 6e    65 74 2f 65 74 63 2f 68    d/cmd-inet/etc/h
0060    6f 73 74 73 2c 76 20 31    2e 31 20 39 31 2f 30 32    osts,v 1.1 91/02
0070    2f 32 38 20 31 36 3a 33    30 3a 33 32 20 63 63 73    /28 16:30:32 ccs
0080    20 45 78 70 20 24 22 0a    23 0a 23 20 49 6e 74 65     Exp $".#.# Inte
0090    72 6e 65 74 20 68 6f 73    74 20 74 61 62 6c 65 0a    rnet host table.
00a0    23 0a 31 32 37 2e 30 2e    30 2e 31 09 6c 6f 63 61    #.127.0.0.1.loca
00b0    6c 68 6f 73 74 09 75 6e    69 78 31 0a                lhost.unix1.
00bc
#_
```

## SEARCHING FOR TEXT WITHIN FILES

The major use of the UNIX operating system over the past thirty years has involved simplifying business and scientific management through database applications; as a result, many commands (referred to as **text tools**) were developed for the UNIX operating system that could search for and manipulate text, such as database information, in many different and advantageous ways. A set of text wildcards was also developed to ease the search for specific text information; these text wildcards are called **regular expressions (regexp)**. They are recognized by several text tools and programming languages including, but not limited to:

- grep
- awk
- sed
- vi
- emacs
- ex
- ed
- C++
- PERL
- Tcl

By combining text tools together, a typical UNIX system can search for and manipulate data in almost every way possible; as a result, regular expressions and the text tools that use them are commonly used in business today.

## Regular Expressions

As mentioned earlier, regular expressions enable you to specify a certain pattern of text within a text document. They work similar to wildcard metacharacters in that they are used to match characters, but they actually have many differences:

- Wildcard metacharacters are interpreted by the shell, whereas regular expressions are interpreted by a text tool program.

- Wildcard metacharacters match characters in filenames (or directory names) on a UNIX filesystem, whereas regular expressions match characters within text files on a UNIX filesystem.

- Wildcard metacharacters typically have different definitions than regular expression metacharacters.

- More regular expression metacharacters are available than wildcard metacharacters.

Regular expression metacharacters are divided into two different categories: common regular expressions and extended regular expressions. Common regular expressions are available to most text tools. Extended regular expressions are less common and only available in certain text tools. Table 5-1 provides definitions and examples of some common and extended regular expressions.

**Table 5-1**    Regular expressions

| Regular Expression | Description | Example | Type |
|---|---|---|---|
| * | Matches zero or more occurrences of the previous character | **letter*** matches lette, letter, letterr, letterrrr, letterrrrr, and so on. | Common |
| ? | Matches zero or one occurrences of the previous character | **letter?** matches lette and letter. | Extended |
| + | Matches one or more occurrences of the previous character | **letter+** matches letter, letterr, letterrrr, letterrrrr, and so on. | Extended |
| . (period) | Matches one character of any type | **letter.** matches lettera, letterb, letterc, letter1, letter2, letter3, and so on. | Common |
| [...] | Matches one character from the range specified within the braces | **letter[1238]** matches letter1, letter2, letter3, letter8. **letter[a-c]** matches lettera, letterb, and letterc. | Common |
| [^...] | Matches one character *not* from the range specified within the braces | **letter[^1238]** matches letter4, letter5, letter6, lettera, letterb, and so on (any character except 1, 2, 3, or 8). | Common |

**Table 5-1**     Regular expressions (continued)

| Regular Expression | Description | Example | Type |
|---|---|---|---|
| { } | Matches a specific number or range of the previous character | **letter{3}** matches letterrr. **letter{2,4}** matches letterr, letterrr, and letterrrr. | Extended |
| ^ | Matches the following characters if they are the first characters on the line | **^letter** matches letter if the letter is the first set of characters in the line. | Common |
| $ | Matches the previous characters if they are the last characters on the line | **letter$** matches letter if letter is the last set of characters in the line. | Common |
| (...\|...) | Matches either of two sets of characters | **(mother\|father)** matches mother or father. | Extended |

## The grep Command

The most common text tool is the **grep command**. It gives a user the ability to search for information using regular expressions. grep stands for Global Regular Expression Print and is used to display lines in a text file that match a certain common regular expression. To display the lines of text that match extended regular expressions, you must use the **egrep command** (or the **-E** option to the grep command). The **fgrep command** (or the **-F** option to the grep command) also exists, which does not interpret any regular expressions and consequently returns results much faster.

Take, for example, the project2 file shown earlier:

```
# cat project2
Hi there, I hope this day finds you well.

Unfortunately we were not able to make it to your dining
room this year while vacationing in Algonquin Park - I
especially wished to see the model of the Highland Inn
and the train station in the dining room.

I have been reading on the history of Algonquin Park but
nowhere could I find a description of where the Highland
Inn was originally located on Cache Lake.

If it is no trouble, could you kindly let me know such that
I need not wait until next year when I visit your lodge?

Regards,
Mackenzie Elizabeth
# _
```

The grep command requires a minimum of two arguments: the first argument specifies which text to search for and the remaining arguments specify which files to search for inside. If a pattern of text is matched, the grep command displays the entire line on the terminal screen. For example, to list only those lines in the file project2 that contain the words "Algonquin Park," enter the following grep command:

```
# grep "Algonquin Park" project2
room this year while vacationing in Algonquin Park - I
I have been reading on the history of Algonquin Park but
# _
```

To list the lines that do not contain the text "Algonquin Park," use the -v option of the grep command to reverse the meaning of the previous command:

```
# grep -v "Algonquin Park" project2
Hi there, I hope this day finds you well.

Unfortunately we were not able to make it to your dining
especially wished to see the model of the Highland Inn
and the train station in the dining room.

nowhere could I find a description of where the Highland
Inn was originally located on Cache Lake.

If it is no trouble, could you kindly let me know such that
I need not wait until next year when I visit your lodge?

Regards,
Mackenzie Elizabeth
# _
```

Keep in mind that the text being searched is case sensitive; to perform a case-insensitive search, use the -i option to the grep command:

```
# grep "algonquin park" project2
# _
# grep -i "algonquin park" project2
room this year while vacationing in Algonquin Park - I
I have been reading on the history of Algonquin Park but
#_
```

Another important note to keep in mind regarding text tools such as grep is that they match only patterns of text; they are unable to discern words or phrases unless they are specified. Say, for example, that you want to search for the lines that contain the word "we;" the following grep command can be used to perform this task:

```
# grep "we" project4
Hi there, I hope this day finds you well.
Unfortunately we were not able to make it to your dining
# _
```

However, notice from the previous output that the first line displayed does not contain the word "we." The word "well" contains the text pattern "we" and is displayed as a result. To display only lines that contain the word "we," type the following to match the word "we" surrounded by spaces:

```
# grep " we " project4
Unfortunately we were not able to make it to your dining
# _
```

None of the previous `grep` examples used regular expression metacharacters to search for text in the project2 file. The remainder of this section provides some examples of using regular expressions when searching (see Table 5-1).

To view lines that contain the words "toe," "the," or "tie," enter the following command:

```
# grep " t.e " project2
especially wished to see the model of the Highland Inn
and the train station in the dining room.
I have been reading on the history of Algonquin Park but
no where could I find a description of where the Highland
# _
```

To view lines that start with the word "I," enter the following command:

```
# grep "^I " project2
I have been reading on the history of Algonquin Park but
I need not wait until next year when I visit your lodge?
#_
```

To view lines that contain the text "lodge" or "lake," you need to use an extended regular expression and the `egrep` command :

```
# egrep "(lodge|lake)" project2
Inn was originally located on Cache lake.
I need not wait until next year when I visit your lodge?
# _
```

## EDITING TEXT FILES

Recall that text files are the most common type of file that UNIX users and administrators will modify; most system configuration is stored in text files as well as common information such as e-mail and program source code. Consequently, many text editors are packaged with most flavors of UNIX and many more are available for UNIX systems via Internet download. The two most common UNIX text editors are pico and vi.

### The pico Text Editor

One of the easiest text editors available for UNIX systems is the **pico (pine composer) text editor**. It was designed to create and edit e-mail messages for use with the pine e-mail client program, but is commonly used today by administrators to edit UNIX configuration files.

To open an existing text file for editing, type `pico filename`, where filename specifies the file to be edited. To open a new file for editing, type pico at the command line as demonstrated here:

```
# pico
```

The pico editor will then run interactively and replace the command-line interface with the following output:

```
UW PICO(tm) 2.9              New Buffer


_



^G Get Help  ^O WriteOut   ^R Read File ^Y Prev Pg   ^K Cut Text    ^C Cur Pos
^X Exit      ^J Justify    ^W Whereis   ^V Next Pg   ^U UnCut Text ^T To Spell
```

When it is opened, the pico editor places a prompt at the top of the screen that enables you to type text. If you are editing an existing file, you may also use the cursor, Page Up, and Page Down keys on the keyboard to navigate the document before inserting text. The bottom of the pico screen shown previously lists the most common functions available. The caret (^) symbol beside each letter represents the Ctrl key. For example, to check for spelling, you could press Ctrl+T, and to exit the pico editor, you could press Ctrl+X. Since function key combinations are not case sensitive, you may use Ctrl+t and Ctrl+x to check spelling and exit the pico editor, respectively. Table 5-2 lists the common pico functions.

**Table 5-2**   Common pico functions

| Key | Description |
|-----|-------------|
| ^C | Displays the current position of the cursor (the line number and character number) |
| ^G | Displays a help screen on pico usage |
| ^J | Justifies (or word wraps) the text |
| ^K | Cuts selected text and places it in a temporary buffer in memory |
| ^O | Saves changes to a file |
| ^R | Reads the contents of a text file on the filesystem into the file at the current cursor position |
| ^T | Checks spelling |
| ^W | Searches for a specified string of text |
| ^X | Exits the pico editor |
| ^U | Pastes the contents of the memory buffer to the current cursor position |
| ^^ | Enables you to mark a selected area of text |
| ^Y | Moves the cursor one page up |
| ^V | Moves the cursor one page down |

**5**

## The vi Text Editor

The **vi text editor** (pronounced "vee-eye") is one of the oldest and most popular visual text editors available for UNIX operating systems. As a result, it is standard on all flavors of UNIX. Although the vi editor is not the easiest of the editors to use when editing text files, it has the advantage of portability. A UnixWare user who is proficient in using the vi editor will find editing files on all other UNIX systems easy as the interface and features of the vi editor are nearly identical across all UNIX systems. In addition to this, the vi editor supports regular expressions and can perform over 1000 different functions for the user. The vi editor is an improvement on an earlier editor called ed. The ed editor is also universal in nature, but is even more difficult to use than vi.

To open an existing text file for editing, type vi filename, where filename specifies the file to be edited. To open a new file for editing, type **vi** at the command line:

```
# vi
```

As with pico, the vi editor will then run interactively and replace the command-line interface with the following output:

```
~
~
~
~
~
~
~
~
~
~
~
~
~
~
~
~
~
~
~
```

The tilde characters (~) shown along the left indicate the end of the file; they will be pushed farther down the screen as text is entered. The vi editor is called a bimodal editor as it functions in one of two modes: **command mode** and **insert mode**. When you first open the vi editor, you are placed in command mode and can use the keys on the keyboard to perform useful functions such as deleting text, copying text, saving changes to a file, and exiting the vi editor. To insert text into the document, you must enter insert mode by typing one of the characters listed in Table 5-3. One way to enter insert mode is to press i on the keyboard while in command mode; the vi editor will then enable the user to enter a sentence such as the following:

```
This is a sample sentence.
~
~
~
~
~
~
~
~
~
~
~
~
~
~
~
~
```

**Table 5-3**   Common keyboard keys used to change to and from insert mode

| Key | Description |
|-----|-------------|
| i | Changes to insert mode and places the cursor before the current character for entering text |
| a | Changes to insert mode and places the cursor after the current character for entering text |
| o | Changes to insert mode and opens a new line underneath the current line for entering text |
| I | Changes to insert mode and places the cursor at the beginning of the current line for entering text |
| A | Changes to insert mode and places the cursor at the end of the current line for entering text |
| O | Changes to insert mode and opens a new line above the current line for entering text |
| Esc | Changes back to command mode while in insert mode |

While in insert mode, you may use the keyboard to type text as required, but must return to command mode by pressing Esc when you are finished to perform other functions via keys on the keyboard. While in command mode, you may navigate to various areas of the document using the cursor keys ( ↑, ↓, →, ←) or the h (left), l (right), j (down), and k (up) keys. Table 5-4 provides a list of other keys useful in command mode and their associated functions.  Once in command mode, to save the text in a file called samplefile in the current directory, press the : character (by pressing Shift+; simultaneously) to reach the : prompt where you can enter a command to save the contents of the current document to a file, as shown in the following output and in Table 5-5.

```
This is a sample sentence.
~
~
~
~
~
~
~
~
~
~
~
~
~
~
~
~
:w samplefile
```

From Table 5-5, you see that you can exit the vi editor by pressing the : character and entering q, which then returns the user to the shell prompt:

```
This is a sample sentence.
~
~
~
~
~
~
~
~
~
~
~
~
~
~
~
:q
# _
```

**Table 5-4**    Key combinations commonly used in command mode

| Key | Description |
| --- | --- |
| w, W, e, and E | Moves the cursor forward one word |
| b and B | Moves the cursor backwards one word |
| 53G | Moves the cursor to line 53 |
| G | Moves the cursor to the last line in the document |
| 0 and ^ | Moves the cursor to the beginning of the line |
| $ | Moves the cursor to the end of the line |
| x | Deletes the character the cursor is on |
| 3x | Deletes three characters starting from the character the cursor is on |
| dw | Deletes one word starting from the character the cursor is on |
| d3w and 3dw | Deletes three words starting from the character the cursor is on |
| dd | Deletes one whole line starting from the line the cursor is on |
| d3d and 3dd | Deletes three whole lines starting from the line the cursor is on |
| d$ | Deletes from the cursor character to the end of the current line |
| d^ and d0 | Deletes from the cursor character to the beginning of current line |
| yw | Copies one word (starting from the character the cursor is on) into a temporary buffer in memory for later use |
| y3w and 3yw | Copies three words (starting from the character the cursor is on) into a temporary buffer in memory for later use |

**Table 5-4**   Key combinations commonly used in command mode (continued)

| Key | Description |
| --- | --- |
| yy | Copies the current line into a temporary buffer in memory for later use |
| y3y and 3yy | Copies three lines (starting from the current line) into a temporary buffer in memory for later use |
| y$ | Copies the current line from the cursor to the end of the line into a temporary buffer in memory for later use |
| y^ and y0 | Copies the current line from the cursor to the beginning of the line into a temporary buffer in memory for later use |
| p | Pastes the contents of the temporary memory buffer underneath the current line |
| P | Pastes the contents of the temporary memory buffer above the current line |
| J | Joins the line underneath the current line to the current line |
| Ctrl+g | Displays the current line statistics |
| u | Undoes the last function (undo) |
| . | Repeats the last function (repeat) |
| /pattern | Searches for the first occurrence of a pattern in the forward direction |
| ?pattern | Searches for the first occurrence of a pattern in the reverse direction |
| n | Repeats the previous search in the forward direction |
| N | Repeats the previous search in the reverse direction |

**Table 5-5**   Key combinations commonly used at the command mode : prompt

| Function | Description |
| --- | --- |
| :q | Exits the vi editor if no changes were made |
| :q! | Exits the vi editor and does not save any changes |
| :wq | Saves any changes to the file and exits the vi editor |
| :w filename | Saves the current document to a file called filename |
| :!date | Executes the date command using a Bourne shell |
| :r !date | Reads the output of the date command into the document under the current line. |
| :r filename | Reads the contents of the text file called filename into the document under the current line |
| :set all | Displays all vi environment settings |
| :set ....... | Sets a vi environment setting to a certain value |
| :s/the/THE/g | Searches for the regular expression "the" and replaces each occurrence globally throughout the current line with the word "THE" |
| :1,$ s/the/THE/g | Searches for the regular expression "the" and replaces each occurrence globally from line 1 to the end of the document with the word "THE" |

The vi editor also offers some advanced features to UNIX users, as depicted in Table 5-5; examples of some of these features will be discussed in the following section using the project2 file shown earlier in this chapter. To edit the project2 file, type vi project2 and view the following screen:

```
Hi there, I hope this day finds you well.

Unfortunately we were not able to make it to your dining
room this year while vacationing in Algonquin Park - I
especially wished to see the model of the Highland Inn
and the train station in the dining room.

I have been reading on the history of Algonquin Park but
nowhere could I find a description of where the Highland
Inn was originally located on Cache Lake.

If it is no trouble, could you kindly let me know such that
I need not wait until next year when I visit your lodge?

Regards,
Mackenzie Elizabeth
~
~
~
~
~
~
~
"project2" 17 lines, 583 characters
```

Note that the name of the file as well as the number of lines and characters in total are displayed at the bottom of the screen (project2 has 17 lines and 583 characters in this example). To insert the current date and time at the bottom of the file, you could move the cursor to the last line in the file and type the following at the : prompt while in command mode:

```
Hi there, I hope this day finds you well.

Unfortunately we were not able to make it to your dining
room this year while vacationing in Algonquin Park - I
especially wished to see the model of the Highland Inn
and the train station in the dining room.

I have been reading on the history of Algonquin Park but
nowhere could I find a description of where the Highland
Inn was originally located on Cache Lake.
```

```
     If it is no trouble, could you kindly let me know such that
     I need not wait until next year when I visit your lodge?

     Regards,
     Mackenzie Elizabeth
     ~
     ~
     ~
     ~
     ~
     ~
     ~
     ~
     :r !date
```

When you press Enter, the output of the **date** command is inserted below the current line:

```
     Hi there, I hope this day finds you well.

     Unfortunately we were not able to make it to your dining
     room this year while vacationing in Algonquin Park - I
     especially wished to see the model of the Highland Inn
     and the train station in the dining room.

     I have been reading on the history of Algonquin Park but
     nowhere could I find a description of where the Highland
     Inn was originally located on Cache Lake.

     If it is no trouble, could you kindly let me know such that
     I need not wait until next year when I visit your lodge?

     Regards,
     Mackenzie Elizabeth
     Tue Sep 17 21:01:19 EDT 2003
     ~
     ~
     ~
     ~
     ~
     ~
```

In addition, to change all occurrences of the word "Algonquin" to "ALGONQUIN," type the following at the : prompt while in command mode:

```
     Hi there, I hope this day finds you well.

     Unfortunately we were not able to make it to your dining
     room this year while vacationing in Algonquin Park - I
     especially wished to see the model of the Highland Inn
     and the train station in the dining room.
```

I have been reading on the history of Algonquin Park but
nowhere could I find a description of where the Highland
Inn was originally located on Cache Lake.

If it is no trouble, could you kindly let me know such that
I need not wait until next year when I visit your lodge?

Regards,
Mackenzie Elizabeth
Tue Sep 17 21:01:19 EDT 2003
~
~
~
~
~
~

```
:1,$ s/Algonquin/ALGONQUIN/g
```

This results in the following output:

Hi there, I hope this day finds you well.

Unfortunately we were not able to make it to your dining
room this year while vacationing in ALGONQUIN Park - I
especially wished to see the model of the Highland Inn
and the train station in the dining room.

I have been reading on the history of ALGONQUIN Park but
nowhere could I find a description of where the Highland
Inn was originally located on Cache Lake.

If it is no trouble, could you kindly let me know such that
I need not wait until next year when I visit your lodge?

Regards,
Mackenzie Elizabeth
Tue Sep 17 21:01:19 EDT 2003
~
~
~
~
~
~
~
~

Another attractive feature of the vi editor is its capability to customize the user environment
through settings that can be altered at the : prompt while in command mode; just type

the words `set all` at this prompt to observe the list of available settings and their current values:

```
:set all
noautoindent          nomodelines              noslowopen
autoprint             nonumber                 tabstop=8
noautowrite           nonovice                 taglength=0
nobeautify            nooptimize               tags=tags /usr/lib/tags
directory=/var/preserve paragraphs=ILP           term=AT386-M-ie
noedcompatible        prompt                   noterse
noerrorbells          readonly                 timeout
noexrc                redraw                   ttytype=AT386-M-ie
flash                 remap                    warn
hardtabs=8            report=5                 window=24
noignorecase          scroll=12                wrapscan
nolisp                sections=NHSHH HUuhsh+c   wrapmargin=0
nolist                shell=/sbin/sh           nowriteany
magic                 shiftwidth=8             recompat
nofullre              noshowmatch
mesg                  noshowmode
[Hit return to continue]
```

Note from the previous output that most settings are set to either on or off; those that are turned off are prefixed with the word "no." In this example, line numbering is turned off (`nonumber` in the output); however, you can turn it on by typing `set number` at the : prompt while in command mode. This results in the following output in vi:

```
 1 Hi there, I hope this day finds you well.
 2
 3 Unfortunately we were not able to make it to your dining
 4 room this year while vacationing in ALGONQUIN Park - I
 5 especially wished to see the model of the Highland Inn
 6 and the train station in the dining room.
 7
 8 I have been reading on the history of ALGONQUIN Park but
 9 nowhere could I find a description of where the Highland
10 Inn was originally located on Cache Lake.
11
12 If it is no trouble, could you kindly let me know such that
13 I need not wait until next year when I visit your lodge?
14
15 Regards,
16 Mackenzie Elizabeth
17 Tue Sep 17 21:01:19 EDT 2003
18
~
~
~
~
~
~

:set number
```

Conversely, to turn line numbering off, type **set nonumber** at the : prompt while in command mode.

 **NOTE** When you use the vi editor and change environment settings at the : prompt, such as :set number to enable line numbering, those changes are lost when you exit the vi editor. To continuously apply the same environment settings, you may choose to put the set commands in a special hidden file in their home directory called .exrc—this .exrc file is then applied each time you open the vi editor.

## CHAPTER SUMMARY

- Text files are the most common file type. Their contents can be viewed by several utilities such as head, tail, cat, more, and pg.

- Binary data files can be viewed using the strings, od, and hd utilities.

- Regular expression metacharacters can be used to specify certain patterns of text when used with certain programming languages and text tool utilities such as grep.

- The vi editor and pico editor are two common text editors available for UNIX systems.

- Although the pico editor is easy to use, the vi editor has several more text functions and is standard on all UNIX systems.

- The vi editor works in one of two modes: command mode and insert mode.

## KEY TERMS

**cat command** — The command used to display (or concatenate) the entire contents of a text file on the screen.

**command mode** — One of the two input modes in vi; it enables a user to perform any available text editing task that is not related to inserting text into the document.

**concatenation** — The joining of text together to make one larger whole. In UNIX, words and strings of text are joined together to form a displayed file.

**egrep command** — A variant of the grep command used to search files for patterns using extended regular expressions.

**fgrep command** — A variant of the grep command that does not allow the use of regular expressions.

**grep command** — The command that searches files for patterns of characters using regular expression metacharacters; grep stands for Global Regular Expression Print.

**hd command** — The command used to display the contents of a file in hexadecimal format.

**head command** — The command that displays the first set of lines of a text file; by default, the head command displays the first 10 lines.

**insert mode** — One of the two input modes in vi; it gives the user the ability to insert text into the document, but does not allow any other functionality.

**more command** — The command used to display a text file page by page and line by line on the terminal screen.

**od command** — The command used to display the contents of a file in octal format.

**pg command** — The command used to display a text file page by page on the terminal screen.

**pico (pine composer) text editor** — A common text editor used with UNIX systems.

**regular expressions (regexp)** — Special metacharacters used to match patterns of text within text files; they are commonly used by many text tool commands such as grep.

**strings command** — The command used to search for and display text characters in a binary file.

**tail command** — The command used to display the last set number of lines of text in a file; by default, the tail command displays the last 10 lines of the file.

**text file** — A file that stores information in a readable text format.

**text tools** — Programs that allow for the creation, modification, and searching of text files.

**vi text editor** — A powerful command-line text editor available on most UNIX systems.

## REVIEW QUESTIONS

1. In which of the following modes can the vi editor function? (Choose all that apply.)
   a. text
   b. command
   c. input
   d. interactive
   e. insert

2. Which of the following commands is used to print the contents of a file, in sequence, to your terminal?
   a. od
   b. hd
   c. ls
   d. cat
   e. dog

3. The pg command offers less functionality than the more command. True or False?

4. Which of the following commands searches for and displays any text contents of a binary file?

   a. text

   b. strings

   c. od

   d. less

5. A user types in the command `tail /poems/mary`. What will be displayed on the terminal screen?

   a. The last line of the file mary

   b. The footer for the file mary

   c. The last 10 lines of the file mary

   d. The first 10 lines of the file mary

   e. The last 20 lines of the file mary

   f. The entire contents of the file mary, but in reverse order from the last line through to the first

6. How can a user switch from insert mode to command mode when using the vi editor?

   a. Press Ctrl+Alt+Del simultaneously.

   b. Press Del.

   c. Type in the : character.

   d. Press Esc.

7. Which of the following methods is valid for switching to insert mode in the vi editor? (Choose all that apply.)

   a. Press I.

   b. Press a.

   c. Press o.

   d. Press O.

8. You want to find all the lines in the file mary that contain the word "we" in them. Which of the following commands would accomplish the task?

   a. grep /etc/hosts "we"

   b. grep "we" /etc/hosts

   c. grep " we " /etc/hosts

   d. grep /etc/hosts " we "

9. Extended regular expressions are more powerful and recognized by more text tools and programming languages than regular expressions. True or False?

10. Which of the following strings will the regular expression file[a-c] match?

    a. filea-c

    b. filea and filec

    c. filea, fileb, and filec

    d. fileabc

11. What will typing q! at the : prompt in command mode do when you are using the vi editor?

    a. Exit, as no changes were made

    b. Exit after saving any changes

    c. Nothing, as the ! is a metacharacter

    d. Exit without saving any changes

12. What will the command tail –12 /etc/hosts display to the terminal screen?

    a. The last 12 lines of the file /etc/hosts

    b. Nothing, as the –12 is undefined and will generate an error

    c. The first 12 lines of the file /etc/hosts

    d. All lines from the 12th to the end of the file /etc/hosts

    e. The first 12 lines appended to the /etc/hosts file since its creation

13. Which of the following commands will display the contents of a file in base 16 or hexadecimal format?

    a. hex

    b. cat base –16

    c. ls –16

    d. od

    e. cat

    f. hd

    g. hd –16

14. A user types in the command head /poems/mary. What will be displayed on the terminal screen?

    a. The first line of the file mary

    b. The header for the file mary

    c. The first 20 lines of the file mary

    d. The last 10 lines of the file mary

    e. The first 10 lines of the file mary

15. How can you specify a text pattern that must be at the beginning of a line of text using a regular expression?

    a. Precede the string with a /.

    b. Follow the string with a \.

    c. Precede the string with a $.

    d. Precede the string with a ^.

16. When the tail command is used to view the contents of a file, the lines are displayed in reverse order, the last line of the file first in the display down through the remaining lines toward the first. True or False?

17. Using regular expressions metacharacters, how can you indicate a character that is *not* an *a*, *b*, *c*, or *d*?

    a. [^abcd]

    b. not [a-d]

    c. [!a-d]

    d. !a-d

18. Which character in vi command mode will join the line underneath the current line to the current line?

    a. a

    b. :join

    c. j

    d. J

19. What will the command head -15 /etc/hosts display on the terminal screen?

    a. The last 15 lines of the file /etc/hosts

    b. Nothing, as the -15 is undefined and will generate an error

    c. The first 15 lines of the file /etc/hosts

    d. All lines from the 15th to the end of the file /etc/hosts

20. Which of the following files can be used to specify vi settings each time the vi editor is opened?

    a. $HOME/.exrc

    b. /.exrc

    c. $HOME/vi.conf

    d. /vi.conf

21. Which of the following variants of the grep command will not interpret regular expressions to speed up execution time?

   a. grep –s

   b. fgrep

   c. ggrep

   d. egrep

22. Which of the following commands displays the contents of a file in base 8 or octal format?

   a. octal

   b. show base –8

   c. ls –8

   d. od

23. What will the command tail +17 /etc/hosts display on the terminal screen?

   a. The last 17 lines of the file /etc/hosts

   b. Nothing, as the +17 is undefined and will generate an error

   c. The first 17 lines of the file /etc/hosts

   d. All lines from the 17th to the end of the file /etc/hosts

   e. The first 17 lines appended to the /etc/hosts file since its creation

## HANDS-ON PROJECTS

These projects should be completed in the order given. All hands-on projects should take a total of three hours to complete. The requirement for this lab includes:

❑ A computer with UnixWare 7 installed according to Project 2-2

### Project 5-1

In this hands-on project, you will display file contents using the cat, head, tail, strings, hd, and od commands.

1. Switch to a command-line terminal (tty2) by pressing **Ctrl+Alt+F2**, and log into the terminal using the username **root** and the password **secret**.

2. At the command prompt, type **cat /etc/hosts** and press **Enter** to view the contents of the file hosts, which resides in the /etc directory.

3. To see the contents of the same file in octal format instead of ASCII text, type **od /etc/hosts** at the command prompt and press **Enter**.

4. At the command prompt, type **cat /etc/inittab** and press **Enter**. Notice the file contains so many lines the display scrolls off your screen.

5.  At the command prompt, type **head /etc/inittab** and press **Enter**. What is displayed on the screen? How many lines are displayed? Which ones are they and why?

6.  At the command prompt, type **head –5 /etc/inittab** and press **Enter**. How many lines are displayed and why? Next, type **head –3 /etc/inittab** and press **Enter**. How many lines are displayed and why? Compare this with what you saw in the last step.

7.  At the command prompt, type **tail /etc/inittab** and press **Enter**. What is displayed on the screen? How many lines are displayed? Which ones are they and why?

8.  At the command prompt, type **tail –5 /etc/inittab** and press **Enter**. How many lines are displayed and why? Compare this with what you saw in the last step. Next, type **tail +55 /etc/inittab** and press **Enter**. How many lines are displayed and why?

9.  At the command prompt, type **head +5 /etc/inittab** and press **Enter**. What error message is displayed and why? Notice that although the tail command can accept numeric arguments using the – or + symbols, the head command can only accept numeric arguments using the – symbol.

10. At the command prompt, type **file /bin/nice** and press **Enter**. What type of file is it? Should you use a text tool command on this file? Caution: Do not use a text tool on a binary file as it can hang your screen.

11. At the command prompt, type **strings /bin/nice** and press **Enter**. Notice that you are able to see some text within this binary file. Next, type **strings /bin/nice | more** to view the same content page by page. When you are finished, press **q** to exit out of the more command.

12. At the command prompt, type **hd /bin/nice | more** and press **Enter**. Notice that in addition to displaying the file in hexadecimal format, you are able to see some ASCII-type characters in the column at the far right of the screen after the columns of numbers. This is an attempt by the system to display the binary content in ASCII format. Press the **spacebar** repeatedly (about 10 to 11 times) until you come to a large section of readable text within the far-right column. Read it and press the **spacebar** to view the next screen. How does this text compare with that displayed by the strings command in the previous step? Why? When you are finished, press **q** to exit out of the more command.

13. Type **exit** and press **Enter** to log out of your shell

**HANDS-ON
PROJECTS**

## Project 5-2

In this hands-on project, you will create and edit text files using the vi editor.

1.  Switch to a command-line terminal (tty2) by pressing **Ctrl+Alt+F2**, and log into the terminal using the username **root** and the password **secret**.

2.  At the command prompt, type **pwd** and press **Enter**. Ensure that / is displayed, showing that you are in the root user's default folder. At the command prompt,

type **vi sample1** and press **Enter** to open the vi editor and create a new text file called sample1. Notice that this name appears at the bottom of the screen along with the indication that it is a new file.

3. At the command prompt, type **My letter** and press **Enter**. Why was nothing displayed on the screen? To switch from command mode to insert mode to allow the typing of text, press **i**. Next, type **My letter** and notice that this text is displayed on the screen. What types of tasks can be accomplished in insert mode?

4. Press **Esc**. Did the cursor move? What mode are you in now? Press the left cursor key [←] two times until the cursor is under the last **t** in **letter**. Press **x**. What happened? Next, type **i** to enter insert mode and type **h**. Did the letter **h** get inserted before or after the cursor?

5. Press **Esc** to switch back to command mode and then move your cursor to the end of the line. Next, type **o** to open a line underneath the current line and enter insert mode.

6. Type **It might look like I am doing nothing, but at the cellular level I can assure you that I am quite busy.** Notice that the line wraps to the next line partway through the sentence. Although this is displayed over two lines on the screen, this sentence is treated as one continuous line of text in vi. Press **Esc** to return to command mode and then press the up cursor key [↑]. Where does the cursor move? Use the cursor keys to navigate to the letter **l** at the beginning of the word **level** and press **i** to enter insert mode. Press **Enter** while in insert mode. Next press **Esc** to return to command mode and press the up cursor key [↑]. Where does the cursor move?

7. Type **dd** three times to delete all lines in the file.

8. Type **i** to enter insert mode. Then type **Hi there, I hope this day finds you well.** and press **Enter**. Press **Enter** again. Type **Unfortunately we were not able to make it to your dining** and press **Enter**. Type **room this year while vacationing in Algonquin Park – I** and press **Enter**. Type **especially wished to see the model of the Highland Inn** and press **Enter**. Type **and the train station in the dining room.** and press **Enter**. Press **Enter** again. Type **I have been reading on the history of Algonquin Park but** and press **Enter**. Type **no where could I find a description of where the Highland** and press **Enter**. Type **Inn was originally located on Cache lake.** and press **Enter**. Press **Enter** again. Type **If it is no trouble, could you kindly let me know such that** and press **Enter**. Type **I need not wait until next year when I visit your lodge?** and press **Enter**. Press **Enter** again. Type **Regards** and press **Enter**. Type **Mackenzie Elizabeth** and press **Enter**. The sample letter used in this chapter should appear on your screen.

9. Press **Esc** to switch to command mode. Next, press **Shift+;** simultaneously to open the **:** prompt at the bottom of the screen. At this prompt, type **w** and press **Enter** to save the changes you have made to the file. What is displayed at the bottom of the file when you are finished?

10. Press **Shift+;** simultaneously to open the **:** prompt at the bottom of the screen again, and type **q** and then press **Enter** to exit the vi editor.

11. At the command prompt, type **ls** and press **Enter** to view the contents of your current directory. Notice that a file called sample1 is now listed.

12. Next, type **file sample1** and press **Enter**. What type of file is sample1? At the command prompt, type **cat sample1** and press **Enter**.

13. At the command prompt, type **vi sample1** and press **Enter** to open the letter again in the vi editor. What is displayed at the bottom of the screen? How does this compare with Step 9?

14. Press **F1** to display a help file for vi and its commands. Use the **Page Down** and **Page Up** keys to navigate the help file. When finished, press **Shift+;** simultaneously to open the **:** prompt at the bottom of the screen again, and type **q** and then press **Enter** to exit the help screen.

15. Use your cursor keys to navigate to the bottom of the document. Press **Shift+;** simultaneously to open the **:** prompt at the bottom of the screen again, and type **!date** and press **Enter**. The current system date and time appears at the bottom of the screen. As indicated, press **Enter** to return to the document. Press **Shift+;** simultaneously again to open the **:** prompt at the bottom of the screen again, and type **r !date** and press **Enter**. What happened and why?

16. Ensure that your cursor is on the line in the document that displays the current date and time, and type **yy** to copy it to the buffer in memory. Next, use your cursor keys to position your cursor on the first line in the document and type **P** (capitalized) to paste the contents of the memory buffer above your current line. Does the original line remain at the bottom of the document?

17. Use the cursor keys to position your cursor on the line at the end of the document that displays the current date and time, and type **dd** to delete it.

18. Use the cursor keys to position your cursor on the **t** in the word **there** on the second line of the file that reads **Hi there, I hope this day finds you well.** and press **dw** to delete the word. Next, type **i** to enter insert mode, type the word **Bob**, and then press **Esc** to switch back to command mode.

19. Press **Shift+;** simultaneously to open the **:** prompt at the bottom of the screen again, and type **w sample2** and press **Enter**. What happened and why?

20. Press **i** to enter insert mode and type the word **test**. Next, press **Esc** to switch to command mode. Press **Shift+;** simultaneously to open the **:** prompt at the bottom of the screen again, and type **q** and press **Enter** to exit the **vi** editor. Were you able exit? Why or why not?

21. Press **Shift+;** simultaneously to open the **:** prompt at the bottom of the screen again, and type **q!** and press **Enter** to exit the **vi** editor and throw away any changes since the last save.

22. At the command prompt, type **ls** and press **Enter** to view the contents of your current directory. Notice that a file called sample2 is now listed, which was created in Step 19.

23. At the command prompt, type **vi sample2** and press **Enter** to open the letter again in the vi editor.

24. Use the cursor keys to position your cursor on the line that reads **Hi Bob, I hope this day finds you well.**

25. Press **Shift+;** simultaneously to open the **:** prompt at the bottom of the screen, and type **s/Bob/Barb/g** and press **Enter** to change all occurrences of **Bob** to **Barb** on the current line.

26. Press **Shift+;** simultaneously to open the **:** prompt at the bottom of the screen again, and type **1,$ s/to/TO/g** and press **Enter** to change all occurrences of **to** to **TO** for the entire file.

27. Press **u** to undo the last function performed. What happened and why?

28. Press **Shift+;** simultaneously to open the **:** prompt at the bottom of the screen again, and type **wq** and press **Enter** to save your document and exit the vi editor.

29. At the command prompt, type **vi sample3** and press **Enter** to open a new file called sample3 in the vi editor. Type **i** to enter insert mode. Next, type **P.S. How were the flies this year?**

30. Press **Shift+;** simultaneously to open the **:** prompt at the bottom of the screen again, and type **wq** and press **Enter** to save your document and exit the vi editor.

31. At the command prompt, type **vi sample1** and press **Enter** to open the file sample1 again, and use the cursor keys to position your cursor on the line that reads **Mackenzie Elizabeth**.

32. Press **Shift+;** simultaneously to open the **:** prompt at the bottom of the screen again, and then type **r sample3** and press **Enter** to insert the contents of the file sample3 below your current line.

33. Press **Shift+;** simultaneously to open the **:** prompt at the bottom of the screen, and type **s/flies/flies and bears/g** and press **Enter**. What happened and why?

34. Press **Shift+;** simultaneously to open the **:** prompt at the bottom of the screen again, and type **:set number** and press **Enter** to turn on the line numbering.

35. Press **Shift+;** simultaneously to open the **:** prompt at the bottom of the screen again, and type **:set nonumber** and press **Enter** to turn off the line numbering.

36. Press **Shift+;** simultaneously to open the **:** prompt at the bottom of the screen again, and type **:set all** and press **Enter** to view all vi parameters. Press **Enter** to advance through the list and return to the vi editor.

37. Press **Shift+;** simultaneously to open the **:** prompt at the bottom of the screen again, and type **:wq** and press **Enter** to save your document and exit the vi editor.

38. Type **exit** and press **Enter** to log out of your shell.

## Project 5-3

In this hands-on project, you will use the grep and egrep commands alongside regular expression metacharacters to explore the contents of text files.

1. Switch to a command-line terminal (tty2) by pressing **Ctrl+Alt+F2**, and log into the terminal using the username **root** and the password **secret**.

2. At the command prompt, type **grep "Inn" sample1** and press **Enter**. What is displayed and why?

3. At the command prompt, type **grep –v "Inn" sample1** and press **Enter**. What is displayed and why? How does this compare to the results from Step 3?

4. At the command prompt, type **grep "inn" sample1** and press **Enter**. What is displayed and why?

5. At the command prompt, type **grep –i "inn" sample1** and press **Enter**. What is displayed and why? How does this compare to the results from Steps 2 and 4?

6. At the command prompt, type **grep "I" sample1** and press **Enter**. What is displayed and why?

7. At the command prompt, type **grep " I " sample1** and press **Enter**. What is displayed and why? How does it differ from the results from Step 6 and why?

8. At the command prompt, type **grep "t.e" sample1** and press **Enter**. What is displayed and why?

9. At the command prompt, type **grep "w...e" sample1** and press **Enter**. What is displayed and why?

10. At the command prompt, type **grep "^I" sample1** and press **Enter**. What is displayed and why?

11. At the command prompt, type **grep "^I " sample1** and press **Enter**. What is displayed and why? How does this differ from the results in Step 10 and why?

12. At the command prompt, type **grep "(we|next)" sample1** and press **Enter**. Is anything displayed? Why?

13. At the command prompt, type **egrep "(we|next)" sample1** and press **Enter**. What is displayed and why?

14. At the command prompt, type **grep "Inn$" sample1** and press **Enter**. What is displayed and why?

15. At the command prompt, type **grep "?$" sample1** and press **Enter**. What is displayed and why? Does the ? metacharacter have special meaning here? Why?

16. At the command prompt, type **grep "^$" sample1** and press **Enter**. Is anything displayed? (*Hint*: Be sure to look closely!) Can you explain the output?

17. Type **exit** and press **Enter** to log out of your shell.

## Project 5-4

In this hands-on project, you will create and edit a text file using the pico editor.

1. Switch to a command-line terminal (tty2) by pressing **Ctrl+Alt+F2**, and log into the terminal using the username **root** and the password **secret**.

2. At the command prompt, type **pwd** and press **Enter**. Ensure that **/** is displayed, showing that you are in the root user's default folder. At the command prompt, type **pico** and press **Enter** to open the pico editor. Observe the functions listed at the bottom of the screen.

3. Type **From the Pirates of Penzance** in the pico editor and press **Enter** to place the cursor on the next line.

4. Next, type **I am the very pattern of a modern Major General. I've informmation vegetable, animal, and mineral. I know the kings of England and I quote the fights historical. From Marathon to Waterloo in order categorical.** in the pico editor. Does the pico editor wrap the words to new lines on the screen?

5. Press **Ctrl+c**. What is displayed?

6. Press **Ctrl+t**. When prompted to edit the word **Penzance**, press **Enter**. When prompted to edit the word **informmation**, change the word to **information** and press **Enter**.

7. Move your cursor to the **F** in the word **From** on line 1. Next, press **Ctrl+^** (which is **Ctrl+Shift+6**). What is displayed at the bottom of the screen? Use the right cursor key to highlight the sentence **From the Pirates of Penzance.**

8. Press **Ctrl+k**. Move your cursor to the last line in the file and press **Ctrl+u**.

9. Press **Ctrl+o** and type the filename **/picosample.txt** when prompted. Press **Enter**.

10. Press **Ctrl+g** and use **Ctrl+v** to page through the help text for the pico editor. When you are finished, press **Ctrl+x** to exit the help screen.

11. Press **Ctrl+x** to exit the pico editor. Do you find the pico editor easier to use than vi?

12. Type **exit** and press **Enter** to log out of your shell.

## DISCOVERY EXERCISES

1. The famous quote "To be or not to be" from Shakespeare's *Hamlet* can be represented by the following regular expression:

   `(2b|[^b]{2})`

   If you used this expression when searching a text file using the egrep command (egrep "(2b|[^b]{2})" filename), what would be displayed? Try this command out on a file that you have created. Why does it display what it does? That is the question.

2. Enter the following text into a new document called question3 using the vi editor and save it. Next, use the vi editor to fix the mistakes in the file using the information in Tables 5-2, 5-3, and 5-4 as well as the examples provided in this chapter:

```
Hi there,
Unfortunately we were not able to make it to your dining room
Unfortunately we were not able to make it to your dining room
this year while vacationing in Algonuin Park - I especially wished
to see the model of the highland inn and the train station in the
dining rooms.

I have been readng on the history of Algonuin Park but
no where could I find a description of where the Highland Inn was
originally located on Cache lake.

If it is not trouble, could you kindly let me that I need
not wait until next year when we visit Lodge?

I hope this day finds you well.
Regard
Elizabeth Mackenzie
```

3. Enter the vi editor and find three environment settings that you would like to change in addition to line numbering (set number). Then create a new file called .exrc in your home directory and enter the four lines changing these vi environment settings (do not start each line with the : character; just enter the set command—set number). When you are finished, test to see whether the settings were applied automatically by opening the vi editor to edit a new file.

4. As discussed earlier, an understanding of the vi editor is valuable to a system administrator since it is supported on almost any UNIX or UNIX computer and modifications of configuration files and scripts are often required on a regular basis when administering the system. However, a learning curve exists with any new topic and the vi editor is no exception. To better gain experience with the vi editor, write a 100-line essay entitled "The Usage of the vi Editor" using the vi editor. Ensure that the essay has no typographical or grammatical errors. Provided you have access to the Internet and a functional Web browser, reference three sources of vi information in the body of the essay from the Internet.

5. As a standard tool, vi is an indispensable multiflavor UNIX tool. Using the Internet or other available resources, research and write a brief essay on the origins of vi. Detail who developed it, when, why, and where the name comes from. By understanding some of its history, you will better understand the tool itself. For an even better understanding and to get used to switching between text and command mode, write an essay using vi. This familiarity will be indispensable in day-to-day UNIX administration and maintenance.

6. Explore the man pages for cat, head, tail, strings, od, hd, grep, vi, and ed. Experiment with what you learn on the files sample1 and Myfile you created in these labs.

# 6

# FILE AND DIRECTORY SECURITY

> **After reading this chapter and completing the exercises, you will be able to:**
> ♦ Modify file and directory ownership
> ♦ Define and change UNIX file and directory permissions
> ♦ Identify the default permissions created on files and directories
> ♦ Modify the Access Control List (ACL) of a file
> ♦ Apply special file and directory permissions

**R**ecall that all users must successfully log in with a username and password to gain access to a UNIX system. Once logged in, users are identified by their username and group memberships. All access to resources depends on whether their username and group memberships have the required permission. Thus, a firm understanding of ownership and permissions is necessary to operate a UNIX system in a secure manner and prevent unauthorized users from accessing sensitive files, directories, and commands. In this chapter, you will learn about file and directory ownership and explore commands that can be used to change it. Next, you will examine standard UNIX permissions and learn how to set them on files and directories. Finally, you will learn how to control the default permissions given to new files and directories, expand the ACL of a file, and assign special UNIX permissions.

# FILE AND DIRECTORY OWNERSHIP

When a user creates a file or directory, that user's name and **primary group** becomes the owner and group owner of the file, respectively. This affects the permission structure as you will see in the next section; however, it also determines who has the ability to modify file and directory **permissions** and ownership. The owner of the file or directory and the root user are the only two users on a UNIX system who can modify permissions on a file or directory or change its ownership.

To view your current username, use the who am i or whoami command, depending on your flavor of UNIX. Similarly, to view your group memberships and primary group, use the groups command. The following output shows an example of viewing the username and group membership while logged in as the root user:

```
# who am i
root          console         Oct 11 19:12
# groups
sys root other bin adm uucp mail tty daemon cron dtadmin priv lp
# _
```

Notice from the previous output that the root user is a member of 13 groups, but the root user's primary group is sys as it is the first group mentioned in the output of the groups command. If this user created a file, then the owner of the file would be root and the group owner of the file would be sys. To quickly create an empty file called file1, use the touch command:

```
# touch file1
# ls -l file1
-rw-r--r--    1 root       sys              0 Oct 11 19:14 file1
# _
```

Notice from this output that the owner of file1 is root and the group owner of file1 is the sys group. To change the ownership of a file or directory, use the **chown (change owner) command**, which takes two arguments (at minimum), the new owner and the files or directories, to change. Both arguments may be absolute or relative pathnames. You can also change permissions recursively throughout the directory tree using the –R option to the chown command. To change the ownership of file1 to user1 and the ownership of the directory Dir1 and all of its contents to user1, enter the following commands:

```
# chown user1 file1
# chown -R user1 Dir1
# ls -l file1
-rw-r--r--    1 user1      sys              0 Oct 11 19:14 file1
# ls -ld Dir1
drwxr-xr-x    2 user1      sys             96 Oct 11 19:16 Dir1
# ls -l Dir1
total 0
```

```
-rw-r--r--      1 user1      sys              0 Oct 11 19:16 file2
-rw-r--r--      1 user1      sys              0 Oct 11 19:16 file3
-rw-r--r--      1 user1      sys              0 Oct 11 19:16 file4
# _
```

 When you change the ownership of a symbolic link, ensure that you use the
–h option to the chown command; otherwise, the permissions on the target
**NOTE** file or directory will be changed.

Recall that the owner of a file or directory and the root user have the ability to change
the ownership of a particular file or directory; if a regular user changed the ownership
of a file or directory that he or she owned, that user cannot gain the ownership back.
Instead, the new owner of that file or directory must change it back to the original user.
However, the previous examples involve the root user, who always has the ability to gain
the ownership back:

```
# chown root file1
# chown -R root Dir1
# ls -l file1
-rw-r--r--      1 root       sys              0 Oct 11 19:14 file1
# ls -ld Dir1
drwxr-xr-x      2 root       sys             96 Oct 11 19:16 Dir1
# ls -l Dir1
total 0
-rw-r--r--      1 root       sys              0 Oct 11 19:16 file2
-rw-r--r--      1 root       sys              0 Oct 11 19:16 file3
-rw-r--r--      1 root       sys              0 Oct 11 19:16 file4
# _
```

Just as you can use the chown command to change the owner of a file or directory, you
can use the **chgrp (change group) command** to change the group owner of a file
or directory. The chgrp command also takes two arguments (at minimum), the new
group owner and the files or directories, to change. As with the chown command, the
chgrp command also accepts the –R option to change group ownership recursively
throughout the directory tree and the –h option to change the group ownership of a
symbolic link. To change the group owner of file1 and the Dir1 directory recursively
throughout the directory tree, execute the following commands:

```
# chgrp bin file1
# chgrp -R bin Dir1
# ls -l file1
-rw-r--r--      1 root       bin              0 Oct 11 19:14 file1
# ls -ld Dir1
drwxr-xr-x      2 root       bin             96 Oct 11 19:16 Dir1
# ls -l Dir1
total 0
```

```
-rw-r--r--    1 root    bin                 0 Oct 11 19:16 file2
-rw-r--r--    1 root    bin                 0 Oct 11 19:16 file3
-rw-r--r--    1 root    bin                 0 Oct 11 19:16 file4
# _
```

Normally, you would change both the ownership and group ownership on a file when that file needs to be maintained by someone else. As a result, you can change both the owner and the group owner at the same time using the **chown** command. To change the owner to user1 and the group to sys for file1 and the directory Dir1 recursively, enter the following commands:

```
# chown user1:sys file1
# chown -R user1:sys Dir1
# ls -l file1
-rw-r--r--    1 user1    sys                 0 Oct 11 19:14 file1
# ls -ld Dir1
drwxr-xr-x    2 user1    sys                96 Oct 11 19:16 Dir1
# ls -l Dir1
total 0
-rw-r--r--    1 user1    sys                 0 Oct 11 19:16 file2
-rw-r--r--    1 user1    sys                 0 Oct 11 19:16 file3
-rw-r--r--    1 user1    sys                 0 Oct 11 19:16 file4
# _
```

Do not insert any spaces before or after the : character in the chown commands shown in the previous output.

The user should own most files that reside in the home directory for good security; some files in a user's home directory (especially the hidden files and directories) require this to function properly.

## FILE AND DIRECTORY PERMISSIONS

Every file and directory file on a UNIX filesystem contains information regarding permissions in its inode. The section of the inode that stores permissions is called the **mode** of the file, which is divided into three sections based on the user(s) receiving the permissions to that file or directory:

- User (owner) permissions
- Group (group owner) permissions
- Other (everyone on the UNIX system) permissions

Furthermore, three regular permissions can be assigned to each user(s):

- **Read**
- **Write**
- **Execute**

## Interpreting the Mode

Recall that the three sections of the mode and the permissions that you can assign to each section are viewed by executing the `ls -l` command. Figure 6-1 provides a detailed depiction of this. It is important to note that the root user supercedes all file and directory permissions; in other words, the root user has all permissions to every file and directory regardless of what the mode of the file or directory indicates.

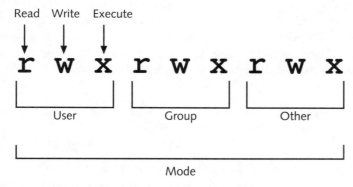

**Figure 6-1**   The mode of a file or directory

Recall that a long directory listing will indicate the permission set (mode) following the file type character:

```
# ls -l
total 19
drwx------      3 root      sys           96 Oct 11 07:12 Dir1
-r---w---x      1 root      sys          282 Oct 11 22:06 file1
-------rwx      1 root      sys          282 Oct 11 22:06 file2
-rwxrwxrwx      1 root      sys          282 Oct 11 22:06 file3
----------      1 root      sys          282 Oct 11 22:06 file4
-rw-r--r--      1 root      sys          282 Oct 11 22:06 file5
-rw-r--r--      1 user1     bin          282 Oct 11 22:06 file6
# _
```

Note from the previous output that all UNIX permissions (shown in Figure 6-1) need not be on a file or directory. If the permission is unavailable, a dash (–) will replace its position in the mode. Be sure not to confuse the character to the left of the mode (which determines the file type) with the mode, as it is unrelated to the permissions on the file or directory. From the previous output, the Dir1 directory gives the **user** or owner of the directory (the root user) read, write, and execute permission, but members of the **group** (the sys group) will not receive any permissions to the directory. In addition, **other** (everyone on the system) does not receive permissions to this directory either.

Permissions are additive; the root user is also a member of the sys group and always a part of the other category; thus, the root user receives the permissions that are available to all three categories of users. In the previous example, this means that the root user will have read, write, and execute permissions to the Dir1 directory.

Along the same lines, the file called file1 in the previous output gives the user or owner of the file (the root user) read permissions, gives members of the group (the sys group) write permissions, and, finally, gives other (everyone on the system) execute permissions. Since permissions are additive and the root user is matched by all three categories of users, the root user will receive read, write, and execute permissions to file1.

The other category seldom contains entries on sensitive files as it refers to all users, and UNIX permissions are additive. Although file2 in our example does not give the user or group any permissions, all users will receive read, write, and execute permissions via the other category; thus, file2 should not contain sensitive data since all users have full access to it. For the same reason, it is bad form to assign all permissions to a file that contains sensitive data, as shown with file3 in the previous example.

On the contrary, it is also possible to have a file that has no permissions assigned to it, as shown in file4; in this case, the only user who has permissions to the file is the root user. Also remember that the owner of the file can change these permissions if needed.

The permission structure chosen for a file or directory may result in too few or too many permissions; general guidelines are available that you may follow to avoid these situations. The owner of a file or directory is typically the person who maintains it; members of the group are typically users in the same company department and must have limited access to the file or directory. As a result, most files and directories encountered on a UNIX filesystem will have more permissions assigned to the user of the file/directory than the group of the file/directory, and the other category will have either the same permissions or less than the group of the file/directory depending on how private that file or directory is. The file file5 in the previous output depicts this common permissions structure. In addition, files in a user's home directory are typically owned by that user; however, you may occasionally find files that are not. For these files, their permission definition changes, as shown in file6. The user or owner of file6 is user1, who has read and write permissions to the file. The group owner of file6 is the bin group; thus, any members of the bin group have read permissions to the file. Finally, everyone on the system receives read permissions to the file via the other category. Regardless of the mode, the root user receives all permissions to this file.

## Interpreting Permissions

Once you understand how to identify the permissions that are applied to user, group, and other on a certain file or directory, you can then interpret the function of those permissions. Permissions for files are interpreted differently than those for directories. In addition, if a user has particular permissions on a directory, that user does not have the same permissions for all files or subdirectories within that directory; file and directory permissions are treated separately by the UNIX system. Table 6-1 shows a summary of the different permissions and their definitions.

**Table 6-1**   Standard UNIX permissions

| Permission | Definition for Files | Definition for Directories |
|---|---|---|
| Read | Enables the user to open and read the contents of a file | Enables the user to list the contents of the directory |
| Write | Enables the user to open, read, and edit the contents of a file | Enables the user to add or remove files to and from the directory |
| Execute | Enables the user to execute the file in memory (if it is a program file) | Enables the user to work with directory contents; revoking this permission revokes all other permissions to the directory and its contents. |

The implications of the permission definitions described in Table 6-1 are important to understand. If a user has read permissions to a text file, then that user could use, among others, the `cat`, `more`, `head`, `tail`, `strings`, `hd`, and `od` commands discussed in Chapter 5 to view its contents. In addition, that same user can open that file using a text editor such as vi; however, the user will not have the ability to save any changes to the document unless that user has write permissions to the file.

Recall from Chapter 4 that some text files contain instructions for the shell to execute and are called shell scripts. Shell scripts are executed in much the same way that binary compiled programs are; the user who executes the shell script must then have execute permissions to that file to execute it as a program.

**NOTE**

It is important to avoid giving execute permissions to files that are not programs or shell scripts. This ensures that these files will not be executed accidentally, causing the shell to interpret the contents.

Also bear in mind that directories are just special files that have an inode and a data section, yet the content of the data section is a list of that directory's contents. If a user wants to read that list, using the `ls` command, for example, then that user requires read permissions to the directory. To modify that list, by adding or removing files, a user requires write permissions to the directory. Thus, if a user wants to create a new file in a directory with a text editor such as vi, that user must have write permissions to that directory. Similarly, when copying a source file to a target directory with the `cp` command, a new file is created in the target directory and that user must have write permissions to the target directory for the copy to be successful. Conversely, to delete a certain file, the user must have write permissions to the directory that contains that file. It is also important to note that a user who has write permissions to a directory has the ability to delete all files and subdirectories within it.

The execute permission on a directory is sometimes referred to as the search permission and works similarly to a light switch. When a light switch is turned on, you can navigate through a room and use the objects within it; however, when a light switch is turned off, you cannot see the objects in the room, or walk around and view them. A user who does not have execute permissions to a directory is prevented from listing the directory's contents, adding and removing files, and working with files and subdirectories inside that directory regardless of what permissions the user has to them. In short, a quick way to deny a user from accessing a directory and all of its contents on a UNIX system is to take away execute permissions on that directory. Since the execute permission on a directory is crucial for user access, it is commonly given to all users via the other category unless the directory must be private.

## Changing Permissions

To change the permissions for a certain file or directory, use the **chmod (change mode) command**. The chmod command takes two arguments at minimum; the first argument specifies the criteria used to change the permissions (Table 6-2) and the remaining arguments indicate the filenames to change.

**Table 6-2**    Criteria used within the chmod command

| Category | Operation | Permission |
|---|---|---|
| u (user) | + (adds a permission) | r (read) |
| g (group) | - (removes a permission) | w (write) |
| o (other) | = (makes a permission equal to) | x (execute) |
| a (all categories) | | |

Take, for example, the directory list used earlier:

```
# ls -l
total 19
drwx------      3 root     sys          96 Oct 11 07:12 Dir1
-r---w---x      1 root     sys         282 Oct 11 22:06 file1
-------rwx      1 root     sys         282 Oct 11 22:06 file2
-rwxrwxrwx      1 root     sys         282 Oct 11 22:06 file3
----------      1 root     sys         282 Oct 11 22:06 file4
-rw-r--r--      1 root     sys         282 Oct 11 22:06 file5
-rw-r--r--      1 user1    bin         282 Oct 11 22:06 file6
#
```

To change the mode of file1 to rw-r--r--, you need to add write permissions to the user of the file, add read permissions and take away write permissions for the group of the file, and add read permissions and take away execute permissions for other.

From the information listed in Table 6-2, use the following command:

```
# chmod u+w,g+r-w,o+r-x file1
# ls -l
total 19
drwx------        3 root        sys           96 Oct 11 07:12 Dir1
-rw-r--r--        1 root        sys          282 Oct 11 22:06 file1
-------rwx        1 root        sys          282 Oct 11 22:06 file2
-rwxrwxrwx        1 root        sys          282 Oct 11 22:06 file3
----------        1 root        sys          282 Oct 11 22:06 file4
-rw-r--r--        1 root        sys          282 Oct 11 22:06 file5
-rw-r--r--        1 user1       bin          282 Oct 11 22:06 file6
# _
```

**NOTE**    Ensure that no spaces appear between any criteria used in the chmod command since all criteria make up the first argument only.

You may also use the = criteria from Table 6-2 to specify the exact permissions to change. To change the mode on file2 in the previous output to the same as file1 (rw-r--r--), use the following chmod command:

```
# chmod u=rw,g=r,o=r file2
# ls -l
total 19
drwx------        3 root        sys           96 Oct 11 07:12 Dir1
-rw-r--r--        1 root        sys          282 Oct 11 22:06 file1
-rw-r--r--        1 root        sys          282 Oct 11 22:06 file2
-rwxrwxrwx        1 root        sys          282 Oct 11 22:06 file3
----------        1 root        sys          282 Oct 11 22:06 file4
-rw-r--r--        1 root        sys          282 Oct 11 22:06 file5
-rw-r--r--        1 user1       bin          282 Oct 11 22:06 file6
# _
```

If the permissions to be changed are identical for the user, group, and other categories, you could use the letter *a* to refer to all categories, as shown in Table 6-2, and the following output when adding execute permissions to user, group, and other for file1:

```
# chmod a+x file1
# ls -l
total 19
drwx------        3 root        sys           96 Oct 11 07:12 Dir1
-rwxr-xr-x        1 root        sys          282 Oct 11 22:06 file1
-rw-r--r--        1 root        sys          282 Oct 11 22:06 file2
-rwxrwxrwx        1 root        sys          282 Oct 11 22:06 file3
----------        1 root        sys          282 Oct 11 22:06 file4
-rw-r--r--        1 root        sys          282 Oct 11 22:06 file5
-rw-r--r--        1 user1       bin          282 Oct 11 22:06 file6
# _
```

However, if no character specifies which category of user to affect, all users are assumed when adding execute permissions to user, group, and other for file2, as shown in the following output:

```
# chmod +x file2
# ls -l
total 19
drwx------     3 root     sys          96 Oct 11 07:12 Dir1
-rwxr-xr-x     1 root     sys         282 Oct 11 22:06 file1
-rwxr-xr-x     1 root     sys         282 Oct 11 22:06 file2
-rwxrwxrwx     1 root     sys         282 Oct 11 22:06 file3
----------     1 root     sys         282 Oct 11 22:06 file4
-rw-r--r--     1 root     sys         282 Oct 11 22:06 file5
-rw-r--r--     1 user1    bin         282 Oct 11 22:06 file6
# _
```

All of the aforementioned `chmod` examples use the symbols listed in Table 6-2 as the criteria used to change the permissions on a file or directory. You may instead choose to use numeric criteria with the `chmod` command to change permissions. All permissions are stored in the inode of a file or directory as binary powers of two:

- Read = $2^2$ = 4
- Write = $2^1$ = 2
- Execute = $2^0$ = 1

Thus, the mode of a file or directory can be represented using the numbers 421421421 instead of rwxrwxrwx. Since permissions are grouped into the categories user, group, and other, you can then simplify this further by using only three numbers, one for each category that represents the sum of the permissions, as depicted in Figure 6-2.

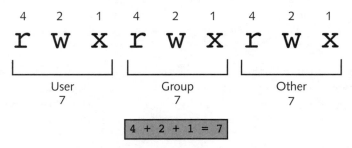

**Figure 6-2**    Representing the mode numerically

Similarly, to represent the mode rw-r--r--, you can use the numbers 644, since user has read and write (4+2=6), group has read (4), and other has read (4). In addition, the mode rwxr-x--- could be represented by the numbers 750 since user has read, write, and execute (4+2+1=7), group has read and execute (4+1=5), and other has nothing (0). Table 6-3 provides a list of the different permissions and their corresponding numbers.

**Table 6-3**   Numeric representations of the permissions in a mode

| Mode (One Section Only) | Corresponding Number |
|---|---|
| rwx | 4 + 2 + 1 = 7 |
| rw- | 4 + 2 = 6 |
| r-x | 4 + 1 = 5 |
| r-- | 4 |
| -wx | 2 + 1 = 3 |
| -w- | 2 |
| --x | 1 |
| --- | 0 |

6

Now, to change the mode of the file1 file used earlier to r-xr-----, use the command `chmod 540 file1` as follows:

```
# chmod 540 file1
# ls -l
total 19
drwx------    3 root      sys            96 Oct 11 07:12 Dir1
-r-xr-----    1 root      sys           282 Oct 11 22:06 file1
-rwxr-xr-x    1 root      sys           282 Oct 11 22:06 file2
-rwxrwxrwx    1 root      sys           282 Oct 11 22:06 file3
----------    1 root      sys           282 Oct 11 22:06 file4
-rw-r--r--    1 root      sys           282 Oct 11 22:06 file5
-rw-r--r--    1 user1     bin           282 Oct 11 22:06 file6
# _
```

Similarly, to change the mode of all files in the directory that start with the word "file" to 644 (which are common permissions for files), issue the following command:

```
# chmod 644 file*
# ls -l
total 19
drwx------    3 root      sys            96 Oct 11 07:12 Dir1
-rw-r--r--    1 root      sys           282 Oct 11 22:06 file1
-rw-r--r--    1 root      sys           282 Oct 11 22:06 file2
-rw-r--r--    1 root      sys           282 Oct 11 22:06 file3
-rw-r--r--    1 root      sys           282 Oct 11 22:06 file4
-rw-r--r--    1 root      sys           282 Oct 11 22:06 file5
-rw-r--r--    1 user1     bin           282 Oct 11 22:06 file6
# _
```

Like the **chown** and **chgrp** commands, the **chmod** command can also be used to change the permission on a directory and all of its contents recursively by using the **-R** option when changing the mode of the Dir1 directory as illustrated here:

```
# chmod -R 755 Dir1
# ls -ld Dir1
```

```
drwxr-xr-x    2 root      sys                    96 Oct 11 19:16 Dir1
# ls -l Dir1
total 0
-rwxr-xr-x    1 root      sys                     0 Oct 11 19:16 file2
-rwxr-xr-x    1 root      sys                     0 Oct 11 19:16 file3
-rwxr-xr-x    1 root      sys                     0 Oct 11 19:16 file4
# _
```

When symbolic links are created, they are given the permissions 777 since the permissions of the target file/directory restrict users on the system. As a result, changing the permissions on a symbolic link will only change the permissions on the target file/directory.

**NOTE**

## DEFAULT PERMISSIONS

Recall that permissions provide security for files and directories by giving only certain users access, and that there are common guidelines for setting permissions on files and directories such that permissions are neither too strict nor too permissive. Also important to maintaining security are the permissions that are given to new files and directories once they are created. New files are given rw-rw-rw- by the system when they are created (since execute should not be given unless necessary) and new directories are given rwxrwxrwx by the system when they are created. These default permissions are too permissive for most files as they provide other full access to directories and nearly full access to files. Hence, a special variable on the system called the **umask (user mask)** takes away permissions on new files and directories immediately after they are created. The most common umask that you will find is 022, specifying that nothing (0) will be taken away from the user, write permissions (2) will be taken away from members of the group, and write permissions (2) will be taken away from other on new files and directories when they are first created and given permissions by the system.

Keep in mind that the umask only applies to newly created files and directories; it will never be used to modify the permissions of existing files and directories. You must use the chmod command to modify existing permissions.

**NOTE**

Figure 6-3 provides an example of how a umask of 022 can be used to alter the permissions of a new file or directory after creation.

To verify the umask used, use the **umask command**. Depending on your flavor of UNIX, the umask command may indicate four numbers instead of three. The first number in this case is just a placeholder for special permissions and should be ignored; thus, the output of 0022 from the umask command indicates a umask of 022.

|  | New files | New directories |
|---|---|---|
| Permissions assigned by system | rw-rw-rw- | rwxrwxrwx |
| - umask | 0 2 2 | 0 2 2 |
| = resulting permissions | rw-r--r-- | rwxr-xr-x |

**Figure 6-3**    Calculating a umask of 022

The umask variable is only valid while your shell is executing. When you exit your shell, your umask is destroyed. When you log in and obtain a new shell, the default umask of 022 is loaded from entries in environment files; these files are discussed later in Chapter 9 of this textbook.

To view the umask using symbols (rwx) instead of numbers, you may use the `umask -S` command.

To ensure that the umask functions as shown in Figure 6-3, create a new file using the `touch` command and a new directory using the `mkdir` command:

```
# umask
0022
# ls -l
total 0
# touch file1
# mkdir Dir1
# ls -l
total 0
drwxr-xr-x    2 root     sys            96 Oct 12 05:47 Dir1
-rw-r--r--    1 root     sys             0 Oct 12 05:46 file1
# _
```

Since the umask is a variable stored in memory, it may be changed. To change the current umask, you can specify the new umask as an argument to the `umask` command. Say, for example, that you change the umask to 007. Figure 6-4 calculates the resulting permissions on new files and directories.

| | New files | New directories |
|---|---|---|
| Permissions assigned by system | rw-rw-rw- | rwxrwxrwx |
| - umask | 0 0 7 | 0 0 7 |
| = resulting permissions | rw-rw---- | rwxrwx--- |

**Figure 6-4**   Calculating a umask of 007

To change the umask to 007 and view its effect, type in the following commands on the command line:

```
# ls -l
total 0
drwxr-xr-x    2 root    sys             96 Oct 12 05:47 Dir1
-rw-r--r--    1 root    sys              0 Oct 12 05:46 file1
# umask 007
# umask
0007
# touch file2
# mkdir Dir2
# ls -l
total 0
drwxr-xr-x    2 root    sys             96 Oct 12 05:47 Dir1
drwxrwx---    2 root    sys             96 Oct 12 05:49 Dir2
-rw-r--r--    1 root    sys              0 Oct 12 05:46 file1
-rw-rw----    1 root    sys              0 Oct 12 05:49 file2
# _
```

## CHANGING THE ACL

The mode of a file or directory is stored in its inode on the filesystem. More specifically, the portion of the inode that stores the mode is known as the **Access Control List (ACL)** as it gives access to three groups of users on the system: user, group, and other.

At times, however, the permissions assigned to user, group, and other might not fit the security needs of the file. Say, for example, that you have a file called acltestfile that should enable the owner of the file (root) and the user bob to read and edit it. Only members of the sys group should be able to read this file and nobody else should have any access to the file at all.

In this situation, the closest mode that you could use is 640, as shown in the following output:

```
# ls -l acltestfile
-rw-r-----    1 root       sys               0 Oct 20 17:45 acltestfile
# _
```

Fortunately, you may add an unlimited number of specific users and groups to the ACL of a file (in addition to user, group, and other) using the **setacl command**. To modify (-m) and recalculate (-r) the ACL on the acltestfile file giving the individual user bob the permissions rw- and view the new mode, use the following command:

```
# setacl -r -m u:bob:rw- acltestfile
# ls -l acltestfile
-rw-rw----+   1 root       sys               0 Oct 20 17:45 acltestfile
# _
```

**NOTE**

To add another group to a file, change the *u* to a *g* and specify a group name instead of a username in the previous command.

Notice from the previous output that bob is not listed in the mode; however, a + indicates that additional users/groups are added to the ACL. Also, on a file where the ACL is expanded, the group permissions indicate the least restrictive permissions given to an additional user/group; in the previous example, the user bob has the permissions rw- and the group permissions are changed to reflect this. To see a full listing of all permissions in the ACL, use the **getacl command**, as shown in the following output:

```
# getacl acltestfile
# file: acltestfile
# owner: root
# group: sys
user::rw-
user:bob:rw-
group::r--
class:rw-
other:---
# _
```

From the previous output, the original permissions for user (rw-), group (r--), and other (---) are preserved; however, the bob user also exists with the permissions rw- and a special group called class exists with the same permissions as bob. The class group only applies to additional users and groups that are added to the ACL and typically specifies the least restrictive permissions for them.

**NOTE**

The class permissions must not be more restrictive than the permissions given to additional users or groups since they override their permission; class permissions of --- will negate any permissions given to an additional user or group on a file.

When a file that has additional users or groups in the ACL is copied or moved, the additional entries in the ACL are lost.

**NOTE**

To remove an additional user or group from the ACL on a file, use the **-d** option to the `setacl` command; the following command will delete the user bob from the acltestfile used earlier:

```
# setacl -d u:bob acltestfile
# ls -l acltestfile
-rw-r-----    1 root      sys            0 Oct 20 17:45 acltestfile
# _
```

The `getacl` and `setacl` commands are named `getfacl` and `setfacl` on Solaris systems.

**NOTE**

---

## SPECIAL PERMISSIONS

Read, write, and execute are the regular file permissions that are used to assign security to files; however, three more special permissions are available that can be optionally used on files and directories:

- **Set user ID (SUID)**
- **Set group ID (SGID)**
- **Sticky bit**

## Defining Special Permissions

The SUID permission has no special function when set on a directory; however, if the SUID is set on a file and that file is executed, then the person who executed the file temporarily becomes the owner of the file while it is executing. Many commands on a typical UNIX system have this special permission set; the **passwd** command (`/usr/bin/passwd`) that is used to change a user's password is one such file. Strictly speaking, only the root user on a UNIX system has the ability to change passwords. Since the /usr/bin/passwd file is owned by the root user, when a regular user executes the **passwd** command, that user temporarily becomes the root user while the **passwd** command is executing in memory. This ensures that any user will be able to change his or her own password.

Like the SUID, the SGID has a function only when applied to files. Just as the SUID enables regular users to execute a binary compiled program and become the owner of the file for the duration of execution, the SGID enables regular users to execute a binary compiled program and become a member of the group that is attached to the file. Thus, if a file is owned by the sys group and also has the SGID permission, then any user who executes that file will be a member of the sys group during execution. If a command or file required the user executing it to have the same permissions applied to the sys group, then setting the SGID on the file would simplify assigning rights to the file for user execution. The SUID and SGID bits are useful for those who develop software programs for use by other users on the same UNIX system. If a certain program file requires access to sensitive files that only the person who developed the software program has permissions to, that person may simply set the SUID and SGID permissions on the executable file. When others execute the file, they will have permissions to access the data while the program is running.

Finally, the sticky bit was used on files in the past to lock them in memory; however, today the sticky bit performs a useful function only on directories. Recall from earlier that write permissions applied to a directory enables you to add and remove any file to or from that directory. Thus, if you had write permissions to a certain directory but no permissions for files within it, you could delete all of those files. Consider a company that requires a common directory that gives all employees the ability to add files; this directory must give everyone write permissions. Unfortunately, the write permission also gives all employees the ability to delete all files and directories within, including the ones that others have added to the directory. If the sticky bit were applied to this common directory in addition to write permissions, then employees may add files to the directory but only delete those files that they have added and not others.

**NOTE**

All special permissions also require the execute permission to work properly; the SUID and SGID work on executable files, and the SGID and sticky bit work on directories (which must have execute permission for access).

## Setting Special Permissions

The mode of a file that is displayed using the `ls -l` command does not have a section for special permissions. However, since special permissions require execute, they mask the execute permission when displayed using the `ls -l` command, as shown in Figure 6-5.

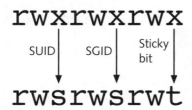

**Figure 6-5** Representing special permissions in the mode

The system enables the setting of special permissions even if the file or directory does not have execute permissions. This will prevent the special permissions from performing their function. If special permissions are set on a file or directory without execute permissions, the special permissions masking the execute permissions in a long listing are capitalized, as shown in Figure 6-6.

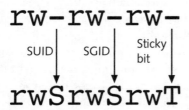

**Figure 6-6**   Representing special permissions without execute permissions

To set the special permissions, visualize them to the left of the mode, as shown in Figure 6-7.

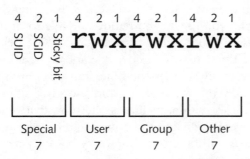

**Figure 6-7**   Setting special permissions

Thus, to set all of the special permissions on a certain file or directory, you could use the command **chmod 7777 name** as indicated in Figure 6-7. However, the SUID and SGID bits are typically set on files. To change the permissions on the file1 file used earlier such that other has the ability to view and execute the file as the owner and a member of the group, use the command **chmod 6755 file1** as follows:

```
# ls -l
total 0
drwxr-xr-x    2 root     sys                 96 Oct 12 05:47 Dir1
drwxrwx---    2 root     sys                 96 Oct 12 05:49 Dir2
-rw-r--r--    1 root     sys                  0 Oct 12 05:46 file1
-rw-rw----    1 root     sys                  0 Oct 12 05:49 file2
# chmod 6755 file1
# ls -l
total 0
drwxr-xr-x    2 root     sys                 96 Oct 12 05:47 Dir1
drwxrwx---    2 root     sys                 96 Oct 12 05:49 Dir2
-rwsr-sr-x    1 root     sys                  0 Oct 12 05:46 file1
-rw-rw----    1 root     sys                  0 Oct 12 05:49 file2
# _
```

Similarly, to set the sticky bit permission on the directory Dir1 used earlier, use the command **chmod 1777 Dir1**. This enables all users (including other) to add files to the Dir1 directory, since you gave write permissions, but only delete the files that they own in Dir1, since you set the sticky bit. Here's an example:

```
# ls -l
total 0
drwxr-xr-x    2 root        sys          96 Oct 12 05:47 Dir1
drwxrwx---    2 root        sys          96 Oct 12 05:49 Dir2
-rwsr-sr-x    1 root        sys           0 Oct 12 05:46 file1
-rw-rw----    1 root        sys           0 Oct 12 05:49 file2
# chmod 1777 Dir1
# ls -l
total 0
drwxrwxrwt    2 root        sys          96 Oct 12 05:47 Dir1
drwxrwx---    2 root        sys          96 Oct 12 05:49 Dir2
-rwsr-sr-x    1 root        sys           0 Oct 12 05:46 file1
-rw-rw----    1 root        sys           0 Oct 12 05:49 file2
# _
```

Also, remember that assigning special permissions without execute renders those permissions useless. If you forget to give execute permission to either user, group, or other and the long listing covers execute permission with a special permission, then the special permission will be capitalized, as shown in the following output, when Dir2 is not given execute underneath the position in the mode that indicates the sticky bit:

```
# ls -l
total 0
drwxrwxrwt    2 root        sys          96 Oct 12 05:47 Dir1
drwxrwx---    2 root        sys          96 Oct 12 05:49 Dir2
-rwsr-sr-x    1 root        sys           0 Oct 12 05:46 file1
-rw-rw----    1 root        sys           0 Oct 12 05:49 file2
# chmod 1770 Dir1
# ls -l
total 0
drwxrwxrwt    2 root        sys          96 Oct 12 05:47 Dir1
drwxrwx—T    2 root        sys          96 Oct 12 05:49 Dir2
-rwsr-sr-x    1 root        sys           0 Oct 12 05:46 file1
-rw-rw----    1 root        sys           0 Oct 12 05:49 file2
# _
```

Although the sticky bit is often used to increase the security on public directories, it is important to use caution when setting the SUID and SGID on files that are owned by the root user or a system group. Say, for example, that the file /bin/tryme is a copy of the Bourne shell that is owned by the root user and has the SUID bit set. Anyone who executes the /bin/tryme file becomes the root user for as long as the program is running. Thus, it is important to periodically check for files that have the SUID or SGID permissions set. The `find` command may be used to do this; for example, to find all files that have a mode that has the SUID (4) or SGID (2) bits set, use the following command:

```
# find / \( -perm -4000 -o -perm -2000 \) -type f
# _
```

## CHAPTER SUMMARY

❑ Each file and directory has an owner and a group owner that are inherited from the creator of the file or directory.

❑ The owner of the file or directory can change permissions and give ownership to others.

❑ Permissions are normally assigned to the user or owner of a file, members of the group of the file, and everyone on the system (other).

❑ Specific users and groups may receive certain permissions to files by expanding the ACL.

❑ There are three regular file and directory permissions (read, write, and execute) and three special file and directory permissions (SUID, SGID, and sticky bit). The definitions of these permissions are separate between files and directories.

❑ Permissions can be changed using the chmod command by specifying symbols or numbers to represent the changed permissions.

❑ To ensure security, new files and directories receive default permissions from the system, less the value of the umask variable.

❑ The root user has all permissions to all files and directories on a UNIX filesystem. Similarly, the root user may change the ownership of any file or directory on a UNIX filesystem.

## KEY TERMS

**Access Control List (ACL)** — The list of permissions on a file/directory and the categories of users that they belong to.

**chgrp (change group) command** — The command used to change the group ownership on a file or directory.

**chmod (change mode) command** — The command used to change the mode (permission set) on a file or directory.

**chown (change owner) command** — The command used to change the ownership on a file or directory.

**execute** — A UNIX permission that enables a user to execute a file (when set on the file) or use a directory and its contents (when set on the directory).

**getacl command** — The command used to view the ACL on a file.

**group** — When used in the mode of a certain file or directory, it refers to group ownership of that file or directory.

**mode** — That part of the inode that stores information on access permissions.

**other** — When used in the mode of a certain file or directory, it refers to all users on the UNIX system.

**permissions** — A list of who can access a file or folder and their levels of access.

**primary group** — The default group to which a user belongs.

**read** — A UNIX permission that enables a user to view the contents of a file (when set on the file) or list the contents of a directory (when set on the directory).

**setacl command** — The command used to change the ACL on a file.

**Set group ID (SGID)** — A special UNIX permission that temporarily changes the current group owner of a file that is executed.

**Set user ID (SUID)** — A special UNIX permission that temporarily changes the current owner of a file that is executed.

**sticky bit** — A special UNIX permission that prevents users from deleting files that they do not own from a directory.

**umask (user mask)** — A system variable used to alter the permissions on all new files and directories by taking select default file and directory permissions away.

**umask command** — The command used to view and change the current umask.

**user** — When used in the mode of a certain file or directory, this refers to the owner of that file or directory.

**write** — A UNIX permission that enables a user to edit the contents of a file (when set on the file) or add/remove files to/from a directory (when set on the directory).

6

## REVIEW QUESTIONS

1. What are the three standard UNIX permissions?

   a. full control, read-execute, and write

   b. read, write, and modify

   c. execute, read, and write

   d. SUID, SGID, and sticky bit

2. What are the three special UNIX permissions?

   a. execute, read, and write

   b. SUID, SGID, and sticky bit

   c. read, write, and sticky bit

   d. full control, read-execute, and write

3. The root user can change permissions on any file or directory. True or False?

4. There is no real difference between the *S* and *s* special permissions when they are displayed using the ls -l command. One just means it is on a file and the other means it is on a directory. True or False?

5. The default permissions given by the system prior to analyzing the umask are _____ for directories and _____ for files.

   a. rw-rw-rw-, rw-rw-rw-

   b. rw-rw-rw-, r--r--r--

   c. rw-rw-rw-, rwxrwxrwx

   d. rwxrwxrwx, rw-rw-rw-

   e. rwxrw-rw-, rwx-rw-rw-

6. A user enters the command to copy the file project1 to the folder /user1; however, when he subsequently enters the command ls –F /user1 he notices that the file was not copied over. Why was the file not copied over?

   a. The user is not the root user.

   b. The command syntax is wrong; it should be cp /home/user1 /home/mary/project1.

   c. The user does not have the write permission to the directory /user1.

   d. The user does not have the write permission to the file project1.

   e. The file was copied, but the ls –F command will show only originals, not copied files.

7. A user utilizes the chgrp command to give ownership of a file to another user. What must she do to regain ownership of the file?

   a. Run chgrp again listing herself as the new owner.

   b. Nothing, as this is a one-way, one-time action.

   c. Have the new owner run chgrp and list the original owner as the new owner.

   d. Run chown and list herself as the new owner.

8. After typing the ls –F command, you see the following line in the output:

   ```
   -rw-r-xr--    1 user1    root        0 Apr 29 15:40 file1
   ```

   What does this mean?

   a. user1 has read and write, members of the root group have read execute, and all others have read permissions to the file.

   b. Members of the root group have read and write, user1 has read and execute, and all others have read permissions to the file.

   c. All users have read and write, members of the root group have read and execute, and user1 has read permissions to the file.

   d. user1 has read and write, all others have read and execute, and members of the root group have read permissions to the file.

9. Access permissions to files and directories are stored in _____.

    a. the mode of the superblock

    b. the mode of the inode

    c. the mode of the filesystem

    d. the user's home directory

10. After typing the command umask 731, the permissions on all subsequently created files and directories will be affected. In this case, what will the permissions on all new files be?

    a. rw-rw-rw-

    b. rwxrw-r--

    c. ----r--rw-

    d. ----wx--x

11. You can use the -h option to the chmod command to change the permissions on a symbolic link. True or False?

12. Jim has rw-rw-rw- to the file resume that resides in the directory jobs. He modifies and prints off a copy, and then wants to delete the file resume but cannot. Why can he not delete the file?

    a. Jim needs execute permission to the file resume.

    b. Jim needs write permission to the directory jobs.

    c. Jim must save the modified file before he can delete it.

    d. Only root users can delete files.

13. The command chmod 317 file1 would produce which of the following lines in the ls command?

    a. --w-r--rwx    1 user1    root      0 Apr 29 15:40 file1

    b. --wx--xrwx    1 user1    root      0 Apr 29 15:40 file1

    c. -rwxrw-r-x    1 user1    root      0 Apr 29 15:40 file1

    d. --w-rw-r-e    1 user1    root      0 Apr 29 15:40 file1

14. In order to see directories' contents, you only need to have execute permission to that directory. True or False?

15. The default permissions given by the system prior to analyzing the umask are _____ for directories and _____ for files.

    a. 666, 666

    b. 666, 444

    c. 666, 777

    d. 777, 666

    e. 766, 766

**6**

16. What command is used to create a new file?

    a. mkfile *filename*

    b. make file *filename*

    c. touch *filename*

    d. take file *filename*

17. Which of the following commands will change the user ownership and group ownership of file1 to user1 and sys, respectively?

    a. chown user1:sys file1

    b. chown user1 : sys file1

    c. It cannot be done as user and group ownership properties of a file must be modified separately.

    d. chown sys:user1file1

    e. chown sys : user1file1

18. The umask variable must be identical for files and directories. True or False?

19. A file has the following permissions: r----x-w-. The command chmod 143 would have the same effect as the command _____. (Choose all that apply.)

    a. chmod u+x-r,g+r-x,o+x file1

    b. chmod u=w,g=rw,o=rx file1

    c. chmod u-r-w,g+r-w,o+r-x file1

    d. chmod u=x,g=r,o=̄wx file1

    e. chmod u+w,g+r-w,o+r-x file1

    f. chmod u=rw,g=r,o=r file1

20. Which of the following commands can be used to set the SGID special permission on a file? (Choose all that apply.)

    a. chmod 777

    b. chmod 7777

    c. chmod 6774

    d. chmod 1737

21. Mary is a member of the adm group. Mary owns a file called project and the group owner is the adm group. This file also has the mode rw-r--r-x. What can Mary do to this file? (Choose all that apply.)

    a. Copy the file to another directory.

    b. Read the file.

    c. Edit the file.

    d. Execute the file.

e. Remove the file.

f. Change the group ownership of the file.

g. Change the ownership of the file.

22. When applied to a directory, the SGID special permission _____.

    a. causes all new files created in the directory to have the same group membership as the directory and not the entity that created them

    b. cannot be done as it is only applied to files

    c. gives users the ability to use more than two groups for files that they create within the directory

    d. does nothing

23. All files have a _____.

    a. superblock

    b. inode

    c. PATH

    d. home directory

24. After typing the command umask 322, the permissions on all subsequently created files and directories will be affected. In this case, what will the permissions on all new directories be?

    a. 455

    b. 344

    c. 322

    d. 433

25. What command would be used to generate the following screen output?

        #    u=rwx,g=rx,o=r

    a. umask

    b. umask –s

    c. umask –S

    d. ls –l

26. Given Question 25, what is the default umask on the system that provided that result?

    a. 666

    b. 777

    c. 754

    d. 023

27. Given Question 25, what would the permission settings on a newly created file on that system be?

    a. 754

    b. 666

    c. 023

    d. 022

28. Which of the following commands can be used to retrieve more information about additional users and groups that are given permission to a file?

    a. setacl

    b. getacl

    c. rmacl

    d. aclinfo

29. Given the following output, what are permissions of the user bob?

    ```
    user::rw-
    user:bob:rw-
    group::r--
    class:---
    other:---
    ```

    a. rwx

    b. rw-

    c. r--

    d. ---

30. Which of the following commands can be used to add a group called acctg with the permissions rwx to a file called file1?

    a. setacl -r -m -g acctg file1 rwx

    b. setacl -r -m u:acctg:rwx file1

    c. setacl -r -m g:acctg:rwx file1

    d. setacl -r -m -u acctg file1 rwx

---

# HANDS-ON PROJECTS

These projects should be completed in the order given. All hands-on projects should take a total of three hours to complete. The requirement for this lab includes:

  ❑ A computer with UnixWare 7.1.1 installed according to Project 2-2

## Project 6-1

In this hands-on project, you will view and modify access permissions on files and directories as well as test their effects.

1. Switch to a command-line terminal (vt02) by pressing **Ctrl+Alt+F2** and log into the terminal using the username **root** and the password **secret**.

2. At the command prompt, type **touch permsample** and press **Enter**. Next, type **chmod 777 permsample** at the command prompt and press **Enter**.

3. At the command prompt, type **ls –l** and press **Enter**. Who has permissions to this file?

4. At the command prompt, type **chmod 000 permsample** and press **Enter**. Next, type **ls –l** at the command prompt and press **Enter**. Who has permissions to this file?

5. At the command prompt, type **rm permsample** and press **Enter**. Were you able to delete this file? Why?

6. At the command prompt, type **cd /** and press **Enter**. Next, type **mkdir forowner** at the command prompt and press **Enter**.

7. At the command prompt, type **ls –ld forowner** and press **Enter** to view the owner, group owner, and permissions on the forowner directory. Who is the owner and group owner? If you were logged in as the user owner, which category would you be placed in (user, group, or other)? What permissions do you have as this category (read, write, or execute)?

8. At the command prompt, type **cd /forowner** and press **Enter** to enter the forowner directory. Next, type **ls –F** at the command prompt and press **Enter**. Are there any files in this directory? Type **cp /etc/hosts .** at the command prompt and press **Enter**. Next, type **ls –F** at the command prompt and press **Enter** to ensure that a copy of the hosts file was made in your current directory.

9. Switch to a different command-line terminal (vt03) by pressing **Ctrl+Alt+F3** and log into the terminal using the username **owner** and the password **secret**.

10. At the command prompt, type **cd /forowner** and press **Enter**. Were you successful? Why? Next, type **ls –F** at the command prompt and press **Enter**. Were you able to see the contents of the directory? Why? Now, type **rm hosts** at the command prompt and press **Enter**. Note the error message you receive.

11. Switch back to your previous command-line terminal (vt02) by pressing **Ctrl+Alt+F2**. Note that you are logged in as the root user on this terminal.

12. At the command prompt, type **chmod o+w /forowner** and press **Enter**. Were you able to change the permissions on the /forowner directory successfully? Why?

13. Switch back to your previous command-line terminal (vt03) by pressing **Ctrl+Alt+F3**. Note that you are logged in as the owner user on this terminal in the /forowner directory.

14. Next, type **rm hosts** at the command prompt and press **Enter**. Were you successful now? Why?

15. Switch back to your previous command-line terminal (vt02) by pressing **Ctrl+Alt+F2**. Note that you are logged in as the root user on this terminal in the /forowner directory.

16. At the command prompt, type **cp/etc/hosts .** and press **Enter** to place another copy of the hosts file in your current directory.

17. At the command prompt, type **ls -l** and press **Enter**. Who is the owner and group owner of this file? If you were logged in as the user owner, which category would you be placed in (user, group, or other)? What permissions do you have as this category (read, write, or execute)?

18. Switch back to your previous command-line terminal (vt03) by pressing **Ctrl+Alt+F3**. Note that you are logged in as the owner user on this terminal in the /forowner directory.

19. Type **cat hosts** at the command prompt and press **Enter**. Were you successful? Why? Next, type **vi hosts** at the command prompt to open the hosts file in the vi editor. Delete the first line of this file and save your changes. Were you successful? Why? Exit the vi editor and discard your changes.

20. Switch back to your previous command-line terminal (vt02) by pressing **Ctrl+Alt+F2**. Note that you are logged in as the root user on this terminal in the /forowner directory.

21. At the command prompt, type **chmod o+w hosts** and press **Enter**.

22. Switch back to your previous command-line terminal (vt03) by pressing **Ctrl+Alt+F3**. Note that you are logged in as the owner user on this terminal on the /forowner directory.

23. Type **vi hosts** at the command prompt to open the hosts file in the vi editor. Delete the first line of this file and save your changes. Why were you successful this time? Exit the vi editor.

24. At the command prompt, type **ls -l** and press **Enter**. Do you have permission to execute the hosts file? Should you make this file executable? Why? Next, type **ls -l /bin** at the command prompt and press **Enter** and note how many of these files you have execute permission to. Type **file /bin/*** at the command prompt and press **Enter** to view the file types of the files in the /bin directory. Should these files have the execute permission?

25. Type **exit** and press **Enter** to log out of your shell.

26. Switch back to your previous command-line terminal (vt02) by pressing **Ctrl+Alt+F2**.

27. Type **exit** and press **Enter** to log out of your shell.

## Project 6-2

In this hands-on project, you will view and manipulate the default file and directory permissions using the umask variable.

1. Switch to a command-line terminal (vt03) by pressing **Ctrl+Alt+F3** and log into the terminal using the username **owner** and the password **secret**.

2. At the command prompt, type **umask** and press **Enter**. What is the default umask variable?

3. At the command prompt, type **touch utest1** and press **Enter**. Next, type **ls –l** at the command prompt and press **Enter**. What are the permissions on the utest1 file? Do these agree with the calculation in Figure 6-3? Create a new directory by typing the command **mkdir udir1** at the command prompt and press **Enter**. Next, type **ls –l** at the command prompt and press **Enter**. What are the permissions on the udir1 directory? Do these agree with the calculation in Figure 6-3?

4. At the command prompt, type **umask 007** and press **Enter**. Next, type **umask** at the command prompt and press **Enter** to verify that your umask variable has been changed to 007.

5. At the command prompt, type **touch utest2** and press **Enter**. Next, type **ls –l** at the command prompt and press **Enter**. What are the permissions on the utest2 file? Do these agree with the calculation in Figure 6-4? Create a new directory by typing the command **mkdir udir2** at the command prompt and press **Enter**. Next, type **ls –l** at the command prompt and press **Enter**. What are the permissions on the udir2 directory? Do these agree with the calculation in Figure 6-4?

6. Type **exit** and press **Enter** to log out of your shell.

## Project 6-3

In this hands-on project, you will view and change the file and directory ownership using the chown and chgrp commands.

1. Switch to a command-line terminal (vt03) by pressing **Ctrl+Alt+F3** and log into the terminal using the username **owner** and the password **secret**.

2. At the command prompt, type **touch ownersample** and press **Enter**. Next, type **mkdir ownerdir** at the command prompt and press **Enter**. Now, type **ls –l** at the command prompt and press **Enter** to verify that the file ownersample and directory ownerdir were created and that owner is the owner and the group other is the group owner of each.

3. At the command prompt, type **chgrp sys owner\*** and press **Enter** to change the group ownership to the sys group for both ownersample and ownerdir. Why were you successful?

4. At the command prompt, type **chown root owner\*** and press **Enter** to change the ownership to the root user for both ownersample and ownerdir. Why were you successful?

5. At the command prompt, type **chown owner owner\*** and press **Enter** to change the ownership back to the owner user for both ownersample and ownerdir. Note the error message that you receive.

6. Switch to a command-line terminal (vt02) by pressing **Ctrl+Alt+F2** and log into the terminal using the username **root** and the password **secret**.

7. At the command prompt, type **cd /home/owner** and press **Enter**. Next, type **chown owner:owner owner\*** at the command prompt and press **Enter**. Next, type **ls -l** at the command prompt and press **Enter** to verify that the file and directory ownership has changed for ownersample and ownerdir, respectively.

7. Type **exit** and press **Enter** to log out of your shell.

8. Switch back to your previous command-line terminal (vt03) by pressing **Ctrl+Alt+F3**. Note that you are logged in as the owner user on this terminal.

9. At the command prompt, type **mv ownersample ownerdir** and press **Enter**. Next, type **ls -lR** at the command prompt and press **Enter** to note that the ownersample file now exists within the ownerdir directory and that both are owned by owner.

10. At the command prompt, type **chown -R root ownerdir** and press **Enter**. Next, type **ls -lR** at the command prompt and press **Enter**. Who owns the ownerdir directory and ownersample file? Why?

11. At the command prompt, type **rm -rf ownerdir** and press **Enter**. Why were you able to delete this directory without being the owner of it?

12. Type **exit** and press **Enter** to log out of your shell.

**HANDS-ON PROJECTS**

## Project 6-4

In this hands-on project, you will add additional users and groups to the ACL of a file.

1. Switch to a command-line terminal (vt02) by pressing **Ctrl+Alt+F2** and log into the terminal using the username **root** and the password **secret**.

2. At the command prompt, type **touch acltestfile** and press **Enter**. Next, type **ls -l acltestfile** and press **Enter**. Who is the owner and group owner for this file? What are the permissions on this file?

3. At the command prompt, type **setacl -r -m u:owner:rw- acltestfile** and press **Enter**. Next, type **ls -l acltestfile** and press **Enter**. What are the group permissions on this file? What special character exists beside the mode?

4. At the command prompt, type **setacl -r -m g:other:rwx acltestfile** and press **Enter**. Next, type **ls -l acltestfile** and press Enter. What are the group permissions on this file?

5. At the command prompt, type **getacl acltestfile** and press **Enter**. Are the original permissions preserved? Who has additional permissions? What are the permissions of the special group class? Why?

6. At the command prompt, type **cp acltestfile acltestfile2** and press **Enter**. Next, type **ls –l acltestfile2**. Are additional users and groups kept on the ACL when a file is copied? Why?

7. At the command prompt, type **setacl –d g:other acltestfile** and press **Enter**.

8. At the command prompt, type **setacl –d u:owner acltestfile** and press **Enter**.

9. At the command prompt, type **ls –l acltestfile** and press **Enter** to verify that the user owner and group other were removed from the ACL.

10. Type **exit** and press **Enter** to log out of your shell.

**HANDS-ON PROJECTS**

## Project 6-5

6

In this hands-on project, you will view and set special permissions on files and directories.

1. Switch to a command-line terminal (vt02) by pressing **Ctrl+Alt+F2** and log into the terminal using the username **root** and the password **secret**.

2. At the command prompt, type **touch specialfile** and press **Enter**. Next, type **ls –l** at the command prompt and press **Enter** to verify that specialfile was created successfully. Who is the owner and group owner of specialfile?

3. At the command prompt, type **chmod 4777 specialfile** and press **Enter**. Next, type **ls –l** at the command prompt and press **Enter**. Which special permission is set on this file? If this file were executed by another user, who would that user be during execution?

4. At the command prompt, type **chmod 6777 specialfile** and press **Enter**. Next, type **ls –l** at the command prompt and press **Enter**. Which special permission is set on this file? If this file were executed by another user, who would that user be during execution and which group would that user be a member of?

5. At the command prompt, type **chmod 6444 specialfile** and press **Enter**. Next, type **ls –l** at the command prompt and press **Enter**. Can you tell if execute is not given underneath the special permission listings? Would the special permissions retain their meaning in this case?

6. At the command prompt, type **mkdir /public** and press **Enter**. Next, type **chmod 1777 /public** at the command prompt and press **Enter**. Which special permission is set on this directory? Who can add or remove files to and from this directory?

7. At the command prompt, type **touch /public/rootfile** and press **Enter**.

8. Type **exit** and press **Enter** to log out of your shell.

9. Switch to a different command-line terminal (vt03) by pressing **Ctrl+Alt+F3** and log into the terminal using the username **owner** and the password **secret**.

8. At the command prompt, type **touch /public/ownerfile** and press **Enter**. Next, type **ls –l /public** at the command prompt and press **Enter**. What files exist in this directory and who are the owners?

9. At the command prompt, type **rm /public/ownerfile** and press **Enter**. Were you successful? Why?

10. At the command prompt, type **rm /public/rootfile** and press **Enter**. When prompted to remove the file, press **y** and press **Enter**. Note the error message you receive.

11. Type **exit** and press **Enter** to log out of your shell.

## DISCOVERY EXERCISES

1. For each of the following modes, write the numeric equivalent (that is, 777):

   a. rw-r--r--

   b. r--r--r--

   c. ---rwxrw-

   d. -wxr-xrw-

   e. rw-rw-rwx

   f. -w-r-----

2. Fill in the following permission table with an x, assuming that all four files are in the directory /public, which has a mode of rwxr-xr-x.

| Filename | Mode | | Read | Edit | Execute | List | Delete |
|----------|------|------|------|------|---------|------|--------|
| sample1 | rw-rw-rw- | User<br>Group<br>Other | | | | | |
| sample2 | r--r----- | User<br>Group<br>Other | | | | | |
| sample3 | rwxr-x--- | User<br>Group<br>Other | | | | | |
| sample4 | r-x------ | User<br>Group<br>Other | | | | | |

3. Fill in the following permission table with an x, assuming that all four files are in the directory /public, which has a mode of rwx--x---.

| Filename | Mode | | Read | Edit | Execute | List | Delete |
|---|---|---|---|---|---|---|---|
| sample1 | rwxr--r-- | User<br>Group<br>Other | | | | | |
| sample2 | r-xr--rw- | User<br>Group<br>Other | | | | | |
| sample3 | --xr-x--- | User<br>Group<br>Other | | | | | |
| sample4 | r-xr--r-- | User<br>Group<br>Other | | | | | |

6

4. For each of the following umasks, calculate the default permissions given to new files and directories:

   a. 017

   b. 272

   c. 777

   d. 000

   e. 077

   f. 027

5. For each of the umasks in Discovery Exercise 4, list the umasks that are reasonable to use to increase security on your UNIX system and explain why.

6. Starting from the UNIX default permissions for file and directories, what umask would you use to ensure that for all new:

   a. directories, the owner would have read, write, and execute, members of the group would have read and execute, and other would have read

   b. files, the owner would have read and execute, the group would have read, write, and execute, and other would have execute

   c. files, the owner would have write, the group would have read, write, and execute, and other would have read and write

   d. directories, the owner would have read, write, and execute, the group would have read, write, and execute, and other would have read, write, and execute

   e. directories, the owner would have execute, the group would have read, write, and execute, and other would have no permissions

   f. files, the owner would have read and write, the group would have no permissions, and other would have write

g. directories, the owner would have read, write, and execute, the group would have read, and other would have read and execute

h. directories, the owner would have write, the group would have read, write, and execute, and other would have read, write, and execute

i. files, the owner would have no permissions, the group would have no permissions, and other would have no permissions

7. What chmod command would you use to impose the following permissions?

a. on a directory such that the owner would have read, write and execute, the group would have read and execute, and other would have read

b. on a file such that the owner would have read and write, the group would have no permissions, and other would have write

c. on a file such that the owner would have write, the group would have read, write, and execute, and other would have read and write

d. on a file such that the owner would have read and execute, the group would have read, write, and execute, and other would have execute

e. on a directory such that the owner would have execute, the group would have read, write, and execute, and other would have no permissions

f. on a directory such that the owner would have write, the group would have read, write, and execute, and other would have read, write, and execute

g. on a directory such that the owner would have read, write, and execute, the group would have read, and other would have read and execute

h. on a directory such that the owner would have read, write, and execute, the group would have read, write, and execute, and other would have read, write, and execute

i. on a file such that the owner would have no permissions, the group would have no permissions, and other would have no permissions

8. Write the commands that can be used to achieve the following permissions for the file called file1 in your current directory that is owned by the root user and the adm group:

|     | root user | adm group | bob user | acctg group |
| --- | --------- | --------- | -------- | ----------- |
| a.  | rw–       | rw–       | rw–      | ---         |
| b.  | rwx       | r--       | ---      | rwx         |
| c.  | rwx       | rwx       | r--      | r---        |
| d.  | rw–       | r--       | r--      | ---         |
| e.  | r--       | r--       | rw–      | ---         |

CHAPTER

# 7

# ADMINISTERING UNIX
# FILESYSTEMS

**After reading this chapter and completing the exercises, you will be able to:**

♦ Describe the structure and characteristics of device files in the /dev directory

♦ Identify disk devices using device files

♦ Use the Device Database to locate information about devices on the system

♦ Understand common UNIX filesystem types and their features

♦ Create filesystems on floppy disks and hard disk slices

♦ Create hard disk partitions and slices

♦ Mount and unmount floppy disks, CD-ROMs, and hard disk slices to and from the UNIX directory tree

♦ Mount and unmount CD-ROM disks to and from the UNIX directory tree

♦ Monitor free space on mounted filesystems

♦ Check filesystems for errors

♦ Use hard disk quotas to limit user space usage

Navigating the UNIX directory tree and manipulating files are common tasks that are performed on a daily basis by all users; however, administrators must provide this directory tree for users as well as manage and fix the disk devices that support it. In this chapter, you will learn about the various device files that represent disk devices and the different filesystems that may be placed on those devices. Next, you will learn how to create, manage, and mount filesystems on disk devices. You will also learn about hard disk partitions and slices. Finally, this chapter concludes with a discussion of disk usage, filesystem errors, and restricting users' ability to store files.

# DEVICE FILES

An understanding of how these disks are specified by the UNIX operating system is fundamental to administering the disks used to store information. Most devices on a UNIX system (such as disks, terminals, and serial ports) are represented by a file on the hard disk called a **device file**; there is one file per device and these files are typically found in the **/dev directory**. For commands that manipulate or utilize disk devices, device files are used within the command to specify the correct device. Before using those commands, however, it is important to learn how to identify and manage device files as well as search their information in the **Device Database**.

## Naming Disk Devices Using Device Files

The name of the device file in the /dev directory specifies the type of device that it refers to. For example, the file /dev/dsk/f03ht specifies the first 3.5-inch high-density floppy disk in UnixWare. Each letter in the device name specifies a different attribute of the device:

- *f* represents a floppy disk.

- 0 represents the first floppy disk in the system (1 represents the second floppy disk in the system).

- 3 represents the 3.5-inch size (5 represents the 5.25-inch size).

- *h* represents high density (*d* stands for double density and *e* stands for extra high density).

- *t* specifies accessing the entire device.

Thus, the second 5.25-inch double-density floppy disk would be represented by the file /dev/dsk/f15dt.

**NOTE**

For simplicity, you may use the files /dev/dsk/f0t and /dev/dsk/f1t to refer to the first floppy disk and second floppy disk detected on your system during installation.

Similarly, the file /dev/cdrom/c1b0t0l0 refers to the first CD-ROM that is attached to the second IDE controller in a UNIX system:

- c1 represents the controller that the CD-ROM is attached to (c0 represents the first SCSI/IDE controller, c1 represents the second SCSI/IDE controller, and so on).

- b0 represents the first SCSI controller bus (b1 represents the second SCSI bus and so on); the number is always 0 for IDE controllers.

- t0 represents the first CD-ROM on the controller (t1 represents the second CD-ROM on the controller and so on).

- l0 represents the Logical Unit Number (LUN) for SCSI CD-ROMs; the number is always 0 for IDE CD-ROMs.

**NOTE**

As with floppy disks, you may use the files /dev/cdrom/cdrom1 and /dev/cdrom/cdrom2 to simplify specifying to the first CD-ROM and second CD-ROM detected on your system during installation.

Data is stored on CD-ROMs and floppy disks in a straightforward manner; however, hard disks require that a UNIX partition and slices within that UNIX partition be created prior to storing files. As a result, you may refer to the first UNIX partition on the first hard disk on the first IDE controller using the device file /dev/dsk/c0b0t0d0p1:

- c0 represents the controller that the hard disk is attached to (c0 represents the first SCSI/IDE controller, c1 represents the second SCSI/IDE controller, and so on).

- b0 represents the first SCSI controller bus (b1 represents the second SCSI bus and so on); the number is always 0 for IDE controllers.

- t0 represents the first hard disk on the controller (t1 represents the second hard disk on the controller and so on).

- d0 represents the LUN for SCSI hard disks; the number is always 0 for IDE hard disks.

- p1 represents the first UNIX partition on the hard disk (p2 represents the second UNIX partition on the hard disk, p3 represents the third UNIX partition on the hard disk, p4 represents the fourth and final UNIX partition on the hard disk, and p0 represents all partitions on the hard disk).

Although you may specify a UNIX partition, recall that there is typically only one UNIX partition created per hard disk and that filesystems are stored only on slices that exist within that UNIX partition. Thus, it is more common to specify slices within the first UNIX partition on a hard disk. For example, the device file /dev/dsk/c0b0t0d0s1 would specify the first slice in the UNIX partition on the first IDE hard disk on the first IDE controller on the system:

- c0 represents the controller that the hard disk is attached to (c0 represents the first SCSI/IDE controller, c1 represents the second SCSI/IDE controller, and so on).

- b0 represents the first SCSI controller bus (b1 represents the second SCSI bus and so on); the number is always 0 for IDE controllers.

- t0 represents the first hard disk on the controller (t1 represents the second hard disk on the controller and so on).

- d0 represents the LUN for SCSI hard disks; the number is always 0 for IDE hard disks.

**7**

■ s1 represents the first slice within the UNIX partition on the hard disk (s2 represents the second slice within the UNIX partition on the hard disk, s3 represents the third slice within the UNIX partition on the hard disk, and so on; s0 represents all slices in the UNIX partition on the hard disk).

Typically, a UNIX partition has more than nine slices; hexadecimal numbers are used for these slices. For the hard disk mentioned earlier, slice 10 would be labeled /dev/dsk/c0b0t0d0sa, slice 11 would be labeled /dev/dsk/c0b0t0d0sb, and so on.

Although device filenames identify the attributes of each device, they also specify how data should be transferred to and from the device. There are two methods for transferring data to and from a device. The first method transfers information character by character to and from the device; devices that transfer data in this fashion are referred to as **character devices**.

Character devices are also called **raw devices**.

The second method transfers chunks or blocks of information at a time by using physical memory to buffer the transfer; devices that use this method of transfer are called **block devices** and can transfer information much faster than character devices. Device files that represent disks such as floppy disks, CD-ROMs, and hard disks typically have both a character device file and a block device file. Block device files for floppy disks and hard disks are stored under the /dev/dsk directory, whereas character device files for these disks are stored under the /dev/rdsk directory. Similarly, block device files for CD-ROMs are stored under the /dev/cdrom directory, whereas character device files for CD-ROMs are stored under the /dev/rcdrom directory.

Tape drives and most nondisk devices are only represented by character device files under the /dev directory.

To see whether a particular device transfers data character by character or block by block, recall from Chapter 4 that the `ls -l` command displays a *c* or *b* character in the type column indicating character and block device files, respectively. The following output lists the block and character device files for the first 3.5-inch high-density floppy disk in the system:

```
# ls -l /dev/dsk/f03ht
brw-rw-rw-    5 root        sys          1,112 Apr  7  1998 /dev/dsk/f03ht
# ls -l /dev/rdsk/f03ht
crw-rw-rw-    5 root        sys          1,112 Apr  7  1998 /dev/rdsk/f03ht #
```

From the far-left character in the previous output, you can see that the /dev/dsk/f03ht is a block device file and /dev/rdsk/f03ht is a character device file. Both of these files represent the same device on the system, but specify different transfer rates.

Recall from Chapter 1 that the largest difference between UNIX flavors is the hardware used. For Solaris and HP-UX, SCSI hard disks and CD-ROMs are standard, and their device names typically do not contain the bus number shown in UnixWare device names. For example, the device file for an SCSI CD-ROM on the first controller would be /dev/dsk/c0t0d0 if it was the first device on that controller with a LUN of 0. Similarly, the raw device file for this CD-ROM would be /dev/rdsk/c0t0d0.

The second SCSI hard disk on the second SCSI controller with a LUN of 0 would be represented by the /dev/dsk/c1t1d0 and /dev/rdsk/c1t1d0 device files. Like UnixWare, Solaris systems divide hard disks into slices; however, the first slice on the hard disk mentioned earlier would be represented by the block device file /dev/dsk/c1t1d0s0, the second slice would be represented by /dev/dsk/c1t1d0s1, and the third slice would be represented by /dev/dsk/c1t1d0s3. All slices are represented by the block device file /dev/dsk/c1t1d0s2. On HP-UX systems, hard disks are typically divided into volume groups that are then further divided into logical volumes; these logical volumes are analogous to slices and may contain a filesystem. The first logical volume in the first volume group will have the device file /dev/vg00/lvol1, the second logical volume in the first volume group will have the device file /dev/vg00/lvol2, and so on.

In addition to this, floppy disks are not commonly found on systems that run HP-UX. If there is a floppy disk in a computer running Solaris, it will be a high-density 3.5-inch floppy disk and will be identified with the block device file /dev/diskette and the character device file /dev/rdiskette.

## The Device Database

During installation, a database of detected devices and their appropriate device file information is created; this database is called the Device Database and resides in the file /etc/device.tab. Originally, the Device Database was used to standardize the naming of devices across UNIX systems; however, today it is used primarily to obtain information about devices on the system.

Each device in the Device Database is given a user-friendly identifier such as diskette1 for the first floppy diskette in the system, disk1 for the first hard disk in the system, and cdrom1 for the first CD-ROM in the system. To see a full list of device identifiers on your system, use the **getdev command**:

```
# getdev | more
arp
cdrom1
disk1
diskette1
hba1
```

```
hba2
icmp
igmp
incf
ip
ipip
llcloop
mdens1HIGH
mdens1LOW
mdens1MEDIUM1
mdens1MEDIUM2
pseudo_master
ptyp0
ptyp1
ptyp10
ptyp11
ptyp12
Standard input
```

To search the Device Database for information about a device in the system including the correct device file, use the **devattr command** followed by the appropriate device identifier. The **-v** option to the `devattr` command also displays the type of information. For example, to view information in the Device Database regarding the first floppy disk in the system, use the following command:

```
# devattr -v diskette1
alias='diskette1'
bdevice='/dev/dsk/f0t'
bdevlist='/dev/dsk/f0'
capacity='2844'
cdevice='/dev/rdsk/f0t'
cdevlist='/dev/rdsk/f0'
copy='true'
desc='Floppy Drive 1'
display='true'
erasecmd='/usr/sadm/sysadm/bin/floperase /dev/rdsk/f0t'
fmtcmd='/usr/sbin/format -v /dev/rdsk/f03ht'
mdensdefault='mdens1HIGH'
mdenslist='mdens1HIGH,mdens1LOW,mdens1MEDIUM1,mdens1MEDIUM2'
mkdtab='true'
mkfscmd='/sbin/mkfs -F s5 /dev/dsk/f0t 2844:711 2 36'
mkvxfscmd='/sbin/mkfs -F vxfs -
o ninode=711 /dev/dsk/f0t 2844'
mountpt='/install'
removable='true'
type='diskette'
volume='diskette'
# _
```

The previous output also indicates useful commands that may be used to format and place filesystems on the first floppy disk device; these commands will be discussed later in this chapter.

## Managing the /dev Directory

After a typical UNIX installation, over 1000 different device files exist in the /dev directory; most of these device files represent devices that may not exist on the particular UNIX system and hence are never used. Providing this large number of redundant device files on a UNIX system does not require much disk space since all device files consist of inodes and no data blocks. As a result, the entire content of the /dev directory is usually less than 50KB in size, which could easily fit on a floppy disk. When using the ls -l command to view device files, the portion of the listing describing the file size in kilobytes is replaced by two numbers: the major number and the minor number. The **major number** of a device file points to the device driver for the device in the UNIX kernel; several different devices can share the same major number if they are of the same general type (that is, two different floppy disk drives can share the same major number). The **minor number** indicates the particular device itself; the first floppy disk drive in the computer will have a different minor number than the second floppy disk drive in the computer. The following output shows that both /dev/dsk/f03ht and /dev/dsk/f13ht share the same major number of 1 since they use the same floppy device driver in the UNIX kernel, but the minor number for /dev/dsk/f03ht is 112 and the minor number for /dev/dsk/f13ht is 113, which differentiates them from one another:

```
# ls -l /dev/dsk/f03ht
brw-rw-rw-    5 root      sys       1,112 Apr  7  1998 /dev/dsk/f03ht
# ls -l /dev/dsk/f13ht
brw-rw-rw-    4 root      sys       1,113 Apr  7  1998 /dev/dsk/f13ht
# _
```

 The major number for devices differs with each UNIX flavor. For UnixWare, floppy disks have a major number of 1, hard disks have a major number of 7679, tape devices have a major number of 111, and CD-ROMs have a major number of 110.

The minor number for most devices is chosen by the UNIX vendor and does not follow any pattern; however, hard disks in UnixWare use the slice number as the minor number:

```
# ls -l /dev/dsk/c0b0t0d0s1
brw-------  1 root  sys  7679, 1 Sep 2 10:47 /dev/dsk/c0b0t0d0s1
# ls -l /dev/dsk/c0b0t0d0s2
brw-------  1 root  sys  7679, 2 Sep 2 10:47 /dev/dsk/c0b0t0d0s2
# ls -l /dev/dsk/c0b0t0d0s3
brw-------  1 root  sys  7679, 3 Sep 2 10:47 /dev/dsk/c0b0t0d0s3
# _
```

Together, the device file type (block or character), the major number (device driver), and the minor number (specific device) make up the unique characteristics of each device file; to create a device file, you need to know these three pieces of information.

If a device file becomes corrupted, it will usually be listed as a regular file instead of a block or character special file; recall from Chapter 4 that the `find /dev -type f` command could be used to search for regular files underneath the /dev directory to identify whether corruption has taken place. If you find a corrupted device file or accidentally delete a device file, the **mknod command** can be used to recreate the device file if you know the type, major number, and minor number. The following is an example of recreating the /dev/dsk/f03ht block device file used earlier with a major number of 1 and a minor number of 112:

```
# ls -l /dev/dsk/f03ht
UX:ls: ERROR: Cannot access /dev/dsk/f03ht: No such file or directory
# mknod /dev/dsk/f03ht b 1 112
# ls -l /dev/dsk/f03ht
brw-rw-rw-    5 root       sys        1,112 Nov  7 2003 /dev/dsk/f03ht
# _
```

Since the device type, major number, and minor number for a device file are stored in its inode, you can safely hard link device files. For example, to create a hard link to /dev/dsk/f03ht called /dev/flopper, use the following command:

```
# ln /dev/dsk/f03ht /dev/flopper
# ls -l /dev/flopper
brw-rw-rw-    5 root       sys        1,112 Nov  7 2003 /dev/dsk/f03ht
# _
```

This hard linking of device files can be used to simplify the device names on your system; you can use the friendly file /dev/flopper instead of /dev/dsk/f03ht while typing commands that specify your floppy disk as an argument.

# FILESYSTEMS

Files need to be organized on the hard disk in a defined format such that the operating system may work with them; this format is called a **filesystem**. Furthermore, the type of filesystem used determines how files are managed on the physical hard disk. Each filesystem can have different methods for storing files and features that make the filesystem robust against errors. Although many different types of filesystems are available, all filesystems share three common components as discussed in Chapter 4: the superblock, the inode table, and data blocks. On a structural level, these three components work together to organize files and allow rapid access to and the retrieval of data. All storage mediums, such as floppy disks, hard disks, and CD-ROMs, need to be formatted with a filesystem before they can be used.

Creating a filesystem on a device is commonly referred to as **formatting**.

## Filesystem Types

Many filesystems are available for use in the UNIX operating system. Each has is own strengths and weaknesses, so some are better suited to some tasks and not others. One benefit of UNIX is that you need not use only one type of filesystem on the system; you may use several different devices formatted with different filesystems under the same directory tree. In addition, files and directories appear the same throughout the directory tree regardless of whether the UNIX system uses 1 filesystem or 20 different filesystems. Table 7-1 lists some common filesystems available for use in UNIX.

**Table 7-1**  Common UNIX filesystems

| Filesystem | Description |
|---|---|
| BFS | Boot Filesystem—a small bootable filesystem used to hold files necessary for system startup |
| CDFS | Compact Disk Filesystem—used to view all tracks and data on a CD-ROM as normal files |
| DOSFS | DOS FAT Filesystem—used to access Windows floppy disks—also called pcfs (Portable Computer Filesystem) in Solaris |
| HFS | High Performance Filesystem—based on the S5 filesystem, this was the traditional filesystem used on HP-UX systems and is the filesystem used to contain the UNIX kernel on current HP-UX systems. |
| NFS | Network Filesystem—used to access filesystems on UNIX computers across a network |
| NUCFS | Netware-UNIX Client Filesystem—used to access Novell Netware filesystems from across a network |
| S5 | System V Filesystem—the filesystem that was released with System V UNIX and the only filesystem that is supported on all UNIX flavors |
| SFS | The Secure Filesystem—a variant of UFS that allows for secure access to files on the filesystem |
| UFS | The UNIX Filesystem—an improved version of the S5 filesystem and the default filesystem used on Solaris systems |
| VxFS | The Veritas Filesystem—a journaling filesystem that offers large file support and extent-based allocation, and supports ACLs (individual user permissions). It is also known as the Journaling Filesystem (JFS) in HP-UX and is the default filesystem for UnixWare and HP-UX systems. |

To see what filesystem resides on a particular device, use the command `fstyp <block_device_file>`.

The VxFS filesystem is the default filesystem used for most slices in UnixWare; it has a maximum size of 1TB, supports large files (over 2GB), and typically creates 1KB blocks to store data; however, it can also create 2KB, 4KB, and 8KB blocks if needed. It is also a journaling filesystem that uses extent-based allocation when storing files on the hard disk.

A **journaling filesystem** (also called an **intent-logging filesystem**) keeps track of the information written to the hard drive in a journal file (also called an intent-log file). If you copy a file on the hard drive from one directory to another, that file must pass into physical memory before it is written to the new location on the hard disk. If the power to the computer is turned off during this process, information may not be transmitted as expected and data may be lost or corrupted; however, with a journaling filesystem, each step required to copy the file to the new location is first written to a journal such that the system can retrace the steps the system took prior to a power outage and complete the file copy.

**Extent-based allocation** causes the data blocks of files to be stored in adjacent areas on the hard disk such that they may be read and written to more efficiently. The only drawback to the VxFS filesystem is that it is not recognized by UNIX bootloaders and cannot contain the kernel of the UNIX operating system as a result. In UnixWare, the kernel of the UNIX operating system instead resides on a slice that is formatted with the BFS.

## Mounting

The term **mounting** originated in the 1960s when information was stored on large tape reels that had to be mounted on computers to make the data available. Today, mounting still refers to making data available; more specifically, it refers to the process whereby a device is made accessible to users via the logical directory tree. This device is attached to a certain directory on the directory tree called a **mount point**. Users may then create files and subdirectories in this mount point directory, which will then be stored on the filesystem that was mounted to that particular directory.

Recall that directories are merely files that do not contain data, but have a list of files and subdirectories contained within them. Thus, it is easy for the UNIX system to cover up directories to prevent user access to that data. This is essentially what happens when a device is mounted to a certain directory; the mount point directory is temporarily covered up by that device while the device remains mounted. Any file contents that were present in the mount point directory prior to mounting are not lost. When the device is unmounted, the mount point directory is uncovered and the previous file contents are revealed. Say, for example, that you mount a floppy device that contains a filesystem to the /mnt directory. Before mounting, the directory structure would resemble that depicted in Figure 7-1. After the floppy is mounted to the /mnt directory, the contents of the /mnt directory would be covered up by the floppy filesystem, as illustrated in Figure 7-2.

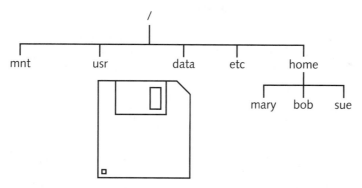

**Figure 7-1**   The directory tree prior to mounting a floppy disk

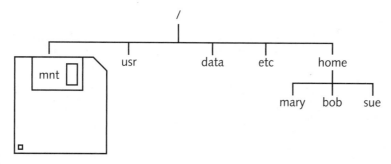

**Figure 7-2**   The directory tree after mounting a floppy disk

If a user then stores a file in the /mnt directory, as shown in Figure 7-2, that file will be stored on the floppy disk device. Similarly, if a user creates a subdirectory under the /mnt directory depicted in Figure 7-2, that subdirectory will be made on the floppy disk.

It is important to note that any existing directory can be used as a mount point; if a user mounts a floppy device to the /sbin directory, then all files in the /sbin directory would be covered up for the duration that floppy disk was mounted, including the command used to unmount the floppy! Thus, it is safe practice to create empty directories used specifically for mounting devices to avoid making existing files inaccessible to users.

When the UNIX system is first turned on, a filesystem present on the hard drive is mounted to the / directory; this is referred to as the **root filesystem** and contains most of the operating system files. Other filesystems present on hard disks inside the computer may also be mounted to various mount point directories underneath the / directory at boot time as well via entries in the **/etc/vfstab** file discussed in the following sections.

Since each filesystem that is mounted to a UNIX directory has its own inode table, inode numbers are unique only between files on the same filesystem. However, three reserved inodes may not be assigned by a filesystem: 0, 1, and 2. An inode of 0 is given to deleted files, an inode of 1 is reserved for future use, and an inode of 2 is given to mount points. Thus, you may identify mount point directories by viewing their inode number using the **-i** option with the **ls** command. Since a filesystem is mounted to the / directory and a separate filesystem is mounted to the /stand directory, they will both share the inode number of 2. However, the /usr directory (which is simply a subdirectory on the / filesystem) will have a different inode number:

```
# ls -id /
    2 /
# ls -id /stand
    2 /stand
# ls -id /usr
   20 /usr
# _
```

Similarly, when you mount a device to a certain directory, the inode number of that directory will be changed to 2 to indicate that it is a mount point on the UNIX system.

The **mount command** is used to mount devices to mount point directories and the **umount command** is used to unmount devices from mount point directories; both of these commands will be discussed throughout the remainder of this chapter.

## WORKING WITH FLOPPY DISKS

When transferring small amounts of information from computer to computer, it is commonplace to use floppy disk removable media to store the files. However, floppy disks must be prepared to store data before they are used in UNIX; this involves placing a filesystem on the floppy disk.

Before placing a filesystem on a floppy disk, it is good form to check the physical structure of the floppy disk to ensure that there are no errors since floppy disks are easily damaged by climate and air conditions over time. To do this, use the **format command** followed by the character device file of the floppy disk. You can also use the **–v** (verbose) option to the format command to view a progress line, as shown in the following output:

```
# format -v /dev/rdsk/f03ht
.................................................................................
................
# _
```

The format command does not place a filesystem on a floppy disk. To create a filesystem on a floppy disk, use the **mkfs (make filesystem) command** and specify the filesystem type using the **–F** option, the block device file representing the floppy disk device, the size of the filesystem to be created (specified in ½KB blocks), and any other desired information following the **–o** option. To create a VxFS filesystem of 1422KB on the first floppy disk that will allow 711 inodes (recall that each file and directory uses one inode), place a floppy disk in the floppy disk drive and type the following command:

```
# mkfs -F vxfs -o ninode=711 /dev/dsk/f03ht 2844
Mkfs: make vxfs file system?
(DEL if wrong)
```

```
        version 4 layout
        2844 sectors, 1422 blocks of size 1024, log size 256 blocks
        711 inodes, largefiles not supported
        1422 data blocks, 1102 free data blocks
        1 allocation units of 32768 blocks, 32768 data blocks
        last allocation unit has 1422 data blocks
    #  _
```

Alternatively, you may specify a different filesystem after the **−F** option such as the S5 filesystem; this will result in different output from the mkfs command as follows:

```
    # mkfs -F s5 /dev/dsk/f03ht 2844
    Mkfs: make s5 file system?
    (DEL if wrong)
    bytes per logical block = 1024
    total logical blocks = 1422
    total inodes = 352
    gap (physical blocks) = 7
    cylinder size (physical blocks) = 400
    Available blocks = 1396
    #  _
```

**NOTE**

The S5 filesystem is commonly placed on floppy disks since it is supported in all flavors of UNIX.

Once a floppy disk has been formatted with a filesystem, it must be mounted on the directory tree before it can be used. A list of currently mounted filesystems can be obtained by using the **mount** command with no options or arguments, which reads the information listed in the **/etc/mnttab** (mount table) file, as shown in the following output:

```
    # mount
    / on /dev/root read/write/setuid on Sat Oct 19 08:39:18 2003
    /stand on /dev/stand read/write on Sat Oct 19 08:39:22 2003
    /proc on /proc read/write on Sat Oct 19 08:40:07 2003
    /dev/fd on /dev/fd read/write on Sat Oct 19 08:40:07 2003
    /system/processor on /processorfs read/write on Sat Oct 19 08:40:12 2003
    /tmp on /tmp read/write on Sat Oct 19 08:40:13 2003
    /var/tmp on /var/tmp read/write on Sat Oct 19 08:40:13 2003
    /dev/_tcp on /dev/_tcp read/write on Sat Oct 19 08:40:13 2003
    # cat /etc/mnttab
    /dev/root    /      vxfs    rw,suid  1035031158
    /dev/stand   /stand   bfs    rw  1035031162
    /proc   /proc   proc   rw  1035031207
    /dev/fd /dev/fd fdfs   rw  1035031207
    /processorfs /system/processor  processorfs  rw  1035031212
    /tmp /tmp  memfs  rw  1035031213
    /var/tmp /var/tmp  memfs  rw  1035031213
    /dev/_tcp /dev/_tcp  specfs  rw  1035031213
    #  _
```

7

As shown in the previous output, the device /dev/root (which is a shortcut to the correct device file for the slice that contains the root filesystem) is mounted on the / directory and contains a VxFS filesystem. Some other filesystems listed in this output such as proc and processors are special filesystems that are used only by the operating system and will be discussed later in Chapter 10 of this textbook.

To mount a device on the directory tree, use the **mount** command with options and arguments to specify the filesystem type, the block device to mount, and the directory to mount the device to (mount point). It is important to ensure that no user is currently using the mount point directory; otherwise, the system will give you an error message and the disk will not be mounted. To check whether the /mnt directory is being used by any users, use the **fuser command** with the -u option, as shown in the following output:

```
# cd /mnt
# pwd
/mnt
# fuser -u /mnt
/mnt:         671c(root)         597c(root)
# cd /
# pwd
/
# fuser -u /mnt
/mnt:
# _
```

The last command in this output indicates that the /mnt directory was not used by any processes since no users were in the directory. To mount the first floppy device with the S5 filesystem to the /mnt directory, type the following command:

```
# mount -F s5   /dev/dsk/f03ht   /mnt
# mount
/ on /dev/root read/write/setuid on Sun Oct 29 05:06:57 2003
/stand on /dev/stand read/write on Sun Oct 29 05:06:59 2003
/proc on /proc read/write on Sun Oct 29 05:07:13 2003
/dev/fd on /dev/fd read/write on Sun Oct 29 05:07:13 2003
/system/processor on /processorfs read/write on Sun Oct 29 05:07:16 2003
/tmp on /tmp read/write on Sun Oct 29 05:07:16 2003
/var/tmp on /var/tmp read/write on Sun Oct 29 05:07:16 2003
/dev/_tcp on /dev/_tcp read/write on Sun Oct 29 05:07:16 2003
/mnt on /dev/dsk/f03ht read/write/setuid on Sun Oct 29 05:33:58 2003
# _
```

Notice that /dev/dsk/f03ht appears to be mounted to the /mnt directory in the output of the previous **mount** command. To access and store files on the floppy device, you can now treat the /mnt directory as the root of the floppy disk.

When a filesystem is created on a disk device using the mkfs command, the **lost+found directory** is created by default, which is used by the fsck command. To explore the recently mounted floppy filesystem, use the following commands:

```
# cd /mnt
# pwd
/mnt
# ls -F
lost+found/
# _
```

To copy files to the floppy device, specify the /mnt directory as the target for the cp command, as shown in the following output:

```
# cd /etc
# cat hosts
#ident   "@(#)hosts       1.2"
#ident "$Header: /sms/sinixV5.4es/rcs/s19-full/usr/src/cmd/cmd-
#inet/etc/hosts,v1.1 91/02/28 16:30:32 ccs Exp $"
#
# Internet host table
#
127.0.0.1        localhost        unix1
# cp hosts /mnt
# cd /mnt
# ls -F
hosts   lost+found/
# cat hosts
#ident   "@(#)hosts       1.2"
#ident "$Header: /sms/sinixV5.4es/rcs/s19-full/usr/src/cmd/cmd-
#inet/etc/hosts,v1.1 91/02/28 16:30:32 ccs Exp $"
#
# Internet host table
#
127.0.0.1        localhost        unix1
# _
```

Similarly, you can also create subdirectories underneath the floppy device to store files; these subdirectories are referenced underneath the mount point directory. To make a directory called workfiles on the floppy mounted in the previous example and copy the /etc/inittab file to it, use the following commands:

```
# pwd
/mnt
# ls -F
hosts   lost+found/
# mkdir workfiles
# ls -F
hosts   lost+found/   workfiles/
# cd workfiles
```

```
# pwd
/mnt/workfiles
# cp /etc/inittab .
# ls -F
inittab
# _
```

Since you may eject the floppy disk from the floppy disk drive without permission from the system, it is important to leave the floppy disk in the system while it is mounted to avoid error messages echoed to the terminal screen. Before a floppy is ejected, it must be properly unmounted using the umount command. The umount command can take the name of the device to unmount or the mount point directory as an argument. Like mounting a floppy disk, unmounting a floppy disk requires that the mount point directory has no users using it. The following output appears when a user tries to unmount the floppy disk mounted to the /mnt directory when that user is still in the directory (and hence using it):

```
# pwd
/mnt
# umount /mnt
UX:umount: ERROR: /mnt busy
# fuser -u /mnt/floppy
/mnt:    1159c(root)    1243c(root)
# cd /
# umount /mnt
# mount
/ on /dev/root read/write/setuid on Sun Oct 29 05:06:57 2003
/stand on /dev/stand read/write on Sun Oct 29 05:06:59 2003
/proc on /proc read/write on Sun Oct 29 05:07:13 2003
/dev/fd on /dev/fd read/write on Sun Oct 29 05:07:13 2003
/system/processor on /processorfs read/write on Sun Oct 29 05:07:16 2003
/tmp on /tmp read/write on Sun Oct 29 05:07:16 2003
/var/tmp on /var/tmp read/write on Sun Oct 29 05:07:16 2003
/dev/_tcp on /dev/_tcp read/write on Sun Oct 29 05:07:16 2003
# _
```

Notice from this output that the user was still using the /mnt directory since it was the current working directory. The fuser command also indicated that the root user had a process using the directory; once the current working directory was changed, the umount command was able to unmount the floppy from the /mnt directory and the output of the mount command indicated that the floppy disk was no longer mounted.

Take careful note of the spelling of the umount command.

TIP

Recall that mounting just attaches a disk device to the UNIX directory tree such that you may treat the device like a directory full of files and subdirectories; a device may be mounted to any existing directory. However, recall that if the directory contains files, those files are made inaccessible by the superblock of the filesystem until the device is unmounted. Say, for example, that you create a directory called /flopper for mounting floppy disks and a file inside called samplefile, as shown in the following output:

```
# mkdir /flopper
# touch /flopper/samplefile
# ls -F /flopper
samplefile
# _
```

If the floppy disk used earlier is mounted to the /flopper directory, then a user who uses the /flopper directory will be using the floppy disk; however, when nothing is mounted to the /flopper directory, the previous contents will be available for use:

```
# mount -F s5  /dev/dsk/f03ht  /mnt
# mount
/ on /dev/root read/write/setuid on Sun Oct 29 05:06:57 2003
/stand on /dev/stand read/write on Sun Oct 29 05:06:59 2003
/proc on /proc read/write on Sun Oct 29 05:07:13 2003
/dev/fd on /dev/fd read/write on Sun Oct 29 05:07:13 2003
/system/processor on /processorfs read/write on Sun Oct 29 05:07:16 2003
/tmp on /tmp read/write on Sun Oct 29 05:07:16 2003
/var/tmp on /var/tmp read/write on Sun Oct 29 05:07:16 2003
/dev/_tcp on /dev/_tcp read/write on Sun Oct 29 05:07:16 2003
/mnt on /dev/dsk/f03ht read/write/setuid on Sun Oct 29 05:49:18 2003
# ls -F /flopper
hosts  lost+found/  workfiles/
# umount /flopper
# ls -F /flopper
samplefile
# _
```

The `mount` command used in the previous output specifies the filesystem type, the device to mount, and the mount point directory. To save time typing on the command line, you can alternatively specify one argument and allow the system to look up the remaining information in the /etc/vfstab (virtual filesystem table) file. The /etc/vfstab file has a dual purpose; it is used to mount devices at boot time and is consulted when a user does not specify enough arguments on the command line when using the `mount` command. The /etc/vfstab file has six fields:

<block> <character> <mount point> <type> <fsck> <auto> <mount options>

The <block> field indicates the full pathname to the block device file, and the <character> field indicates the full pathname to the character device file that will be mounted. The mount point specifies where to mount the device. The <type> field indicates the type of filesystem. The <fsck> is used by the `fsck` command (discussed later in this chapter) when checking filesystems at boot time for errors; filesystems with a 1 in this field are checked, and filesystems with a 0 are not checked. If yes appears in the <auto> field, then the filesystem will be automatically mounted at boot time. Any other options that may be passed to the mount command may be listed in the <mount options> field. Two common options include ro to mount the filesystem read-only or mincache= closesync to enable all changes to files in memory to be saved immediately to the disk. A complete list of options that the mount command accepts can be found by viewing the manual page for the mount command.

The following output displays the contents of the /etc/vfstab file:

```
# cat /etc/vfstab
/dev/root  /dev/rroot  /       vxfs  1  no  mincache=closesync
/dev/stand /dev/rstand /stand bfs   1  no  -
/proc  -   /proc proc   -   no  -
/processorfs  -  /system/processor  profs  -  yes  -
/dev/fd   -   /dev/fd fdfs   -   no  -
/dev/dsk/f0t  /dev/rdsk/f0t  /install  s5  -  no  -
/dev/dsk/f1t  /dev/rdsk/f1t  /install  s5  -  no  -
/dev/dsk/f0   /dev/rdsk/f0   /install  s5  -  no  -
/dev/dsk/f1   /dev/rdsk/f1   /install  s5  -  no  -
/tmp  -  /tmp  memfs  -  yes  swapmax=10485760
/var/tmp  -  /var/tmp  memfs  -  yes  swapmax=4194304
/dev/_tcp  -  /dev/_tcp  specfs  -  yes  dev=tcp
# _
```

**NOTE**

The / and /stand filesystems are not mounted automatically at boot time from entries in /etc/vfstab; this is because they are already mounted before this file is interpreted.

Thus, to mount the S5 filesystem on the first floppy device (/dev/dsk/f0t) to the /install directory, you need to specify enough information for the mount command to find the appropriate line in the /etc/vfstab file:

```
# mount /dev/dsk/f0t
# mount
/ on /dev/root read/write/setuid on Sun Oct 29 05:06:57 2003
/stand on /dev/stand read/write on Sun Oct 29 05:06:59 2003
/proc on /proc read/write on Sun Oct 29 05:07:13 2003
/dev/fd on /dev/fd read/write on Sun Oct 29 05:07:13 2003
/system/processor on /processorfs read/write on Sun Oct 29 05:07:16 2003
/tmp on /tmp read/write on Sun Oct 29 05:07:16 2003
/var/tmp on /var/tmp read/write on Sun Oct 29 05:07:16 2003
/dev/_tcp on /dev/_tcp read/write on Sun Oct 29 05:07:16 2003
/install on /dev/dsk/f0t read/write on Sun Oct 29 07:12:07 2003
# _
```

The mount command in the previous output succeeded because there is a line in /etc/vfstab that describes the mounting of the /dev/dsk/f0t device.

Alternatively, you could specify the mount point as an argument to the `mount` command to mount the same device via the correct entry in /etc/vfstab:

```
# umount /tmp
# mount
/ on /dev/root read/write/setuid on Sun Oct 29 05:06:57 2003
/stand on /dev/stand read/write on Sun Oct 29 05:06:59 2003
/proc on /proc read/write on Sun Oct 29 05:07:13 2003
/dev/fd on /dev/fd read/write on Sun Oct 29 05:07:13 2003
/system/processor on /processorfs read/write on Sun Oct 29 05:07:16 2003
/var/tmp on /var/tmp read/write on Sun Oct 29 05:07:16 2003
/dev/_tcp on /dev/_tcp read/write on Sun Oct 29 05:07:16 2003
/install on /dev/dsk/f0t read/write on Sun Oct 29 07:12:07 2003
# mount /tmp
# mount
/ on /dev/root read/write/setuid on Sun Oct 29 05:06:57 2003
/stand on /dev/stand read/write on Sun Oct 29 05:06:59 2003
/proc on /proc read/write on Sun Oct 29 05:07:13 2003
/dev/fd on /dev/fd read/write on Sun Oct 29 05:07:13 2003
/system/processor on /processorfs read/write on Sun Oct 29 05:07:16 2003
/tmp on /tmp read/write on Sun Oct 29 07:17:11 2003
/var/tmp on /var/tmp read/write on Sun Oct 29 05:07:16 2003
/dev/_tcp on /dev/_tcp read/write on Sun Oct 29 05:07:16 2003
/install on /dev/dsk/f0t read/write on Sun Oct 29 07:12:07 2003
# _
```

Table 7-2 shows some useful commands you can use when mounting and unmounting filesystems.

**Table 7-2**    Useful commands when mounting and unmounting filesystems

| Command | Description |
|---|---|
| mount | Displays mounted filesystems |
| mount -F <type> <device> <mount point> | Mounts a <device> of a certain <type> to a <mount point> directory |
| fuser -u <directory> | Displays the users using a particular directory |
| umount <mount point> or umount <device> | Unmounts a <device> from a certain <mount point> directory |

Although the commands listed in Table 7-2 give you complete control over the mounting process, you can also mount floppy devices using a GUI. The SCO Admin Filesystem Manager shown in Figure 7-3 may be used to mount and unmount devices that are listed in /etc/vfstab.

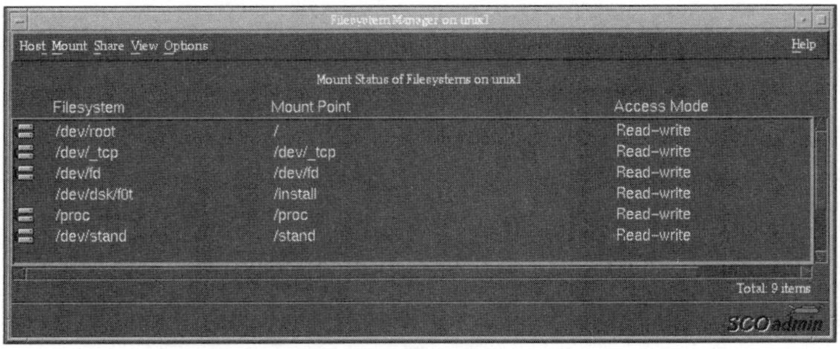

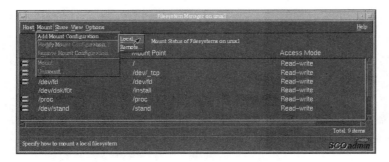

**Figure 7-3** Filesystem Manager

The mounted filesystems in Figure 7-3 have an icon to the left of their device name. To add a line to the /etc/vfstab file, add a local mount configuration from the Mount menu shown in Figure 7-4 and supply the appropriate information, as depicted in Figure 7-5.

**Figure 7-4** Adding a mount configuration

**Figure 7-5** Specifying the mount configuration

When you are finished, highlight the filesystem and mount or unmount it using the Mount menu, as shown in Figure 7-6.

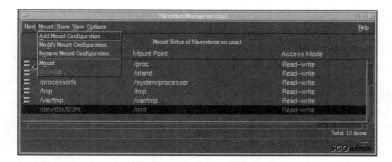

**Figure 7-6**    Mounting a filesystem

7

## WORKING WITH CD-ROMs

Most software that is not downloaded from the Internet is packaged on CD-ROM disks as they have a much larger storage capacity than floppy disks; one CD-ROM disk can store more than 500 times the data a floppy disk can store. Like floppies, CD-ROMs can be mounted with the **mount** command and unmounted with the **umount** command, as shown in Table 7-2; however, the device file and filesystem type used with these commands is different. In addition, since CD-ROMs are read-only filesystems, you must also use the **-r** option to the **mount** command when mounting the CD-ROM:

```
# mount -r -F cdfs /dev/cdrom/cdrom1 /mnt
# mount
/ on /dev/root read/write/setuid on Sun Oct 20 16:19:45 2003
/stand on /dev/stand read/write on Sun Oct 20 16:19:49 2003
/proc on /proc read/write on Sun Oct 20 16:20:35 2003
/dev/fd on /dev/fd read/write on Sun Oct 20 16:20:35 2003
/system/processor on /processorfs read/write on Sun Oct 20 16:20:40 2003
/tmp on /tmp read/write on Sun Oct 20 16:20:40 2003
/var/tmp on /var/tmp read/write on Sun Oct 20 16:20:40 2003
/dev/_tcp on /dev/_tcp read/write on Sun Oct 20 16:20:40 2003
/mnt on /dev/cdrom/cdrom1 read only/setuid/susp/rrip on Sun Oct 20
16:21:07 2003
# _
```

As with floppies, you can specify only a single argument to the **mount** command to mount a CD-ROM via an entry in the /etc/vfstab file. Also, you can use the **umount** command to unmount the CD-ROM from the directory tree, and the Filesystem Manager to both mount and unmount the CD-ROM.

Like floppy disks, the mount point directory must not be in use to successfully mount or unmount CD-ROM disks; the **fuser** command can be used to verify this. However, unlike floppy disks, CD-ROM disks cannot be ejected from the CD-ROM drive until the CD-ROM is properly unmounted since the `mount` command locks the CD-ROM device as a precaution.

## WORKING WITH HARD DISKS

On a physical level, hard disks are circular metal platters that spin at a fast speed. Data is read off of these disks in concentric circles called **tracks**; each track is divided into **sectors** of information and sectors are combined into more usable **blocks** of data when a filesystem is formatted on it, as shown in Figure 7-7. Most hard disk drives have several platters inside them organized on top of each other such that they may be written to simultaneously speed up data transfer. A series consisting of the same concentric track on all of the metal platters inside a hard disk drive is known as a **cylinder**.

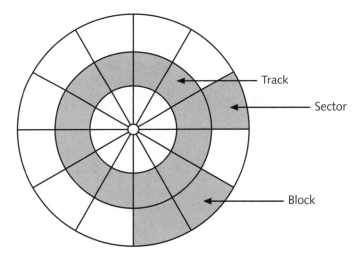

**Figure 7-7**    Physical disk geometry

In addition, hard disks have the largest storage capacity of any device that you would use to store information on a regular basis. This also poses some problems; as the size of a disk increases, organization becomes more difficult and the chance of error increases. To solve these problems, recall that you usually divide a hard disk into smaller, more usable sections called partitions. Since there can only be up to four partitions on a hard disk, each partition may further be divided into a maximum of 184 slices. Each slice may contain a filesystem that can be mounted to the directory tree and accessed in the same way that CD-ROM and floppy disks are accessed. Dividing a hard disk into partitions and slices has further advantages, including:

- The separation of different types of data—home directory data is stored on a filesystem on a separate slice mounted to /home.

- The ability to use more than one type of filesystem on one hard disk drive—some filesystems are tuned for database use.

- A reduced chance that filesystem corruption will render a system unusable; if the filesystem on the slice that is mounted to the /home directory becomes corrupted, it does not affect the system as operating system files are stored on a separate filesystem on a slice mounted to the / directory.

- Faster access to stored data by keeping filesystems as small as possible

## Hard Disk Partitioning

The fdisk utility can be used to create and manage partitions on hard disks; just specify the character device file of the hard disk as an argument to the **fdisk command**. To manage all the partitions on the first IDE hard disk on the first IDE controller, use the `fdisk /dev/rdsk/c0b0t0d0p0` command, which results in the following interactive screen:

```
        Total disk size is 2088 cylinders (16378.8 MB)

                                    Cylinders              Approx
    Partition  Status      Type      Start   End   Length   %     MB
    =========  ======  ===========   =====   ===   ======  ===  ======
        1      Active  UNIX System     0    2087    2088   100  16378.7




    SELECT ONE OF THE FOLLOWING:

        0.    Overwrite system master boot code
        1.    Create a partition
        2.    Change Active (Boot from) partition
        3.    Delete a partition
        4.    Exit (Update disk configuration and exit)
        5.    Cancel (Exit without updating disk configuration)
    Enter Selection: _
```

You can then use the menu selections to create and delete partitions as well as change the active partition. Choosing to overwrite the master boot code (MBR) in the previous output will delete all partitions on the disk since the table of partitions and their sizes is stored in the master boot code. After changing partition information in the fdisk utility for the hard disk that contains the currently active UnixWare operating system, you will need to reboot the computer to activate the changes. After changing the partition information for other hard disks, a reboot is not required.

## Viewing and Creating Slices within a Partition

During a UnixWare installation, 16 slices are created by default inside the UNIX partition (s0 through s15); each slice may contain a filesystem to store information organized by directory or alternatively store information in a raw format directly on the slice itself. Recall from Chapter 2 that the table that stores a list of slices for a UNIX partition is called the **Volume Table of Contents (VTOC)** and is located on a special slice within the UNIX partition; this slice is called the **BOOT slice**.

 The VTOC is also called the Physical Disk INFO (PDINFO).

**NOTE**

Since the BOOT slice does not contain a filesystem, it cannot be mounted to the directory tree and its contents cannot be viewed using standard UNIX utilities. Instead, to view the VTOC on the BOOT slice, you must use the **prtvtoc (print VTOC) command**, which understands how to access the VTOC on the BOOT slice.

To view all slices in the VTOC in the UNIX partition on the first IDE hard disk on the first IDE controller, specify the appropriate character device file as an argument to the `prtvtoc` command:

```
# prtvtoc /dev/rdsk/c0b0t0d0s0
slice 0:     DISK      permissions:  VALID UNMOUNTABLE
   starting sector: 63 (cyl 0)   length: 33543657 (2088.0 cyls)
slice 1:     ROOT      permissions:  VALID
   starting sector: 385560 (cyl 24) length: 32515560 (2024.0 cyls)
slice 2:     SWAP      permissions:  VALID UNMOUNTABLE
   starting sector: 64260 (cyl 4)   length: 321300 (20.00 cls)
slice 7:     BOOT      permissions:  VALID UNMOUNTABLE
   starting sector: 63 (cyl 0)       length: 34 (0.00 cyls)
slice 8:     ALT SEC/TRK   permissions:    VALID UNMOUNTABLE
   starting sector: 97 (cyl 0)       length: 15968 (0.99 cyl)
slice 10:    STAND     permissions:    VALID
   starting sector: 16065 (cyl 1)   length: 48195 (3.00 cyl)
slice 15:    VOLPRIVATE  permissions:    VALID UNMOUNTABLE
   starting sector: 32901120 (cyl 2048)  length: 16065 (.00 cyls)
Total disk size is 2088 cylinders (16378.8 MB)

# _
```

As shown in the previous output, not all 16 slices need to be used. In addition, the numbers given to the slices shown previously are standard when created during the installation program; slice 0 always refers to the entire UNIX partition (DISK), slice 1 always refers to the slice that contains the / filesystem (ROOT), and so on.

To add or change slices, it is good form to first find the total number of cylinders and sectors for the UNIX partition your hard disk. This information is also stored in the VTOC and may be viewed using the **-p** option of the **prtvtoc** command:

```
# prtvtoc -p /dev/rdsk/c0b0t0d0s0
        Device /dev/rdsk/c0b0t0d0s0
device type:           1 (DPT_WINI)
cylinders:             2088          heads:           255
sectors/track:         63            bytes/sector:    512
number of partitions:  16            size of alts table:    204
8
media stamp:           "EBmyHdByeYRS"
# _
```

Next, you can print the VTOC to a text file that can be edited later; to save the VTOC in an easy-to-edit format to the file /tmp/vtoc.tmp, use the following command:

```
# prtvtoc -f /tmp/vtoc.tmp /dev/rdsk/c0b0t0d0s0
# cat /tmp/vtoc.tmp
#SLICE   TAG      FLAGS     START      SIZE
  0      0x5      0x201     63         33543657
  1      0x2      0x200     385560     32515560
  2      0x3      0x201     64260      321300
  3      0x0      0x0       0          0
  4      0x0      0x0       0          0
  5      0x0      0x0       0          0
  6      0x0      0x0       0          0
  7      0x1      0x201     63         34
  8      0xd      0x201     97         15968
  9      0x0      0x0       0          0
 10      0x9      0x200     16065      48195
 11      0x0      0x0       0          0
 12      0x0      0x0       0          0
 13      0x0      0x0       0          0
 14      0x0      0x0       0          0
 15      0xf      0x201     32901120   16065
# _
```

7

Each slice has a starting cylinder (START) and size in ½KB sectors (SIZE). In addition, TAG in this output indicates the type of slice:

- 0x01 represents the BOOT slice.

- 0x02 represents the root filesystem.

- 0x03 represents the swap slice.

- 0x05 represents the entire UNIX partition.

- 0x09 represents the /stand slice.

- 0x0d represents the ALTS TABLE.

- 0x0f represents the Volprivate slice.

FLAGS indicates the status of the slice:

- 0x0 indicates it is not used.
- 0x200 indicates it contains a mountable filesystem.
- 0x201 indicates it is does not contain a mountable filesystem.

**NOTE**    For a full list of TAGs and FLAGs, consult the manual page for the `prtvtoc` command.

The /tmp/vtoc.tmp file can be edited to include additional slices provided that room is available within the UNIX partition on the hard disk. After editing this file, you may over-write the VTOC on the BOOT slice of the first IDE hard disk on the first IDE controller with the /tmp/vtoc.tmp file by using the command `edvtoc -f /tmp/vtoc.tmp / dev/rdsk/c0b0t0d0s0` at a command prompt.

## Creating Filesystems on Slices

Once slices have been created within a UNIX partition, you can use the `mkfs` com-mand to create filesystems on those slices using the same syntax shown earlier with floppy disks. Since hard disks store much more information than floppy disks, it is impor-tant to carefully choose the filesystem to place on a device. The two most common filesystems used on UNIX slices are VxFS and UFS. VxFS is the preferred filesystem in UnixWare as it is a very versatile filesystem due to its support of various block sizes, maximum size of 1TB, extent-based allocation, and journaling capabilities. The file that stores most of the default settings used when creating or using a VxFS filesystem is **/etc/default/vxfs**:

```
# cat /etc/default/vxfs
#ident   "@(#)pdi.cmds:dflt.d/vxfs.dflt   1.4"
BLKSIZE=1024,2048,4096,8192
MNTOPT=mincache=closesync
MKFSTYP=4
LABELIT=YES
MAXSIZE=2147483648
# _
```

MAXSIZE in the previous output indicates that a VxFS filesystem is limited to 1TB (2147483648 ½KB blocks). However, you may not store files on a VxFS filesystem that are larger than 2GB by default. Certain applications such as databases might need to create files that are larger than 2GB; thus, it is important to enable **large filesystem support** when creating filesystems that will store files larger than 2GB. Individual files will then have a maximum possible size of 1TB. You can only specify large file support when creating a filesystem. To enable large file support afterwards, you will need to recreate the filesystem with `mkfs` (which destroys all data on the original filesystem).

To see whether a filesystem has large file support enabled, use the −m option to the mkfs command followed by the appropriate block device file:

```
# mkfs -m /dev/dsk/c0b0t0d0s1
mkfs -F vxfs -o ninode=unlimited,bsize=1024,version=4,inosize=256,logsize=1024,
nolargefiles /dev/dsk/c0b0t0d0s1 32515560
# _
```

The nolargefiles keyword in the previous output indicates that large file support is not enabled for the filesystem.

To create a 1GB VxFS filesystem with large file support on the fourth slice on the first IDE hard disk on the first IDE controller, use the following command:

```
# mkfs -F vxfs -o largefiles /dev/dsk/c0b0t0d0s4 2048000
Mkfs: make vxfs file system?
(DEL if wrong)
    version 4 layout
    2048000 sectors, 1024000 blocks of size 1024, log size 256 blocks
    unlimited inodes, largefiles supported
    2048000 data blocks, 2039081 free data blocks
    1 allocation units of 32768 blocks, 32768 data blocks
    last allocation unit has 1024000 data blocks
# _
```

7

## Mounting Slices

Like floppy disks and CD-ROMs, hard disks can be mounted with the mount command and unmounted with the umount command; simply specify the appropriate filesystem type, block device file, and mount point:

```
# mount -F vxfs /dev/dsk/c0b0t0d0s4 /data
# mount
/ on /dev/root read/write/setuid on Sun Oct 20 16:19:45 2003
/stand on /dev/stand read/write on Sun Oct 20 16:19:49 2003
/proc on /proc read/write on Sun Oct 20 16:20:35 2003
/dev/fd on /dev/fd read/write on Sun Oct 20 16:20:35 2003
/system/processor on /processorfs read/write on Sun Oct 20 16:20:40 2003
/tmp on /tmp read/write on Sun Oct 20 16:20:40 2003
/var/tmp on /var/tmp read/write on Sun Oct 20 16:20:40 2003
/dev/_tcp on /dev/_tcp read/write on Sun Oct 20 16:20:40 2003
/data on /dev/dsk/c0b0t0d0s4 read/write/setuid on Sun Oct 20 21:11:03 2003
# _
```

Since hard disks are not removable media like floppy disks and CD-ROMs, they are rarely mounted to the /mnt directory; instead they are mounted to their own directory and configured to mount automatically at boot time using entries in the /etc/vfstab file. The filesystem mounted in the previous output can be mounted automatically at each boot by entering the line /dev/dsk/c0b0t0d0s4  /dev/rdsk/c0b0t0d0s4 /data vxfs 1 yes - in the /etc/vfstab file.

## Adding a New Hard Disk to the System

As your UNIX system is used to store more data or programs, you may find that you need another hard disk. This hard disk will need to be partitioned, the VTOC will need to be edited to create slices, filesystems will need to be created on the slices, and the /etc/vfstab file will need to be edited such that the slices are mounted automatically at boot time.

 If your system had only SCSI disk drives during UnixWare installation, you can only add SCSI disk drives to the system as the IDE driver will not exist in the UnixWare kernel.

**NOTE**

To simplify these tasks in UnixWare, use the **diskadd command**. The diskadd command invokes a program that is an interactive wizard that prompts the user for all information needed to partition, slice, format, and mount hard disks. It uses fdisk to create partitions and then runs the **disksetup command** to create slices in the partition, create filesystems within the slices, mount the slices, and update the /etc/vfstab file. If you have recently added a second hard disk to the first IDE controller on your system, use the command diskadd /dev/dsk/c0b0t1d0 to start the wizard for that hard disk.

## MONITORING FILESYSTEMS

Once filesystems are created on disk devices and those disk devices are mounted to the directory tree, they should be checked periodically for errors and disk space usage. This minimizes the problems that can occur as a result of a damaged filesystem and reduces the likelihood that a file cannot be saved due to insufficient disk space. The type of filesystem on unmounted devices can be determined via the **fstyp command**.

## Disk Usage

Recall that several filesystems may be mounted to the directory tree; the more filesystems that are used, the less likely a corrupted filesystem can interfere with normal system operations. Conversely, having more filesystems typically results in less hard disk space per filesystem and can result in system errors if certain filesystems fill up with data. Many users create filesystems for the /, /home, and /var directories during installation. The /home directory contains home directories for regular users on a UNIX system, and should have enough space for all the users of the filesystem and the files they intend to work with. The /var directory grows in size continuously as it stores log files; old log files should be removed periodically to leave room for new ones. The / filesystem is the most vital of these and should always contain a great deal of free space, which will be used as working space for the operating system. As a result, the / filesystem should be monitored frequently; if free space on the / filesystem falls below 15%, the system may suffer from poorer performance.

The easiest method for monitoring free space by mounted filesystem is to use the **df (disk free space) command**. By default, the df command prints sizes in ½KB blocks; to print sizes in 1KB blocks, use the **-k** option to the df command as follows:

```
# df -k
filesystem              kbytes    used      avail      capacity  mounted on
/dev/root               16257780  1428680   14829100   9%        /
/dev/stand              24097     5583      18514      24%       /stand
/proc                   0         0         0          0%        /proc
/dev/fd                 0         0         0          0%        /dev/fd
/processorfs            0         0         0          0%        /system/pr
ocessor
/tmp                    10240     4         10236      1%        /tmp
/var/tmp                40960     0         40960      0%        /var/tmp
/dev/_tcp               0         0         0          0%        /dev/_tcp
/dev/cdrom/cdrom1       667514    667514    0          100%      /mnt
# _
```

From the previous output, the only filesystem used is the / filesystem; the /home and /var directories are simply directories on the / filesystem, which increases the importance of monitoring the / filesystem. Since the / filesystem is 9% used in the previous output, there is no immediate concern; however, log files, user files, and software installed in the future will increase this number and may warrant the purchase of an additional hard disk for data to reside on.

Also, UnixWare provides a more user-friendly version of the df command called the **dfspace command**, which indicates disk space in megabytes and does not show any special filesystems used only by the UNIX kernel:

```
# dfspace
/          : Disk space: 14481.54 MB of 15876.73 MB available(91.21%)
/stand     : Disk space:    18.08 MB of    23.53 MB available(76.83%)
/tmp       : Disk space:     9.99 MB of     9.99 MB available(99.96%)
/var/tmp   : Disk space:    39.99 MB of    39.99 MB available(100.00%)
/dev/_tcp  : Disk space:     0.00 MB of     0.00 MB available( 0.00%)
/mnt       : Disk space:     0.00 MB of   651.86 MB available( 0.00%)

Total Disk Space: 14549.61 MB of 16602.14 MB available (87.64%).
# _
```

If a filesystem is approaching full capacity, it may be useful to examine which directories on that filesystem are taking up the most disk space such that you may remove or move files from that directory to another filesystem that has sufficient space. To view the size of a directory and its contents in kilobytes, use the **-k** option to the **du (directory usage) command**. If the directory is large, you should use either the pg or more command to view the output page by page, as shown with the following /var directory:

```
# du -k /var | more
34        /var/adm/log
0         /var/adm/passwd
1036      /var/adm/sa
0         /var/adm/streams
0         /var/adm/acct/fiscal
0         /var/adm/acct/nite
0         /var/adm/acct/sum
2         /var/adm/acct
6         /var/adm/isl/morepkgs
16        /var/adm/isl
1187      /var/adm
0         /var/tmp
35        /var/options
0         /var/sadm/pkg/UnixWare/install
18        /var/sadm/pkg/UnixWare
4         /var/sadm/pkg/base/install/base
48        /var/sadm/pkg/base/install
50        /var/sadm/pkg/base
1         /var/sadm/pkg/cdfs
1         /var/sadm/pkg/dfm
1         /var/sadm/pkg/mouse
1         /var/sadm/pkg/qt
1         /var/sadm/pkg/sys
19        /var/sadm/pkg/lp/install
Standard input
```

To view only a summary of the total size of a directory, use the **-s** option to the du command, as shown with the following /var directory:

```
# du -ks /var
8588 /var
# _
```

Also, certain users use more disk space than other users; this may lead to disk space problems on a filesystem. To identify the number of kilobytes of data that users own on a filesystem, use the **quot command**, as shown in the following output:

```
# quot -F vxfs /
/dev/rroot:
216654   bin
207881   bob
204748   root
 1727    lp
 1367    sys
  681    #43996
```

```
635    uucp
241    nobody
196    adm
 18    owner
  5    user1
  3    mhsmail
#  _
```

From the previous output, the user bob has a great deal of files on the / filesystem. To free up space, you could move many of those files to a separate filesystem that has enough free space.

## Checking Filesystems for Errors

Filesystems themselves may accumulate errors over time; these errors are often referred to as **filesystem corruption** and are common on most filesystems over time. Those filesystems that are accessed frequently are more prone to corruption than those that are not; as a result, those filesystems should be checked regularly for errors. The most common filesystem corruption occurs because a system was not shut down properly using the shutdown command typically due to a power outage. Data is stored in memory for a short period of time before it is written to a file on the hard disk; this process of saving data to the hard disk is called **syncing**. If the power is turned off on the computer, data is memory may not be synced over from memory properly to the hard disk and corruption may occur. Filesystem corruption may also occur if the hard disks are used frequently for time-intensive tasks such as database access; as the usage of any system increases, the possibility for operating system errors when writing to the hard disks increases. Along the same lines, the physical hard disks themselves are mechanical in nature and can wear over time. Some areas of the disk may become unusable if they cannot hold a magnetic charge; these areas are known as **bad blocks**. When the operating system finds a bad block, it puts a reference to that bad block in the ALTS TABLE slice in the UNIX partition. Entries in the ALTS TABLE are not used for any future disk storage.

To check a filesystem for errors, use the **fsck (filesystem check) command**, which can check filesystems of many different types. The fsck command takes an option specifying the filesystem type and an argument specifying the device to check. It is also important to note that the filesystem being checked must be unmounted beforehand for the fsck command to work properly, as shown in the following output:

```
# fsck -F vxfs /dev/rdsk/f03ht
UX:vxfs fsck: ERROR: /dev/rdsk/f03ht already mounted
# umount /dev/dsk/f03ht
# fsck -F vxfs /dev/rdsk/f03ht
file system is clean - log replay is not required
#  _
```

**NOTE**

Since the / filesystem cannot be unmounted, you should only run the `fsck` command on the / filesystem in single-user mode, which is discussed in Chapter 8.

Notice from the previous output that the `fsck` command does not give lengthy output on the terminal screen when checking the filesystem; this is because the `fsck` command only checks the journaling file (also called the intent log) for errors unless the `-o full` option is used to perform a full check, as shown in the following output:

```
# fsck -F vxfs -o full /dev/rdsk/f03ht
log replay in progress
pass0 - checking structural files
pass1 - checking inode sanity and blocks
pass2 - checking directory linkage
pass3 - checking reference counts
pass4 - checking resource maps
OK to clear log? (ynq)y
set state to CLEAN? (ynq)y
# _
```

If the `fsck` command finds a corrupted file, it displays a message to the user asking whether to fix the error. To avoid these messages, use the `-y` option to specify that the `fsck` command should automatically repair any corruption. If there are files that the `fsck` command cannot repair, it will place them in the lost+found directory on that filesystem and rename the file to the inode number. Recall that the lost+found directory is automatically created when a filesystem is created by the `mkfs` command.

To view the contents of the lost+found directory, mount the device and view the contents of the lost+found directory immediately underneath the mount point. Since it is difficult to identify lost files by their inode number, most users delete the contents of this directory periodically. However, if you suspect that the corrupted file was hard linked, then you can use the `find` command or **ncheck command** to locate other files that have the same inode number to obtain a copy of the data.

## HARD DISK QUOTAS

If several users are on a UNIX system, enough hard disk space must be available to support the files that each user stores on the hard disk. However, if hard disk space is limited or company policy limits disk usage, you should impose limits on filesystem usage. These restrictions are called hard disk **quotas**, and most UNIX filesystems support them. Furthermore, quotas may restrict how many files and directories a user can create (that is, restrict the number of inodes created) on a particular filesystem or the total size of all files that a user can own on a filesystem. Two types of quota limits exist: soft limits and hard limits. **Soft limits** enable the user to extend them for a certain period of time, whereas **hard limits** are rigid and will prevent the user from going past them. Quotas are typically enabled at boot time if the quota mount option exists for the filesystem in

/etc/vfstab, but can also be turned on and off by using the **quotaon command** and **quotaoff command**, respectively.

To set up quotas for a VxFS filesystem and restrict user1, carry out the following steps:

1. Run the command `touch /quotas` to create a file in the root of the / filesystem called quotas.

2. Run the command **quotaon –F vxfs /** to turn on quotas for the / filesystem. This step calculates the ownership for all files on the filesystem and places this information in the /quotas file.

3. Run the command **edquota –F vxfs user1** to edit quotas for user1. This will bring up the vi editor and enable the user to set soft and hard quotas for the number of blocks a user may own on the filesystem (typically, 1 block represents 1KB) and the total number of inodes (files and directories) that a user can own on the filesystem. A soft limit and hard limit of zero indicates that there is no limit. To set a hard limit of 20Mb (20,480KB) and 1000 inodes, as well as a soft limit of 18Mb (18,432KB) and 900 inodes, enter the following into the vi editor:

```
fs / blocks (soft = 18432, hard = 20480) inodes (soft = 900, hard = 1000)
~
~
~
~
~
~
~
~
~
~
~
~
~
~
"/tmp/EdP.a000Cx" 1 line, 61 characters
```

4. Edit the time limit for which users may go beyond soft quotas by using the `edquota –F vxfs –t` command. This command uses the vi editor to edit time limit parameters for extending a soft limit for the number of blocks and the number of inodes (files) that you can store:

```
fs / blocks time limit = 5.00 mins, files time limit = 5.00 mins
~
~
~
~
~
~
~
```

```
~
~
~
~
~
~
~
~
"/tmp/EdP.a000De" 1 line, 69 characters
```

5. Ensure that quotas were updated properly by gathering a report for quotas by user on the / filesystem using the **repquota command**, as shown in the following output:

```
# repquota -F vxfs /
                         Block limits                    File limits
User            used   soft   hard    timeleft   used   soft   hard
timeleft
user1    --      3   18432  20480                  7    900   1000
# _
```

After quotas have been set up on a VxFS filesytem, use the **quota command** to view the quota limits for individual users:

```
# quota -F vxfs -v user1
Disk quotas for user1 (uid 100):
Filesystem  usage  quota  limit timeleft  files  quota  limit timeleft
/             5   18432  20480                8    900   1000
# _
```

## CHAPTER SUMMARY

◻ Disk devices are represented by device files that reside in the /dev directory; these device files specify the type of data transfer, the major number of the device driver in the UNIX kernel, and the minor number of the specific device.

◻ The Device Database can be used to locate information regarding disk devices in your UNIX system.

◻ Each disk device must contain a filesystem that is then mounted to the UNIX directory tree for usage using the mount command and can later be unmounted using the umount command. The directory used to mount the device must not be used by any logged-in users for mounting and unmounting to take place.

◻ Hard disks must be partitioned and sliced into distinct sections before filesystems are created on those slices. The table of all partitions on a hard disk is stored in the MBR and the table of all slices within a UNIX partition is stored in the VTOC.

❐ Many different filesystems are available to UNIX; each filesystem is specialized for a certain purpose and several different filesystems can be mounted to different mount points on the directory tree. You can create a filesystem on a device using the mkfs command.

❐ It is important to monitor disk usage using the df, du, and quot commands to avoid running out of storage space. Similarly, it is important to check disks for errors using the fsck command.

❐ If hard disk space is limited, you can use hard disk quotas to limit the space that each user has on a filesystem.

## KEY TERMS

**/dev directory** — The directory under the root where device files are typically stored.

**/etc/default/vxfs** — The file that contains default values used when creating or mounting a VxFS filesystem.

**/etc/vfstab** — A file used to specify which filesystems to mount automatically at boot time and is queried by the mount command if an insufficient number of arguments are specified.

**/etc/mnttab** — A file that stores a list of currently mounted filesystems.

**bad blocks** — Those areas of a storage medium unable to properly store data.

**block** — The unit of data commonly used by filesystem commands—a block may contain several sectors.

**block devices** — Storage devices that transfer data to and from the system in chunks of many data bits by caching the information in RAM. They are represented by block device files.

**BOOT slice** — The slice in a UNIX partition that contains the VTOC.

**character devices** — Storage devices that transfer data to and from the system one data bit at a time. They are represented by character device files. *See also* Raw devices.

**cylinder** — A series of tracks on a hard disk that are written to simultaneously by the magnetic heads in a hard disk drive.

**devattr command** — The command used to list device information for a certain device listed in the Device Database.

**Device Database** — A database of devices detected during installation and information regarding their device files and usage.

**device file** — A file that represents a specific device on the system and is used by UNIX commands that require devices to be specified. These files do not have a data section, and use major and minor numbers to reference the proper driver and specific device on the system, respectively.

**df (disk free space) command** — The command that displays disk free space by filesystem.

**dfspace command** — The command used to print a user-friendly list of mounted filesystems.

7

**diskadd command** — The command used to add an additional hard disk to the system. It calls the fdisk and disksetup commands.

**disksetup command** — The command used to create slices within a partition, create filesystems on those slices, and mount them.

**du (directory usage) command** — The command that displays directory usage.

**edquota command** — The command used to specify quota limits for users.

**edvtoc command** — The command used to edit the VTOC on a UNIX partition.

**extent-based allocation** — An attribute of certain filesystems where information is written to adjacent areas of the filesystem.

**fdisk command** — The command used to create, delete, and manipulate partitions on hard disks.

**filesystem** — The organization imposed on a physical storage medium that is used to manage the storage and retrieval of data.

**filesystem corruption** — Errors in a filesystem structure that prevent the retrieval of stored data.

**format command** — The command used to redefine the tracks on a floppy disk and check for structural errors.

**formatting** — The process where a filesystem is placed on a disk device.

**fsck (filesystem check) command** — The command used to check the integrity of a filesystem and repair damaged files.

**fstyp command** — The command used to determine the type of filesystem on a certain device.

**fuser command** — The command used to identify any users or processes using a particular file or directory.

**getdev command** — The command used to show all devices listed in the Device Database.

**hard limit** — A limit imposed that cannot be exceeded.

**intent-logging filesystem** — *See also* Journaling filesystem.

**journaling filesystem** — A filesystem that writes pending filesystem changes to a journal file on the filesystem.

**large filesystem support** — A filesystem feature that enables files larger than 2GB to be stored on the filesystem.

**lost+found directory** — A directory that exists on filesystems created by the mkfs command and is used by the fsck command to store files that cannot be repaired.

**major number** — A number used by the kernel to identify what device driver to call to properly interact with a given category of hardware. Hard disk drives, CD-ROMs, and video cards are all categories of hardware. Similar devices share a common major number.

**minor number** — A number used by the kernel to identify which specific hardware device within a given category to use the specified driver to communicate with. *See also* Major number.

**mkfs (make filesystem) command** — The command used to format or create filesystems.

**mknod command** — The command used to recreate a device file provided the major number, minor number, and type (character or block) are known.

**mount command** — The command used to mount filesystems on devices to mount point directories.

**mount point** — The directory in a file structure to which something is mounted.

**mounting** — The process used to associate a device with a directory in the logical directory tree such that users may store data on that device.

**ncheck command** — The command used to identify files on a filesystem by inode number.

**partition** — A physical division of a hard disk drive.

**prtvtoc (print VTOC) command** — The command used to view the VTOC on a UNIX partition.

**quot command** — The command used to list filesystem usage for each user on the system.

**quota command** — The command used to view disk quotas imposed on a user.

**quotaoff command** — The command used to deactivate disk quotas.

**quotaon command** — The command used to activate disk quotas.

**quotas** — Limits on the number of files or total storage space on a filesystem imposed on system users.

**raw devices** — *See also* Character devices.

**repquota command** — The command used to produce a report on quotas for a particular filesystem.

**root filesystem** — The filesystem that contains most files that make up the operating system; it should have enough free space to prevent errors and slow performance.

**sectors** — The smallest unit of data storage on a hard disk; they are arranged into concentric circles called tracks and can be grouped into blocks for use by the system.

**soft limit** — A limit imposed that can be exceeded for a certain period of time.

**syncing** — The process of writing data to the hard disk drive that was stored in RAM.

**tracks** — The area on a hard disk that forms a concentric circle of sectors.

**umount command** — The command used to break the association between a device and a directory in the logical directory tree.

**Volume Table of Contents (VTOC)** — A list of slices within a UNIX partition. It is stored on the BOOT slice of the UNIX partition.

# REVIEW QUESTIONS

1. You can only mount and unmount CD-ROMs and floppy disk drives from the command line. True or False?

2. You find that a device file in the /dev directory has become corrupted. You know that this device is /dev/dsk/c0b0t0d0s5. What should you do?

   a. Run the command mknod /dev/dsk/c0b0t0d0s5 b 5 7679.

   b. Run the command mknod /dev/dsk/c0b0t0d0s5 c 5 7679.

   c. Run the command mknod /dev/dsk/c0b0t0d0s5 b 7679 5.

   d. Run the command mknod /dev/dsk/c0b0t0d0s5 c 7679 5.

3. Once a slice within a UNIX partition is formatted with a filesystem, all slices in that UNIX partition must use the same filesystem. True or False?

4. You want to see the hard disk filesystems that are currently in use on the system. Which of the following commands could you use? (Choose all that apply.)

   a. df

   b. cat /etc/vfstab

   c. cat /etc/mnttab

   d. mount

5. Jim has just purchased two new SCSI hard disk drives and a controller card for them. He properly installs the hardware in his machine. Before he can use them for data storage and retrieval, what must he do?

   a. Mount the two hard drives so they are accessible by the operating system.

   b. Use diskadd to create partitions, slices, and filesystems on each of the hard disk drives and mount them to the directory tree.

   c. Mount a filesystem to each of the hard disk drives.

   d. Use the fdisk command to create one or more partitions on each of the hard disk drives.

   e. Mount all partitions on the two hard drives such that they are accessible by the operating system.

   f. Format the partitions on the hard disk with a valid filesystem recognized by UNIX.

6. Given the following output from /etc/vfstab, which filesystems will be automatically mounted at boot time from entries in this file?

```
/dev/root    /dev/rroot    /         vxfs    1    no     mincache=closesnc
/dev/stand   /dev/rstand   /stand    bfs     1    no     -
/tmp         -             /tmp      memfs   -    yes    -
/var/tmp     -             /var/tmp  memfs   -    yes    -
```

   a. none

   b. / and /stand

   c. /tmp and /var/tmp

   d. all of them

7. A user mounts a device to a mount point directory and realizes afterwards there are files previously found within the mount point directory that are needed. What should this user do?

   a. The files are lost and cannot ever be accessed.

   b. The files could not have been there as you can only mount to empty directories.

   c. Unmount the device from the directory.

   d. Run the fsck command to recover the file.

   e. Look in the lost+found directory for the file.

8. Which of the following commands can be used to view the VTOC on the UNIX partition on the first hard disk on the second controller of your UNIX system?

   a. prtvtoc /dev/rdsk/c0b0t0d0s0

   b. prtvtoc /dev/rdsk/c1b0t0d0s0

   c. prtvtoc /dev/rdsk/c1b0t1d0s0

   d. prtvtoc /dev/rdsk/c0b0t1d0s0

9. Which of the following commands can be used to display how much free space exists on a filesystem?

   a. fsck

   b. quota

   c. du

   d. df

10. You have just mounted a CD-ROM device to the /mycd directory. What inode number will you see for this directory if you execute the command ls –lid /mycd?

   a. 0

   b. 1

   c. 2

   d. The inode number cannot be predicted.

11. Character devices transfer data _____.

   a. sector by sector

   b. always in a error-free manner

   c. only between floppy disk drives and hard disk drives

   d. character by character

7

12. What must you do to successfully run the fsck command on a filesystem?

    a. Run the fsck command with the –u switch to automatically unmount the filesystem first.

    b. When warned that running fsck on a mounted filesystem may cause damage and asked if you want to continue, answer yes.

    c. Unmount the filesystem.

    d. Ensure that the filesystem is mounted.

13. Character devices typically transfer data more quickly than block devices. True or False?

14. Jim wants to know the major number for the first floppy disk drive he has attached to his machine. How does he find it?

    a. Display the contents of the file /dev/ds/f03ht and read the major number from it.

    b. Go to the manufacturer's Web site to locate the driver used for that floppy disk drive.

    c. Use the ls –l /dev/dsk/f03ht command and read the first number in what would normally be the file size column.

    d. Use the ls –l /dev/dsk/f03ht command and read the second number in what would normally be the file size column.

15. What does the du –s /var command do?

    a. shows which users are connected to the /var directory

    b. shows the size of the /var directory in blocks

    c. shows the amount of free space in the /var directory

    d. shows the size of the /var directory in kilobytes

16. Where is the VTOC stored?

    a. in the /etc/vfstab file

    b. on the BOOT slice

    c. in the /stand/vtoc.tmp file

    d. in the /tmp/vtoc.tmp file

17. In a device file, the minor number points to a specific device on the system and the major number indicates the device driver to be used. True or False?

18. Which of the following commands lists the device names used by the Device Database?

    a. cat /etc/vfstab

    b. devattr

    c. getdev

    d. cat /tmp/vtoc.tmp

19. The first floppy drive on the system is not responding. You enter the file /dev/ dsk/f03ht command and receive the following output. What is the problem?

```
# file /dev/dsk/f03ht
/dev/dsk/f03ht:  ASCII text
# _
```

   a. The floppy drive cable has come loose.

   b. There is no floppy disk in the drive.

   c. The device file has become corrupted.

   d. The floppy drive is seen as a character device.

20. Which of the following statements is true? (Choose all that apply.)

   a. Quotas may only limit user space.

   b. Quotas may only limit the number of files a user may own.

   c. Quotas may limit both user space and the number of files a user may own.

   d. Hard limits can never be exceeded.

   e. Hard limits allow a user to exceed them for a certain period of time.

   f. Soft limits can never be exceeded.

   g. Soft limits allow a user to exceed them for a certain period of time.

   h. Either a hard limit or a soft limit may be set, but not both concurrently.

21. Which of the following is supported by the VxFS filesystem? (Choose all that apply.)

   a. extent-based allocation

   b. intent logging

   c. logical block size of 1KB, 2KB, 4KB, and 8KB

   d. large file support

   e. enhanced data integrity using the mincache=closesync mount option

22. You attempt to mount a floppy disk drive to the /home/jim directory and receive a warning stating the operation cannot be completed. Why?

   a. You can only mount floppy disk drives to the /mnt directory.

   b. The directory /home/jim is not empty.

   c. A file in the directory /home/jim is being accessed by a user.

   d. The directory /home/jim is not formatted with the mnt filesystem.

23. What does the repquota command do?

   a. activates quotas on a VxFS filesystem

   b. deactivates quotas on a VxFS filesystem

   c. edits the quotas for a certain user on a VxFS filesystem

   d. gives a report on quota usage for a VxFS filesystem

7

24. A device file _____. (Choose all that apply.)

    a. has no inode section

    b. has no data section

    c. has no size

    d. displays a major and minor number in place of a file size

    e. has a fixed size of 300KB

25. If the filesystem type is not specified with the mkfs command, the mkfs command _____.

    a. prompts the user for the filesystem to use

    b. will not work

    c. uses the VxFS filesystem by default

    d. uses the UFS filesystem by default

26. What will be the result if at the command prompt Jim types mount /mnt?

    a. The system will respond with a message prompting for more information.

    b. The system will respond with a message that the command failed due to missing parameters.

    c. The command will succeed if a line with the necessary parameters exists in /etc/vfstab.

    d. The command will succeed because floppy disks are always mounted to the /mnt directory.

27. A user runs the fsck command on a filesystem that is showing signs of corruption. How would that user locate any files the system was unable to repair?

    a. The system would prompt the user for a location to save the file when it comes across a file it cannot repair.

    b. Mount the filesystem and check the lost+found directory underneath the mount point.

    c. Use the ncheck command.

    d. View the contents of the /lost+found directory.

28. Which of the following commands is used to create a filesystem on a slice within a UNIX partition on a hard disk?

    a. mount

    b. format

    c. mkfs

    d. make FS

29. Which of the following commands can be used to display the pathname to the device file for the first CD-ROM on your system?

   a. ls -l /dev/dsk/cdrom*

   b. devattr -v cdrom1

   c. getdev | grep cdrom1

   d. cat /etc/default/vxfs

30. You find a floppy disk and wonder what is on it. What must you do to view its contents? (Choose all that apply.)

   a. Run the fstyp command to find the filesystem type for the floppy device.

   b. Mount the floppy using the mount command.

   c. Check the floppy for disk errors using fsck.

   d. View the contents of the mount point.

---

## HANDS-ON PROJECTS

These projects should be completed in the order given. All hands-on projects should take a total of three hours to complete. The requirements for this lab include:

❑ A computer with UnixWare 7.1.1 installed according to Project 2-2

❑ A 3.5-inch floppy disk

**HANDS-ON PROJECTS**

## Project 7-1

In this hands-on project, you will view and create device files.

1. Turn on your computer. Once your UNIX system has been loaded, you will be placed at a graphical terminal (vt01). Switch to a command-line terminal (vt02) by pressing **Ctrl+Alt+F2**, and log into the terminal using the username **root** and the password **secret**.

2. At the command prompt, type **ls -l /dev/dsk/f03***  and press **Enter**. What devices are listed (block or character)? What major number is shared by all devices? Why?

3. At the command prompt, type **ls -l /dev/rdsk/f03***  and press **Enter**. What devices are listed (block or character)? What major number is shared by all devices? Why?

4. At the command prompt, type **ls -l /dev/dsk/f03ht** and press **Enter**. What is the major and minor number for this block device?

5. At the command prompt, type **rm /dev/dsk/f03ht** and press **Enter**. Next, type **ls -l /dev/dsk/f03ht** at the command prompt and press **Enter**. Was the file removed successfully?

6. Type the command **mknod /dev/dsk/f03ht b 1 112** at the command prompt and press **Enter**. What did this command do? Next, type **ls -l /dev/dsk/f03ht** at the command prompt and press **Enter**. Was the file recreated successfully?

7. At the command prompt, type **ln /dev/dsk/f03ht /dev/myfloppy** and press **Enter**. What did this command do? Next, type **ls -l /dev/myfloppy** at the command prompt and press **Enter**. What type (block or character), major number, and minor number does this device have? Why?

8. At the command prompt, type **find /dev** and press **Enter** to list all of the filenames underneath the /dev directory. Are there many files? Next, type **du -ks /dev** at the command prompt and press **Enter**. How large in kilobytes are all files within the /dev directory? Why?

9. At the command prompt, type **getdev | more** and press **Enter** to list all of the devices in the Device Database. Which name represents your floppy disk? Which name represents your CD-ROM? Which name represents your first hard disk? Press **q** to exit the more utility.

10. At the command prompt, type **devattr -v diskette1** and press **Enter** to list information from the Device Database for your first floppy device. What is the block device file? What command can be used to create a S5 filesystem on the floppy disk? What command can be used to create a VxFS filesystem on the floppy disk?

11. At the command prompt, type **devattr -v disk1** and press **Enter** to list information from the Device Database for your first hard disk device. What is the block device file? Is there a command listed that may be used to create a VxFS filesystem on the hard disk? Why?

12. At the command prompt, type **devattr -v cdrom1** and press **Enter** to list information from the Device Database for your first CD-ROM device. What is the block device file? Is there a command listed that may be used to create a VxFS filesystem on the CD-ROM? Why?

13. Type **exit** and press **Enter** to log out of your shell.

**HANDS-ON PROJECTS**

## Project 7-2

In this hands-on project, you will create filesystems on floppy disks, mount them to the directory tree, and view their contents.

1. Switch to a command-line terminal (vt02) by pressing **Ctrl+Alt+F2**, and log into the terminal using the username **root** and the password **secret**.

2. At the command prompt, type **mkdir /mymount** and press **Enter** to create a new mount point directory. Next, type **ls -F /mymount** at the command prompt and press **Enter**. Are there any files in the /mymount directory? Now, type **cp /etc/hosts /mymount** at the command prompt and press **Enter**. Next, type **ls -F /mymount** at the command prompt and press **Enter** to verify that the hosts file was copied successfully.

3. Place a floppy disk into the floppy disk drive of your computer and type **format -v /dev/rdsk/f03ht** at the command prompt and press **Enter**. Next, type **mkfs -F vxfs -o ninode=711 /dev/dsk/f03ht 2844** at the command prompt and press **Enter**. Observe the message displayed, but do not press any keys; in a few seconds, your floppy will be formatted.

4. At the command prompt, type **mount -F vxfs /dev/dsk/f03ht /mymount** and press **Enter**. Next, type **mount** at the command prompt and press **Enter**. Was the floppy disk successfully mounted to the /mymount directory?

5. At the command prompt, type **ls -F /mymount** and press **Enter**. What file do you see? Why? What happened to the hosts file? Next, type **cp /etc/inittab /mymount** at the command prompt and press **Enter**. Did the light on the floppy disk drive of your computer turn on? At the command prompt, type **ls -F /mymount** and press **Enter** to verify that the file was copied to the floppy successfully.

6. At the command prompt, type **cd /mymount** and press **Enter**. Next, type **umount /mymount** at the command prompt and press **Enter**. What error message do you receive? Why?

7. At the command prompt, type **fuser -u /mymount** and press **Enter**. Who is using the /mymount directory? Next, type **cd /** at the command prompt and press **Enter**.

8. At the command prompt, type **umount /mymount** and press **Enter**. Next, type **mount** at the command prompt and press **Enter**. Was the floppy disk successfully unmounted from the /mymount directory?

9. At the command prompt, type **ls -F /mymount** and press **Enter**. What file do you see? Why? What happened to the inittab file and lost+found directory? Is the hosts file present?

10. Switch to the graphical terminal (vt01) by pressing **Ctrl+Alt+F1**, and log into the CDE desktop using the username **root** and the password **secret**.

11. Open **SCO Admin**. From the SCO Admin menu, select the **Filesystem Manager**. What filesystems are listed? What filesystems are mounted? What file is read by the Filesystem Manager?

12. From the Mount menu, select **Add Mount Configuration** and then **Local**.

13. At the information screen, enter **/dev/dsk/f03ht** in the Device File box and use your mouse to highlight the **Mount Point** text box. Click **Continue**. The system will attempt to detect the type of filesystem on the floppy disk. When you are finished, enter **/mymount** in the Mount Point text box. Next, use your mouse to deselect **Now** and **At System Startup** and click **OK** when you are finished.

14. Is there a line describing the information required to mount your floppy disk in Filesystem Manager? Ensure that the line is highlighted, select the **Mount** menu, and then **Mount**.

15. Next, select the **Mount** menu and choose **Unmount**. Click **Yes** when prompted. Close the Filesystem Manager and SCO Admin. Log out of the CDE desktop.

16. Switch back to your command-line terminal (vt02) by pressing **Ctrl+Alt+F2**. Note that you are logged in as the root user on this terminal.

17. At the command prompt, type **cat /etc/vfstab** and press **Enter**. Is there a line representing the Mount Configuration that you added in Filesystem Manager? Is this floppy mounted automatically at boot time? Why?

18. At the command prompt, type **mount /mymount** and press **Enter**. Next, type **mount** at the command prompt and press **Enter**. Is your floppy mounted? Explain.

19. At the command prompt, type **ls –F /mymount** and press **Enter**. What files do you see and why? Next, type **umount /mymount** at the command prompt and press **Enter**. Type **mount** at the command prompt and press **Enter** to verify that the floppy was successfully unmounted from the /mymount directory.

20. Remove the floppy disk from your computer's floppy disk drive. Keep this floppy disk in a safe place as it will be used in an exercise in a later chapter.

21. Type **exit** and press **Enter** to log out of your shell.

**HANDS-ON PROJECTS**

# Project 7-3

In this hands-on project, you will mount CD-ROM disks to the directory tree and view their contents.

1. Switch to a command-line terminal (vt02) by pressing **Ctrl+Alt+F2**, and log into the terminal using the username **root** and the password **secret**.

2. At the command prompt, type **ls –l /dev/cdrom/cdrom1** and press **Enter**. What type of device is it (block or character)? What is the major number? What is the minor number?

3. Next, insert the first UnixWare 7.1.1 installation CD-ROM in your computer's CD-ROM drive. At the command prompt, type **mount –r –F cdfs /dev/cdrom/cdrom1 /mnt** and press **Enter**. Next, type **mount** at the command prompt and press **Enter**. Was the CD-ROM disk successfully mounted to the /mymount directory?

4. At the command prompt, type **ls –F /mymount** and press **Enter**. Are there many files and directories on this CD-ROM? Next, type **cd /mnt/UnixWare** at the command prompt and press **Enter**. At the command prompt, type **ls –F** and press **Enter** to view the files in this directory. Next, type **cat pkginfo** at the command prompt and press **Enter**. What is the name of the package contained within this directory on the CD-ROM?

5. At the command prompt, type **cd** and press **Enter** to return to your home directory. Next, type **umount /mnt** at the command prompt and press **Enter**. Was the CD-ROM disk successfully unmounted from the /mnt directory? Type the **mount** command at a command prompt and press **Enter** to verify this.

6. Switch to the graphical terminal (vt01) by pressing **Ctrl+Alt+F1**, and log into the CDE desktop using the username **root** and the password **secret**.

7. Open **SCO Admin**. From the SCO Admin menu, select the **Filesystem Manager**.

8. From the Mount menu, select **Add Mount Configuration** and then **Local**.

9. At the information screen, enter **/dev/cdrom/cdrom1** in the Device File box and use your mouse to highlight the **Mount Point** text box. Press **Continue.** The system will attempt to detect the type of filesystem on the CD-ROM. When finished, enter **/mnt** in the Mount Point text box. Next, use your mouse to deselect **Now** and **At System Startup** and press **OK** when you are finished.

10. Is there a line describing the information required to mount your CD-ROM in Filesystem Manager? Ensure that the line is highlighted, and select the **Mount** menu and then **Mount**. Try to eject the CD-ROM using the button on your CD-ROM drive. Were you successful? Why or why not?

11. Next, select the **Mount** menu and choose **Unmount**. Click **Yes** when prompted. Eject the CD-ROM disk from the CD-ROM disk drive. Why were you successful?

12. Close the Filesystem Manager and SCO Admin. Log out of the CDE desktop.

13. Switch back to your command-line terminal (vt02) by pressing **Ctrl+Alt+F2**.

14. Type **exit** and press **Enter** to log out of your shell.

**HANDS-ON PROJECTS**

## Project 7-4

In this hands-on project, you will examine hard disk partitions, slices, and filesystems.

1. Switch to a command-line terminal (vt02) by pressing **Ctrl+Alt+F2**, and log into the terminal using the username **root** and the password **secret**.

2. At the command prompt, type **fdisk /dev/rdsk/c0b0t0d0p0** and press **Enter**. How many partitions are configured on the system? What type of partition is it? Is it marked active? Press **5** and then press **Enter**. when you are finished to exit the fdisk utility.

3. At the command prompt, type **prtvtoc /dev/rdsk/c0b0t0d0s0** and press **Enter** to display all of the slices within the UNIX partition on the first hard disk. Answer the following:

   What slice number is the / filesystem? _____

   What slice number is the /stand filesystem? _____

   What slice number is the swap slice? _____

   What slice number is used for the ALTS TABLE? _____

   What slice number is used for the /home filesystem? _____

   What slice number is used for the BOOT slice? _____

   What slice refers to the entire UNIX partition? _____

4. At the command prompt, type **prtvtoc –f /tmp/vtoc.tmp/dev/rdsk/c0b0t0d0s0** and press **Enter** to save a copy of the VTOC to the /tmp/vtoc.tmp file. Next, type **cat /tmp/vtoc.tmp** at the command prompt and press **Enter**. Which of the slices on the VTOC are mountable (that is, contain a filesystem)?

5. At the command prompt, type **prtvtoc –p /dev/rdsk/c0b0t0d0s0** and press **Enter** to view the disk geometry. How many cylinders does your hard disk have? How many slices (called partitions in the command output) are there in the UNIX partition by default?

6. At the command prompt, type **df** and press **Enter**. What hard disk filesystems are displayed? Can you see the swap slice? Why?

7. At the command prompt, type **ls –F /home** and press **Enter**. What slice are you observing?

8. Next, type the **ls –id /home** command and press **Enter**. What is the inode of the /home directory? Why?

9. At the command prompt, type **cat /etc/vfstab** and press **Enter**. Is there a line in this file that mounts the /home filesystem automatically at boot time?

10. At the command prompt, type **umount /home** and press **Enter**. Next, type the **mount** command and press **Enter** to verify that the /home filesystem was unmounted successfully.

11. At the command prompt, type **ls –F /home** and press **Enter**. What happened to the files that were observed in Step 7? What slice are you observing?

12. Next, type the **ls –id /home** command and press **Enter**. What is the inode of the /home directory? Compare this to the number observed in Step 8. Why are they different?

13. At the command prompt, type **mount /home** and press **Enter**. Next, type the **mount** command and press **Enter** to verify that the /home filesystem was mounted successfully from the appropriate entry in /etc/vfstab.

14. At the command prompt, type **fstyp /dev/dsk/c0b0t0d0sc** and press **Enter**. What filesystem is on the /home filesystem?

15. At the command prompt, type **mkfs –m /dev/dsk/c0b0t0d0s4** and press **Enter**. Does the /home filesystem have large file support enabled? How could you enable it?

16. Type **exit** and press **Enter** to log out of your shell.

## Project 7-5

In this hands-on project, you will create errors on a floppy disk and repair those errors using the fsck command.

1. Switch to a command-line terminal (vt02) by pressing **Ctrl+Alt+F2**, and log into the terminal using the username **root** and the password **secret**.

2. Place the floppy diskette created in Project 7-2 into your floppy disk drive.

3. Type the command **fsdb –F vxfs /dev/dsk/f03ht** at the command prompt and press **Enter**. At the following interactive prompt, type **4i** and press **Enter**. At the next interactive prompt, type **ln=0** and press **Enter**. At the following interactive

prompt, type **q** and press **Enter**. You have just changed the link count to zero (an impossible link count) for the inittab file (the inode number is 4) on the floppy disk.

4. At the command prompt, type **fsck –F vxfs /dev/rdsk/f03ht** and press **Enter**. What message do you receive? Why?

5. At the command prompt, type **fsck –F vxfs –o full /dev/rdsk/f03ht** and press **Enter**.

6. When prompted to change the link count for inode number 4 to 1, press **y**.

7. Press **y** and **Enter** when prompted to clear the (intent) log and press **y** and **Enter** again when prompted to set the state to CLEAN.

8. Type **exit** and press **Enter** to log out of your shell.

# Project 7-6

7

In this hands–on project, you will view disk usage by user as well as enable, set, and view disk quotas for the /home filesystem.

1. Switch to a command-line terminal (vt02) by pressing **Ctrl+Alt+F2**, and log into the terminal using the username **root** and the password **secret**.

2. At the command prompt, type **quot –F vxfs /home** to view the ownership of files in the /home filesystem. Who owns the most files?

3. At the command prompt, type **quot –F vxfs /** to view the ownership of files in the / filesystem. Who owns the most files?

4. At the command prompt, type **touch /home/quotas** to create the quota database in the root of the /home filesystem.

5. At the command prompt, type **quotaon –F vxfs /home** and press **Enter**.

6. At the command prompt, type **edquota –F vxfs owner** and press **Enter**. When the vi editor opens, edit the default information to match:

    ```
    fs /home blocks (soft = 1024, hard = 2048) inodes (soft = 100, hard = 200)
    ```

    Save your changes and exit the vi editor when finished.

7. At the command prompt, type **edquota –F vxfs –t** and press **Enter**. When the vi editor opens, edit the default information to match:

    ```
    fs /home blocks time limit = 2.00 mins, files time limit = 2.00 mins
    ```

    Save your changes and exit the vi editor when finished.

8. At the command prompt, type **repquota –F vxfs /home** and press **Enter**. Are the quota changes you made for the user owner visible? How many files has owner stored on this filesystem so far?

9. At the command prompt, type **quota –F vxfs –v owner** and press **Enter**. Compare this to the output from Step 8.

10. Type **exit** and press **Enter** to log out of your shell.

## DISCOVERY EXERCISES

1. Answer the following questions regarding your system by using the commands listed in this chapter. For each question, write the command you used to obtain the answer:

   a. What filesystems are currently mounted on your system?

   b. What filesystems are available to be mounted on your system?

   c. What filesystems will be checked automatically at boot?

   d. What filesystems will be mounted automatically at boot?

2. List the major numbers for the following devices:

   a. /dev/dsk/f03ht

   b. /dev/rdsk/f15dt

   c. /dev/dsk/c0b0t0d0s5

   d. /dev/rdsk/c0b0t0d0sa

   e. /dev/dsk/c0b0t1d0s3

   f. /dev/dsk/c1b0t1d0s1

   How do they compare? Is there a pattern? Why or why not?

3. Provided you have access to a functional Web browser and Internet connection, gather information on four filesystems compatible with UNIX. For each filesystem, list the situations for which the filesystem was designed and the key features that the filesystem provides.

4. You are planning a UNIX installation. The department manager wants to use the UNIX computer to run a database application that will be used by 100 users. The database application and the associated data will take up over 5GB of hard disk space. In addition, these 100 users will store their personal files on the hard disk of the system. Each user must have a maximum of 5GB of storage space. The department manager has made it very clear that this system must not exhibit any downtime as a result of hard disk errors. How much hard disk space would you require, and what slices and filesystems would you need to ensure that the system will perform as needed? To which directory would the filesystems be mounted? What quotas would you implement? What commands would you need to run and what entries to /etc/vfstab would you have? Justify your answers.

5. You have several filesystems on your hard disk that are mounted to separate directories on the UNIX directory tree. The /dev/dsk/c0b0t0d0s9 filesystem was unable to be mounted at boot time. What could have caused this? What commands could you use to find more information about the nature of the problem?

6. Add a second hard disk to your system and run the diskadd wizard without arguments. Follow the prompts to create three slices with filesystems that will be automatically mounted to the /slice1, /slice2, and /slice3 directories. When the wizard is finished, use the df command to verify that they are mounted. Next, use the

prtvtoc –f /tmp/vtoc *<device>* (where *<device>* is the raw device file for the hard disk) to dump the VTOC to a file called /tmp/vtoc. Edit the /tmp/vtoc file so that there are two equal-sized slices instead of three. Save your changes to the VTOC by running the edvtoc –f /tmp/vtoc *<device>* (where *<device>* is the raw device file for the hard disk). Next, use mkfs to create filesystems and mount those filesystems to the /slice1 and /slice2 directories as well as configure them to automatically mount at boot time using the /etc/vfstab file.

7

# 8

# SYSTEM INITIALIZATION, RUNLEVELS, AND SAF

**After reading this chapter and completing the exercises, you will be able to:**

♦ Summarize the major steps necessary to initialize a UNIX system

♦ Detail the different bootstrap programs and boot loaders available to UNIX systems

♦ Use and manage the Boot Command Processor (BCP)

♦ Describe the different UNIX runlevels available and how to change them

♦ Identify how the init daemon initializes the system at boot time

♦ Configure daemons to start and stop upon entering a runlevel

♦ Understand how Service Access Facility (SAF) enables users to log into the system

♦ Enable and disable port monitor daemons and virtual terminals

The ability to configure system services to start during system startup and stop during system shutdown is fundamental to administering a UNIX system. This chapter details how a UNIX system is initialized to start system services and give users the opportunity to log into the system. More specifically, this chapter begins by outlining the system initialization process and explaining how daemons are organized by runlevel. Next, you will learn how to configure the UnixWare boot loader as well as the init daemon to start and stop daemons. Finally, this chapter outlines the process by which users receive terminals to log into the system.

## OVERVIEW OF SYSTEM INITIALIZATION

Since different hardware architectures are used by different UNIX flavors, the system initialization process varies from one UNIX flavor to another. Although this chapter discusses the system initialization process for Solaris, HP-UX, and UnixWare, it focuses on UnixWare system initialization. Regardless of your UNIX flavor, system initialization involves three main components that occur in this order:

1. Bootstrapping
2. Kernel loading
3. Daemon initialization

## Bootstrapping

When a computer is turned on, hardware components must be initialized and a program that can load the operating system on a disk device must be located and executed. This procedure is called **bootstrapping**, a term coined from the American idiom "pulling yourself up by your own bootstraps."

On the Intel architecture, bootstrapping is performed by the BIOS on the motherboard. The BIOS first initializes all hardware components to ensure that there are no hardware failures; this is called a power-on self test (POST). Following the POST, the BIOS checks its configuration stored on a CMOS chip on the motherboard for devices (called **boot devices**) to search for programs that can execute the UNIX kernel. Computers typically search floppy and CD-ROM devices if they are present in the computer and have disks inside them; this ensures that the installation of an operating system from CD-ROM or floppy disk may occur at boot time. After these two devices are checked, the computer usually checks the Master Boot Record (MBR) on the first hard disk inside the computer.

 You may alter the order that boot devices are checked in the configuration program for the computer BIOS.

**NOTE**

The MBR contains a pointer to a partition on the system that contains a program that loads the UNIX kernel on the first sector; the partition that the MBR points to is referred to as the **active partition**.

 On HP-UX systems, bootstrapping is performed by the **Processor Dependent Code (PDC)** stored in a CMOS computer chip on the motherboard. The PDC also enables you to configure the boot device via a series of commands and menus.

**NOTE**

On Sun systems that run Solaris, bootstrapping is performed by the **OpenBoot programmable read-only memory (PROM)** stored in a CMOS computer chip on the motherboard. Like the BIOS and PDC, the OpenBoot PROM enables you to configure the boot device.

## Kernel Loading

The bootstrap program cannot directly load the UNIX kernel; instead, it loads a program on the boot device that loads the UNIX kernel. This program is called the **boot loader**. The boot loader used by UnixWare is called the **Boot Command Processor (BCP)**; it is loaded by the computer BIOS. Once loaded, it mounts the filesystem on the slice that contains the UNIX kernel (the **/stand** filesystem) and then executes that UNIX kernel in memory (**/stand/unix**).

The PDC on HP-UX systems load the **Initial System Loader (ISL)** boot loader. This boot loader then mounts the /stand filesystem and executes the hpux program to load the UNIX kernel **/stand/vmunix**.

**8**

The OpenBoot PROM on Solaris systems load the boot loader program bookblk. This boot loader then mounts the /kernel filesystem and executes the ufsboot program to load the UNIX kernel **/kernel/genunix**.

## Daemon Initialization

Once the UNIX kernel is loaded into memory, the boot loader is no longer active; instead, the UNIX kernel continues to initialize the system by executing programs that mount filesystems from entries in /etc/vfstab, set the system time, configure the system hostname, and load daemons into memory. A **daemon** is a system process that performs useful tasks such as printing, scheduling, and operating system maintenance. The first daemon process on a UnixWare system is called sysproc; it loads the **init (initialize) daemon**, which is responsible for loading all other daemons on the system required to bring the system to a useable state where users may log in and interact with services. Figure 8-1 depicts the entire UnixWare system initialization process.

After loading the init daemon, the sysproc daemon handles the transfer of information to and from the swap slice as well as process scheduling; as a result, it is typically called the **swapper daemon** on HP-UX systems and the **sched daemon** on Solaris systems.

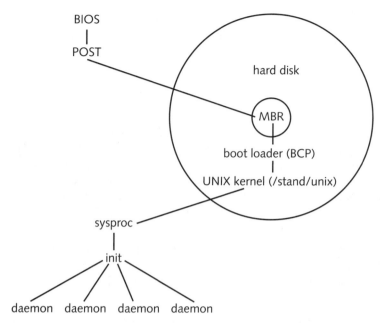

**Figure 8-1** The UnixWare system initialization process

# RUNLEVELS

Since several daemons may need to be started by the init daemon on a typical UNIX system, the init daemon categorizes the system into runlevels. A **runlevel** defines the number and type of daemons that are loaded into memory and executed by the kernel on a particular system. A UNIX system can be in any one of seven standard run levels at any one time. Table 8-1 defines these runlevels.

**Table 8-1** UNIX runlevels

| Runlevel | Common Name | Description |
|---|---|---|
| 0 | Shutdown | A system that has no daemons active in memory and is ready to be powered off |
| 1<br>s<br>S | **Single-user mode** | A system that has only enough daemons to enable you to log in and perform system maintenance tasks |
| 2 | **Multiuser mode** | A system that has most daemons started and enables multiple users to log in and use system services. The CDE desktop and most common network services are available in this runlevel as well. |
| 3 | **Extended multi-user mode** | A system that has the same abilities as multiuser mode, but with all extra networking services started (such as NFS) |
| 4 | Not used | Not normally used, but may be defined manually if needed |

**Table 8-1**    UNIX runlevels (continued)

| Runlevel | Common Name | Description |
|----------|-------------|-------------|
| 5 | Shutdown | A system that has no daemons active in memory and is ready to be powered off. It is the same as runlevel 0. |
| 6 | Reboot | A special runlevel used to reboot the system |

**NOTE**   Runlevel 3 is the default runlevel that UnixWare, HP-UX, and Solaris systems enter during system initialization.

**NOTE**   Since the init daemon is responsible for starting and stopping daemons and hence changing runlevels, runlevels are often also called **initstates**.

**NOTE**   Runlevels 5 and 6 are not used on HP-UX systems.

8

## Viewing and Changing Runlevels

To see the current runlevel of the system as well as the number of times that the system has entered this runlevel (if runlevels have been changed since system startup) and the most recent runlevel, use the **who  -r** command, as shown in the following output:

```
# who -r
     .         run-level 3  Oct 27 12:33    3    0    S
#
```

The previous command indicates that the system is currently in runlevel 3, has never been in this runlevel before (0), and the most recent runlevel was single-user mode (S).

To change the runlevel on a running system, you need to specify the **init command** followed by the new runlevel. To change from runlevel 3 to runlevel 1 to perform system maintenance tasks, use the following command and log into the system as the root user:

```
# init 1

Welcome to UnixWare 7, Release 7.1.1
The system's name is unix1.

Console Login: root
Password:

Last login: Sun Oct 27 12:34:10 2002 on console
You have mail
```

```
# who -r
    .          run-level 1  Oct 27 12:33    1    0    3
# _
```

The **telinit command** is a shortcut to the `init` command; thus, the command `telinit 1` can be used instead to switch to single-user mode.

**NOTE**

You can also change runlevels by specifying the target runlevel after the `-i` option to the `shutdown` command. For example, to change to runlevel 1 using the `shutdown` command, use the command `shutdown -i1`.

**NOTE**

Switching to runlevel 0, 1, 5, or 6 will terminate the sessions for logged-in users. Because of this, it is good practice to warn all users that the system is shutting down using the **wall (warn all) command**. After executing this command, specify the message to send to all users and press Ctrl-d on a new line when you are finished:

```
# wall
Please save any changes to files and log off the system.   The system
will be shut down in 5 minutes for maintenance.   Thankyou.
Ctrl-d

Broadcast Message from root (console) on unix1 Tue Oct 29 20:26:16...
Please save any changes to files and log off the system.   The system
will be shut down in 5 minutes for maintenance.   Thankyou.
# _
```

# CONFIGURING THE BOOT COMMAND PROCESSOR (BCP)

As discussed earlier, the primary function of boot loaders during the boot process is to load the UNIX kernel into memory. However, boot loaders can also perform other functions, including passing information to the kernel during system startup and booting other operating systems that are present on the hard disk.

Only one operating system may be active at any one time.

**NOTE**

Recall that the BCP is the standard boot loader used on UnixWare systems. The first half of the BCP resides on the boot slice (the first sector of the active UNIX partition); it mounts the BFS-formatted /stand filesystem. The second half of the BCP resides on the /stand filesystem. Once both components of the BCP are loaded into memory, a splash screen, which is shown in Figure 8-2, is displayed for five seconds before the default UNIX kernel (/stand/unix) is loaded.

**Figure 8-2**    The UnixWare splash screen

If you press Enter at the splash screen before the five seconds transpires, you will reach a [boot] prompt where you can alter the BCP as follows:

```
Bootstrap Command Processor
Ready for boot commands... [? for help]

[boot] _
```

The ? or help commands can be typed at the [boot] prompt to obtain a list of commands and variables that may be used at the [boot] prompt, as shown in the following output. This information is stored in the /stand/help.txt file, which can be viewed after the system has initialized:

```
[boot] ?
Available BOOT commands:
  ? -or- help -- Display this message
  boot [<filename>] -- Load and run specified program; default is BOOTPROG
  dir [<dev>] -- List all files in /stand directory; default device is BOOTDEV
  logo -- Display the logo image until a key is pressed
  logo off -- Don't display logo
  show [-a | <param>] -- Show boot parameter values
       -a -- Show all boot parameters, even messages
       <param> -- Show only the specified boot parameter
  <param>=<value> -- Set the value of a boot parameter
  <param>+=<value> -- Append the value to a boot parameter, inserting a comma

Parameters that are recognized by BOOT:
ALIGN=<num> -- Alignment requirement for FILES images
```

```
AUTOBOOT=yes|no|<num> -- Minimum time (sec) to wait while loading BOOTPROG
BLM=<filename>{,<filename>} -- Bootstrap Loadable Modules loaded into BOOT
BOOTDEV=<dev> -- Device BOOTPROG is loaded from
BOOTMSG1=<text> -- Message displayed when starting to boot
BOOTMSG2=<text> -- Message displayed when entering interactive mode
BOOTMSG3=<text> -- String displayed at beginning of command line
BOOTMSG4=<text> -- String displayed when waiting to display more
BOOTPROG=<filename> -- Filename of kernel or other program to load and run
CONSOLE=<dev> -- Device used by BOOT and BOOTPROG for console I/O
```

[MORE]

Most features of the BCP are represented by variables that may be changed using the syntax VARIABLENAME=value at the [boot] prompt. To see a list of default variables in the BCP, type the **show command**, as shown in the following output:

```
[boot] show
AUTOBOOT=5
BLM=dcmp.blm,stage3.blm,platform.blm,hd.blm
BOOTDEV=hd(0,1)
BOOTPROG=unix
BOOTSTAMP=EBmyHdByeYRS
BUSTYPES=PCI2.10,ISA,PnP1.0
FILES=resmgr,license
HDPARM0=1023,255,63
MEMORY=0-2K:reserved,2K-639K:boot,639K-640K:reserved,1M-
1048740:boot,1048740-12
M
ROOTFS=vxfs
TZ_OFFSET=14400

[boot] _
```

Most variables shown in the previous output should not be changed, as they represent boot loader files (BLM and FILES), hardware parameters (HDPARM0, BUSTYPES, and MEMORY), and boot loader identifiers (BOOTSTAMP). However, other variables can be changed or new variables can be created to alter how the BCP loads the UNIX kernel. Table 8-2 lists these variables.

**Table 8-2**   Common BCP variables

| BCP Variable | Description |
| --- | --- |
| AUTOBOOT=5 | Gives the user five seconds to press Enter at the UnixWare splash screen before loading the default UNIX kernel. If this number is set to the number 0 or the word "no," then you will always see the [boot] prompt during system initialization. |
| BOOTDEV=hd(0,1) | Specifies that the operating system or boot loader to load resides on the first partition (1) on the first hard disk (0) |

**Table 8-2**   Common BCP variables (continued)

| BCP Variable | Description |
|---|---|
| BOOTPROG=unix.old | Specifies to load an alternate UNIX kernel from the /stand directory called unix.old (when the kernel is changed by the system, the old kernel is saved as /stand/unix.old). To see a list of files within the /stand directory, type dir at the [boot] prompt. |
| DISABLE_CACHE=yes | Disables the use of memory caches |
| ENABLE_4GB_MEM=yes | Enables kernel support for memory sizes over 4GB. The BCP passes this information to the UNIX kernel when it is loaded. |
| INITSTATE=1 | Specifies that the system should enter runlevel 1 (instead of 3). The BCP passes this information to the UNIX kernel; the UNIX kernel then passes it to the init daemon. |
| ROOTFS=vxfs | Specifies that the / filesystem is VxFS such that the UNIX kernel can mount it once loaded |
| TIMEOUT=20 | Continues to boot the default UNIX kernel if you do not enter any commands at the [boot] prompt in 20 seconds |
| TZ_OFFSET=14400 | Specifies the time zone offset of four hours (in seconds) for daylight-saving time |

Any variables that are changed at the [boot] prompt affect the current boot only. The default variables and their values used by the BCP are listed in the **/stand/boot** file, which can be edited or viewed only at a UNIX shell prompt:

```
# cat /stand/boot
#ident   "@(#)stand:common/boot/conf/boot.hd     1.3"
#ident   "$Header: $"

BLM=hd.blm
files=resmgr,license
rootfs=vxfs
TZ_OFFSET=18000

# _
```

Thus, to boot into single-user mode by default on each boot, place the line INITSTATE=1 in the /stand/boot file.

**NOTE**

Boot loaders on HP-UX and Solaris also enable you to configure how the UNIX kernel is loaded. For example, to boot into single-user mode during HP-UX system initialization, type hpux -is at the ISL prompt. Similarly, to boot into single-user mode during Solaris initialization, type boot -s at the OpenBoot PROM prompt.

The BCP also has variables that represent the messages that are printed to the terminal screen on system startup. Since they do not affect the operation of the BCP, they are not shown by the show command unless the **-a** option is used:

```
Bootstrap Command Processor
Ready for boot commands... [? for help]

[boot] show -a
ALIGN=4096
AUTOBOOT=5
AUTOMSG=Automatic Boot Procedure
BLM=dcmp.blm,stage3.blm,platform.blm,hd.blm
BOOTCONS=200208,200240
BOOTDEV=hd(0,1)
BOOTMSG1=Starting UnixWare...
BOOTMSG2=Bootstrap Command Processor\
Ready for boot commands... [? for help]
BOOTMSG3=[boot]
BOOTMSG4=[MORE]
BOOTPROG=unix
BOOTSTAMP=EBmyHdByeYRS
BUSTYPES=PCI2.10,ISA,PnP1.0
COPYRIGHT=Copyright (c) 1976-1998 The Santa Cruz Operation, Inc. and\
its suppliers. All Rights Reserved.\
\
RESTRICTED RIGHTS LEGEND:\
\
When licensed to a U.S., State, or Local Government, all Software \
produced by SCO is commercial computer software as defined in \
[MORE]
```

Note from the previous output that variables that use multiple lines use the \ character to protect the new line character and that the BCP displays a [MORE] prompt when the output is too large for the terminal screen. From this prompt, press Enter to advance to the next page of output.

Default message variables and their values used by the BCP are listed in the **/stand/bootmsgs** file. Like /stand/boot, this file can only be edited or viewed at a UNIX shell prompt:

```
# head /stand/bootmsgs
#ident  "@(#)stand:common/boot/conf/msgs/bootmsgs        1.5"
#ident  "$Header: $"
BOOTMSG1=Starting UnixWare...
BOOTMSG2=Bootstrap Command Processor\
Ready for boot commands... [? for help]\
```

```
TITLE=UnixWare 7, based on UNIX System V Release 5 from SCO
COPYRIGHT=Copyright (c) 1976-1998 The Santa Cruz Operation, Inc. and \
its suppliers.  All Rights Reserved.\
\

# _
```

If you change a variable while in the BCP, the system will not continue the boot process immediately. Instead, it provides another [boot] prompt for you to enter other commands or change other variables. To continue the boot process, you must enter the **boot command** at the [boot] prompt.

**NOTE**

Alternatively, you can use the commands b, go, or g at the [boot] prompt to continue the boot process.

For example, to specify /stand/unix.old as the kernel loaded and continue to boot that kernel, type the following:

```
Bootstrap Command Processor
Ready for boot commands... [? for help]

[boot] BOOTPROG=unix.old
[boot] boot
```

The **boot** command also takes arguments that can be used to boot another operating system that has a boot loader on a certain partition on the hard disk. This process is sometimes called **dual booting**. For example, to specify that the BCP should load the boot loader present on the first partition (1) on the first hard disk in the system (0), use the following command at the [boot] prompt:

```
Bootstrap Command Processor
Ready for boot commands... [? for help]

[boot] boot hd(0,1)
```

If the Windows operating system was installed on this partition, then the Windows boot loader will be loaded to complete the rest of the Windows boot process.

**NOTE**

If you want to dual boot the Windows operating system with UnixWare, you must first install the Windows operating system on a partition that is less than 8GB in size (such that it ends before the 1024th cylinder) and leave enough free space outside this partition for the installation of UnixWare. You can then install UnixWare and boot into the Windows operating system by specifying the correct command, such as b hd(0,1), at the BCP prompt.

## The init Daemon

Recall that once a boot loader loads the UNIX operating system kernel into memory, the kernel resumes control and executes the first daemon process on the system called sysproc. The **sysproc daemon** then loads the init daemon, which uses its configuration file **/etc/inittab** (init table) to load other daemons on the system. These daemons are organized by runlevel and provide system services that ultimately enable users to log in and use the system. Furthermore, the init daemon is responsible for unloading daemons when the system is halted or rebooted.

## The /etc/inittab File

When the init daemon needs to change the runlevel of the system by starting or stopping daemons, it consults the /etc/inittab file. This file is also consulted when the system is brought to a certain runlevel at boot time. The following depicts an example of a /etc/inittab file:

```
# cat /etc/inittab
#
# WARNING: THIS FILE IS AUTOMATICALLY GENERATED.
# Any changes made directly to this file may be overwritten
# at the next system reboot.
# Permanent changes should also be made to files in the
# /etc/conf/init.d directory.
# See Init(4) and idmkinit(1M) for more information.
#
fr::sysinit:/sbin/fixroot >/dev/sysmsg 2>&1
vol1::sysinit:/etc/init.d/vxvm-sysboot </dev/sysmsg > /dev/sysmsg 2>&1 ##vxvm
swp1::sysinit:/sbin/swap -a /dev/swap >/dev/sysmsg 2>&1
cr::sysinit:/sbin/ckroot >/dev/sysmsg 2>&1
pdi0::sysinit:/etc/scsi/sdistatic -B >/dev/sysmsg 2>&1
mi::sysinit:/sbin/sh -c '[ -x /sbin/macinit ] && /sbin/macinit' >/dev/sysmsg 2>
1
mm::sysinit:/etc/conf/bin/idmodreg -c `/etc/conf/bin/idkname -c` >/dev/null 2>&
ap::sysinit:/sbin/autopush -f /etc/ap/chan.ap
ak::sysinit:/sbin/wsinit >/etc/wsinit.err 2>&1
ls::sysinit:/sbin/loadfont >/dev/console 2>&1
cm1::sysinit:/sbin/ckmount /stand >/dev/console 2>&1
dcun::sysinit:/sbin/dcu -N >/dev/console 2>&1
pdi1::sysinit:/etc/scsi/pdiunits -a >/dev/console 2>&1
ldmd::sysinit:/etc/conf/bin/idmodload >/dev/console 2>&1
vol2::sysinit:/etc/init.d/vxvm-startup </dev/sysmsg >/dev/sysmsg 2>&1 ##vxvm
pdi2::sysinit:/etc/scsi/pdiunits -o >/dev/console 2>&1
ac::sysinit:/sbin/aconf1_sinit >/dev/console 2>&1
bu::sysinit:/etc/conf/bin/idrebuild reboot </dev/console >/dev/console 2>&1
me::sysinit:/etc/conf/bin/idmkenv >/dev/console 2>&1
nd::sysinit:/etc/conf/bin/idmknodd -r `/etc/conf/bin/idkname -c` >/dev/console
```

```
>&1
pdi4::sysinit:/etc/scsi/pdi_timeout -b >/dev/console 2>&1
cm2::sysinit:/sbin/ckmount /var >/dev/console 2>&1
iks0::sysinit:/sbin/initsock -d >/dev/console 2>&1
swp2::sysinit:/sbin/swap -c >/dev/console 2>&1
bchk::sysinit:/sbin/bcheckrc </dev/console >/dev/console 2>&1
vol3::sysinit:/etc/init.d/vxvm-reconfig </dev/console >/dev/sysmsg 2>&1 ##vxvm
xdc::sysinit:/sbin/sh -c 'if [ -x /etc/rc.d/es_setup ] ; then /etc/rc.d/es_setu
  ; fi' >/dev/console 2>&1
ia::sysinit:/sbin/creatiadb </dev/console >/dev/console 2>&1
metr::sysinit:/sbin/sh -c '[ -x /sbin/metreg ] && /sbin/metreg' >/dev/console 2
&1
pmd0::sysinit:/etc/ifor_pmd -k >/dev/console 2>&1
pmd::sysinit:/etc/ifor_pmd < /dev/null > /var/adm/pmd.log 2>&1
is:3:initdefault:
bd:56:wait:/etc/conf/bin/idrebuild </dev/console >/dev/console 2>&1
r0:0:wait:/sbin/rc0 off >/dev/console 2>&1 </dev/console
r1:1:wait:/sbin/rc1 >/dev/console 2>&1 </dev/console
r2:23:wait:/sbin/rc2 >/dev/console 2>&1 </dev/console
r3:3:wait:/sbin/rc3  >/dev/console 2>&1 </dev/console
r5:5:wait:/sbin/rc0 firm >/dev/console 2>&1 </dev/console
r6:6:wait:/sbin/rc0 reboot >/dev/console 2>&1 </dev/console
sd:0:wait:/sbin/uadmin 2 0 >/dev/console 2>&1 </dev/console
fw:5:wait:/sbin/uadmin 2 2 >/dev/console 2>&1 </dev/console
rb:6:wait:/sbin/uadmin 2 1 >/dev/console 2>&1 </dev/console
sc:234:respawn:/usr/lib/saf/sac -t 300
co:12345:respawn:/usr/lib/saf/ttymon -g -p "Console Login: " -d /dev/console -l
console
d2:23:wait:/sbin/dinit >/dev/console 2>&1 </dev/console
# _
```

The format of entries in the /etc/inittab file are as follows:

label : runlevel : action : process

The label is just an identifier that enables the init daemon to examine this file in alphabetical order, the runlevel specifies which runlevel or runlevels the line in /etc/inittab corresponds to, the action tells the init daemon how to execute the command, and the process tells the init daemon what to execute when entering the runlevel. Many different actions can be used. Table 8-3 lists these actions and their definitions.

**Table 8-3**    Common action keywords

| Action | Description |
|--------|-------------|
| sysinit | Executes the process before the init daemon processes runlevels |
| initdefault | Specifies the default runlevel during system initialization |
| boot | Executes a process only when the /etc/inittab is read at boot time |

**Table 8-3** Common action keywords (continued)

| Action | Description |
|--------|-------------|
| bootwait | Executes a process only when switching from single-user mode to multiuser mode at boot time |
| wait | Executes a process and waits for its termination before proceeding to the next line in /etc/inittab |
| once | Executes a process and immediately proceeds to the next line in /etc/inittab |
| respawn | Executes a process and restarts the process if the process is terminated |
| off | Used to comment an entry in /etc/inittab—lines that contain this action are ignored. |

Thus, the line :3:initdefault: in the /etc/inittab file tells the init daemon that runlevel 3 is the default runlevel to boot to when initializing the UNIX system at system startup.

**NOTE**

If the INITSTATE variable has been passed to the kernel by the BCP, it overrides the default runlevel specified in /etc/inittab.

In addition, the `bchk::sysinit:/sbin/bcheckrc </dev/console >/dev/console 2>&1` line tells the init daemon to run the program `/sbin/bcheckrc` before entering a runlevel at system initialization and redirect the stdout and stderr to the file /dev/console. The `bcheckrc` program checks filesystems listed in /etc/vfstab with the fsck utility provided they have a 1 in the fsck field of the file.

Since the default runlevel is 3, the line `r2:23:wait:/sbin/rc2 >/dev/console 2>&1 </dev/console` will be executed as the number 3 is listed in the runlevel field. This line executes the `/sbin/rc2` command and waits for it to finish before proceeding to the rest of the /etc/inittab file. All stdin, stdout, and stderr is redirected to the /dev/console file. The `/sbin/rc2` command executes all files that start with *S* or *K* in the /etc/rc2.d/ directory. Each file in this directory is a script that loads a certain daemon and each of these files is executed in ASCII order; the *S* or *K* indicates whether to start or kill the daemon upon entering this runlevel, respectively.

**NOTE**

ASCII order is similar to alphabetical order using the ASCII code; space characters and numbers are first, followed by capital letters, followed by lowercase letters.

Here are some sample contents of the /etc/rc2.d/ directory:

```
# ls /etc/rc2.d
K20nfs           S15nd            S70Rnuc          S88ldap
S01MOUNTFSYS     S15static_conf   S70pf            S90sysinfo2html
S02PRESERVE      S42ls            S70unixtsa       S93scohelphttp
S02audit         S51domain        S71ppp           S95vxvm-recover
S02mse           S65loopback      S73snmp          S96isapnp
```

```
S05RMTMPFILES    S69inet         S75rpc          S98vesa
S10dstsync       S70Nnwip        S80nis          S99dtlogin
S15mkdtab        S70Pnw          S81sendmail     s74netbios
#  _
```

In the previous output, the init daemon starts the sendmail daemon (`S81sendmail`) upon entering this runlevel and kills the nfs daemon (`K20nfs`) if it exists in memory upon entering this runlevel. The file s74netbios will be ignored since it does not start with *S* or *K*.

Next, the init daemon will interpret the line `r3:3:wait:/sbin/rc3 >/dev/ console 2>&1 </dev/console` in the /etc/inittab file. This line executes the `/sbin/rc3` command and waits for it to finish before proceeding to the rest of the /etc/inittab file. All stdin, stdout, and stderr is redirected to the /dev/console file. Similar to the `/sbin/rc2` process, the `/sbin/rc3` command executes all files that start with *S* or *K* in the /etc/rc3.d/ directory. Recall that runlevel 3 is identical to runlevel 2, but has extra networking services started; thus, few files exist in the /etc/rc3.d/ directory:

```
# ls /etc/rc3.d
S22nfs
#  _
```

After the scripts in the /etc/rc3.d/ directory are executed, the init daemon loads processes that allow for user logins on virtual terminals (`sc:234:respawn:/usr/lib/ saf/sac -t 300`) and the system console (`co:12345:respawn:/usr/lib/ saf/ttymon -g -p "Console Login: " -d /dev/console -l console`). This process will be discussed later in this chapter.

Finally, the init daemon progresses to interpret the line `d2:23:wait:/sbin/ dinit >/dev/console 2>&1 </dev/console` in the /etc/inittab file. This line executes the `/sbin/dinit` command (redirecting all stdin, stdout, and stderr to /dev/console) and waits for it to finish. The `/sbin/dinit` process executes all files that start with *S* or *K* in the **/etc/dinit.d/** directory. The /etc/dinit.d/directory was originally created to speed up the boot process. It contains scripts to load daemons that provide services that are less essential to system startup and may be loaded after users are given the ability to log into the system:

```
# ls /etc/dinit.d
S23ttymap        S70uucp         S80cs           S81np
S69keymaster     S75cron         S80lp           S85perf
#  _
```

Recall that runlevel 1 (single-user mode) contains only enough daemons for a single user to log in and perform system tasks; if a user tells the init daemon to change to this runlevel using the init 1 command, the init daemon will find the appropriate entry in /etc/init-tab (`r1:1:wait:/sbin/rc1 >/dev/console 2>&1 </dev/console`) and proceed to execute every file that starts with *S* or *K* in the /etc/rc1.d/ directory. Since few daemons are started in single-user mode, most files in this directory start with *K*:

```
# ls /etc/rc1.d
```

8

```
K00ANNOUNCE   K40nfs      K68Nnuc       K69inet      S02mse
K10dtlogin    K40ppp      K68Pnw        K80nis       S10dstsync
K19np         K44ldap     K68Rnwip      K85nd        S42ls
K20lp         K67snmp     K68sendmail   S01MOUNTFSYS
#  _
```

Likewise, when the system is shut down, the init daemon uses the line `r0:0:wait:/sbin/rc0 off >/dev/console 2>&1 </dev/console` in /etc/inittab to execute the scripts in the /etc/rc0.d directory. All of these scripts start with *K* such that all daemons are killed:

```
# ls /etc/rc0.d
K00ANNOUNCE   K10dstsync   K20lp    K44ldap    K68Rnwip     K69inet
K02audit      K10dtlogin   K40nfs   K68Nnuc    K68netbios   K80nis
K02mse        K19np        K40ppp   K68Pnw     K68sendmail  K85nd
#  _
```

## Configuring Daemon Startup and Shutdown

Recall from the previous section that most daemons that are loaded upon system startup are executed from entries in /etc/inittab that run the **/sbin/rc***n* commands (where *n* refers to the runlevel) at system startup to load daemons from files that start with *S* in the appropriate **/etc/rc***n***.d/** directory (where *n* is either runlevel 1, 2, or 3). In addition, some scripts that start with *K* in the /etc/rc0.d/ directory are used to kill daemons when the system is shut down or rebooted.

**NOTE**

To temporarily disable a daemon from starting via a file that starts with *S* in the /etc/rc*n*.d/ directory, rename it such that it begins with a lowercase *s*. Only files that begin with uppercase *S* or *K* characters are executed by the init daemon.

These scripts typically process two arguments: start and stop. When the filename starts with an *S*, the start argument is passed to the script by the appropriate /sbin/rc*n* script in /etc/inittab (where *n* represents the runlevel). Alternatively, when the filename starts with *K*, the stop argument is passed to the script by the /sbin/rc*n* script in /etc/inittab (where *n* represents the runlevel).

The **/etc/rc2.d/S88ldap** script shown in the following output indicates that the ldap daemons will be started (using the **/usr/sbin/ldapstart** program) when the first argument is start and will be stopped (using the **/usr/sbin/ldapstop** program) when the first argument is stop:

```
# cat /etc/rc2.d/S88ldap
# LDAP start up script
```

```
if [ -z "$LC_ALL" -a -z "$LC_MESSAGES" ]
then
        if [ -z "$LANG" ]
        then
                LNG=`defadm locale LANG 2>/dev/null`
                if [ "$?" != 0 ]
                then LANG=C
                else eval $LNG
                fi
        fi
        export LANG
fi


case "$1" in
start)
        /usr/bin/ldapstart boot
        ;;
stop)
        /usr/bin/ldapstop all
        ;;
*)
        exit 1
esac

# _
```

**NOTE**

The variable $1 refers to the first argument given when executing the shell script on the command line.

Using script files that accept start and stop arguments enables you to use the same script in the /etc/rc0.d/ directory to kill a daemon process on system shutdown; just ensure that the first letter of the filename starts with *K*. For example, the /etc/rc0.d/ K44ldap script is identical to the /etc/rc2.d/S88ldap script, as shown in the following output. The *S* and *K* characters in the filenames determine which argument is used with the script and whether the ldap daemons will start or stop:

```
# cat /etc/rc0.d/K44ldap
# LDAP start up script

if [ -z "$LC_ALL" -a -z "$LC_MESSAGES" ]
then
        if [ -z "$LANG" ]
        then
                LNG=`defadm locale LANG 2>/dev/null`
                if [ "$?" != 0 ]
                then LANG=C
```

```
                      else eval $LNG
                      fi
            fi
            export LANG
    fi


    case "$1" in
    start)
            /usr/bin/ldapstart boot
            ;;
    stop)
            /usr/bin/ldapstop all
            ;;
    *)
            exit 1
    esac

    # _
```

To manually start the ldap daemon, run the command `/etc/rc2.d/`
`S881dap start`. To manually stop the ldap daemon, run the command
`/etc/rc2.d/S881dap stop`. Fortunately, UnixWare keeps a copy of all the scripts
used to start and stop daemons in the /etc/init.d/ directory so you can easily locate
them. The files in this directory do not start with K or S; instead, they are named to
describe their service:

```
# ls /etc/init.d
ANNOUNCE       dstsync      mkdtab      nuc        sysinfo2html
MOUNTFSYS      dtlogin      mse         nw         ttymap
PRESERVE       inetinit     nd          nwip       unixtsa
README         isapnp       netbios     pccard     uucp
RMTMPFILES     keymaster    nfs         perf       vxvm-mirstand
audit          ldap         nis         rpc        vxvm-reconfig
cron           loopback     nprinter    sendmail   vxvm-recover
cs             lp           nsadmin     snmp       vxvm-startup
domain         ls           nsfast      soundon    vxvm-sysboot
# _
```

Thus, to start and stop the ldap daemons manually, type the commands `/etc/init.d/`
`ldap start` and `/etc/init.d/ldap stop`, respectively.

If you want to configure a daemon to start automatically upon entering runlevel 3, create
a script file that processes the words "start" and "stop" in the /etc/init.d/ directory, as
shown in the following example using a sample daemon called mydaemon:

```
# cat /etc/init.d/mydaemon
# A sample start up script

case "$1" in
start)
```

```
        place command here to start daemon
        ;;
stop)
        place command here to stop daemon
        ;;
*)
        exit 1
esac

# _
```

Next, you can create hard or symbolic links to this file in the appropriate /etc/rcn.d/ directories to enable it to start or stop when the system enters the appropriate runlevel (*n*). To configure mydaemon to start only in runlevel 3 and stop in all other runlevels, run the following commands:

```
# ln /etc/init.d/mydaemon /etc/rc3.d/S99mydaemon
# ln /etc/init.d/mydaemon /etc/rc2.d/K10mydaemon
# ln /etc/init.d/mydaemon /etc/rc1.d/K10mydaemon
# ln /etc/init.d/mydaemon /etc/rc0.d/K10mydaemon
# _
```

HP-UX systems store scripts in the /sbin/init.d/ directory and link them to files that start with *S* or *K* in the /sbin/rcn.d/ directories to start and stop daemons upon changing runlevels.

## Modifying the /etc/inittab File

The /etc/inittab file is rebuilt by the system each time the kernel is changed or rebuilt. As a result, if you add lines to the /etc/inittab file, they will be lost when the system creates a new /etc/inittab file.

When rebuilding the /etc/inittab file, the system combines any files in the **/etc/conf/init.d/** directory together. Hardware and software vendors can then add files to this directory that will load daemons on system startup. At least one file called kernel in this directory contains system-related information and comprises most of the lines seen in the /etc/inittab file earlier. Thus, if you make changes to the /etc/inittab file, ensure that you also make those same changes to the **/etc/conf/init.d/kernel** file to avoid future problems if the /etc/inittab file is rebuilt by the system.

Alternatively, you can make the changes to /etc/conf/init.d/kernel file only and run the **/etc/conf/bin/idmkinit** command to create a new inittab file in the /etc/conf/cf.d/ directory. Simply copy the new /etc/conf/cf.d/inittab file to the /etc directory (overwriting the old /etc/inittab file) and run the command init q to force the init daemon to query the new /etc/inittab file.

Before changing important configuration files such as /etc/inittab and /etc/conf/init.d/kernel, it is good practice to create backup copies of them.

## ALLOWING USERS TO LOG INTO THE SYSTEM

Recall that init daemon loads daemons that enable users to log into a terminal and obtain a shell. On HP-UX systems, these daemons (getty) are started directly from in the /etc/inittab file. On Solaris and UnixWare systems, the **Service Access Facility (SAF)** enables users to log into the system. The first component of SAF is called the **Service Access Controller (sac)** daemon and is started by the init daemon (via the line `sc:234:respawn:/usr/lib/saf/sac -t 300` in the /etc/inittab file). The sac daemon first checks for configuration information in the **/etc/saf/_sysconfig** file and then proceeds to load other daemons via entries in the **/etc/saf/_sactab** (sac table) file that enable users to log into the system.

Daemons that enable users to log into terminals on the system are called **port monitor daemons**. Three port monitor daemons are loaded by default on UnixWare systems from entries in the /etc/saf/_sactab file: **listen**, **inetd**, and **ttymon**. The listen and inetd daemons allow for network logins, whereas the ttymon daemon allows for logins across serial ports (i.e., dumb terminals) and virtual terminals. Each of these port monitor daemons runs a process called **login** on each terminal that it monitors. If a user logs in with a valid username and password, the `login` program loads the **shserv** program, which starts a shell for the user. Figure 8-3 depicts the entire SAF process.

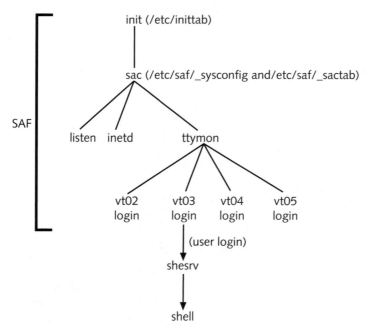

**Figure 8-3**    The SAF process

To see which port monitors are active, run the `sacadm -l` command:

```
# sacadm -l
PMTAG       PMTYPE    FLGS RCNT STATUS   COMMAND
tcp         listen    -    3    NO_SAC   /usr/lib/saf/listen
inetd       inetd     -    0    NO_SAC   /usr/sbin/inetd
nbcots      listen    -    0    NO_SAC   /usr/lib/saf/listen nbcots
contty      ttymon    -    0    NO_SAC   /usr/lib/saf/ttymon
# _
```

The previous output indicates the name used to identify the port monitor daemon process (PMTAG), the type of port monitor daemon (PMTYPE), the flags used during startup (FLAGS), the number of times that the sac daemon will restart the daemon if it fails (RCNT), and the status and pathname to its executable file (COMMAND).

You can also use the **sacadm command** to disable a port monitor. To disable the ttymon port monitor (and prevent any logins across virtual terminals), use the `sacadm -d -p contty` command at a command prompt. Conversely, to enable the ttymon port monitor, use the `sacadm -e -p contty` command.

The **pmadm command** is used to view and configure ports monitored by port monitor daemons. To see which ports are monitored by port monitor daemons, use the `pmadm -l` command:

```
# pmadm -l
PMTAG       PMTYPE    SVCTAG    FLGS ID        SCHEME    <PMSPECIFIC
contty      ttymon    2         u    -         login   /dev/vt02 - -
/usr/bin/shserv - console - Login (vt02):   - - - -   #
contty      ttymon    3         u    -         login   /dev/vt03 - -
/usr/bin/shserv - console - Login (vt03):   - - - -   #
contty      ttymon    4         u    -         login   /dev/vt04 - -
/usr/bin/shserv - console - Login (vt04):   - - - -   #
contty      ttymon    5         u    -         login   /dev/vt05 - -
/usr/bin/shserv - console - Login (vt05):   - - - -   #
contty      ttymon    6         u    -         login   /dev/vt06 - -
/usr/bin/shserv - console - Login (vt06):   - - - -   #
contty      ttymon    7         u    -         login   /dev/vt07 - -
/usr/bin/shserv - console - Login (vt07):   - - - -   #
contty      ttymon    8         u    -         login   /dev/vt08 - -
/usr/bin/shserv - console - Login (vt08):   - - - -   #
nbcots      listen    0         -    root      -         - - c - /usr/
ib/saf/nlps_server #NLPS server
tcp         listen    ttdbserverd - root      -         - 100083,1 cd
- /usr/dt/bin/rpc.ttdbserverd #
tcp         listen    0         -    root      -         \x10020ACE000
00000000000000000000 - c - /usr/lib/saf/nlps_server #
tcp         listen    lp        -    root      -         - - p - /var/
pool/lp/fifos/listenS5 #
tcp         listen    lpd       -    root      -         \x10020203000
```

8

```
00000000000000000000 - p - /var/spool/lp/fifos/listenBSD #
tcp        listen    10103    -    nuucp    -    - - c - /usr/
ib/uucp/uucico -r 0 -u nuucp -i TLI #uucp
tcp        listen    cu       u    root     -    - - c - /usr/
ib/saf/ttymon -g -h -m ntty,tirdwr,ldterm #cu
# _
```

**NOTE**

The configuration of the listen and inetd daemons is beyond the scope of this textbook.

The virtual terminals that are monitored by the ttymon daemon are listed in the **/etc/saf/contty/_pmtab** file on UnixWare systems; the first field in this file labels each virtual terminal:

```
# cat /etc/saf/contty/_pmtab
# VERSION=2
2:u::reserved:reserved:login:/dev/vt02:::/usr/bin/shserv::console::Login (vt02)
: :::::#
3:u::reserved:reserved:login:/dev/vt03:::/usr/bin/shserv::console::Login (vt03)
: :::::#
4:u::reserved:reserved:login:/dev/vt04:::/usr/bin/shserv::console::Login (vt04)
: :::::#
5:u::reserved:reserved:login:/dev/vt05:::/usr/bin/shserv::console::Login (vt05)
: :::::#
6:u::reserved:reserved:login:/dev/vt06:::/usr/bin/shserv::console::Login (vt06)
: :::::#
7:u::reserved:reserved:login:/dev/vt07:::/usr/bin/shserv::console::Login (vt07)
: :::::#
8:u::reserved:reserved:login:/dev/vt08:::/usr/bin/shserv::console::Login (vt08)
: :::::#
# _
```

To disable a virtual terminal for login, use the command **pmadm -d -p contty -s <label>** where <label> is the first field of the /etc/saf/contty/_pmtab file. For example, to disable logins on vt08, run the command **pmadm -d -p contty -s 8** at a command prompt. Alternatively, to enable logins on vt08, run the command **pmadm -e -p contty -s 8**.

## CHAPTER SUMMARY

❑ System initialization involves three components: bootstrapping, kernel loading, and daemon initialization.

❑ The bootstrap program and boot loader vary between different UNIX flavors.

◻ The boot loader used to load the UnixWare kernel is the BCP; it displays a [boot] prompt that you can use to specify the operating system to load as well as the options such as the runlevel to enter.

◻ Seven standard runlevels are used to categorize a UNIX system based on the number and type of daemons loaded in memory.

◻ The init daemon is responsible for loading and unloading daemons using its configuration file /etc/inittab.

◻ Scripts that start daemons are typically stored in the etc/init.d directory and loaded at system startup from entries in the /etc/rc*.d directories.

◻ The /etc/inittab file is rebuilt from the file contents of the /etc/conf/init.d directory when the kernel is changed.

◻ The SAF is started by the init daemon and uses port monitor daemons to provide terminals that users can use to log into the system.

**8**

## KEY TERMS

**/etc/conf/bin/idmkinit** — The program that creates a new inittab file using the contents of the /etc/conf/init.d directory.

**/etc/conf/init.d/** — The directory in which files used to rebuild /etc/inittab are stored.

**/etc/conf/init.d/kernel** — The main file used to build the /etc/inittab file.

**/etc/dinit.d/** — The directory that contains the script used to start daemons after runlevels have been reached.

**/etc/init.d/** — The directory that contains a copy of startup scripts such that you may manually start and stop daemons.

**/etc/inittab** — The configuration file for the init daemon.

**/etc/rcn.d/** — The directories used to start and kill daemons upon entering runlevel *n*.

**/etc/saf/_sactab** — The file that lists the port monitor daemons that are loaded by the sac daemon.

**/etc/saf/_sysconfig** — The file used to store configuration information for the sac daemon.

**/etc/saf/contty/_pmtab** — The file that lists the virtual terminals monitored by ttymon.

**/kernel/genunix** — The pathname to the UNIX kernel on Solaris systems.

**/sbin/rcn** — The script that executes files in the /etc/rcn.d/ directories.

**/stand/** — The directory containing the kernel and boot-related files on UnixWare and HP-UX systems.

**/stand/boot** — A file that holds the default variables used by the BCP.

**/stand/bootmsgs** — A file that holds the default boot message variables used by the BCP.

**/stand/unix** — The pathname to the UNIX kernel on UnixWare systems.

**/stand/vmunix** — The pathname to the UNIX kernel on HP-UX systems.

**active partition** — The partition searched by a bootstrap program for a boot loader.

**boot command** — The command used at the BCP [boot] prompt to continue the boot process.

**Boot Command Processor (BCP)** — The boot loader used on UnixWare systems.

**boot device** — A device such as a hard disk that contains a boot loader.

**boot loader** — A program used to load an operating system.

**bootstrapping** — The process where a computer initializes hardware and locates a boot loader after being turned on.

**daemon** — A UNIX system process that provides a certain service.

**dual booting** — The process of booting more than one operating system using a boot loader.

**extended multiuser mode** — Also called runlevel 3; it provides most daemons and a full set of networking daemons.

**inetd** — A port monitor daemon that enables users to log into network services such as FTP and Telnet.

**init command** — The command used to change the operating system from one runlevel to another.

**init (initialize) daemon** — A system utility loaded by the sysproc daemon; it is responsible for starting and stopping other daemons on the system.

**Initial System Loader (ISL)** — The boot loader used on HP-UX systems.

**initstate** — *See* Runlevel.

**listen** — A port monitor daemon that accepts connections from users across a network.

**login** — A program that presents users with the login prompt.

**multiuser mode** — Also called runlevel 2; it provides most daemons and a partial set of networking daemons.

**OpenBoot programmable read-only memory (PROM)** — The boot loader used on Solaris systems.

**pmadm command** — The command used to view and configure ports monitored by port monitor daemons.

**port monitor daemons** — Daemons that enable users to connect to the system via terminals.

**Processor Dependent Code (PDC)** — The bootstrap program used on HP-UX systems.

**runlevel** — A term that defines a certain type and number of daemons on a UNIX system.

**sacadm command** — The command used to view and manage port monitors on the system.

**sched daemon** — The first process started by the UNIX kernel on Solaris systems; it is analogous to the sysproc daemon in UnixWare.

**Service Access Controller (sac) daemon** — The daemon that loads port monitor daemons.

**Service Access Facility (SAF)** — The set of daemons and files on a UnixWare or Solaris system that enable users to gain access to the system.

**show command** — The command used at the BCP [boot] prompt to show the values of BCP variables.

**shserv** — The utility called by the login program after a successful login to provide the user with a shell.

**single-user mode** — Also called runlevel 1; it provides a single terminal and a limited set of services.

**swapper daemon** — The first process started by the UNIX kernel in HP-UX; it is analogous to the sysproc daemon in UnixWare.

**sysproc daemon** — The first process started by the UNIX kernel in UnixWare; it is responsible for starting the init daemon, scheduling processes and managing information transferred to and from the swap slice.

**telinit command** — A symbolic link to the init command.

**ttymon** — The port monitor daemon that enables users to log into virtual terminals and serial connections.

**wall (warn all) command** — The command used to send a message to all users logged into the system.

8

---

## Review Questions

1. You can interact with boot loaders and pass them commands to alter the boot process. True or False?

2. When a computer first powers on, what does it typically perform?
   a. POST
   b. CMOS
   c. BIOS
   d. BCP

3. Which runlevel is used when shutting down the system?
   a. 1
   b. 6
   c. 0
   d. S

4. What file does init reference on startup to determine what to configure for a given runlevel?
   a. /etc/initstate
   b. /inittab
   c. /etc/init
   d. /etc/inittab

5. What does action respawn indicate for a process when specified in the /etc/inittab file?

   a. Create it.

   b. Kill it.

   c. Cause it to regenerate should it be killed.

   d. There is no such value in /etc/inittab.

6. What does the MBR point to that holds part or all of a boot loader?

   a. POST

   b. CMOS

   c. BIOS

   d. active partition

7. What file would you edit to change the messages the system can display to the screen during the boot process on a UnixWare system?

   a. /stand/boot

   b. /inittab/bootmsgs

   c. /boot/msgs

   d. /stand/bootmsgs

8. The /etc/dinit.d directory, which contains scripts that load less essential daemons after user login, was created to speed up the boot process. True or False?

9. Which runlevel do UNIX systems boot to by default when they enable all services available?

   a. 1

   b. 6

   c. 0

   d. 3

10. Only one kernel can be available to load on any given UNIX system. True or False?

11. What is the name of the directory that contains the configuration information for runlevel 2?

    a. /etc/rc2.d

    b. /rc.d/rc2.d

    c. /etc/rc.d/2

    d. /etc/init/rc2.d

    e. /etc/inittab/rc2.d

12. In what directory is the UNIX kernel stored on a UnixWare system?

    a. /boot

    b. /kernel

c. /bin

d. /

e. /stand

13. The order in which devices are checked for boot information on a computer is fixed and not changeable. True or False?

14. The first process generated on a UnixWare system is _____.

a. initstate

b. inittab

c. init

d. sysproc

15. In UnixWare, what do you enter at the BCP [boot] prompt to continue the boot process? (Choose all that apply.)

a. boot

b. g

c. b

d. start

e. init

f. go

16. Which of the following will boot a kernel called emerg on a UnixWare system from the BCP [boot] prompt? (Choose all that apply.)

a. b hd(0,emerg)

b. BOOTPROG=emerg

c. boot

d. BOOTDEV=emerg

17. Which runlevel in UnixWare specifies to reboot the system?

a. 1

b. 6

c. 0

d. s

e. r

18. What command is used to view the variable values used by BCP during the boot process on a UnixWare system?

a. var

b. boot

c. show

d. echo $BOOTVAR

8

19. Your system has more than one operating system installed. From the BCP [boot] prompt, how do you specify to execute the boot loader that resides on the second partition of third hard disk drive?

    a. boot hd(2,3)

    b. boot hd (2,2)

    c. boot (3,2)

    d. boot hd–3/2

20. What port monitor is used to allow users to log into virtual terminals?

    a. contty

    b. listen

    c. sacadm

    d. pmadm

    e. ttymon

21. What command will cause the system to enter single-user mode?

    a. init 0

    b. initstate 1

    c. init 1

    d. initstate 5

22. The timeout value in the BCP configuration file is measured in _____.

    a. seconds

    b. 1/10 of a minute

    c. 1/10 of a second

    d. 1/100 of a second

    e. minutes

23. Scripts starting with an *S* in the /etc/rc2.d/ directory will start the services they reference upon entering runlevel 2. True or False?

24. What command in UnixWare can be used to display your current runlevel, most recent runlevel, and the number of times the present run has been invoked?

    a. runlevel

    b. init –r

    c. initstate

    d. who –r

25. The files in the /etc/rcn.d directory for the appropriate runlevel (*n*) are executed in _____ order.

    a. numeric

    b. ASCII

c. alphabetic

d. the order in which they are listed, top to bottom

26. What is the name of the default kernel on a UnixWare system?

a. kernel

b. unix

c. sysproc

d. genunix

e. vmunix

27. Once loaded, what daemon is responsible for loading all other daemons, thus bringing the system up to a usable state?

a. initstate

b. genesis

c. inittab

d. init

e. sysproc

28. What command is used to enable, disable, and view port monitors?

a. contty

b. listen

c. sacadm

d. pmadm

e. ttymon

29. Where are the kernels available to be booted stored on a UnixWare system?

a. /

b. /boot

c. /bin

d. /stand

e. /unix

30. How do you access the boot prompt on a UnixWare system?

a. Press Ctrl+Alt+Del simultaneously.

b. Press Del immediately after powering in the system.

c. Press Enter once the UnixWare splash screen is displayed.

d. Use the command init –boot.

# HANDS-ON PROJECTS

These projects should be completed in the order given. All hands-on projects should take a total of three hours to complete. The requirement for this lab includes:

❑ A computer with UnixWare 7.1.1 installed according to Hands-on Project 2-2

## Project 8-1

In this hands-on project, you will explore runlevels and the /etc/inittab file, as well as the contents of the /etc/rcn.d, /etc/dinit.d, and /etc/init.d directories.

1. Switch to a command-line terminal (vt02) by pressing **Ctrl+Alt+F2**, and log into the terminal using the username **root** and the password **secret**.

2. At the command prompt, type **who –r** and press **Enter**. What is your current runlevel? What is the most recent runlevel?

3. At the command prompt, type **more /etc/inittab** and press **Enter**. Navigate through the file using the Enter key. What line in this file determines the default runlevel at boot time? Can this be changed?

    What line indicates that the /sbin/rc0 script is run upon entering runlevel 0?

    What line indicates that the /sbin/rc1 script is run upon entering runlevel 1?

    What line indicates that the /sbin/rc2 script is run upon entering runlevel 2 or 3?

    What line indicates that the /sbin/rc3 script is run upon entering runlevel 3?

    What line indicates that the /sbin/rc0 script is run upon entering runlevel 5?

    What line indicates that the /sbin/rc0 script is run upon entering runlevel 6?

    What line indicates that the /sbin/dinit script is run upon entering runlevel 2 or 3?

    What do these scripts do?

    Press **q** to exit the more utility.

4. At the command prompt, type **ls /etc/rc2.d** and press **Enter**. What files do you see? When will these files be executed and in what order? Are there more files that start with *K* rather than *S*? Are there any that will be ignored? Explain.

5. At the command prompt, type **ls /etc/rc3.d** and press **Enter**. What file do you see? Is there a big difference between runlevel 2 and runlevel 3 on your system? If you were to boot your system to runlevel 2, what service would not be available?

6. At the command prompt, type **ls /etc/rc1.d** and press **Enter**. What files do you see? When will these files be executed? Are there more files that start with *K* rather than *S*? Explain.

7. At the command prompt, type **ls /etc/rc0.d** and press **Enter**. What files do you see? When are they executed? What character does each file start with? Why?

8. At the command prompt, type **ls /etc/dinit.d** and press **Enter**. What files do you see? When will these files be executed? Are there more files that start with *K* rather than *S*? Explain.

9. At the command prompt, type **init 2** and press **Enter**. Was anything displayed on your terminal screen? Are any daemons started? Are any daemons stopped? Why? Are you required to log in? Explain.

10. Next type **who –r** at the command prompt and press **Enter**. What is your current runlevel? What is the most recent runlevel?

11. At the command prompt, type **init 1** and press **Enter**. What is displayed on your terminal screen? Are any daemons started? Are any daemons stopped? Why? Are you required to log in? Why?

12. Next type **who –r** at the command prompt and press **Enter**. What is your current runlevel? What is the most recent runlevel?

13. At the command prompt, type **init 3** and press **Enter**. What is displayed on your terminal screen? Are any daemons started? Are any daemons stopped? Why? What is displayed after switching to runlevel 3?

14. Switch to a command-line terminal (vt02) by pressing **Ctrl+Alt+F2**, and log into the terminal using the username **root** and the password **secret**.

15. Next, type **who –r** at the command prompt and press **Enter**. What is your current runlevel? What is the most recent runlevel?

16. At the command prompt, type **ls /etc/init.d** and press **Enter**. What files do you see? Do they start with *S* or *K*? Why?

17. At the command prompt, type **ls –li /etc/init.d/inetinit** and press **Enter** to view the inode number for the script that starts and stops your TCP/IP network. What number do you see?

18. At the command prompt, type **ls –li /etc/rc2.d/S69inet** and press **Enter** to view the inode number for the script that starts your TCP/IP network upon entering runlevel 2 or 3. What number do you see? Compare this to the inode number in the previous step. Explain.

19. At the command prompt, type **ls –li /etc/rc0.d/K69inet** and press **Enter** to view the inode number for the script that stops your TCP/IP network upon entering runlevel 0, 5, or 6. What number do you see? Compare this to the inode number in the previous step. Explain.

20. Type **exit** and press **Enter** to log out of your shell.

**HANDS-ON PROJECTS**

## Project 8-2

In this hands-on project, you will start and stop system services as well as configure them to start and stop automatically upon entering certain runlevels.

1. Switch to a command-line terminal (vt02) by pressing **Ctrl+Alt+F2**, and log into the terminal using the username **root** and the password **secret**.

2. At the command prompt, type **/etc/init.d/sendmail stop** and press **Enter** to stop the sendmail daemon.

8

3. At the command prompt, type **/etc/init.d/sendmail start** and press **Enter** to start the sendmail daemon.

4. At the command prompt, type **cat /etc/init.d/sendmail** and press **Enter**. Do you see any lines that accept the start and stop arguments?

5. At the command prompt, type **vi /etc/init.d/sample** and press **Enter** to create a fake daemon startup script in the /etc/init.d directory.

6. Enter the following information in the vi editor. When you are finished, save your changes and exit the vi editor.

**NOTE**

The following script will print information to the file /startfile when executed with the start argument and will print information to the file /stopfile when executed with the stop argument:

```
case "$1" in
start)
        echo The sample daemon has started at `date` > /startfile
        ;;
stop)
        echo The sample daemon has stopped at `date` > /stopfile
        ;;
esac
```

7. At the command prompt, type **ln /etc/init.d/sample /etc/rc0.d/K80sample** and press **Enter**. What does this command do? What will happen when you enter runlevel 0, 5, or 6?

8. At the command prompt, type **ln /etc/init.d/sample /etc/rc1.d/K80sample** and press **Enter**. What does this command do? What will happen when you enter runlevel 1?

9. At the command prompt, type **ln /etc/init.d/sample /etc/rc2.d/S80sample** and press **Enter**. What does this command do? What will happen when you enter runlevel 2 or 3?

10. At the command prompt, type **shutdown –g0 –y –i6** and press **Enter** to reboot the system. Allow the system to boot normally.

11. When the system has booted successfully, switch to a command-line terminal (vt02) by pressing **Ctrl+Alt+F2**, and log into the terminal using the username **root** and the password **secret**.

12. At the command prompt, type **cat /stopfile** and press **Enter**. What are the contents? Why?

13. At the command prompt, type **cat /startfile** and press **Enter**. What are the contents? Why?

14. Type **exit** and press **Enter** to log out of your shell.

## Project 8-3

In this hands-on project, you will change the default runlevel by editing the /ec/inittab file.

1. Switch to a command-line terminal (vt02) by pressing **Ctrl+Alt+F2**, and log into the terminal using the username **root** and the password **secret**.

2. At the command prompt, type **ls /etc/conf/init.d** and press **Enter**. What files are listed? View the contents of each file. Which file contains the most information present in the /etc/inittab file? Why?

3. At the command prompt, type **vi /etc/conf/init.d/kernel** and press **Enter**. Change the line:

   ```
   is:3:initdefault:
   ```

   such that it reads:

   ```
   is:2:initdefault:
   ```

   When you are finished, save your changes and exit the vi editor.

4. At the command prompt, type **/etc/conf/bin/idmkinit** to create a new inittab file in the /etc/conf/cf.d/ directory.

5. At the command prompt, type **cp /etc/conf/cf.d/inittab /etc** and press **Enter** to overwrite the existing /etc/inittab file.

6. At the command prompt, type **init q** and press **Enter** to force the init daemon to query the new /etc/inittab file.

7. At the command prompt, type **shutdown –g0 –y –i6** and press **Enter** to reboot the system. Allow the system to boot normally.

8. When the system has booted successfully, switch to a command-line terminal (vt02) by pressing **Ctrl+Alt+F2**, and log into the terminal using the username **root** and the password **secret**.

9. At the command prompt, type **who –r** and press **Enter**. What is your current runlevel? Why?

10. Type **exit** and press **Enter** to log out of your shell.

## Project 8-4

In this hands-on project, you will interact with and configure the BCP.

1. Switch to a command-line terminal (vt02) by pressing **Ctrl+Alt+F2**, and log into the terminal using the username **root** and the password **secret**.

2. At the command prompt, type **ls /stand** and press **Enter**. What files are listed? Which one is the default UNIX kernel? Is there another UNIX kernel available for use?

3. At the command prompt, type **more /stand/help.txt** and press **Enter**. Which option to the show command will display all variables including message variables? Navigate through the rest of the help.txt file and exit the more utility when you are finished.

4. At the command prompt, type **shutdown –g0 –y –i6** and press **Enter** to reboot the system. When the UnixWare 7 splash screen appears, press the **Enter** to obtain a [boot] prompt.

5. At the [boot] prompt, type the command **dir** and press **Enter**. Do you recognize the files displayed? What filesystem are you viewing? Has the UNIX kernel been loaded yet?

6. At the [boot] prompt, type the command **help** and press **Enter**. Do you recognize the output on the terminal screen? What file is being displayed? Press **Enter** until the file is no longer displayed on the terminal screen.

7. At the [boot] prompt, type the command **show** and press **Enter**. What is the default UNIX kernel loaded if one is not specified? How many seconds do you have to interrupt the BCP before this kernel is loaded?

8. At the [boot] prompt, type the command **show –a** and press **Enter**. Do you recognize any of the boot message variables? When are they displayed? Press **Enter** to finish displaying the variable list.

9. At the [boot] prompt, type the command **INITSTATE=1** and press **Enter**. Does anything happen? Next, type **show** at the [boot] prompt and press **Enter**. Was the INITSTATE variable set properly? If you continue the boot process, what runlevel will be entered?

10. At the [boot] prompt, type the command **boot** and press **Enter**. What other commands could you use to continue the boot process from the [boot] prompt?

11. When the system has booted, log into the terminal using the username **root** and the password **secret**.

12. At the command prompt, type **who –r** and press **Enter**. What runlevel are you in and why?

13. At the command prompt, type **grep initdefault /etc/inittab** and press **Enter**. If you reboot the system now and do not interrupt the BCP, what runlevel will be entered?

14. At the command prompt, type **vi /stand/boot** and press **Enter**. Add the following line to the bottom of the file:

    ```
    INITSTATE=3
    ```

    When you are finished, save your changes and exit the vi editor.

15. At the command prompt, type **vi /stand/bootmsgs** and press **Enter**. Edit the line that reads:

    ```
    RESTRICTED RIGHTS LEGEND:\
    ```

    such that it reads:

    ```
    THE NEW RESTRICTED RIGHTS LEGEND:\
    ```

    When you are finished, save your changes and exit the vi editor.

16. At the command prompt, type **shutdown -g0 -y -i6** and press **Enter** to reboot the system. Do not interrupt the BCP; instead, observe the boot messages displayed during the boot process. Do you see your modified copyright message? Why?

17. When the system has fully loaded, switch to a command-line terminal (vt02) by pressing **Ctrl+Alt+F2**, and log into the terminal using the username **root** and the password **secret**.

18. At the command prompt, type **who -r** and press **Enter**. What runlevel are you in and why?

19. Type **exit** and press **Enter** to log out of your shell.

## Project 8-5

In this hands-on project, you will view and change the configuration of SAF.

1. Switch to a command-line terminal (vt02) by pressing **Ctrl+Alt+F2**, and log into the terminal using the username **root** and the password **secret**.

2. At the command prompt, type **grep sac /etc/inittab** and press **Enter**. In which runlevels is the sac daemon started?

3. At the command prompt, type **grep ttymon /etc/inittab** and press **Enter**. In which runlevel is the ttymon daemon started directly from /etc/inittab? Explain.

4. At the command prompt, type **sacadm -l** and press **Enter**. What port monitor daemons are currently active? What does each do?

5. At the command prompt, type **pmadm -l | more** and press **Enter**. Navigate through the file using the Enter key. What ports are monitored on the system? What virtual terminals are monitored on the system? Press **q** to exit the more utility.

6. Press the **Ctrl+Alt+F8** key combination to switch to vt08. Next, press the **Ctrl+Alt+F9** key combination to switch to vt09. Why were you not successful? Press the **Ctrl+Alt+F2** key combination to switch back to vt02.

7. At the command prompt, type **vi /etc/saf/contty/_pmtab** and press **Enter**. Add the following line to the bottom of the file:

    ```
    9:u::reserved:reserved:login:/dev/vt09:::/usr/bin/shserv::console::Login(vt09)\:
    :::::#
    ```

    When you are finished, save your changes and exit the vi editor.

8. At the command prompt, type **pmadm -e -p contty -s 9** and press **Enter**.

9. Press the **Ctrl+Alt+F9** key combination to switch to vt09, and log into the terminal with the username **root** and password **secret**. Why were you successful?

10. Type **exit** and press **Enter** to log out of your shell.

11. Press the **Ctrl+Alt+F2** key combination to switch back to vt02.

12. At the command prompt, type **pmadm -d -p contty -s 9** and press **Enter**. What does this command do?

13. Press the **Ctrl+Alt+F9** key combination to switch to vt09, and attempt to log into the terminal with the username **root** and password **secret**. Why were you not successful?

14. Press the **Ctrl+Alt+F2** key combination to switch back to vt02.

15. At the command prompt, type **pmadm -e -p contty -s 9** and press **Enter**. What does this command do?

16. Press the **Ctrl+Alt+F9** key combination to switch to vt09, and attempt to log into the terminal with the username **root** and password **secret**. Why were you successful?

17. Type **exit** and press **Enter** to log out of your shell.

18. Press the **Ctrl+Alt+F2** key combination to switch back to vt02.

19. Type **exit** and press **Enter** to log out of your shell.

## DISCOVERY EXERCISES

1. Describe what would happen if you edited the /etc/inittab file and changed the line that read id:3:initdefault: to read id:6:initdefault:.

2. You have created a daemon called mydaemon that performs database management tasks on the system; however, you want to have this daemon start only in runlevel 1. This daemon should not exist in memory when the system is in any other runlevel. What directory should you place this daemon in? What links should you create to this daemon? Write the commands you would use to have this daemon start and stop automatically on the system.

3. Provided you have a copy of the Windows operating system, install it on a hard disk drive leaving adequate free space outside the Windows partition for the installation of UNIX. Next, install UnixWare and specify a UNIX partition on the second primary partition. When you are finished, what operating system is loaded by default? What command can you use at the BCP [boot] prompt to load the Windows operating system? Try this command at the [boot] prompt to verify your answer.

4. Runlevel number 4 is typically not used on most UNIX systems. What file defines this runlevel? How could you start daemons in this runlevel if you needed to? Outline the steps required to utilize runlevel 4; it should load all daemons from runlevel 3 plus some special database daemons.

5. Examine the /sbin/bcheckrc shell script. What does this script do? What keyword is in the action field of /etc/inittab and what does this action indicate? Why must this file be run before the files in the /etc/rc*.d directories? Examine some other scripts that are executed from /etc/inittab using the same action. Briefly describe what each script does to initialize the system before most daemons are loaded.

## CHAPTER 9

# THE SHELL ENVIRONMENT

> **After reading this chapter and completing the exercises, you will be able to:**
> ♦ Understand the file descriptors stdin, stdout, and stderr
> ♦ Redirect the input and output of a command
> ♦ Pipe the output of one command to another
> ♦ Identify and manipulate common shell environment variables
> ♦ Create and export new shell variables
> ♦ Use command aliases to create shortcuts to commands
> ♦ Edit environment files to create variables upon shell startup

A solid understanding of shell features is vital to both administrators and users as they interact with the shell on a daily basis. The first part of this chapter explores the different shells found on UNIX systems and their features. Next, you will discover how the shell can manipulate command input and output using redirection and pipe shell metacharacters. Finally, you will explore the different types of variables present in a shell after login as well as their purpose and usage.

## SHELL FEATURES

Recall from Chapter 3 that your shell is responsible for providing your user interface and interpreting commands entered on the command line. In addition to this, your shell may offer other features; however, these features differ from shell to shell. The four most common shells used on UNIX systems are the Bourne, POSIX, Korn, and C shells; Table 9-1 lists their features.

**Table 9-1**    Common shell features

| Feature | Bourne | Korn | POSIX | C |
|---------|--------|------|-------|---|
| I/O redirection and piping | Yes | Yes | Yes | Yes |
| Environment variables | Yes | Yes | Yes | Yes |
| Command aliases | No | Yes | Yes | Yes |
| Integer arithmetic | No | Yes | Yes | No |
| Command history | No | Yes | Yes | Yes |
| Background process control | No | Yes | Yes | Yes |
| Command-line editing | No | Yes | Yes | Yes |

As shown in Table 9-1, all shells support I/O **redirection** and piping as well as environment variables. These features will be discussed in separate sections throughout this chapter.

In addition, all shells enable users to run commands in the background. This enables you to execute other commands without having to wait for the previous command to finish. However, only the Korn, POSIX, and C shells can manipulate these background commands after execution; this feature is called **background process control** and is discussed in Chapter 10. The Korn and POSIX shells also enable you to perform integer arithmetic using the let shell function; this is useful when creating shell scripts to automate tasks.

The Korn, POSIX, and C shells offer features such as command aliases, command history, and command-line editing. **Command aliases** are special **variables** used to execute commands; they are discussed in the section "Other Variables." The **command history** feature enables you to recall previous commands typed on the command line. For example, to see the last five commands entered on the command line in a Korn shell, use the `history` command followed by the `-5` option:

```
# history -5
82      du -ks /dev
83      ls
84      df
85      cd /etc
86      ls -F
87      history -5
# _
```

To recall a previously entered command, use the r command followed by the number displayed by the `history` command. To recall command 84 from the previous output, use the following:

```
# r 84
df
/                     (/dev/root   ): 29658800 blocks 3954489 files
/stand                (/dev/stand  ):    37029 blocks      78 files
/proc                 (/proc       ):        0 blocks     393 files
/dev/fd               (/dev/fd     ):        0 blocks       0 files
/system/processor     (/processorfs):        0 blocks       0 files
/tmp                  (/tmp        ):    20480 blocks   32766 files
/var/tmp              (/var/tmp    ):    81920 blocks   32766 files
/dev/_tcp             (/dev/_tcp   ):        0 blocks       0 files
# _
```

**Command-line editing** enables you to use editor commands to correct mistakes on a command line without having to use the Backspace key to remove characters. This feature is already enabled in the C shell and uses common key combinations from the emacs editor to edit command-line text. For the Korn and POSIX shells, you must first run the command `set -o <editorname>` to choose the editor from which common key combinations are to be taken. To enable command-line editing in the Korn shell and use key combinations from the vi editor, you can do the following:

```
# set -o vi
# _
```

Now, press Esc to enter command mode and use the *h* and *l* keys to move the cursor on the command line left and right, respectively. Following this, you can use standard vi keys to manipulate text; for example, you can use the *x* key to delete a character on the command line or the *i* key to enter insert mode where you can insert characters.

The shell that you receive after login is defined in the properties of your user account (discussed in Chapter 13); however, you can start a new shell after login by executing the appropriate file on the command line. The pathnames to these files on a UnixWare system are as follows:

- /usr/bin/sh (Bourne shell)
- /usr/bin/posix/sh (POSIX shell)
- /usr/bin/ksh (Korn shell)
- /usr/bin/csh (C shell)

## COMMAND INPUT AND OUTPUT

Your shell can manipulate command input and output, provided you specify certain shell metacharacters on the command line alongside the command. Command input and output are represented by labels known as **file descriptors**. Each command that can be manipulated by your shell has three file descriptors:

- Standard input (stdin)
- Standard output (stdout)
- Standard error (stderr)

**Standard input** refers to the information that is processed by the command during execution and is often in the form of user input typed on the keyboard. **Standard output** refers to the normal output of a command, whereas **standard error** refers to any error messages generated by the command. Both standard output and standard error are displayed on the terminal screen by default. Figure 9-1 depicts all three components.

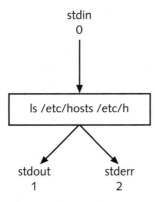

**Figure 9-1**   File descriptors

Figure 9-1 also shows that each file descriptor is represented by a number; stdin is represented by the number 0, stdout is represented by the number 1, and stderr is represented by the number 2.

Although all three components are available to any command, not all commands use every component. The `ls /etc/hosts /etc/h` command used in Figure 9-1 gives standard output (the listing of the /etc/hosts file) and standard error (an error message indicating that the /etc/h file does not exist) to the terminal screen, as shown in the following output:

```
# ls /etc/hosts /etc/h
UX:ls: ERROR: Cannot access /etc/h: No such file or directory
/etc/hosts
# _
```

## Redirection

You can use the shell to redirect standard output and standard error from the terminal screen to a file on the filesystem using the > shell metacharacter followed by the absolute or relative pathname of the file. To redirect only the standard output to a file called goodoutput for the command used in Figure 9-1, simply append the number of the file descriptor (1) followed by the redirection symbol > and the file to redirect the standard output to (goodoutput), as shown in the following output:

```
# ls /etc/hosts /etc/h1>goodoutput
UX:ls: ERROR: Cannot access /etc/h: No such file or directory
# _
```

 You may put a space character after the > metacharacter, but it is not necessary.

Notice from the previous output that the standard error was still displayed to the terminal screen as it was not redirected to a file. The listing of /etc/hosts was not displayed as it was redirected to a file called goodoutput in the current directory. If the goodoutput file did not exist prior to running the command in the previous output, then it will be created automatically; however, if the goodoutput file did exist prior to the redirection, then the shell will clear its contents before executing the command. To see if the standard output was redirected to the goodoutput file, run the following commands:

```
# ls g*
goodoutput
# cat goodoutput
/etc/hosts
# _
```

Similarly, you can redirect the standard error of a command to a file; just specify file descriptor number 2, as shown in the following output:

```
# ls /etc/hosts /etc/h  2>badoutput
/etc/hosts
# cat badoutput
UX:ls: ERROR: Cannot access /etc/h: No such file or directory
# _
```

In the previous output, only the standard error was redirected to a file called badoutput; thus, the standard output (a listing of /etc/hosts) was displayed on the terminal screen.

Because redirecting the standard output to a file for later use is more common than redirecting the standard error to a file, the shell assumes standard output in the absence of a numeric file descriptor:

```
# ls /etc/hosts /etc/h  >goodoutput
UX:ls: ERROR: Cannot access /etc/h: No such file or directory
# cat goodoutput
/etc/hosts
# _
```

You can also redirect both standard output and standard error to separate files at the same time, as shown in the following output:

```
# ls /etc/hosts /etc/h  >goodoutput  2>badoutput
# cat goodoutput
/etc/hosts
# cat badoutput
UX:ls: ERROR: Cannot access /etc/h: No such file or directory
# _
```

**NOTE**

The order of redirection on the command line does not matter; the command ls /etc/hosts /etc/h >goodoutput 2>badoutput is the same as ls /etc/hosts /etc/h 2>badoutput >goodoutput.

**TIP**

To avoid displaying error messages that are generated by a command, simply redirect the stderr to the file /dev/null. Any data sent to /dev/null will be deleted.

It is important to use separate filenames to hold the contents of standard output and standard error; using the same filename for both would result in a loss of data since the system writes to the file at the same time:

```
# ls /etc/hosts /etc/h  >goodoutput  2>goodoutput
# cat goodoutput
/etc/hosts
R: Cannot access /etc/h: No such file or directory
# _
```

To redirect both standard output and standard error to the same file without any loss of data, you must use special notation. To specify that standard output be sent to the file goodoutput and standard error be sent to the same place as standard output, do the following:

```
# ls /etc/hosts /etc/h  >goodoutput  2>&1
# cat goodoutput
UX:ls: ERROR: Cannot access /etc/h: No such file or directory
/etc/hosts
# _
```

Alternatively, you can specify that the standard error be sent to the file badoutput and the standard output be sent to the same place as standard error:

```
# ls /etc/hosts /etc/h  2>badoutput  >&2
# cat badoutput
UX:ls: ERROR: Cannot access /etc/h: No such file or directory
/etc/hosts
# _
```

In all of the examples used earlier, the contents of the files used to store the output from commands were cleared prior to use by the shell. The following output shows another example of this when redirecting the standard output of the date command to the file dateoutput:

```
# date >dateoutput
# cat dateoutput
Mon May  4 13:57:05 EST 2003
# date >dateoutput
# cat dateoutput
Mon May  4 13:58:11 EST 2003
# _
```

To prevent the file from being cleared by the shell and append output to the existing output, specify two > metacharacters alongside the file descriptor:

```
# date >dateoutput
# cat dateoutput
Mon May  4 13:58:40 EST 2003
# date >>dateoutput
# cat dateoutput
Mon May  4 13:58:40 EST 2003
Mon May  4 13:59:55 EST 2003
# _
```

Also, you can redirect a file to the standard input of a command using the < metacharacter. Because only one file descriptor is available for input, it is not necessary to specify the number 0 before the < metacharacter to indicate the standard input, as shown in the following output:

```
# cat </etc/hosts
#ident   "@(#)hosts        1.2"
#ident "$Header: /sms/sinixV5.4es/rcs/s19-full/usr/src/cmd/cmd-
#inet/etc/hosts,v1.1 91/02/28 16:30:32 ccs Exp $"
#
# Internet host table
#
127.0.0.1        localhost        unix1
# _
```

In the previous output, the shell located and sent the /etc/hosts file to the cat command as the standard input. Since the cat command normally takes the filename to be displayed as an argument on the command line (that is, cat /etc/hosts), you do not need to use standard input redirection with the cat command as you did in the previous example; however, some commands on the UNIX system only accept files when they are passed by the shell through standard input. The **tr command** is one such command that can be used to replace characters in a file sent via standard input. To translate all of the lowercase *l* characters in the /etc/hosts file to uppercase *L* characters, run the following command:

```
# tr l L /etc/hosts
UX:tr: ERROR: Incorrect usage
UX:tr: TO FIX: Usage:
        tr [-cs] string1 string2
        tr -s[-c] string1
        tr -d[-c] string1
        tr -ds[-c] string1 string2
# tr l L </etc/hosts
#ident   "@(#)hosts       1.2"
#ident "$Header: /sms/sinixV5.4es/rcs/s19-fuLL/usr/src/cmd/cmd-
#inet/etc/hosts,v1.1 91/02/28 16:30:32 ccs Exp $"
#
# Internet host tabLe
#
127.0.0.1        LocaLhost        unix1
# _
```

The previous command does not modify the /etc/hosts file; it just takes a copy of the /etc/hosts file, manipulates it, and then sends the standard output to the terminal screen. To save a copy of the standard output for later use, you can use both standard input and standard output redirection together:

```
# tr l L </etc/hosts >newhosts
# cat newhosts
#ident   "@(#)hosts       1.2"
#ident "$Header: /sms/sinixV5.4es/rcs/s19-fuLL/usr/src/cmd/cmd-
#inet/etc/hosts,v1.1 91/02/28 16:30:32 ccs Exp $"
#
# Internet host tabLe
#
127.0.0.1        LocaLhost        unix1
# _
```

As with redirecting standard output and standard error in the same command, you should use different filenames when redirecting standard input and standard output. This is because the shell clears a file that already exists before performing the redirection. Here is an example:

```
# sort <newhosts>newhosts
# cat newhosts
# _
```

The newhosts file has no contents when displayed in the previous output. Since the shell saw that output redirection was indicated on the command line, it cleared the contents of the file newhosts, and then sorted the blank file and saved the output (nothing in our example) into the file newhosts. Because of this feature of shell redirection, UNIX administrators commonly use the command >filename at the command prompt to clear the contents of a file.

**NOTE**

The contents of logfiles are typically cleared periodically using the command >/path/to/logfile.

Table 9-2 provides a summary of the different types of redirection shown in this section.

**Table 9-2**  Common examples of redirection

| Command | Description |
|---|---|
| command  1>file<br>command   >file | The standard output of the command is sent to a file instead of the terminal screen. |
| command  2>file | The standard error of the command is sent to a file instead of the terminal screen. |
| command  1>fileA<br>2>fileB<br>command   >fileA<br>2>fileB | The standard output of the command is sent to fileA instead of the terminal screen, and the standard error of the command is sent to fileB instead of the terminal screen. |
| command  1>file  2>&1<br>command   >file  2>&1<br>command  1>&2  2>file<br>command   >&2  2>file | Both the standard output and the standard error are sent to the same file instead of the terminal screen. |
| command  1>>file<br>command   >>file | The standard output of the command is appended to a file instead of being sent to the terminal screen. |
| command  2>>file | The standard error of the command is appended to a file instead of being sent to the terminal screen. |
| command  0<file<br>command   <file | The standard input of a command is taken from a file. |

## Pipes

Note from Table 9-2 that redirection only occurs from a command to a file, and vice versa. You can also send the standard output of one command to another command as standard input. To do this, use the | shell metacharacter and specify commands on either side. The shell will then send the standard output of the command on the left to the command on the right, which then interprets the information as standard input. Figure 9-2 depicts this process.

**NOTE**

The string of commands that includes the I metacharacter is commonly referred to as a **pipe**.

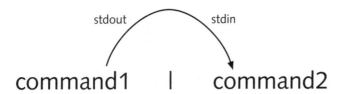

stdout          stdin

## command1   |   command2

**Figure 9-2** Sending information across a pipe

For example, the standard output of the `ls -l /etc` command is too large to fit on one terminal screen. To send the standard output of this command to the **more** command, which views standard input page by page, use the following command:

```
# ls -l /etc | more
total 1722
-rw-rw-r--    1 root  sys     4619 Sep  2 09:24 Odevice.tab
-r-xr-xr-x    1 root  sys       25 Sep  1 19:18 TIMEZONE
drwxrwxr-x    8 root  sys     2048 Sep  1 19:21 TZ
drwxrwxr-x    2 adm   adm       96 Sep  1 19:21 acct
-r--r--r--    1 root  sys     1405 Apr  3  1998 addrpool.samp
-rw-r--r--    1 bin   bin     3488 Apr  3  1998 admpe.tlib
-rw-r--r--    1 bin   bin      170 Apr  3  1998 admpe.tndx
drwxr-xr-x    2 bin   bin       96 Sep  1 19:26 ap
lrwxrwxrwx    1 root  sys       14 Sep  1 19:22 autopush
lrwxrwxrwx    1 root  sys       14 Sep  1 19:22 bcheckrc
-r--r--r--    1 root  sys     9216 Apr  7  1998 boot
lrwxrwxrwx    1 root  sys       18 Sep  1 19:33 bootptab
lrwxrwxrwx    1 root  sys       15 Sep  1 19:22 brand
lrwxrwxrwx    1 root  sys        9 Sep  1 19:22 brc
-rw-r--r--    1 root  sys      828 Apr  7  1998 bupsched
-rw-rw-r--    1 root  sys       10 Apr  7  1998 checklist
lrwxrwxrwx    1 root  sys       16 Sep  1 19:39 chroot
-rwxr-xr-x    1 bin   bin      173 Oct 12  1999 clean_screen
Standard input
```

**NOTE**

You do not need to insert spaces around the | metacharacter; the commands `ls -l /etc|more` and `ls -l /etc | more` are equivalent.

A common use of piping is to reduce the amount of information displayed on the terminal screen from commands that reveal too much information. Recall the **prtvtoc** command used earlier:

```
# prtvtoc /dev/rdsk/c0b0t0d0s0
slice 0:     DISK      permissions:  VALID UNMOUNTABLE
   starting sector: 63 (cyl 0)  length: 33543657 (2088.0 cyls)
slice 1:     ROOT      permissions:  VALID
   starting sector: 385560 (cyl 24) length: 32515560 (2024.0 cyls)
```

```
slice 2:      SWAP      permissions:  VALID UNMOUNTABLE
   starting sector: 64260 (cyl 4)    length: 321300 (20.00 cls)
slice 7:      BOOT      permissions:  VALID UNMOUNTABLE
   starting sector: 63 (cyl 0)       length: 34 (0.00 cyls)
slice 8:      ALT SEC/TRK  permissions:   VALID UNMOUNTABLE
   starting sector: 97 (cyl 0)       length: 15968 (0.99 cyl)
slice 10:     STAND     permissions:    VALID
   starting sector: 16065 (cyl 1)    length: 48195 (3.00 cyl)
slice 15:     VOLPRIVATE    permissions:    VALID UNMOUNTABLE
   starting sector: 32901120 (cyl 2048)  length: 16065 (.00 cyls)
Total disk size is 2088 cylinders (16378.8 MB)
# _
```

To find out which slice number is used for the swap slice, send the standard output of the prtvtoc command to the **grep (Global Regular Expression Print) command** as standard input, as shown in the following output:

```
# prtvtoc /dev/rdsk/c0b0t0d0s0 | grep SWAP
slice 2:      SWAP      permissions:  VALID UNMOUNTABLE
# _
```

The **grep** command in the previous output receives the full output from the **prtvtoc** command and then displays only those lines that have SWAP in them. The **grep** command normally takes two arguments; the first specifies the text to search for and the second specifies the filename(s) to search within. This **grep** command requires no second argument since the material to search comes from standard input (the **prtvtoc** command) instead of a file.

Furthermore, you can use more than one | metacharacter on the command line to pipe information from one command to another command in much the same fashion as an assembly line in a factory. A manufacturing factory usually contains several departments, each of which does a specialized task very well. One department might assemble the product, another might paint the product, and yet another might package the product. Every product must pass through each department in order to be complete.

Similarly, UNIX has several commands that can manipulate data in some manner. The piping of each of these commands can be compared to the flow of a manufacturing factory. Information is manipulated by one command, and then that manipulated information is sent to another command that manipulates it further. After being manipulated by several commands in this fashion, the information is in a form that the user desires. Figure 9-3 depicts this process.

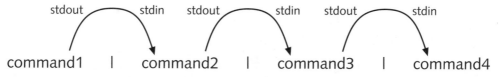

**Figure 9-3**  Using several commands in a pipe

Any command that can take from standard input and give to standard output is called a **filter**. It is important to note that commands such as `ls` and `prtvtoc` are not filter commands since they do not accept standard input from other commands, but instead find information from the system and display it to the user. As a result, these commands must be at the beginning of a pipe. Other commands such as the vi editor are interactive and as such cannot exist within a pipe as they cannot take from standard input and give to standard output.

Several hundred filter commands are available to UNIX users; Table 9-3 lists some common filter commands that are used throughout this textbook.

**Table 9-3**    Common filter commands

| Command | Description |
|---|---|
| sort | Sorts lines in a file (ASCII) |
| sort -r | Reverse sorts lines in a file (ASCII) |
| wc | Counts the number of lines, words, and characters in a file |
| wc -l | Counts the number of lines in a file |
| wc -w | Counts the number of words in a file |
| wc -c | Counts the number of characters in a file |
| pr | Formats a file for printing (has several options available); it places a date and page number at the top of each page. |
| pr -d | Formats a file double spaced |
| tr | Replaces characters in the text of a file |
| grep | Displays lines in a file that match a regular expression |
| nl | Numbers lines in a file |

Take, for example, the prologue from Shakespeare's *Romeo and Juliet*:

```
# cat prologue
Two households, both alike in dignity,
In fair Verona, where we lay our scene,
From ancient grudge break to new mutiny,
Where civil blood makes civil hands unclean.
From forth the fatal loins of these two foes
A pair of star-cross'd lovers take their life;
Whole misadventured piteous overthrows
Do with their death bury their parents' strife.
The fearful passage of their death-mark'd love,
And the continuance of their parents' rage,
Which, but their children's end, nought could remove,
Is now the two hours' traffic of our stage;
The which if you with patient ears attend,
What here shall miss, our toil shall strive to mend.
# _
```

If you want to replace all lowercase *a* characters with uppercase *A* characters in the previous file, sort the contents by the first character on each line, and then double space the output and view the results page by page, use the following pipe:

```
# cat prologue | tr a A | sort | pr -d | more
```
```
2003-05-30 09:32                                          Page 1
```
```
And the continuAnce of their pArents' rAge,

A pAir of stAr-cross'd lovers tAke their life;

Do with their deAth bury their pArents' strife.

From Ancient grudge breAk to new mutiny,

From forth the fAtAl loins of these two foes

In fAir VeronA, where we lAy our scene,

Is now the two hours' trAffic of our stAge;

The feArful pAssAge of their deAth-mArk'd love,

The which if you with pAtient eArs Attend,

Two households, both Alike in dignity,
Standard input
```

The command used in the previous example displays the final standard output to the terminal screen via the **more** command. In many cases, a user may want to display the results of the pipe as well as have a saved copy in a file on the hard disk. As a result, a filter command called the **tee command** can be used. This command takes information from standard input and sends that information to a file as well as to standard output.

To save a copy of the manipulated prologue before displaying it on the terminal screen with the **more** command, use the following command:

```
# cat prologue | tr a A | sort | pr -d | tee newfile | more
```
```
2003-05-30 09:32                                          Page 1
```
```
And the continuAnce of their pArents' rAge,

A pAir of stAr-cross'd lovers tAke their life;

Do with their deAth bury their pArents' strife.

From Ancient grudge breAk to new mutiny,

From forth the fAtAl loins of these two foes

In fAir VeronA, where we lAy our scene,

Is now the two hours' trAffic of our stAge;

The feArful pAssAge of their deAth-mArk'd love,
```

```
The which if you with pAtient eArs Attend,

Two households, both Alike in dignity,
Standard input q
# _
# cat newfile

2003-05-30 09:58                                              Page 1

And the continuAnce of their pArents' rAge,

A pAir of stAr-cross'd lovers tAke their life;

Do with their deAth bury their pArents' strife.

From Ancient grudge breAk to new mutiny,

From forth the fAtAl loins of these two foes

In fAir VeronA, where we lAy our scene,

Is now the two hours' trAffic of our stAge;

The feArful pAssAge of their deAth-mArk'd love,

The which if you with pAtient eArs Attend,

Two households, both Alike in dignity,

WhAt here shAll miss, our toil shAll strive to mend.

Where civil blood mAkes civil hAnds uncleAn.

Which, but their children's end, nought could remove,

Whole misAdventured piteous overthrows

# _
```

You can also combine redirection and piping together; however, input redirection must occur at the beginning of the pipe and output redirection must occur at the end of the pipe. The following output shows an example that replaces all lowercase *a* characters with uppercase *A* characters in the prologue file used in previous example, sorts the file, numbers each line, and saves the output to a file called newprologue instead of sending the output to the terminal screen:

```
# tr a A <prologue | sort | nl >newprologue
# cat newprologue
     1  And the continuAnce of their pArents' rAge,
     2  A pAir of stAr-cross'd lovers tAke their life;
     3  Do with their deAth bury their pArents' strife.
     4  From Ancient grudge breAk to new mutiny,
     5  From forth the fAtAl loins of these two foes
     6  In fAir VeronA, where we lAy our scene,
     7  Is now the two hours' trAffic of our stAge;
```

```
 8   The feArful pAssAge of their deAth-mArk'd love,
 9   The which if you with pAtient eArs Attend,
10   Two households, both Alike in dignity,
11   WhAt here shAll miss, our toil shAll strive to mend.
12   Where civil blood mAkes civil hAnds uncleAn.
13   Which, but their children's end, nought could remove,
14   Whole misAdventured piteous overthrows
# _
```

# SHELL VARIABLES

Every shell has several variables in memory at any one time. Recall from Chapter 3 that a variable is a reserved portion of memory containing information that may be accessed. Most variables in a given shell are referred to as **environment variables** because they are typically set by the system and contain information that the system and programs access regularly. Users can also create their own custom variables; these variables are called **user-defined variables**. In addition to these two types of variables, other special variables are useful when executing commands and creating new files and directories.

## Environment Variables

Many environment variables are set by default in the shell. To see a list of these variables and their current values, use the **set command**, as shown in the following output:

```
# set
HOME=/
HZ=100
IFS=
KEYBOARD=C/US
LANG=C
LOGNAME=root
MAILCHECK=600
MAPCHAN=/usr/lib/mapchan/88591.dk
NUMLOCK=no
OPTIND=1
PATH=/sbin:/usr/sbin:/usr/bin:/etc:/usr/ccs/bin
PS1=#
PS2=>
SHELL=/sbin/sh
SHIFTDOWN=yes
TERM=AT386-M-ie
TERMCAP=/etc/termcap
TFADMIN=
TIMEOUT=0
TZ=:US/Eastern
XKEYBOARD=C/US
XMODIFIERS=@im=Local
```

9

```
XNLSPATH=/usr/X/lib/Xsi/C/US
# _
```

Some of the environment variables shown in the previous output are used by programs that require information about the system; the TZ (time zone) and SHELL (pathname to shell) variables are two examples. Other variables are used to set the user's working environment. The most common of these include:

- PS1—the default shell prompt
- HOME—the absolute pathname to the user's home directory
- PWD—the present working directory in the directory tree
- PATH—a list of directories to search for executable programs

The PS1 variable represents the shell prompt. To view the contents of this variable only, recall from Chapter 3 that you can use the echo command and specify the variable name prefixed by the $ shell metacharacter, as shown in the following output:

```
# echo $PS1
#
# _
```

To change the value of a variable in a Bourne, POSIX, or Korn shell, specify the variable name immediately followed by an equal sign (=) and the new value. To change the value of a variable in the C shell, you must use the **setenv command** followed by the variable name and the new value.

The following output demonstrates how you can change the value of the PS1 variable in the Bourne shell. The new prompt will take effect immediately and allow the user to type commands:

```
# PS1="This is the new prompt: #"
This is the new prompt: # _
This is the new prompt: # date
Mon May  4 14:22:15 EST 2003
This is the new prompt: # _
This is the new prompt: # who
root       tty2       Nov  4 13:52
This is the new prompt: # _
This is the new prompt: # PS1="#"
# _
```

The HOME variable is used by programs that require the pathname to the current user's home directory to store or search for files. As a result, it should not be changed. If the root user logs into the system, then the HOME variable is set to /; alternatively, the HOME variable is set to /home/user1 if the user named user1 logs into the system.

Like the HOME variable, the PWD variable is vital to the user's environment and should not be changed. PWD stores the current user's location in the directory tree; it is affected by the cd command and used by other commands such as pwd when the current directory needs to be identified. The following output demonstrates how this variable works:

```
# pwd
/
# echo $PWD
/
# cd /etc
# pwd
/etc
# echo $PWD
/etc
# _
```

The PATH variable is one of the most important variables in a shell as it enables users to execute commands by typing the command name alone. Recall from Chapter 4 that every command is represented by an executable file on the hard drive typically organized into directories named bin or sbin throughout the UNIX directory tree. To execute the ls command, you could either type the absolute or relative pathname to the file (that is, /usr/bin/ls or ../../usr/bin/ls), or type the letters *ls* and enable the system to search the directories listed in the PATH variable for a command named ls. The following is an example of the contents of the PATH variable:

```
# echo $PATH
/sbin:/usr/sbin:/usr/bin:/etc:/usr/ccs/bin
# _
```

From the previous output, if the user types the command ls at the command prompt and presses Enter, the shell will notice that there is no / character in the pathname and proceed to search for the file ls in the /sbin directory, the /usr/sbin directory, and the /usr/bin directory before finding the ls executable file. If no ls file was found in any directory in the PATH variable, the shell will return the following error message with a misspelled command:

```
# lss
UX:sh: ERROR: lss: Not found
# _
```

Thus, if a command is located within a directory that is listed in the PATH variable, then you can type the name of the command on the command line to execute it as the shell will be able to find the appropriate executable file on the filesystem. All the commands used in this textbook up until this section have been located in directories listed in the PATH variable. However, if the executable file is not in a directory listed in the PATH variable, then the user must specify either the absolute or relative pathname to the executable file. The following output shows an example of this using the myprogram file in the / directory (a directory that is not listed in the PATH variable):

```
# pwd
/
```

```
# ls -F my*
myprogram*
# myprogram
UX:sh: ERROR: myprogram: Not found
# /myprogram
This is a sample program.
# ./myprogram
This is a sample program.
# cp myprogram /usr/bin
# myprogram
This is a sample program.
# _
```

Once the myprogram executable file was copied to the /usr/bin directory in the previous output, the user was able to execute it by typing its name since the /usr/bin directory is listed in the PATH variable.

Table 9-4 lists the environment variables used in most shells.

**Table 9-4**    Common environment variables

| Variable | Description |
|----------|-------------|
| DISPLAY | Redirects the output of X Windows to another computer or device |
| ENV | Specifies the absolute pathname to a runtime configuration file |
| HOME | The absolute pathname of the current user's home directory |
| LOGNAME | The username of the current user used when logging into the shell |
| LPDEST | The name of the default printer |
| MAIL | The location of the mailbox file (where e-mail is stored) |
| MANPATH | The absolute pathnames to directories that contain manual pages |
| PATH | The directories to search for executable program files in the absence of an absolute or relative pathname containing a / character |
| PS1 | The current shell prompt |
| PS2 | The shell prompt used if a command requires more information or if a quote character is used to specify information that spans more than one line on the terminal |
| PWD | The current working directory |
| SHELL | The absolute pathname of the current shell |
| TERM | Determines the terminal settings from an entry in the terminal database |
| TERMCAP | The absolute pathname to the database that stores all terminal settings |
| TZ | The time zone for the system |

## User-Defined Variables

Users can set their own variables using the same method discussed earlier to change the contents of existing environment variables. To set a new variable in the Bourne, POSIX, or Korn shell, specify the name of the variable (known as the **variable identifier**) immediately followed by the equal sign (=) and the new contents. To set a new variable in the C shell, specify the `setenv` command followed by the variable identifier and the new contents.

When creating new variables, it is important to note the following features of variable identifiers:

- They can contain alphanumeric characters (0–9, A–Z, and a–z), the dash (-) character, or the underscore (_) character.

- They must not start with a number.

- They are typically capitalized to follow convention (such as HOME, PATH, and so on).

To create a variable called MYVAR with the contents "This is a sample variable" and display its contents in the Bourne shell, use the following commands:

```
# MYVAR="This is a sample variable"
# echo $MYVAR
This is a sample variable
# _
```

The previous command created a variable that is available to the current shell. Most commands that are run by the shell are run in a separate shell that is created by the current shell called a **subshell**; any variables created in the current shell are not available to those subshells and the commands running within them. Thus, if a user creates a variable to be used within a certain program such as a database editor, then that variable should be exported to all subshells using the **export command** to ensure that all programs started by the current shell have the capability to access the variable.

Recall from earlier that all environment variables in the shell may be listed using the `set` command; user-defined variables are also indicated in this list. Similarly, to see a list of all exported environment and user-defined variables in the shell, use the **env command**. Because the outputs of `set` and `env` are typically large, you commonly redirect the standard output of these commands to the `grep` command to display certain lines only.

To see the difference between the `set` and `env` commands as well as export the MYVAR variable created earlier, perform the following commands:

```
# set | grep MYVAR
MYVAR=This is a sample variable
# env | grep MYVAR
# _
# export MYVAR
# env | grep MYVAR
MYVAR=This is a sample variable
# _
```

Not all environment variables are exported; the PS1 variable is an example of a variable that does not need to be available to subshells and is not exported as a result. However, it is good form to export user-defined variables since they will likely be used by processes that run in subshells.

In the Korn and POSIX shells, use the `export` command to create and export a variable all at once. For example, to create and export a user-defined variable called MYVAR2, use the command `export MYVAR2="This is another sample variable"` at a command prompt.

Environment variables are automatically exported in the C shell.

## Other Variables

Other variables are available that are not displayed by the **set** or **env** commands; these variables perform specialized functions in the shell.

The umask variable introduced in Chapter 6 is an example of a special variable available in all shells that reduces the permissions on new files and directories. Also recall that you must set the UMASK variable with the **umask** command.

Recall from earlier that the Korn, POSIX, and C shells enable users to create command aliases. Command aliases are shortcuts to commands stored in special variables that can be created and viewed using the **alias command**. To create an alias to the command `mount -F vxfs /dev/dsk/f03ht /mnt` called `mf` and view it, use the following commands:

```
# alias mf="mount -F vxfs /dev/dsk/f03ht /mnt"
# alias
2d='set -f; _2d'
autoload='typeset -fu'
command='command '
fc=hist
float='typeset -E'
functions='typeset -f'
hash='alias -t --'
history='hist -l'
integer='typeset -i'
mf='mount -F vxfs /dev/dsk/f03ht /mnt'
nameref='typeset -n'
nohup='nohup '
r='hist -s'
redirect='command exec'
stop='kill -s STOP'
suspend='kill -s STOP $$'
times='{ { time;} 2>&1;}'
type='whence -v'
# _
```

Now, you just need to run the mf command to mount a floppy device that contains an ext2 filesystem to the /mnt/floppy directory, as shown in the following output:

```
# mf
# mount
/ on /dev/root read/write/setuid on Tues Nov 5 02:06:57 2003
/stand on /dev/stand read/write on Tues Nov 5 02:06:59 2003
/proc on /proc read/write on Tues Nov 5 02:07:13 2003
/dev/fd on /dev/fd read/write on Tues Nov 5 02:07:13 2003
/system/processor on /processorfs read/write on Tues Nov 5 02:07:16 2003
/tmp on /tmp read/write on Tues Nov 5 02:07:16 2003
/var/tmp on /var/tmp read/write on Tues Nov 5 02:07:16 2003
/dev/_tcp on /dev/_tcp read/write on Tues Nov 5 02:07:16 2003
/mnt on /dev/dsk/f03ht read/write on Tues Nov 5 07:02:07 2003
# _
```

You can also create aliases to multiple commands provided they are separated by the ; metacharacter introduced in Chapter 3. To create and test an alias called dw that runs the date command followed by the who command, do the following:

```
# alias dw="date;who"
# alias
2d='set -f; _2d'
autoload='typeset -fu'
command='command '
dw='date;who'
fc=hist
float='typeset -E'
functions='typeset -f'
hash='alias -t --'
history='hist -l'
integer='typeset -i'
mf='mount -F vxfs /dev/dsk/f03ht /mnt'
nameref='typeset -n'
nohup='nohup '
r='hist -s'
redirect='command exec'
stop='kill -s STOP'
suspend='kill -s STOP $$'
times='{ { time;} 2>&1;}'
type='whence -v'
# dw
Tue Nov  5 07:07:00 EST 2002
root        vt02        Nov  5 06:59
# _
```

**NOTE**

It is important to use unique alias names since the shell searches for them before it searches for executable files. If you create an alias called who, then that alias would be used instead of the who command on the filesystem.

## Environment Files

Recall that variables are stored in memory. When users exit their shell, all variables stored in memory are destroyed along with the shell itself. Thus, to ensure that variables are accessible to a shell at all times, you must place variables in a file that is executed each time you log in and start a shell. These files are called **environment files**. Table 9-5 lists some common shell environment files and the order in which they are executed.

**Table 9-5**    Shell environment files

| Shell | Environment Files |
| --- | --- |
| Bourne and POSIX | /etc/profile and $HOME/.profile |
| Korn | /etc/profile, $HOME/.profile, and $HOME/.kshrc |
| C | /etc/cshrc, $HOME/.cshrc, and $HOME/.login |

For Bourne shell users, the /etc/profile file is always executed immediately after login and sets most environment variables such as HOME and PATH. After /etc/profile finishes executing, the user's home directory is searched for the hidden environment file .profile. If this file exists, it will be executed.

Korn shell users also execute the /etc/profile and $HOME/.profile files after login; however, they will also execute the $HOME/.kshrc (Korn shell runtime configuration) file if it exists. This Korn shell runtime configuration file is also executed each time a new Korn shell is started after login.

**NOTE**    The ENV environment variable sets the path to the Korn shell runtime configuration file.

After login, C shell users first execute the /etc/cshrc (C shell runtime configuration) file followed by the $HOME/.cshrc and $HOME/.login files if they exist. Like the $HOME/.kshrc file, the /etc/cshrc and $HOME/.cshrc files are executed each time a new C shell is created after login.

Only the root user can edit the /etc/profile and /etc/cshrc files; however, all users have the ability to edit the hidden environment files in their home directory to set their own customized variables independent of shells used by other users on the system. Any values assigned to variables in these files override those set in /etc/profile and /etc/cshrc due to the order of execution.

To add a variable to any of these files, add a line that has the same format as the command used on the command line. To add the MYVAR2 variable used previously to the .profile file, edit the file using a text editor such as vi and add the line `MYVAR2="This is another sample variable"` to the file. Additionally, you can add the line `export MYVAR2` to export the MYVAR2 variable.

Variables are not the only type of information that can be entered into an environment file; any command that can be executed on the command line can also be placed inside any environment file. If a user wants to set the UMASK to 077, display the date after each login, and create an alias, that user could add the following lines to one of the hidden environment files in his or her home directory:

```
umask 077
date
alias dw="date;who"
```

## CHAPTER SUMMARY

- ❏ Three components are available to commands: standard input, standard output, and standard error. Not all commands use every component.

- ❏ Standard input is typically user input taken from the keyboard, whereas standard output and standard error are sent to the terminal screen by default.

- ❏ You can redirect the standard output and standard error of a command to a file using redirection symbols. Similarly, you can use redirection symbols to redirect a file to the standard input of a command.

- ❏ To redirect the standard output from one command to the standard input of another, you must use the pipe symbol (|).

- ❏ Most variables available to the shell are environment variables that are loaded into memory after login from environment files.

- ❏ Users can create their own variables in the shell and export them such that they are available to programs started by the shell. These variables may also be placed in environment files such that they are loaded into memory on every shell login.

- ❏ The umask variable and command aliases are special variables that must be set using a certain command.

## KEY TERMS

| — A shell metacharacter used to pipe standard output from one command to the standard input of another command.

< — A shell metacharacter used to obtain standard input from a file.

> — A shell metacharacter used to redirect standard output and standard error to a file.

**alias command** — A command used to create command aliases.

**background process control** — A feature of the shell that enables background commands to be manipulated.

**command aliases** — Special variables that are shortcuts to longer command strings.

**command history** — A feature of the shell that enables users to recall commands that were previously typed into the command line.

**command-line editing** — A feature of the shell that enables users to edit the text on a command line using editor key combinations.

**env command** — A command used to display a list of exported variables present in the current shell except special variables.

**environment files** — Files used immediately after logon to execute commands—they are typically used to load variables into memory.

**environment variables** — Variables that store information commonly accessed by the system or programs executing on the system—together these variables form the user environment.

**export command** — A command used to send variables to subshells.

**file descriptors** — Numeric labels used to define command input and command output.

**filter** — A command that can take from standard input and send to standard output—in other words, a filter is a command that can exist in the middle of a pipe.

**grep (Global Regular Expression Print) command** — A program used to search one or more text files for a desired string of characters.

**pipe** — A string of commands connected by | metacharacters.

**redirection** — The process of changing the default locations of standard input, standard output, and standard error.

**set command** — A command used to view all variables in the shell except special variables.

**setenv command** — A command used to create or modify variables in the C shell.

**standard error** — Represents any error messages generated by a command.

**standard input** — Represents information inputted to a command during execution.

**standard output** — Represents the desired output from a command.

**subshell** — A shell started by the current shell.

**tee command** — A command used to take from standard input and send to both standard output and a specified file.

**tr command** — A command used to transform or change characters received from standard input.

**user-defined variables** — Variables that are created by the user and are not used by the system—these variables are typically exported to subshells.

**variable** — An area of memory that is used to store information—variables are created from entries in environment files when the shell is first created after login and are destroyed when the shell is destroyed upon logout.

**variable identifier** — The name of a variable.

# REVIEW QUESTIONS

1. Since standard error and standard output represent the results of a command and standard input represents the input required for a command, only standard error and standard output can be redirected to a file. True or False?

2. Before a user-defined variable can be used by processes that run in subshells, that variable must be _____.

   a. imported

   b. validated by running the env command

   c. exported

   d. redirected to theshell

3. The alias command can only be used to make a shortcut to a single command. True or False?

4. What environment variable is used to define where to look for executable commands when the absolute or relative pathname is not listed on the command line?

   a. COM

   b. PATH

   c. TERM

   d. EXEC

5. Which of the following files is always executed immediately after a user logs into a UNIX system and receives a Korn shell?

   a. /etc/profile

   b. $HOME/.profile

   c. $HOME/.login

   d. $HOME/.kshrc

6. Which shell supports command history? (Choose all that apply.)

   a. Bourne

   b. Korn

   c. POSIX

   d. C

7. Which of the following is a file descriptor? (Choose all that apply.)

   a. standard output

   b. Standard Deviation

   c. Standard Settings

   d. standard error

8. Which of the following commands could you use to see a list of all environment and user-defined shell variables as well as their current values?

   a. env

   b. set

   c. grep

   d. echo

9. Which of the following commands displays the current value for the HOME variable?

   a. setenv $HOME

   b. set $HOME

   c. echo $HOME

   d. echo "HOME"

10. What must be done prior to using the command-line editing feature in the Korn and POSIX shells?

    a. Disable command aliases.

    b. Run the command set -o vi.

    c. Edit the LINE variable.

    d. Run the command setenv vi.

11. A pipe is a temporary software connection between two commands that takes the stdout of the first command and uses it as the stdin of the second. True or False?

12. What does 2>&1 accomplish when it is entered on the command line after a command?

    a. appends standard output to the existing contents of the specified file

    b. redirects both standard error and standard output to the same file

    c. redirects both standard error and standard input to the same file

    d. sends standard error to the same location as standard output

    e. redirects both standard input and standard output to the same file

13. Which of the following file descriptors represents stdout?

    a. 2

    b. 0

    c. 1

    d. 3

14. Due to their contradictory nature, standard output and standard error can never be redirected to the same file. True or False?

15. Environment variables _____.

    a. are set by the user depending on his or her environment

    b. are set by the system and are not modifiable

    c. are set by the system and are not viewable by any user but root

    d. are normally set by the system but can be modified if desired

16. Which of the following does not use correct command syntax?

    a. command >> file

    b. command 2> file

    c. command | file

    d. command 2>&1

17. Which of the following is true regarding I/O redirection?

    a. File descriptor 2 identifies stdin.

    b. By default, stdin refers to your keyboard, and stdout and stderr refer to your terminal screen.

    c. stdout and stderr share file descriptor 1.

    d. stderr sends error messages to /dev/null by default.

18. Which one of the following commands will not be successful?

    a. who | sort >wholog

    b. sort fruit | tee salad | more

    c. sort file1 | grep mother | file2

    d. grep mother file1 | sort

19. Which of the following results in a Bourne shell command prompt of [:{)?

    a. PS1 [:{)

    b. PS1=[:{)

    c. PS1="[:{)"

    d. PS1 "[:{)"

20. You desire to redirect all standard error to a central file called /var/Errors for review at a later time instead of viewing the errors on the terminal screen. To accomplish this, you generate the command ls /home/user1 2>/var/Errors. What will happen if you run the command for the first time and the Errors file does not exist?

    a. The operation will fail as the file to which the information is to be stored does not exist, and you will be informed of this by an error message on the screen.

    b. The operation will fail as the file to which the information is to be stored does not exist, but you will not know this as you have prevented standard error from being displayed on the screen.

    c. The system will prompt you to create the file Errors and then place the error messages, if any, into it.

    d. The system will automatically create the necessary file without user intervention and place any error messages generated into it automatically.

21. What would be the effect of using the alias command to make an alias for the date command named cat in honor of your favorite pet?

    a. It cannot be done as an environment variable cat is already associated with the cat command.

    b. It cannot be done as a command cat already exists on the system.

    c. When you use the cat command at the command prompt with the intention of viewing a text file, the date will appear instead.

    d. There will be no effect until the alias is imported as it is a user-defined variable.

22. Which shell does not support command aliases?

    a. Bourne

    b. Korn

    c. POSIX

    d. C

23. You have redirected standard error to a file called Errors. You view the contents of this file afterwards and notice that there are six error messages. After repeating the procedure, you notice that there are only two error messages in this file. Why?

    a. Once you open the file and view the contents, the contents are lost.

    b. The system generated different standard output.

    c. You did not append the standard error to the Error file; as a result, it was overwritten when the command was run a second time.

    d. You must specify a new file each and every time you redirect as the system creates the specified file by default.

24. Which variable sets the default shell prompt?

    a. ENV

    b. PATH

    c. TERM

    d. PS1

    e. SHELL

25. What is wrong with the command string ls /etc/hosts>listofhostfile?

    a. nothing

    b. The file descriptor was not declared, and unless 1 is indicated for standard output or 2 is indicated for standard error, the command will fail.

    c. The ls command is one of the commands that cannot be used with redirection; you must use | to pipe instead.

    d. The file listofhostfile will always only contain standard error as a file descriptor was not declared.

26. Which of the following is not necessarily generated by every command on the system? (Choose all that apply.)

   a. standard input

   b. standard deviation

   c. standard output

   d. standard error

27. A variable identifier must _____.

   a. not begin with a number

   b. not begin with an uppercase letter

   c. start with a number

   d. start with an underscore (_)

28. What does >> accomplish when it is entered on the command line after a command?

   a. It is a double redirect, and redirects both standard error and standard output to the same location.

   b. Nothing, it is a typo; you just hit the same key twice in error.

   c. It is a double redirect, and redirects standard error and standard input to the same location.

   d. It appends standard output to a file.

9

## HANDS-ON PROJECTS

These projects should be completed in the order given. All hands-on projects should take a total of three hours to complete. The requirement for this lab includes:

❑ A computer with UnixWare 7.1.1 installed according to Project 2-2

**HANDS-ON PROJECTS**

### Project 9-1

In this hands-on project, you will use command history and command-line editing features of the Korn shell to recall commands and edit commands on the command line.

1. Switch to a command-line terminal (vt02) by pressing **Ctrl+Alt+F2**, and log into the terminal using the username **root** and the password **secret**.

2. At the command prompt, type **history** and press **Enter**. What happened?

3. At the command prompt, type **echo $SHELL** and press **Enter**. What shell do you have?

4. At the command prompt, type **ksh** and press **Enter** to start a Korn shell.

5. At the command prompt, type **date** and press **Enter**. Next, type **who** at the command prompt and press **Enter**.

6. At the command prompt, type **history** and press **Enter**. How many commands are listed? Do you see the date and who commands? What is the number for the date command?

7. At the command prompt, type **r #** (where # is the number that you recorded in Step 5) and press **Enter**. Did the date command reexecute?

8. At the command prompt, type **r** and press **Enter**. What happens if you do not specify an argument to the r command?

9. At the command prompt, type **set -o vi** and press **Enter**. What does this command do?

10. Next, type the command **echo This is a somple sentence.** without pressing **Enter**. What is wrong with this command?

11. Press **Esc** to enter command mode. Next, press **h** to move the cursor to the *o* character in the word **somple** and press **x**. What happened? Why?

12. Next, press **i** to enter input mode and type **a** to insert the *a* character.

13. When you are finished, press **Enter** to execute the command. Did it work?

14. Type **exit** and press **Enter** to log out of your shell.

# Project 9-2

In this hands-on project, you will use the shell to redirect the standard output and standard error to a file and take standard input from a file.

1. Switch to a command-line terminal (vt02) by pressing **Ctrl+Alt+F2**, and log into the terminal using the username **root** and the password **secret**.

2. At the command prompt, type **touch sample1 sample2** and press **Enter** to create two new files named sample1 and sample2 in your home directory. Verify their creation by typing **ls -F sample\*** at the command prompt and press **Enter**.

3. At the command prompt, type **ls -l sample1 sample2 sample3** and press **Enter**. Is any standard output displayed on the terminal screen? Is any standard error displayed on the terminal screen? Why or why not?

4. At the command prompt, type **ls -l sample1 sample2 sample3> file** and press **Enter**. Is any standard output displayed on the terminal screen? Is any standard error displayed on the terminal screen? Why or why not?

5. At the command prompt, type **cat file** and press **Enter**. What are the contents of file and why?

6. At the command prompt, type **ls -l sample1 sample2 sample32> file** and press **Enter**. Is any standard output displayed on the terminal screen? Is any standard error displayed on the terminal screen? Why or why not?

7. At the command prompt, type **cat file** and press **Enter**. What are the contents of file and why? Were the previous contents retained? Why or why not?

8. At the command prompt, type **ls –l sample1 sample2 sample3> file2>file2** and press **Enter**. Is any standard output displayed on the terminal screen? Is any standard error displayed on the terminal screen? Why or why not?

9. At the command prompt, type **cat file** and press **Enter**. What are the contents of file and why?

10. At the command prompt, type **cat file2** and press **Enter**. What are the contents of file2 and why?

11. At the command prompt, type **ls –l sample1 sample2 sample3> file2>&1** and press **Enter**. Is any standard output displayed on the terminal screen? Is any standard error displayed on the terminal screen? Why or why not?

12. At the command prompt, type **cat file** and press **Enter**. What are the contents of file and why?

13. At the command prompt, type **ls –l sample1 sample2 sample3>&22>file2** and press **Enter**. Is any standard output displayed on the terminal screen? Is any standard error displayed on the terminal screen? Why or why not?

14. At the command prompt, type **cat file2** and press **Enter**. What are the contents of file2 and why?

15. At the command prompt, type **date> file** and press **Enter**.

16. At the command prompt, type **cat file** and press **Enter**. What are the contents of file and why?

17. At the command prompt, type **date>> file** and press **Enter**.

18. At the command prompt, type **cat file** and press **Enter**. What are the contents of file and why? Can you tell when each date command was run?

19. At the command prompt, type **tr o O /etc/hosts** and press **Enter**. What error message do you receive and why?

20. At the command prompt, type **tr o O </etc/hosts** and press **Enter**. What happened and why?

21. Type **exit** and press **Enter** to log out of your shell.

## Project 9-3

In this hands-on project, you will redirect standard output and standard input using pipe metacharacters.

1. Switch to a command-line terminal (vt02) by pressing **Ctrl+Alt+F2**, and log into the terminal using the username **root** and the password **secret**.

2. At the command prompt, type **cat /etc/inittab** and press **Enter** to view the /etc/inittab file. Next, type **cat /etc/inittab | more** at the command prompt and press **Enter** to perform the same task page by page. Explain what the | metacharacter does in the previous command. How is this different from the more /etc/inittab command?

3. At the command prompt, type **cat /etc/inittab | grep rc** and press **Enter**. How many lines are displayed? Why did you not need to specify a filename with the grep command?

4. At the command prompt, type **cat /etc/inittab | grep rc | tr o O** and press **Enter**. Explain the output on the terminal screen.

5. At the command prompt, type **cat /etc/inittab | grep rc | tr o O | sort –r** and press **Enter**. Explain the output on the terminal screen.

6. At the command prompt, type **cat /etc/inittab | grep rc | tr o O | sort –r | tee file** and press **Enter**. Explain the output on the terminal screen. Next, type **cat file** at the command prompt and press **Enter**. What are the contents? Why? What does the tee command do in the previous pipe?

7. At the command prompt, type **cat /etc/inittab | grep rc | tr o O | sort –r | tee file | wc –l** and press **Enter**. Explain the output on the terminal screen. Next, type **cat file** at the command prompt and press **Enter**. What are the contents? Why?

8. Type **exit** and press **Enter** to log out of your shell.

# Project 9-4

In this hands-on project, you will view and change existing shell variables. You will also export user-defined variables and load variables automatically upon shell startup.

1. Switch to a command-line terminal (vt02) by pressing **Ctrl+Alt+F2**, and log into the terminal using the username **root** and the password **secret**.

2. At the command prompt, type **set | more** and press **Enter** to view the shell environment variables currently loaded into memory. Scroll through this list by pressing **Enter**. When you are finished, press **q** to exit the more utility.

3. At the command prompt, type **env | more** and press **Enter** to view the exported shell environment variables currently loaded into memory. Scroll through this list by pressing **Enter**. Is this list larger or smaller than the list generated in Step 2? Why? When you are finished, press **q** to exit the more utility.

4. At the command prompt, type **PS1="Hello There: "** and press **Enter**. What happened and why? Next, type **echo $PS1** at the command prompt and press **Enter** to verify the new value of the PS1 variable.

5. At the command prompt, type **exit** and press **Enter** to log out of the shell. Next, log into the terminal using the username **root** and the password **secret**. What prompt did you receive and why? How could you ensure that the "Hello There: " prompt occurs at every login?

6. At the command prompt, type **vi .profile** and press **Enter**. Add the following lines to the file. When you are finished, save and exit the vi editor:

```
echo Hello root,
echo Welcome to your Shell Environment.
echo Today is `date`
```

Explain what the previous lines will perform after each login.

7. At the command prompt, type **exit** and press **Enter** to log out of the shell. Next, log into the terminal using the username **root** and the password **secret**. What appeared on the terminal screen before you received your shell prompt? Why?

8. At the command prompt, type **MYVAR="My sample variable"** and press **Enter** to create a variable called MYVAR. Verify its creation by typing **echo $MYVAR** at the command prompt and press **Enter**.

9. At the command prompt, type **set | grep MYVAR** and press **Enter**. Is the MYVAR variable listed? Why or why not?

10. At the command prompt, type **env | grep MYVAR** and press **Enter**. Is the MYVAR variable listed? Why or why not?

11. At the command prompt, type **export MYVAR** and press **Enter**. Next, type **env | grep MYVAR** at the command prompt and press **Enter**. Is the MYVAR variable listed now? Why or why not?

12. At the command prompt, type **exit** and press **Enter** to log out of the shell. Next, log into the terminal using the username **root** and the password **secret**.

13. At the command prompt, type **echo $MYVAR** and press **Enter** to view the contents of the MYVAR variable. What is listed and why?

14. At the command prompt, type **vi .profile** and press **Enter**. At the bottom of the file, add the following lines. When you are finished, save and exit the vi editor:

```
MYVAR="My sample variable"
export MYVAR
```

15. At the command prompt, type **exit** and press **Enter** to log out of the shell. Next, log into the terminal using the username **root** and the password **secret**.

16. At the command prompt, type **echo $MYVAR** and press **Enter** to list the contents of the MYVAR variable. What is listed and why?

17. At the command prompt, type **alias** and press **Enter**. What aliases are displayed?

18. At the command prompt, type **alias asample="cd /etc ; cat hosts ; cd / ; ls -F"** and press **Enter**. What does this command do?

19. At the command prompt, type **asample** and press **Enter**. What happened and why?

20. At the command prompt, type **ksh** and press **Enter**. What shell are you using now?

21. At the command prompt, type **asample** and press **Enter**. What happened and why?

22. At the command prompt, type **alias asample="cd /etc ; cat hosts ; cd / ; ls -F"** and press **Enter**.

23. At the command prompt, type **asample** and press **Enter**. What happened and why?

24. Type **exit** and press **Enter** to log out of your shell.

## DISCOVERY EXERCISES

1. Which command can be used to:

    a. create an alias called dt, which displays only the free space on the /tmp filesystem?

    b. create and export a variable called NEWHOME that is equivalent to the value contained in the HOME variable?

    c. find all files that start with the word "host" starting from the /etc directory and save the standard output to a file called file1 and the standard error to the same file?

    d. display only the lines from the output of the set command that start with the letter *P*? This output on the terminal screen should be sorted alphabetically.

2. Make a copy of /etc/hosts called /file. Verify that /file exists and has contents. Next, execute the following command and examine the contents of /file:

    ```
    tr a A </file | sort -r | pr -d >/file
    ```

    Did you get what you expected? Explain what went wrong.

3. Provided you have Internet access and a functional Web browser, research three more shells that were not discussed in this text. Summarize their features and list the UNIX flavors that support them.

4. Recall that only standard output can be sent across a pipe to another command. Using the information presented in this chapter, how could you send standard error across the pipe in the following command?

    ```
    ls /etc/hosts /etc/h|trhH
    ```

# 10

# PROCESS ADMINISTRATION

> ## After reading this chapter and completing the exercises, you will be able to:
>
> ♦ Categorize the different types of processes on a UNIX system
> ♦ Identify the common attributes of every process
> ♦ View processes using command-line and graphical utilities
> ♦ Illustrate the difference between common kill signals
> ♦ Send kill signals to processes using command-line and graphical utilities
> ♦ Describe how binary programs and shell scripts are executed
> ♦ Create and manipulate background processes
> ♦ Use standard UNIX utilities to modify the priority of a process
> ♦ Schedule commands to execute in the future using the at command
> ♦ Schedule commands to execute repetitively using the crontab command
> ♦ Create and view process accounting reports

A typical UNIX system can run thousands of processes simultaneously, including those that were explored in previous chapters. This chapter focuses on viewing and managing processes. The first part discusses the different types of processes on a UNIX system and how to view and terminate them. You will then discover how processes are executed on a system, run in the background, and prioritized. Finally, this chapter introduces you to the various methods used to schedule commands to execute in the future.

## UNIX PROCESSES

Throughout the previous chapters of this textbook as well as in the workplace, the terms "program" and "process" are used interchangeably; however, a definite but fine difference exists between these two terms. A program is an executable file on the hard disk that can be run when the user executes it. A process refers to a program that is running in memory and on the CPU; in other words, a process is a program in action.

If a process is started by a user who is logged into a terminal, then that process runs in that terminal and is labeled a **user process**; examples of user processes include ls, grep, find, and most other commands that have been executed throughout this textbook. Recall that a system process that is not associated with a terminal is called a **daemon process**. These processes are typically started on system startup, but may also be started manually by a user. Most daemon processes provide system services such as printing, scheduling, and system maintenance, as well as network server services such as Web servers, database servers, file servers, and print servers.

Every process has a unique **process ID (PID)** that enables the kernel to identify them. Each process can additionally start an unlimited number of other processes, which are called **child processes**. Conversely, each process must have been started by an existing process called a **parent process**. As a result, each process has a **parent process ID (PPID)** that identifies the process that started it. Figure 10-1 depicts an example of the relationship between parent and child processes.

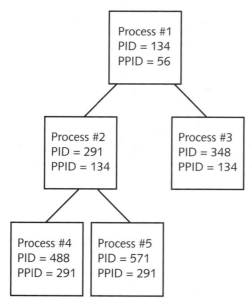

**Figure 10-1**    Parent and child processes

PIDs are not given to new processes in sequential order; each PID is randomly generated from free entries in a process table used by the UNIX kernel.

**NOTE**

Remember that although each process can have an unlimited number of child processes, it can only have one parent process.

**NOTE**

As mentioned earlier in Chapter 8, the first process started by the UnixWare kernel is the sysproc daemon. It has a PID of 0 and starts the init daemon, which has a PID of 1. The init daemon then starts most other daemons including those that allow for user logins. Once a user logs into the system, a shell is started to interpret user commands and starts all user processes. Thus, each process on the UNIX system can be traced back to the sysproc daemon by examining the series of PPIDs, as shown in Figure 10-2.

10

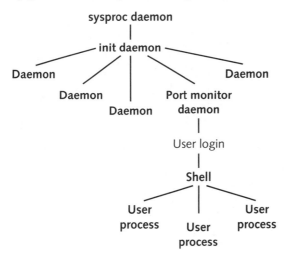

**Figure 10-2**   Process lineage

The init daemon is often referred to as the "grandfather of all user processes" because it starts most daemons, including those that allow for user logins.

**NOTE**

# VIEWING PROCESSES

Although several UNIX utilities can view processes, the most versatile and common utility is the **ps command**. Without arguments, the **ps** command displays a list of processes that are running in the current shell. The following output shows an example of this while logged into the terminal:

```
#ps
     PID   CLS   PRI   TTY    TIME    COMD
```

```
        601   TS   70   vt02   0:00   sh
        618   TS   29   vt02   0:01   ps
    #  _
```

The previous output shows that two processes were running in the terminal vt02 when the **ps** command executed. The command that started each process (COMD) is listed along with its PID, terminal (TTY), and the time it has taken on the CPU (TIME). Also listed are the **process priority** (PRI) and class (CLS). Process priority (PRI) is the priority used by the kernel for the process; it is measured between 0 (high priority) and 127 (low priority). In addition, classes are used to group process types together by priority; Fixed Class (FC) and Time Sharing (TS) classes share the lowest priority, System (SYS) classes have moderate priority and are used to run kernel processes, and Fixed Priority (FP) classes have the most priority on the system.

To find out more about these processes, use the –f option with the ps command, as shown in the following:

```
# ps -f
        UID   PID PPID CLS PRI C   STIME    TTY   TIME   COMD
        root  601 131  TS  70  0 09:19:03  vt02  0:00    -sh
        root  619 601  TS  57  0 09:22:18  vt02  0:00  ps -f
    #  _
```

This listing provides more information about each process. It displays the user who started the process (UID), the PPID, the time it was started (STIME), and the CPU utilization (C), which starts at zero and is incremented with each processor cycle the process runs on the CPU.

The most valuable information from the **ps –f** command is each process's PPID and lineage. The **sh** process (PID = 601) interprets user commands; it started the **ps –f** process (PID = 619) since the **ps –f** process had a PPID of 601.

Because daemon processes are not associated with a terminal, they are not displayed by the **ps –f** command. To display an entire list of processes across all terminals including daemons, add the **–e** option to any **ps** command, as shown in the following output:

```
    # ps -ef
UID    PID PPID CLS PRI C STIME    TTY TIME COMD
root     0    0 SYS  79 0 00:50:30  ?  0:04 sysproc
root     1    0 TS   70 0 00:50:30  ?  0:00 /sbin/init
root  1010 1009 TS   80 0 00:51:13  ?  0:00 /etc/sco_cpd
root   616    1 TS   70 0 00:50:49  ?  0:00 /etc/ifor_pmd
root  1056    1 TS   85 0 00:51:14  ?  0:00 /usr/lib/saf/sac -t300
root  1011 1009 TS   80 0 00:51:13  ?  0:00 /etc/ifor_sld
root   640    1 TS   88 0 00:50:52  ?  0:00 /usr/lib/mousemgr
root   824    1 TS   80 0 00:51:03  ?  0:00 hostmibd
root  1061 1056 TS   80 0 00:51:15  ?  0:00 /usr/lib/saf/ttymon
root   751    1 TS   80 0 00:50:57  ?  0:00 in.snmpd
root   685    1 TS   80 0 00:50:54  ?  0:00 /usr/sbin/in.routed
```

```
root   745    1   TS   70 0 00:50:57 pts/0 0:00 /usr/sbin/pppd
root   779    1   TS   80 0 00:51:01 ?   0:00 /usr/lib/sendmail
root   870    1   TS   80 0 00:51:09 ?   0:00 /usr/dt/bin/dtlogin
root   703    1   TS   80 0 00:50:55 ?   0:00 /usr/sbin/syslogd
root   759    1   TS   80 0 00:50:59 ?   0:00 /usr/sbin/rpcbind
root  1057    1   TS   80 0 00:51:14 console 0:00 /usr/lib/saf/ttymon
-g -p Console Login: -d /dev/syscon -l console
root  1009  616   TS   80 0 00:51:13 ?   0:00 /etc/ifor_pmd
root   878    1   TS   80 0 00:51:09 ?   0:00 cat /dev/osm
root   907    1   TS   80 0 00:51:10 ?   0:00 /usr/lib/nfs/lockd
root   908    1   TS   80 0 00:51:10 ?   0:00 /usr/lib/nfs/pcnfsd
root   906    1   TS   80 0 00:51:10 ?   0:00 /usr/lib/nfs/statd
root   896    1   TS   80 0 00:51:10 ?   0:00 /usr/lib/nfs/biod
root   897    1   TS   80 0 00:51:10 ?   0:00 /usr/lib/nfs/nfsd -a
root   898    1   TS   80 0 00:51:10 ?   0:00 /usr/lib/nfs/nfsd -a
root   909    1   TS   80 0 00:51:11 ?   0:00 /usr/lib/nfs/mountd -n
root  1062 1056   TS   80 0 00:51:15 ?   0:00 /usr/sbin/inetd
root  1067  870   TS   80 0 00:51:15 vt01 0:00 /usr/bin/X11/X :0 -
noexit -auth /var/dt/Atester:0-2000Da
root  1155 1079   TS   80 0 00:51:21 ?   0:00 dtgreet -
display tester:0
root  1160 1061   TS   70 0 00:55:05 vt03 0:00 -sh
root   601  131   TS   70 0 09:19:03 vt02 0:00 -sh
root  1071 1056   TS   80 0 00:51:15 ?   0:00 /usr/lib/saf/listen
nbcots
root  1072 1056   TS   80 0 00:51:16 ?   0:00 /usr/lib/saf/listen -m
inet/tcp0 tcp 2>/dev/null
root  1122    1   TS   80 0 00:51:18 ?   0:00 /usr/lib/lpsched
root  1079  870   TS   85 0 00:51:17 ?   0:00 /usr/dt/bin/dtlogin -
daemon
root  1176 1160   TS   59 0 00:59:59 vt02 0:00 ps -ef
root  1101    1   TS   80 0 00:51:17 ?   0:00 /usr/sbin/cron
root  1098    1   TS   80 0 00:51:17 ?   0:00 /usr/sbin/keymaster -n
root  1132 1122   TS   80 0 00:51:18 ?   0:00 lpNet
root  1112    1   TS   80 0 00:51:17 ?   0:00 /usr/sbin/cs
# _
```

As shown in the previous output, the init daemon (PID=1) starts most other daemons since those daemons have a PPID of 1. Additionally, a ? appears in the TTY column for daemons because they do not run on a terminal.

Because the output of the ps -ef command can be several hundred lines long on a UNIX server, the output is usually piped to the more command to send the output to the terminal screen page by page or to the grep command, which can be used to display lines containing only certain information. For example, to display only the Bourne shells in the previous output, use the following command:

```
# ps -ef | grep sh
root   1160 1061   TS 70 0 00:55:05 vt03 0:00 -sh
```

10

```
root    601  131  TS 70 0 09:19:03 vt02 0:00 -sh
root    621  601  TS 85 0 09:26:04 vt02 0:00 grep sh
#  _
```

Notice that the `grep sh` command is also displayed alongside any Bourne shells in the previous output because it was running in memory at the time the `ps` command was executed. This may not always be the case since the UNIX kernel schedules commands to run based on a variety of different factors.

The `-e` and `-f` options are the most common options used with the `ps` command; however, many other options are available. The `-l` option to the `ps` command lists even more information about each process than the `-f` option. The following output shows an example of using this option to view the processes in the terminal vt02:

```
# ps -l
F  S UID PID PPID CLS PRI NI C    ADDR SZ    WCHAN TTY  TIME COMD
42 S   0 601  131  TS  70 20 0 c7dbe550 30 c7dbe8fc vt02 0:00  sh
42 O   0 623  601  TS  59 20 0 c7dbf540 45          vt02 0:00  ps
#  _
```

The process flag (F) indicates particular features of the process; the flag of 42 is the sum of flags 4 (not traced), 8 (primary memory), 10 (locked), and 20 (cannot be swapped). The **process state** (S) column is the most valuable to system administrators as it indicates what the process is currently doing. If a process is not being run on the processor at the current time, then you will see an *S* (sleeping) in the process state column. Processes are in this state most of the time, as shown with *sh* in the previous output. You will see an *R* in this column if the process is ready to run on the processor, an *O* if the process is currently running on the processor, an *X* if it is waiting for memory, an *I* if it is being created, or a *T* if it has stopped or is being traced by another process. In addition to these, you might also see a *Z* in this column indicating a **zombie process**. When a process finishes executing, the parent process must check to see if it executed successfully and then release the child process's PID so that it can be used again. Although a process is waiting for its parent process to release the PID, the process is said to be in a zombie state as it has finished but still retains a PID. On a busy UNIX server, zombie processes may accumulate and prevent new processes from being created. If this occurs, kill the parent process of the zombies, as discussed in the next section.

**NOTE**

Zombie processes are also known as defunct processes.

The nice value (NI) can be used to affect the process priority (PRI) indirectly; it is measured between 0 (a greater chance of a high priority) and 39 (a greater chance of a lower priority). The ADDR in the previous output indicates the memory address of the process, whereas the WCHAN indicates what the process is waiting for while sleeping. The size of the process in memory (SZ) is also listed and measured in kilobytes; it is roughly equivalent to the size of the executable file on the filesystem.

Some large processes such as the sysproc daemon are further divided into **Lightweight Processes (LWPs)** that share the same PID yet have a unique LWP identification number. These LWPs can share memory and system resources yet be scheduled separately by the UNIX kernel to improve performance. To view LWPs, use the **-L** option with the **ps** command, as shown in the following output:

```
# ps -eL
    PID LWP   CLS PRI TTY     LTIME   COMD
      0   2   SYS  79 ?       0:00    sysproc
      0   3   SYS  79 ?       0:00    mod_noti
      0   4   SYS  79 ?       0:06    fsflush
      0   5   SYS  79 ?       0:00    bdelay
      0   6   SYS  79 ?       0:00    adtflush
      0   7   SYS  79 ?       0:00    strdaemo
      0   8   SYS  94 ?       0:00    swapin
      0   9   SYS  94 ?       0:00    sleeper_
      0  10   SYS  94 ?       0:01    wallcloc
      0  11   SYS  94 ?       0:00    swapout
      0  12   SYS  79 ?       0:00    autounlo
      0  13   SYS  79 ?       0:06    fsflush_
      0  14   SYS  94 ?       0:00    kma_give
      0  15   SYS  94 ?       0:01    poolrefr
      0  16   SYS  93 ?       0:00    pageout
      0  17   SYS  79 ?       0:03    vx_sched
      0  18   SYS  64 ?       0:00    vx_workl
      0  19   SYS  64 ?       0:00    vx_workl
      0  20   SYS  64 ?       0:00    vx_workl
      0  21   SYS  64 ?       0:01    vx_workl
      0  22   SYS  64 ?       0:00    vx_workl
      0  23   SYS  64 ?       0:00    vx_workl
      0  24   SYS  64 ?       0:00    vx_workl
Standard input
# _
```

The **ps** command has several options that can be used to display processes and their attributes. Table 10-1 lists the most common of these.

**Table 10-1**    Common options to the **ps** command

| Option | Description |
|--------|-------------|
| -e | Displays all processes running on terminals as well as processes that do not run on terminals (daemons) |
| -f | Displays a full list of information about each process, including the UID, PID, PPID, CPU utilization, start time, terminal, processor time, and command name |

**10**

**Table 10-1**    Common options to the ps command (continued)

| Option | Description |
|---|---|
| -l | Displays a long list of information about each process including the flag, state, UID, PID, PPID, CPU utilization, priority, nice value, address, size, WCHAN, terminal, and command name |
| -L | Displays the LWP ID for each process |
| -t terminal | Displays only those processes that are running on a certain terminal (such as vt02) |
| -u user | Displays only those processes that are run by a certain user (username or UID) |

You can also view processes using the SCO Admin Process Manager, as shown in Figure 10-3.

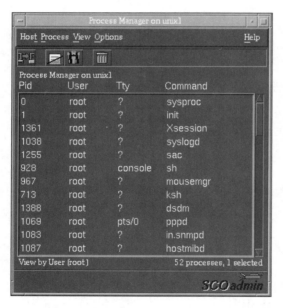

**Figure 10-3**    The SCO Admin Process Manager

Four attributes of each process are displayed by default in the Process Manager. To display more attributes, select Attributes from the View menu in the Process Manager and select the attributes to view, as depicted in Figure 10-4.

The Process Manager enables you to select individual attributes or sets of attributes based on their function (Ownership, Times, Scheduling, Size, or Full Command). For example, selecting Ownership from Figure 10-4 will result in the process attributes shown in Figure 10-5.

**Figure 10-4**     Selecting process attributes

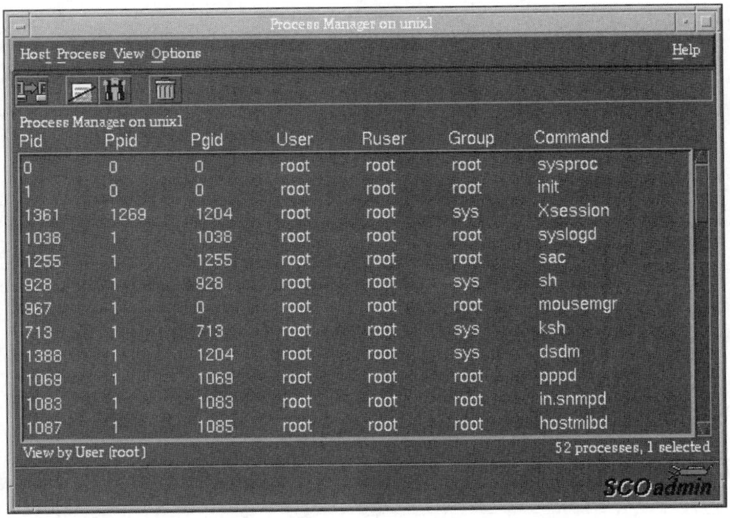

**Figure 10-5**     Viewing ownership attributes

# KILLING PROCESSES

You might encounter a process that has encountered an error during execution and con-tinuously uses up system resources. These processes are referred to as **rogue processes** and will have a large value in the TIME column of the `ps` command. Recall that zom-bie processes can also use up system resources. Because of this, rogue and zombie processes should be sent a **kill signal** to terminate them and increase overall system performance. The most common command used to send kill signals is the **kill command**. The `kill` command can send 34 different signals to a certain process; each signal operates in a dif-ferent manner. To view the different kill signal names in order, use the **-l** option with the `kill` command, as shown in the following output:

```
# kill -l
HUP    INT     QUIT ILL  TRAP ABRT EMT  FPE    KILL   BUS
```

```
SEGV  SYS      PIPE ALRM TERM USR1 USR2 CHLD    PWR    WINCH
URG   POLL     STOP TSTP CONT TTIN TTOU VTALRM PROF   XCPU
XFSZ  WAITING LWP  AIO
# _
```

Most of the kill signals listed in this output are not useful for system administrators. Table 10-2 lists the five most common kill signals used for administration.

**Table 10-2**  Common administrative kill signals

| Name | Number | Description |
|------|--------|-------------|
| HUP | 1 | Also known as the hang-up signal, it stops a process and then restarts it with the same PID. If you edit the configuration file used by a running daemon, that daemon may be sent a HUP signal to restart it; when the daemon starts again, it will read the new configuration file. |
| INT | 2 | This signal sends an interrupt signal to a process. Although this signal is one of the weakest kill signals, it works most of the time. When a user presses Del in a command-line terminal (or presses Ctrl+c in a graphical terminal) to kill a currently running process, an INT signal is actually being sent to the process. |
| QUIT | 3 | Also known as a core dump, the QUIT signal terminates a process by taking the process information in memory and saving it to a file called core.<PID_of process> on the hard disk in the current working directory . You can press Ctrl+\ to send a QUIT signal to a process that is currently running. |
| TERM | 15 | The software termination signal is the most common kill signal used by programs to kill other processes. This is the default kill signal used by the `kill` command. |
| KILL | 9 | Also known as the absolute kill signal, it forces the UNIX kernel to stop executing the process by sending the processes resources to a special device file called /dev/null. |

To send a kill signal to a process, specify the kill signal to send as an option to the `kill` command, followed by the appropriate PID of the process or processes that will be killed. For example, to send a QUIT signal to a process called `sample`, use the following commands to locate and terminate the process:

```
# ps -ef | grep sample
root    646    601   TS 59 0 09:32:57 vt02 0:00 /sbin/sample
# kill -3 646
# _
# ps -ef | grep sample
# _
```

**NOTE**

Alternatively, you could have used the command `kill -QUIT 646` to do the same as the `kill -3 646` command used in the previous output.

**NOTE** If you do not specify the kill signal when using the `kill` command, the `kill` command will use a TERM signal, as it is the default kill signal.

Some processes have the capability to ignore certain kill signals that are sent to them; this is known as **trapping** a signal. The only kill signal that cannot be trapped by any process is the KILL signal. If an INT, QUIT, and TERM signal do not terminate a stubborn process, then you can use a SIGKILL to terminate it; however, you should only use SIGKILL as a last resort because it prevents a process from closing temporary files and other resources properly.

If you send a kill signal to a process that has child processes, then that parent process will terminate all of its child processes before terminating itself. Thus, to kill several related processes, send a kill signal to their parent process. To kill zombie processes, it is often necessary to send a kill signal to its parent process.

The SCO Admin Process Manager can also be used to send kill signals to processes; just highlight the correct process in the Process Manager, select Signal from the Process menu, and choose the kill signal, as shown in Figure 10-6.

**10**

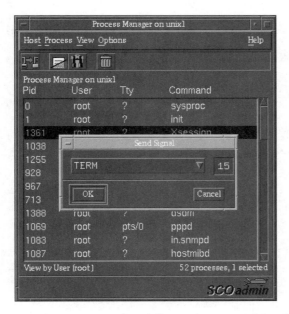

**Figure 10-6**    Sending kill signals using SCO Admin

## PROCESS EXECUTION

You can execute three main types of commands:

- Binary programs
- Shell scripts
- Shell functions

Most commands such as `ls`, `find`, and `grep` are **binary programs** that exist on the filesystem until executed. They were written in a certain programming language and compiled into a binary format that only the computer can understand. Other commands such as `cd` and `exit` are built into the shell running in memory; they are called **shell functions**. In addition, **shell scripts** are text files that can contain a list of binary programs, shell functions, and special constructs for the shell to execute in order.

When executing compiled programs or shell scripts, the shell that interprets the command typed in by the user creates a new shell. This process is known as **forking** and is carried out by the fork function in the shell. This new subshell then executes the binary program or shell script using its exec function. Once the binary program or shell script has completed, the new shell uses its exit function to kill itself and return control to the original shell. The original shell uses its wait function to wait for the new shell to carry out the aforementioned tasks before returning a prompt to the user. Figure 10-7 depicts this process when a user types the `date` command at the command line.

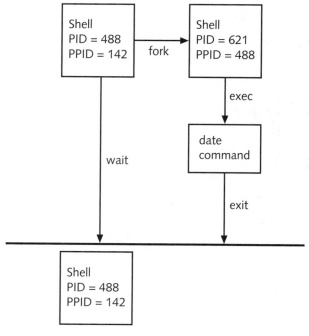

**Figure 10-7**    Process forking

# RUNNING PROCESSES IN THE BACKGROUND

As discussed in the previous section, the shell forks a subshell to execute most commands on the UNIX system. Unfortunately, the original shell must wait for the command in the subshell to finish before displaying a shell prompt to accept new commands; commands run in this fashion are known as **foreground processes**.

Alternatively, you can omit the wait function shown in Figure 10-7 by appending an ampersand (&) character to the command; commands run in this fashion are known as **background processes**. When a command is run in the background, the shell immediately returns the shell prompt for the user to enter another command. To run the `sample` command in the background, enter the following command:

```
# sample &
2583
# _
```

Inserting spaces between the command and & is optional; the command `sample&` is equivalent to the command `sample &` used previously.

The shell returns the PID (2583 in the previous example) such that the user may kill the process after it has been started without having to use the `ps` command to find the correct PID of the process.

The Bourne shell can run processes in the background; however, it cannot manipulate them afterwards as the C, POSIX, and Korn shells can. The following output starts a Korn shell and runs the `sample` process in the background:

```
# ksh
# sample &
[1]   2661
# _
```

The Korn shell returns the PID of the background process as well as a background job ID (1 in the previous example) so that the user can manipulate the background job after it has been run. To view background jobs after they have been started, use the **jobs command**:

```
# jobs
[1] + Running        sample &
# _
```

To terminate the background process, you can either send a kill signal to the PID, as seen earlier in this chapter, or to the background job ID. Background job IDs must be prefixed by the % character. To send an INT signal to the `sample` background process created earlier, use the following `kill` command:

```
# kill -2 %1
[1] + Terminated      sample &
```

**10**

```
# jobs
# _
```

Once a background process has been started, it can be moved to the foreground by using the **fg (foreground) command** followed by the background job ID. Similarly, a foreground process can be paused using the Ctrl+z key combination and sent to the background with the **bg (background) command**. Pressing Ctrl+z assigns the foreground process a background job ID that is then used as an argument to the **bg** command. To start a sample process and move it to the foreground, and then pause it and move it to the background again, use the following commands:

```
# sample &
[1] 7519
# fg %1
sample


Ctrl-z
[1] +  Stopped     sample
# bg %1
[1]                sample &
# jobs
[1] +  Running     sample &
# _
```

When multiple background processes are executing in the shell, the `jobs` command will indicate the most recent process with the + symbol and the second most recent process with the - symbol. If a user places the %% notation in a command in place of the background job ID, then the command will operate on the most recent background process. The following output shows an example of this in which four sample processes are started and sent QUIT kill signals using the %% notation:

```
# sample &
[1] 7605
# sample2 &
[2] 7613
# sample3 &
[3] 7621
# sample4 &
[4] 7629
# jobs
[1]    Running       sample &
[2]    Running       sample2 &
[3]-   Running       sample3 &
[4]+   Running       sample4 &
# kill -3 %%
[4] + Terminated     sample4 &
# jobs
[1]    Running       sample &
[2]-   Running       sample2 &
```

```
[3]+  Running            sample3 &
# kill -3 %%
[3] + Terminated         sample3 &
# jobs
[1]-  Running            sample &
[2]+  Running            sample2 &
# kill -3 %%
[2] + Terminated         sample2 &
# jobs
[1]+  Running            sample &
# kill -3 %%
[1] + Terminated         sample &
# jobs
# _
```

## PROCESS PRIORITIES

Recall that UNIX is a multitasking operating system; it can perform several different tasks at the same time. Because most computers contain only a single CPU, UNIX executes small amounts of each process on the processor in series. This enables processes to seem as if they are executing simultaneously to the user. The amount of time a process has to use the CPU is called a **time slice**; the more time slices a process has, the more time it has to execute on the CPU and the faster it will execute. Time slices are typically measured in milliseconds; thus, several hundred processes can be executing on the processor in a single second.

Recall from earlier that the `ps` command lists the UNIX kernel priority (PRI) of a process. This value is directly related to the amount of time slices a process will have on the CPU. A PRI of 0 is the most likely to get time slices on the CPU, and a PRI of 127 is the least likely to receive time slices on the CPU. The following is an example of this command:

```
# ps -l
F  S UID  PID PPID CLS PRI NI C ADDR       SZ WCHAN    TTY  TIME COMD
42 S   0  601    1  TS  72 20 0 c7dbe550   31 c7dbe8fc vt02 0:01 sh
 2 S   0  713  601  TS  70 20 0 c4da9530  230 c0435060 vt02 0:00 ksh
42 O   0  732  713  TS  60 20 0 c7dbeaa0   45          vt02 0:00 ps
# _
```

The `sh`, `ksh`, and `ps` processes all have different PRI values since the kernel automatically assigns time slices based on several factors. You cannot change the PRI directly, but you can influence it indirectly by assigning a certain **nice value** to a process. A lower nice value will increase the likelihood that the process will receive more time slices, whereas a higher nice value will do the opposite. Figure 10-8 depicts the range of nice values.

All users can be nice to other users of the same computer by lowering the priority of their own processes by increasing their nice value; however, only the root user has the ability to increase the priority of a process by lowering its nice value.

| 0 | 20 | 39 |
|---|---|---|
| Most likely to receive time slices; the PRI will be closer to 0. | The default nice value for new processes | Least likely to receive time slices; the PRI will be closer to 127. |

**Figure 10-8**    The nice value scale

Processes are started with a nice value of 20 by default, as shown in the NI column of the `ps -l` output. To start a process with a nice value of 39 (low priority), use the **nice command** and specify to increase the default nice value 19 units using the **-n** option followed by the command to start. If the **-n** option is omitted, a nice value increase of 10 units will be assumed. To start the `ps -l` command with a nice value of 39, issue the following command:

```
# nice -n 19 ps -l
F  S UID PID PPID CLS PRI NI C ADDR        SZ WCHAN    TTY  TIME COMD
42 S   0 601    1  TS   72 20 0 c7dbe550   31 c7dbe8fc vt02 0:01 sh
 2 S   0 713  601  TS   70 20 0 c4da9530  230 c0435060 vt02 0:00 ksh
42 O   0 738  713  TS   74 39 0 c7dbeaa0   45          vt02 0:00 ps
# _
```

Notice from the previous output that NI is 39 for the `ps` process as compared to 20 for the `sh` and `ksh` processes. Furthermore, the PRI of 74 for the `ps` process will result in fewer time slices than the PRI of 72 for the `sh` process and the PRI of 70 for the `ksh` process.

Conversely, to increase the priority of the `ps -l` command, use the following command:

```
# nice -n -20 ps -l
F  S UID PID PPID CLS PRI NI C ADDR        SZ WCHAN    TTY  TIME COMD
42 S   0 601    1  TS   72 20 0 c7dbe550   31 c7dbe8fc vt02 0:01 sh
 2 S   0 713  601  TS   70 20 0 c4da9530  230 c0435060 vt02 0:00 ksh
42 O   0 741  713  TS   58  0 0 c7dbeaa0   45          vt02 0:00 ps
# _
```

Note from the previous output that the nice value of 0 for the `ps` command resulted in a PRI of 58, which is more likely to receive time slices than the `sh` and `ksh` processes, which have PRI values of 72 and 70, respectively.

**NOTE**    Background processes are given a nice value of 23 (4 units lower than the default) to lower the chance they will receive time slices.

After a process has been started, a user can change his or her priority by using the **renice command** and specify the change to the nice value as well as the PID of the processes to change. Say, for example, three `sample` processes are currently executing on a terminal:

```
# ps -l
F  S UID PID PPID CLS PRI NI C ADDR     SZ WCHAN    TTY  TIME COMD
42 S   0 601    1  TS  72 20 0 c7dbe550 31 c7dbe8fc vt02 0:01 sh
42 R   0 744  601  TS  58 20 0 c4da7550 45 c7dbe8fc vt02 0:00 sample
42 R   0 746  601  TS  58 20 0 c4da9530 45 c4da839c vt02 0:00 sample
42 R   0 748  601  TS  58 20 0 c4da7aa0 45 c0435060 vt02 0:00 sample
42 O   0 752  601  TS  58 20 0 c4da7000 45 c0435060 vt02 0:00 ps
# _
```

To lower the priority of the first two sample processes by changing the nice value from 20 to 25 and view the new values, execute the following commands:

```
# renice -n 5 744 746
744: old priority 20, new priority 25
746: old priority 20, new priority 25
# ps -l
F  S UID PID PPID CLS PRI NI C ADDR     SZ WCHAN    TTY  TIME COMD
42 S   0 601    1  TS  72 20 0 c7dbe550 31 c7dbe8fc vt02 0:01 sh
42 R   0 744  601  TS  58 25 0 c4da7550 45 c7dbe8fc vt02 0:00 sample
42 R   0 746  601  TS  58 25 0 c4da9530 45 c4da839c vt02 0:00 sample
42 R   0 748  601  TS  58 20 0 c4da7aa0 45 c0435060 vt02 0:00 sample
42 O   0 754  601  TS  58 20 0 c4da7ty0 45 c0435060 vt02 0:00 ps
# _
```

**NOTE**

As with the `nice` command, only the root user can reduce the nice value of a process using the `renice` command.

**NOTE**

You can only use the `nice` and `renice` commands to alter the priority of a process that is in the Time Sharing (TS) class.

**NOTE**

The default nice value for processes on Solaris systems is 0 and nice values range from -20 (high priority) to 20 (low priority).

You can also change the priority of processes using the SCO Admin Process Manager. To do this, select the correct process, select Priority from the Process menu, and enter the appropriate change to the nice value, as shown in Figure 10-9.

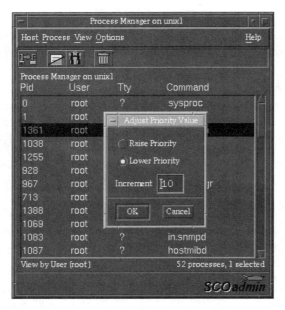

**Figure 10-9**    Changing the nice value using SCO Admin

## SCHEDULING PROCESSES

Although most processes are begun by users executing commands while logged into a terminal, at times you might want to schedule a command to run at some point in the future. Scheduling system maintenance commands to run during nonworking hours is good practice as it will not disrupt normal business activities.

The **cron daemon** is used to schedule commands. It can be used to schedule a command to execute once in the future, or it can be used to schedule a command to execute repeatedly in the future.

### Scheduling Commands Using the at Command

To schedule a command or set of commands to execute at a later time using the cron daemon, you can specify the time as an argument to the **at command**. Table 10-3 lists some common time formats used with the `at` command.

**Table 10-3**    Common `at` commands

| Command | Description |
|---|---|
| `at 1015pm` | Schedules commands to run at 10:15 P.M. on the current date |
| `at 10:15pm July 15` | Schedules commands to run at 10:15 P.M. on July 15 |
| `at 22:15 July 15` | Schedules commands to run at 10:15 P.M. on July 15 |

**Table 10-3**   Common at commands (continued)

| Command | Description |
|---|---|
| at 10 pm Friday | Schedules commands to run at 10:00 P.M. on Friday |
| at now next day | Schedules commands to run at the current time the next day |
| at now + 5 minutes | Schedules commands to run in five minutes |
| at now + 10 hours | Schedules commands to run in ten hours |
| at now + 4 days | Schedules commands to run in four days |
| at now + 2 weeks | Schedules commands to run in two weeks |
| at now or batch | Schedules commands to run immediately |

Once it is invoked, the at command will display a blank prompt enabling you to type in commands to be executed, one per line. Once the commands have been entered, use the Crtl+d key combination to schedule the commands using the cron daemon.

**NOTE** The cron daemon will use the current shell's environment when executing scheduled commands; the shell environment and scheduled commands are stored in the **/var/spool/cron/atjobs** directory.

**NOTE** If the standard output of any command scheduled using the cron daemon has not been redirected to a file, it will be mailed to the user. You can check your local mail by using the **mail command**. More information about the mail utility can be found in its man page.

To schedule the commands date and who to run at 10:15 P.M. on July 20, use the following commands:

```
# at 10:15pm July 15
date > /atfile
who >> /atfile
Ctrl-d
UX:at: INFO: Job 1058321700.a.0 at Tue Jul 15 22:15:00 2003
# _
```

As shown in the previous output, the at command returns an at job ID (1058321700.a.0 in the example) such that the user may subsequently query or remove the scheduled command. To display a list of at job IDs, specify the -l option to the at command or use the atq command:

```
# at -l
1058321700.a.0 Tue Jul 15 22:15:00 2003
# atq
 Rank   Execution Date   Owner   Job          Queue Job Name
   1st Jul 15, 2003 22:15 root   1058321700.a.0  a       stdin
# _
```

When running the `at -1` or `atq` commands, a regular user will only see his or her scheduled `at` jobs; however, the root user will see all scheduled `at` jobs.

To see the contents of the `at` job listed in the previous output alongside the shell environment at the time the `at` job was scheduled, use the **-d** option with the `at` command and specify the appropriate `at` job ID:

```
# at -d 1058321700.a.0
### BEGIN     1058321700.a.0     BEGIN ###
: at job
: jobname: stdin
: notify by mail: no
export HOME; HOME='/'
export HZ; HZ='100'
export KEYBOARD; KEYBOARD='C/US'
export LANG; LANG='C'
export LOGNAME; LOGNAME='root'
export MAPCHAN; MAPCHAN='/usr/lib/mapchan/88591.dk'
export NUMLOCK; NUMLOCK='no'
export PATH; PATH='/sbin:/usr/sbin:/usr/bin:/etc:/usr/ccs/bin'
export SHELL; SHELL='/sbin/sh'
export SHIFTDOWN; SHIFTDOWN='yes'
export TERM; TERM='AT386-M-ie''
export TERMCAP; TERMCAP='/etc/termcap'
export TFADMIN; TFADMIN=' '
export TZ; TZ=':US/Eastern'
export XKEYBOARD; XKEYBOARD='C/US'
export XMODIFIERS; XMODIFIERS='@im=Local'
export XNLSPATH; XNLSPATH='/usr/X/lib/Xsi/C/US'
cd /
#ident "@(#)adm:common/cmd/.adm/.proto 1.2.3.1"
#ident "Header: /sms/sinixV5.4es/rcs/s19-full/usr/src/cmd/.adm/.proto,v
1.1 91/
2/28 15:51:58 ccs Exp "
cd /
ulimit 2097151
umask 22
date > /atfile
who >> /atfile

### END     1058321700.a.0     END ###
# _
```

To remove the `at` job used in the previous example, use the `atrm` command followed by the `at` job ID. Alternatively, you may specify the `-r` option to the `at` command followed by the `at` job ID, as shown in the following output:

```
# at -r 1058321700.a.0
# at -l
# _
```

If many commands will be scheduled using the `at` command, it is beneficial to place these commands in a shell script and schedule the shell script to execute at a later time using the `-f` option with the `at` command. The following output is an example of scheduling a shell script called myscript using the `at` command:

```
# cat myscript
#this is a sample shell script
date > /atfile
who >> /atfile
# at -f myscript 10:15pm July 15
UX:at: INFO: Job 1058321700.a.0 at Tue Jul 15 22:15:00 2003
# _
```

By default, only the root user is allowed to schedule tasks using the `at` command. To give this ability to other users, create an **/etc/cron.d/at.allow** file and add the names of users allowed to use the `at` command, one per line. Conversely, use the **/etc/cron.d/at.deny** file to deny certain users access to the `at` command; any user not listed in this file is then allowed to use the `at` command. If both files exist, then the system first checks the /etc/cron.d/at.allow file and does not process the entries in the /etc/cron.d/at.deny file.

**NOTE**

On UnixWare systems, only an /etc/cron.d/at.deny file exists by default after installation. Because this file is initially left blank, all users are allowed to use the `at` command to schedule processes using the cron daemon.

## Scheduling Commands with the crontab Command

The `at` command is useful for scheduling tasks to occur on a certain date in the future, but is ill suited for scheduling repetitive tasks since each task will require its own at job ID. Fortunately, the cron daemon is well suited for repetitive tasks; it can use configuration files called **cron tables** to specify when a command should be executed.

Cron tables have six fields separated by space or tab characters. The first five fields specify the times to run the command, and the sixth field is the absolute pathname to the command to be executed. As with the `at` command, you can place commands in a shell script and schedule the shell script to run repetitively; in this case, the sixth field will be the absolute pathname to the shell script. Figure 10-10 depicts each field in a cron table.

**10**

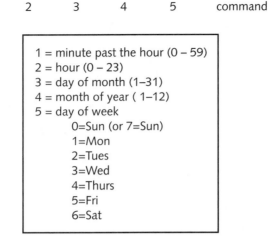

**Figure 10-10** The format of a cron table

Thus, to execute the /myscript shell script at 5:20 P.M. and 5:40 P.M. Monday through Friday regardless of the day of the month or month of the year, you could use the cron table depicted in Figure 10-11.

| 1 | 2 | 3 | 4 | 5 | command |
|---|---|---|---|---|---------|
| 20,40 | 17 | * | * | 1–5 | /myscript |

**Figure 10-11** A sample cron table

The first field in Figure 10-11 specifies the minute past the hour. Because the command must be run at 20 minutes and 40 minutes past the hour, this field has two values that are separated by a comma. The second field specifies the time in 24-hour format; 5 P.M. is the 17th hour. The third and fourth fields specify the day of the month and month of the year to run the command, respectively. Because the command can run during any month regardless of the day of the month, both of these fields use the * wildcard metacharacter to match all values. The final field indicates the day of the week to run the command. As with the first field, the command must be run on multiple days, but a range of days was specified (day 1 to day 5).

Alternatively, you can use the cron table depicted in Figure 10-12 to execute the /myscript shell script at midnight (0 minutes past the hour at the 0th hour) on the first and second days of every month regardless of the day of the week.

| 1 | 2 | 3 | 4 | 5 | command |
|---|---|---|---|---|---------|
| 0 | 0 | 1,2 | * | * | /myscript |

**Figure 10-12** A sample cron table not specifying the day

Cron tables are stored in **/var/spool/cron/crontabs** and given the same name as the user for whom tasks are scheduled. By default, this directory contains five files—one for the root user and four for the daemon processes:

```
# ls /var/spool/cron/crontabs
adm    lp    root  sys   uucp
# _
```

As the root user, you can edit or create files in this directory; however, normal users must use the `crontab -e` command to create or edit their own cron table. By default, the **crontab command** uses the ed editor to edit files; however, you can set the VISUAL or EDITOR variable in your shell to the value /usr/bin/vi to force the use of the vi editor with the `crontab` command. If you run the command `crontab -e` as the root user with the VISUAL variable set to /usr/bin/vi, you will see the following output, where you may add, edit, or remove lines from your cron table:

```
#ident  "@(#)adm:common/cmd/.adm/root   1.1.11.1"
#ident  "$Header: root 1.2 91/07/24 $"
#
# The root crontab should be used to perform accounting data collection.
#
1,30 * * * * $TFADMIN /usr/bin/ps -p $$ >/dev/null
5 4 * * * /usr/lib/dstime/dst_sync
30 4 * * 5 /bin/command1
0 14 1 * * /bin/command2
~
~
~
~
~
~
~
~
~
~
~
~
~
~
~
~
~
"/tmp/crontab000CA" 7 lines, 249 characters
```

**10**

To schedule the command /bin/command1 to run at 4:30 A.M. every Friday and /bin/command2 to run at 2:00 P.M. on the first day of every month, add the following lines while in the vi editor:

```
#ident "@(#)adm:common/cmd/.adm/root  1.1.11.1"
#ident "$Header: root 1.2 91/07/24 $"
#
# The root crontab should be used to perform accounting data collection.
#
1,30 * * * * $TFADMIN /usr/bin/ps -p $$ >/dev/null
5 4 * * * /usr/lib/dstime/dst_sync
30 4 * * 5 /bin/command1
0 14 1 * * /bin/command2
~
~
~
~
~
~
~
~
~
~
~
~
~
~
~
~
"/tmp/crontab000CA" 9 lines, 293 characters
```

As with the **at** command, you can use the **/etc/cron.d/cron.allow** file to list users who have the ability to schedule tasks using the **crontab** command; all other users will be denied. Conversely, you can create an **/etc/cron.d/cron.deny** file to list those users who are denied the ability to schedule tasks using the **crontab** command; any users not listed in this file are allowed to schedule tasks only. If both files exist, then only the /etc/cron.d/cron.allow file will be processed.

To list your cron table, use the **-l** option to the **crontab** command. The following output lists the cron table created earlier:

```
# crontab -l
#ident "@(#)adm:common/cmd/.adm/root  1.1.11.1"
#ident "$Header: root 1.2 91/07/24 $"
#
# The root crontab should be used to perform accounting data collection.
#
1,30 * * * * $TFADMIN /usr/bin/ps -p $$ >/dev/null
5 4 * * * /usr/lib/dstime/dst_sync
```

```
30 4 * * 5 /bin/command1
0 14 1 * * /bin/command2
# _
```

Furthermore, to remove a cron table and all scheduled jobs, use the −r option with the crontab command as follows:

```
# crontab -r
# crontab -l
UX:crontab: ERROR: Cannot open crontab file: No such file or directory
# _
```

The root user can edit, list, or remove any other user's cron table by using the −u option with the crontab command followed by the username. For example, to edit the cron table for the user mary, the root user could use the command crontab -e -u mary at the command prompt. Similarly, to list and remove mary's cron table, the root user could execute the commands crontab -l -u mary and crontab -r -u mary, respectively.

## PROCESS ACCOUNTING

10

In the 1980s, computers that ran the UNIX operating system were expensive by today's standards. As a result, one UNIX computer typically supported several different departments in a company, and the cost of the UNIX computer was divided among the departments that used it. Because the cost was representative of each department's usage, process accounting daemons tracked each process run by users. For example, if users in the Marketing Department ran 30% of the processes on the UNIX computer during the year, they incurred 30% of the cost of the UNIX computer.

Process accounting daemons are disabled by default because they log a great deal of information. To enable them, you can select Enable/Disable from the Accounting menu of the SCO Admin Reports Manager in the System folder of SCO Admin, as shown in Figure 10-13.

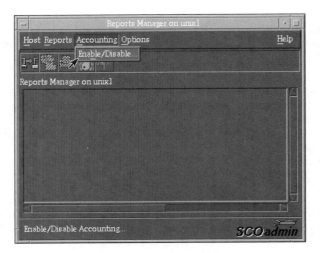

**Figure 10-13**   Enabling and disabling process accounting daemons using SCO Admin

Once process accounting has been enabled, all process activity is logged to the file /var/adm/pacct. To view the contents of this file afterwards, select Accounting Summary from the Reports menu of the SCO Admin Reports Manager and choose to display a Daily or Monthly report, as shown in Figure 10-14.

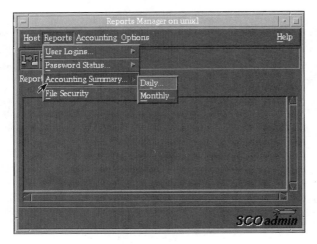

**Figure 10-14**   Selecting process accounting reports using SCO Admin

Selecting Daily from Figure 10-14 will provide the information shown in Figure 10-15.

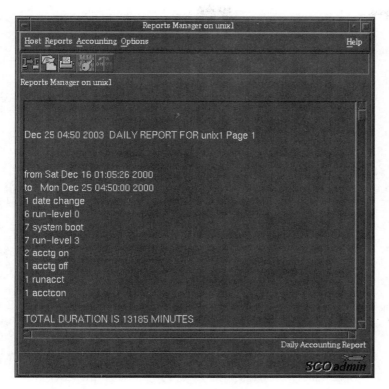

**Figure 10-15**  A sample daily accounting report

Alternatively, you can use the `acctcom` command to view the contents of the /var/adm/pacct file:

```
# acctcom | more
COMMAND                    START     END       REAL    CPU     MEAN
NAME       USER TTYNAME    TIME      TIME      (SECS)  (SECS)  SIZE(K)
#accton    root ?          00:20:11  00:20:11  0.08    0.04    299.00
turnacct   adm  ?          00:20:10  00:20:10  0.60    0.09    128.89
rm         adm  ?          00:20:11  00:20:11  0.08    0.05    189.60
rm         adm  ?          00:20:11  00:20:11  0.04    0.03    220.00
rm         adm  ?          00:20:11  00:20:11  0.05    0.03    226.67
#startup   adm  ?          00:20:10  00:20:11  1.08    0.21    181.33
#cp        root ?          00:20:11  00:20:11  0.12    0.07    355.43
ln         root ?          00:20:11  00:20:11  0.13    0.05    295.20
accounti   root ?          00:20:08  00:20:11  3.47    0.16    888.25
sendmail   adm  ?          00:20:12  00:20:12  0.09    0.04    1516.00
#sendmail  adm  ?          00:20:10  00:20:12  2.10    0.60    1374.40
#slocal    adm  ?          00:20:13  00:20:13  0.34    0.22    1083.64
#sendmail  adm  ?          00:20:12  00:20:13  1.47    0.16    1503.75
#sendmail  root ?          00:20:37  00:20:37  0.19    0.09    1475.56
uname      root ?          00:20:39  00:20:39  0.19    0.07    1610.86
pkginfo    root ?          00:20:39  00:20:39  0.07    0.07    859.43
```

```
expr        root  ?       00:20:39 00:20:39  0.06   0.04    435.00
uname       root  ?       00:20:39 00:20:39  0.07   0.04    550.00
hostname    root  ?       00:20:40 00:20:40  0.08   0.01    600.00
grep        root  ?       00:20:39 00:20:39  0.11   0.07    497.14
hostname    root  ?       00:20:39 00:20:39  0.48   0.19   1178.53
wc          root  ?       00:20:43 00:20:43  0.30   0.17   1892.94
Standard input
```

To view only those processes associated with a certain user, use the command `acctcom -u <username>`, where <username> is the login name or UID of a user on the system:

```
# acctcom -u adm | more
COMMAND                   START    END      REAL   CPU    MEAN
NAME      USER  TTYNAME   TIME     TIME     (SECS) (SECS) SIZE(K)
turnacct  adm   ?         00:20:10 00:20:10 0.60   0.09   128.89
rm        adm   ?         00:20:11 00:20:11 0.08   0.05   189.60
rm        adm   ?         00:20:11 00:20:11 0.04   0.03   220.00
rm        adm   ?         00:20:11 00:20:11 0.05   0.03   226.67
#startup  adm   ?         00:20:10 00:20:11 1.08   0.21   181.33
sendmail  adm   ?         00:20:12 00:20:12 0.09   0.04   1516.00
#sendmail adm   ?         00:20:10 00:20:12 2.10   0.60   1374.40
#slocal   adm   ?         00:20:13 00:20:13 0.34   0.22   1083.64
#sendmail adm   ?         00:20:12 00:20:13 1.47   0.16   1503.75
rm        adm   ?         00:21:02 00:21:02 0.05   0.04   197.00
id        adm   ?         00:21:02 00:21:02 0.08   0.06   337.33
crontab   adm   ?         00:21:03 00:21:03 0.09   0.07   440.00
awk       adm   ?         00:21:03 00:21:03 0.14   0.11   561.82
cmp       adm   ?         00:21:03 00:21:03 0.07   0.04   333.00
crontab   adm   ?         00:21:03 00:21:03 0.12   0.08   451.50
cat       adm   ?         00:21:03 00:21:03 0.06   0.05   192.80
cat       adm   ?         00:21:03 00:21:03 0.07   0.04   304.00
date      adm   ?         00:21:03 00:21:03 0.07   0.05   276.80
mailx     adm   ?         00:21:03 00:21:03 0.54   0.30   888.80
rm        adm   ?         00:21:04 00:21:04 0.06   0.04   208.00
#acct_ena adm   ?         00:21:02 00:21:03 1.49   0.36   152.56
acctwtmp  adm   ?         00:21:04 00:21:04 0.05   0.03   220.00
Standard input
```

Similarly, to view only those processes that have been started by members of a group, use the command `acctcom -g <groupname>`, where <groupname> is the name or GID of a valid group on the system.

## CHAPTER SUMMARY

❒ Processes are programs that are executing on the system; their attributes can be viewed using the ps command or the SCO Admin Process Manager.

❒ User processes are run in the same terminal as the user who executed them, whereas daemon processes are system processes that do not run on a terminal.

❏ Every process has a parent process associated with it and optionally several child processes.

❏ Zombie and rogue processes that exist for long periods of time use up system resources and should be killed to improve system performance.

❏ You may send kill signals to a process using the kill commands and the SCO Admin Process Manager.

❏ UNIX shells fork a subshell to execute most commands.

❏ Processes can be run in the background by appending an & to the command name; most shells assign each background process a background job ID such that it can be manipulated afterwards.

❏ The priority of a process can be affected indirectly by altering its nice value; nice values range from 0 (high priority) to 39 (low priority). Only the root user can increase the priority of a process.

❏ Commands can be scheduled to run at a later time by the cron daemon. The at command schedules tasks to occur at a later time, whereas the crontab command uses cron tables to schedule tasks to occur repetitively in the future.

10

# KEY TERMS

**/etc/cron.d/at.allow** — A file listing all users who can use the at command.

**/etc/cron.d/at.deny** — A file listing all users who cannot access the at command.

**/etc/cron.d/cron.allow** — A file listing all users who can use the cron command.

**/etc/cron.d/cron.deny** — A file listing all users who cannot access the cron command.

**/var/spool/cron/atjobs** — A directory that stores the information used to schedule processes configured by the at command.

**/var/spool/cron/crontabs** — A directory that stores cron tables.

**at command** — The command used to schedule commands and tasks to run at a preset time in the future.

**background processes** — A process that does not require the shell to wait for its termination; upon execution, the user receives the shell prompt immediately.

**bg (background) command** — The command used to run a foreground process in the background.

**binary program** — An executable file that contains binary data.

**child process** — A process that was started by another process (parent process).

**cron table** — A file specifying tasks to be run by the cron daemon.

**cron daemon** — The system daemon that executes tasks in the future—it may be configured using the at and crontab commands.

**crontab command** — The command used to view and edit cron tables.

**daemon process** — A system process that is not associated with a terminal.

**fg (foreground) command** — The command used to run a background process in the foreground.

**foreground processes** — A process for which the shell that executed it must wait for its termination.

**forking** — The act of creating a new shell child process from a parent shell process.

**jobs command** — The command used to see the list of background processes running in the current shell.

**kill command** — The command used to kill or terminate a process.

**kill signal** — The type of signal sent to a process by the kill command; different kill signals affect processes in different ways.

**Lightweight Process (LWP)** — A small part of a larger process that shares a PID with other parts of the larger process, but may be scheduled individually.

**mail command** — The traditional e-mail reader on UNIX systems.

**nice command** — The command used to change the priority of a process as it is started.

**nice value** — The value that indirectly represents the priority of a process; the higher the value, the lower the priority.

**parent process** — A process that has started other processes (child processes).

**parent process ID (PPID)** — The PID of the parent process that created the current process.

**process** — A program currently loaded into physical memory and running on the system.

**process ID (PID)** — A unique identifier assigned to every process as it begins.

**process priority** — A number assigned to a process used to determine how many time slices on the processor time it will receive; the higher the number, the lower the priority.

**process state** — The current state of the process on the processor; most processes are in the sleeping state.

**program** — A structured set of commands stored in an executable file on a filesystem; it may be executed to create a process.

**ps command** — The command used to obtain information about processes currently running on the system.

**renice command** — The command used to alter the nice value of a process currently running on the system.

**rogue process** — A process that has become faulty in some way and continues to consume far more system resources than it should.

**shell function** — A special variable in memory created by the shell that can be executed to perform a certain task.

**shell script** — A text file that contains commands and constructs that are interpreted by the shell upon execution.

**time slice** — The amount of time a process is given on a CPU on a machine using a multiprocessing operating system.

**trapping** — The process of ignoring a kill signal.

**user process** — A process begun by a user that runs on a terminal.

**zombie process** — A process that has finished executing, but whose parent has not yet released its PID; it still retains a spot in the kernel's process table.

## REVIEW QUESTIONS

1. A program is an executable or set of executables stored on physical storage media that can be loaded into physical memory and run. True or False?

2. Which command entered without arguments is used to display a list of processes running on the current shell?

    a. ppid

    b. list

    c. pid

    d. ps

3. Only system processes or daemons can be run in the background; all user-initiated processes must be associated with a terminal and run in the foreground. True or False?

4. What is the only kill signal that cannot be trapped by a process?

    a. KILL

    b. QUIT

    c. INT

    d. TERM

5. If the nice command is run and no value is specified, what default value will the system assume?

    a. 0

    b. 19

    c. –20

    d. 10

6. Which of the following statements is true? (Choose all that apply.)

    a. If /etc/cron.d/at.allow exists, only users listed in it can use the at command.

    b. If /etc/cron.d/cron.allow exists, only users listed in it can use the crontab command.

   c. If /etc/cron.d/cron.deny exists and /etc/cron.d/cron.allow does not exist, then any user not listed in /etc/cron.d/cron.deny can use the crontab command.

   d. If /etc/cron.d/cron.allow and /etc/cron.d/cron.deny exist, only users listed in the former can use the crontab command and any listed in the latter are denied access to the crontab command.

   e. If a user is listed in both /etc/cron.d/cron.allow and /etc/cron.d/cron.deny, then /etc/cron.d/cron.deny takes precedence and the user cannot access the crontab command.

7. Where are individual user tasks scheduled to run with the cron daemon stored?

   a. /etc/crontab

   b. /etc/cron/<username>

   c. /var/spool/cron/crontabs

   d. /var/spool/cron/crontabs/<username>

8. Which process will always have a PID of 1 and a PPID of 0?

   a. ps

   b. init

   c. top

   d. sysproc

9. What command can be used to view process accounting reports by group?

   a. acctcom

   b. acctcom -g <groupname>

   c. groupcom

   d. groupcom -g <groupname>

10. The term used to describe a process spawning or initiating another process is referred to as _____.

   a. child process

   b. forking

   c. branching

   d. parenting

11. Only the root user can lower the nice values of processes and hence raise their priority. True or False?

12. A process is a/an _____.

   a. program loaded into physical memory and running

   b. predefined way of doing something

   c. executable or set of executables stored on a hard disk drive

   d. program that must be initiated by a user logged into a terminal

13. As daemon processes are not associated with a terminal, you have to use the -e switch with ps to view them. True or False?

14. Which of the following commands will most increase the chance of a process receiving more time slices?

   a. renice –n 0

   b. renice –n 15

   c. renice –n –12

   d. renice –n 19

15. How do you bypass the wait function and send a process to the background?

   a. This cannot happen once a process is executing; it can only be done when the command is entered by placing an ampersand (&) after it.

   b. Only daemon processes can run in the background.

   c. by using the ps command

   d. by using the bg command

16. The at command is used to _____.

   a. schedule processes to run periodically in the background

   b. schedule processes to run periodically on a recurring basis in the future

   c. schedule processes to run at a single instance in the future

   d. schedule processes to run in the foreground

17. Every process on a UNIX system including the init daemon has a PID and a PPID. True or False?

18. The higher the priority of a process, the more time slices it has on the CPU. True or False?

19. What command is used to view and modify user jobs scheduled to run with cron?

   a. crontab

   b. cron

   c. ps

   d. sched

20. When the at command is used to schedule a process to run, where is the information on what shell to use when executing the process stored?

   a. /var/spool/atjobs

   b. /var/spool/cron/atjobs

   c. /etc/atjobs

   d. /etc/at/shell

**10**

21. Every process has a PID and a _____.

    a. fork process

    b. daemon

    c. child process

    d. PPID

22. What is the preferred way to kill a zombie process?

    a. Kill its parent process.

    b. Use the -9 option with the kill command.

    c. Use the -15 option with the kill command.

    d. Zombie processes cannot be killed.

23. Nice values used to affect process priorities range between _____.

    a. 0 and 20

    b. 0 and 39

    c. -19 and 20

    d. 0 and 127

24. What is the name given to a process not associated with a terminal?

    a. child process

    b. parent process

    c. user process

    d. daemon process

25. In order to kill a process running in the background, you must place a % character before its PID. True or False?

26. What kill level signal cannot be trapped?

    a. 1

    b. 9

    c. 3

    d. 15

27. A runaway process that is faulty and consuming mass amounts of system resources _____.

    a. is a zombie process

    b. is an orphaned process

    c. has a PID of 1

    d. has a PPID of 0

    e. is a rogue process

28. When you run the ps command, how are daemon processes recognized?

    a. The terminal is listed as tty0.

    b. A question mark appears in the TTY column.

    c. There is no way to do this with ps; you must use the top command.

    d. The letter *d* for daemon appears in the terminal identification column.

29. When renice is used to affect a process's priority by lowering the nice value, it has _____ than it had before.

    a. more priority

    b. less priority

    c. the same priority

    d. This does not work; the nice command is used to do this, not the renice command.

30. What command can be used to see processes running in the background?

    a. bg

    b. jobs

    c. ps –%

    d. They cannot be seen or listed as they are running in the background; only foreground processes can be seen.

## HANDS-ON PROJECTS

These projects should be completed in the order given. All hands-on projects should take a total of three hours to complete. The requirement for this lab includes:

❏ A computer with UnixWare 7.1.1 installed according to Project 2-2

**HANDS-ON PROJECTS**

### Project 10-1

In this hands-on project, you will view the characteristics of processes and change their priority.

1. Turn on your computer. Once your UNIX system has been loaded, switch to a command-line terminal (vt02) by pressing **Ctrl+Alt+F2**, and log into the terminal using the username **root** and the password **secret**.

2. At the command prompt, type **ps –ef | more** and press **Enter** to view the first processes started on the entire UNIX system.

3. Fill in the following information from the data displayed on the terminal screen after typing the command:

    a. Which process has a PID of 0? _____

    b. Which process has a PID of 1? _____

   c. What character do most processes have in the terminal column (TTY)?

   _____

   d. What does the character in the terminal column indicate? _____

   e. Which user started most of these processes? _____

   f. Most processes that are displayed on the screen are started by a certain parent process indicated in the PPID column. Which process is the parent to most processes? _____

   Type **q** to exit the more utility.

4. At the command prompt, type **ps -el | more** and press **Enter** to view the process states for the first processes started on the entire UNIX system.

5. Fill in the following information from the data displayed on the terminal screen after typing the command:

   a. What character exists in the state (S) column for most processes, and what does this character indicate? _____

   b. What range of numbers is possible to have in the nice (NI) column?

   _____

> You may notice that the values in the NI column are all 0 regardless of the actual nice value; this is a fault with the ps command in UnixWare 7.1.1 and will likely be fixed in future versions of UnixWare.

**NOTE**

   c. What class of process is sysproc? What class of process are most other processes that appear on the screen? What does this tell you about the priority of the sysproc process compared to most daemons? _____

   Type **q** to exit the more utility.

6. At the command prompt, type **ps -el | grep Z** and press **Enter** to display zombie processes on your UNIX system. Are any zombie processes indicated in the state (S) column?

7. Type **exit** and press **Enter** to log out of your shell.

8. Switch to the graphical terminal (vt01) by pressing **Ctrl+Alt+F1**, and log into the CDE desktop using the username **root** and the password **secret**.

9. Open the SCO Admin Process Manager. What process attributes are listed by default? Open the **View** menu and select **Attributes**. Add **Ppid** to the selected list of attributes and press **OK** when you are finished.

10. Observe the new PPID column. What is the PPID for most processes listed? What is listed in the TTY column for most processes listed? Why? Compare this to the information collected in Step 3.

11. Highlight the **init** daemon, open the **Process** menu, and select **Priority**. At the Adjust Priority Value screen, ensure that a lower priority is selected and enter the number **19** in the dialog box. Press **OK** when you are finished. What nice value does the init daemon have now?

12. Close all programs and log out of the CDE desktop.

## Project 10-2

In this hands-on project, you will use the kill command and SCO Admin Process Manager to terminate processes on your system.

1. Switch to a command-line terminal (vt02) by pressing **Ctrl+Alt+F2**, and log into the terminal using the username **root** and the password **secret**.

2. At the command prompt, type **ps -ef | grep sh** and press **Enter** to view the Bourne shells that are running in memory on your computer. Record the PID of the bash shell running in your terminal (vt02): _____

3. At the command prompt, type **kill -l** and press **Enter** to list the available kill signal that you can send to a process. Which number is associated with INT? Which number is associated with QUIT?

4. At the command prompt, type **kill -2 PID** (where PID is the PID that you recorded in Step 2) and press **Enter**. Did your shell terminate?

5. At the command prompt, type **kill -3 PID** (where PID is the PID that you recorded in Step 2) and press **Enter**. Did your shell terminate?

6. At the command prompt, type **kill -15 PID** (where PID is the PID that you recorded in Step 2) and press **Enter**. Did your shell terminate?

7. At the command prompt, type **kill -9 PID** (where PID is the PID that you recorded in Step 2) and press **Enter**. Did your shell terminate? Why did this command work when the others did not?

8. Switch to the graphical terminal (vt01) by pressing **Ctrl+Alt+F1**, and log into the CDE desktop using the username **root** and the password **secret**.

9. Open SCOAdmin and double-click **Process Manager**.

10. After Process Manager has opened, highlight the process named **Xsession**. This process is the parent process of all CDE desktop processes.

11. Use your mouse to open the **Process** menu and select **Signal** from the list.

12. At the Send Signal dialog box, choose a kill signal and press **OK**. What happened?

## Project 10-3

In this hands-on project, you will run processes in the background and kill them using the kill command.

1. Switch to a command-line terminal (vt02) by pressing **Ctrl+Alt+F2**, and log into the terminal using the username **root** and the password **secret**.

10

2. At the command prompt, type **sleep 6000** and press **Enter** to start the sleep command, which waits 6000 seconds in the foreground. Do you get your prompt back once you enter this command? Why or why not? Send the process an INT signal by pressing **Delete**.

3. At the command prompt, type **sleep 6000&** and press **Enter** to start the sleep command, which waits 6000 seconds in the background. Observe the PID that is returned. Did you receive a background job ID? Why or why not? If you got a PID, note it.

4. At the command prompt, type **kill <PID>** (where <PID> is the PID that was shown in the previous step) and press **Enter**. What kill signal was sent?

5. At the command prompt, type **ksh** and press **Enter** to start a Korn shell.

6. At the command prompt, type **sleep 6000&** and press **Enter**. Observe the PID and background job ID that is returned.

7. Bring the background sleep process to the foreground by typing **fg %1** at the command prompt and pressing **Enter**. Send the process an INT signal by pressing **Delete**.

8. Place another sleep command in memory by typing the **sleep 6000&** command and press **Enter**. Repeat this command three more times to place a total of four sleep commands in memory.

9. At the command prompt, type **jobs** and press **Enter** to view the jobs running in the background. What does the + symbol indicate?

10. At the command prompt, type **kill %%** and press **Enter** to terminate the most recent process and view the output.

11. At the command prompt, type **kill %1** and press **Enter** to terminate background job 1 and view the output.

12. Type **exit** and press **Enter** to log out of your Korn shell.

13. Type **exit** and press **Enter** to log out of your Bourne shell.

## Project 10-4

HANDS-ON
PROJECTS

In this hands-on project, you will schedule processes by using the at and crontab utilities.

1. Switch to a command-line terminal (vt02) by pressing **Ctrl+Alt+F2**, and log into the terminal using the username **root** and the password **secret**.

2. Schedule processes to run one minute in the future by typing the command **at now + 1 minute** at the command prompt and pressing **Enter**.

3. When the blank prompt appears, type the word **date** and press **Enter**.

4. When the second blank prompt appears, type the word **who** and press **Enter**.

5. When the third blank prompt appears, press **Ctrl+d** to finish the scheduling and observe the output. When will your job run? Where will the output of the date and who commands be sent?

6. In approximately one minute, check your mail by typing **mail** at the command line and pressing **Enter**. Look for the most recent e-mail (the one with the highest e-mail number) and record the number: _____

7. At the ? prompt, type the number that corresponds to the e-mail in the previous question, press **Enter**, and observe the output. When you are finished, type **q** at the ? prompt and press **Enter** to exit the mail program.

8. At the command prompt, type **crontab -l** and press **Enter** to list your cron table. Do you have one?

9. At the command prompt, type **VISUAL=/usr/bin/vi** and press **Enter**. Next, type **export VISUAL** at the command prompt and press **Enter**.

10. At the command prompt, type **crontab -e** and press **Enter** to edit your cron table. When the vi editor appears, add the following line:

```
30 20 *   *   5  /bin/false
```

When you are finished, save your changes and exit the vi editor.

11. At the command prompt, type **crontab -l** and press **Enter** to list your cron table. When will the /bin/false command run?

12. At the command prompt, type **cat /var/spool/cron/crontabs/root** and press **Enter** to list your cron table from the cron directory. Is it the same as the output from the previous command?

13. Type **exit** and press **Enter** to log out of your shell.

## Project 10-5

In this hands-on project, you will enable and view process accounting reports.

1. Switch to the graphical terminal (vt01) by pressing **Ctrl+Alt+F1**, and log into the CDE desktop using the username **root** and the password **secret**.

2. Open SCO Admin and navigate to the **System** folder to select the **Reports Manager**.

3. In the Reports Manager, select the **Accounting** menu and choose **Enable/Disable**. What warning do you receive?

4. Press **OK** at the warning screen and press **OK** again to close the confirmation screen. Leave the Reports Manager screen open.

5. Use your mouse to click open SCOhelp from the CDE desktop toolbar.

6. Next, close SCOhelp and use your mouse to highlight the **Reports Manager**.

7. In the Reports Manager, select the **Accounting** menu and choose **Enable/Disable**.

8. Press **OK** at the warning screen and press **OK** again to close the confirmation screen.

9. Close all programs and log out of the CDE desktop.

10. Switch to a command-line terminal (vt02) by pressing **Ctrl+Alt+F2**, and log into the terminal using the username **root** and the password **secret**.

11. At the command prompt, type **acctcom | more** and press **Enter** to list the information recorded in the /var/adm/pacct file. How much information is there? How much information do you estimate will be logged to this file on a busy UnixWare computer in one hour? Press **q** to quit the more utility.

12. Type **exit** and press **Enter** to log out of your shell.

## DISCOVERY EXERCISES

1. Type the command **sleep 5** at a command prompt and press **Enter**. When did you receive your shell prompt back? Explain the events that occurred by referencing Figure 10-7. Next, type **exec sleep 5** at a command prompt and press **Enter**. What happened? Can you explain the results using Figure 10-7? Redraw Figure 10-7 to indicate what happens when a command is directly executed.

2. Using the man pages or SCOhelp, research four more options to the ps command. What processes does each option display? What information is given about each process?

3. Log into the CDE desktop and open a command-line terminal. At the shell prompt, type **xcalc** to execute the X Windows calculator. Does the terminal window stay open? Click on the terminal window to bring it to the foreground. Do you see your shell prompt? Why or why not? Close your terminal window by double-clicking on the upper-left corner. What happened to the X Windows calculator? Why? Next, open another command-line terminal and type **xcalc&** at the command prompt to execute the X Windows calculator in the background. Click on the terminal window to bring it to the foreground. Do you see your shell prompt? Why or why not? Close your terminal window by double-clicking on the upper-left corner. What happened to the X Windows calculator? Why?

4. You are the system administrator for a large trust company. Most of the UNIX servers in the company host databases that are accessed frequently by company employees. One particular UNIX server has been reported as being very slow today. Upon further investigation using the ps command, you have found a rogue process that is wasting a great deal of system resources. Unfortunately, the rogue process is a database maintenance program and should be killed with caution. Which kill signal would you send this process and why? If the rogue process traps this signal, which other kill signals would you try? Which command could you use as a last resort to kill the rogue process?

5. Write the lines that someone could use in his or her user cron table to schedule the /bin/myscript command to run:

   a. every Wednesday afternoon at 2:15 P.M.

   b. every hour on the hour every day of the week

   c. every 15 minutes on the first of every month

   d. only on February 25 at 6:00 P.M.

   e. on the first Monday of every month at 12:10 P.M.

# 11

# PACKAGE AND LOG FILE MANAGEMENT

**After reading this chapter and completing the exercises, you will be able to:**

◆ Indentify installed software packages and package sets

◆ Install software packages and verify their integrity

◆ Spool software packages for future installation

◆ Create a software depot and install software from this depot across a network

◆ Use SCO Admin to install and manage software packages

◆ Identify common log files and their location on the system

◆ Manage the contents of log files on the system using command-line utilities and the System Logs Manager

◆ Configure system logging using the system log daemon

In Chapter 4, you learned how to manage the various files present on a UNIX filesystem, and in Chapter 6, you learned how to alter their security. The focus of this chapter is on the management of log files and files that comprise software packages. First, this chapter outlines terminology related to software packages and discusses how to list, add, and remove them. Following this, you will learn how to identify common log files on a UNIX system and how the system log daemon can be used to log system events. Finally, this chapter discusses how to manage log files and use the System Logs Manager in SCO Admin.

# PACKAGE MANAGEMENT

One of the primary responsibilities of most UNIX administrators is the installation and maintenance of software packages. **Software packages** consist of a series of files and system settings that comprise a program on the system. For example, the nd package contains all network drivers, whereas the scohelp package contains the SCOhelp graphical help system.

Software packages that share a similar function are often categorized into **package sets**. For example, the NSComm4 package set contains all the packages that comprise Netscape Communicator, whereas the UnixWare package set contains all the packages that comprise the UnixWare operating system.

 **NOTE**  Because UNIX is a proprietary operating system, most software that runs on UNIX systems is proprietary. As a result, most software packages must be purchased from the vendor of the software.

 **NOTE**  Several free software programs (commonly called open source software) are available for Linux systems by Internet download. As a result, many UNIX vendors have adapted these programs to their UNIX flavor and made them available on the Internet. To obtain free software packages for UnixWare systems, visit *www.sco.com/skunkware*.

 **NOTE**  Package sets are often called **Set Installation Packages (SIPs)**.

When software packages are installed on a UNIX system, the system records all file information for them in the /var/sadm/install/contents file. For example, the following command will display information about the /usr/sbin/prtvtoc file as well as identify the package to which it belongs:

```
# grep "/usr/sbin/prtvtoc" /var/sadm/install/contents
/usr/sbin/prtvtoc f sysutil 0500 root bin 23160 39878 891989344 base
# _
```

The previous output indicates that the file /usr/sbin/prtvtoc is a file (f) that belongs to the sysutil package and the base package. It also indicates that the file has a mode of 0500 (r-x------), an owner of bin, a group owner of bin, a size of 23,160 bytes, and a **checksum** of 39,878. It was last modified April 7, 1998 (891,989,344 seconds since January 1, 1970).

 **NOTE**  You can use the **sum command** to return the checksum of a file; for example, the command sum /usr/sbin/prtvtoc will return the checksum number 39,878.

Over time, administrators can alter or remove files that belong to certain packages. To check the integrity of installed packages against the entries in the /var/sadm/install/contents file, use the **pkgchk command**:

```
# pkgchk
UX:pkgchk: ERROR: /dev/dsk/f03ht
    permissions <0666> expected <0644> actual
UX:pkgchk: ERROR: /dev/dsk/f0q18dt
    pathname not properly linked to </dev/dsk/f03ht>
UX:pkgchk: ERROR: /dev/fd0135ds18
    pathname not properly linked to </dev/dsk/f03ht>
UX:pkgchk: ERROR: /dev/fd096ds18
    pathname not properly linked to </dev/dsk/f03ht>
UX:pkgchk: ERROR: /dev/tty01
    major/minor device <3,2> expected <3,4> actual
UX:pkgchk: ERROR: /dev/vt00
    permissions <0666> expected <0620> actual
UX:pkgchk: ERROR: /etc/conf/autotune.d/dlpibase
    group name <sys> expected <root> actual
UX:pkgchk: ERROR: /etc/conf/cf.d/res_major
    file size <1273> expected <1304> actual
    file cksum <34143> expected <23252> actual
UX:pkgchk: ERROR: /etc/conf/init.d/kernel
    file size <2553> expected <2941> actual
    file cksum <20169> expected <36709> actual
# _
```

**NOTE** As shown in the previous output, common errors that are reported by the pkgchk command include permissions on files and directories that have been changed since installation to improve security, as well as files that have increased in size since they were installed. These errors are the result of normal system activity and can be safely ignored.

**NOTE** If the pkgchk command reports that a file has been removed, simply reinstall the package to replace the file.

**NOTE** After executing the pkgchk command on a UnixWare system, you should run the command /etc/security/tools/setpriv -x to ensure that security files have not been altered.

**NOTE** HP-UX systems use the **swverify command** to verify the integrity of installed software packages.

Other information regarding tasks that must be performed before package installation, such as checking prerequisite packages, as well as tasks that must be performed prior to package removal are listed within files that reside in the /var/sadm/pkg/<package_name> directory. For example, the /var/sadm/pkg/base directory contains the information required for installing and removing the base package that contains the /usr/sbin/prtvtoc command shown earlier.

## Viewing Installed Packages

The information in the /var/sadm/install/contents file is difficult to read; as a result, you must use various commands to list its contents. The **displaypkg command** displays a list of package names page by page using the pg command:

```
# displaypkg

        The following software packages have been installed:

UnixWare Documentation
UnixWare Manual Pages
Netscape FastTrack Server 2.01 Documentation
Netscape Communicator 4.61 for UnixWare 7
TriTeal Enterprise Desktop (CDE Desktop)
CDE Desktop Postscript Manuals
CDE Online Help
CDE Login Manager
CDE Manual Pages
Core Systems Services
Access Control List Utilities
Enhanced Application Compatibility
Audio Subsystem
Auditing Subsystem
Base System
X11R6 Base X Runtime System
Bash - GNU Bourne Again SHell
BSD Compatibility
Advanced Commands
BSD compatibility package
Distributed File System Utilities
:q
# _
```

Unfortunately, the displaypkg command does not list the full package information from the /var/sadm/install/contents file. To view this information, you must use the **pkginfo command**. Without arguments, the pkginfo command displays a list of all installed package names as well as their type and description:

```
# pkginfo | more
application BASEdoc      UnixWare Documentation
application BASEman      UnixWare Manual Pages
```

```
system       DLPI              BUILT IN TO NETWORK INTERFACE CARD SUPPORT,
CANNOT BE REMOVED.
application FTRKdoc            Netscape FastTrack Server 2.01 Documentation
system       MDI               BUILT IN TO NETWORK INTERFACE CARD SUPPORT,
CANNOT BE REMOVED.
application TEDdesk            TriTeal Enterprise Desktop (CDE Desktop)
application TEDdocs            CDE Desktop Postscript Manuals
application TEDhelp            CDE Online Help
application TEDlogin           CDE Login Manager
application TEDman             CDE Manual Pages
system       acl               Access Control List Utilities
system       acp               Enhanced Application Compatibility
system       audio             Audio Subsystem
system       audit             Auditing Subsystem
system       base              Base System
graphics     basex             X11R6 Base X Runtime System
system       bsdcompat         BSD Compatibility
system       cdfs              BUILT INTO THE BASE, CANNOT BE REMOVED.
system       cmds              Advanced Commands
system       compat            BUILT INTO BSD COMPATIBILITY, CANNOT BE
REMOVED.
system       dfm               BUILT INTO THE BASE, CANNOT BE REMOVED.
utilities    dfs               Distributed File System Utilities
Standard input q
# _
```

Since over 100 packages are installed on a typical UNIX system, you can specify the package name as an argument to the `pkginfo` command to display information about a single package:

```
# pkginfo base
system       base              Base System
# _
```

To see only the package sets that are installed on the system, use the following command:

```
# pkginfo -c set
set          NScomm4           Netscape Communicator 4.61 for UnixWare 7
set          NSfast2           Netscape FastTrack server 2.01a for UnixWare
7
set          UnixWare          Core Systems Services
set          doc               Documentation Services
# _
```

The `pkginfo` command can also be used to obtain extended information about each package. To see the version and architecture of an installed package, use the `-x` option with the `pkginfo` command followed by the package name:

```
# pkginfo -x base
base              Base System
```

```
                      (IA32) 7.0.0u
   #  _
```

Similarly, to obtain a full list of information about an installed package, use the **-l** option
with the `pkginfo` command followed by the package name:

```
# pkginfo -l base
   PKGINST:  base
      NAME:  Base System
  CATEGORY:  system
      ARCH:  IA32
   VERSION:  7.0.0u
    VENDOR:  SCO
   SETINST:  UnixWare
   SETNAME:  Core Systems Services
      DESC:  Base Operating System, commands and utilities.
    PSTAMP:  UW7 04/07/98
  INSTDATE:  Sep 01 2002 11:19 PM
    STATUS:  completely installed
     FILES:    4536 installed pathnames
               1121 shared pathnames
                359 linked files
                175 symbolic links
                512 directories
                707 executables
                 31 setuid/setgid executables
              77051 blocks used (38525K)(approx)

   #  _
```

You can also display package information using the **Application Installer** inside the
Software_Management folder of SCO Admin, as shown in Figure 11-1.

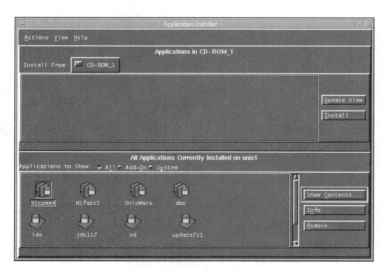

**Figure 11-1**   Viewing packages and package sets using the SCO Admin Application Installer

In Figure 11-1, the Application Installer displays installed package sets and packages in the lower pane. Package sets are represented by icons that consist of two boxes, whereas packages are represented by icons that consist of a single box. You can then use the Info button to obtain information about a package or package set, as shown in Figure 11-2.

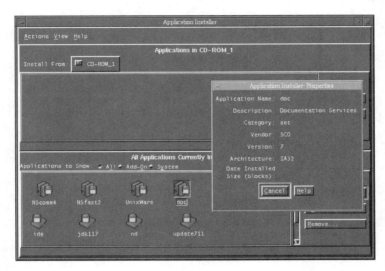

**Figure 11-2**    Viewing information for the doc package set

Alternatively, you can use the Show Contents button to display the packages within a package set. Figure 11-3 lists the contents of the doc package set.

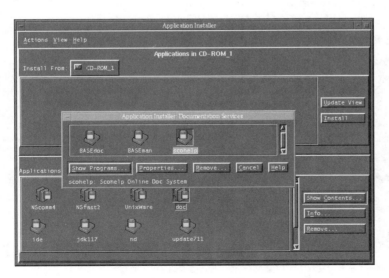

**Figure 11-3**    Viewing the contents of the doc package set

**11**

Select the Properties button from Figure 11-3 to display the package information for the highlighted package, as depicted in Figure 11-4.

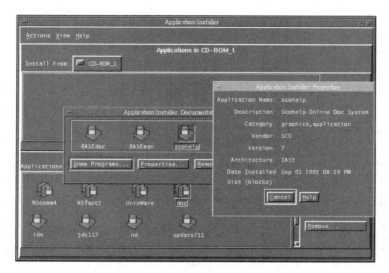

**Figure 11-4**    Viewing the properties of the scohelp package

The Show Programs button from Figure 11-3 displays the executable files within a package, as shown in Figure 11-5. These executable files can then be copied to alternate locations on the filesystem.

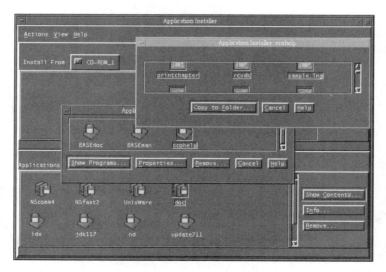

**Figure 11-5**    Viewing the programs within the scohelp package

HP-UX systems use the **swlist command** to list installed software packages.

# Installing Software

Additional software programs can be installed on a UNIX system from a variety of different media including CD-ROMs, floppy disks, and FTP servers across a network. To list the software packages on a media device, specify the **-d** option to the `pkginfo` command followed by the appropriate device file. To list the packages on the first CD-ROM on the system, use the following command and insert the CD-ROM into the CD-ROM drive when prompted:

```
# pkginfo -d /dev/cdrom/cdrom1

Insert CD into SCSI CD-Rom Drive 1.
Type [go] when ready,
  or [q] to quit: (default: go)

skunkware    xpdf         Xpdf - An X11 viewer for Adobe(tm) PDF files
skunkware    xpm          xpm - X11 pixmap library
skunkware    xpool        Xpool - X Pool
skunkware    xquote       Xquote - Stock quote retrieval
skunkware    xrolodex     xrolodex - X11 rolodex program
skunkware    xsane        xsane - scanner frontend for SANE
skunkware    xscavenge    Scavenger for X Window System
skunkware    xt           xt - communications program using telnet
skunkware    xwave        XWave X11 audio player, recorder, editor
skunkware    xwpe         xwpe - programming environment and editor
skunkware    yabasic      Yabasic - Yet Another Basic
skunkware    yodl         YODL pre-document language and tools
skunkware    zircon       zircon - Tcl/Tk IRC client
skunkware    zsh          The Z shell, a UNIX command interpreter
# _
```

The `pkginfo` command also accepts device identifiers listed in the device database; thus, the `pkginfo -d cdrom1` command is identical to the `pkginfo -d /dev/cdrom/cdrom1` command used earlier.

To install the xpdf package from the CD-ROM, use the **pkgadd command**:

```
# pkgadd -d /dev/cdrom/cdrom1 xpdf

Insert CD into SCSI CD-Rom Drive 1.
Type [go] when ready,
  or [q] to quit: (default: go)
```

11

```
Installation in progress.  Do not remove the CD.

PROCESSING:
Package: Xpdf - An X11 viewer for Adobe(tm) PDF files (xpdf) from
</dev/cdrom/cdrom1>.

Xpdf - An X11 viewer for Adobe(tm) PDF files
(i386) Version 0.90
Using </> as the package base directory.
SCO
## Processing package information.
## Processing system information.
## Verifying package dependencies.
## Verifying disk space requirements.

Installing Xpdf - An X11 viewer for Adobe(tm) PDF files as <xpdf>

## Installing part 1 of 1.
/usr/local/bin/pdfimages
/usr/local/bin/pdfinfo
/usr/local/bin/pdftopbm
/usr/local/bin/pdftops
/usr/local/bin/pdftotext
/usr/local/bin/xpdf
/usr/local/man/cat1/pdfimages.1
/usr/local/man/cat1/pdfinfo.1
/usr/local/man/cat1/pdftopbm.1
/usr/local/man/cat1/pdftops.1
/usr/local/man/cat1/pdftotext.1
/usr/local/man/cat1/xpdf.1
## Installing part 1 of 1.
/usr/local/bin/pdfimages
/usr/local/bin/pdfinfo
/usr/local/bin/pdftopbm
/usr/local/bin/pdftops
/usr/local/bin/pdftotext
/usr/local/bin/xpdf
/usr/local/man/cat1/pdfimages.1
/usr/local/man/cat1/pdfinfo.1
/usr/local/man/cat1/pdftopbm.1
/usr/local/man/cat1/pdftops.1
/usr/local/man/cat1/pdftotext.1
/usr/local/man/cat1/xpdf.1
/usr/local/man/man1/pdfimages.1
/usr/local/man/man1/pdfinfo.1
/usr/local/man/man1/pdftopbm.1
/usr/local/man/man1/pdftops.1
/usr/local/man/man1/pdftotext.1
```

```
/usr/local/man/man1/xpdf.1
[ verifying class <xpdf> ]

Installation of Xpdf - An X11 viewer for Adobe(tm) PDF files (xpdf)
was successful.
# _
```

**NOTE** Like the `pkginfo` command, `pkgadd` also accepts device identifiers listed in the device database; thus, the `pkgadd -d cdrom1 xpdf` command is identical to the `pkgadd -d /dev/cdrom/cdrom1 xpdf` command used earlier.

Some packages prompt you for information during the installation procedure. To simplify the installation of these packages to several computers, use the **pkgask command** to store the answers to the questions in a file that can be reused with the `pkgadd` command. Say, for example, that your CD-ROM has a package called samplepackage that prompts the user for several questions during installation. If you run the command `pkgask -r /answerfile -d /dev/cdrom/cdrom1 samplepackage` at a command prompt, the system will simulate an installation, read your responses to the questions, and store the answers in a file called /answerfile. Then you can run the command `pkgadd -r /answerfile -d /dev/cdrom/cdrom1 samplepackage` to install the package without being prompted to answer questions during the installation. The /answerfile can then be used on other systems to perform the same installation.

You can also install packages using the SCO Admin Application Installer. Simply choose the media that contains the software packages in the drop box next to the Install From: section in Figure 11-1 and select Update View to display the packages available, as shown in Figure 11-6.

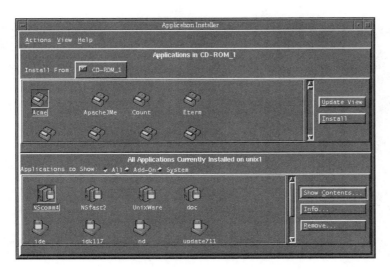

**Figure 11-6**   Viewing packages on a CD-ROM

You can then highlight a package and choose Install to start the installation process. You may also be prompted for information during the installation. Figure 11-7 shows the screen that appears when you install the bash package from within the SCO Admin Application Installer.

**Figure 11-7** Installing the bash package

When the installation of the bash package is complete, you will see an icon representing the bash package in the lower pane of the Application Installer, as shown in Figure 11-8.

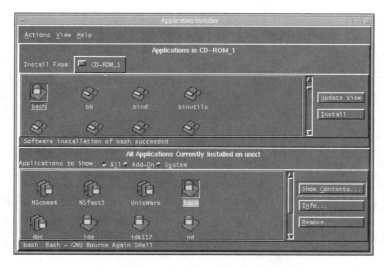

**Figure 11-8** Viewing the installed bash package

HP-UX systems use the **swinstall command** to install software packages.

## Spooling Software

Instead of installing a software package from installation media, you can copy the software package to the filesystem so that it may be installed at a later time. This process is called **software spooling**. Software is spooled to the /var/spool/pkg directory by default. You can then install the software later from this directory using the pkgadd command.

To spool the bash package from the CD-ROM device to the /var/spool/pkg directory, use the −s option to the pkgadd command:

```
# pkgadd -s -d /dev/cdrom/cdrom1 bash
UX:pkgadd: ERROR: unable to transfer package to file system format
     use the -s option to transfer package in datastream format
UX:mailx: WARNING: No message !?!
#
```

Notice from the previous output that the bash package could not be spooled. This is because it is in **datastream format** (compressed) on the CD-ROM. Software packages must be in **filesystem format** (uncompressed) before they can be spooled to the filesystem.

To uncompress and spool the bash package from the CD-ROM device to the /var/spool/pkg directory, use the **pkgtrans command** instead:

```
# pkgtrans /dev/cdrom/cdrom1 /var/spool/pkg bash

Insert CD into SCSI CD-Rom Drive 1.
Type [go] when ready,
  or [q] to quit: (default: go)
Transferring <bash> package instance to
        </var/spool/pkg> in file system format
# ls -F /var/spool/pkg
bash/
#
```

To install the bash package from this directory, use the pkgadd command; without options or arguments, the pkgadd command displays the packages present in the /var/spool/pkg directory and prompts you to install some or all of them:

```
# pkgadd

The following packages are available:
  1  bash     Bash - GNU Bourne Again SHell
               (i386) Version 2.03
```

11

```
Select package(s) you wish to process (or 'all' to process
all packages). (default: all) [?,??,quit]: 1

PROCESSING:
Package: Bash - GNU Bourne Again SHell (bash) from </var/spool/pkg>.

Bash - GNU Bourne Again SHell
(i386) Version 2.03
Using </> as the package base directory.
SCO
## Processing package information.
## Processing system information.
## Executing preinstall script.
## Installing part 1 of 1.
/usr/bin/bash
/usr/bin/bashbug
/usr/local/bin/bash <symbolic link>
/usr/local/bin/bashbug <symbolic link>
/usr/local/info/bash.info
/usr/local/man/cat1/bash.1
/usr/local/man/cat1/bashbug.1
/usr/local/man/html/bash/bash.html
/usr/local/man/html/bash/bashref.html
/usr/local/man/man1/bash.1
/usr/local/man/man1/bashbug.1
[ verifying class <bash> ]
## Executing postinstall script.

Installation of Bash - GNU Bourne Again SHell (bash) was successful.

The following packages are available:
  1  bash      Bash - GNU Bourne Again SHell
               (i386) Version 2.03

Select package(s) you wish to process (or 'all' to process
all packages). (default: all) [?,??,quit]: quit
# _
```

## Removing Software

The **pkgrm command** can be used to remove software packages from the system; simply specify the package name as an argument. To remove the bash package installed earlier, use the following command and confirm the deletion:

```
# pkgrm bash

The following package is currently installed:
   bash            Bash - GNU Bourne Again SHell
                   (i386) Version 2.03
```

```
Do you want to remove this package [yes,no,?,quit] y

## Removing installed package instance <bash>
## Verifying package dependencies.
## Processing package information.

## Removing pathnames in <bash> class
/usr/local/man/man1/bashbug.1
/usr/local/man/man1/bash.1
/usr/local/man/man1 <shared pathname not removed>
/usr/local/man/html/bash/bashref.html
/usr/local/man/html/bash/bash.html
/usr/local/man/html/bash
/usr/local/man/html
/usr/local/man/cat1/bashbug.1
/usr/local/man/cat1/bash.1
/usr/local/man/cat1 <shared pathname not removed>
/usr/local/man <shared pathname not removed>
/usr/local/info/bash.info
/usr/local/info
/usr/local/bin/bashbug
/usr/local/bin/bash
/usr/local/bin <shared pathname not removed>
/usr/local <shared pathname not removed>
/usr/bin/bashbug
/usr/bin/bash
/usr/bin <shared pathname not removed>
/usr <shared pathname not removed>
## Executing postremove script.
## Updating system information.


Removal of <bash> was successful.
# _
```

As with the installation of a software package, the removal of a software package may prompt you for information.

**NOTE**

Alternatively, you can remove software using the SCO Admin Application Installer. To remove the bash package, highlight the bash icon in the lower pane and choose Remove to start the removal procedure, as shown in Figure 11-9.

HP-UX systems use the **swremove command** to remove software packages.

**NOTE**

**Figure 11-9** Removing the bash package

## Configuring a Software Depot

If there are several UNIX computers on a network, you may want to centralize the storage of software packages by storing them on one UNIX computer to make them available to the other UNIX computers. The computer that holds the software packages is called a **software depot** (or **install server**). This computer can contain packages that comprise the UNIX operating system (called **system packages**) or additional software packages that are not related to the UNIX operating system (called **add-on packages**). System packages can be used to install the UNIX operating system across a network, and add-on packages are typically used to distribute software to other UNIX computers. Packages on the software depot are typically spooled to the /var/spool/dist directory.

To load the operating system software packages, insert the first UnixWare CD-ROM, run the **installsrv command** with the **–ue** option to spool the UnixWare package set to the /var/spool/dist directory, and enable the software depot. Following this, you can spool any add-on packages to the /var/spool/dist directory using the command `pkgadd -d <device> -s /var/spool/dist <package_name>` if the package is in filesystem format or the command `pkgtrans <device> /var/spool/dist <package_name>` if the package is in datastream format.

Alternatively, you can use the Install Server tool in the Software_Management folder of SCO Admin, as shown in Figure 11-10.

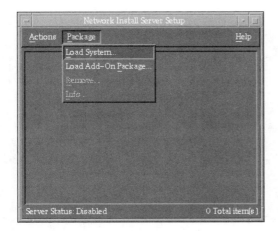

**Figure 11-10**    Adding packages to a software depot

If you choose Load System from the Package menu in Figure 11-10, you will load system packages from the first UnixWare CD-ROM. However, if you choose to Load Add-On Package from Figure 11-10, you will be prompted to choose the device and packages to spool to /var/spool/dist, as shown in Figure 11-11.

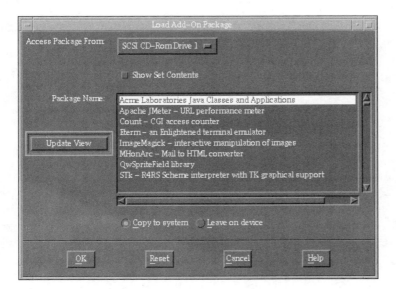

**Figure 11-11**    Selecting add-on packages

After you have chosen all packages to share, the software depot is enabled automatically; however, you can manually enable or disable it by choosing Enable or Disable from the Actions menu, as shown in Figure 11-12.

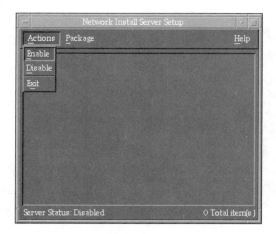

**Figure 11-12**    Enabling and disabling a software depot

Once a software depot has been created, other UNIX computers can install add-on software across the network using the **pkginstall command**. For example, to install the xpdf package from the computer depot.course.com across the network, use the command `pkginstall -s depot.course.com:/var/spool/dist xpdf` at a command prompt.

Alternatively, you can specify to install from a network server called depot.course.com in the SCO Admin Application Installer, as shown in Figure 11-13.

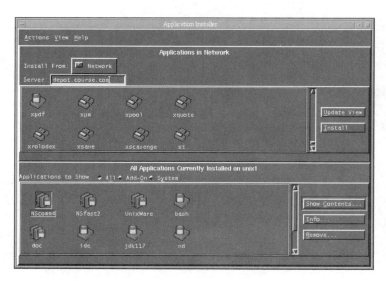

**Figure 11-13**    Viewing packages on a software depot

# LOG FILE MANAGEMENT

To identify and troubleshoot problems on a UNIX system, you must view the events that occur over time. Since it is impossible to observe all events that take place on a UNIX system as they occur, most daemons record information and error messages to files stored on the filesystem. These files are referred to as **log files**, which are typically stored in the /var/adm and /var/adm/log directories. For example, the /var/adm/log/ppp.log file contains events from the Point-to-Point Protocol (PPP) daemon.

Table 11-1 lists and describes some common log files.

**Table 11-1**    Common UNIX log files

| Log File | Description |
|---|---|
| /var/adm/wtmp | Contains an entry for each user login. The /etc/wtmp file is symbolically linked to /var/adm/wtmp. |
| /var/adm/loginlog | Contains unsuccessful user login attempts |
| /var/adm/sulog | Contains successful and unsuccessful user logins obtained by using the su command (discussed in the next chapter) |
| /var/adm/log/osmlog | Contains important operating system messages |
| /var/adm/utmp | Contains the most recent user login.  The /etc/utmp file is symbolically linked to /var/adm/utmp. |
| /var/adm/syslog | Contains error messages detected by the system log daemon (syslogd) |

**11**

## The System Log Daemon (syslogd)

The logging of most system-related events is handled centrally in UNIX via the **system log daemon (syslogd)**. When this daemon is loaded upon system startup, it listens for information sent to the /dev/log device file and saves it to the appropriate log file according to entries in the /etc/syslog.conf file. The following output shows the default /etc/syslog.conf file on a UnixWare system:

```
# cat /etc/syslog.conf
#ident  "@(#)syslog.conf       1.4"
#
# Portions Copyright (C) 1992 The Santa Cruz Operation, Inc.
# All Rights Reserved.
# The information in this file is provided for the exclusive use of
# the licensees of The Santa Cruz Operation, Inc.  Such users have the
# right to use, modify, and incorporate this code into other products
# for purposes authorized by the license agreement provided they
# include this notice and the associated copyright notice with any
# such product.
# The information in this file is provided "AS IS" without warranty.
#
#
```

```
*.info;*.debug                       /usr/adm/syslog
local0.notice                        /var/adm/syslog
kern.warn                            /dev/console
kern.notice                          /dev/console

#  _
```

Any line that starts with the # character is a comment in the /etc/syslog.conf file; all other entries have the following format:

```
facility.priority          /var/log/logfile
```

The **facility** is the area of the system to listen to, whereas the **priority** refers to the importance of the information. For example, a facility of kern and a priority of warn indicates that the system log daemon should listen for kernel messages that have the priority warning and more serious. When these messages are found, the system log daemon will send them to the /var/log/logfile file. The aforementioned entry would read:

```
kern.warning               /var/log/logfile
```

To only log warning messages from the kernel to /var/log/logfile, use the following entry instead:

```
kern.=warning              /var/log/logfile
```

Alternatively, you can log all error messages from the kernel to /var/log/logfile by using the * wildcard, as shown in the following entry:

```
kern.*                     /var/log/logfile
```

You can also specify multiple facilities and priorities. To log all error messages from the kernel and mail daemons to /var/log/logfile, use the following entry:

```
kern.*;mail.*              /var/log/logfile
```

To log all warnings and more serious from all facilities except for the kernel, use the none keyword, as shown in following entry:

```
*.warn;kern.none           /var/log/logfile
```

Table 11-2 lists and describes the different facilities available.

**Table 11-2**   Facilities used by the system log daemon

| Facility | Description |
|----------|-------------|
| auth | Specifies messages from the login system, such as the login program, the getty program, and the su command |
| cron | Specifies messages from the cron daemon |
| daemon | Specifies messages from system daemons, such as the FTP daemon |
| kern | Specifies messages from the UNIX kernel |

**Table 11-2**    Facilities used by the system log daemon (continued)

| Facility | Description |
|----------|-------------|
| mail | Specifies messages from the e-mail system (sendmail) |
| mark | Used internally only; it specifies timestamps used by syslogd. |
| news | Specifies messages from the Inter Network News daemon and other Usenet daemons |
| user | Specifies messages from user processes |
| uucp | Specifies messages from the uucp (UNIX-to-UNIX copy) daemon |
| local0-7 | Specifies local messages; these are not used by default, but can be defined for custom use. |

Table 11-3 lists the different priorities available in ascending order.

**Table 11-3**    Priorities used by the system log daemon

| Priority | Description |
|----------|-------------|
| debug | Indicates all information from a certain facility |
| info | Indicates normal information messages as a result of system operations |
| notice | Indicates information that should be noted for future reference, yet does not indicate a problem |
| warning or warn | Indicates messages that may be the result of an error, but are not critical to system operations |
| err or error | Indicates all other error messages not described by other priorities |
| crit | Indicates system-critical errors such as hard disk failure |
| alert | Indicates an error that should be rectified immediately, such as a corrupt system database |
| emerg | Indicates very serious system conditions that would normally be broadcast to all users |

**NOTE**

Notice from the /etc/syslog.conf file shown earlier that UnixWare systems send most system error messages to the /usr/log/syslog file. Since the /usr/log directory is symbolically linked to the /var/log directory on UnixWare systems, you can view the /var/log/syslog file to read these error messages. Also, most kernel messages are sent to the system console terminal (/dev/console).

## Viewing Log Files

Typical log files may contain hundreds or thousands of entries. Fortunately, you can use standard UNIX utilities to extract only the information that you require from log files.

For example, to display only error messages generated by the sendmail daemon in the /var/adm/log/osmlog file, use the following command:

```
# grep sendmail /var/adm/log/osmlog
Nov 14 15:42:30 sendmail[1069]: PAA01067: to=root, ctladdr=root (0/3),
delay=00:00:01, xdelay=00:00:01, mailer=local, stat=Sent
Nov 14 15:42:30 sendmail[1069]: PAA01067: to=owner, ctladdr=owner
(101/1), delay=00:00:01, xdelay=00:00:00, mailer=local, stat=Sent
Nov 18 17:46:27 sendmail[1183]: My unqualified host name (localhost)
unknown; sleeping for retry
Nov 18 17:46:27 sendmail[1185]: RAA01183: to=root, ctladdr=root (0/3),
delay=00:00:00, xdelay=00:00:00, mailer=local, stat=Sent
Nov 18 17:46:28 sendmail[1185]: RAA01183: to=owner, ctladdr=owner
(101/1), delay=00:00:01, xdelay=00:00:01, mailer=local, stat=Sent
Nov 18 18:00:00 sendmail[1477]: My unqualified host name (localhost)
unknown; sleeping for retry
Nov 18 18:00:00 sendmail[1477]: unable to qualify my own domain name
(localhost -- using short name
Nov 18 18:00:02 sendmail[1477]: alias database /etc/mail/aliases rebuilt
by root
Nov 18 18:00:02 sendmail[1477]: /etc/mail/aliases: 2 aliases, longest 10
bytes,37 bytes total
Nov 18 18:00:02 sendmail[1482]: My unqualified host name (localhost)
unknown; sleeping for retry
Nov 18 18:00:02 sendmail[1482]: unable to qualify my own domain name
(localhost -- using short name
Nov 18 18:00:03 sendmail[1483]: starting daemon (8.9.3):
SMTP+queueing@00:01:00
Nov 22 23:45:36 sendmail[2504]: My unqualified host name (localhost)
unknown; sleeping for retry
Nov 22 23:45:36 sendmail[2504]: unable to qualify my own domain name
(localhost -- using short name
Nov 22 23:45:37 sendmail[2504]: XAA02504: from=uucp, size=202, class=0,
pri=3022, nrcpts=1, msgid=<200211190445.XAA02504@localhost>,
relay=uucp@localhost
Nov 22 23:45:39 sendmail[2507]: XAA02504: to=uucp, ctladdr=uucp (5/5),
delay=00:00:03, xdelay=00:00:01, mailer=local, stat=Sent
# _
```

Most log files indicate the date and time of each event; thus, to display only sendmail error messages from November 14 in the /var/adm/log/osmlog file, use the following command:

```
# grep sendmail /var/adm/log/osmlog | grep "Nov 14"
Nov 14 15:42:30 sendmail[1069]: PAA01067: to=root, ctladdr=root (0/3),
delay=00:00:01, xdelay=00:00:01, mailer=local, stat=Sent
Nov 14 15:42:30 sendmail[1069]: PAA01067: to=owner, ctladdr=owner
(101/1), delay=00:00:01, xdelay=00:00:00, mailer=local, stat=Sent
# _
```

Also, since log files are typically appended to, you can use the **-f** option with the **tail** command to view the last 10 lines of a log file and keep the file contents open on the terminal screen so that new entries will be viewed as they are added.

## Managing Log Files

Although log files may contain important system information, they can take up unnecessary space on the filesystem over time. Thus, it is important to clear the contents of log files over time.

**NOTE**

Do not remove log files; if you do, the permissions and ownership will also be removed.

Before clearing log files, it is good form to preserve them by copying them to removable media such as a floppy disk or print them and store them in a safe place for future reference. To clear a log file, recall that you can use the > redirection symbol. The following commands display the size of the /var/adm/log/osmlog log file before and after it has been printed and cleared:

```
# ls -l /var/adm/log/osmlog
-rw-r--r--  1 root  root     2766 Nov 19 06:20 /var/adm/log/osmlog
# > /var/adm/log/osmlog
# ls -l /var/adm/log/osmlog
-rw-r--r--  1 root  root        0 Nov 19 14:29 /var/adm/log/osmlog
# _
```

You can also schedule commands to print and clear log files on a repetitive basis using the cron daemon.

Alternatively, you can use the **System Logs Manager** in the System folder of SCO Admin to manage log files, as shown in Figure 11-14.

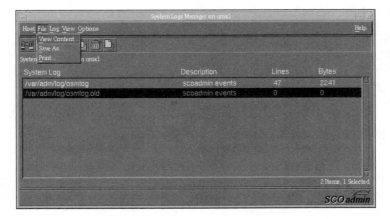

**Figure 11-14**    The System Logs Manager

**11**

The File menu in Figure 11-14 enables you to print, save, or view the contents of log files. Selecting View Content from Figure 11-14 enables you to view and search the contents of the file, as shown in Figure 11-15.

**Figure 11-15**     Viewing the contents of a log file

You can also choose Clear Log on the Log menu of the System Logs Manager to clear the contents of a log file, as shown in Figure 11-16.

**Figure 11-16**     Including, excluding, and clearing a log file

By default, the System Logs Manager only displays the /var/adm/log/osmlog and /var/adm/log/osmlog.old files. However, you can select Include Log on the Log menu shown in Figure 11-16 to include other log files; simply specify the path to the log file and an optional description, as shown in Figure 11-17.

**Figure 11-17** Adding a log file to the System Logs Manager

You can also choose Exclude Log on the Log menu shown in Figure 11–16 to exclude a log file from the list displayed in the System Logs Manager.

## CHAPTER SUMMARY

- ❐ Software programs on a UNIX system are grouped into packages and package sets.

- ❐ Package information is stored in a file that may be queried later using the pkginfo command or SCO Admin Application Installer.

- ❐ Packages can be installed on the system or spooled to the hard disk for future installation; the default directory for spooled packages is /var/spool/pkg.

- ❐ A software depot can be used to hold software packages; these packages can be later installed across a computer network. The default directory used to store these packages is /var/spool/dist.

- ❐ System and daemon events are recorded in log files that reside in the /var/adm or /var/adm/log directories; these log files should be cleared periodically to save disk space.

- ❐ The system log daemon can be used to record different system events via entries in the /etc/syslog.conf file.

- ❐ The SCO Admin System Logs Manager can be used to view, search, print, copy, and clear log files.

## KEY TERMS

**add-on packages** — Packages that are not part of the UNIX operating system.

**Application Installer** — An SCO Admin utility that can be used to install, manage, and remove software packages.

**checksum** — A number that represents the contents of a file; it is different for different files.

**datastream format** — A package that has been compressed.

**displaypkg command** — The command used to display a list of installed software packages on the system.

**facility** — When used with the syslog daemon, this term refers to the area of the system from which events will be logged.

**filesystem format** — A package that is not compressed.

**install server** — An SCO Admin utility that can be used to create and manage a software depot.

**installsrv command** — The command used to create a software depot.

**log files** — Files that contain system events.

**package set** — A group of software packages that share a similar function. *See also* Set Installation Packages (SIPs).

**pkgadd command** — A command-line utility used to install packages.

**pkgask command** — The command used to create an answer file for use with future installations of a given package.

**pkgchk command** — The command used to check the integrity of the /var/sadm/ install/contents file.

**pkginfo command** — A command that can be used to list installed software packages and package sets as well as their attributes.

**pkginstall command** — A command used to install software packages from a software depot on the computer network.

**pkgrm command** — A command used to remove software packages currently installed on a system.

**pkgtrans command** — A command used to uncompress a package that is in datastream format.

**priority** — When used with the syslog daemon, this term refers to the relative importance of the event being monitored.

**Set Installation Packages (SIPs)** — *See also* Package sets.

**software depot** — A server on the network that holds packages available to be installed on other computers on the network.

**software packages** — A series of related files that together comprise a program that can be installed on a computer.

**software spooling** — The copying of a software package to a filesystem for installation at a later time.

**sum command** — The command used to calculate a unique checksum for a file based on its contents.

**swinstall command** — The command used to install software packages on an HP-UX system.

**swlist command** — The command used to display software packages currently installed on an HP-UX system.

**swremove command** — The command used to remove packages currently installed on an HP-UX system.

**swverify command** — The command used to verify the integrity of packages installed on an HP-UX system.

**system log daemon (syslogd)** — A daemon initialized on system startup that is responsible for monitoring selected portions of the system and generating log files from the results.

**System Logs Manager** — An SCO Admin tool that can be used to manage and clear log files.

**system packages** — Packages that contain programs that comprise the UNIX operating system.

## REVIEW QUESTIONS

1. A package set is also referred to as a Set Installation Package. True or False?

2. Where is all the information pertinent to packages currently installed on a system stored?

   a. /var/temp/log/pkgs

   b. /var/sadm/install/contents

   c. /var/sadm/install/packages

   d. /var/pkgs/installed

3. On an SCO UNIX system, package installation, modification, maintenance, and removal can only be done via the command line. True or False?

4. Which of the following commands is used to check the integrity of an installed package on an SCO UNIX machine?

   a. sum

   b. pkgverify

   c. swverify

   d. pkgchk

5. The process of storing software packages on a filesystem for installation at a later date is referred to as _____.

   a. package staging

   b. software staging

   c. software spooling

   d. package stacking

**11**

6. Which of the following statements is true? (Choose all that apply.)

    a. To create an answer file called /unattended for use with future installations of a package, you use the pkgadd –r /unattended <package_name> command.

    b. When you create an answer file for use with future installations, you must perform a mock installation and answer all relevant questions.

    c. To create an answer file called unattended for use with future installations of a package, you use the pkgask –r /answerfile <package_name> command.

    d. The answer files you create for use with packages are for single use and are installation specific; they just exist so inexperienced users can install packages properly.

    e. To use an answer file called unattended for use with future installations of a package, you use the pkgadd –r /unattended <package_name> command.

7. What daemon loaded during system startup monitors information sent to the /dev/log device file and saves it to the proper log file?

    a. sortlogd

    b. /var/log

    c. syslogd

    d. logd

8. Which of the following commands would you use to change a package from datastream format to filesystem format during the spooling process?

    a. unpack

    b. decompress

    c. pkgepnd

    d. pkgtrans

9. What priority level indicates a severe system concern of which all users should be notified?

    a. alert

    b. warn

    c. crit

    d. emerg

10. When referring to system logging via the syslog daemon, the terms "facility" and "priority" are used. Facility refers to _____, whereas priority refers to _____.

    a. the importance of the message, the area of the system to monitor for messages

    b. the area of the system to monitor for messages, the importance of the message

    c. the area of the system to monitor for messages, the log file

    d. the log file, the area of the system to monitor for messages

11. You should always copy or print log files before clearing them. True or False?

12. Log files can be very large and contain extensive information. Which of the following utilities is useful when locating specific lines within a log file?

    a. head

    b. cat

    c. sort

    d. grep

13. What is the name of the utility in SCO Admin that enables you to print, view, search, and clear log files?

    a. System Logs Manager

    b. syslogd

    c. log viewer

    d. Sysloger

14. How could you clear log files automatically on a repetitive basis?

    a. Use the logrotate manager of SCO Admin.

    b. Use the System Logs Manager.

    c. Configure the appropriate cron table to perform the >log file command.

    d. Configure the syslog daemon to perform automatic clearing based on entries in the /etc/syslog.conf file.

15. To simplify log file management, you can remove log files on the system on a periodic basis. True or False?

16. The displaypkg command displays more attributes regarding software packages than the pkginfo command. True or False?

17. What command can be used to remove a package from a UnixWare system?

    a. pkgadd -rm

    b. pkgrm

    c. pkgremove

    d. swremove

18. In UNIX, most log files are stored in the _____ and _____ directories.

    a. /var/adm

    b. /usr/adm/logs

    c. /usr/log

    d. /var/adm/log

    e. /var

**11**

19. When creating a software depot, what type of package represents software that is not integral to or part of the operating system?

    a. system package

    b. sw package

    c. primary package

    d. add–on package

20. The file /etc/syslog.conf contains the following line:

    ```
    mail.=warn                          /var/log/logfile
    ```

    What is the effect of that line?

    a. The syslog daemon will monitor the mail facility for all messages and redirect them to /var/log/logfile.

    b. The syslog daemon will monitor the mail facility for messages and warn, or ask, the user before redirecting the messages to the /var/log/logfile.

    c. The syslog daemon will monitor the mail facility for messages and redirect only messages of a level of warn to the /var/log/logfile.

    d. The syslog daemon will monitor the mail facility for messages and redirect only messages of a level of warn or higher to the /var/log/logfile.

21. A software package is _____.

    a. a file used to install a program on a computer

    b. a compressed program that must be uncompressed before being used on a computer

    c. a collection of files and system settings used to define a program on a computer

    d. a collection of related programs offering similar functionality

22. Which of the following commands could be used to copy a package to a filesystem for later installation? (Choose all that apply.)

    a. This cannot be done; you have to install packages to filesystems.

    b. pkgtrans

    c. pkgspl

    d. pkgdd

    e. pkgcopy

    f. pkgadd –s

23. Which of the following statements is true? (Choose all that apply.)

    a. Datastream format refers to files that are in uncompressed format.

    b. Packages must be in datastream format before package spooling can be used.

    c. Filesystem format refers to files that are in compressed format.

    d. Packages must be in filesystem format before package spooling can be used.

e. Datastream format refers to files that are in compressed format.

f. Filesystem format refers to files that are in uncompressed format.

24. On an SCO UNIX system, if you are using the Application Installer of SCO Admin, how can you tell the difference between an installed package and an installed package set?

   a. You cannot; this can only be done via pkginfo from the command line.

   b. There is no difference.

   c. Packages appear as a single box and package sets appear as two boxes.

   d. Packages appear in a normal font and package sets are bolded.

25. Which of the following commands can be used to install packages on an HP-UX system?

   a. packageinstall

   b. pkginstall

   c. pkgadd

   d. swinstall

---

## HANDS-ON PROJECTS

These projects should be completed in the order given. All hands-on projects should take a total of three hours to complete. The requirement for this lab includes:

❏ A computer with UnixWare 7.1.1 installed according to Project 2-2

**HANDS-ON PROJECTS**

## Project 11-1

In this hands-on project, you will view and check software installed on your system using command-line and graphical utilities.

1. Turn on your computer. Once your UNIX system has been loaded, switch to a command-line terminal (vt02) by pressing **Ctrl+Alt+F2**, and log into the terminal using the username **root** and the password **secret**.

2. At the command prompt, type **pkginfo –c set** and press **Enter**. What does this command do?

3. At the command prompt, type **pkginfo doc** and press **Enter** to display the contents of the doc package set. What packages are inside the doc package set?

4. At the command prompt, type **pkginfo –x doc** and press **Enter**. What extra information is provided about each package in the doc package set?

5. At the command prompt, type **pkginfo –l doc | more** and press **Enter** to view a full list of information about the packages within the doc package set. Observe the different categories of information displayed. Press **q** when finished to quit the more utility.

6. At the command prompt, type **displaypkg | grep CDE** and press **Enter**. How many packages related to the CDE desktop are installed?

7. At the command prompt, type **pkginfo -x | grep CDE** and press **Enter**. What are the actual package names for each CDE package? Does each package name contain the letters CDE?

8. At the command prompt, type **pkgchk** and press **Enter**. What does this command do?

9. At the command prompt, type **/etc/security/tools/setpriv -x** and press **Enter**. What does this command do? If you receive any warnings from this command, you can safely ignore them.

10. Type **exit** and press **Enter** to log out of your shell.

11. Switch to the graphical terminal (vt01) by pressing **Ctrl+Alt+F1**, and log into the CDE desktop using the username **root** and the password **secret**.

12. Open the Application Installer in the Software_Management folder of SCO Admin. How can you tell which icons represent packages and package sets?

13. Highlight the **UnixWare** package set and click on the **Info** button. What is the full description of this package set? Click **Cancel**.

14. Highlight the **UnixWare** package set and click on the **Show Contents** button to view the packages in the UnixWare package set. Highlight the **scoadmin** package and click on the **Properties** button. What is the full description of this package? When was it installed? Press **Cancel** to close the dialog window. Press **Cancel** to close the UnixWare package set window.

15. Close all programs and log out of the CDE desktop.

# Project 11-2

In this hands-on project, you will add and remove software packages using command-line utilities.

1. Switch to a command-line terminal (vt02) by pressing **Ctrl+Alt+F2**, and log into the terminal using the username **root** and the password **secret**.

2. Place the second UnixWare 7.1.1 CD-ROM in your CD-ROM drive.

3. At the command prompt, type **pkginfo -d cdrom1 | more** and press **Enter**. When prompted, press **Enter** again to search the CD-ROM for packages. View the list of packages on your CD-ROM device and press **q** to exit the more utility.

4. At the command prompt, type **pkginfo -d cdrom1 | grep lxrun** and press **Enter**. When prompted, press **Enter** again to search the CD-ROM for packages. What two packages are displayed?

5. At the command prompt, type **pkgadd -d cdrom1 lxrun** and press **Enter**. Press **Enter** again to start the installation of the lxrun package. Observe the output on the screen indicating the installed files. What is the pathname to the lxrun executable file?

6. At the command prompt, type **pkginfo | grep lxrun** and press **Enter**. Is the package installed?

7. At the command prompt, type **pkgadd –d cdrom1 –s lxrunlibs** and press **Enter**. Press **Enter** again to start the spooling of the lxrun package. What error message do you receive? Why?

8. At the command prompt, type **pkgtrans cdrom1 /var/spool/pkg lxrunlibs** and press **Enter**. To what directory will this package be spooled? Press **Enter**.

9. At the command prompt, type **ls –F /var/spool/pkg** and press **Enter**. What do you see and why?

10. At the command prompt, type **pkgadd** and press **Enter**. What spooled packages in the /var/spool/pkg directory are available to be installed? Press **Enter** to install all packages. When the installation of the lxrunlibs package has completed, type **q** and press **Enter** to exit the utility.

11. At the command prompt, type **pkginfo | grep lxrunlibs** and press **Enter**. Is the package installed?

12. At the command prompt, type **pkgrm lxrun** and press **Enter**. Type **y** and press **Enter** to confirm the removal of the lxrun package.

13. At the command prompt, type **pkgrm lxrunlibs** and press **Enter**. Type **y** and press **Enter** to confirm the removal of the lxrunlibs package.

14. Remove the CD-ROM from your CD-ROM drive.

15. Type **exit** and press **Enter** to log out of your shell.

**HANDS-ON PROJECTS**

## Project 11-3

In this hands-on project, you will add and remove software packages using SCO Admin.

1. Switch to the graphical terminal (vt01) by pressing **Ctrl+Alt+F1**, and log into the CDE desktop using the username **root** and the password **secret**.

2. Open the Application Installer in the Software_Management folder of SCO Admin.

3. Observe the lower pane of the Application Installer. Are the lxrun and lxrunlibs packages listed?

4. Place the second UnixWare 7.1.1 CD-ROM in your CD-ROM drive.

5. Ensure that **CD-ROM_1** is selected in the Install From: drop box and press the **Update View** button.

6. Highlight the **lxrun** package and press the **Install** button.

7. Highlight the **lxrunlibs** package and press the **Install** button.

8. Observe the lower pane of the Application Installer. Are the lxrun and lxrunlibs packages listed?

9. Highlight the **lxrun** package in the lower pane of the Application Installer and press the **Remove** button. Type **y** and press **Enter** to confirm the package removal.

10. Highlight the **lxrunlibs** package in the lower pane of the Application Installer and press the **Remove** button. Type **y** and press **Enter** to confirm the package removal.

11. Close all programs and log out of the CDE desktop.

## Project 11-4

In this hands-on project, you will create a software depot using command-line and graphical utilities. Next, you will install the lxrun package from the software depot.

1. Switch to a command-line terminal (vt02) by pressing **Ctrl+Alt+F2**, and log into the terminal using the username **root** and the password **secret**.

2. Insert the first UnixWare 7.1.1 CD-ROM into your CD-ROM drive.

3. At the command prompt, type **installsrv –ue** and press **Enter**. What packages are being spooled to the system? To which directory are they spooled? Is the installation server started?

4. At the command prompt, type **ls –F /var/spool/dist** and press **Enter**. What files or directories are present? Why?

5. Remove the CD-ROM from the CD-ROM drive. If the CD-ROM does not eject, you will need to run the command umount /installr at the command prompt and press **Enter** before removal.

6. Type **exit** and press **Enter** to log out of your shell.

7. Switch to the graphical terminal (vt01) by pressing **Ctrl+Alt+F1**, and log into the CDE desktop using the username **root** and the password **secret**.

8. Open the Install Server in the Software_Management folder of SCO Admin. Is the software depot enabled? What packages are available?

9. Select the **Package** menu and select **Load Add-On Package**.

10. Insert the second UnixWare 7.1.1 CD-ROM into the CD-ROM drive and select the **Update View** button. After a few moments, the package contents of this CD-ROM will be displayed and the selected packages will have a white background.

11. Use your mouse to select the **Linux Application Environment Emulator** and deselect the **Netscape Communicator 4.61 for UnixWare 7** option.

12. Press **OK** to spool the Linux Application Environment Emulator to the /var/spool/dist directory.

13. Press **Cancel** to exit the Load Add-On Package window.

14. What packages are available in the Install Server window? Is the software depot enabled?

15. Open the Application Installer in the Software_Management folder of SCO Admin. In the drop box beside Install From:, select **Network** and enter the IP address **127.0.0.1** in the dialog box provided (the IP address 127.0.0.1 is a special IP address that refers to the local computer). When you are finished, press the **Update View** button.

16. What packages are available? Explain.

17. Highlight the **lxrun** package and press the **Install** button.

18. Observe the lower pane of the Application Installer. Is the lxrun package listed?

19. Highlight the **lxrun** package in the lower pane of the Application Installer and press the **Remove** button. Type **y** and press **Enter** to confirm the package removal.

20. Close all programs and log out of the CDE desktop.

**HANDS-ON PROJECTS**

## Project 11-5

In this hands-on project, you will view and manage log files using command-line and graphical utilities.

1. Switch to a command-line terminal (vt02) by pressing **Ctrl+Alt+F2**, and log into the terminal using the username **root** and the password **secret**.

2. At the command prompt, type **ls –F /var/adm** and press **Enter**. What log files are listed?

3. At the command prompt, type **ls –F /var/adm/log** and press **Enter**. What log files are listed?

4. At the command prompt, type **cat /etc/syslog.conf** and press **Enter**. What log files are created by the syslog daemon and what events are logged to them?

5. At the command prompt, type **more /var/adm/syslog** and press **Enter**. Observe the entries and press **q** to exit the more utility.

6. At the command prompt, type **grep IPX /var/adm/syslog | more** and press **Enter**. Are any messages in this log related to the IPX protocol? Why or why not? Was IPX installed during installation in Chapter 2? Observe the entries and press **q** to exit the more utility.

7. At the command prompt, type **cp /var/adm/syslog /var/adm/syslog.old** and press **Enter**. Next, type **>/var/adm/syslog** at the command prompt and press **Enter**. What does this command do?

8. At the command prompt, type **cat /var/adm/syslog** and press **Enter**. What are the contents? Why?

9. Type **exit** and press **Enter** to log out of your shell.

10. Switch to the graphical terminal (vt01) by pressing **Ctrl+Alt+F1**, and log into the CDE desktop using the username **root** and the password **secret**.

11. Open the System Logs Manager in the System folder of SCO Admin. What two log files are listed by default? How many lines and bytes does each have?

12. Select the **Log** menu and choose **Include Log**. In the Location box, type **/var/adm/log/ppp.log** and in the Description box, type **PPP events** and click **OK** when you are finished. Does the /var/adm/log/ppp.log appear in the list of log files?

**11**

13. Double-click the **/var/adm/log/osmlog**. Observe the contents. In the Search box, type **sendmail** and press **Enter**. What was the first line that contained the word **sendmail**? Use the Next arrow to scroll through the other lines that contain the word **sendmail** and press **OK** when you are finished.

14. Highlight the **/var/adm/log/osmlog** entry, select the **File** menu, and select **Save As**. In the Selection box, ensure that the pathname is /var/adm/log/osmlog.backup and press **OK**. Was it successful? Click **OK** again to close the confirmation window.

15. Highlight the **/var/adm/log/osmlog** entry, select the **Log** menu, and select **Clear Log**. Click the **Yes** button to confirm the action. How many lines and bytes does the /var/adm/log/osmlog file have now?

16. Close all programs and log out of the CDE desktop.

## DISCOVERY EXERCISES

1. Provided you have Internet access and a functional Web browser, download and install two freely available UnixWare applications. Valuable Internet Web sites for this task include *www.sco.com*, *www.freebird.org*, and *www.google.com*.

2. Which entry could you add to /etc/syslog.conf to do the following?

   a. Log all critical messages from the kernel to /var/adm/alert.

   b. Log all messages from the user processes to /var/adm/userlog.

   c. Log all debug messages and more serious from the uucp daemon to /var/adm/uuerrors.

   d. Log all messages more serious than notices from the mail daemon to /var/adm/mailman.

   e. Log all alerts and critical error messages to /var/adm/serious.

   f. Log all warnings and errors from the kernel and the cron daemon to /var/adm/shared.

3. Examine the log files present on your system. Given that your system is not a production server, how large do you expect typical log files to reach in one day? Which log files will likely contain more information and which will contain less information? Use Internet resources or SCOhelp to support your answer. Based on your findings, create a chart listing at least five common log files and their expected growth per day on a typical production server. Also include an estimated interval for clearing each log file. Use your table to write cron table entries that can be used to automatically back up and clear each log file.

## CHAPTER 12

# ARCHIVING AND
# COMPRESSING DATA

> **After reading this chapter and completing the exercises, you will be able to:**
> ♦ Outline the features of common UNIX archiving utilities
> ♦ Identify tape device files used for archiving data
> ♦ Create, view, and extract archives using the tar utility
> ♦ Create, view, and extract archives using the cpio utility
> ♦ Archive whole filesystems using the vxdump utility
> ♦ Compress and uncompress UNIX files

Maintaining the integrity of data is a core job responsibility for most UNIX administrators. In order to maintain this properly, administrators must store existing files for use when data is lost and compress files to save disk space. This chapter first discusses the process of archiving and examines the tape devices commonly used to store the archives. Next, this chapter explores the usage and syntax of the tar, cpio, and vxdump backup utilities. Finally, this chapter ends with a discussion of file compression and the compress utility.

# PERFORMING SYSTEM BACKUPS

Files and directories can be copied to an alternate location at regular intervals; these backup copies can then be distributed to other computers or used to restore files if a system failure occurs that results in a loss of information. This entire process is known as **system backup** or **archiving**, and the backup copies of files and directories are called **archives**.

Archives can be created within a file on the filesystem (called an **archive file**) or a media device. Many different types of media such as tapes, zip disks, floppy disks, and CD-RW disks can be used to store an archive. The most common and cost-effective medium used to back up data is tape. The device files that represent tape devices differ between UNIX flavors. On UnixWare systems, tape device files typically reside in the /dev/rmt (raw magnetic tape) directory and are categorized based on their rewind and retension capabilities.

 Tapes lose tension over time. As a result, some tape drives can manually tighten or retension the tape.

**NOTE**

Table 12-1 lists some common UnixWare device files.

**Table 12-1**   Common UnixWare tape device files

| Device File | Description |
|---|---|
| /dev/rmt/ctape1 | First nonretensioning, rewinding tape device |
| /dev/rmt/ctape2 | Second nonretensioning, rewinding tape device |
| /dev/rmt/ctape3 | Third nonretensioning, rewinding tape device |
| /dev/rmt/ntape1 | First nonretensioning, nonrewinding tape device |
| /dev/rmt/nrtape1 | First retensioning, nonrewinding tape device |
| /dev/rmt/rtape1 | First retensioning, rewinding tape device |

The **tapecntl (tape controller) command** can be used to manipulate tape devices or prepare a tape for system backup; for example, to rewind the first nonretensioning, rewinding tape device on a system, use the `tapecntl -w /dev/rmt/ctape1` command. Table 12-2 lists some common options used with the `tapecntl` command.

**Table 12-2**   Common options used with the `tapecntl` command

| Option | Description |
|---|---|
| -w | Rewinds the tape |
| -r | Resets the tape; it rewinds the tape and then forwards it to the beginning of the tape for writing. |
| -t | Retensions the tape |
| -e | Erases the tape |

**NOTE**

If you do not specify a tape device when using the `tapecntl` command, it assumes the /dev/rmt/ntape1 device file.

A typical UNIX system may have hundreds of thousands of files on it; not all of these files need to be included in an archive. Temporary files in the /tmp and /var/tmp directories do not need to be included, nor do any cached Internet content found in the .netscape (for the Netscape Navigator Web browser) directory under each user's home directory.

As a general rule of thumb, you should back up user files from home directories and any important system configuration files such as /etc/inittab. In addition to this, you may want to back up files used by system services; for example, you would back up Web site files if the UNIX computer was used as a Web server. Programs on the filesystem such as grep and vi do not need to be backed up since they can be restored from the original installation media in the event of a system failure.

Once files have been selected for system backup, you can use a backup utility to copy the files to the appropriate media. Several backup utilities are available to UNIX administrators. The most common backup utilities are:

- tar
- cpio
- vxdump

**NOTE**

You can schedule backup utilities to occur repeatedly using the cron daemon to automate the process of creating archives.

**12**

## THE TAR UTILITY

The tar (tape archive and restore) utility is one of the oldest and most common backup utilities. It can create an archive in a file on a filesystem or directly on a device such as a tape or zip drive.

The tar utility accepts options to determine the location of the archive and the action to perform on the archive. Any arguments specified to the **tar command** list the file(s) to place in the archive. Table 12-3 lists the common options used with the `tar` command.

**Table 12-3**  Common options used with the tar utility

| Option | Description |
| --- | --- |
| -A | When restoring files from an archive, they will be restored using relative pathnames instead of absolute pathnames. |
| -c | Creates a new archive |

**Table 12-3**   Common options used with the tar utility (continued)

| Option | Description |
|---|---|
| -f *FILENAME* | Specifies the location of the archive (*FILENAME*); it can be a file on a filesystem or a device file. |
| -h or -L | Will prevent tar from backing up symbolic links; instead, tar will back up the target files of symbolic links. |
| -r | Appends files to an existing archive |
| -t | Lists the filename contents (table of contents) of an existing archive |
| -u | Appends files to an existing archive only if they are newer than the same filename inside the archive |
| -v | Displays verbose output (file and directory information) when manipulating archives |
| -x | Extracts the contents of an archive |

To create an archive file called /backup.tar that contains the contents of the current directory (/projects) and view the results, use the following command:

```
# pwd
/projects
# tar -cvf /backup.tar *
a Newfiles/ 0 tape blocks
a Newfiles/project1 7 tape blocks
a Newfiles/project2 7 tape blocks
a Newfiles/project3 7 tape blocks
a Newfiles/sampleproject 1 tape block
a email.txt 1 tape block
a myscript2 1 tape block
# ls -l /backup.tar
-rw-r--r--   1 root      sys       17920 Nov 25 14:21 /backup.tar
# _
```

Note from the previous command, that the **-f** option is followed by the pathname of the archive file and that the * metacharacter indicates that all files in the current directory will be added to this archive. Also note that files are backed up recursively by default and stored using relative pathnames.

The filename used for an archive does not need to have an extension; however, it is good practice to name archive files with an extension to identify their contents, as shown with /backup.tar in the previous example.

**NOTE**

To back up the target file that symbolic links point to, you must use the –h or –L option with the tar command.

**NOTE**

**NOTE** The tar utility was designed to write to tapes in defined sections or blocks. As a result, the tar utility will use one tape block for files that are very small and do not use one tape block. This might result in archive files that are much larger in size compared to the combined size of the files within.

**NOTE** The tar utility cannot back up device files—files larger than 2GB in size or files with filenames longer than 255 characters.

You can view the detailed contents of an archive after creation by specifying the -t (table of contents) option to the tar command and the archive to view; for example, to view the detailed contents of the /backup.tar archive created earlier, issue the following command:

```
# tar -tvf /backup.tar
UX:tar: INFO: blocksize = 20
drwxr-xr-x    0/3            0 Nov 25 14:20 2002 Newfiles/
-r--r--r--    0/3         3204 Nov 25 14:20 2002 Newfiles/project1
-r--r--r--    0/3         3204 Nov 25 14:20 2002 Newfiles/project2
-r--r--r--    0/3         3204 Nov 25 14:20 2002 Newfiles/project3
-r--r--r--    0/3          188 Nov 25 14:20 2002 Newfiles/sampleproject
-r--r--r--    0/3          188 Sep 19 16:03 2002 email.txt
-rwxr-xr-x    0/3          188 Sep 17 19:57 2002 myscript2
# _
```

The -x option can be used with the tar command to extract a specified archive. To extract the contents of the /backup.tar file to a new directory called /tartest and view the results, issue the following commands:

```
# mkdir /tartest
# cd /tartest
# tar -xvf /backup.tar
UX:tar: INFO: blocksize = 20
x Newfiles/, 0 bytes, 0 tape blocks
x Newfiles/project1, 3204 bytes, 7 tape blocks
x Newfiles/project2, 3204 bytes, 7 tape blocks
x Newfiles/project3, 3204 bytes, 7 tape blocks
x Newfiles/sampleproject, 188 bytes, 1 tape block
x email.txt, 188 bytes, 1 tape block
x myscript2, 188 bytes, 1 tape block
# ls -F
Newfiles/    email.txt    myscript2*
# _
```

Notice that the files within the archive were restored using relative pathnames; this is because their relative pathnames were used when the archive was created. If you use absolute pathnames when specifying files to be added to an archive, those files will also be stored using absolute pathnames. Say, for example, that you create the /backup.tar

**12**

archive instead from the contents of the /projects directory specifying the absolute path-name to the files that should be placed in the archive:

```
# tar -cvf /backup.tar /projects
a /projects/ 0 tape blocks
a /projects/Newfiles/ 0 tape blocks
a /projects/Newfiles/project1 7 tape blocks
a /projects/Newfiles/project2 7 tape blocks
a /projects/Newfiles/project3 7 tape blocks
a /projects/Newfiles/sampleproject 1 tape block
a /projects/myscript2 1 tape block
a /projects/email.txt 1 tape block
# _
```

The contents of the /backup.tar file created in the previous output contain the absolute pathname to each file under the /projects directory. If you restore the contents of this archive, then the files will be restored using absolute pathnames to their original locations in the directory tree (overwriting any existing files):

```
# tar -xvf /backup.tar
UX:tar: INFO: blocksize = 20
x /projects/, 0 bytes, 0 tape blocks
x /projects/Newfiles/, 0 bytes, 0 tape blocks
x /projects/Newfiles/project1, 3204 bytes, 7 tape blocks
x /projects/Newfiles/project2, 3204 bytes, 7 tape blocks
x /projects/Newfiles/project3, 3204 bytes, 7 tape blocks
x /projects/Newfiles/sampleproject, 188 bytes, 1 tape block
x /projects/myscript2, 188 bytes, 1 tape block
x /projects/email.txt, 188 bytes, 1 tape block
# _
```

To suppress absolute pathnames during a restore, simply use the -A option with the tar command when restoring files:

```
# mkdir /tartest2
# cd /tartest2
# tar -xAvf /backup.tar
UX:tar: INFO: Suppressing absolute pathnames
UX:tar: INFO: blocksize = 20
x projects/, 0 bytes, 0 tape blocks
x projects/Newfiles/, 0 bytes, 0 tape blocks
x projects/Newfiles/project1, 3204 bytes, 7 tape blocks
x projects/Newfiles/project2, 3204 bytes, 7 tape blocks
x projects/Newfiles/project3, 3204 bytes, 7 tape blocks
x projects/Newfiles/sampleproject, 188 bytes, 1 tape block
x projects/myscript2, 188 bytes, 1 tape block
x projects/email.txt, 188 bytes, 1 tape block
# ls -F
projects/
```

```
# ls -F projects
Newfiles/   email.txt   myscript2*
# _
```

Backing up files to an archive file is useful when archiving small numbers of files, but it is ill suited for backing up large amounts of data for system recovery. Devices such as tapes are better suited for this task. To back up files to a device, use the -f option with the tar command to specify the pathname to the appropriate character device file; files will then be transferred character by character to the device, overwriting any other data or filesystems that might be present.

For example, to create an archive on the first rewinding, nonretensioning tape device containing the contents of the /projects directory, use the following command:

```
# tar -cvf /dev/rmt/ctape1 /projects
a /projects/ 0 tape blocks
a /projects/Newfiles/ 0 tape blocks
a /projects/Newfiles/project1 7 tape blocks
a /projects/Newfiles/project2 7 tape blocks
a /projects/Newfiles/project3 7 tape blocks
a /projects/Newfiles/sampleproject 1 tape block
a /projects/myscript2 1 tape block
a /projects/email.txt 1 tape block
# _
```

You can then view the contents of the archive on the tape device used in the previous example using the command tar -tvf /dev/rmt/ctape1 or extract the contents of the archive on the tape device using the command tar -xvf /dev/rmt/ctape1 in a similar fashion to the examples shown earlier.

**12**

To simplify specifying the device file when creating an archive on a media device, you can use numbers in place of the -f option to refer to devices that are listed in the /etc/default/tar file. The following output shows an example of an /etc/default/tar file:

```
# cat /etc/default/tar
#ident  "@(#)unixsrc:usr/src/common/cmd/tar/tar.dfl /main/uw7_nj/2"
#         device        block    size    tape
archive0=/dev/rdsk/f0q15dt    15      1200    n
archive1=/dev/rdsk/f1q15dt    15      1200    n
archive2=/dev/rdsk/f05ht      15      1200    n
archive3=/dev/rdsk/f15ht      15      1200    n
archive4=/dev/rdsk/f03dt      18      720     n
archive5=/dev/rdsk/f13dt      18      720     n
archive6=/dev/rdsk/f03ht      18      1440    n
archive7=/dev/rdsk/f13ht      18      1440    n
archive8=/dev/rmt/ctape1      20      0       y
#archive9=/dev/null #reserved
#
# The default device in the absence of a numeric or "-f device" argument
archive=/dev/rdsk/f0t         18      1440    n
# _
```

Since archive6 refers to the /dev/rdsk/f03ht device file in the /etc/default/tar file shown in the previous output, you can use the following command to create an archive of the /projects directory on the first floppy disk:

```
# tar -cv6 /projects
a /projects/ 0 tape blocks
a /projects/Newfiles/ 0 tape blocks
a /projects/Newfiles/project1 7 tape blocks
a /projects/Newfiles/project2 7 tape blocks
a /projects/Newfiles/project3 7 tape blocks
a /projects/Newfiles/sampleproject 1 tape block
a /projects/myscript2 1 tape block
a /projects/email.txt 1 tape block
# _
```

If you do not specify a number or an -f option to the tar command, it will assume the device specified by the archive= line in the /etc/default/tar file. Because the /etc/default/tar file shown earlier contains the line archive=/dev/rdsk/f0t and /dev/rdsk/f0t is a copy of /dev/rdsk/f03ht on most systems after installation, you can use the following command to create an archive of the /projects directory on the first floppy disk:

```
# tar -cv /projects
a /projects/ 0 tape blocks
a /projects/Newfiles/ 0 tape blocks
a /projects/Newfiles/project1 7 tape blocks
a /projects/Newfiles/project2 7 tape blocks
a /projects/Newfiles/project3 7 tape blocks
a /projects/Newfiles/sampleproject 1 tape block
a /projects/myscript2 1 tape block
a /projects/email.txt 1 tape block
# _
```

Similarly, you can use the tar -tv and tar -xv commands to view and extract the contents of the archive on the floppy disk, respectively.

Since tape devices may hold large amounts of information, you might want to add to a tar archive that already exists on the tape device. To do this, replace the -c option with either the -r option to append files or the -u option to append files if they do not exist when using the tar utility. For example, to create an archive of the /projects directory on the first rewinding, nonretensioning tape and afterwards append a file called sample-file to the archive and view the results, use the following commands:

```
# tar -cvf /dev/rmt/ctape1 /projects
UX:tar: INFO: Volume ends at 1439K, blocking factor = 1K
UX:tar: INFO: seek = 1K a /projects/ 0K
UX:tar: INFO: seek = 1K a /projects/Newfiles/ 0K
UX:tar: INFO: seek = 1K a /projects/Newfiles/project1 4K
UX:tar: INFO: seek = 5K a /projects/Newfiles/project2 4K
UX:tar: INFO: seek = 9K a /projects/Newfiles/project3 4K
```

```
UX:tar: INFO: seek = 13K  a /projects/Newfiles/sampleproject 1K
UX:tar: INFO: seek = 14K  a /projects/myscript2 1K
UX:tar: INFO: seek = 15K  a /projects/email.txt 1K
# tar -uvf /dev/rmt/ctape1 /samplefile
UX:tar: INFO: Volume ends at 1439K, blocking factor = 1K
UX:tar: INFO: seek = 16K   a /samplefile 1K
# tar -tvf /dev/rmt/ctape1
drwxr-xr-x  0/3     0 Nov 25 14:27 2002 /projects/
drwxr-xr-x  0/3     0 Nov 25 14:20 2002 /projects/Newfiles/
-r--r--r--  0/3 3204 Nov 25 14:20 2002 /projects/Newfiles/project1
-r--r--r--  0/3 3204 Nov 25 14:20 2002 /projects/Newfiles/project2
-r--r--r--  0/3 3204 Nov 25 14:20 2002 /projects/Newfiles/project3
-r--r--r--  0/3  188 Nov 25 14:20 2002 /projects/Newfiles/sampleproject
-rwxr-xr-x  0/3  188 Sep 17 19:57 2002 /projects/myscript2
-r--r--r--  0/3  188 Sep 19 16:03 2002 /projects/email.txt
-r--r--r--  0/3  188 Nov 25 14:41 2002 /samplefile
# _
```

# THE CPIO UTILITY

Another common backup utility is cpio (copy in/out). Although this utility uses similar options as the tar utility, cpio has some added features including the capability to back up device files and files greater than 2GB in size.

Since the primary use of the cpio utility is to back up files in case of a system failure, it is good form to use absolute pathnames when archiving. cpio normally takes a list of files to archive from standard input and sends the files out to an archive specified by the −O option. Conversely, when extracting an archive, the −I option must be specified to indicate the archive from which to read files.

Table 12-4 lists and describes some commonly used options with the **cpio** command.

**Table 12-4**    Common options used with the cpio utility

| Option | Description |
|---|---|
| −A | Appends files to an existing archive |
| −B | Changes the default block size from 512 bytes to 5KB, thus speeding up the transfer of information |
| −c | Uses a storage format (SVR4) that is widely recognized by different versions of cpio |
| −d | Creates directories as needed during extraction |
| −i | Reads files from an archive |
| −I *FILENAME* | Represents the input archive; it is the file or device file of the archive used when viewing or extracting files. |
| −k | Attempts to skip any corrupted information |
| −L | Will prevent cpio from backing up symbolic links; instead, cpio will back up the target files of symbolic links. |

12

**Table 12-4** Common options used with the cpio utility (continued)

| Option | Description |
|---|---|
| -m | Preserves the original modification time when backing up files |
| -o | Creates a new archive |
| -O *FILENAME* | Represents the output archive; it is the file or device file of the target archive when backing up files. |
| -t | Lists the filename contents (table of contents) of an existing archive |
| -u | Overwrites existing files during extraction |
| -v | Displays verbose output (file and directory information) when manipulating archives |

To create an archive using cpio, a list of filenames must first be generated. This can be accomplished using the **find** command. To list all filenames underneath the /projects directory, use the following command:

```
# find /projects
/projects
/projects/Newfiles
/projects/Newfiles/project1
/projects/Newfiles/project2
/projects/Newfiles/project3
/projects/Newfiles/sampleproject
/projects/myscript2
/projects/email.txt
# _
```

Now, you can send this list via standard input to the **cpio command**. For example, to verbosely back up all files in /projects to the first rewinding, nonretensioning tape device using a block size of 5KB and a common format, use the following command:

```
# find /projects | cpio -vocB -O /dev/rmt/ctape1
/projects
/projects/Newfiles
/projects/Newfiles/project1
/projects/Newfiles/project2
/projects/Newfiles/project3
/projects/Newfiles/sampleproject
/projects/myscript2
/projects/email.txt
30 blocks
# _
```

To view the verbose table of contents of this archive, use the following command:

```
# cpio -ivBt -I /dev/rmt/ctape1
drwxr-xr-x   3 root  sys   0       Nov 25 14:27 2002, /projects
drwxr-xr-x   2 root  sys   0       Nov 25 14:20 2002, /projects/Newfiles
```

```
-r--r--r--  1 root   sys    3204   Nov 25 14:20 2002, /projects/Newfiles/
project1
-r--r--r--  1 root   sys    3204   Nov 25 14:20 2002, /projects/Newfiles/
project2
-r--r--r--  1 root   sys    3204   Nov 25 14:20 2002, /projects/Newfiles/
project3
-r--r--r--  1 root   sys    188    Nov 25 14:20 2002, /projects/Newfiles/
sampleproject
-rwxr-xr-x  1 root   sys    188    Sep 17 19:57 2002, /projects/myscript2
-r--r--r--  1 root   sys    188    Sep 19 16:03 2002, /projects/email.txt
30 blocks
# _
```

Following this, you can extract the archive on /dev/rmt/ctape1, creating directories and overwriting files as needed by using the following command:

```
# cpio -vicduB -I /dev/rmt/ctape1
/projects
/projects/Newfiles
/projects/Newfiles/project1
/projects/Newfiles/project2
/projects/Newfiles/project3
/projects/Newfiles/sampleproject
/projects/myscript2
/projects/email.txt
30 blocks
# _
```

Like tar, the cpio command can be used to create an archive file on the filesystem. To do this, simply specify the filename after the –O option. To create an archive file called /sample.cpio that contains the files from the directory /projects, using a block size of 5KB as well as a common header, and view the results, issue the following commands:

```
# find /projects | cpio -vocB -O /sample.cpio
/projects
/projects/Newfiles
/projects/Newfiles/project1
/projects/Newfiles/project2
/projects/Newfiles/project3
/projects/Newfiles/sampleproject
/projects/myscript2
/projects/email.txt
30 blocks
# ls -l /sample.cpio
-rw--r--r--  1 root        sys            15360 Nov 25 15:25 /sample.cpio
# _
```

As with the tar utility, cpio archive filenames need not have an extension to identify their contents; however, it is good practice to use extensions, as shown with /sample.cpio in the previous example.

12

## THE VXDUMP UTILITY

Like the tar and cpio utilities, the vxdump utility can be used to back up files and directories to a device or to a device file on the filesystem; however, the vxdump utility can only work with files on VxFS filesystems.

Although the vxdump utility can be used to back up only certain files and directories, it was designed to back up entire VxFS filesystems to an archive and keep track of these filesystems in a file called **/etc/dumpdates**. Since archiving all data on a filesystem (known as a **full backup**) may take a long time, you can choose to perform a full backup only on weekends and run incremental backups each evening during the week. An **incremental backup** only backs up the data that has been changed since the last backup. In the case of a system failure, you must restore the information from the full backup and then restore the information from all subsequent incremental backups in sequential order. You can also perform up to nine different incremental backups using the vxdump utility. Number 0 represents a full backup, whereas numbers 1 through 9 represent incremental backups.

Say, for example, that you perform a full backup of the VxFS filesystem in the /dev/dsk/c0b0t0d0s1 slice on Sunday, perform incremental backups from Monday to Wednesday (shown in Figure 12-1), and on Thursday the /dev/dsk/c0b0t0d0s1 filesystem becomes corrupted.

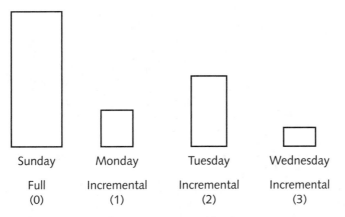

**Figure 12-1**    Full and incremental backups

Once the filesystem has been recreated, you should restore the full backup (0) followed by the first incremental backup (1), the second incremental backup (2), and the third incremental backup (3) to ensure that data has been properly recovered.

Similar to the tar and cpio utilities, many options are available for the vxdump utility. Table 12-5 lists some of these options.

**Table 12-5**    Common options used with the vxdump utility

| Option | Description |
|--------|-------------|
| -# | Specifies the type of backup when used with the **vxdump command**; if # is 0, a full backup is performed. If # is 1 through 9, then the appropriate incremental backup is performed. |
| -b *NUM* | Specifies a certain block size to use in kilobytes; the default block size is 63KB. |
| -f *FILENAME* | Specifies the pathname to the archive; the *FILENAME* can be a file on a filesystem or a device file. |
| -u | Specifies to update the /etc/dumpdates file after a successful backup |
| -n | Notifies the user if any errors occur and when the backup has completed |

Say, for example, that you wanted to perform a full backup of the / filesystem (/dev/dsk/c0b0t0d0s1) to the first rewinding, nonretensioning tape device and update the /etc/dumpdates file when completed. To do this, issue the following command:

```
# vxdump -0uf /dev/rmt/ctape1 /dev/dsk/c0b0t0d0s1
vxdump: Date of this level 0 dump: Tue Nov 26 04:19:48 2003
vxdump: Date of last level 0 dump: the epoch
vxdump: Dumping /dev/rdsk/c0b0t0d0s1 to /dev/rmt/ctape1
vxdump: mapping (Pass I) [regular files]
vxdump: mapping (Pass II) [directories]
vxdump: estimated 997590 blocks (487.10MB).
vxdump: dumping (Pass III) [directories]
vxdump: dumping (Pass IV) [regular files]
vxdump: 16.53% done, finished in 0:25
vxdump: 33.44% done, finished in 0:19
vxdump: 48.80% done, finished in 0:15
vxdump: 62.69% done, finished in 0:11
vxdump: 73.91% done, finished in 0:08
vxdump: 87.86% done, finished in 0:04
vxdump: vxdump: 499057 tape blocks on 1 volumes(s)
vxdump: level 0 dump on Tue Nov 26 04:19:48 2003
vxdump: Closing /dev/rmt/ctape1
vxdump: vxdump is done
# _
```

12

**NOTE**

Alternatively, you can specify the filesystem mount point when using the vxdump command; the command vxdump -0uf /dev/rmt/ctape1 / is equivalent to the one used in the previous example.

The contents of the /etc/dumpdates file will now indicate that a full backup has taken place:

```
# cat /etc/dumpdates
/dev/rdsk/c0b0t0d0s1 <UNNAMED> 0 Tue Nov 26 04:19:48 2003
# _
```

To perform the first incremental backup and view the contents of the /etc/dumpdates file, place a new tape into the tape drive and issue the following commands:

```
# vxdump -1uf /dev/rmt/ctape1 /dev/dsk/c0b0t0d0s1
vxdump: Date of this level 1 dump: Tue Nov 26 04:56:20 2003
vxdump: Date of last level 0 dump: Tue Nov 26 04:19:48 2003
vxdump: Dumping /dev/rroot (/) to /dev/rmt/ctape1
vxdump: mapping (Pass I) [regular files]
vxdump: mapping (Pass II) [directories]
vxdump: estimated 997594 blocks (487.11MB).
vxdump: dumping (Pass III) [directories]
vxdump: dumping (Pass IV) [regular files
vxdump: vxdump: 5961 tape blocks on 1 volumes(s)
vxdump: level 1 dump on Tue Nov 26 04:56:20 2003
vxdump: Closing /dev/rmt/ctape1
vxdump: vxdump is done
# cat /etc/dumpdates
/dev/rdsk/c0b0t0d0s1 <UNNAMED> 0 Tue Nov 26 04:19:48 2003
/dev/rdsk/c0b0t0d0s1 <UNNAMED> 1 Tue Nov 26 04:56:20 2003
# _
```

**NOTE**

You can use the ufsdump utility on UnixWare and Solaris systems to archive a UFS filesystem. Similarly, the dump utility on HP-UX systems can be used to archive an HFS filesystem. The **ufsdump command** and the **dump command** both use the same options and syntax that the vxdump command uses.

To view or extract the contents of an archive created with the **vxdump** command, you must use the **vxrestore command**. Like vxdump, the **vxrestore** command can use many options. Table 12-6 lists the most common of these options.

**Table 12-6**  Common options used with the vxrestore utility

| Option | Description |
|---|---|
| -b *NUM* | Specifies a certain block size to use in kilobytes; if a block size is not specified, the **vxrestore** command will attempt to detect it from the archive. |
| -f *FILENAME* | Specifies the pathname to the archive; the *FILENAME* can be a file on a filesystem or a device file. |
| -r | Specifies to extract the entire archive |
| -x *FILENAME* | Used to extract a certain file or files represented by *FILENAME* |
| -i | Presents a prompt where you may restore files interactively |

**Table 12-6**   Common options used with the vxrestore utility (continued)

| Option | Description |
|--------|-------------|
| -t | Lists the filename contents (table of contents) of an existing archive |
| -v | Displays verbose output (file and directory information) when viewing and extracting archives |

Thus, to view the contents of an archive, specify the **-t** option to the **b** command followed by the archive information. To view the contents of the full backup performed earlier, place the appropriate tape into the tape drive and execute the following command:

```
# vxrestore -tf /dev/rmt/ctape1 | more
Dump    date: Tue Nov 26 04:56:20 2003
Dumped from: the epoch
           2      .
           3      ./lost+found
           4      ./etc
           6      ./etc/vfstab
           8      ./etc/inst
           9      ./etc/inst/locale
          10      ./etc/inst/locale/C
          11      ./etc/inst/locale/C/menus
          12      ./etc/inst/locale/C/menus/help
          15      ./etc/inst/locale/C/menus/help/pla.hcf
         125      ./etc/inst/locale/C/menus/NScomm4
         126      ./etc/inst/locale/C/menus/NScomm4/set.1
         127      ./etc/inst/locale/C/menus/NScomm4/set.2
         128      ./etc/inst/locale/C/menus/NScomm4/set.3
         129      ./etc/inst/locale/C/menus/NScomm4/set.4
         130      ./etc/inst/locale/C/menus/NScomm4/set.5
         131      ./etc/inst/locale/C/menus/NScomm4/set.6
         132      ./etc/inst/locale/C/menus/NScomm4/set.7
         134      ./etc/inst/locale/C/menus/NScomm4/set.8
         139      ./etc/inst/locale/C/menus/NScomm4/set.9
         546      ./etc/inst/locale/C/menus/base
         549      ./etc/inst/locale/C/menus/base/chknode.1
Standard input q
#  _
```

To extract the full backup shown in the previous output, specify the **-r** option to the **vxrestore** command followed by the archive information. Additionally, you can specify the **-v** option to list the filenames restored, as shown in the following output:

```
# vxrestore -vrf /dev/rmt/ctape1 | more
Verify tape and initialize maps
Tape block size is 63
Dump    date: Tue Nov 26 04:56:20 2003
Dumped from: the epoch
```

**12**

```
level 0 dump of / on /dev/rroot
Begin level 0 restore
Initialize symbol table.
Extract directories from tape
Calculate extraction list.
./lost+found
./etc
./etc/inst
./etc/inst/locale
./etc/inst/locale/C
./etc/inst/locale/C/menus
./etc/inst/locale/C/menus/help
./etc/inst/locale/C/menus/NScomm4
./etc/inst/locale/C/menus/base
./etc/inst/locale/C/menus/upgrade
./etc/inst/locale/C/menus/nsu
./etc/inst/locale/C/menus/inet
./etc/inst/locale/C/menus/inet/help
./etc/inst/locale/C/menus/update711
./etc/inst/locale/C/menus/nd
./etc/inst/save
./etc/inst/save/etc
./etc/inst/save/etc/acct
./etc/inst/save/etc/ap
./etc/inst/save/etc/cron.d
Standard input q
# _
```

**NOTE**    You can use the ufsrestore utility on UnixWare and Solaris systems to view and extract an archive created with ufsdump. Similarly, the restore utility on HP-UX systems can be used to view and extract an archive created with the dump utility. The **ufsrestore command** and the **restore command** both use the same options and syntax that the vxrestore command uses.

# FILE COMPRESSION

At times, you may want to reduce the size of a large file due to infrequent usage or limited disk space. You may also want to compress files such as tar archive files before they are sent across a computer network such as the Internet to decrease transfer time. In either case, several utilities are available that can perform a standard set of instructions on a file to reduce its size by stripping out characters. This procedure is called **compression**, and the standard set of instructions used to compress a file is known as a **compression algorithm**. To decompress a file, you can simply run the compression algorithm in reverse.

Since compression utilities use different compression algorithms, they achieve different rates of compression for similar types of files. The rate of compression is known as a **compression ratio**. If a compression utility compressed a file to 52% of its original size, it has a compression ratio of 48%.

Although many compression utilities for UNIX are available for download, compress is the standard compression utility available on most UNIX systems. It uses a compression algorithm called Adaptive Lempel-Ziv-Welch coding (LZW) and has an average compression ratio of 40% to 50%.

To compress a file using the compress utility, specify the files to compress as arguments to the **compress command**. Each file will be renamed with a .Z filename extension to indicate that they are compressed. Additionally, you can use the **-v** (verbose) option with the compress command to display the compression ratio during compression. The following output displays the filenames and size of samplefile and samplefile2 before and after compression:

```
# ls -l
total 10
-rw-r--r--     1 root       sys                 3204 Nov 26 18:38 samplefile
-r--r--r--     1 root       sys                  555 Nov 26 18:39 samplefile2
# compress -v samplefile samplefile2
UX:compress: INFO: samplefile: Compression: 51.99%
-- replaced with samplefile.Z
UX:compress: INFO: samplefile2: Compression: 34.23%
-- replaced with samplefile2.Z
# ls -l
total 6
-rw-r--r--     1 root       sys                 1538 Nov 26 18:38 samplefile.Z
-r--r--r--     1 root       sys                  365 Nov 26 18:39 samplefile2.Z
# _
```

**12**

The compress utility preserves the original ownership, modification, and access time for each file that it compresses.

By default, the compress utility will not compress very small files; to force the compress utility to compress these files, you must use the -f option.

Once compressed, the **zcat command** can be used to display the contents of a compressed file, as shown in the following output:

```
# zcat samplefile2.Z
Hi there, I hope this day finds you well.
```

Unfortunately we were not able to make it to your dining
room this year while vacationing in Algonquin Park - I
especially wished to see the model of the Highland Inn
and the train station in the dining room.

I have been reading on the history of Algonquin Park but
nowhere could I find a description of where the Highland
Inn was originally located on Cache Lake.

If it is no trouble, could you kindly let me know such that
I need not wait until next year when I visit your lodge?

Regards,
Mackenzie Elizabeth

\#  _

To decompress files that have been compressed with the compress utility, use the
**uncompress command** followed by the names of the files to be decompressed; this
will restore the original filename. The following output decompresses and displays the
filenames for the samplefile.Z and samplefile2.Z files created earlier:

```
# uncompress -v samplefile.Z samplefile2.Z
UX:uncompress: INFO: samplefile.Z:  -- replaced with samplefile
UX:uncompress: INFO: samplefile2.Z:  -- replaced with samplefile2
# ls -l
total 10
-rw-r--r--    1 root      sys              3204 Nov 26 18:38 samplefile
-r--r--r--    1 root      sys               555 Nov 26 18:39 samplefile2
#  _
```

**NOTE**  The user will be prompted for confirmation if any existing files will be overwritten during decompression. To prevent this, use the −f option with the
uncompress command.

You can omit the .Z extension when using the uncompress command; the command
uncompress −v samplefile samplefile2 achieves the same results as the command shown in the previous output.

Furthermore, the compress utility is a filter command that can take information from
standard input and send it to standard output. For example, to send the output of the
ps −ef command to the compress utility and save the compressed information to a file
called file.Z, execute the following command:

```
# ps -ef | compress -v >file.Z
Compression: 38.99%
#  _
```

Following this, you can display the contents of file.Z using the `zcat` command or decompress it using the `uncompress` command, as shown in the following output:

```
# zcat file.Z
   UID    PID  PPID  CLS PRI  C     STIME TTY        TIME COMD
   root     0     0  SYS  79  0  16:47:36 ?          0:13 sysproc
   root     1     0   TS  70  0  16:47:37 ?          0:02 /sbin/init -s 1
   root   738   737   TS  59  0  18:46:27 console    0:00 ps -ef
   root   737   667   TS  59  0  18:46:27 console    0:00 -sh
   root   667     1   TS  70  0  16:59:12 console    0:01 -sh
   root   594     1   TS  88  0  16:48:46 ?          0:00 /usr/lib/mousemgr
# uncompress -v file.Z
UX:uncompress: INFO: file.Z:  -- replaced with file
# _
```

---

## CHAPTER SUMMARY

❑ System backup is necessary to maintain the integrity of a UNIX system in case of a hard drive failure or data corruption.

❑ Files and directories can be backed up to an archive on a device or an archive file on a filesystem.

❑ The most common medium used to store archives is tape.

❑ Standard UNIX archiving utilities include tar, cpio, and vxdump; each utility uses a series of options to create and manipulate archives.

❑ The vxdump utility can perform full and incremental backups of VxFS filesystems.

❑ Files can be compressed using a compression utility; these compression utilities use a compression algorithm to reduce the size of a file.

❑ The standard UNIX compression utility is compress.

**12**

---

## KEY TERMS

**/etc/dumpdates** — The file used to store information about incremental and full backups for use by the dump utility.

**archive** — A backup copy of files and directories; it is typically created by a backup utility and may reside on a device or within an archive file.

**archive file** — A file on a filesystem that contains an archive.

**archiving** — The act of creating an archive.

**compress command** — The command used to compress files using an LZW compression algorithm; it is the standard compression utility on UNIX systems.

**compression** — The process in which files are reduced in size by a compression algorithm.

**compression algorithm** — The set of instructions used to systematically reduce the contents of a file.

**compression ratio** — The amount of compression that occurred during compression.

**cpio command** — A common backup utility.

**dump command** — A common utility used to create full and incremental backups on HP-UX systems.

**full backup** — An archive of an entire filesystem.

**incremental backup** — An archive of a filesystem that contains only files that were modified since the last archive was created.

**restore command** — The command used to extract archives created with the dump command.

**system backup** — The process whereby files are copied to an archive. *See also* Archiving.

**tapecntl (tape controller) command** — The command used to manipulate tape devices or prepare a tape for system backup.

**tar command** — The most common utility used to create archives.

**ufsdump command** — A backup utility used to create archives from information stored on UFS filesystems; it is common on UnixWare and Solaris systems.

**ufsrestore command** — The command used to restore information archived with the ufsdump command.

**uncompress command** — The command used to decompress files compressed using the compress command.

**vxdump command** — A backup utility used to create archives from data stored on VxFS filesystems.

**vxrestore command** — The command used to restore information archived with the vxdump utility.

**zcat command** — The command used to view the contents of an archive created with the compress command.

---

# REVIEW QUESTIONS

1. Which dump level indicates a full backup?

   a. 0

   b. 9

   c. 1

   d. f

2. Files that have been compressed using the compress utility typically have the _____ extension.

   a. .tar

   b. .gz

   c. .Z

   d. .cpio

3. You have created a full backup and four incremental backups. In which order must you restore these backups?

   a. 0, 1, 2, 3, 4

   b. 0, 4, 3, 2, 1

   c. 4, 3, 2, 1, 0

   d. 1, 2, 3, 4, 0

4. Which of the following commands will extract an archive?

   a. cpio –vocBL /dev/rmt/ctape1

   b. cpio –vicdu –I /dev/rmt/ctape1

   c. cpio –vicdu –O /dev/rmt/ctape1

   d. cpio –vti –I /dev/rmt/ctape1

5. How many dump levels are there for use with the dump command?

   a. 1

   b. 5

   c. 9

   d. 10

6. Which file contains full and incremental backup information for use with the dump utility?

   a. /etc/dumps

   b. /etc/dumpdates

   c. /etc/dumpfile

   d. /etc/dump.conf

7. Which of the following represents the first nonrewinding, retensioning tape device on a UnixWare system?

   a. /dev/rmt/ctape1

   b. /dev/rmt/nrtape1

   c. /dev/rmt/utape1

   d. /dev/rmt/ntape1

8. Which of the following commands will create an archive?

   a. tar –cvf /dev/fd0

   b. tar –xvf /dev/fd0

   c. tar –tvf /dev/fd0

   d. tar –cvf /dev/fd0 *

9. The tar utility can compress symbolically linked files and device files. True or False?

**12**

10. Which of the following utilities can be used to rewind a tape device?

    a. tapecntl

    b. tapef

    c. rtape

    d. utape1

11. What will be the result if the tapecntl command is used without arguments?

    a. Nothing—it must have arguments to function.

    b. It will perform an incremental backup.

    c. It will perform a differential backup.

    d. It will use the device /dev/rmt/ntape1.

12. When performing a system backup, you must ensure that all data on every filesystem is archived. True or False?

13. Which of the following files will the tar utility fail to back up? (Choose all that apply.)

    a. new files that have not been archived before

    b. files larger than 5GB in size

    c. files that are less than 1GB in size

    d. a device file

14. If an archive has been generated by the tar utility, what utility can be used to restore the archive information?

    a. untar

    b. restore

    c. tar

    d. uncompress

15. Because of their size, archives can be generated on all devices except floppy drives. True or False?

16. The cpio utility can create an archive for files that are over 2GB in size. True or False?

17. Which of the following utilities can create archives from data stored on a VxFS filesystem only?

    a. tar

    b. compress

    c. cpio

    d. uxdump

    e. vxdump

18. How many incremental backups can be scheduled to run using vxdump?

    a. one

    b. zero

    c. seven

    d. nine

19. If you have files stored on a UFS filesystem, you must use the uxdump utility to back them up. True or False?

20. Compression algorithms all produce the same compression ratio. True or False?

21. Which of the following commands can be used to list the files contained within an archive created with ufsdump?

    a. ufsrestore

    b. restore

    c. uxread

    d. uxlist

22. You uncompress a file and check the file ownership. Who will be listed as the owner?

    a. your user account since you uncompressed it

    b. the root user

    c. the original owner of the file before compression

    d. the nobody user

23. You have compressed a 1000MB file. Its new size is 750MB. What is the compression ratio?

    a. It depends on the compression algorithm used.

    b. You do not have enough data to calculate.

    c. 25%

    d. 75%

24. Which of the following commands can be used to view the contents of a compressed file?

    a. restore

    b. lscompress

    c. un_compress

    d. zcat

**12**

## HANDS-ON PROJECTS

These projects should be completed in the order given. All hands-on projects should take a total of three hours to complete. The requirements for this lab include:

❑ A computer with UnixWare 7.1.1 installed according to Project 2-2

❑ A blank floppy disk

### Project 12-1

In this hands-on project, you will create archive files using the tar utility, as well as view and extract their contents.

1. Switch to a command-line terminal (tty2) by pressing **Ctrl+Alt+F2**, and log into the terminal using the username **root** and the password **secret**.

2. At the command prompt, type **cd /home/owner** and press **Enter**. Next, type **ls –a** at the command prompt and press **Enter** to view the contents of the owner's home directory.

3. At the command prompt, type **tar –cvf /owner.tar .** and press **Enter** to create an archive called owner.tar in the root directory that contains the contents of the current directory. Did you use absolute or relative pathnames when creating this archive?

4. Next, type **ls –l /owner.tar** at the command prompt and press **Enter**. Was the file successfully created?

5. At the command prompt, type **tar –tvf /owner.tar** and press **Enter**. What is displayed?

6. At the command prompt, type **mkdir /new1** and press **Enter**. Next, type **cd /new1** at the command prompt and press **Enter** to change the current directory to the /new1 directory.

7. At the command prompt, type **tar –xvf /owner.tar** and press **Enter** to extract the contents of the /owner.tar archive. Next, type **ls –aF** at the command prompt and press **Enter** to view the contents of the /new1 directory. Was the extraction successful?

8. At the command prompt, type **rm /owner.tar** and press **Enter** to remove the archive file.

9. At the command prompt, type **tar –cvf /owner.tar /home/owner** and press **Enter** to create an archive called owner.tar in the root directory that contains the /home/owner directory and its contents. Did you use absolute pathnames when creating this archive?

10. Next, type **ls –l /owner.tar** at the command prompt and press **Enter**. Was the file successfully created?

11. At the command prompt, type **tar –tvf /owner.tar** and press **Enter**. What is displayed?

12. At the command prompt, type **tar -xvf /owner.tar** and press **Enter**. Where were the contents of /owner.tar extracted to? Why?

13. At the command prompt, type **mkdir /new2** and press **Enter**. Next, type **cd /new2** at the command prompt and press **Enter** to change the current directory to the /new2 directory.

14. At the command prompt, type **tar -xAvf /owner.tar** and press **Enter** to extract the contents of the /owner.tar archive and suppress absolute pathnames. Next, type **ls -F** at the command prompt and press **Enter** to view the contents of the /new2 directory. Was the extraction successful? What directory is present?

15. At the command prompt, type **ls -F home** and press **Enter**. What is displayed? Next, type **ls -aF home/owner** and press **Enter**. Were the files restored successfully?

16. At the command prompt, type **cd** and press **Enter** to return to your home directory.

17. At the command prompt, type **rm /owner.tar** and press **Enter** to remove the archive file. Next, type **rm -r /new[12]** at the command prompt and press **Enter** to remove the directories created earlier and their contents.

18. Type **exit** and press **Enter** to log out of your shell.

**HANDS-ON PROJECTS**

## Project 12-2

In this hands-on project, you will place files within an archive on a floppy disk using the tar utility, as well as view and extract its contents.

1. Switch to a command-line terminal (tty2) by pressing **Ctrl+Alt+F2**, and log into the terminal using the username **root** and the password **secret**.

2. Insert a floppy disk into the floppy disk drive of your computer.

3. At the command prompt, type **cat /etc/default/tar** and press **Enter**. What archive number corresponds to /dev/rdsk/f03ht? What is the default archive device if a number is not displayed?

4. At the command prompt, type **cd /home/owner** and press **Enter**.

5. At the command prompt, type **tar -cv6 .** and press **Enter** to create an archive on the device /dev/rdsk/f03ht, which contains the contents of the current directory using relative pathnames.

6. At the command prompt, type **tar -tv6** and press **Enter**. What is displayed?

7. At the command prompt, type **tar -rv6 /etc/issue** and press **Enter** to append the /etc/issue file to the archive on the device /dev/rdsk/f03ht.

8. At the command prompt, type **tar -tv6** and press **Enter**. Is the /etc/issue file displayed? Does it use a relative or absolute pathname?

9. At the command prompt, type **mkdir /new3** and press **Enter**. Next, type **cd /new3** at the command prompt and press **Enter** to change the current directory to the /new3 directory.

12

10. At the command prompt, type **tar –xv6** and press **Enter** to extract the contents of the archive stored on the floppy disk. Next, type **ls –aF** at the command prompt and press **Enter** to view the contents of the /new3 directory. Was the extraction successful? Is the /etc/issue file present? Where was it extracted to? How could you extract this file to your current directory?

11. At the command prompt, type **cd** and press **Enter** to return to your home directory. Next, type **rm –r /new3** at the command prompt and press **Enter** to remove the /new3 directory.

12. Remove the floppy disk from your floppy disk drive. Type **exit** and press **Enter** to log out of your shell.

HANDS-ON
PROJECTS

## Project 12-3

In this hands-on project, you will create, view, and extract archives using the cpio utility.

1. Switch to a command-line terminal (tty2) by pressing **Ctrl+Alt+F2**, and log into the terminal using the username **root** and the password **secret**.

2. At the command prompt, type **cd /home/owner** and press **Enter**.

3. At the command prompt, type **find . | cpio –ovcBL –O /owner.cpio** and press **Enter** to create an archive file called /owner.cpio, which contains the contents of owner's home directory. Did you use absolute pathnames when creating this archive?

4. At the command prompt, type **ls –l /owner.cpio** and press **Enter**. Was the archive file created successfully?

5. At the command prompt, type **cpio –ivtB –I /owner.cpio** and press **Enter**. What is displayed? What does each option indicate in the aforementioned command?

6. At the command prompt, type **mkdir /new4** and press **Enter**. Next, type **cd /new4** at the command prompt and press **Enter** to change the current directory to the /new4 directory.

7. At the command prompt, type **cpio –ivcdumB –I /owner.cpio** and press **Enter** to extract the contents of the archive file created earlier. Next, type **ls –aF** and press **Enter**. Were the files restored successfully?

8. At the command prompt, type **cd** and press **Enter** to return to your home directory. Next, type **rm –r /new4** at the command prompt and press **Enter** to remove the /new4 directory.

9. Insert a floppy disk into the floppy disk drive of your computer.

10. At the command prompt, type **find /home/owner | cpio –ovcBL –O /dev/rdsk/f03ht** and press **Enter** to create an archive on your floppy disk that contains owner's home directory. Did you use absolute pathnames when creating this archive?

11. At the command prompt, type **cpio –ivtB –I /dev/rdsk/f03ht** and press **Enter**. What is displayed?

12. At the command prompt, type **cpio –ivcdumB –I /dev/rdsk/f03ht** and press **Enter** to extract the contents of the archive on the first floppy device. Where were the files extracted to?

13. Remove the floppy disk from your floppy disk drive. Type **exit** and press **Enter** to log out of your shell.

## Project 12-4

In this hands-on project, you will create archives using the vxdump command, as well as view and extract those archives using the vxrestore command.

1. Switch to a command-line terminal (tty2) by pressing **Ctrl+Alt+F2**, and log into the terminal using the username **root** and the password **secret**.

2. At the command prompt, type **cat /etc/mnttab** and press **Enter**. What type of filesystem is mounted to the /home directory?

3. At the command prompt, type **vxdump –0uf /home0.dump /home** and press **Enter** to create an archive of the /home filesystem in the archive file /home0.dump. What type of backup was performed? Will the /etc/dumpdates file be updated?

4. At the command prompt, type **cat /etc/dumpdates** and press **Enter**. View the contents.

5. At the command prompt, type **cp /etc/issue /home/owner** and press **Enter**.

6. At the command prompt, type **vxdump –1uf /home1.dump /home** and press **Enter** to create an archive of the /home filesystem in the archive file /home1.dump. What type of backup was performed? Will the /etc/dumpdates file be updated? Will the issue file that was copied to /home/owner earlier be archived?

7. At the command prompt, type **cat /etc/dumpdates** and press **Enter**. View the contents.

8. At the command prompt, type **vxrestore –tf /home0.dump** and press **Enter**. What was displayed? Are the pathnames used absolute or relative pathnames?

9. At the command prompt, type **vxrestore –tf /home1.dump** and press **Enter**. What was displayed? Are the pathnames used absolute or relative pathnames?

10. At the command prompt, type **vxrestore –rf /home0.dump** and press **Enter** to restore the contents of the /home filesystem from the /home0.dump archive file.

11. At the command prompt, type **vxrestore –rf /home1.dump** and press **Enter** to restore the contents of the /home filesystem from the /home1.dump archive file.

12. Type **exit** and press **Enter** to log out of your shell.

**12**

## Project 12-5

In this hands-on project, you will use the compress utility to compress single files and view their compression ratio as well compress the contents of a directory.

1. Turn on your computer. Once your Linux system has been loaded, switch to a command-line terminal (tty2) by pressing **Ctrl+Alt+F2**, and log into the terminal using the username **root** and the password **secret**.

2. At the command prompt, type **cp /etc/security/ia/master /testfile1** and press **Enter**. Next, type **cp /etc/device.tab /testfile2** at the command prompt and press **Enter**. These two test files will be used to test compression in the following steps.

3. At the command prompt, type **file /testfile\*** and press **Enter**. What type of data is in /testfile1 and /testfile2?

4. At the command prompt, type **ls –l /testfile\*** and press **Enter**. How large are /testfile1 and /testfile2?

5. At the command prompt, type **compress –v /testfile\*** and press **Enter** to compress the two test files. Which one achieved more compression? Next, type **ls –l** at the command prompt and press **Enter**. What extension does each file have? What are their sizes?

6. At the command prompt, type **zcat /testfile2.Z | more** and press **Enter** to view the contents of the compressed /testfile2.Z text file. Press **q** to exit the more utility.

7. At the command prompt, type **uncompress –v /testfile\*** and press **Enter** to decompress the two test files. Next, type **ls –l /testfile\*** at the command prompt. Do these files have an extension? What are their sizes?

8. At the command prompt, type **rm /testfile\*** and press **Enter** to remove the two test files from the filesystem.

9. At the command prompt, type **du –ks /stand** and press **Enter** to view the total size of the files within the /stand filesystem.

10. At the command prompt, type **tar –cvf /stand.backup /stand** and press **Enter** to create an archive of the /stand filesystem in the archive file /stand.backup.

11. At the command prompt, type **ls –l /stand.backup** and press **Enter**. What is the size of the /stand.backup file? Compare this to the size displayed in Step 9. Explain the large size difference.

12. At the command prompt, type **compress –v /stand.backup** and press **Enter** to compress the /stand.backup archive file. What compression ratio was given?

13. At the command prompt, type **ls –l /stand.backup.Z** and press **Enter**. Next, type **rm /stand.backup.Z** and press **Enter** to remove the archive file.

14. Type **exit** and press **Enter** to log out of your shell.

## DISCOVERY EXERCISES

1. Write the command that can be used to perform the following:

   a. Back up the contents of the /var directory (which contains symbolically linked files) to the first nonretensioning, nonrewinding tape device on the system using the tar utility.

   b. Append the /etc/inittab file to the archive created in Step a.

   c. Use the cpio utility to back up all files in the /var directory (which contains symbolically linked files) to the first retensioning, rewinding tape device with a block size of 5KB.

   d. Perform a full filesystem backup of the /var filesystem to the first nonretensioning, rewinding tape device using the vxdump utility and record the event in the /etc/dumpdates file.

   e. View the contents of the archives created in Steps a, c, and d.

   f. Extract the contents of the archive created in Step a to the /tmp directory.

   g. Extract the contents of the archives created in Steps c and d to their original locations.

2. The pax (portable archive interchange) utility may be used to interpret tar and cpio archives of different versions. Use the manual pages to list the usage of the pax command and summarize it in a table. Next, create a tar and cpio archive file, and use the pax command to view and extract the contents to a temporary directory.

3. The dd (direct device access) utility is often used to perform rapid backups of partitions because it can perform a block-by-block copy of files without interpreting them first. View the manual page for this utility and list the usage of it in a table. Next, use the manual page or Internet resources to summarize the advantages and disadvantages of using the dd command for system backups. Following this, use the dd command to create an archive file called /home.dd from the contents of the /home filesystem.

4. Use the Internet, library, or other sources of information to research two other compress utilities that are available for UNIX systems. For each utility, list their benefits, compression ratio, and usage. Also list the location on the Internet where each can be downloaded. Download and use these two utilities to compress a copy of the /etc/device.tab file. Compare the compression ratio to the one obtained for testfile2 in Step 5 of Project 12-5. Do they offer better compression ratios than the compress utility?

12

# USER AND GROUP ADMINISTRATION

**After reading this chapter and completing the exercises, you will be able to:**

♦ Describe the process of authentication

♦ Define the format of the user and group database files

♦ Change user accounts and primary group membership

♦ Create, modify, and delete user accounts using command-line utilities

♦ Create, modify, and delete group accounts using command-line utilities

♦ Use SCO Admin to manage users and groups

♦ Assign administrative rights to users using command-line utilities and SCO Admin

In previous chapters of this textbook, you logged in using the root or owner user accounts that were created during installation. This chapter focuses on the creation of additional user accounts and user account management. More specifically, you will explore user and group account databases, and learn how to switch your user account and primary group. Next, you will learn how to create, modify, and delete user accounts as well as assign user accounts administrative rights. Finally, this chapter shows you how to create and manage groups on the system.

## USER AND GROUP ACCOUNTS

You must log into a UNIX system with a valid username and password before a shell is granted; this process is called **authentication** since the username and password are authenticated against a system database that contains all **user account** information. Authenticated users are then granted access to files, directories, and other resources on the system based on their user account.

The system database that contains user account information typically consists of two files: **/etc/passwd** and **/etc/shadow**. Every user typically has a line that describes the user account in /etc/passwd and a line that contains the encrypted password and expiry information in /etc/shadow.

Older UNIX systems stored the encrypted password in the /etc/passwd file and did not use the /etc/shadow file at all. This is considered poor security today since processes often require access to the user information in /etc/passwd. Storing the encrypted password in a separate file that cannot be accessed by processes prevents a process from obtaining all user account information.

Each line of the /etc/passwd file has the following colon-delimited format:

```
name:password:UID:GID:GECOS:homedirectory:shell
```

The name in the previous output refers to the name of the user. Usernames can be a maximum of 254 characters long and must not include a colon character. If an /etc/shadow is not used, then the password field contains the encrypted password for the user; otherwise, it just contains an *x* as a placeholder for the password stored in /etc/shadow.

The **user identifier (UID)** specifies the unique numeric UID that is assigned to each user. Typically, UIDs that are less than 100 refer to user accounts that are used by daemons when logging into the system. The root user always has a UID of 0.

The **group identifier (GID)** is the primary numeric GID for the user; each user can be a member of several groups, but only one of those groups can be the **primary group**. The primary group of a user is the group that becomes the group owner of any file or directory that the user creates. Similarly, when a user creates a file or directory, that user becomes the owner of that file or directory.

The **GECOS (General Electric Comprehensive Operating System)** field represents a text description of the user and is typically left blank. This information was originally used in the General Electric Comprehensive Operating System. The last two fields represent the absolute pathname to the user's home directory and the shell, respectively.

The following output shows an example of an /etc/passwd file:

```
# cat /etc/passwd
root:x:0:3:0000-Admin(0000):/:/sbin/sh
daemon:x:1:12:0000-Admin(0000):/:
bin:x:2:2:0000-Admin(0000):/usr/bin:
sys:x:3:3:0000-Admin(0000):/:
adm:x:4:4:0000-Admin(0000):/var/adm:
```

```
uucp:x:5:5:0000-uucp(0000):/usr/lib/uucp:
mail:x:6:6:Mail Processes:/etc/mail:
nuucp:x:10:10:0000-uucp(0000):/var/spool/uucppublic:/usr/lib/uucp/uucico
nobody:x:60001:60001:uid no body:/:
noaccess:x:60002:60002:uid no access:/:
lp:x:7:9:0000-LP(0000):/var/spool/lp:/usr/bin/sh
listen:x:37:4:Network Admin:/usr/net/nls:/usr/bin/ksh
mhsmail:x:61:6:MHS Admin Processes:/var/spool/smf:/usr/bin/ksh
owner:x:101:1:system owner account:/home/owner:/usr/bin/ksh
# _
```

The root user is usually listed at the top of the /etc/passwd file, as shown previously, followed by the user accounts used by daemons when logging into the system, followed by the regular user accounts. The last line of the previous output indicates that the user owner has a UID of 101, a primary GID of 1, a GECOS of system owner account, and a home directory of /home/owner. The user owner also uses the Korn shell (/usr/bin/ksh).

Like /etc/passwd, the /etc/shadow file is colon delimited, but it has the following format:

**name:password:lastchange:min:max:warn:inactive:expiry:flag**

Although the first two fields in the /etc/shadow file are the same as those in the /etc/passwd file, the contents of the password field will be different. The password field in /etc/shadow will contain the encrypted password, whereas the password field in /etc/passwd will contain an *x*, as it is not used.

The lastchange field represents the date of the most recent password change. It is measured in the number of days since January 1, 1970.

**NOTE**  Traditionally, a calendar date was represented by a number indicating the number of days since January 1, 1970; today, many calendar dates found in configuration files follow the same convention.

**13**

To prevent unauthorized access to a UNIX system, it is good form to change passwords for user accounts regularly; thus, passwords may be set to expire at certain intervals. The next three fields of the /etc/shadow file indicate information about password expiry: min represents the number of days users must wait before they change their password after receiving a new one, max represents the number of days users can use the same password without changing it, and warn represents the number of days before a password expires that users are warned to change their password.

**NOTE**  By default on UnixWare systems, no values are set for min, max, and warn.

You can expire the password for user accounts if they are not used for a long period of time. The inactive field in /etc/shadow indicates the number of days of inactivity before a user account is locked. In addition, you can choose a set expiry date for user accounts. This expiry date is entered in the expiry field of /etc/shadow and is indicated using the number of days since January 1, 1970.

The flag field in the /etc/shadow file is rarely used, but it may contain options used by a password generator. The following output shows an example of an /etc/shadow file:

```
# cat /etc/shadow
root:9Fu6GyZyMwL1.:11932:::::::
daemon:NP:6445:::::::
bin:NP:6445:::::::
sys:NP:6445:::::::
adm:NP:6445:::::::
uucp:NP:6445:::::::
mail:NP:6445:::::::
nuucp:NP:6445:::::::
nobody:NP:6445:::::::
noaccess:NP:6445:::::::
lp:*LK*:::::::
listen:*LK*:::::::
mhsmail:*LK*:::::::
owner:vEpM4yrPnEK66:11932:::::::
# _
```

Note from the previous output that most user accounts used by daemons do not receive an encrypted password; instead, their password field indicates NP (Not Provided) or *LK* (Locked). This is to prevent users from accidentally logging into the system with daemon accounts.

Although every user must have a primary group listed in the /etc/passwd file, each user may be a member of multiple groups. All groups and their members are listed in the **/etc/group** file. The /etc/group file has the following colon-delimited fields:

```
name:password:GID:members
```

The first field is the name of the group, which may be a maximum of eight characters, followed by a group password. The password field usually contains an *x* as group passwords are rarely used today.

The GID represents the unique GID for the group, and the members field indicates the list of user accounts that are members of the group. The following output shows an example of an /etc/group file:

```
# cat /etc/group
root::0:root
other::1:root
bin::2:root,bin,daemon
sys::3:root,bin,sys,adm
```

```
adm::4:root,adm,daemon
uucp::5:root,uucp
mail::6:root
tty::7:root,adm
audit::8:root
nuucp::10:root,nuucp
daemon::12:root,daemon
cron::23:root
dtadmin::25:root
priv::47:root
nobody::60001:
noaccess::60002:
lp::9:root,lp
dos::100:
# _
```

From the previous output, the bin group has a GID of 2 and three users as members: root, bin, and daemon.

Recall from Chapter 5 that the **groups** command displays the groups that you are a member of. To further display your UID, primary GID, and all GIDs for the groups that you belong to, use the **id command**. The primary group is always the first group listed by each command. The following output shows the output of these commands when executed by the root user:

```
# groups
sys root other bin adm uucp mail tty audit nuucp daemon cron
dtadmin priv lp
# id
uid=0(root) gid=3(sys) groups=0(root),1(other),2(bin),3(sys),
4(adm),5(uucp),6(mail),7(tty),8(audit),10(nuucp),12(daemon),
23(cron),25(dtadmin),47(priv),9(lp)
# _
```

In the previous output, the primary group for the root user is the sys group. This group will be attached as the group owner for all files that are created by the root user, as shown in the following output:

```
# touch samplefile1
# ls -l samplefile1
-rw-r--r--    1 root      sys      0 Dec  6 17:29 samplefile1
# _
```

To change your primary group temporarily to another group that you are a member of, use the **newgrp command**. Any new files created afterwards will reflect your new primary group. The following output demonstrates how changing the primary group for the root user affects file ownership:

```
# newgrp other
# id
uid=0(root) gid=1(other) groups=0(root),1(other),2(bin),3(sys),
4(adm),5(uucp),6(mail),7(tty),8(audit),10(nuucp),12(daemon),
23(cron),25(dtadmin),47(priv),9(lp)
# touch samplefile2
# ls -l samplefile2
-rw-r--r--        1 root    other 0 Dec   6 17:29 samplefile2
# _
```

You may also change your user account after login by using the **su (switch user) command** followed by the target user account. The root user may switch to any other user account without specifying a password; however, regular users must supply the correct password for the target user account when using the **su** command. Also, the **–** option can be used to run the target user's environment files. To switch from the root account to the owner account and execute the owner's environment files, use the following command:

```
# su - owner

You have mail
$ _
```

If a username is not specified as an argument to the **su** command, the root user is assumed. For example, to switch from the owner account to the root account and execute root's environment files, use the following command and supply the root user's password:

```
$ su -
Password:

You have mail
# _
```

When executing the su command, password characters are not displayed on the terminal screen when they are typed.

**NOTE**

The su command opens a new shell each time it changes users. To return the previous user account, use the exit command or the Ctrl+d key combination at a command prompt.

**NOTE**

It is important to use the root user account only when necessary. Most administrators create a regular user account for daily use and then use the su command when logged into that account to become the root user as needed.

**NOTE**

# CREATING USER ACCOUNTS

You can create user accounts on a UNIX system by using the **useradd command**. To create a user named bobg and his home directory, use the following command:

```
# useradd -m bobg
#
```

In this case, all other information required to create the user account is taken from a file on the filesystem. This file is called **/etc/default/useradd** and contains information regarding the default primary group, the location and mode of home directories, the default number of days to disable inactive accounts, the expiry date, the shell used, and the skeleton directory used. The **skeleton directory** used by the useradd command is **/etc/skel** and contains files that are copied to all new user's home directories when the home directory is created. Most of these files are environment files such as .profile.

The following output provides an example of an /etc/default/useradd file:

```
# cat /etc/default/useradd
#ident   "@(#)useradd.dfl        1.3"
#ident   "$Header: useradd.dfl 2.0 91/07/13 $"
SHELL=/usr/bin/ksh
HOMEDIR=/home
SKELDIR=/etc/skel
GROUPID=1
INACT=
EXPIRE=
HOME_MODE=755
#
```

The previous /etc/default/useradd file indicates that all new users will use the Korn shell (/usr/bin/ksh) and have a home directory of the same name created underneath /home that has the permission 755 and contains files from /etc/skel. Also, each new user will be a member of the group called other (GID = 1) and will not have values in the inactive or expiry fields of /etc/shadow.

Although you can edit the /etc/default/useradd file using a text editor such as vi, you can also use the defadm command. The defadm command can edit any file in the /etc/default directory; simply specify the name of the file and the line to change as arguments. For example, to change the default shell for all new users to the Bourne shell, use the following commands:

```
# defadm useradd SHELL=/bin/sh
# cat /etc/default/useradd
#ident   "@(#)useradd.dfl        1.3"
#ident   "$Header: useradd.dfl 2.0 91/07/13 $"
SHELL=/bin/sh
HOMEDIR=/home
```

13

```
SKELDIR=/etc/skel
GROUPID=1
INACT=
EXPIRE=
HOME_MODE=755
#  _
```

**NOTE**
You can also use the System Defaults Manager in the System folder of SCO Admin to edit files in the /etc/default directory.

To override any of the default parameters specified in the /etc/default/useradd file when creating users, specify the options to the **useradd** command. For example, to create a user named maryj with a UID of 762 and the shell /bin/csh, use the following command:

```
# useradd -u 762 -s /bin/csh maryj
#  _
```

Table 13-1 lists and describes some common options available to the **useradd** command.

**Table 13-1**    Common options to the **useradd** command

| Option | Description |
|---|---|
| -c "*description*" | Adds a description for the user to the GECOS field of /etc/passwd |
| -d *homedirectory* | Specifies the absolute pathname to the user's home directory |
| -e *expirydate* | Specifies a date to disable the account from logging in; it populates the expiry field of /etc/shadow. |
| -f *days* | Specifies the number of days that an inactive account will be disabled; it populates the inactive field of /etc/shadow. |
| -g *group* | Specifies the primary group for the user account |
| -G *group1, group2,etc.* | Specifies all other group memberships for the user account |
| -i | When used with the –u option, it allows a UID that is being aged to be used (discussed later in this chapter). |
| -k *directory* | Specifies the skeleton directory used when copying files to a new home directory |
| -m | Specifies that a home directory should be created for the user account |
| -o | When used with the –u option, it allows a UID to be duplicated on the system. |
| -s *shell* | Specifies the absolute pathname to the shell used for the user account |
| -u *UID* | Specifies the UID of the user account |

Once a user account has been added, the password field in the /etc/shadow file will contain *LK*, indicating that no password has been set for the user account. To set the password, type the **passwd command** followed by the name of the new user account at a command prompt and supply the appropriate password when prompted. The following output shows an example of setting the password for the user bobg :

```
# passwd bobg
New password:
Re-enter new password:
# _
```

When executing the passwd command, password characters are not displayed on the terminal screen when they are typed.

**NOTE**

All user accounts must have a password set before they are used to log into the system.

**NOTE**

The root user can set the password on any user account using the passwd command; however, regular users can use the passwd command to change the password on their account only.

**NOTE**

The default minimum password length for regular users on a UnixWare system is different for different security profiles. It is defined by the PASSLENGTH parameter in the **/etc/default/passwd** file. This parameter is set to zero characters for low security, three characters for traditional security, six characters for improved security, and eight characters for high security.

**NOTE**

**13**

Passwords should be difficult to guess and contain a combination of uppercase, lowercase, and special characters to increase system security; an example of a good password to choose is C2Jr1;Pwr.

**NOTE**

You can also create user accounts using the SCO Admin **Account Manager**. By default, the Account Manager displays a list of user accounts on the system, as shown in Figure 13-1.

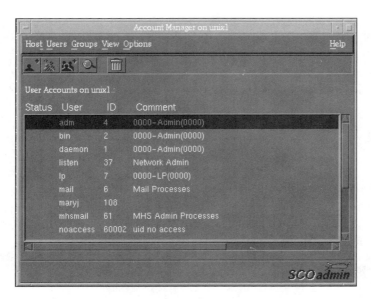

**Figure 13-1**   The Account Manager

If you select Show Status from the Options menu in Figure 13-1, you will see symbols in the Status column, as shown in Figure 13-2.

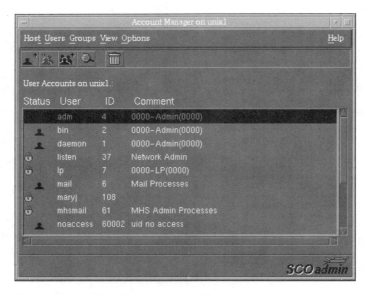

**Figure 13-2**   Viewing the account status

A lock symbol beside a user account in Figure 13-2 indicates that the password has been locked. A black user symbol indicates a regular user account, and a red user symbol indicates an account with superuser rights (root).

To add a new user account using the Account Manager, select Add New User from the Users menu and you will be prompted to enter the appropriate account information, as shown in Figure 13-3.

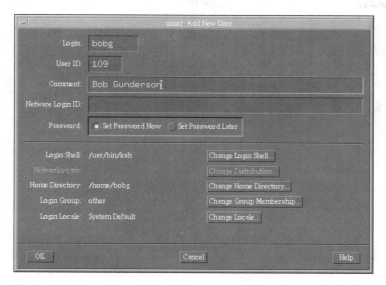

**Figure 13-3**    Adding a new user account

The next available UID above 100 is automatically displayed when creating new users using the Account Manager. The Comment (GECOS) and Netware Login ID fields are optional. Also, a home directory is automatically created for the user account and default information from the /etc/default/useradd file is displayed at the bottom of the screen; you can accept this information or change it before creating the user account.

Since all user accounts must have a password to log in and use the system, you are prompted to set the password immediately following the creation of the user account (Set Password Now) or at a later time (Set Password Later). If you select Set Password Now, then you will receive the screen depicted in Figure 13-4.

Also, you can set or change the password for a user account by selecting Change Password from the Users menu in the Account Manager.

**NOTE**

The skeleton directory used by the Account Manager when creating users is **/usr/lib/scoadmin/account/skel**.

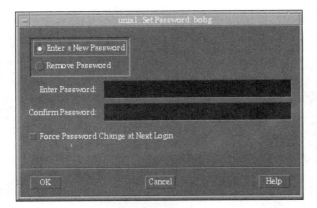

**Figure 13-4**   Supplying a password

To ease the creation of several user accounts, edit the information in the /etc/default/user-add file. You can also modify this file by selecting User Defaults from the Options menu in the Account Manager, as shown in Figure 13-5.

**Figure 13-5**   Editing account defaults

## MODIFYING USER ACCOUNTS

To modify the information regarding a user account after creating it, you can edit the /etc/passwd or /etc/shadow file; however, this is not recommended practice since typographical errors in these files may prevent the system from functioning.

If you manually change the entries in the /etc/passwd file, you should run the **pwck command** afterwards to check the format of /etc/passwd and ensure that no structural errors have occurred.

The **usermod command** can be used to safely modify most information regarding user accounts; for example, to change the login name of the user bobg to barbg, use the −l option with the usermod command:

```
# usermod -l barbg bobg
# _
```

Table 13-2 provides a complete list of options used with the usermod command to modify user accounts.

**Table 13-2**    Common options to the usermod command

| Option | Description |
| --- | --- |
| −c "description" | Specifies a new description for the user in the GECOS field of /etc/passwd |
| −d homedirectory | Specifies the absolute pathname to a new home directory |
| −e expirydate | Specifies a date to disable the account from logging in; it modifies the expiry field of /etc/shadow. |
| −f days | Specifies the number of days that an inactive account will be disabled; it modifies the inactive field of /etc/shadow. |
| −g group | Specifies a new primary group for the user account |
| −G group1, group2,etc. | Specifies all other group memberships for the user account |
| −l name | Specifies a new login name |
| −s shell | Specifies the absolute pathname to a new shell used for the user account |
| −u UID | Specifies a new UID for the user account |

**13**

It might be necessary in certain situations to prevent a user from logging in temporarily; this is commonly called **locking an account**. To lock a user account, you can use the passwd −l username command. This clears the password field for the user in the /etc/shadow file and replaces it with the character *LK*. To unlock a user account, assign a new password for the user using the passwd −u username command.

Yet another method commonly used to lock a user account is to change the shell specified in /etc/passwd for a user account to an invalid shell such as /bin/false. Without a valid shell, a user will not be able to use the system. To lock a user account this way, edit the /etc/passwd file and make the appropriate change, or use the −s option with the usermod command. The following example uses the usermod command to change the shell to /bin/false for the user bobg:

```
# usermod -s /bin/false bobg
# _
```

You can also modify user account information in the SCO Admin Account Manager by selecting the user account and choosing Modify from the Users menu. Figure 13-6 shows the properties of the bobg user account.

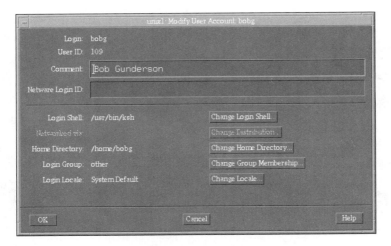

**Figure 13-6**  Modifying a user account

Note from Figure 13-6 that you may not modify the login name and UID of an account using the Account Manager; you must instead use the `usermod` command to modify them.

To lock a user account from the Account Manager, select Lock from the Users menu. Conversely, to unlock a user account, select Unlock from the Users menu and supply a new password when prompted.

The Account Manager also enables you to change the expiry, inactive, min, max, and warn field in the /etc/shadow file for a user account; simply choose Expiration from the Users menu and supply the desired information, as shown in Figure 13-7.

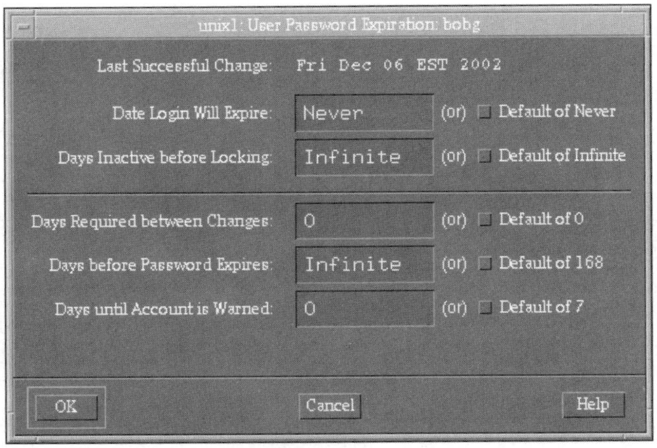

**Figure 13-7**  Account expiration

## DELETING USER ACCOUNTS

To delete a user account, you can use the **userdel command** and specify the username as an argument. This will remove entries from both /etc/passwd and /etc/shadow corresponding to the user account. Furthermore, you may specify the **-r** option to the `userdel` command to remove the home directory for the user and all of its contents.

When a user account is deleted, any files that were previously owned by the user become owned by the number that represents the UID of the deleted user. Any future user account that is given the same UID then becomes the owner of those files.

Just as the `useradd` command searches the contents of the /etc/default/useradd file, the `userdel` command searches the contents of the /etc/default/userdel file. There is only one parameter in the /etc/default/userdel file that is used to specify the number of months before a deleted user's UID can be used for another user:

```
# cat /etc/default/userdel
#ident   "@(#)userdel.dfl          1.2"
#ident   "$Header: userdel.dfl 2.0 91/07/13 $"
UIDAGE=12
# _
```

Since UIDAGE has a value of 12 in the previous output, the UIDs for all deleted users must reside in the /etc/security/ia/ageduid file for 12 months before being reused. If UIDAGE has a value of 0, then UIDs may be reused immediately. Conversely, if UIDAGE has a value of –1, then UIDs must reside in the /etc/security/ia/ageduid file forever and may never be reused.

The **-n** option with the `userdel` command can be used to override the UIDAGE parameter in the /etc/default/userdel file. Say, for example, that the user bobg leaves the company. To delete bobg's user account and immediately reuse the UID, use the following command:

```
# userdel -n 0 bobg
# _
```

Since the **-r** option was not used, bobg's home directory was not removed. Any files that bobg owned before his user account was deleted will now be owned by his previous UID:

```
# ls -l /home/bobg
total 6
drwxr-xr-x    2 107      other       96 Dec  6 16:44 Projects
drwxrwxr-x    5 107      other       96 Dec  6 16:44 Reports
-rw-r--r--    1 107      other        0 Sep  1 19:22 Update
-rw-r--r--    1 107      other      630 Apr  7  1998 project1
-rw-r--r--    1 107      other      664 Oct 12  1999 project2
-rw-r--r--    1 107      other       51 Apr  3  1998 project3
# _
```

**13**

In the previous output, the old UID of the user bobg was 107. If the user sueb was hired by the company to replace bobg, you can assign the UID of 107 to her user account such that she may own all of bobg's old files and reuse them as needed.

The following output creates the user sueb with a UID of 107 and lists the ownership of the files in bobg's home directory:

```
# useradd -u 107 -m sueb
# ls -l /home/bobg
total 6
drwxr-xr-x   2 sueb     other     96 Dec  6 16:44 Projects
drwxrwxr-x   6 sueb     other     96 Dec  6 17:22 Reports
-rw-r--r--   1 sueb     other      0 Sep  1 19:22 Update
-rw-r--r--   1 sueb     other    630 Apr  7  1998 project1
-rw-r--r--   1 sueb     other    664 Oct 12  1999 project2
-rw-r--r--   1 sueb     other     51 Apr  3  1998 project3
#
```

Since the **-m** option was used with the **useradd** command in the previous output, sueb will have her own home directory (/home/sueb). Since she also owns the files within /home/bobg, she may copy the files that she needs and remove any that she does not.

To delete users from the SCO Admin Account Manager, highlight the user and choose Delete from the Users menu; you will be prompted to confirm the deletion and choose whether to remove the home directory for the user, as shown in Figure 13-8.

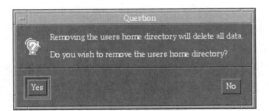

**Figure 13-8**    Removing the home directory

# GRANTING ADMINISTRATIVE RIGHTS TO USERS

By default, only the root user has the ability to perform all administrative tasks on a UNIX system. The system owner account created during UnixWare installation has all administrative rights while using SCO Admin only. All other user accounts have no administrative rights and cannot manage system resources.

As a UNIX administrator, you may not be available at all times to perform administrative tasks; thus, you may want to assign limited rights to other user accounts. For example, the manager of a department in a company may be responsible for creating user accounts or system backups when you are unavailable.

It is poor security to give the system owner account to others who must perform system administration because the system owner account has the ability to change the root user's password.

The SCO Admin Account Manager enables you to assign predefined sets of administrative rights called **authorizations** to user accounts. Users with authorizations must then use SCO Admin to perform administrative tasks. To assign authorizations to a user, select the user account and choose Authorizations from the Users menu in the Account Manager. Figure 13-9 shows the authorizations for the new user bobg.

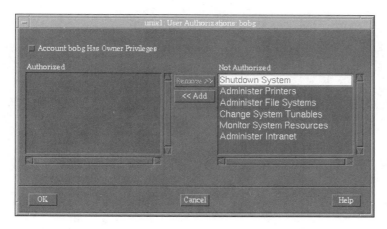

**Figure 13-9**    User account authorizations

Note from Figure 13-9 that you may assign a user six authorizations. Table 13-3 lists each of these authorizations.

**13**

**Table 13-3**    UnixWare authorizations

| Authorization | Description |
|---|---|
| Shutdown System | Shut down or reboot the system using the SCO Admin System Shutdown Manager. |
| Administer Intranet | Configure the TCP/IP Protocol using the SCO Admin Network Configuration Manager. |
| Administer Filesystems | Create, mount, and manage filesystems using the SCO Admin Filesystem Manager. |
| Administer Printers | Create, modify, and remove printers using the SCO Admin Printer Setup Manager. |
| Change System Tunables | Change UNIX kernel parameters using the SCO Admin System Tuner. |
| Monitor System Resources | View the utilization of system resources using the SCO Admin System Monitor. |

Selecting Account bobg Has Owner Privileges from Figure 13-9 will assign all of the authorizations to bobg, as shown in Figure 13-10; however, it will also assign all other administrative rights to SCO Admin in the CDE desktop.

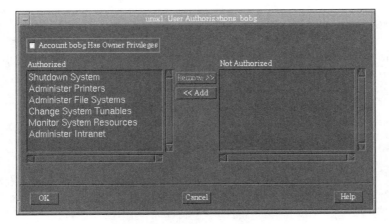

**Figure 13-10**    Assigning owner privileges

You can also use the `/usr/lib/scoadmin/account/make-owner bobg` command to assign bobg the same administrative rights as the system owner.

**NOTE**

To assign individual rights or rights that are not listed in Figure 13-9, you must use the **adminrole command** to create a role that has administrative rights and then the **adminuser command** to assign that role to a user account.

Say, for example, that you want to allow the manager of a department to create user accounts when people are hired by the company. First, you must create a new role using the `adminrole` command:

```
# adminrole -n MANAGER
# _
```

Next, you must assign the role privileges to the `/usr/sbin/useradd` command:

```
# adminrole -a useradd:/usr/sbin/useradd:allprivs MANAGER
# _
```

Finally, you must assign the role to a user account using the **adminuser** command. If the manager's user account is called bobg, you can assign the MANAGER role using the following command:

```
# adminuser -n -o MANAGER bobg
# _
```

The user bobg may now add user accounts using the `useradd` command; however, bobg must use the **tfadmin (Trusted Facility Administrator) command** (/sbin/tfadmin) when creating user accounts with the `useradd` command, as shown in the following output:

```
$ who am i
bobg          vt02       Dec   7 15:22
$ useradd -m royc
UX:useradd: ERROR: Permission denied
$ /sbin/tfadmin useradd -m royc
$ _
```

 If you are unable to execute the /sbin/tfadmin command, it is likely that the file rights database (/etc/security/tcb/privs) has been corrupted. To fix this database, run the /etc/security/tools/setpriv -x command.

**TIP**

## Managing Groups

By far the easiest method to add groups to a system is to edit the /etc/group file using a text editor and add the appropriate line for the group.

 If you manually change the entries in the /etc/group file, you should run the **grpck command** afterwards to check the format of /etc/group and ensure that no structural errors have occurred.

**TIP**

Alternatively, you can use the **groupadd command** to add groups to the /etc/group file. To add a group called group1 to the system and assign it a GID of 492, use the following command:

```
# groupadd -g 492 group1
# _
```

**13**

Next, you can use the –G option with the `usermod` command to add members to the group. To add the user maryj to this group and view the addition, use the following `usermod` command:

```
# usermod -G group1 maryj
# cat /etc/group
root::0:root,owner
other::1:root
bin::2:root,bin,daemon
sys::3:root,bin,sys,adm
adm::4:root,adm,daemon
uucp::5:root,uucp
mail::6:root
tty::7:root,adm
```

```
audit::8:root
nuucp::10:root,nuucp
daemon::12:root,daemon
cron::23:root
dtadmin::25:root
priv::47:root
nobody::60001:
noaccess::60002:
lp::9:root,lp
dos::100:
group1::492:maryj
# _
```

The **groupmod command** can be used to modify the group name and GID, and the **groupdel command** can be used to remove groups from the system.

The SCO Admin Account Manager can also be used to manage groups. Recall that the Account Manager displays all user accounts on the system by default. Selecting By Groups from the View menu will display all group accounts on the system, as shown in Figure 13-11.

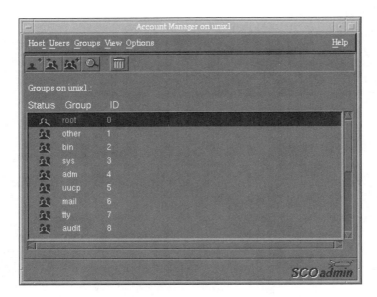

**Figure 13-11**    Viewing groups

To add a group account to the system, select Add New Group from the Groups menu shown in Figure 13-11 and you will be prompted to enter the parameters for the group, as depicted in Figure 13-12.

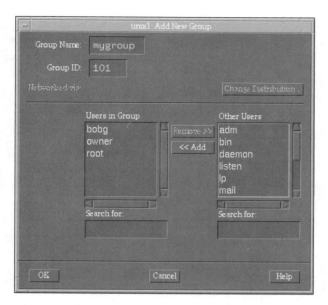

**Figure 13-12**    Adding a new group account

As shown in Figure 13-12, the Account Manager automatically chooses the next available GID above 100 and enables you to add members to the group. You can modify the group membership afterwards by selecting Modify from the Groups menu or delete a group by choosing Delete from the Groups menu in the Account Manager.

## CHAPTER SUMMARY

- User and group account information is stored in the /etc/passwd, /etc/shadow, and /etc/group files.

- All user accounts must have a valid password before they can gain access to a UNIX system.

- You can change your user account and primary group after login using the su and newgrp commands, respectively.

- You can use the useradd command to create user accounts and the groupadd command to create group accounts.

- User accounts can be modified with the usermod and passwd commands; group accounts can be modified with the groupmod command.

- The userdel and groupdel commands can be used to remove users and groups from the system, respectively.

❏ The SCO Admin Account Manager is a graphical utility that can manage users and groups on the system.

❏ Administrative rights can be assigned using the Account Manager or the adminrole and adminuser utilities.

## KEY TERMS

**/etc/default/passwd** — The file that contains the default minimum password length used when changing passwords.

**/etc/default/useradd** — The file that contains default values for user creation.

**/etc/group** — The file that contains a list of valid groups on the system.

**/etc/passwd** — The file that contains user account information.

**/etc/shadow** — The file that contains the encrypted password and account expiry parameters for each user account.

**/etc/skel** — The skeleton directory used by the useradd command when creating user accounts.

**/usr/lib/scoadmin/account/skel** — The skeleton directory used by the SCO Admin Account Manager when creating user accounts.

**Account Manager** — The graphical SCO Admin manager used to manage users and groups on the system.

**adminrole command** — The command used to create a role and assign it administrative rights on the system.

**adminuser command** — The command used to assign a role created with the adminrole command to a user on the system.

**authentication** — The act of verifying a user's identity by comparing a username and password to a system database (/etc/passwd and /etc/shadow).

**authorizations** — Sets of administrative rights that can be assigned to users using SCO Admin.

**GECOS (General Electric Comprehensive Operating System) field** — The field in the /etc/passwd file that contains a description of the user account.

**group identifier (GID)** — A unique number given to each group.

**groupadd command** — The command used to add a group to the system.

**groupdel command** — The command used to delete a group from the system.

**groupmod command** — The command used to modify the name or GID of a group on the system.

**grpck command** — The command that checks the structural integrity of the /etc/group database.

**id command** — The command that displays your UID(s) and GID(s).

**locking an account** — The process of making an account temporarily unusable by altering its password information stored on the system.

**newgrp command** — The command used to temporarily change the primary group of a user.

**passwd command** — The command used to modify the password associated with a user account.

**primary group** — The group that is specified for a user in the /etc/passwd file and specified as group owner for all files created by a user.

**pwck command** — The command that checks the structural integrity of the /etc/passwd database.

**skeleton directory** — A directory that contains files that are copied to all new user's home directories upon creation.

**su (switch user) command** — The command used to change your user account after login.

**tfadmin (Trusted Faculty Administrator) command** — The command that enables users with administrative rights to run administrative commands on the command line.

**user account** — Information regarding a user that is stored in a system database that may be used to log into the system and gain access to system resources.

**user identifier (UID)** — A unique number assigned to each user account.

**useradd command** — The command used to add a user account to the system.

**userdel command** — The command used to remove a user account from the system.

**usermod command** — The command used to modify the properties of a user account on the system.

## REVIEW QUESTIONS

13

1. What is the name used to describe the process whereby a user provides a user account name and password to log onto a system?

   a. validation

   b. logon

   c. authentication

   d. confirmation

2. What file contains information on a given user's minimum password length?

   a. /etc/skel

   b. /etc/passwd

   c. /etc/default/passwd

   d. /etc/default useradd

3. Although both users and groups may have passwords attached to them, groups typically do not have passwords assigned to them. True or False?

4. What command can be used to add an administrative role to the system?

   a. adminrole

   b. adminuser

   c. useradd

   d. tfadmin

5. What command can you use to lock a user account?

   a. lock *username*

   b. passwd -l *username*

   c. usermod -l *username*

   d. useradd -l *username*

6. What command can be used to alter the primary group associated with a given user temporarily?

   a. There is no such command.

   b. chggrp

   c. gpasswd

   d. newgrp

7. You look at the appropriate field in /etc/shadow to see when a password was last changed and observe a value indicating 11000. What does this value indicate?

   a. You are looking at the wrong field.

   b. You are looking in the wrong file; this field should be in /etc/passwd.

   c. the number of hours since January 1, 1980

   d. the number of days since January 1, 1970

8. When creating a user from the GUI, you cannot specify the UID; this can only be done from the command line. True or False?

9. What file contains default information used when creating user accounts?

   a. /etc/skel

   b. /etc/passwd

   c. /etc/default/useradd

   d. /etc/default/passwd

10. What is the name of the file that contains a listing of all users on the system and their home directories?

    a. /etc/passwd

    b. /etc/passwrd

    c. /etc/users/conf

    d. /etc/shadow

11. UIDs and GIDs are unique to the system and once used can never be reused. True or False?

12. You can lock a user account by changing the default login shell to an invalid shell in /etc/passwd. True or False?

13. How can you change the default values contained in the /etc/default/userdel file? (Choose all that apply.)

    a. the Account Manager

    b. the vi editor

    c. the defadm command

    d. the usermod command

14. Which of the following commands can be used to check the integrity of the /etc/group file after it has been manually edited?

    a. pwck

    b. tfadmin

    c. grpck

    d. defadm

15. What command can be used to assign an administrative role to a user?

    a. adminrole

    b. adminuser

    c. useradd

    d. tfadmin

16. How can you add users to groups on the system? (Choose all that apply.)

    a. the newgrp command

    b. vi /etc/group

    c. the Account Manager

    d. the groupadd command

17. The primary group for a user account is listed in /etc/passwd and all other group membership for a user is listed in /etc/group. True or False?

**13**

18. What command would you use to unlock a user account?

    a. unlock *username*

    b. open *username*

    c. enable *username*

    d. passwd *username*

19. Where will you find the variable that sets the default time that a deleted UID is aged?

    a. /etc/default/useradd

    b. /etc/default/passwd

    c. /etc/default/userdel

    d. /etc/security/ia/ageduid

20. Account Manager can be used to assign predefined sets of rights to users called
    _____.

    a. authorizations

    b. privileges

    c. rights

    d. properties

21. You have installed a UNIX operating system and have not changed any of the default settings. You delete the user jims who had a UID of 354 and immediately issue the command useradd -u 354 janem. Unfortunately, you receive an error message. What should you do?

    a. Set the UIDAGE parameter in /etc/default/userdel.

    b. Run the /etc/security/tools/setpriv -x command.

    c. Remove the line for the UID in /etc/security/ia/ageduid.

    d. Manually edit the /etc/passwd and /etc/shadow files.

22. The skeleton directory used when creating user accounts with Account Manager is /etc/skel. True or False?

23. Along with a listing of user accounts, the /etc/passwd file also contains information on account expiry. True or False?

24. What command is used to delete a user account and remove the home directory?

    a. usermod -r *username*

    b. usermod -m *username*

    c. userdel -r *username*

    d. userdel -m *username*

25. You can add users to groups on the system by modifying the last field in /etc/group. True or False?

# HANDS-ON PROJECTS

These projects should be completed in the order given. All hands-on projects should take a total of three hours to complete. The requirement for this lab includes:

❏  A computer with UnixWare 7.1.1 installed according to Project 2-2

## Project 13-1

In this hands-on project, you will observe user account databases and create a user account using command-line utilities.

1. Switch to a command-line terminal (vt02) by pressing **Ctrl+Alt+F2**, and log into the terminal using the username **root** and the password **secret**.

2. At the command prompt, type **cat /etc/passwd** and press **Enter**. Where is the line that describes the root user located in this file? Where is the line that describes the owner user in this file? How many daemon accounts are present? What is in the password field for all accounts?

3. At the command prompt, type **ls –l /etc/passwd** and press **Enter**. Who is the owner and group owner of this file? Who has permission to read this file?

4. At the command prompt, type **cat /etc/shadow** and press **Enter**. What is in the password field for the root user and owner user accounts? What is in the password field for most daemon accounts?

5. At the command prompt, type **ls –l /etc/shadow** and press **Enter**. Who is the owner and group owner of this file? Who has permission to read this file? Compare the permissions for /etc/shadow to those of /etc/passwd obtained in Step 3 and explain the difference.

6. At the command prompt, type **cat /etc/default/useradd** and press **Enter**. What is the default shell used when creating users? What is the default skeleton directory? Where are user home directories created by default? What permissions will new home directories have?

7. At the command prompt, type **ls –a /etc/skel** and press **Enter**. What files are stored in this directory? What is the purpose of this directory when creating users?

8. At the command prompt, type **touch /etc/skel/policies.txt** and press **Enter** to create a sample file in the /etc/skel directory.

9. At the command prompt, type **useradd –m –u 666 bozo** and press **Enter**. What does the –m option specify? From where is the default shell and home directory information taken?

10. At the command prompt, type **cat /etc/passwd** and press **Enter**. What shell and home directory does bozo have? What is bozo's UID?

11. At the command prompt, type **cat /etc/shadow** and press **Enter**. Does bozo have a password? Can bozo log into the system?

13

12. At the command prompt, type **passwd bozo** and press **Enter**. Enter the password **secret** and press **Enter**. Enter the password **secret** again to confirm and press **Enter**.

13. At the command prompt, type **ls -a /home/bozo** and press **Enter**. How many files are in this directory? Compare this list to the one obtained in Step 7. Is the policies.txt file present?

14. Type **exit** and press **Enter** to log out of your shell.

**HANDS-ON PROJECTS**

## Project 13-2

In this hands-on project, you will modify user accounts using command-line utilities.

1. Switch to a command-line terminal (vt02) by pressing **Ctrl+Alt+F2**, and log into the terminal using the username **root** and the password **secret**.

2. At the command prompt, type **cat /etc/passwd** and press **Enter**. Record the line used to describe the user bozo: _____

3. At the command prompt, type **cat /etc/shadow** and press **Enter**. Record the line used to describe the user bozo: _____

4. At the command prompt, type **usermod –l bozo2 bozo** and press **Enter** to change the login name for the user bozo to bozo2. Next, type **cat /etc/passwd** at the command prompt and press **Enter**. Was the login name changed from bozo to bozo2? Was the UID changed? Was the home directory changed?

5. At the command prompt, type **usermod –l bozo bozo2** and press **Enter** to change the login name for the user bozo2 back to bozo.

6. At the command prompt, type **usermod –u 666 bozo** and press **Enter** to change the UID of the user bozo to 666. Next, type **cat /etc/passwd** at the command prompt and press **Enter**. Was the UID changed?

7. At the command prompt, type **usermod –f 14 bozo** and press **Enter** to expire bozo's user account after 14 days of inactivity. Next, type **cat /etc/shadow** at the command prompt and press **Enter**. Which field was changed?

8. At the command prompt, type **usermod –e "01/01/2009" bozo** and press **Enter** to expire bozo's user account on January 1, 2009. Next, type **cat /etc/shadow** at the command prompt and press **Enter**. Which field was changed? What does the number represent in this field?

9. At the command prompt, type **vi /etc/shadow** and press **Enter**. Use the format of this file as defined in this chapter when performing the following step.

10. Enter the number **2** in the min field of bozo's account line such that the user bozo must wait at least two days before password changes. Next, enter the number **40** in the max field of bozo's account line such that the user bozo must change passwords every 40 days. Next, enter the number **5** in the warn field

to warn the user bozo five days in advance before a password change is required. When you are finished, save your changes and exit the vi editor.

To save a read-only file, recall that you must use w! at the : prompt.

11. Type **exit** and press **Enter** to log out of your shell.

## Project 13-3

In this hands-on project, you will lock and unlock user accounts using command-line utilities.

1. Switch to a command-line terminal (vt02) by pressing **Ctrl+Alt+F2**, and log into the terminal using the username **root** and the password **secret**.

2. At the command prompt, type **cat /etc/shadow** and press **Enter**. Record the encrypted password for bozo's user account: _____

3. At the command prompt, type **passwd –l bozo** and press **Enter** to lock bozo's user account.

4. At the command prompt, type **cat /etc/shadow** and press **Enter**. What has been changed regarding the original encrypted password recorded in Step 2?

5. Switch to a command-line terminal (vt05) by pressing **Ctrl+Alt+F5**, and attempt to log into the terminal using the username **bozo** and the password **secret**. Were you successful?

6. Switch back to the command-line terminal (vt02) by pressing **Ctrl+Alt+F2**.

7. At the command prompt, type **passwd bozo** and press **Enter**. Enter the password **secret** and press **Enter**. Enter the password **secret** again to confirm and press **Enter**.

8. At the command prompt, type **cat /etc/shadow** and press **Enter**. Compare the encrypted password for bozo's user account to the one recorded in Step 2.

9. Switch to a command-line terminal (vt05) by pressing **Ctrl+Alt+F5**, and attempt to log into the terminal using the username **bozo** and the password **secret**. Were you successful?

10. Type **exit** and press **Enter** to log out of your shell.

11. Switch back to the command-line terminal (vt02) by pressing **Ctrl+Alt+F2**.

12. At the command prompt, type **usermod –s /bin/false bozo** and press **Enter** to change bozo's shell to /bin/false. Type **cat /etc/passwd** at the command prompt to verify that the shell was changed to /bin/false for bozo's user account.

13. Switch to a command-line terminal (vt05) by pressing **Ctrl+Alt+F5**, and attempt to log into the terminal using the username **bozo** and the password **secret**. Were you successful?

14. Switch back to the command-line terminal (vt02) by pressing **Ctrl+Alt+F2**.

13

15. At the command prompt, type **usermod –s /usr/bin/ksh bozo** and press **Enter** to change bozo's shell to /usr/bin/ksh.

16. Switch to a command-line terminal (tty5) by pressing **Ctrl+Alt+F5**, and attempt to log into the terminal using the username **bozo** and the password **secret**. Were you successful?

17. Type **exit** and press **Enter** to log out of your shell.

18. Switch back to the command-line terminal (vt02) by pressing **Ctrl+Alt+F2**.

19. Type **exit** and press **Enter** to log out of your shell.

**HANDS-ON
PROJECTS**

# Project 13-4

In this hands-on project, you will remove a user account and create a new user account in its place using command-line utilities.

1. Switch to a command-line terminal (vt02) by pressing **Ctrl+Alt+F2**, and log into the terminal using the username **root** and the password **secret**.

2. At the command prompt, type **ls –la /home/bozo** and press **Enter**. Who owns most files in this directory? Why?

3. At the command prompt, type **userdel bozo** and press **Enter**. Was the home directory removed for bozo removed as well?

4. At the command prompt, type **ls –la /home/bozo** and press **Enter**. Who owns the most files in this directory? Why?

5. At the command prompt, type **useradd –m –u 666 bozoette** and press **Enter**. What error do you receive?

6. At the command prompt, type **cat /etc/default/userdel** and press **Enter**. What is the value of the UIDAGE parameter? What does this indicate?

7. At the command prompt, type **cat /etc/security/ia/ageduid** and press **Enter**. What line is present? What do you think the second number represents?

8. At the command prompt, type **> /etc/security/ia/ageduid** and press **Enter** to clear the contents of the /etc/security/ia/ageduid file.

9. At the command prompt, type **useradd –m –u 666 bozoette** and press **Enter**. Why were you successful?

10. At the command prompt, type **passwd bozoette** and press **Enter**. Enter the password **secret** and press **Enter**. Enter the password **secret** again to confirm and press **Enter**.

11. At the command prompt, type **cat /etc/passwd** and press **Enter**. What is bozoette's home directory? What is bozoette's UID?

12. At the command prompt, type **ls –la /home/bozo** and press **Enter**. Who owns the most files in this directory? Why? Can bozoette manage these files?

13. Type **exit** and press **Enter** to log out of your shell.

## Project 13-5

In this hands-on project, you will create, use, and delete groups using command-line utilities.

1. Switch to a command-line terminal (vt02) by pressing **Ctrl+Alt+F2**, and log into the terminal using the username **root** and the password **secret**.

2. At the command prompt, type **vi /etc/group** and press **Enter** to open the /etc/group file in the vi editor. Add a line to the bottom of this file that reads:

   ```
   groupies:x:1234:root,bozoette
   ```

   This will add a group to the system with a GID of 1234 and the members root and bozoette. When you are finished, save the changes and exit the vi editor.

3. At the command prompt, type **grpck** and press **Enter** to ensure that you have not made any structural errors in the /etc/group file.

4. Switch to a command-line terminal (vt05) by pressing **Ctrl+Alt+F5**, and log into the terminal using the username **bozoette** and the password **secret**.

5. At the command prompt, type **groups** and press **Enter**. Which groups is bozoette a member of?

6. At the command prompt, type **id** and press **Enter**. Which group is the primary group for the user bozoette?

7. At the command prompt, type **touch file1** and press **Enter** to create a new file called file1 in the current directory.

8. At the command prompt, type **ls –l** and press **Enter**. Who is the owner and group owner of the file file1? Why?

9. At the command prompt, type **newgrp groupies** and press **Enter** to temporarily change bozoette's primary group to groupies.

10. At the command prompt, type **touch file2** and press **Enter** to create a new file called file2 in the current directory.

11. At the command prompt, type **ls –l** and press **Enter**. Who is the owner and group owner of the file file2? Why?

12. Type **exit** and press **Enter** to log out of your shell.

13. Switch back to the command-line terminal (vt02) by pressing **Ctrl+Alt+F2**.

14. At the command prompt, type **groupdel groupies** and press **Enter** to remove the group groupies from the system. Which file is edited by the groupdel command?

15. Type **exit** and press **Enter** to log out of your shell.

**13**

## Project 13-6

In this hands-on project, you will assign administrative rights to a user account using command-line utilities.

1. Switch to a command-line terminal (vt02) by pressing **Ctrl+Alt+F2**, and log into the terminal using the username **root** and the password **secret**.

2. At the command prompt, type **useradd -m shutdownuser** and press **Enter**.

3. At the command prompt, type **passwd shutdownuser** and press **Enter**. Enter the password **secret** and press **Enter**. Enter the password **secret** again to confirm and press **Enter**.

4. Type **exit** and press **Enter** to log out of your shell. Next, log into the terminal using the username **shutdownuser** and the password **secret**.

5. At the command prompt, type **cd /** and press **Enter** to change to the / directory.

6. At the command prompt, type **shutdown -g0 -y -i6** and press **Enter** to shut down and reboot the system immediately. What error did you receive?

7. Type **exit** and press **Enter** to log out of your shell. Next, log into the terminal using the username **root** and the password **secret**.

8. At the command prompt, type **adminrole -n TEST** and press **Enter**.

9. At the command prompt, type **adminrole -a shutdown:/sbin/shutdown:allprivs TEST** and press **Enter**.

10. At the command prompt, type **adminuser -n -o TEST shutdownuser** and press **Enter**.

11. Type **exit** and press **Enter** to log out of your shell. Next, log into the terminal using the username **shutdownuser** and the password **secret**.

12. At the command prompt, type **cd /** and press **Enter** to change to the / directory.

13. At the command prompt, type **shutdown -g0 -y -i6** and press **Enter** to shut down and reboot the system immediately. What error did you receive?

14. At the command prompt, type **/sbin/tfadmin shutdown -g0 -y -i6** and press **Enter** to shut down and reboot the system immediately.

## Project 13-7

In this hands-on project, you will manage users and groups using the SCO Admin Account Manager.

1. Switch to the graphical terminal (vt01) by pressing **Ctrl+Alt+F1**, and log into the CDE desktop using the username **root** and the password **secret**.

2. Open the SCO Admin Account Manager. What is displayed?

3. Click on the **Options** menu and select **Show Status**.

If you receive an error message, you may safely ignore it and press **OK** on the error message screen.

4. Click on the **Options** menu and select **Refresh**. What is displayed in the Status column of Account Manager?

5. Click on the **Users** menu and select **Add New User**. What default information is provided? Enter the name **sample** in the Login dialog box, the number **555** in the User ID dialog box, and the name **sample user** in the Comment dialog box.

6. Click on the **Change Login Shell** button and use the drop box to select the shell **/bin/ksh** and click **OK**.

7. Ensure that **Set Password Now** is selected and click **OK**. Type in the password **secret** in the two boxes provided and click **OK** when you are finished.

8. Ensure that the line representing the sample user is highlighted, and click on the **Users** menu and select **Modify**. What information cannot be modified using Account Manager?

9. Click on the **Change Group Membership** button. What primary group is listed at the top of the screen? Select the group **sys** in the Other Groups dialog box and click on the **Add** button. Click **OK** to close the current window and click **OK** again to modify the user account.

10. Click on the **Users** menu and select **Expiration**. Enter the following values in the spaces provided:

    **Date Login Will Expire: 01/01/2009**

    **Days Inactive before Locking: 30**

    **Days Required between Changes: 1**

    **Day before Password Expires: 60**

    **Days until Account is Warned: 7**

    What will each entry do? Click **OK** when you are finished.

11. Click on the **Users** menu and select **Authorizations**. Choose **Shutdown System** under the Not Authorized dialog box and press the **Add** button. Click **OK** when you are finished.

12. Click on the **View** menu and select **By Groups**.

13. Click on the **Groups** menu and select **Add New Group**. Enter the name **mygroup** in the Group Name dialog box and the number **444** in the Group ID dialog box.

14. Select the user **sample** in the Other Users dialog box and press the **Add** button. Next, select the user **root** in the Other Users dialog box and press the **Add** button. Click **OK** when you are finished to create the group.

15. Exit all programs and log out of the CDE desktop.

16. Switch to a command-line terminal (vt02) by pressing **Ctrl+Alt+F2**, and log into the terminal using the username **root** and the password **secret**.

17. At the command prompt, type **cat /etc/passwd** and press **Enter**. What is the UID, GECOS, and shell for the sample user?

18. At the command prompt, type **cat /etc/shadow** and press **Enter**. What are the account expiration parameters?

13

19. At the command prompt, type **cat /etc/group** and press **Enter**. Who are the members of mygroup? Is the sample user a member of the sys group?

20. Type **exit** and press **Enter** to log out of your shell.

21. Switch to the graphical terminal (vt01) by pressing **Ctrl+Alt+F1**, and log into the CDE desktop using the username **sample** and the password **secret**.

22. Open the System Shutdown Manager in the System folder of SCO Admin. Ensure that **0** appears in the Minutes dialog box and select **Begin Shutdown** from the Shutdown menu. Click **OK** to confirm the action. Why were you able to shut down your system?

---

## DISCOVERY EXERCISES

1. Write commands to accomplish the following (use the manual pages or SCOhelp if necessary):

   a. Create a user with a login name of bsmith, a UID of 733, a GECOS field entry of accounting manager, and a password of Gxj234.

   b. Delete the user jdoe, but leave the home directory intact.

   c. Change the properties of the existing user wjones such that the user has a new comment field of shipping and an account expiry of March 23, 2011.

   d. Lock the account of wjenkins.

   e. Change the password of bsmith to We34Rt.

   f. Change the properties of the existing user tbanks such that the user is a member of the managers group and has a login name of artbanks.

   g. Create a user with the same UID and primary group as root and a login name of wjones.

   h. Create a new user with a login name of jdoe who has a password of he789R and no home directory.

   i. Change the primary group of the user wsmith to root.

   j. Add the users tbanks and jdoe to the group acctg.

2. If you change the UID for a user account, what repercussions will that have on existing files? Explain.

   Create a new user account called utest, log in as this user account, and create some files in utest's home directory. Next, do a long listing of these files. Who is the owner of them? Now, change the UID of utest to 900 using the command usermod -u 900 utest and view the ownership of the files in utest's home directory. Who owns them? Explain.

Use the manual page for the usermod command to find out what the -U option does to the file that it references. Create a new user account called utest2, log in as this user account, and create some files in this user's home directory. Next, log in as the root user and change the UID of utest2 to 901 using the command usermod -u 901 -U utest and view the ownership of the files in utest2's home directory. Who owns them and why?

3. Many files in the /etc/default directory are used by commands on the filesystem. Examine the /etc/default/login file. This file is used to determine the parameters used by the login process during authentication. Use the manual pages, SCOhelp, or the Internet to define the following lines in this file:

PASSREQ=YES

MANDPASS=NO

UMASK=022

MAXTRYS=99

LOGFAILURES=1

DISABLETIME=10

TIMEOUT=60

Next, use the defadm command to change the value of DISABLETIME to 5. Following this, use the SCO Admin System Defaults Manager to change the value of LOGFAILURES to 1. Use the command >/var/adm/loginlog to create the log file used to record LOGFAILURES. Now, switch to another terminal and log in unsuccessfully as the root user with a blank password several times. Return to your previous terminal and view the contents of /var/adm/loginlog. What do they indicate?

4. You may obtain summary information about various areas of your system using the Reports Manager in the System folder of SCO Admin. Use the Reports Manager to generate a report on the following:

a. the password status for all users on the system

b. the password status only for the users that you have created in this chapter

c. the user logins that have occurred for all users on the system

d. the user logins that have occurred only for the users that you have created in this chapter

**13**

# 14

# PRINTER ADMINISTRATION

**After reading this chapter and completing the exercises, you will be able to:**

♦ Outline the print process

♦ Create and manage printers using command-line utilities

♦ Create and manage printers using the Printer Setup Manager

♦ Send print jobs to the print queue

♦ Manage print jobs in the print queue using command-line utilities

♦ Manage print jobs in the print queue using the Print Job Manager

♦ Alter print job priorities and print priority ranges for users

♦ Describe how print jobs are managed within the print queue

M ost users on a UNIX system usually need to have the ability to print work files. Printing log files and system configuration information is good procedure in case of a system failure. Thus, a firm understanding of how to set up, manage, and print to printers is vital for those who set up and administer UNIX servers. This chapter first introduces you to the print process and how to create printers, followed by a discussion of how to print documents and manage printer devices. Finally, this chapter ends with a discussion of print priority and the management of the spool directory.

# THE PRINT PROCESS

Understanding the process by which information is sent to a printer is fundamental to printing on a UNIX system. A set of information that is sent to a printer at the same time is called a **print job**. Print jobs can consist of a file, several files, or the output of a command. To send a print job to a printer, you must use the **lp (line printer) command** and specify what to print.

Next, the **line printer scheduler (lpsched) daemon** assigns the print job a unique **print job ID** and places a copy of the print job into a temporary directory on the filesystem called the **print queue**, provided the printer is an **accepted printer**. If the printer is a **rejected printer**, then the lpsched daemon will print an error message stating that the printer is not accepting print jobs.

Accepting print jobs into a print queue is commonly called **spooling**.

The lpsched daemon is started in runlevel 2 and 3 on UnixWare systems. To manually start the lpsched daemon, you may run the **/usr/lib/lpsched command** at a command prompt. Conversely, to manually stop the lpsched daemon, you may run the **/usr/lib/lpshut command** at the command prompt.

The print queue for a printer is typically the **/var/spool/lp/tmp/*hostname* directory**, where *hostname* is the hostname of the computer. Regardless of how many printers you have configured on a computer, they all share the same print queue directory.

To view your hostname, use the uname –n command.

Once a print job is in the print queue, it is ready to be printed. If the printer is an **enabled printer** and ready to receive the print job, the lpsched daemon then sends the print job from the print queue to the printer and removes the copy of the print job in the print queue. Conversely, if the printer is a **disabled printer**, the print job will remain in the print queue.

Sending print jobs from a print queue to a printer is commonly called **printing**.

Figure 14-1 illustrates an example of this process for a printer called printer1.

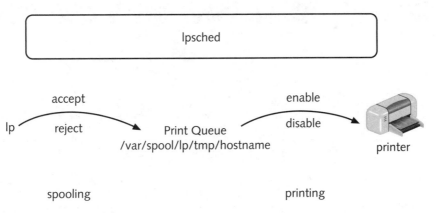

**Figure 14-1** The print process

 When the ink or toner cartridge for a printer needs to be replaced, it is good practice to disable the printer. This will enable users to print to the queue while the cartridge is being replaced. After a few minutes when the cartridge has been replaced, you may then enable the printer. Any print jobs in the print queue will then be printed.

 If a printer is unavailable for a long period of time due to a mechanical failure, you should reject the printer. Any user who attempts to send a print job to the printer will immediately receive an error message indicating that the printer is not accepting requests.

## CREATING AND MANAGING PRINTERS

After a UNIX installation, no printers are configured on the system. To create a printer, use the **lpadmin command** followed by options that specify the:

- Printer name
- Printer destination
- Interface script

The printer destination may be a printer that is attached to a computer on the network or a device file that identifies a local printer port to which a printer is attached. Table 14-1 lists some common printer device files.

**14**

**Table 14-1**    Common printer device files

| Option | Description |
|---|---|
| /dev/lp0<br>or<br>/dev/lp | The first 25-pin parallel/serial port (LPT1), which uses IRQ 7 and I/O address 0x378-37f |
| /dev/lp1 | The first 25-pin parallel port (LPT1), which uses IRQ 7 and I/O address 0x3bc-3be. This device is typically used by older Compaq computers. |
| /dev/lp2 | The second 25-pin parallel port (LPT2), which uses IRQ 5 and I/O address 0x278-27a |
| /dev/term/00h | The first 9-pin serial port on the system (COM1) connected to a printer that uses RTS/CTS flow control |
| /dev/term/01h | The second 9-pin serial port on the system (COM2) connected to a printer that uses RTS/CTS flow control |
| /dev/term/00s | The first 9-pin serial port on the system (COM1) connected to a printer that uses XON/XOFF flow control |
| /dev/term/01s | The second 9-pin serial port on the system (COM2) connected to a printer that uses XON/XOFF flow control |

**NOTE**

You may use the Device Configuration Utility to view the IRQ and I/O addresses used by devices on your UnixWare system; simply type dcu at the command prompt.

The **interface script** is used by the lpsched daemon to initialize the printer device, format data before it is sent to the printer device, and process options to the `lp` command that specify print layout. Sample printer interface scripts are stored in the **/etc/lp/ model directory**, and the /etc/lp/model/standard printer interface script is used for most industry standard printers. When a printer is created, the appropriate interface script is copied from the /etc/lp/model directory to the **/etc/lp/interfaces directory** and renamed the same name as the printer.

**NOTE**

The /etc/lp/model directory is a symbolic link to the /usr/lib/lp/model directory.

To create a printer called printer1 that uses the /etc/lp/model/standard interface script and prints to the first 25-pin parallel/serial printer port on the computer, use the following command:

```
# lpadmin -p printer1 -m standard -v /dev/lp0
# _
```

To further make printer1 the default printer on the system when a printer is not specified in a print command, specify the **–d** option to the `lpadmin` command:

```
# lpadmin -d printer1
#
```

Table 14-2 summarizes some common options used with the `lpadmin` command.

**Table 14-2**    Common options used with the `lpadmin` command

| Option | Description |
|--------|-------------|
| -d *printername* | Specifies the default printer name (*printername*) that will be used with print commands if none is specified |
| -m *filename* | Specifies the name of the printer interface script file (*filename*) in the /etc/lp/model directory that will be used for the printer |
| -p *printername* | Specifies the name of the printer (*printername*) that will be used by print commands |
| -s *servername!printername* | Specifies to print to a printer called *printername* across a computer network on a computer called *servername* |
| -v *devicefile* | Specifies the local device file (*devicefile*) that represents the port that attaches to the printer |
| -x *printername* | Specifies to remove the printer *printername* from the system |

**TIP**    To ensure that the device used to connect a printer is functional, redirect the output of a command to its device file. For example, the command `date > /dev/lp0` should print the output of the `date` command on the printer if a printer is connected to the first 25-pin parallel/serial port (LPT1).

To see a list of all printers on the system as well as their print jobs and status, use the **–t** (total) option with the **lpstat command**, as shown in the following output:

```
# lpstat -t
scheduler is running
system default destination: printer1
device for printer1: /dev/lp0
printer1 not accepting requests since Mon Dec 2 20:10:44 EST 2003 -
        new destination
printer printer1 disabled since Mon Dec 2 20:10:44 EST 2003. available.
        new printer
#
```

The previous output indicates that only one printer on the system called printer1 prints to the device /dev/lp0. It is the default printer for all users and its print queue has no print jobs. The lpsched daemon is running but not accepting jobs into the print queue for this printer and will not send jobs from this print queue to printer1 since it is disabled.

**14**

Without arguments, the `lpstat` command displays your print jobs only; however, it accepts many options that may be used to display information about printers on the system. Table 14-3 summarizes these options.

**Table 14-3**    Common options used with the `lpstat` command

| Option | Description |
|---|---|
| `-a` | Displays a list of printers that are accepting requests on the system |
| `-d` | Displays the system default printer |
| `-o` *printername* | Displays print jobs for a specified printer (*printername*) only |
| `-p`<br>`-p` *printername* | Displays a short description of all printers or a specified printer (*printername*) |
| `-r` | Displays whether or not the lpsched daemon is running |
| `-s` | Displays a short status for all printers on the system |
| `-t` | Displays the total status for all printers on the system |
| `-u` *username* | Displays print jobs for a certain user (*username*) |

You can manipulate the status of the printer using the **accept, reject, enable,** and **disable commands.** To accept and enable the printer called printer1, use the following commands:

```
# accept printer1
UX:accept: INFO: destination "printer1" now accepting requests
# enable printer1
UX:enable: INFO: printer "printer1" now enabled
# lpstat -t
scheduler is running
system default destination: printer1
device for printer1: /dev/lp0
printer1 accepting requests since Mon Dec  2 20:32:01 EST 2003
printer printer1 is idle. enabled since Mon Dec  2 20:32:05 EST 2003.
available.
# _
```

When rejecting or disabling printers using the `reject` and `disable` commands, respectively, use the `-r` option to specify a reason. The following output disables a printer called printer1 with a reason and views the reason afterwards:

```
# disable -r "Toner cartridge is being replaced" printer1
UX:disable: INFO: printer "printer1" now disabled
# lpstat -t
scheduler is running
system default destination: printer1
device for printer1: /dev/lp0
printer1 accepting requests since Mon Dec  2 20:32:01 EST 2002
printer printer1 disabled since Mon Dec  2 20:38:12 EST 2002.
available.
        Toner cartridge is being replaced
# _
```

You can also use the SCO Admin **Printer Setup Manager** to create and manage printers on a UnixWare system. By default, the Printer Setup Manager displays all printers that have been configured on the system, as shown in Figure 14-2.

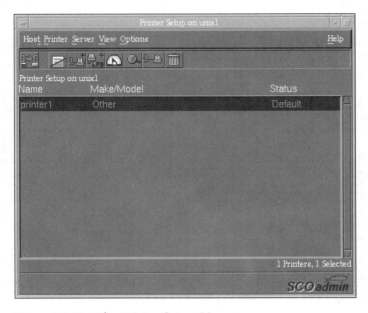

**Figure 14-2**     The Printer Setup Manager

To create a new local printer, choose Add Local Printer from the Printer menu shown in Figure 14-2.You will then be prompted for the appropriate information regarding the printer name, device, and interface script, as shown in Figure 14-3.

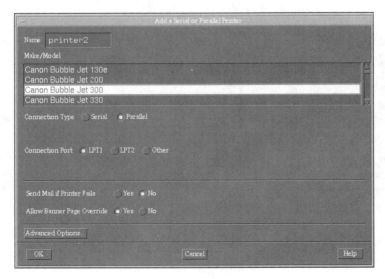

**Figure 14-3**     Creating a new printer

To simplify the selection of the correct interface script, a list of printer models is provided in Figure 14-3. Each printer model is mapped to the correct printer interface script from the /etc/lp/model directory via information in the /usr/lib/scoadmin/printer/model.stz file. Most printer models listed use the /etc/lp/model/standard interface script. To further set the paper settings for the printer, select Advanced Options from Figure 14-3 and supply the correct information, as shown in Figure 14-4.

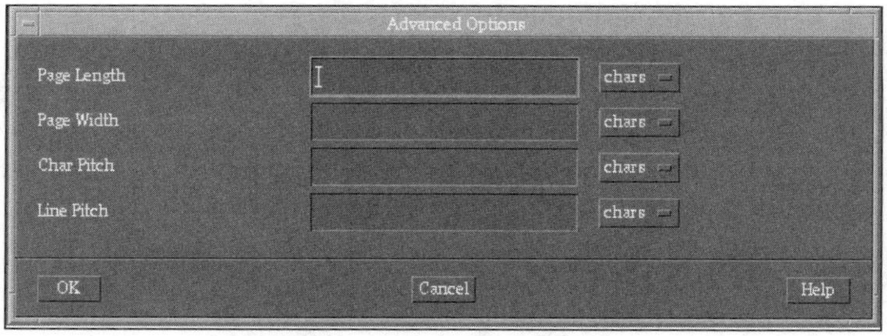

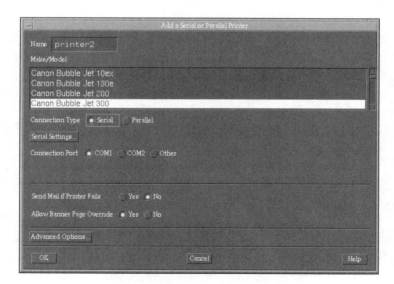

**Figure 14-4**    Setting page properties

As shown Figure 14-3, printers use the first parallel port device, do not send mail to the user if printing errors have occurred, and enable users to override the printing of a banner (title) page. If you select Serial from Figure 14-3, you can choose the serial port that the printer is on, as shown in Figure 14-5.

**Figure 14-5**    Specifying a serial printer

Selecting the Serial Settings button from Figure 14-5 enables you to configure the specific settings of the serial port, as depicted in Figure 14-6.

**Figure 14-6**    Selecting serial port settings

You can also use the Printer Setup Manager to create a printer on a local computer that prints to another printer across a TCP/IP computer network such as the Internet. Simply choose Add TCP/IP Printer from the Printer menu shown in Figure 14-2 and you will be prompted for the printer name, interface script, and connection information, as shown in Figure 14-7.

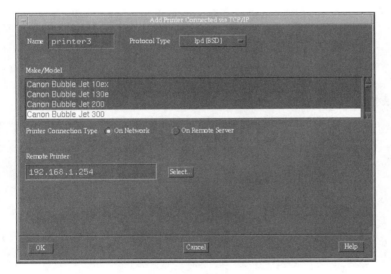

**Figure 14-7**    Creating a TCP/IP printer

Note from Figure 14-7 that the default style of TCP/IP printing is lpd(BSD); however, you may also choose to use System V (legacy) by selecting the Protocol Type drop box. By default, Figure 14-7 requires the hostname or IP address of a printer that is directly connected to the network; however, you may also select On Remote Server to print to a printer that is attached to another computer on the network, as shown in Figure 14-8.

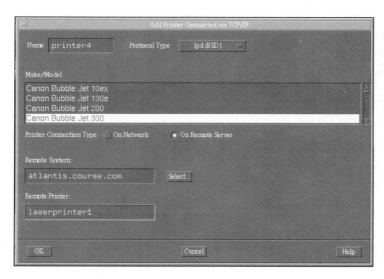

**Figure 14-8**    Selecting a printer on a remote computer

Once configured, the Printer Setup Manager displays the printer, as shown in Figure 14-9.

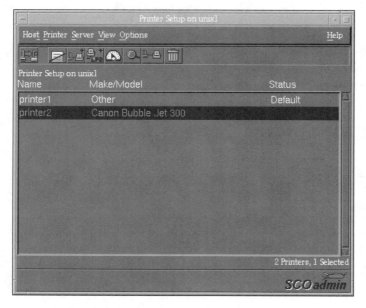

**Figure 14-9**    Viewing printers after creation

After printer creation, you may manipulate printer configuration using the Printer menu. Selecting Properties from the Printer menu enables you to change the settings that you chose earlier for the printer, and selecting Control from the Printer menu enables you to manipulate spooling and printing, as shown in Figure 14-10.

**Figure 14-10**    Controlling printing and spooling for a printer

By default, printers enable all users to print to them from the local computer, but you can alter this by selecting Set User Access from the Printer menu. Similarly, you can control which remote computers can print to local printers by selecting Set Remote Access from the Printer menu of the Printer Setup Manager.

If you want to make a certain printer the default printer on the system, highlight the printer and choose Make Default from the Printer menu in Figure 14-9. The Printer Setup Manager can also stop and start the lpsched daemon; select Halt and Start from the Server menu in Figure 14-9.

## CREATING AND MANAGING PRINT JOBS

Recall that you must use the **lp** command to create a print job. To print a copy of the /etc/inittab file to the printer printer1 shown in earlier examples, use the following command:

```
# lp -d printer1 /etc/inittab
request id is printer1-1 (1 file)
# _
```

**NOTE**

By default, a banner page that describes the print job, the user who printed it, and the time it was printed is printed before each print job. This helps identify print jobs that are printed on a printer that is shared by many people.

The **lp** command returns a print job ID after each print request, which consists of the printer name and the print job number; the print job ID in the previous output is printer1-1, which indicates that it prints to printer1 and is the first print job on the system. Also note that the **-d** option specifies the printer name. If this option is omitted, the **lp** command will assume the default printer on the system; since printer1 is the default printer on the system, the command **lp /etc/inittab** is equivalent to the one used in the previous output.

14

**NOTE**    Each user on a UNIX system can specify his or her own default printer by using the **LPDEST variable**. To specify printer2 as the default printer, add the following lines to an environment file in your home directory such as .profile:

    LPDEST=printer2
    export LPDEST

Table 14-4 lists some common options used with the lp command that are used when printing files.

**Table 14-4**    Common options used with the lp command

| Option | Description |
|---|---|
| -d *printername* | Prints to a specified destination printer (*printername*) |
| -n X | Prints *x* copies of the file; for example, -n 5 would print five copies. |
| -t '*string*' | Prints a specified *string* on the banner page |
| -m | E-mails you when the pr28762int job has completed |
| -c | Sends a copy of the file to be printed to the queue directory |
| -i *printjobID* | Used to manipulate a print job (*printjobID*) in the print queue |
| -H *action* | When used with the -i option, it specifies an action to take on a print job in the print queue. Actions include hold, resume, and immediate. |
| -q n | Specifies to print the job with a priority of *n*, where *n* is between 0 (high priority) and 39 (low priority) |
| -R | Removes the file after printing |
| -o *option* | Formats the print job using a specified option. Common options include: *double* (specifies double-sided printing) *land* (specifies landscape format) *length=n* (specifies page length of *n* lines) *lm=n* (specifies a left margin of *n* characters) *nobanner* (prevents the printing of a banner page) *port* (specifies portrait format) *postscript* (specifies PostScript printing) *rm=n* (specifies a right margin of *n* characters) *width=n* (specifies the page width of *n* characters) |
| -w | Sends a message to your terminal when the print job has completed |

You can also specify several files to be printed using a single lp command by specifying the files as arguments; in this case, only one print job is created to print all of the files. To print the files /etc/hosts and /etc/issue to the printer printer1, execute the following command:

```
# lp -d printer1 /etc/hosts /etc/inittab
request id is printer1-2 (2 files)
# _
```

The `lp` command accepts information from standard input; thus, you may place the `lp` command at the end of a pipe to print information. For example, to print a list of logged in users, use the following pipe:

```
# who | lp -d printer1
request id is printer1-3 (standard input)
# _
```

To see a list of your print jobs in the print queue, use the `lpstat` command without any options:

```
# lpstat
printer1-1        root         3204     Wed Dec   4 20:00:48 EST 2003
printer1-2        root         3392     Wed Dec   4 20:02:19 EST 2003
printer1-3        root           37     Wed Dec   4 20:02:53 EST 2003
# _
```

The `lp` command can also be used to manipulate a print job in the print queue if you use the `-i` option to specify the print job ID. For example, to place the first print job ID in the previous output (printer1-1) on hold, use the following command:

```
# lp -i printer1-1 -H hold
# lpstat
printer1-1        root         3204     Thu Dec   5 09:05:13 EST 2003 being held
printer1-2        root         3392     Wed Dec   4 20:02:19 EST 2003
printer1-3        root           37     Wed Dec   4 20:02:53 EST 2003
# _
```

This print job will then remain in the print queue while other print jobs are printed. To resume normal printing of this print job, use the following command:

```
# lp -i printer1-1 -H resume
# lpstat
printer1-1        root         3204     Thu Dec   5 09:07:07 EST 2003
printer1-2        root         3392     Wed Dec   4 20:02:19 EST 2003
printer1-3        root           37     Wed Dec   4 20:02:53 EST 2003
# _
```

By default, jobs are printing in a first-in-first-out manner; thus, the print job ID printer1-1 in the previous output will print before the print job ID printer1-2, which will in turn print before print job ID printer1-3. If you are the root user, you can use the following command to print the print job ID printer1-3 immediately:

```
# lp -i printer1-1 -H immediate
# lpstat
printer1-3        root           37     Thu Dec   5 09:08:48 EST 2003
printer1-1        root         3204     Thu Dec   5 09:07:07 EST 2003
printer1-2        root         3392     Wed Dec   4 20:02:19 EST 2003
# _
```

**14**

Note from the `lpstat` output that print job ID printer1-3 was moved to the top of the print queue.

If you have several printers configured on a system, you can transfer a print job from one printer to another by specifying to change the destination of a print job in the queue. This may be necessary if a printer needs physical repair and has print jobs waiting in the print queue. To change the destination of the print job ID printer1-1 to printer2, use the following command:

```
# lp -i printer1-1 -d printer2
# lpstat
printer1-3      root         37   Thu Dec  5 09:08:48 EST 2003
printer1-1      root       3204   Thu Dec  5 09:10:31 EST 2003 on printer2
printer1-2      root       3392   Wed Dec  4 20:02:19 EST 2003
# _
```

You can delete print jobs from the print queue by using the **cancel command** followed by the appropriate print job IDs. To cancel the print job IDs printer1-1 and printer1-2 in the previous output, use the following command:

```
# cancel printer1-1 printer1-2
Request "printer1-1" canceled.
Request "printer1-2" canceled.
# lpstat
printer1-3          root          37   Thu Dec 5 09:08:48 EST 2002
# _
```

Normally, users may modify or delete their own print jobs only; however, as the root user, you may modify or delete any print job. For example, to delete all print jobs for the user mary, you can use the command `cancel -u mary`. Similarly, you can use the command `cancel -u all` to cancel all print jobs.

The **Print Job Manager** in SCO Admin may also be used to modify or delete print jobs. By default, the Print Job Manager displays all print jobs in the print queue, as shown in Figure 14-11.

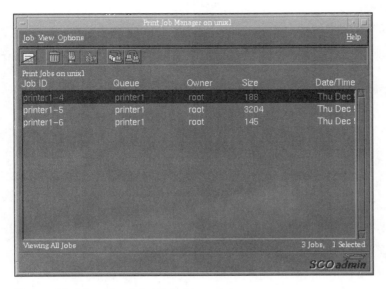

**Figure 14-11** The Print Job Manager

You can then use the Job menu to Delete, Hold, Resume, Promote, or Transfer print jobs, as shown in Figure 14-12.

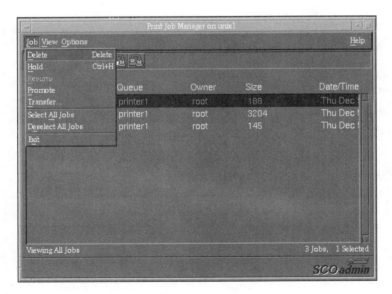

**Figure 14-12** Manipulating print jobs using the Job menu

14

## PRINT JOB PRIORITIES

Every print job has a default priority of 20 when printed. As a result, print jobs are printed in first-in-first-out order. However, you may alter the **print priority** of a print job to increase or decrease the likelihood that it will be printed before existing print jobs.

Print priories range from 0 (high priority) to 39 (low priority). To print a copy of the /etc/inittab file with a priority of 35 (lower than the default), use the following command:

```
# lp -q 35 /etc/inittab
request id is printer1-7 (1 file)
# _
```

In addition, you may also modify the print priority of a print job in the print queue; simply specify the print job ID and the new priority, as shown in the following output:

```
# lp -i printer1-7 -q 25
# _
```

To list the print priority for all users on the system, use the −l option with the **lpusers command**:

```
# lpusers -l
Default priority: 20
        Priority limit for users not listed below: 0
        Priority  Users
# _
```

The previous output indicates that the default priority for new print jobs is 20 and that all users can print with a maximum priority of 0. In other words, all users can print using print priorities in the range 0 to 39.

As the root user, you may limit users to using a certain print priority range. To change the default print priority range for the user mary such that she can print files using a priority between 10 and 39, use the following command:

```
# lpusers -u mary -q 10
# lpusers -l
Default priority: 20
        Priority limit for users not listed below: 0
        Priority  Users
        10        mary
# _
```

To change the default print priority range for the user mary back to the default range of 0 to 39, use the following command:

```
# lpusers -u mary
# lpusers -l
Default priority: 20
        Priority limit for users not listed below: 0
```

```
                Priority  Users
    #  _
```

You may also use the **−d** option with the **lpusers** command to change the default print priority for new print jobs. The following command changes the default print priority from 20 to 30:

```
# lpusers -d 30
# lpusers -l
Default priority: 30
        Priority limit for users not listed below: 0
        Priority  Users
#  _
```

## MANAGING THE PRINT QUEUE

Recall that the print queue directory is /var/spool/lp/tmp/*hostname* regardless of how many printers are installed on the system. When you print files using the **lp** command, a file is placed in this directory that ends with -0. Say, for example, the /etc/inittab file is printed on a computer that has the hostname unix1 and the contents of the print queue are viewed:

```
# lp -d printer1 /etc/inittab
request id is printer1-8 (1 file)
# cd /var/spool/lp/tmp/unix1
# ls
8-0
#  _
```

Since the print job number was 8 in the previous output, the file that was placed in the print queue directory is 8-0. This file is not a copy of the /etc/inittab file; instead, it contains information about the print job:

```
# cat 8-0
C 1
D printer1
F /etc/inittab
O locale=C
P 20
t simple
U root
s   0000
#  _
```

The previous file specifies that the lpsched daemon should print one copy of the file /etc/inittab to the printer called printer1 with a priority of 20 and a simple layout. Also, the user who printed this file is root and the default C locale is used when printing text. The last line in this output indicates the status of the print job; a status of 0000 indicates that it has not been printed yet.

**14**

When the lpsched daemon is ready to send the print job to the printer, it will use this file to locate the /etc/inittab file and print it. If, however, you print a file and then modify its contents shortly thereafter, the lpsched daemon may print the modified file if the print job remains in the queue for a long time.

To solve this problem, you may send a copy of the file to the print queue using the **-c** option with the **lp** command. To print the /etc/inittab file and send a copy to the queue, use the **lp** command in the following output:

```
# lp -c -d printer1 /etc/inittab
request id is printer1-9 (1 file)
# cd /var/spool/lp/tmp/unix1
# ls
8-0   9-0   9-1
# _
```

Note from the previous output that two more files were added to the print queue; these files are named 9-0 and 9-1 since the print job number is 9. The 9-0 file contains information about the print job and the 9-1 file is a copy of the /etc/inittab file. Furthermore, the 9-0 file lists the 9-1 file as the file to print instead of /etc/inittab, as shown in the following output:

```
# cat 9-0
C 1
D printer1
F /var/spool/lp/tmp/unix1/9-1
O locale=C
P 20
t simple
U root
s   0000
# head 9-1
#
# WARNING: THIS FILE IS AUTOMATICALLY GENERATED.
# Any changes made directly to this file may be overwritten
# at the next system reboot.
# Permanent changes should also be made to files in the
# /etc/conf/init.d directory.
# See Init(4) and idmkinit(1M) for more information.
#
fr::sysinit:/sbin/fixroot >/dev/sysmsg 2>&1
vol1::sysinit:/etc/init.d/vxvm-sysboot </dev/sysmsg > /dev/sysmsg 2>&1
# head /etc/inittab
#
# WARNING: THIS FILE IS AUTOMATICALLY GENERATED.
# Any changes made directly to this file may be overwritten
# at the next system reboot.
# Permanent changes should also be made to files in the
# /etc/conf/init.d directory.
# See Init(4) and idmkinit(1M) for more information.
#
fr::sysinit:/sbin/fixroot >/dev/sysmsg 2>&1
vol1::sysinit:/etc/init.d/vxvm-sysboot </dev/sysmsg > /dev/sysmsg 2>&1
# _
```

If you print information from standard input, two files are also created in the print queue: a file that ends in -0, which contains information about the print job, and a file that ends in -1, which contains the standard input. The following lp command accepts the standard output of the who command as standard input and creates two files in the print queue directory:

```
# who | lp -d printer1
request id is printer1-10 (standard input)
# cd /var/spool/lp/tmp/unix1
# ls
10-0   10-1   8-0    9-0    9-1
# _
```

The 10-0 file in the previous output contains information about the tenth print job and the 10-1 file contains the output of the who command:

```
# cat 10-0
C 1
D printer1
F /var/spool/lp/tmp/unix1/10-1
O locale=C
P 20
t simple
U root
s    0000
# cat 10-1
root          console      Dec   5 14:39
root          vt02         Dec   5 15:11
# _
```

Other files may be created in the print queue directory. For example, a file named F10-1 would contain a copy of the data from the tenth print job in PostScript format and a file named 10 would contain errors that were encountered while trying to print the tenth print job.

When print jobs have been removed from the print queue, their information is recorded in the **/var/lp/logs/requests file**:

```
# cancel -u all
Request "printer1-8" canceled.
Request "printer1-9" canceled.
Request "printer1-10" canceled.
# tail -30 /var/lp/logs/requests
= printer1-8, uid 0, gid 3, lid 0, size 3204, Thu Dec  5 14:53:40 EST
2003
z printer1
C 1
D printer1
F /etc/inittab
O locale=C
P 20
t simple
```

14

```
U root
s 0x0040
= printer1-9, uid 0, gid 3, lid 0, size 3204, Thu Dec  5 15:01:54 EST
2003
z printer1
C 1
D printer1
F /var/spool/lp/tmp/unix1/9-1
O locale=C
P 20
t simple
U root
s 0x0040
= printer1-10, uid 0, gid 3, lid 0, size 37, Thu Dec  5 15:06:34 EST
2003
z printer1
C 1
D printer1
F /var/spool/lp/tmp/unix1/10-1
O locale=C
P 20
t simple
U root
s 0x0040

# _
```

Each print job that is recorded in the /var/lp/logs/requests file is indicated by a line that contains the print job ID and date followed by the information from the -0 file. Note from the previous output that the status of each print job (printer1-8, printer1-9, and printer1-10) is 0x0040; this indicates that these print jobs were cancelled by the user. Alternatively, a status of 0x0010 indicates a successful printing and a status of 0x0100 indicates a failure to print.

**NOTE**    The /var/lp/logs/requests file may grow quickly in size if files are printed regularly. As a result, it is good practice to clear this log file on a regular basis to save disk space.

## Chapter Summary

❑ Print jobs are spooled to a print queue before being printed to a printer.

❑ You may use the accept and reject commands to control spooling as well as the enable and disable commands to control printing.

❑ Print jobs are created and manipulated using the lp command, may be viewed in the print queue using the lpstat command, and removed from the print queue using the cancel command.

❑ You may create and manage local and remote printers using the Printer Setup Manager in SCO Admin.

- ❐ Print jobs can be manipulated using the Print Job Manager in SCO Admin.

- ❐ Print jobs priorities range from 0 (high) to 39 (low); all print jobs have a priority of 20 by default.

- ❐ Normally, only one file is created in the print queue for print jobs that describes the print job information; if you print standard input or use the −c option with the lp command, then another file will be created in the print queue that contains the data to be printed.

- ❐ All print jobs are logged to the file /var/lp/logs/requests after being removed from the print queue directory.

## KEY TERMS

**/etc/lp/interfaces directory** — The directory that stores printer interface scripts.

**/etc/lp/model directory** — The directory that stores sample printer interface scripts.

**/usr/lib/lpsched command** — The command used to start the lpsched daemon.

**/usr/lib/lpshut command** — The command used to stop the lpsched daemon.

**/var/lp/logs/requests file** — A log file that stores information about print jobs that have been removed from the print queue directory.

**/var/spool/lp/tmp/*hostname* directory** — The print queue directory (where *hostname* is the hostname of the computer).

**accept command** — The command used to enable spooling for a printer.

**accepted printer** — When managing the print process, it refers to a printer that will accept print jobs into the print queue.

**cancel command** — The command used to remove print jobs from the print queue.

**disable command** — The command used to disable printing for a printer.

**disabled printer** — When managing the print process, it refers to a printer that will not send print jobs from the print queue to a printer.

**enable command** — The command used to enable printing for a printer.

**enabled printer** — When managing the print process, it refers to a printer that will send print jobs from the print queue to a printer.

**interface script** — A shell script that is used by the lpsched daemon to format data sent to the print device.

**line printer scheduler (lpsched) daemon** — The daemon that accepts print jobs into the print queue and prints them to the printer.

**lp (line printer) command** — The command used to create and manipulate print jobs in the print queue.

**lpadmin command** — The command used to create printers on the system.

**LPDEST variable** — A variable used to specify the default printer for a user.

14

**lpstat command** — The command used to view the contents of print queues and printer status.

**lpusers command** — The command used to modify print priority ranges for users on the system as well as the default print job priority.

**print job** — Information sent to a printer for printing.

**print job ID** — A unique identifier used to mark and distinguish each print job; it is comprised of the printer name and a unique number.

**Print Job Manager** — A SCO Admin manager that can be used to manage and cancel print jobs.

**print priority** — A number between 0 and 39 that is used by the lpsched daemon to increase or decrease the likelihood that a print job is to be printed before other print jobs in the print queue.

**print queue** — A directory on the filesystem that holds print jobs that are waiting to be printed.

**Printer Setup Manager** — A SCO Admin manager that can be used to create and control printers on the system.

**printing** — The process by which print jobs are sent from a print queue to a printer.

**reject command** — The command used to disable spooling for a printer.

**rejected printer** — When managing the print process, it refers to a printer that will not accept print jobs into the print queue.

**spooling** — The process of accepting a print job into a print queue.

# Review Questions

1. If a system has three printers attached to it, only one can be designated as the default printer and this default printer applies to all users on the system. True or False?

2. How would you set the default print priority for all print jobs to 25?

   a. lpadm –d 25

   b. lpusers –l 25

   c. lpusers –d 25

   d. lpusers –q 25

3. When you redirect standard output to a printer, how many files are generated in the print queue?

   a. zero

   b. one

   c. two

   d. three

4. The process of sending print jobs from the print queue to the printer is called
   _____ .

   a. spooling

   b. queuing

   c. sending

   d. printing

5. When a printer is disabled, _____ .

   a. the print queue will not accept jobs and send a message to the user noting that the printer is unavailable

   b. the print queue will accept jobs into the print queue and hold them there until the printer is enabled again

   c. the printer will appear as offline in the output of the lpstat −t command

   d. the print queue will redirect all print jobs sent to it to /dev/null

6. What is the default priority assigned to a print job submitted by a regular user?

   a. 10

   b. 0

   c. 39

   d. 20

7. What command can be used to send a file to the default printer named Printer1? (Choose all that apply.)

   a. lp −d Printer1 *file*

   b. lp Printer1 *file*

   c. lp *file*

   d. lpstat Printer1 *file*

8. What command is used to view the status of printers on the system?

   a. lpqst

   b. lpstat

   c. lpsched

   d. lp −s

9. When a printer is rejected, _____ .

   a. the print queue will not accept jobs and send a message to the user noting that the printer is unavailable

   b. the print queue will accept jobs into the print queue and hold them there until the printer is enabled again

   c. the printer will appear as offline in the output of the lpstat −t command

   d. the print queue will redirect all print jobs sent to it to /dev/null

**14**

10. What command would print five copies of the resume file in the /home/bobg directory to the default printer and notify you when the print job was ready?

    a. lp –d –5 /home/bobg/resume

    b. lp –d –n 5 /home/bobg/resume

    c. lp –n 5 /home/bobg/resume

    d. lp –n 5 -m /home/bobg/resume

    e. lp –n 5 -mail /home/bobg/resume

11. What is the background process responsible for printing on UNIX systems?

    a. lpstat

    b. lpd

    c. lpsched

    d. sysproc

12. As the root user, you send a print job to the print queue. Later, you view the contents of the print queue and find that your boss has 25 files waiting to print ahead of yours. What can you do to quickly print your print job?

    a. Use the cancel –u all command.

    b. Resort the files in the /var/spool/lp/tmp/hostname directory.

    c. Issue the command lp –i <printjobID> –H immediate.

    d. Reprint the job using the command lp with the –c switch.

13. You use lpstat and determine that a user named user1 has placed two large print jobs in the queue for printer1 that have yet to start printing. They have print job IDs of printer1-455 and printer1-457, respectively. What command would you use to remove these two jobs from the print queue?

    a. lp –i printer1-455 printer1-457 –d /dev/null

    b. cancel printer1-455 printer1-457

    c. cancel –u all

    d. lp –i printer1-455 printer1-457 –r

14. The process of sending print jobs to the print queue to be held until the printer is ready is called _____.

    a. spinning

    b. queuing

    c. spooling

    d. sorting

15. In addition to printing a file or several files, you can also redirect output from commands to printers as print jobs. True or False?

16. When a UNIX system is started at any level above runlevel 1, the lpsched daemon makes the shared printers on it available over the network. Without switching to runlevel 1, how could you stop the lpsched daemon?

    a. disable command

    b. /usr/lib/lpshut command

    c. reject command

    d. /usr/lib/lpsched stop command

17. Which print device file uses a parallel/serial port and an IRQ of 7? (Choose all that apply.)

    a. /dev/lp0

    b. /dev/lp2

    c. /dev/lp1

    d. /dev/lp

18. Which of the following print device files uses a serial port connection?

    a. /dev/lp0l

    b. /term/010h

    c. /dev/serial/00s

    d. /dev/term/00h

19. Which of the following commands may be used to view IRQs and I/O addresses in use by devices on an SCO UnixWare system?

    a. lp

    b. dcu

    c. irq

    d. irqview

20. What could you do if you wanted to see what print jobs were printed two days ago?

    a. nothing, since logging is disabled by default

    b. View the /var/spool/lp/tmp/printername file.

    c. View the /var/lp/logs/requests file.

    d. View the /etc/lp/logs/requests/printername file.

21. Which of the following print priorities is more likely to be printed before other jobs in the queue that use the default print priority? (Choose all that apply.)

    a. 1

    b. 17

    c. 7

    d. 25

    e. 30

14

22. Normal system users can only affect print jobs they themselves have sent to the print queue. True or False?

23. You have gone into the print queue and placed a print job with an ID of printer1-53 on hold. What command could you use to resume printing of this job?

    a. lp −i printer1-53 −R resume

    b. enable printer1-53

    c. accept printer1-53

    d. lp −i printer1-53 −H resume

24. What command would make a printer named printer1 the default printer on the system for all users?

    a. lpdef −printer1

    b. lpadm −d printer1

    c. default −p printer1

    d. lpadmin −d printer1

    e. printer1 default

25. What command can be used to create a new printer?

    a. lpadd

    b. lpadmin

    c. lpprinter

    d. lpconfigure

26. Which of the following commands will display the default printer on a system?

    a. lpdefault

    b. lpadmin -d

    c. lpdisplay

    d. lpstat -d

27. What command can be used to delete a printer named Printer1 from the server?

    a. lprm

    b. lpadmin

    c. printerdel

    d. lpconfigure

28. Which of the following managers in SCO Admin can be used to reject a printer?

    a. Printer Setup Manager

    b. Print Job Manager

    c. Print Control Manager

    d. Print Manager

29. What will be the result of the command lpusers −u bobg −q 12?

    a. The user bobg will have a default print job priority of 12.

    b. The user bobg will be limited to a maximum of 12 jobs in the print queue.

    c. The user bobg will only be able to raise the priority on his print jobs in the queue to a maximum of 12.

    d. The user bobg will only be able to lower the priority on his print jobs in the queue to a maximum of 12.

30. The /var/lp/logs/requests file will clear itself on a regular basis to save disk space. True or False?

---

# Hands-on Projects

These projects should be completed in the order given. All hands-on projects should take a total of three hours to complete. The requirement for this lab includes:

❑ A computer with UnixWare 7.1.1 installed according to Project 2-2

## Project 14-1

In this hands-on project, you will create a local printer using the lpadmin command and view its configuration.

1. Switch to a command-line terminal (tty2) by pressing **Ctrl+Alt+F2**, and log into the terminal using the username **root** and the password **secret**.

2. At the command prompt, type **lpstat -t** and press **Enter**. What is displayed? Why?

3. At the command prompt, type **lpadmin −m standard −p p1 −v /dev/null** and press **Enter** to create a printer called p1 on the system that prints to a special device /dev/null using a standard interface script.

Any data sent to /dev/null is deleted.

**NOTE**

4. Next, type **lpadmin −d p1** at the command prompt and press **Enter** to make p1 the default printer on the system.

5. At the command prompt, type **cd /etc/lp/model** and press **Enter**. Next, type **ls −l** at the command prompt and press **Enter**. What is the size of the standard interface script?

6. At the command prompt, type **cd /etc/lp/interfaces** and press **Enter**. Next, type **ls −l** at the command prompt and press **Enter**. What is the size of the p1 file? Explain.

7. Type **exit** and press **Enter** to log out of your shell.

**14**

## Project 14-2

In this hands-on project, you will control printer status, create print jobs, and manipulate and delete those print jobs.

1. Switch to a command-line terminal (tty2) by pressing **Ctrl+Alt+F2**, and log into the terminal using the username **root** and the password **secret**.

2. At the command prompt, type **lpstat** and press **Enter**. What is the default printer on the system? Is it accepting requests? Is it enabled?

3. At the command prompt, type **accept p1** and press **Enter**. What warning message did you receive and why?

4. At the command prompt, type **enable p1** and press **Enter**.

5. At the command prompt, type **lpstat** and press **Enter**. Is p1 accepting requests? Is it enabled?

6. At the command prompt, type **lp /etc/hosts** and press **Enter**. What printer will this file be printed to and why? What is the print job ID for your print job?

7. At the command prompt, type **lpstat** and press **Enter**. Is anything displayed? Explain.

8. At the command prompt, type **disable –r "Stopping jobs from leaving the queue" p1** and press **Enter**.

9. At the command prompt, type **lpstat –t** and press **Enter**. Is p1 enabled? Do you see your reason?

10. At the command prompt, type **lp /etc/hosts** and press **Enter**. What is the print job ID for your print job?

11. At the command prompt, type **lpstat** and press **Enter**. Is your print job displayed? Why or why not?

12. At the command prompt, type **lp –n3 –dp1 –m /etc/hosts** and press **Enter** to print three copies of the /etc/hosts file to p1 and mail confirmation after printing. What is the print job ID for your print job?

13. At the command prompt, type **lp –oland –w /etc/hosts** and press **Enter** to print /etc/hosts in landscape format to the default printer and send a message to the terminal after printing. What is the print job ID for your print job?

14. At the command prompt, type **lpstat** and press **Enter**. What print jobs are displayed?

15. At the command prompt, type **lp –i p1-3 –H immediate** and press **Enter**. Next, type **lpstat** and press **Enter**. What is displayed?

16. At the command prompt, type **lp –i p1-3 –H hold** and press **Enter**. Next, type **lpstat** and press **Enter**. What is displayed?

17. At the command prompt, type **lp –i p1-3 –H resume** and press **Enter**. Next, type **lpstat** and press **Enter**. What is displayed?

18. At the command prompt, type **cancel p1-3** and press **Enter**. Next, type **lpstat** and press **Enter**. Was the job removed successfully?

19. At the command prompt, type **cancel −u all** and press **Enter**. What jobs were cancelled? Next, type **lpstat** and press **Enter**. Were the jobs removed successfully?

20. At the command prompt, type **reject −r "Printer unavailable" p1** and press **Enter**. Next, type **lpstat −t** at the command prompt and press **Enter**. Is p1 accepting requests?

21. At the command prompt, type **lp /etc/hosts** and press **Enter**. What message do you receive? Next, type **lpstat −a** at the command prompt and press **Enter**. What reason is displayed?

22. At the command prompt, type **accept p1** and press **Enter**.

23. Type **exit** and press **Enter** to log out of your shell.

**HANDS-ON PROJECTS**

## Project 14-3

In this hands-on project, you will create a network printer using the Printer Setup Manager and test its configuration.

1. Switch to the graphical terminal (tty1) by pressing **Ctrl+Alt+F1**, and log into the CDE desktop using the username **root** and the password **secret**.

2. Open the Printer Setup Manager from SCO Admin. What printer is displayed? Is it the default printer?

3. Double-click on the line that represents p1. Is p1 accepting requests? Is it enabled? Click **Cancel**.

4. Open the **Printer** menu and select **Add TCP/IP Printer**.

5. In the Name dialog box, enter the name **p2**. Ensure that the Make/Model is Cannon Bubble Jet 10ex and that the Protocol Type is lpd (BSD).

6. Select **On Remote Server** beside Printer Connection Type. In the Remote System dialog box, type **localhost**. In the Remote Printer dialog box, type **p1**. Press **OK** when you are finished. The p2 printer will print across the network to the p1 printer on the local computer.

7. Double-click on the line that represents p2. Is p2 accepting requests? Is it enabled? Click **Cancel**.

8. Highlight the line that represents the printer p1, open the **Printer** menu, and choose **Set Remote Access**. Select **localhost** in the Host List and click the **Add** button to place it in the Allow List. Click **OK** when you are finished. The printer p1 will now accept print requests from the computer localhost (the local computer).

9. Close all programs and log out of the CDE desktop.

10. Switch to a command-line terminal (tty2) by pressing **Ctrl+Alt+F2**, and log into the terminal using the username **root** and the password **secret**.

11. At the command prompt, type **lpstat −t** and press **Enter**. What is displayed?

**14**

12. At the command prompt, type **lp –d p2 /etc/hosts** and press **Enter**. Where will the /etc/hosts file be printed?

13. At the command prompt, type **lpstat** and press **Enter**. What is displayed? Why?

14. At the command prompt, type **enable p1** and press **Enter**. Wait 30 seconds. Next, type **lpstat** at the command prompt and press **Enter**. What is displayed? Why?

15. At the command prompt, type **disable p1** and press **Enter**.

16. Type **exit** and press **Enter** to log out of your shell.

**HANDS-ON PROJECTS**

# Project 14-4

In this hands-on project, you will use the LPDEST variable to specify a default printer as well as manage print jobs using the Print Job Manager.

1. Switch to a command-line terminal (tty2) by pressing **Ctrl+Alt+F2**, and log into the terminal using the username **root** and the password **secret**.

2. At the command prompt, type **lp /etc/hosts** and press **Enter**. What printer received the request?

3. At the command prompt, type **vi .profile** and add the following lines to the bottom of the file:

   ```
   LPDEST=p2
   export LPDEST
   ```

   When you are finished, save your changes and exit the vi editor.

4. Type **exit** and press **Enter** to log out of your shell. Next, log into the terminal using the username **root** and the password **secret**.

5. At the command prompt, type **lp /etc/hosts** and press **Enter**. What printer was the file sent to?

6. At the command prompt, type **lp –dp1 /etc/issue** and press **Enter**.

7. At the command prompt, type **lp –dp1 /etc/inittab** and press **Enter**.

8. At the command prompt, type **lpstat** and press **Enter**. How many print jobs are listed?

9. Switch to the graphical terminal (tty1) by pressing **Ctrl+Alt+F1**, and log into the CDE desktop using the username **root** and the password **secret**.

10. Open the Print Job Manager from SCO Admin. How many print jobs are displayed? Compare this to the number you saw in Step 8 and explain any differences.

11. Highlight the print job at the bottom of the list and select **Promote** from the Job menu. Where is this job displayed now?

12. Highlight the print job at the top of the list and select **Hold** from the Job menu to place the print job on hold. Next, highlight the print job at the top of the list and select **Resume** from the Job menu.

13. Highlight the print job at the top of the list and select **Transfer** from the Job menu. At the Transfer to Queue screen, select **p2** and click **OK**. How many print jobs are displayed now and why? Press **q** to exit the more utility.

14. Choose **Select All Jobs** from the Job menu. Next, choose **Delete** from the Job menu to remove all print jobs. Click **OK** to confirm the deletion. If you receive an error message, you may safely ignore it and press **OK**; this error is the result of printing across the network to a local printer.

15. Close all programs and log out of the CDE desktop.

## Project 14-5

In this hands-on project, you will examine the print queue directory, modify print job priorities, and change the default print priority range for users on the system.

1. Switch to a command-line terminal (tty2) by pressing **Ctrl+Alt+F2**, and log into the terminal using the username **root** and the password **secret**.

2. At the command prompt, type **lpstat** and press **Enter**. Are there any print jobs in the print queue?

3. At the command prompt, type **cd /var/spool/lp/tmp/unix1** and press **Enter**. Next, type the command **ls** at the command prompt and press **Enter**. Are there any files in this directory?

4. At the command prompt, type **lp –dp1 /etc/hosts** and press **Enter**. Note the print job ID returned. Next, type the command **ls** at the command prompt and press **Enter**. What is the name of the file created? Why? View the contents of this file. What file is being printed? What user printed it? What priority does it have?

5. At the command prompt, type **lp –c –dp1 /etc/hosts** and press **Enter**. Note the print job ID returned. Next, type the command **ls** at the command prompt and press **Enter**. What are the names of the two files created? Why? View the contents of each file. What file is being printed? What user printed it? What priority does it have?

6. At the command prompt, type **date | lp –dp1** and press **Enter**. Note the print job ID returned. Next, type the command **ls** at the command prompt and press **Enter**. What are the names of the two files created? Why? View the contents of each file. What file is being printed? What user printed it? What priority does it have?

7. At the command prompt, type **cancel –u all** and press **Enter** to cancel all print jobs.

8. At the command prompt, type **tail -31 /var/lp/logs/requests | more** and press **Enter**. Can you tell whether these print jobs were cancelled? Why?

9. At the command prompt, type **lp –q 0 –d p1 /etc/hosts** and press **Enter** to print a copy of the /etc/hosts file with a high print priority. Record the print job ID that you received: _____

10. Next, type the command **ls** at the command prompt and press **Enter**. What is the name of the file created? View the contents of this file. What priority does the print job have? Why?

14

11. At the command prompt, type **lp –i printjobID –q 10** and press **Enter** (where printjobID is the print job ID you recorded in the previous step). Did this raise or lower the previous priority?

12. View the contents of the file that you viewed in Step 9. What priority does the print job have now? Why?

13. At the command prompt, type **lpusers –l** and press **Enter**. What is the default print priority for all print jobs? What is the highest priority that users may use when printing files?

14. At the command prompt, type **lpusers –u owner –q 15** and press **Enter**. Next, type **lpusers –l** at the command prompt and press **Enter**. What is the print priority range for the owner user account?

15. Switch to a command-line terminal (tty5) by pressing **Ctrl+Alt+F5**, and log into the terminal using the username **owner** and the password **secret**.

16. At the command prompt, type **lp –q 0 –d p1 /etc/hosts** and press **Enter**. What error message do you receive? Why?

17. Switch back to the command-line terminal (tty2) by pressing **Ctrl+Alt+F2**.

18. At the command prompt, type **lpusers –u owner** and press **Enter**. Next, type **lpusers –l** at the command prompt and press **Enter**. What is the print priority range for the owner user account?

19. Switch back to the command-line terminal (tty5) by pressing **Ctrl+Alt+F5**.

20. At the command prompt, type **lp –q 0 –d p1 /etc/hosts** and press **Enter**. Why were you successful?

21. Type **exit** and press **Enter** to log out of your shell.

22. Switch back to the command-line terminal (tty2) by pressing **Ctrl+Alt+F2**.

23. Type **exit** and press **Enter** to log out of your shell.

## Discovery Exercises

1. Write commands to perform the following:

   a. Disable the printer laserjet1 with the reason Changing Toner Cartridge.

   b. Print five copies of the file /etc/sample to the printer laserjet5 and send a copy of the file to the print queue.

   c. List all of the print jobs in the print queue for the printer laserjet1 only.

   d. Enable the printer laserjet1.

   e. Change the priority of the print job laserjet5-49 to 35.

   f. Determine whether the lpsched daemon is running.

   g. Print two copies of the /etc/sample file to the printer laserjet1 with the title Corporate Sales on the banner page.

   h. Place the print job laserjet5-49 on hold.

2. Many HP brand printers have an NIC in them and are directly connected to the network. To print to these printers, you must specify their IP address or hostname, as shown in Figure 14-7. To configure the IP address on these printers, run the /usr/lib/hpnp/hpnpinstall and /usr/lib/hpnp/hpnpcfg commands. Use manual pages, the Internet, or SCOhelp to find information on how to use these utilities and summarize your findings.

3. The print system described in this chapter is commonly called the AT&T style of printing and is the standard printing system used on System V UNIX systems. However, another similar method of printing is available called the BSD style of printing, which is used on BSD UNIX systems and most Linux systems. This style of printing uses the lpr, lpq, lpc, and lprm commands to create and manipulate print jobs. Use the Internet to research the commands, daemons, configuration, and maintenance of this printing system. Next, prepare a table that lists the differences and similarities between the BSD and AT&T styles of printing.

4. An open source printing system called Common Unix Printing System (CUPS) was recently created and made available to all Linux and UNIX systems. This printing system is similar to the AT&T-style printing system used on System V UNIX systems, yet offers some improvements. Use the Internet to research the commands, daemons, configuration, and maintenance of this printing system. Next, prepare a table that lists the differences and similarities between the CUPS and AT&T styles of printing.

14

# Glossary

**.** — A special metacharacter used to indicate the user's current directory in the directory tree.

**..** — A special metacharacter used to represent the user's parent directory in the directory tree.

**|** — A shell metacharacter used to pipe standard output from one command to the standard input of another command.

**<** — A shell metacharacter used to obtain standard input from a file.

**>** — A shell metacharacter used to redirect standard output and standard error to a file.

**/dev directory** — The directory under the root where device files are typically stored.

**/etc/conf/bin/idmkinit** — The program that creates a new inittab file using the contents of the /etc/conf/init.d directory.

**/etc/conf/init.d/** — The directory in which files used to rebuild /etc/inittab are stored.

**/etc/conf/init.d/kernel** — The main file used to build the /etc/inittab file.

**/etc/cron.d/at.allow** — A file listing all users who can use the at command.

**/etc/cron.d/at.deny** — A file listing all users who cannot access the at command.

**/etc/cron.d/cron.allow** — A file listing all users who can use the cron command.

**/etc/cron.d/cron.deny** — A file listing all users who cannot access the cron command.

**/etc/default/passwd** — The file that contains the default minimum password length used when changing passwords.

**/etc/default/useradd** — The file that contains default values for user creation.

**/etc/default/vxfs** — The file that contains default values used when creating or mounting a VxFS filesystem.

**/etc/dinit.d/** — The directory that contains the script used to start daemons after runlevels have been reached.

**/etc/dumpdates** — The file used to store information about incremental and full backups for use by the dump utility.

**/etc/group** — The file that contains a list of valid groups on the system.

**/etc/init.d/** — The directory that contains a copy of startup scripts such that you may manually start and stop daemons.

**/etc/inittab** — The configuration file for the init daemon.

**/etc/lp/interfaces directory** — The directory that stores printer interface scripts.

**/etc/lp/model directory** — The directory that stores sample printer interface scripts.

**/etc/mnttab** — A file that stores a list of currently mounted filesystems.

**/etc/passwd** — The file that contains user account information.

**/etc/rcn.d/** — The directories used to start and kill daemons upon entering runlevel *n*.

**/etc/saf/_sactab** — The file that lists the port monitor daemons that are loaded by the sac daemon.

**/etc/saf/_sysconfig** — The file used to store configuration information for the sac daemon.

**/etc/saf/contty/_pmtab** — The file that lists the virtual terminals monitored by ttymon.

**/etc/shadow** — The file that contains the encrypted password and account expiry parameters for each user account.

**/etc/skel** — The skeleton directory used by the useradd command when creating user accounts.

**/etc/vfstab** — A file used to specify which filesystems to mount automatically at boot time and is queried by the mount command if an insufficient number of arguments are specified.

**/kernel/genunix** — The pathname to the UNIX kernel on Solaris systems.

**/sbin/rcn** — The script that executes files in the /etc/rcn.d/ directories.

**/stand/** — The directory containing the kernel and boot-related files on UnixWare and HP-UX systems.

**/stand/boot** — A file that holds the default variables used by the BCP.

**/stand/bootmsgs** — A file that holds the default boot message variables used by the BCP.

**/stand/unix** — The pathname to the UNIX kernel on UnixWare systems.

**/stand/vmunix** — The pathname to the UNIX kernel on HP-UX systems.

**/usr/lib/lpsched command** — The command used to start the lpsched daemon.

**/usr/lib/lpshut command** — The command used to stop the lpsched daemon.

**/usr/lib/scoadmin/account/skel** — The skeleton directory used by the SCO Admin Account Manager when creating user accounts.

**/var/lp/logs/requests file** — A log file that stores information about print jobs that have been removed from the print queue directory.

**/var/spool/cron/atjobs** — A directory that stores the information used to schedule processes configured by the at command.

**/var/spool/cron/crontabs** — A directory that stores cron tables.

**/var/spool/lp/tmp/*hostname* directory** — The print queue directory (where *hostname* is the hostname of the computer).

**absolute pathname** — The full pathname to a certain file or directory starting from the root directory.

**accept command** — The command used to enable spooling for a printer.

**accepted printer** — When managing the print process, it refers to a printer that will accept print jobs into the print queue.

**Access Control List (ACL)** — The list of permissions on a file/directory and the categories of users that they belong to.

**Account Manager** — The graphical SCO Admin manager used to manage users and groups on the system.

**active partition** — The partition searched by a bootstrap program for a boot loader.

**add-on packages** — Packages that are not part of the UNIX operating system.

**adminrole command** — The command used to create a role and assign it administrative rights on the system.

**adminuser command** — The command used to assign a role created with the adminrole command to a user on the system.

**alias command** — A command used to create command aliases.

**ALTS TABLE** — The slice on a UNIX partition that is used to record any bad blocks on the physical hard disk so that they are not used in the future.

**application** — Software that runs on an operating system and provides the user with specific functionality, such as word processing or financial calculation.

**application independence** — A program's capability to be easily adapted to hardware platforms other than the one for which it was originally written.

**Application Installer** — An SCO Admin utility that can be used to install, manage, and remove software packages.

**archive** — A backup copy of files and directories; it is typically created by a backup utility and may reside on a device or within an archive file.

**archive file** — A file on a filesystem that contains an archive.

**archiving** — The act of creating an archive.

**argument** — Text that appears after a command name, does not start with a dash (-) character, and specifies information the command requires to work properly.

**asymmetric multiprocessing (ASMP)** — The process by which an operating system uses multiple processors yet assigns different tasks to each.

**at command** — The command used to schedule commands and tasks to run at a preset time in the future.

**authentication** — The act of verifying a user's identity by comparing a username and password to a system database (/etc/passwd and /etc/shadow).

**authorizations** — Sets of administrative rights that can be assigned to users using SCO Admin.

**background process control** — A feature of the shell that enables background commands to be manipulated.

**background processes** — A process that does not require the shell to wait for its termination; upon execution, the user receives the shell prompt immediately.

**bad blocks** — Those areas of a storage medium unable to properly store data.

**basic input/output system (BIOS)** — A program used to locate and initialize the operating system on an Intel computer.

**bg (background) command** — The command used to run a foreground process in the background.

**binary data file** — A file that contains machine language (binary 1s and 0s) and stores information (such as common functions and graphics) used by binary compiled programs.

**binary program** — An executable file that contains binary data.

**block** — The unit of data commonly used by filesystem commands—a block may contain several sectors.

**block devices** — Storage devices that transfer data to and from the system in chunks of many data bits by caching the information in RAM. They are represented by block device files.

**boot command** — The command used at the BCP [boot] prompt to continue the boot process.

**Boot Command Processor (BCP)** — The boot loader used on UnixWare systems.

**boot device** — A device such as a hard disk that contains a boot loader.

**boot loader** — A program used to load an operating system.

**BOOT slice** — The slice in a UNIX partition that contains the VTOC.

**bootstrapping** — The process where a computer initializes hardware and locates a boot loader after being turned on.

**bootstrap program** — A program used to locate and initialize the operating system on a non-Intel computer.

**C2** — A level of security defined by the U.S. Department of Defense Trusted Computer System Evaluation Criteria (TCSEC).

**cancel command** — The command used to remove print jobs from the print queue.

**cat command** — The command used to display (or concatenate) the entire contents of a text file on the screen.

**cd (change directory) command** — The command used to change the current directory in the directory tree.

**certification exam** — A standard benchmark of technical ability administered by an authorized testing center, recognized in industry, and sought after by many companies.

**character devices** — Storage devices that transfer data to and from the system one data bit at a time. They are represented by character device files. *See also* Raw devices.

**checksum** — A number that represents the contents of a file; it is different for different files.

**chgrp (change group) command** — The command used to change the group ownership on a file or directory.

**child process** — A process that was started by another process (parent process).

**chmod (change mode) command** — The command used to change the mode (permission set) on a file or directory.

**chown (change owner) command** — The command used to change the ownership on a file or directory.

**cluster** — Several smaller computers linked together to function as one large supercomputer.

**command** — A program that may be executed when typed on the command line.

**command aliases** — Special variables that are shortcuts to longer command strings.

**command history** — A feature of the shell that enables users to recall commands that were previously typed into the command line.

**command-line editing** — A feature of the shell that enables users to edit the text on a command line using editor key combinations.

**command-line interface** — A text-based user interface that requires that the user type commands to instruct the operating system.

**command-line terminal** — An interface that enables a user to interact with a command-line shell.

**command mode** — One of the two input modes in vi; it enables a user to perform any available text editing task that is not related to inserting text into the document.

**Common Desktop Environment (CDE)** — One of the two default desktop environments provided with SCO UnixWare 7.1.1; it is also the standard desktop environment on UNIX.

**Compatible Hardware Web Pages (CHWP)** — An Internet resource provided by SCO that lists hardware that is compatible with the UnixWare operating system.

**Complex Instruction Set Computing (CISC)** — The hardware architecture type commonly used by the Intel architecture.

**compress command** — The command used to compress files using an LZW compression algorithm; it is the standard compression utility on UNIX systems.

**compression** — The process in which files are reduced in size by a compression algorithm.

**compression algorithm** — The set of instructions used to systematically reduce the contents of a file.

**compression ratio** — The amount of compression that occurred during compression.

**concatenation** — The joining of text together to make one larger whole. In UNIX, words and strings of text are joined together to form a displayed file.

**cpio command** — A common backup utility.

**cron daemon** — The system daemon that executes tasks in the future—it may be configured using the at and crontab commands.

**cron table** — A file specifying tasks to be run by the cron daemon.

**crontab command** — The command used to view and edit cron tables.

**cylinder** — A series of tracks on a hard disk that are written to simultaneously by the magnetic heads in a hard disk drive.

**daemon** — A UNIX system process that provides a certain service.

**daemon process** — A system process that is not associated with a terminal.

**data blocks** — These store the information of a certain file and the filename.

**datastream format** — A package that has been compressed.

**default router** — Also known as the default gateway or gateway of last resort, this is where information is sent on a network that is not destined for the local network.

**desktop environment** — A set of programs that provide a standard appearance for X Windows.

**devattr command** — The command used to list device information for a certain device listed in the Device Database.

**Device Database** — A database of devices detected during installation and information regarding their device files and usage.

**device driver** — Software that contains instructions that the operating system uses to control and interact with a specific type of computer hardware.

**device file** — A file that represents a specific device on the system and is used by UNIX commands that require devices to be specified. These files do not have a data section, and use major and minor numbers to reference the proper driver and specific device on the system, respectively.

**df (disk free space) command** — The command that displays disk free space by filesystem.

**dfspace command** — The command used to print a user-friendly list of mounted filesystems.

**directory file** — A special file on the filesystem used to organize other files into a logical directory tree structure.

**disable command** — The command used to disable printing for a printer.

**disabled printer** — When managing the print process, it refers to a printer that will not send print jobs from the print queue to a printer.

**diskadd command** — The command used to add an additional hard disk to the system. It calls the fdisk and disksetup commands.

**disksetup command** — The command used to create slices within a partition, create filesystems on those slices, and mount them.

**displaypkg command** — The command used to display a list of installed software packages on the system.

**domain name** — The name of the network, company, or organization that is registered on a DNS server.

**Domain Name Service (DNS) server** — A server on a computer network that resolves names to IP addresses.

**du (directory usage) command** — The command that displays directory usage.

**dual booting** — The process of booting more than one operating system using a boot loader.

**dump command** — A common utility used to create full and incremental backups on HP-UX systems.

**Dynamic Host Configuration Protocol (DHCP) server** — A server on a computer network that can assign most TCP/IP configuration settings to other computers.

**edition license** — A license that determines the hardware, software, and user support for the UnixWare operating system.

**edquota command** — The command used to specify quota limits for users.

**edvtoc command** — The command used to edit the VTOC on a UNIX partition.

**egrep command** — A variant of the grep command used to search files for patterns using extended regular expressions.

**electrically erasable programmable read-only memory (EEPROM)** — A specialized chip that is able to retain information in the absence of power and whose information store can be altered. Also referred to as nonvolatile RAM (NVRAM).

**enable command** — The command used to enable printing for a printer.

**enabled printer** — When managing the print process, it refers to a printer that will send print jobs from the print queue to a printer.

**env command** — A command used to display a list of exported variables present in the current shell except special variables.

**environment files** — Files used immediately after logon to execute commands—they are typically used to load variables into memory.

**environment variables** — Variables that store information commonly accessed by the system or programs executing on the system—together these variables form the user environment.

**executable program file** — A file that can be executed by the UNIX operating system to run in memory as a process and perform a useful function.

**execute** — A UNIX permission that enables a user to execute a file (when set on the file) or use a directory and its contents (when set on the directory).

**Explicitly Parallel Instruction Computing (EPIC)** — A hardware architecture type that computes all tasks in parallel.

**export command** — A command used to send variables to subshells.

**extended multiuser mode** — Also called runlevel 3; it provides most daemons and a full set of networking daemons.

**extent-based allocation** — An attribute of certain filesystems where information is written to adjacent areas of the filesystem.

**ezcp utility** — A Windows utility provided on the first UnixWare 7.1.1 CD-ROM that can be used to create installation floppy disks.

**facility** — When used with the syslog daemon, this term refers to the area of the system from which events will be logged.

**fdisk command** — The command used to create, delete, and manipulate partitions on hard disks.

**fg (foreground) command** — The command used to run a background process in the foreground.

**fgrep command** — A variant of the grep command that does not allow the use of regular expressions.

**file command** — The command that displays the file type of a specified filename.

**file descriptors** — Numeric labels used to define command input and command output.

**filename** — The user-friendly identifier given to a file.

**filename extension** — A series of identifiers following a period (.) at the end of a filename used to denote the type of file; the filename extension .txt denotes a text file.

**filesystem** — The organization imposed on a physical storage medium that is used to manage the storage and retrieval of data.

**filesystem corruption** — Errors in a filesystem structure that prevent the retrieval of stored data.

**filesystem format** — A package that is not compressed.

**Filesystem Hierarchy Standard (FHS)** — A standard outlining the location of set files and directories on a UNIX system.

**filter** — A command that can take from standard input and send to standard output—in other words, a filter is a command that can exist in the middle of a pipe.

**foreground processes** — A process for which the shell that executed it must wait for its termination.

**forking** — The act of creating a new shell child process from a parent shell process.

**format command** — The command used to redefine the tracks on a floppy disk and check for structural errors.

**formatting** — The process where a filesystem is placed on a disk device.

**Frequently Asked Questions (FAQs)** — A list, usually posted on a Web site, where answers to commonly posed questions can be found.

**fsck (filesystem check) command** — The command used to check the integrity of a filesystem and repair damaged files.

**fstyp command** — The command used to determine the type of filesystem on a certain device.

**full backup** — An archive of an entire filesystem.

**Fully Qualified Domain Name (FQDN)** — The full name used to identify a computer on networks such as the Internet; it consists of the system node name and domain name of a computer.

**fuser command** — The command used to identify any users or processes using a particular file or directory.

**GECOS (General Electric Comprehensive Operating System) field** — The field in the /etc/passwd file that contains a description of the user account.

**getacl command** — The command used to view the ACL on a file.

**getdev command** — The command used to show all devices listed in the Device Database.

**GNU Object Model Environment (GNOME)** — One of the GUI environments that is available on some flavors of UNIX.

**grep command** — The command that searches files for patterns of characters using regular expression metacharacters; grep stands for Global Regular Expression Print.

**grep (Global Regular Expression Print) command** — A program used to search one or more text files for a desired string of characters.

**graphical terminal** — An interface that enables a user to log in and start X Windows and a desktop environment.

**graphical user interface (GUI)** — The GUI is the component of an operating system that provides a user-friendly interface, comprising graphics or icons to represent desired tasks. Users can point and click to execute a command rather than having to know and use proper command-line syntax.

**group** — When used in the mode of a certain file or directory, this refers to group ownership of that file or directory.

**groupadd command** — The command used to add a group to the system.

**groupdel command** — The command used to delete a group from the system.

**group identifier (GID)** — A unique number given to each group.

**groupmod command** — The command used to modify the name or GID of a group on the system.

**grpck command** — The command that checks the structural integrity of the /etc/group database.

**hard limit** — A limit imposed that cannot be exceeded.

**hard link** — A file joined to other files on the same filesystem that share the same inode.

**hardware** — The tangible parts of a computer, such as the network boards, video card, hard disk drives, printers, and keyboards.

**hardware architecture** — A configuration of computer hardware that has a specific type of CPU; three types of hardware architectures are available: RISC, CISC, and EPIC.

**hardware platform** — *See also* Hardware architecture.

**hd command** — The command used to display the contents of a file in hexadecimal format.

**head command** — The command that displays the first set of lines of a text file; by default, the head command displays the first 10 lines.

**hidden files** — Files that are not normally revealed to the user via common filesystem commands.

**home directory** — A directory on the filesystem set aside for users to store personal files and information.

**host bus adapter (HBA) diskette** — A diskette that contains UNIX device drivers used during the installation process.

**id command** — The command that displays your UID(s) and GID(s).

**incremental backup** — An archive of a filesystem that contains only files that were modified since the last archive was created.

**inetd** — A port monitor daemon that enables users to log into network services such as FTP and Telnet.

**init command** — The command used to change the operating system from one runlevel to another.

**init (initialize) daemon** — A system utility loaded by the sysproc daemon; it is responsible for starting and stopping other daemons on the system.

**Initial System Loader (ISL)** — The boot loader used on HP-UX systems.

**initstate** — *See* Runlevel.

**inode** — The portion of a file that stores information on the files attributes, access permissions, location, ownership, and file type.

**inode table** — The collection of inodes for all files and directories on a filesystem.

**insert mode** — One of the two input modes in vi; it gives the user the ability to insert text into the document, but does not allow any other functionality.

**install server** — An SCO Admin utility that can be used to create and manage a software depot.

**installsrv command** — The command used to create a software depot.

**intent-logging filesystem** — *See also* Journaling filesystem.

**interface script** — A shell script that is used by the lpsched daemon to format data sent to the print device.

**Internet Packet Exchange/Sequence Packet Exchange (IPX/SPX) protocol** — A method used to format information for use on a computer network commonly used on Novell networks.

**Internet Protocol (IP) address** — The unique number that each computer participating on the Internet must have.

**jobs command** — The command used to see the list of background processes running in the current shell.

**journaling filesystem** — A filesystem that writes pending filesystem changes to a journal file on the filesystem.

**K Desktop Environment (KDE)** — One of the GUIs available for some flavors of UNIX.

**kernel** — The core component of the UNIX operating system.

**kill command** — The command used to kill or terminate a process.

**kill signal** — The type of signal sent to a process by the kill command; different kill signals affect processes in different ways.

**large filesystem support** — A filesystem feature that enables files larger than 2GB to be stored on the filesystem.

**l command** — An equivalent to the ls -l command; it gives a long file listing.

**license** — Information that enables you to use an operating system.

**Lightweight Process (LWP)** — A small part of a larger process that shares a PID with other parts of the larger process, but may be scheduled individually.

**line printer scheduler (lpsched) daemon** — The daemon that accepts print jobs into the print queue and prints them to the printer.

**linked file** — Files that represent the same data.

**Linux** — A widely used UNIX flavor originated by Linus Torvalds.

**listen** — A port monitor daemon that accepts connections from users across a network.

**locale** — Refers to the world region that determines the character set that an operating system will use to display text characters.

**locking an account** — The process of making an account temporarily unusable by altering its password information stored on the system.

**log files** — Files that contain system events.

**login** — A program that presents users with the login prompt.

**lost+found directory** — A directory that exists on filesystems created by the mkfs command and is used by the fsck command to store files that cannot be repaired.

**lpadmin command** — The command used to create printers on the system.

**lp (line printer) command** — The command used to create and manipulate print jobs in the print queue.

**LPDEST variable** — A variable used to specify the default printer for a user.

**lpstat command** — The command used to view the contents of print queues and printer status.

**lpusers command** — The command used to modify print priority ranges for users on the system as well as the default print job priority.

**ls command** — The command used to list the files in a given directory.

**mail command** — The traditional e-mail reader on UNIX systems.

**major number** — A number used by the kernel to identify what device driver to call to properly interact with a given category of hardware. Hard disk drives, CD-ROMs, and video cards are all categories of hardware. Similar devices share a common major number.

**manual pages** — The most common set of local command syntax documentation, available by typing the man command-line utility—also known as man pages.

**Master Boot Record (MBR)** — The area of a hard disk outside of a partition that stores partition information.

**metacharacter** — A single character that is interpreted by the shell as having specific or special meaning; the shell interprets several metacharacters specially.

**minor number** — A number used by the kernel to identify which specific hardware device within a given category to use the specified driver to communicate with. *See also* Major number.

**mkfs (make filesystem) command** — The command used to format or create filesystems.

**mknod command** — The command used to recreate a device file provided the major number, minor number, and type (character or block) are known.

**mode** — The part of the inode that stores information on access permissions.

**monitor** — The part of the bootstrap program that halts an operating system if any hardware or software problems are detected.

**more command** — The command used to display a text file page by page and line by line on the terminal screen.

**mount command** — The command used to mount filesystems on devices to mount point directories.

**mounting** — The process used to associate a device with a directory in the logical directory tree such that users may store data on that device.

**mount point** — The directory in a file structure to which something is mounted.

**multitasking** — An operating system's capability to run two or more tasks at one time; the operating system then regulates the time each process has to execute on the processor.

**multiuser** — An operating system's capability to allow access by more than one user at a time.

**multiuser mode** — Also called runlevel 2; it provides most daemons and a partial set of networking daemons.

**named pipe** — A temporary connection that sends information from one command or process in memory to another; it can also be represented by a file on the filesystem.

**ncheck command** — The command used to identify files on a filesystem by inode number.

**netmask** — Also known as the network mask or subnet mask, this specifies which portion of the IP address identifies the logical network the computer is on.

**Network File System (NFS)** — A distributed file system designed by Sun Microsystems that allows computers to share data stored on them with other computers on the network.

**Network Information Service (NIS)** — A service that enables multiple UNIX computers to share configuration information across a computer network.

**Network Information System (NIS)** — A network service designed by Sun Microsystems that enables UNIX computers to share configuration information with other computers on the network.

**network interface card (NIC)** — Hardware device used to connect a computer to a network of other computers and communicate or exchange information on it.

**newgrp command** — The command used to temporarily change the primary group of a user.

**newsgroup** — A group of messages that users may add or respond to. The worldwide collection of newsgroups is called Usenet.

**nice command** — The command used to change the priority of a process as it is started.

**nice value** — The value that indirectly represents the priority of a process; the higher the value, the lower the priority.

**od command** — The command used to display the contents of a file in octal format.

**OpenBoot programmable read-only memory (PROM)** — The boot loader used on Solaris systems.

**operating system** — Software used to control and directly interact with computer hardware components.

**options** — Specific letters that start with one dash (-) or two dashes (--) and appear after the command name to alter the way the command works.

**other** — When used in the mode of a certain file or directory, it refers to all users on the UNIX system.

**owner** — The user whose name appears in a long listing of a file or directory and who has the ability to change permissions on that file or directory.

**package set** — A group of software packages that share a similar function. *See also* Set Installation Packages (SIPs).

**Panorama desktop environment** — One of the two default desktop environments provided with SCO UnixWare 7.1.1.

**parent process** — A process that has started other processes (child processes).

**parent process ID (PPID)** — The PID of the parent process that created the current process.

**partition** — A physical division of a hard disk drive.

**passwd command** — The command used to modify the password associated with a user account.

**PATH variable** — A variable that stores a list of directories that will be searched in order when commands are executed without an absolute or relative pathname.

**permissions** — A list of who can access a file or folder and their levels of access.

**pg command** — The command used to display a text file page by page on the terminal screen.

**pico (pine composer) text editor** — A common text editor used with UNIX systems.

**pipe** — A string of commands connected by | metacharacters.

**pkgadd command** — A command-line utility used to install packages.

**pkgask command** — The command used to create an answer file for use with future installations of a given package.

**pkgchk command** — The command used to check the integrity of the /var/sadm/install/ contents file.

**pkginfo command** — A command that can be used to list installed software packages and package sets as well as their attributes.

**pkginstall command** — A command used to install software packages from a software depot on the computer network.

**pkgrm command** — A command used to remove software packages currently installed on a system.

**pkgtrans command** — A command used to uncompress a package that is in datastream format.

**pmadm command** — The command used to view and configure ports monitored by port monitor daemons.

**Portable Operating System Interface (POSIX)** — An IEEE standard that has led to the standardization of many operating systems including most UNIX flavors.

**port monitor daemons** — Daemons that enable users to connect to the system via terminals.

**power-on self test (POST)** — The initialization of hardware components by the BIOS when the computer is first turned on.

**pre-installation checklist** — A list of hardware and software information useful during a UNIX installation.

**primary group** — The group that is specified for a user in the /etc/passwd file and specified as group owner for all files created by a user.

**print job** — Information sent to a printer for printing.

**print job ID** — A unique identifier used to mark and distinguish each print job; it is comprised of the printer name and a unique number.

**Print Job Manager** — A SCO Admin manager that can be used to manage and cancel print jobs.

**print priority** — A number between 0 and 39 that is used by the lpsched daemon to increase or decrease the likelihood that a print job is to be printed before other print jobs in the print queue.

**print queue** — A directory on the filesystem that holds print jobs that are waiting to be printed.

**Printer Setup Manager** — A SCO Admin manager that can be used to create and control printers on the system.

**printing** — The process by which print jobs are sent from a print queue to a printer.

**priority** — When used with the syslog daemon, this term refers to the relative importance of the event being monitored.

**process** — A program loaded into memory and running on the processor performing a specific task.

**process ID (PID)** — A unique identifier assigned to every process as it begins.

**Processor Dependent Code (PDC)** — The bootstrap program used on HP-UX systems.

**process priority** — A number assigned to a process used to determine how many time slices on the processor time it will receive; the higher the number, the lower the priority.

**process state** — The current state of the process on the processor; most processes are in the sleeping state.

**program** — A structured set of commands stored in an executable file on a filesystem; it may be executed to create a process.

**prtvtoc (print VTOC) command** — The command used to view the VTOC on a UNIX partition.

**ps command** — The command used to obtain information about processes currently running on the system.

**pwck command** — The command that checks the structural integrity of the /etc/passwd database.

**pwd (print working directory) command** — The command used to display the current directory in the directory tree.

**quota command** — The command used to view disk quotas imposed on a user.

**quotaoff command** — The command used to deactivate disk quotas.

**quotaon command** — The command used to activate disk quotas.

**quotas** — Limits on the number of files or total storage space on a filesystem imposed on system users.

**quot command** — The command used to list filesystem usage for each user on the system.

**raw devices** — *See also* Character devices.

**read** — A UNIX permission that enables a user to view the contents of a file (when set on the file) or list the contents of a directory (when set on the directory).

**recursive** — Referring to itself and its own contents. A recursive search includes all subdirectories in a directory and their contents.

**redirection** — The process of changing the default locations of standard input, standard output, and standard error.

**Reduced Instruction Set Computing (RISC)** — A hardware architecture type that is commonly used today on computers that require high performance.

**regular expressions (regexp)** — Special metacharacters used to match patterns of text within text files; they are commonly used by many text tool commands such as grep.

**reject command** — The command used to disable spooling for a printer.

**rejected printer** — When managing the print process, it refers to a printer that will not accept print jobs into the print queue.

**relative pathname** — The pathname of a target directory relative to your current directory in the tree.

**renice command** — The command used to alter the nice value of a process currently running on the system.

**repquota command** — The command used to produce a report on quotas for a particular filesystem.

**restore command** — The command used to extract archives created with the dump command.

**rogue process** — A process that has become faulty in some way and continues to consume far more system resources than it should.

**root filesystem** — The filesystem that contains most files that make up the operating system; it should have enough free space to prevent errors and slow performance.

**runlevel** — A term that defines a certain type and number of daemons on a UNIX system.

**sacadm command** — The command used to view and manage port monitors on the system.

**scalability** — The ability for a system to increase its performance as the number of processors increase.

**sched daemon** — The first process started by the UNIX kernel on Solaris systems; it is analogous to the sysproc daemon in UnixWare.

**search engine** — An Internet Web site such as *www.google.com* or *www.dogpile.com* where a person types in a phrase representing what is being searched for and receives a list of Web sites that contain relevant material.

**sectors** — The smallest unit of data storage on a hard disk; they are arranged into concentric circles called tracks and can be grouped into blocks for use by the system.

**security profile** — Indicates a general selection of security-related system parameters.

**server** — A computer configured with network services. Other computers may access these services from across a computer network.

**Service Access Controller (sac) daemon** — The daemon that loads port monitor daemons.

**Service Access Facility (SAF)** — The set of daemons and files on a UnixWare or Solaris system that enable users to gain access to the system.

**setacl command** — The command used to change the ACL on a file.

**set command** — A command used to view all variables in the shell except special variables.

**setenv command** — A command used to create or modify variables in the C shell.

**Set group ID (SGID)** — A special UNIX permission that temporarily changes the current group owner of a file that is executed.

**Set Installation Packages (SIPs)** — *See also* Package sets.

**Set user ID (SUID)** — A special UNIX permission that temporarily changes the current owner of a file that is executed.

**shell** — A user interface that accepts input from the user and passes the input to the kernel for processing.

**shell function** — A special variable in memory created by the shell that can be executed to perform a certain task.

**shell script** — A text file that contains commands and constructs that are interpreted by the shell upon execution.

**show command** — The command used at the BCP [boot] prompt to show the values of BCP variables.

**shserv** — The utility called by the login program after a successful login to provide the user with a shell.

**shutdown command** — A command used to safely shut down the UNIX operating system.

**single-user mode** — Also called runlevel 1; it provides a single terminal and a limited set of services.

**skeleton directory** — A directory that contains files that are copied to all new user's home directories upon creation.

**slice** — Used to divide up a UNIX partition into smaller areas for ease of use. There may be 184 slices per UNIX partition.

**small footprint server** — A system profile that consists of the bare minimum set of software packages in a UnixWare system.

**socket** — A named pipe connecting processes on two different computers; it can also be represented by a file on the filesystem.

**soft limit** — A limit imposed that can be exceeded for a certain period of time.

**software** — Programs stored on a storage device in a computer that provide a certain function when executed.

**software depot** — A server on the network that holds packages available to be installed on other computers on the network.

**software packages** — A series of related files that together comprise a program that can be installed on a computer.

**software spooling** — The copying of a software package to a filesystem for installation at a later time.

**source file/directory** — The portion of a command that refers to file or directory from which information is taken.

**special device file** — A file used to identify hardware devices such as hard disks and serial ports.

**spooling** — The process of accepting a print job into a print queue.

**standard error** — Represents any error messages generated by a command.

**standard input** — Represents information inputted to a command during execution.

**standard output** — Represents the desired output from a command.

**sticky bit** — A special UNIX permission that prevents users from deleting files that they do not own from a directory.

**strings command** — The command used to search for and display text characters in a binary file.

**subdirectory** — A directory that resides within another directory in the directory tree.

**subshell** — A shell started by the current shell.

**su (switch user) command** — The command used to change your user account after login.

**sum command** — The command used to calculate a unique checksum for a file based on its contents.

**superblock** — The portion of a filesystem that stores critical information such as the inode table and block size.

**swapper daemon** — The first process started by the UNIX kernel in HP-UX; it is analogous to the sysproc daemon in UnixWare.

**swinstall command** — The command used to install software packages on an HP-UX system.

**swlist command** — The command used to display software packages currently installed on an HP-UX system.

**swremove command** — The command used to remove packages currently installed on an HP-UX system.

**swverify command** — The command used to verify the integrity of packages installed on an HP-UX system.

**symbolic link** — A pointer to another file on the same or another filesystem; commonly referred to as a shortcut.

**symmetric multiprocessing (SMP)** — The process by which an operating system uses multiple processors to perform a single task.

**syncing** — The process of writing data to the hard disk drive that was stored in RAM.

**sysproc daemon** — The first process started by the UNIX kernel in UnixWare; it is responsible for starting the init daemon, scheduling processes and managing information transferred to and from the swap slice.

**system backup** — The process whereby files are copied to an archive. *See also* Archiving.

**system log daemon (syslogd)** — A daemon initialized on system startup that is responsible for monitoring selected portions of the system and generating log files from the results.

**System Logs Manager** — An SCO Admin tool that can be used to manage and clear log files.

**system node name** — Also known as a hostname, this is the logical identifier given to a computer.

**system packages** — Packages that contain programs that comprise the UNIX operating system.

**system profile** — The system software chosen for a UnixWare installation.

**system services** — Applications that are integral to the operating system and enable it to perform specialized tasks.

**tail command** — The command used to display the last set number of lines of text in a file; by default, the tail command displays the last 10 lines of the file.

**tapecntl (tape controller) command** — The command used to manipulate tape devices or prepare a tape for system backup.

**tar command** — The most common utility used to create archives.

**target file/directory** — The portion of a command that refers to the file or directory to which information is directed.

**TCP/IP protocol** — A method used to format information for use on a computer network; this is the most common protocol used on computer networks and the protocol used on the Internet.

**tee command** — A command used to take from standard input and send to both standard output and a specified file.

**telinit command** — A symbolic link to the init command.

**terminal** — A channel that enables a user to log in and gain access to a UNIX system.

**text file** — A file that stores information in a readable text format.

**text tools** — Programs that allow for the creation, modification, and searching of text files.

**tfadmin (Trusted Faculty Administrator) command** — The command that enables users with administrative rights to run administrative commands on the command line.

**time slice** — The amount of time a process is given on a CPU on a machine using a multiprocessing operating system.

**tracks** — The area on a hard disk that forms a concentric circle of sectors.

**trapping** — The process of ignoring a kill signal.

**tr command** — A command used to transform or change characters received from standard input.

**ttymon** — The port monitor daemon that enables users to log into virtual terminals and serial connections.

**ufsdump command** — A backup utility used to create archives from information stored on UFS filesystems; it is common on UnixWare and Solaris systems.

**ufsrestore command** — The command used to restore information archived with the ufsdump command.

**umask command** — The command used to view and change the current umask.

**umask (user mask)** — A system variable used to alter the permissions on all new files and directories by taking select default file and directory permissions away.

**umount command** — The command used to break the association between a device and a directory in the logical directory tree.

**uncompress command** — The command used to decompress files compressed using the compress command.

**UNIX** — The first true multitasking, multiuser operating system, developed by Ken Thompson and Dennis Ritchie.

**UNIX Filesystem (UFS)** — The default filesystem used by Solaris.

**UNIX flavors** — Different versions of the UNIX operating system.

**Usenet** — A worldwide system used to exchange ideas and information in forums called newsgroups.

**user** — When used in the mode of a certain file or directory, this refers to the owner of that file or directory.

**user account** — Information regarding a user that is stored in a system database that may be used to log into the system and gain access to system resources.

**useradd command** — The command used to add a user account to the system.

**user-defined variables** — Variables that are created by the user and are not used by the system—these variables are typically exported to subshells.

**userdel command** — The command used to remove a user account from the system.

**user identifier (UID)** — A unique number assigned to each user account.

**user interface** — The program that a human uses to interact with an operating system.

**usermod command** — The command used to modify the properties of a user account on the system.

**user process** — A process begun by a user that runs on a terminal.

**variable** — An area of memory that is used to store information—variables are created from entries in environment files when the shell is first created after login and are destroyed when the shell is destroyed upon logout.

**variable identifier** — The name of a variable.

**vendor-neutral certification** — Certification that is broad based and not restricted to one type of operating system.

**vendor-specific certification** — Certification that is focused and restricted to one type of operating system.

**Veritas Filesystem (VxFS)** — The default filesystem used by UnixWare and HP-UX.

**virtual memory** — An area on a hard disk (swap partition) that can be used to store information that normally resides in physical memory (RAM) if the physical memory is being used excessively.

**virtual terminals** — Terminals located and accessed locally on the UNIX server.

**vi text editor** — A powerful command-line text editor available on most UNIX systems.

**Volume Table of Contents (VTOC)** — A list of slices within a UNIX partition. It is stored on the BOOT slice of the UNIX partition.

**vxdump command** — A backup utility used to create archives from data stored on VxFS filesystems.

**vxrestore command** — The command used to restore information archived with the vxdump utility.

**wall (warn all) command** — A command used to send a message to all users currently logged into the system.

**wall (warn all) command** — The command used to send a message to all users logged into the system.

**wildcard metacharacters** — Metacharacters used to match certain characters in a file or directory name; they are often used to specify multiple files.

**write** — A UNIX permission that enables a user to edit the contents of a file (when set on the file) or add/remove files to/from a directory (when set on the directory).

**X Windows** — The component of the UNIX GUI that displays graphics to windows on the terminal screen.

**zcat command** — The command used to view the contents of an archive created with the compress command.

**zombie process** — A process that has finished executing, but whose parent has not yet released its PID; it still retains a spot in the kernel's process table.

# Index

Note: Boldface numbers indicate illustrations and tables.

## A